Get started with your **Connected Casebook**

Redeem your code below to access the **e-book** with search, highlighting, and note-taking capabilities; **case briefing** and **outlining** tools to support efficient learning; and more.

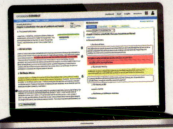

1. Go to www.casebookconnect.com
2. Enter your access code in the box and click **Register**
3. Follow the steps to complete your registration and verify your email address

If you have already registered at CasebookConnect.com, simply log into your account and redeem additional access codes from your Dashboard.

ACCESS CODE:

Scratch off with care.

Is this a used casebook? Access code already redeemed? Purchase a digital version at **CasebookConnect.com/catalog**.

If you purchased a digital bundle with additional components, your additional access codes will appear below.

"I liked being able to search quickly while in class."

"Being able to highlight and easily create case briefs was a fantastic resource and time saver for me!"

"I loved it! I was able to study on the go and create a more effective outline."

PLEASE NOTE: Each access code can only be used once. Access codes expire one year after the discontinuation of the corresponding print or bundle title and must be redeemed before then. CCH reserves the right to discontinue this program at any time for any business reason. For further details, please see the CasebookConnect End User License Agreement at CasebookConnect.com/terms.

For technical support, please visit http://support.wklegaledu.com.

9999

10072344-0001

CIVIL RIGHTS ENFORCEMENT

ASPEN CASEBOOK SERIES

CIVIL RIGHTS ENFORCEMENT

SCOTT MICHELMAN

Legal Co-Director, American Civil Liberties Union of the District of Columbia
Lecturer on Law (Spring Terms 2015-21), Harvard Law School

Wolters Kluwer

Published by Wolters Kluwer in New York.

Wolters Kluwer Legal & Regulatory U.S. serves customers worldwide with CCH, Aspen Publishers, and Kluwer Law International products. (www.WKLegaledu.com)

To contact Customer Service, e-mail customer.service@wolterskluwer.com, call 1-800-234-1660, fax 1-800-901-9075, or mail correspondence to:

Wolters Kluwer
Attn: Order Department
PO Box 990
Frederick, MD 21705

Printed in the United States of America.

2 3 4 5 6 7 8 9 0

ISBN 978-1-5438-1366-1

Library of Congress Cataloging-in-Publication Data

Names: Michelman, Scott, author.
Title: Civil rights enforcement / Scott Michelman, Legal Co-Director,
  American Civil Liberties Union of the District of Columbia [and]
  Lecturer on Law (Spring Terms 2015-21), Harvard Law School
Description: New York : Wolters Kluwer, 2019. | Series: Aspen casebook
  series | Includes bibliographical references and index. | Summary: "Law
  school casebook covering a broad range of civil rights/liberties
  issues" — Provided by publisher.
Identifiers: LCCN 2019040460 | ISBN 9781543813661 (hardcover) | ISBN
  9781543817126 (ebook)
Subjects: LCSH: Civil rights — United States. | Actions and defenses — United
  States. | LCGFT: Casebooks (Law)
Classification: LCC KF4748 .M53 2019 | DDC 342.7308/5 — dc23
LC record available at https://lccn.loc.gov/2019040460

About Wolters Kluwer Legal & Regulatory U.S.

Wolters Kluwer Legal & Regulatory U.S. delivers expert content and solutions in the areas of law, corporate compliance, health compliance, reimbursement, and legal education. Its practical solutions help customers successfully navigate the demands of a changing environment to drive their daily activities, enhance decision quality and inspire confident outcomes.

Serving customers worldwide, its legal and regulatory portfolio includes products under the Aspen Publishers, CCH Incorporated, Kluwer Law International, ftwilliam.com and MediRegs names. They are regarded as exceptional and trusted resources for general legal and practice-specific knowledge, compliance and risk management, dynamic workflow solutions, and expert commentary.

*I dedicate this book to my students, to my clients, and to my little mouse N.C.M.,
in the hope that something in these pages will help to bend, or help them to bend,
the arc of our nation's moral universe toward justice.*

Summary of Contents

Contents

PART II
CONSTITUTIONAL TORT CLAIMS — LIMITATIONS AND DEFENSES

CHAPTER 5

Municipal Liability

Preface

This book arises from the confluence of my fourteen years as a civil rights litigator — mostly spent at or in partnership with national or local offices of the American Civil Liberties Union — and more than a dozen semesters as a clinical or classroom law school instructor, including five teaching Civil Rights Litigation at Harvard Law School. The book began as a set of supplemental materials to an existing textbook, created to fill what I saw as gaps in the textbook's coverage of civil rights litigation *as it is practiced*. With each year I taught Civil Rights Litigation, I found myself expanding my materials, sometimes in response to thoughtful questions from my students, sometimes in response to my own sense that I had taken just a few steps down a road that needed to be followed to its end. Ultimately, after my third semester teaching the course, I expanded my materials into a manuscript for this complete textbook. I subsequently revised the manuscript in response to student feedback, advice from Dean Erwin Chemerinsky and several other brilliant academic reviewers, and my experiences in both the classroom and the courtroom.

The title of this book, *Civil Rights Enforcement*, reflects what I think is an important distinction between this book and others in this field: This book attempts to maintain a rigorous focus on doctrines concerning the enforcement of civil rights (rather than the content of those rights) and on the aspects of those doctrines of most central concern to those doing, or opposing, the enforcement: attorneys at civil rights organizations, at plaintiff-side firms with a civil rights practice, in government at any level, and at firms of any kind that maintain a civil rights pro bono practice or a practice representing governments. Put another way, this is a book with a practical bent that will hopefully speak not only to students interested in studying civil rights law for its rich lessons in statutory interpretation, the relationship between rights and remedies, and tradeoffs between the values of federalism and judicial review, but also to students who see themselves as potential practitioners in this area of law.

I must note that it is a particular type of enforcement that I cover here: the enforcement of civil rights *through civil actions brought by non-governmental parties* (as opposed to enforcement by government or through criminal laws). Within the field of private civil actions to enforce civil rights, I focus on doctrines relevant to the enforcement of many kinds of civil rights rather than specialized fields with their own unique statutory schemes (such the Voting Rights Act).

From the book's orientation toward a pragmatic understanding of private civil actions to enforce civil rights, several of the book's characteristics follow:

1. **Detailed problems, application notes, and practical as well as theoretical questions.** At the end of each chapter, I include "Chapter Problems" that give students a chance to apply their knowledge to specific factual settings. Many of these are drawn from or inspired by real cases (including some of my own). In my experience, students get a lot out of tackling these problems — solidifying and testing their knowledge, thinking through how legal theory plays out in practice, and building strategic thinking skills. Some of my best class discussions have arisen out of these problems, which may be discussed in a wide range of formats, from small-group brainstorming to individual student presentations to full class debates with half the class assigned to argue the plaintiff's perspective and half the class the defendant's. Additionally, many problems in later chapters refer back to prior problems or include questions reviewing prior material, to help students see how doctrines and issues interrelate — in real life, of course, most cases do not fit neatly into a single box but instead require the application of multiple doctrines at the same time.

   Along similar lines, a number of notes following principal cases take the form of "Application" sections in which I identify key follow-up cases extending or qualifying the main case and lower-court decisions applying it. Like the problems, the applications help students see the effects of the rules laid down in the principal cases.

   Finally, I begin with, and weave throughout, larger strategic questions about the uses of civil rights litigation and the closely related subject of impact litigation. My post-case notes and questions are designed to prompt students to think about the practical effects of civil-rights enforcement doctrines in litigation and by extension their effects on government policies and practices. How do these doctrines interact with each other? How do they contribute to gaps between rights and remedies? What incentives do they create? How can litigators anticipate obstacles in their cases and prepare to meet them? In anonymous surveys, my students report that they appreciate being challenged to think through these types of questions instead of considering only more esoteric ones.

2. **Exploration of the interrelationship between constitutional and statutory civil rights enforcement.** Although 42 U.S.C. § 1983 doctrines account for a substantial fraction of the material in the book, real-world legal problems do not divide themselves into constitutional and non-constitutional cases, and I think litigators should understand the statutory rights and causes of action that complement and sometimes surpass in effectiveness claims brought to remedy constitutional violations. Indeed, in practice, many civil rights cases consist of both constitutional and statutory claims. Therefore, I cover several enforcement doctrines in the latter category: those relevant to employment discrimination law, Titles VI and IX, and the use of § 1983

to assert rights provided by other federal statutes. Studying these additional areas not only helps provide comprehensive coverage for students who might one day practice in the field, but it also introduces remedial models other than the § 1983 framework and facilitates fruitful comparisons (for instance, institutional liability under *Ellerth* as compared with *Gebser/Davis* as compared with *Monell*; or the Court's approach to congressional intent in the context of implied rights of action, § 1983 enforcement of statutory rights, and *Bivens*). For comprehensiveness, I also identify types of parallel state-law claims that civil rights litigators often include alongside the federal ones that are the book's focus.

3. **A litigator's organization and a litigator's selection of cases.** I organize the materials the way a litigator might think about a constitutional civil rights case: (1) What's the cause of action? (2) What defenses should I anticipate? (3) What statutory claims can I add to the case and what rules govern their enforcement? and (4) What relief can I obtain for my client? (The remedies question, I recognize, could logically arise either first or last.) A non-doctrinal Prologue, which could be assigned as an introduction, an interlude between doctrinal topics, or an epilogue, situates private civil rights enforcement litigation within its social and historical context and invites students to consider its uses, successes, and shortcomings.

I recognize some instructors may prefer other sequences for the various topics. Accordingly, I introduce topics that often lead off this type of course — like sovereign immunity and remedies—in a manner that would facilitate starting a course with them instead of with the book's opening chapter on the interpretation of § 1983.

In my choice of principal cases, I seek to expose students not just to the most challenging or analytically complex cases on a topic but also to the leading and foundational cases that reveal a doctrine's origins, rationale, and basic contours. Thus, students can become familiar with the cases that litigators in the field know and begin at the beginning of the law's development rather than partway through.

4. **A focus on enforcement in case selection and editing.** Because this book is about the relationship between rights and remedies and the tools used by civil rights litigators, not the substance of the underlying rights themselves, I do not emphasize topics that are primarily about *what* a constitutional or statutory right protects as opposed to *how* and *to what extent* these protections can be *enforced*. Although the book includes many cases in which constitutional rights are enforced, my goal is not to teach the content of substantive constitutional rights, such as what constitutes excessive force or cruel and unusual punishment. Likewise, in employment discrimination, I focus on the standards for holding an employer liable rather than, for instance, the treatment of mixed motives or what constitutes a reasonable accommodation. I have edited the cases with the doctrines we're studying in mind and seek to avoid such long excerpts that an instructor is forced to

choose between devoting an entire class session to just one or two cases or skipping important cases entirely. I don't think students are well served by reading sprawling excerpts that range deeply into peripheral topics, and, as an instructor, I find that students come better prepared to understand the part of the case that matters to the subject at hand if they are reading shorter passages focused on that subject.

My attempt to avoid treading into merits doctrines raises an important pedagogical question: How much constitutional law must students have studied as a prerequisite to courses using this book? None, I believe. If substantive constitutional knowledge were required to understand the mechanics of civil rights enforcement, courses in this field would have too many prerequisites to be feasible, as the key cases address circumstances in which plaintiffs attempt to enforce their rights under the First, Fourth, Fifth, Eighth, and Fourteenth Amendments. Instead of requiring knowledge of all these doctrines, I have edited the cases keeping in mind students who lack substantive constitutional law knowledge (or knowledge of civil rights statutes like Title VII). To the extent students may find a bit of background on the relevant substantive law helpful as they read, the book includes as a reference a brief glossary describing in the most basic manner most of the substantive constitutional concepts that appear in the cases excerpted. I have found over several semesters that a glossary of this kind provides enough reference material to enable students to understand the material without any prerequisites other than Civil Procedure.

A few notes about formatting: I use ellipses and other editorial punctuation within cases to indicate where I have chosen to omit material so that readers can look up the original sources and also know where the text provided is edited. The three exceptions to this general practice are a case's internal citations, footnotes, and section headings — these I retain only where I think they are of pedagogical value; otherwise, I truncate or omit them without comment. Relatedly, where a case cites 42 U.S.C. § 1983 as it used to be known, "Rev. Stat. § 1979," I have replaced these citations with the modern § 1983. All footnotes that appear are the sources' notes. I use square brackets like this — [] — to indicate alterations I have made in excerpted sources for clarity or conciseness or where I summarize a portion of a case.

Finally, having spent several pages describing the book's orientation toward issues arising in practice, I should add a few words about theory. The pragmatic focus of this book does not mean that the book shies away from important philosophical and policy questions in order to hammer on black-letter law alone. Quite the contrary: Because this field is such a heavily contested one in which many of the rules are malleable or in flux, I believe a solid grounding in the history, philosophy, and policy implications of the doctrine is critical for litigators working on this variable terrain. Running throughout the materials are several themes and arguments that recur in this area of law. These include the plaintiff-side goals of compensation and deterrence; defendant-side concerns about fairness and the chilling of officers' performance of their duties; and structural questions about institutional competence, federalism, the proper role of courts, and the *Marbury* principle that remedy should follow right. I have edited the cases with these themes in mind and highlight them in the notes and questions. I also flag instances in which a legal-realist or critical-studies approach might have the most explanatory power given certain doctrines' twists and turns and the rightward shift of the Supreme Court in the past half-century. Additionally, I treat *Bivens* in more detail than many text-books, both because the cause of action, though in decline, is still regularly invoked to enforce constitutional rights against federal officials, and because the debate over *Bivens* exemplifies the clash among many of the principles — theoretical as well as practical — that have been central to shaping civil rights enforcement doctrines. Indeed, many of the Supreme Court's opinions in this area provide the most explicit articulations of the competing values at stake. It is my hope that by connecting the theoretical and policy underpinnings of the relevant doctrines directly to the practice of civil rights litigation, students will develop a deep understanding of how the rules governing this field have developed, have been applied, and may yet be revised.

November 2019

Scott Michelman

Acknowledgments

It gives me great pleasure to acknowledge all the people whose advice, encouragement, mentorship, expertise, and friendship have made this book a reality: Kathy and Peter Michelman, who have always supported me and believed in me, and in particular encouraged me to write; Anne McCunney, who modeled for me what magic an engaged teacher could work in the lives of her students; Amy Perlin, who taught me to value *tikkun olam*; Alexa Shabecoff and Judy Murciano, who helped me break into the field of civil rights litigation; the late Judge Betty Binns Fletcher, an exemplar of wisdom and compassion on the bench who taught me never to lose sight of the law's impact on human beings; Ben Wizner, Baher Azmy, Jay Rorty, and Art Spitzer, four brilliant lawyers and mentors who showed me how to practice law; Jon Gould, for the impetus behind my course proposal at Harvard; Martha Minow, John Manning, Catherine Claypoole, and the entire Harvard Law faculty, for the incredible honor of an appointment to teach Civil Rights Litigation at Harvard Law School; Dick Fallon, who has been my model for clarity, organization, and passion in legal teaching and who taught me the critical lesson that as a teacher one should only ever be oneself; all my students, whose questions and insights have helped shape my teaching and these materials, and in particular Alyx Darensbourg, both for valuable observations in the classroom and for diligent research assistance outside of it; Mike Kirkpatrick, Catherine Crump, and Art Spitzer, for crucial quality control on the chapter problems and the glossary; Aaron Caplan, Jon Gould, Alex Reinert, David Rudovsky, Joanna Schwartz, Steve Vladeck, and Chris Walker, whose deep engagement with the draft manuscript and incisive feedback sparked countless improvements large and small; Joe Terry, Kathy Langone, Sarah Hains, and the entire team at Wolters Kluwer for their expert guidance through the publication process; Erwin Chemerinsky, the Dean of Berkeley Law School and Dean of Civil Rights Litigation, who continues to inspire me as the model of a litigator-teacher and whose advice on the content and organization of my course and my draft manuscript have been indispensable; and Alison Sizer, the love of my life, who encouraged me to expand my supplemental materials into a complete stand-alone manuscript.

Foreword

Over the years, I have many times taught a course in Civil Rights Litigation. But I always have been frustrated that there was not a casebook that approached the material from the perspective of civil rights litigators — whether representing plaintiffs or defendants in civil rights cases. I tried using existing casebooks and adapting them to my structure, but it never quite worked. It always is difficult for students to use a book totally out of its order and also none focused on how civil rights cases are actually litigated.

Scott Michelman, a terrific civil rights lawyer who has been teaching Civil Rights Litigation at Harvard Law School for many years, kindly shared his course materials with me. I was stunned at how similar his approach was to what I had been trying to do. Exactly like my course, he focuses on four questions: (1) What's the cause of action? (2) What are the defenses and procedural bars? (3) In light of the obstacles, what statutory causes of action are there and what doctrines govern the enforcement of civil rights through these types of claims? and (4) What relief is possible? I always begin my course with the last question, but otherwise I structure the course the same as Professor Michelman (and his book easily allows covering remedies first). These are the questions that any lawyer dealing with a civil rights case must focus on in preparing and litigating the matter.

As soon as I read Professor Michelman's materials, I strongly encouraged him to publish them as a casebook. He has done a superb job of organizing and editing the key cases. The hypotheticals he has written will provide a great basis for students to explore the topics by dealing with realistic problems and also will offer an excellent opportunity for class discussion. The book is comprehensive, yet manageable. It can be easily adapted to law school courses of different credit hours. It is clear and accessible, yet challenging for students. It does not assume prior knowledge, such as of constitutional law or remedies, on the part of the students. It is inspiring, such as in the initial material on *Brown v. Board of Education* and some recent civil rights cases, but also realistic in presenting all of the obstacles plaintiffs pursuing civil rights cases face.

In every way, Professor Michelman has written a superb book on Civil Rights Enforcement that will be of great value in teaching the next generation of civil rights lawyers.

Erwin Chemerinsky
Dean and Jesse H. Choper Distinguished Professor of Law
University of California, Berkeley School of Law

Glossary of Relevant Constitutional Concepts

This glossary provides a reference for readers who may find a bit of context on constitutional concepts helpful to understanding certain cases. In light of its function as a reference guide for the cases *in this book* rather than as a mini-Constitutional Law primer, the glossary is not comprehensive and simplifies certain concepts. Terms within an entry that have their own separate entries appear in bold.

Brady. *Brady v. Maryland*, 373 U.S. 83 (1963), requires that prosecutors turn any material (i.e., consequential) **exculpatory evidence** over to the defense. This rule, part of the constitutional requirement of **due process**, is among the most important guarantees of fairness in criminal proceedings.

Collateral review. See **habeas corpus**.

Conditions of confinement. Refers to the circumstances in which a person is detained, whether civilly, pretrial, or after conviction of a crime. The Constitution requires that such conditions meet minimum standards. For instance, prison officials "must ensure that prisoners receive adequate food, clothing, shelter, and medical care, and must take reasonable measures to guarantee the safety of the inmates." *Farmer v. Brennan*, 511 U.S. 825, 832 (1994) (citation and internal quotation marks omitted).

Consent. Voluntary agreement. For example, a person's consent renders a **search** or **seizure** constitutional even if it would otherwise be forbidden.

Cruel and unusual punishment. The Eighth Amendment prohibits "cruel and unusual punishments." In addition to restricting certain applications and methods of capital punishment (the Eighth Amendment context that receives the most popular attention), the bar on cruel and unusual punishment, among other things, requires minimum standards for **conditions of confinement** and prohibits the use of **excessive force** against people incarcerated for having committed a crime.

Disparate impact. Practices or policies that have a disproportionate *effect* on a particular group, even though there has been no showing of *intent* to discriminate against that group. For instance, a business's requirement that all its employees work on Saturdays (the Jewish day of rest) would have a disparate impact on religious Jews seeking employment even if no one intended to discriminate. Contrast **disparate treatment**.

Disparate treatment. Discrimination *because of* a certain characteristic; that is, *intentional* discrimination based on that characteristic. For instance, a business with a sign saying "Help wanted — no Jews need apply" is engaging in disparate treatment based on religion. Contrast **disparate impact**.

Due process. A constitutional right that encompasses an array of protections. Due process may be violated where a person is subjected to unfair procedures at trial (such as a ***Brady*** violation), where a person is deprived of a liberty or property interest without adequate procedures (which is a violation of "procedural due process"), or where the person is deprived of certain personal liberties ranked as fundamental. This last category, called "substantive due process," covers the right to abortion, the right to use contraception, the right to refuse medical treatment, the right to make parenting decisions, the right to privacy of information (according to some courts of appeals), the right to choose a sexual partner, and the right to choose a marital partner, among others. As applied to civil and pretrial detainees, due process protects against **excessive force** and inhumane **conditions of confinement**. Additionally, the Supreme Court has held that the Fifth Amendment's Due Process Clause, which applies to the federal government, implicitly guarantees **equal protection**. (Fifth Amendment equal protection is necessary because the Fourteenth Amendment, which contains an explicit equal protection guarantee, applies only to states, not the federal government.)

Equal protection. A constitutional right to be free from legal distinctions that are irrational, are based on certain identity-related characteristics, or arise from group-related animosity, and also to be free from certain types of *intentional* discrimination (that is, **disparate treatment**, not **disparate impact**). In applying equal protection, courts view certain types of identity-based distinctions as more inherently "suspect" than others. For instance (to take just three examples), distinctions based on race are treated as highly suspect and therefore likely unconstitutional; distinctions based on sex are also quite suspect (but not quite as suspect as race); distinctions based on age are not suspect but can be successfully challenged if they are irrational or based on animosity toward older persons. One prominent application of equal protection is to forbid segregation by race in public schools. Equal protection also forbids discrimination with respect to certain fundamental rights like voting, whether or not a "suspect" classification is involved.

Excessive force. A constitutional violation characterized by unnecessary violence. A use of excessive force by law enforcement outside of the jail or prison context is a type of **unreasonable search or seizure** that violates the Fourth Amendment; in jail or prison, it is a violation of **due process** as to civil or pretrial detainees or a prohibited instance of **cruel and unusual punishment** as to individuals incarcerated for a crime. Whether excessive force has occurred for purposes of the Fourth Amendment or due-process protections for civil or pretrial detainees depends on a reasonableness inquiry: "the question is whether the officers' actions are 'objectively reasonable' in light of the facts and circumstances confronting them, without regard to their underlying intent or motivation."

Graham v. Connor, 490 U.S. 386, 397 (1989); *see also Kingsley v. Hendrickson*, 135 S. Ct. 2466, 2473 (2015) (adopting *Graham* standard for due process claim). The standard under the Eighth Amendment for excessive force against individuals incarcerated for crimes is whether force was used "maliciously and sadistically to cause harm" instead of in a good-faith effort to maintain discipline. *Hudson v. McMillian*, 503 U.S. 1, 7 (1992).

Exclusionary rule. Constitutional rule of criminal procedure under which unlawfully obtained evidence cannot be used at a criminal trial. Enforced by a **motion to suppress**.

Exculpatory evidence. Information that tends to suggest the innocence of a person accused of a crime, whether because it makes it appear less likely that the person committed a crime or because it casts doubt on the testimony of a witness who says the person *did* commit a crime ("impeachment evidence"). Material (i.e., consequential) exculpatory evidence known to prosecutors or police must be turned over to the defense under ***Brady***.

Fourteenth Amendment, § 5. The provision of the Fourteenth Amendment authorizing Congress to enact legislation to protect constitutional rights.

Habeas corpus. A type of legal action, long predating the Constitution, to challenge a person's detention as unlawful. The availability of habeas is guaranteed (with some limits) by the Constitution, Art. I, § 9, cl. 2. Habeas originally could be used only to challenge a detention without legal process. (It is still sometimes used this way—for instance, by detainees at Guantanamo Bay.) It is also used in modern times to challenge criminal convictions alleged to violate the convicted person's constitutional rights. This second usage, which is also called **collateral review**, is roughly analogous to an additional but more difficult appeal process that is pursued after a standard appeal fails. Concretely: Someone convicted of a state crime may first ask for review by a state appeals court ("direct appeal"). If that is unsuccessful, the person may file a new civil action for habeas relief in the state courts and then if *that* is unsuccessful file yet another civil action for habeas relief in the federal courts. The procedure is somewhat more streamlined, but similar, for federal habeas relief from *federal* convictions.

Incorporation. The settled understanding that the Fourteenth Amendment, in addition to guaranteeing the rights to **due process** and **equal protection**, also extended most of the rights protected by the first ten amendments to the Constitution (the Bill of Rights), to restrain the conduct of state and local governments. (These rights originally restrained only the conduct of the federal government.) Thus, a claim against an official for violating the "Fourth and Fourteenth Amendments" usually means a claim that a state or local official (as opposed to a federal one) violated the Fourth Amendment, not a claim as to the substance of both amendments.

Motive-based claims. A type of constitutional claim that depends on the defendant's reason for taking the challenged action. Examples are **equal protection** claims and First Amendment **retaliation** claims, both of which challenge actions that might be lawful if taken for permissible reasons but are unconstitutional if taken for impermissible reasons (such as a person's race or to punish a person for engaging in speech). Because what separates the constitutional from the unconstitutional in these examples is the reason (the motive) behind the challenged action, these claims are called motive-based claims.

Motion to suppress. A request for a criminal court to apply the **exclusionary rule** to forbid the use at trial of unlawfully obtained evidence.

Retaliation. A claim that a person has been punished for engaging in protected activity. For instance, a First Amendment retaliation claim is a claim that the government has unconstitutionally punished a person (including, under certain circumstances, a government employee) because of the person's speech. This is a type of **motive-based claim**: the retaliatory action must have occurred *because of* the speech. Many antidiscrimination statutes (covered in Chapters 6 and 7) also prohibit retaliation for having opposed, complained of, or sought remedies for discrimination.

Search. Although sometimes the word is used in the ordinary, colloquial sense of looking for something, for a "search" to trigger Fourth Amendment scrutiny, it must fit within this more specific category: invasions of a person's "reasonable expectation of privacy." Examples include entering a person's home, rummaging in a person's bag, patting a person down, or eavesdropping on a phone call.

Seizure. The halting or moving of a person or item, however temporary, that occurs either through intentional application of physical force or a show of authority to which a person submits.

State action. Constitutional rights generally protect individuals only from "state action" — usually action by federal, state, or local governments or officials. Occasionally, as covered in Chapter 1, Section B, activities of private parties can amount to "state action" that is constrained by the Constitution. (Certain *statutes* covered in Chapters 6 and 7 prohibit discrimination by private parties in circumstances that the Constitution doesn't reach.)

Unreasonable search or seizure. The Fourth Amendment protects against "unreasonable **searches** and **seizures**." Searches of a person or dwelling without a **warrant** are presumptively "unreasonable searches," although there are various exceptions to this principle, such as **consent** by the person being searched. Types of "unreasonable seizures" include arrests without warrants or probable cause, temporary detentions of individuals without "reasonable suspicion" (reason to suspect a person is armed and/or dangerous), and uses of **excessive force**.

Warrant. A judge's authorization (to conduct a search or arrest).

Why Civil Rights Litigation?

This book is about the legal doctrines that individuals can invoke, and the obstacles they face, in enforcing their civil rights through civil actions. By "civil rights," I mean rights guaranteed by the U.S. Constitution and by statutes animated by constitutional values like equal protection of the laws. Questions about the substance of these rights—such as what the freedom of speech protects, when a search or seizure is unreasonable, and what constitutes discrimination in employment—are left to other courses like Constitutional Law, Criminal Procedure, and Employment Discrimination. The book also does not cover civil rights enforcement, civil or criminal, by governmental entities. Instead, this book is about *how*, and in some cases *whether*, these rights can be enforced *by private parties through civil litigation*.

Placing civil rights litigation in historical context is crucial to understanding its importance and its development as a field of law. Central to that historical context is the experience of African-Americans, who as a group endured nearly 250 years of slavery in the American colonies and subsequently the United States, then an additional century or so of widespread, systemic, and explicit state-sponsored discriminatory treatment combined with pervasive governmental and private racist violence. This period was followed by decades, extending into the present, in which government policies and practices, though less often overtly racist, have been carried out or constructed in ways that continue to disadvantage African-Americans—including criminal justice policy, economic policy, and limitations on the right to vote—even as race-based violence continues.

African-Americans are not, of course, the only group in the United States subjected to systemic discrimination, violence, and denials of their personhood. Native Americans, women, Latino/a/x individuals, Asian-Americans, religious minorities, immigrants in general, individuals with disabilities, and members of the LGBTQ community, to name a few, have all faced and continue to face discrimination and hardship based on their identities. But the experience of African-Americans is particularly significant as background to our study because combatting race-based

1

violence and discrimination was the primary goal of most of our nation's civil rights laws.

Enforcement of the Constitution's equal protection mandate is not the only purpose or use of civil rights laws. Causes of action for violations of constitutional rights may be invoked to redress deprivations of all kinds of rights, such as the freedom of speech, the prohibition against unreasonable searches and seizures, the guarantee of due process, and the prohibition against cruel and unusual punishment. Indeed, cases involving these rights all figure prominently in the development of constitutional civil rights litigation. Nonetheless, the experience of African-Americans in the United States provided both the impetus for the enactment of the civil rights laws we will study and the primary imperative for their early interpretation and enforcement.

The archetypal story of civil rights litigation is *Brown v. Board of Education*. The decades-long strategic campaign for the eradication of racial segregation in public education is both a model and a cautionary tale for civil rights litigators. *Brown* is an exemplar of what is today known as "impact litigation"—a strategic case or set of cases designed not just to vindicate the rights of a small and discrete group of litigants but also to bring about change in laws, policies, practices, and even societal norms themselves. *Brown* demonstrates both the potential power of impact litigation and also its limitations, including how difficult large-scale legal and social change can be to enforce and sustain, and how court action can be (*should be*, in the view of some; *will inevitably be*, in the view of others) limited by considerations of institutional competence, deference to other branches of government, and political will.

Although this book is primarily about the laws and doctrines that govern civil rights enforcement through private civil actions, not the long and sobering story of race relations in the United States, the history of *Brown* and the meaning of impact litigation provide important context for our study of civil rights enforcement—its goals, its promise, its importance, and its limitations. We therefore begin by considering the story of *Brown*—not as law but as history, context, and model for civil rights enforcement through private civil actions. We then contrast the model of institutional reform litigation exemplified by *Brown* with more common uses of civil rights litigation to pursue law reform through injunctions against specific statutes or practices and through damages actions. Our introduction concludes with critiques of impact litigation.

A. INSTITUTIONAL REFORM LITIGATION AND THE ROAD TO *BROWN*

To understand the conditions that gave rise to the *Brown* campaign, recall the central role of race in the development of American society and government—a role that persisted following the Civil War. As legal scholar Michelle Alexander recounts:

> It may be impossible to overstate the significance of race in defining the basic structure of American society. The structure and content of the original Constitution was based largely on the effort to preserve a racial caste system—slavery—while at the

same time affording political and economic rights to whites, especially propertied whites. The Southern slaveholding colonies would agree to form a union only on the condition that the federal government would not be able to interfere with the right to own slaves. . . . Consequently, the Constitution was designed so the federal government would be weak, not only in its relationship to private property, but also in relationship to the rights of states to conduct their own affairs. The language of the Constitution itself was deliberately colorblind (the words *slave* or *Negro* were never used), but the document was built upon a compromise regarding the prevailing racial caste system. Federalism—the division of power between the states and the federal government—was the device employed to protect the institution of slavery and the political power of slaveholding states. Even the method for determining proportional representation in Congress and identifying the winner of a presidential election (the electoral college) were specifically developed with the interest of slaveholders in mind. Under the terms of our country's founding document, slaves were defined as three-fifths of a man, not a real, whole human being. . . .

The history of racial caste in the United States would end with the Civil War if the idea of race and racial difference had died when the institution of slavery was put to rest. But during the four centuries in which slavery flourished, the idea of race flourished as well. Indeed, the notion of racial difference—specifically the notion of white supremacy—proved far more durable than the institution that gave birth to it.

White supremacy, over time, became a religion of sorts. Faith in the idea that people of the African race were bestial, that whites were inherently superior, and that slavery was, in fact, for blacks' own good, served to alleviate the white conscience and reconcile the tension between slavery and the democratic ideals espoused by whites in the so-called New World. There was no contradiction in the bold claim made by Thomas Jefferson in the Declaration of Independence that "all men are created equal" if Africans were not really people. Racism operated as a deeply held belief system based on "truths" beyond question or doubt. This deep faith in white supremacy not only justified an economic and political system in which plantation owners acquired land and great wealth through the brutality, torture, and coercion of other human beings; it also endured, like most articles of faith, long after the historical circumstance that gave rise to the religion passed away. . . . After the death of slavery, the idea of race lived on.

Michelle Alexander, *The New Jim Crow* 25-26 (2010).

Reconstruction—the dozen years following the Civil War—marked a period of significant advancement for African-Americans. Three constitutional amendments were added to the Constitution (the Thirteenth, outlawing slavery; the Fourteenth, requiring equal protection of the laws, among other things; and the Fifteenth, prohibiting discrimination in voting based on race); new civil rights statutes were passed (some still highly relevant today, as we'll see through our study); and a new federal agency (the Freedman's Bureau) to assist formerly enslaved individuals.

But at the same time, African-Americans faced acts of terrorism designed to reduce them to, or replicate, their former enslaved status—or simply to kill them outright. Atrocities were abetted by white-supremacist state and local governments, which refused to prevent or punish racist violations of the law and which enacted and enforced discriminatory laws themselves. In the debates over the federal civil rights legislation known as the Ku Klux Klan Act of 1871, members of Congress sympathetic to the plight of newly freed individuals decried "whippings and lynchings and banishment [that] have been visited upon unoffending American citizens" with no response from local white authorities; incidents in which "[m]en were murdered, houses were burned, women were outraged, men were scouraged [sic], and officers of the law shot down; and the State made no successful effort to bring the guilty to punishment or afford protection or redress to the outraged and innocent"; and "outrages committed upon loyal men . . . under the forms of law." *Monroe v. Pape*, 365 U.S. 167, 175-76 (1961) (citation and internal quotation marks omitted).

The disputed election of 1876 ended with a compromise that handed the White House to Republicans (the party that had championed Reconstruction) in exchange for the withdrawal of federal troops from the South. As journalist Ta-Nehisi Coates recounts:

> The dream of Reconstruction died. For the next century, political violence was visited upon blacks wantonly, with special treatment meted out toward black people of ambition. Black schools and churches were burned to the ground. Black voters and the political candidates who attempted to rally them were intimidated, and some were murdered. At the end of World War I, black veterans returning to their homes were assaulted for daring to wear the American uniform. . . . Organized white violence against blacks continued into the 1920s—in 1921 a white mob leveled Tulsa's "Black Wall Street" and in 1923 another one razed the black town of Rosewood, Florida—and virtually no one was punished.

Ta-Nehisi Coates, *The Case for Reparations*, The Atlantic, June 2014, *reprinted in* Ta-Nehisi Coates, *We Were Eight Years in Power* 185 (2017).

Complementing these extra-legal horrors was the re-imposition of a regime of legal disabilities for black Americans that cut them out of vast swaths of national life and any hope of political power:

> By the turn of the twentieth century, every state in the South had laws on the books that disenfranchised blacks and discriminated against them in virtually every sphere of life, lending sanction to a racial ostracism that extended to schools, churches, housing, jobs, restrooms, hotels, restaurants, hospitals, orphanages, prisons, funeral homes, morgues, and cemeteries. Politicians competed with each other by proposing and passing ever more stringent, oppressive, and downright ridiculous legislation (such as laws specifically prohibiting blacks and whites from playing chess together). . . .
>
> The new racial order, known as Jim Crow—a term apparently derived from a minstrel show character—was regarded as the "final settlement," the "return to sanity," and "the permanent system."

Alexander, *supra*, at 35.

During the century of formalized, state-sanctioned subjugation of African-Americans that followed the Civil War, few avenues of redress were open to African-Americans. The courts, like the rest of U.S. society, were not inclined to upset the nation's racial order. Nonetheless, civil rights activists sought the courts' aid, using careful planning and framing their plight in the most sympathetic terms to attempt to overcome the ethos of white supremacy that pervaded the national culture.

Legal historian Peter Irons discusses the contours of this strategy by reference to two of its most famous participants—Homer Plessy, arrested in 1892 for boarding a train car reserved for whites, and Rosa Parks, arrested in 1955 for refusing to give up her seat on a Montgomery, Alabama, bus for a white man. Plessy's action ended in the notorious case *Plessy v. Ferguson*, 163 U.S. 537 (1896), upholding segregation in public transportation under the theory that the Constitution required no more than "separate but equal" accommodations. Parks's action sparked the Montgomery bus boycott led by Rev. Dr. Martin Luther King, Jr.; a year later, bus segregation in Montgomery was struck down. *See Browder v. Gayle*, 142 F. Supp. 707, 717 (M.D. Ala.), *summarily aff'd*, 352 U.S. 903 (1956). Irons observes:

> Whatever their personal motives for refusing to change seats, both had affiliations with civil rights groups that supported challenges to Jim Crow laws. Plessy was a friend of Rodolphe Desdunes . . . [who] helped to organize a "Citizens' Committee to Test the Constitutionality of the Separate Car Law," and most likely he recruited Plessy to challenge the law. Rosa Parks had been an active member and secretary of the Montgomery chapter of the National Association for the Advancement of Colored People. . . . It is likely that Rosa Parks understood—or even welcomed—the probable reaction to her act. She later said that "this is what I wanted to know: when and how could we ever determine our rights as human beings?"
>
> We know a great deal about Rosa Parks, who has been honored many times since her act of defiance, but we know very little about Homer Plessy, not even his occupation. . . . Despite his personal obscurity, Plessy deserves recognition because his case represented one of the first examples of "interest group" litigation, in which organizations like the New Orleans citizens' committee bring "test cases" to expand—or defend—the constitutional rights of their members and constituents. Since the *Plessy* case, the NAACP, founded in 1909 by blacks and sympathetic whites, and another important organization, the American Civil Liberties Union, formed in 1920, have brought more Bill of Rights cases before the Supreme Court than all other groups combined. Many of these cases are carefully planned and prepared. . . . [T]hese "test case" clients allow their sponsors to bring constitutional issues before the courts . . . .

Peter Irons, *A People's History of the Supreme Court* 223 (2006).

Of course, the best known "test case" was *Brown v. Board of Education*. *Brown* wasn't a single isolated case; the *Brown* opinion resolved four different cases brought in Kansas, South Carolina, Virginia, and Delaware, and these, in turn, represented the culmination of a campaign that took decades.

Pulitzer Prize–winning author Richard Kluger traces the origins of the NAACP's strategy in shaping the *Brown* campaign back to a debate within the organization more than twenty years before the Supreme Court issued its famous opinion. Initially, the organization considered a proposal to fund a wave of lawsuits against school districts that underfunded schools for black children relative to schools for white children. The goal was not to challenge the "separate" in separate-but-equal, but to try to make officials live up to the "equal" requirement. The hope was to make the cost of a dual school system prohibitive by challenging each instance of unequal funding. But in 1930, the NAACP hired Nathan Margold to shape the campaign's strategy, and he doubted the efficacy of single-district lawsuits: Each victory would have no binding effect on other districts, whose inequalities would have to be separately documented and separately challenged. Margold proposed instead that the NAACP challenge state *laws* permitting unequal funding, which plaintiffs could show produced systems in which white schools were funded at twice, five times, or even ten times the rate of black schools. *See* Richard Kluger, *Simple Justice* 131-35 (2004). The goal of this approach would be to obtain legal rulings that could require reform of state spending practices more broadly.

Building on Margold's original blueprint, Charles Hamilton Houston, who had been the first African-American to serve on the Harvard Law Review and who preceded Thurgood Marshall as the NAACP's top lawyer in the 1930s, added an important strategic nuance that would help put the NAACP campaign into action. Kluger describes the plan:

> The black attack ought to begin in the area where the whites were most vulnerable and least likely to respond with anger. That segregation had produced blatantly discriminatory and unequal school systems, Houston calculated, was most obvious at the level of graduate and professional schools: aside from Howard [Law School in Washington, D.C.] and Meharry Medical College in Nashville, there were *no* graduate or professional schools at any black college in the South. . . . Here was an area where the educational facilities for blacks were neither separate nor equal but nonexistent. The Supreme Court . . . would have trouble turning its back on so plain a discrimination and denial of equal protection. The South would either have to build and operate separate graduate schools for blacks or admit them to white ones. The first alternative, while costly, would not require the sort of massive expenditure that would be likely to engender a violent backlash; the second alternative—admitting Negroes to existing graduate and professional schools—was unthinkable on the face of it, but, in view of the relatively small number of blacks who would be involved and their maturity, the step was not likely to prove convulsive. At the very least, a legal drive at the graduate level promised to result in improved all-black facilities; at the most, it would demonstrate that blacks and whites could attend school together to the mutual benefit of the students as well as the state treasury. . . . The point now was to establish a real beachhead. If graduate schools were peaceably desegregated, then the NAACP could turn to undergraduate colleges. And then secondary schools. And grade schools. Each new gain would help the advance to the next stage.

Kluger, *supra*, at 136-37.

The NAACP's graduate school cases produced a series of Supreme Court decisions between 1938 and 1950 that chipped away at the legal foundation for segregated schools, as Professor Charles Ogletree chronicles:

> The NAACP won its first major federal victory in a case on behalf of Lloyd Gaines, an honors graduate from Lincoln University, who was denied admission to the University of Missouri Law School. . . . [T]he Missouri Supreme Court ruled that Missouri's offer to supply Gaines with an out-of-state scholarship satisfied the state's obligation to provide equal graduate training for black students. In 1938, in *Missouri ex rel. Gaines v. Canada*, the Supreme Court provided Houston and the NAACP a major precedent setting victory. Justice Hughes's decision found that the right to equal protection was a personal one, which one state could not pass off to another.

The Court held that Missouri had an obligation to provide Gaines with a graduate education, and it ordered the admission of Gaines to the in-state law school. . . .

After World War II, the number of black applicants seeking admission to state college and graduate programs increased substantially and provided the NAACP with a wealth of plaintiffs from which to choose. In one major postwar victory, *Sipuel v. Oklahoma*, a young black woman named Ada Louise Sipuel sought admission to the University of Oklahoma Law School. In 1948, the Supreme Court, relying on *Gaines*, ruled that Oklahoma had an obligation to provide Sipuel with an education on the same basis as white students. The Regents of the University of Oklahoma tried to respond by hastily establishing a separate law school for black students in three rooms in the state capitol building. Marshall challenged this arrangement, but the Supreme Court neglected to take any action. Sipuel was admitted to the white law school in 1949 when prohibitive costs for maintaining a separate school for one student caused the state to close the black law school.

In the late 1940s, Houston, Marshall, and the NAACP won two major victories that cleared the way for a direct attack on educational segregation. Herman Marion Sweatt was denied admission to the University of Texas Law School. When Marshall filed suit, the state legislature allocated $100,000 to construct a separate black law school. The state court ruled that the state had satisfied its obligation by using a substantial amount of money to construct this separate law school. At the same time, a sixty-eight-year-old professor at the black Langston College in Oklahoma applied to the University of Oklahoma's Graduate School of Education. The state allowed Professor McLaurin to attend the white school, but he was forced to sit in a room adjoining the main classroom roped off with a sign that read "colored section." The state courts held that Dr. McLaurin's admission with separate treatment satisfied the state's obligation.

Both cases—*Sweatt v. Painter* and *McLaurin v. Oklahoma*—were appealed to the Supreme Court, and decisions were handed down in 1950 on the same day. In *Sweatt*, the Court assumed that there was equality between the two physical plants, but found that this was not sufficient. It held that there was more to legal education than a physical plant and that Texas could not replicate in the black school the learning environment, the established reputation, and the alumni contacts of the white school. In *McLaurin*, the Court found that the University of Oklahoma's arrangement for separate treatment within the graduate school stigmatized Dr. McLaurin and handicapped him in his ability to pursue his education.

These two cases together—one stating that physical equality was still insufficient to meet the requirements of equal protection and the other finding that actual equality with separate arrangements imposed a stigma and was therefore unconstitutional—opened up the opportunity for a direct attack on segregation and paved the way to the *Brown* decision. Marshall reacted to the Court's rulings by declaring, "The decisions . . . are replete with road markings telling us where to go next."

Charles J. Ogletree, Jr., *All Deliberate Speed* 121-22 (2004).

As the graduate school cases were reaching their climax, the NAACP was already lining up the test cases that would reach the core of educational segregation. The first of these—one of the four ultimately consolidated for decision in *Brown*— arose in Clarendon County, South Carolina, which Thurgood Marshall selected in part for the starkness of the disparity in educational spending and facilities. The county spent four times as much per white pupil as per black pupil. Most of the black schools lacked plumbing or electricity.

An initial attempt at a Clarendon lawsuit faltered. Levi Pearson, a Clarendon County farmer with three children who had to attend school nine miles from home, sued in early 1948 to get the local school board to provide bus transportation to black children, as it did for white children. But the suit was dismissed because Pearson's property was almost precisely on the boundary between two school districts, and he paid his property taxes to one but sent his children to a school in the other, so the court ruled that he lacked standing (that is, a personal stake in the case). Pearson found that after attempting unsuccessfully to stand up for his rights, the white-owned banks and stores in the area cut off his credit. *See* Kluger, *supra*, at 14-17.

But Marshall and the black community of Clarendon County did not give up. In early 1949, Marshall proposed a suit seeking broader relief on behalf of a group of twenty plaintiffs, to spread the risk of retaliation. It took local organizers, led by the Reverend J.A. DeLaine, eight months to round up that number, and many of them suffered for their courage—being fired, denied credit, or having their properties foreclosed on. *See* Irons, *supra*, 385-86.

The case went to trial before a three-judge district court in May 1951, and the school board's lawyer Robert Figg surprised the plaintiffs at the outset by admitting that inequalities existed; however, he argued, the state legislature had now passed legislation aimed at rectifying the disparities, and so the school district should be granted a "reasonable time" to provide a plan to bring the black schools' funding up to par. Figg's concession and proposal did not keep the court from hearing the NAACP's witnesses, who created a thorough record of the inequalities between the black and white schools in Clarendon County, but Figg's gambit did shape the court's order the following month. The court held that *Plessy* had recognized the constitutionality of segregation; invoking the principle of separate-but-equal, the court ordered the defendants to report back to the court in six months on their progress toward equal funding. Kluger, *supra*, at 347-67.

The NAACP asked the Supreme Court to review the case, but it punted, sending the case back to the district court to respond to the school district's progress report. The report, which proposed to build a new high school by the following September and two new grade schools after that, and to equalize teacher salaries, school equipment, and transportation, was convincing to the district court. Thurgood Marshall proposed that, in the meantime, the court should order the schools integrated so that black children could begin receiving education immediately on an equal basis. *See* Kluger, *supra*, at 533-36.

The court's opinion dismissed that suggestion out of hand:

> There can be no doubt that as a result of the program in which defendants are engaged the educational facilities and opportunities afforded Negroes within the district will, by the beginning of the next school year in September 1952, be made equal to those afforded white persons. Plaintiffs contend that because they are not now equal we should enter a decree abolishing segregation and opening all the schools of the district at once to white persons and Negroes. A sufficient answer is

that the defendants have complied with the decree of this court to equalize conditions as rapidly as was humanly possible . . . .

The court should not use its power to abolish segregation in a state where it is required by law if the equality demanded by the Constitution can be attained otherwise. This much is demanded by the spirit of comity which must prevail in the relationship between the agencies of the federal government and the states if our constitutional system is to endure.

Briggs v. Elliott, 103 F. Supp. 920, 922-23 (E.D.S.C. 1952).

The plaintiffs again sought Supreme Court review. The resulting decision follows.

Brown v. Board of Education ("Brown I")
347 U.S. 483 (1954)

■ *Mr. Chief Justice* WARREN *delivered the opinion of the Court.*

These cases come to us from the States of Kansas, South Carolina, Virginia, and Delaware. They are premised on different facts and different local conditions, but a common legal question justifies their consideration together in this consolidated opinion.

In each of the cases, minors of the Negro race, through their legal representatives, seek the aid of the courts in obtaining admission to the public schools of their community on a nonsegregated basis. In each instance, they have been denied admission to schools attended by white children under laws requiring or permitting segregation according to race. This segregation was alleged to deprive the plaintiffs of the equal protection of the laws under the Fourteenth Amendment. . . .

[The Court found the history of the Fourteenth Amendment's adoption "inconclusive" on the question presented.]

In the first cases in this Court construing the Fourteenth Amendment, decided shortly after its adoption, the Court interpreted it as proscribing all state-imposed discriminations against the Negro race. The doctrine of "separate but equal" did not make its appearance in this court until 1896 in the case of *Plessy v. Ferguson*, involving not education but transportation. American courts have since labored with the doctrine for over half a century. In this Court, there have been six cases involving the "separate but equal" doctrine in the field of public education. In *Cumming v. Board of Education of Richmond County*, and *Gong Lum v. Rice*, the validity of the doctrine itself was not challenged. In more recent cases, all on the graduate school level, inequality was found in that specific benefits enjoyed by white students were denied to Negro students of the same educational qualifications. *State of Missouri ex rel. Gaines v. Canada*; *Sipuel v. Board of Regents of University of Oklahoma*; *Sweatt v. Painter*; *McLaurin v. Oklahoma State Regents*. In none of these cases was it necessary to re-examine the doctrine to grant relief to the Negro plaintiff. And in *Sweatt v. Painter*, the

Court expressly reserved decision on the question whether *Plessy v. Ferguson* should be held inapplicable to public education.

In the instant cases, that question is directly presented. Here, unlike *Sweatt v. Painter*, there are findings below that the Negro and white schools involved have been equalized, or are being equalized, with respect to buildings, curricula, qualifications and salaries of teachers, and other "tangible" factors. Our decision, therefore, cannot turn on merely a comparison of these tangible factors in the Negro and white schools involved in each of the cases. We must look instead to the effect of segregation itself on public education.

In approaching this problem, we cannot turn the clock back to 1868 when the Amendment was adopted, or even to 1896 when *Plessy v. Ferguson* was written. We must consider public education in the light of its full development and its present place in American life throughout the Nation. Only in this way can it be determined if segregation in public schools deprives these plaintiffs of the equal protection of the laws.

Today, education is perhaps the most important function of state and local governments. Compulsory school attendance laws and the great expenditures for education both demonstrate our recognition of the importance of education to our democratic society. It is required in the performance of our most basic public responsibilities, even service in the armed forces. It is the very foundation of good citizenship. Today it is a principal instrument in awakening the child to cultural values, in preparing him for later professional training, and in helping him to adjust normally to his environment. In these days, it is doubtful that any child may reasonably be expected to succeed in life if he is denied the opportunity of an education. Such an opportunity, where the state has undertaken to provide it, is a right which must be made available to all on equal terms.

We come then to the question presented: Does segregation of children in public schools solely on the basis of race, even though the physical facilities and other "tangible" factors may be equal, deprive the children of the minority group of equal educational opportunities? We believe that it does.

In *Sweatt v. Painter*, in finding that a segregated law school for Negroes could not provide them equal educational opportunities, this Court relied in large part on "those qualities which are incapable of objective measurement but which make for greatness in a law school." In *McLaurin v. Oklahoma State Regents*, the Court, in requiring that a Negro admitted to a white graduate school be treated like all other students, again resorted to intangible considerations: "* * * his ability to study, to engage in discussions and exchange views with other students, and, in general, to learn his profession." Such considerations apply with added force to children in grade and high schools. To separate them from others of similar age and qualifications solely because of their race generates a feeling of inferiority as to their status in the community that may affect their hearts and minds in a way unlikely ever to be undone. The effect of this separation on their educational opportunities was well stated by a finding in the Kansas case by a court which nevertheless felt compelled to rule against the Negro plaintiffs:

"Segregation of white and colored children in public schools has a detrimental effect upon the colored children. The impact is greater when it has the sanction of the law; for the policy of separating the races is usually interpreted as denoting the inferiority of the negro group. A sense of inferiority affects the motivation of a child to learn. Segregation with the sanction of law, therefore, has a tendency to (retard) the educational and mental development of Negro children and to deprive them of some of the benefits they would receive in a racial(ly) integrated school system."

Whatever may have been the extent of psychological knowledge at the time of *Plessy v. Ferguson*, this finding is amply supported by modern authority. Any language in *Plessy v. Ferguson* contrary to this finding is rejected.

We conclude that in the field of public education the doctrine of "separate but equal" has no place. Separate educational facilities are inherently unequal. Therefore, we hold that the plaintiffs and others similarly situated for whom the actions have been brought are, by reason of the segregation complained of, deprived of the equal protection of the laws guaranteed by the Fourteenth Amendment. . . .

Because these are class actions, because of the wide applicability of this decision, and because of the great variety of local conditions, the formulation of decrees in these cases presents problems of considerable complexity. . . . [T]he cases will be restored to the docket, and the parties are requested to present further argument [regarding remedies]. . . .

It is so ordered.

Notes and Questions

1. Consider Nathan Margold's insights in developing the NAACP's core strategy and Charles Hamilton Houston's and Thurgood Marshall's key innovations in implementing it. What factors influenced the NAACP's choices about which cases to bring, where, and when?

2. Note the role of the NAACP's prior victories in the *Brown* opinion itself. What does the sequencing of cases reveal about impact litigation campaigns?

3. What strategies did the various defendants and their allies employ? Which if any of these strategies are legitimate for a lawyer to advise a client to pursue? Which strategies were the most effective, and why? What lessons should counsel advising institutional defendants (like local and state agencies, police departments, and school boards) today draw from the *Brown* campaign? What types of defenses and tactics should impact litigators be prepared to counter?

4. Consider the relationship between the plaintiffs and the lawyers in the cases on the road to *Brown*. Whose cases were these? For whose ends? What sacrifices did the plaintiffs make to participate in the NAACP campaign?

5. Now consider the aftermath of *Brown*. The decision was powerful in many ways—in rejecting formal, legal separation by race in education; recognizing the stigmatic harm of segregation to black children; rejecting the separate-but-equal

doctrine in education and paving the way for its ultimate repudiation across the board; and helping create momentum for further civil rights victories to follow, including new federal statutes aimed at securing equality in voting, employment, and housing. Yet the legacy of *Brown* is mixed. The year after *Brown I*, the Court held in *Brown II* that the implementation of desegregation would be the responsibility of local district courts throughout the country, proceeding with "all deliberate speed." This oxymoronic phrase turned out to presage more deliberation than speed, and the next decade and a half of desegregation efforts were marred by what became known as "massive resistance"—a combination of gamesmanship, delay, and outright defiance on the part of school authorities, which mostly succeeded in thwarting the mandate of *Brown* for years. A decade after *Brown*, less than 2 percent of African-American students were attending school with white students. *See* Erwin Chemerinsky, *The Segregation and Resegregation of American Public Education: The Courts' Role*, 81 N.C. L. Rev. 1597, 1603 (2003).

By the end of the 1960s, the courts were taking a more aggressive approach to recalcitrant school districts, and the pace of desegregation increased. But the Court now faced political backlash, in part due to its desegregation efforts. Beginning in 1974, the Supreme Court, now with four new Nixon appointees, began to limit the types of desegregation remedies courts could impose, and decisions in the 1980s and 1990s from an increasingly conservative Court marked out a path for school boards to have desegregation orders lifted. These court decisions, together with demographic shifts brought about by the decisions of white city dwellers to move to suburbs ("white flight"), halted the progress of school integration, which reached its peak in the late 1980s. By the 1990s, schools were becoming increasingly re-segregated. *See id.* at 1598 (citing Gary Orfield, The Civil Rights Project, Harvard University, *Schools More Separate: Consequences of a Decade of Resegregation* (2001)).

We'll study the legal doctrines governing institutional reform litigation in Chapter 12, but this brief overview of *Brown*'s implementation offers an important cautionary note about the promise of institutional reform litigation. Decades of careful planning, organizing, strategizing, and litigating won a great legal victory in 1954, but many of the NAACP's goals for circumstances on the ground were stalled for years, and subsequent gains reversed. Based on this history, what additional strategies would you advise today's would-be Thurgood Marshalls to pursue alongside their legal advocacy?

B. BEYOND INSTITUTIONAL REFORM: TARGETING LAWS OR POLICIES

The litigation seeking to desegregate the nation's schools sought not only to change the shape of the law but also to transform the structure and operation of a set of governmental institutions. Not all impact litigation seeks institutional reform. Some of the most momentous impact litigation efforts in recent years have aimed solely at changing the interpretation of the law, usually principles of constitutional law. And some impact litigation can have far-reaching effects simply by obtaining a decision applying legal rules already in force to strike down a government policy or practice of particular import.

This section introduces examples of non-institutional impact litigation through injunctive relief aimed at law reform or halting particular policies or practices. As you consider the examples discussed, compare the strategies, tactics, and goals of the litigators and plaintiffs here to those of their counterparts in institutional reform litigation.

1. CHANGING THE LAW

Non-structural injunctions can create change in a variety of ways—such as by recognizing new rights, extending existing ones, or cabining or overturning existing legal precedents.

(a) **Marriage equality litigation.** Cases aimed at making marriage available to same-sex couples were attempted at least as early as the 1970s, *see Baker v. Nelson*, 191 N.W.2d 185 (Minn. 1971) (rejecting constitutional claims), *appeal dismissed*, 409 U.S. 810 (1972); the modern campaign began with state-court litigation in the 1990s and early 2000s. Advocates targeted states in which they thought they could establish state constitutional entitlements to same-sex civil unions or marriages; although these rights would be limited to certain states, they would, because of their grounding in state law, be insulated from review by a conservative Supreme Court. A Hawaii trial court held that denying recognition to a same-sex marriage violated the state constitution, *Baehr v. Miike*, 1996 WL 694235 (Haw. Cir. Ct. Dec. 3, 1996), but that decision was overridden by state constitutional amendment in 1998, Haw. Const. art. I, § 23. A Vermont case succeeded in requiring the state to recognize same-sex civil unions, *Baker v. State*, 744 A.2d 864 (Vt. 1999), and then a Massachusetts decision required state recognition of same-sex marriage itself, *Goodridge v. Dep't of Pub. Health*, 798 N.E.2d 941 (Mass. 2003).

As with the *Brown* campaign, political backlash was significant. In addition to the Hawaii constitutional amendment just mentioned, Congress, spurred by the Hawaii litigation (and probably also election-year politics) passed the Defense of Marriage Act (DOMA) in 1996. That law defined marriage for all federal-law purposes as limited to opposite-sex marriages. Following the Massachusetts court decision, voters in eleven states amended their state constitutions on Election Day 2004 to ban same-sex marriage. *See* James Dao, *Same-Sex Marriage Issue Key to Some G.O.P. Races*, N.Y. Times, Nov. 4, 2004. However, the marriage-equality campaign continued to progress, notching victories through the political process as well as in court. By the time the issue of same-sex marriage reached the Supreme Court, a dozen states recognized same-sex marriage.

Against this backdrop, consider the factual context in which marriage-equality advocates finally presented their case to the Supreme Court in *United States v. Windsor*, 570 U.S. 744 (2013), which challenged DOMA:

Edith Windsor and Thea Spyer met in New York City in 1963 and began a long-term relationship. Windsor and Spyer registered as domestic partners when New York City gave that right to same-sex couples in 1993. Concerned about Spyer's health, the couple made the 2007 trip to Canada for their marriage, but they continued to reside in New York City. The State of New York deems their Ontario marriage to be a valid one.

Spyer died in February 2009, and left her entire estate to Windsor. Because DOMA denies federal recognition to same-sex spouses, Windsor did not qualify for the marital exemption from the federal estate tax, which excludes from taxation "any interest in property which passes or has passed from the decedent to his surviving spouse." Windsor paid $363,053 in estate taxes and sought a refund. The Internal Revenue Service denied the refund, concluding that, under DOMA, Windsor was not a "surviving spouse." Windsor commenced this refund suit . . . [arguing] that DOMA violates the guarantee of equal protection . . . .

DOMA had far-reaching effects, the Court explained:

By its great reach, DOMA touches many aspects of married and family life, from the mundane to the profound. It prevents same-sex married couples from obtaining government healthcare benefits they would otherwise receive. It deprives them of the Bankruptcy Code's special protections for domestic-support obligations. It forces them to follow a complicated procedure to file their state and federal taxes jointly. It prohibits them from being buried together in veterans' cemeteries. . . .

DOMA also brings financial harm to children of same-sex couples. It raises the cost of health care for families by taxing health benefits provided by employers to their workers' same-sex spouses. And it denies or reduces benefits allowed to families upon the loss of a spouse and parent, benefits that are an integral part of family security.

In *Windsor*, the Supreme Court struck down DOMA as violating equal protection and due process principles.

Two years later, in *Obergefell v. Hodges*, 135 S. Ct. 2584 (2015), the Supreme Court held that *states'* refusal to recognize same-sex marriages was likewise unconstitutional. The Supreme Court described the plaintiffs in that case as follows:

Petitioner James Obergefell . . . met John Arthur over two decades ago. They fell in love and started a life together, establishing a lasting, committed relation. In 2011, however, Arthur was diagnosed with amyotrophic lateral sclerosis, or ALS. This debilitating disease is progressive, with no known cure. Two years ago, Obergefell and Arthur decided to commit to one another, resolving to marry before Arthur died. To fulfill their mutual promise, they traveled from Ohio to Maryland, where same-sex marriage was legal. It was difficult for Arthur to move, and so the couple were wed inside a medical transport plane as it remained on the tarmac in Baltimore. Three months later, Arthur died. Ohio law does not permit Obergefell to be listed as the surviving spouse on Arthur's death certificate. By statute, they must remain strangers even in death, a state-imposed separation Obergefell deems "hurtful for the rest of time." He brought suit to be shown as the surviving spouse on Arthur's death certificate.

April DeBoer and Jayne Rowse . . . celebrated a commitment ceremony to honor their permanent relation in 2007. They both work as nurses, DeBoer in a neonatal unit and Rowse in an emergency unit. In 2009, DeBoer and Rowse fostered and then adopted a baby boy. Later that same year, they welcomed another son into their family. The new baby, born prematurely and abandoned by his biological mother, required around-the-clock care. The next year, a baby girl with special needs joined their family. Michigan, however, permits only opposite-sex married couples or single individuals to adopt, so each child can have only one woman as his or her legal parent. If an emergency were to arise, schools and hospitals may treat the three children as if they had only one parent. And, were tragedy to befall either DeBoer or Rowse, the other would have no legal rights over the children she had not been permitted to adopt. . . .

Army Reserve Sergeant First Class Ijpe DeKoe and his partner Thomas Kostura . . . fell in love. In 2011, DeKoe received orders to deploy to Afghanistan. Before leaving, he and Kostura married in New York. A week later, DeKoe began his deployment, which lasted for almost a year. When he returned, the two settled in Tennessee, where DeKoe works full-time for the Army Reserve. Their lawful marriage is stripped from them whenever they reside in Tennessee, returning and disappearing as they travel across state lines.

In what way does this campaign echo the *Brown* campaign in terms of strategies and methods of proceeding? In what ways does it differ?

What characteristics of the plaintiffs in *Windsor* and *Obergefell* do you think contributed to making these cases successful?

Brown was unanimous; *Windsor* and *Obergefell* were 5-4. Yet the resistance to *Windsor* and *Obergefell* has been much shorter and less widespread than the resistance to *Brown*. What do you think accounts for the relative speed and success of the marriage equality campaign as compared with *Brown*? The degree to which each campaign's victories imposed burdens on those who oppose it? The strategies and tactics employed? Differences in the degree of society's hostility to the ends sought? Something else?

(b) Establishing an individual right to bear arms. Impact litigation is not solely the domain of causes or organizations identified with the political left. One of the most successful law-reform campaigns in recent years is one identified with the political right: obtaining protection for an individual right to bear arms.

Prior to the early 2000s, federal courts of appeals had consistently ruled that the Second Amendment did not establish an individual right to possess and use firearms; the Supreme Court's last significant treatment of the question had unanimously rejected a Second Amendment defense to a federal prosecution for unlawfully transporting a sawed-off shotgun across state lines. *See United States v. Miller*, 307 U.S. 174, 178 (1939) ("In the absence of any evidence tending to show that possession or use of a 'shotgun having a barrel of less than eighteen inches in length' at this time has some reasonable relationship to the preservation or efficiency of a well regulated militia, we cannot say that the Second Amendment guarantees the right to keep and bear such an instrument.").

Beginning in the 1980s and 1990s, a growing body of legal scholarship, some funded by the National Rifle Association, but others published by left-leaning academics, argued for a more robust reading of the provision. More than a hundred articles on the Second Amendment were published after 1980, a majority of which argued that the Second Amendment established an individual right. *See* Peter Finn, *NRA Money Helped Reshape Gun Law*, Wash. Post, Mar. 13, 2013.

Consider the context in which libertarian advocates sought to bring this history to the Supreme Court and ask for recognition of an individual right. As the Court recited the facts in *District of Columbia v. Heller*, 554 U.S. 570 (2008):

> The District of Columbia generally prohibits the possession of handguns. It is a crime to carry an unregistered firearm, and the registration of handguns is prohibited. Wholly apart from that prohibition, no person may carry a handgun without a license, but the chief of police may issue licenses for 1-year periods. District of Columbia law also requires residents to keep their lawfully owned firearms, such as registered long guns, "unloaded and dissembled or bound by a trigger lock or similar device" unless they are located in a place of business or are being used for lawful recreational activities.
>
> Respondent Dick Heller is a D.C. special police officer authorized to carry a handgun while on duty at the Thurgood Marshall Judiciary Building. He applied for a registration certificate for a handgun that he wished to keep at home, but the District refused. He thereafter filed a lawsuit in the Federal District Court for the District of Columbia seeking, on Second Amendment grounds, to enjoin the city from enforcing the bar on the registration of handguns, the licensing requirement insofar as it prohibits the carrying of a firearm in the home without a license, and the trigger-lock requirement insofar as it prohibits the use of "functional firearms within the home."

Relying on historical analysis, the Court in *Heller* recognized an individual right to bear arms and struck down the District's ban. The Court subsequently held that the Second Amendment restrained the actions of states as well as that of federal actors and territories. *McDonald v. City of Chicago*, 561 U.S. 742 (2010).

What lessons does this brief history of gun-rights litigation provide about the tools available to impact litigators? In what types of legal contexts are academic articles likely to be most effective as building blocks toward impact litigation? Would a slew of articles have helped advocates for school desegregation or marriage equality? Why or why not?

What aspects of the facts in *Heller* do you think made the case attractive to impact litigators? What risks did they run in choosing the case they did?

What do the facts of *Heller* have in common with *Windsor* and cases on the road to *Brown*? What generalizations can you make about the types of elements present in successful impact litigation?

In the years following *Heller* and *McDonald*, gun-rights advocates have challenged additional gun restrictions, but with limited success: "[T]he broader trend in the courts has been to uphold most forms of gun control," Adam Winkler, *Is the Second Amendment Becoming Irrelevant?* 93 Ind. L.J. 253, 256 (2018), and some Justices have decried "the treatment of the Second Amendment as a disfavored right." *Peruta v. California*, 137 S. Ct. 1995, 1999 (2017) (Thomas, J., dissenting from denial of certiorari). (The Court did, however, agree to hear a Second Amendment case in its October 2019 Term.) Based on the lessons of school desegregation and marriage equality, how would you advise gun-rights advocates to proceed? What types of cases should they bring? How do public opinion regarding gun control and the mass-shooting epidemic in the United States affect their chances for further progress?

(c) Setting up impact litigation to target precedents. Sometimes precedent-setting litigation can be engineered by prospective litigation *defendants*.

For instance, in 2019, several states enacted anti-abortion legislation that appears inconsistent with the Supreme Court's current abortion jurisprudence. Yet proponents of the new laws seem eager to see them tested in court, hoping that the Supreme Court will overturn or further narrow its 1973 *Roe v. Wade* decision recognizing constitutional protection for abortion. *See* K.K. Rebecca Lai, *Abortion Bans: 9 States Have Passed Bills to Limit the Procedure This Year*, N.Y. Times, May 29, 2019. Effectively, this strategy entails setting up impact cases from the *defendant's* side: Because what advocates are trying to overturn is a court decision rather than a statute or policy, they need to pass a law that will be challenged so that the precedent they are targeting can be revisited.

Challenges to precedents can sometimes be engineered through litigation strategy as well as legislation: A party can disclaim what might be a winning litigation position in order to test the validity of the underlying legal rule. For instance, consider the proceedings in *United States v. Flores-Montano*, 541 U.S. 149 (2004). There, a U.S. customs official at the California-Mexico border tapped a vehicle attempting to enter the United States and noticed that the gas tank sounded solid. The official then called a mechanic to disassemble the gas tank; the wait for the mechanic and subsequent disassembly took between thirty and sixty minutes. The search yielded more than eighty pounds of marijuana. In the ensuring criminal prosecution, the car owner successfully moved to suppress the evidence:

> Relying on [*United States v. Molina-Tarazon*, 279 F.3d 709 (9th Cir. 2002)], respondent filed a motion to suppress the marijuana recovered from the gas tank. In *Molina-Tarazon*, a divided panel of the Court of Appeals held, inter alia, that removal of a gas tank requires reasonable suspicion in order to be consistent with the Fourth Amendment.
>
> The Government advised the District Court that it was not relying on reasonable suspicion as a basis for denying respondent's suppression motion, but that it believed *Molina-Tarazon* was wrongly decided. The District Court, relying on *Molina-Tarazon*, held that reasonable suspicion was required to justify the search and, accordingly, granted respondent's motion to suppress. The Court of Appeals, citing *Molina-Tarazon*, summarily affirmed the District Court's judgment.

The government sought review in the Supreme Court, which reversed, holding that the Fourth Amendment permitted removal of a gas tank as part of a border search without reasonable suspicion. By forgoing reliance on reasonable suspicion (which might well have existed, given the agent's initial tapping on the side of the car), the government increased its risk of losing the case, in exchange for the possibility of winning a more important victory. The government's gamble paid off.

In what sense is *Flores-Montano* impact litigation? How does the government's use of impact litigation principles and tactics differ from the use of these principles and tactics by non-governmental advocacy organizations? How do government and nonprofit impact litigation differ from each other in terms of the potential for misalignment between the goals of counsel and client?

What lessons, if any, can impact litigators seeking to attack precedents draw from the other examples of impact litigation we have considered?

2. Injunctions against specific statutes, policies, and practices

Suits to enforce civil rights can have a significant impact without establishing or redefining a constitutional right. In recent years, advocates seeking to enforce various civil and constitutional rights have won major victories, often in lower courts, in the form of injunctions against wide-ranging or symbolically important statutes, policies, and practices alleged to violate various civil rights. A sampling of prominent examples over the course of the past fifteen years includes:

- *J.D. v. Azar*, 925 F.3d 1291 (D.C. Cir. 2019) (affirming classwide injunction against federal policy of refusing to permit undocumented, unaccompanied immigrant minors in federal custody to leave the facilities at which they were held to access abortion services);
- *Ms. L. v. U.S. Immigration & Customs Enforcement*, 310 F. Supp. 3d 1133 (S.D. Cal. 2018), *modified*, 330 F.R.D. 284 (S.D. Cal. 2019) (enjoining, as violation of due process, federal policy of separating parents in immigration detention from their children), *appeal pending*;
- *Stout by Stout v. Jefferson Cty. Bd. of Educ.*, 882 F.3d 988 (11th Cir. 2018) (rejecting racially motivated attempt by Alabama town to secede from school district under continuing desegregation order);
- *Trinity Lutheran Church of Columbia, Inc. v. Comer*, 137 S. Ct. 2012 (2017) (holding that exclusion of church preschool from state program providing grants to purchase rubber playground surfaces violated Free Exercise Clause of the First Amendment);
- *Whitaker v. Kenosha Unified Sch. Dist. No. 1 Bd. of Educ.*, 858 F.3d 1034 (7th Cir. 2017) (affirming injunction, on equal protection and statutory grounds, requiring school to permit transgender boy to use boys' restroom);
- *Lebron v. Sec'y of Fla. Dep't of Children & Families*, 772 F.3d 1352, 1355 (11th Cir. 2014) (affirming injunction, on Fourth Amendment grounds, against Florida law mandating suspicionless drug testing of applicants for welfare benefits);
- *Burwell v. Hobby Lobby Stores, Inc.*, 573 U.S. 682 (2014) (holding that administrative regulations requiring closely-held businesses to provide their employees with health-insurance coverage for contraception, in contravention of business owners' religious beliefs, violated Religious Freedom Restoration Act);

- *Lozano v. City of Hazleton*, 724 F.3d 297 (3d Cir. 2013) (enjoining, as pre-empted by federal law, local ordinances prohibiting renting housing to or employing undocumented immigrants);
- *Melendres v. Arpaio*, 695 F.3d 990 (9th Cir. 2012) (in case alleging racial profiling of Latino drivers by Maricopa County, Arizona, Sheriff's Office, affirming injunction, on Fourth Amendment grounds, against detaining any individual based only on knowledge or belief that the individual is unlawfully present in the United States);
- *John Doe, Inc. v. Mukasey*, 549 F.3d 861 (2d Cir. 2008) (upholding in part injunction, on First Amendment grounds, against enforcement of provisions of USA PATRIOT Act imposing non-disclosure requirements on recipients of investigative demands known as "National Security Letters"); and
- *Kitzmiller v. Dover Area Sch. Dist.*, 400 F. Supp. 2d 707 (M.D. Pa. 2005) (enjoining, as violation of the Establishment Clause of the First Amendment, high school's teaching of "intelligent design").

Which constraints on broader campaigns like those of *Brown*, *Windsor*, and *Heller* are less likely to apply to suits seeking more targeted injunctions? What lessons of the broader campaigns do you think advocates should consider when building cases like the ones listed?

C. IMPACT THROUGH DAMAGES SUITS

Unlike injunctions against unconstitutional laws or policies, money damages cannot directly halt unconstitutional activity, only compensate the victims of such activity after the fact. Nonetheless, damages, like injunctions, can have effects extending beyond the parties to the litigation.

Damages may serve as a deterrent to future misconduct. Potential repeat-player defendants who have the capacity to violate rights over and over—government agencies, cities, school boards, and law enforcement officers—should logically respond to a damages award for unconstitutional behavior by changing that behavior, lest they be once again dragged into court, forced to spend time and money defending themselves, and exposed to additional liability.

Courts frequently cite deterrence of wrongdoers (alongside compensation of victims) as a core of purpose of damages in civil rights cases, and courts assume damages awards will influence future conduct. *See, e.g., City of Riverside v. Rivera*, 477 U.S. 561, 575 (1986) (plurality opinion) ("[T]he damages a plaintiff recovers contribute[] significantly to the deterrence of civil rights violations in the future."); *Carlson v. Green*, 446 U.S. 14, 21 (1980) ("It is almost axiomatic that the threat of damages has a deterrent effect[.]"). If damages are awarded against an institutional actor rather than an individual, the entity may respond by changing policies and retraining or discharging rogue officials. *See, e.g., City of Newport v. Fact Concerts, Inc.*, 453 U.S. 247, 269 (1981); Richard H. Fallon, Jr. & Daniel J. Meltzer, *New Law, Non-Retroactivity, and Constitutional Remedies*, 104 Harv. L. Rev. 1731, 1788 (1991);

Pamela S. Karlan, *The Paradoxical Structure of Constitutional Litigation*, 75 Fordham L. Rev. 1913, 1918 (2007).

Some commentators have challenged these assumptions about how damages operate as a deterrent: Police departments and municipalities, they argue, do not respond to financial incentives alone; for instance, they may have political incentives to tolerate or even reward "tough" policing that crosses the constitutional line. *See, e.g.,* Barbara E. Armacost, *Organizational Culture and Police Misconduct*, 72 Geo. Wash. L. Rev. 453, 475 (2004); Daryl J. Levinson, *Making Government Pay: Markets, Politics, and the Allocation of Constitutional Costs*, 67 U. Chi. L. Rev. 345, 347 (2000). Further, the ultimate payouts in litigation may not be near enough in time to the incidents giving rise to them, or large enough relative to the entire budget of a police department, to induce policymakers to change course in response. *See* Armacost, *supra,* at 474-75.

Which set of assumptions more accurately describes damages' deterrent effect (or lack thereof)? Professor Joanna Schwartz has researched the degree to which police departments track and respond to litigation about their conduct. The results of her study of twenty-six law enforcement agencies across the country suggest that in many departments, the mechanisms through which lawsuits could produce a deterrent effect are absent:

> Most police departments lack sufficient information about past suits to draw any sensible lessons. Some police departments completely ignore information from law-suits. Other departments try to gather information from suits, but their efforts are frustrated by technological problems, human error, and efforts to obfuscate relevant information.

Joanna C. Schwartz, *Myths and Mechanics of Deterrence: The Role of Lawsuits in Law Enforcement Decisionmaking*, 57 UCLA L. Rev. 1023, 1085 (2010). Accordingly, Professor Schwartz contends:

> Officials may pay attention to lawsuits that lead to large judgments or political repercussions. But most departments ignore lawsuits that do not inspire front-page newspaper stories, candlelight vigils, or angry meetings with the mayor. The city attorney will defend these suits, any settlement or judgment will be paid out of the city's coffer, and the department will not keep track of which officers were named, what claims were alleged, what evidence was amassed, what resolution was reached, or what amount was paid.

Joanna C. Schwartz, *What Police Learn from Lawsuits*, 33 Cardozo L. Rev. 841, 844 (2012).

Nonetheless, Professor Schwartz has also found encouraging results among the handful of departments that *do* seek to learn from litigation against them:

> [L]awsuits have notified officials of misconduct allegations that did not surface through these other reporting systems. For example, the Los Angeles Sheriff's Department's review of lawsuit claims revealed clusters of improper vehicle pur-suits, illegal searches, and warrantless home entries. These vehicle pursuits, searches, and home entries did not appear in officers' use-of-force reports because the events—while potentially serious constitutional violations—did not involve the

application of force as defined by department policies and so did not trigger reporting requirements. . . .

Even when a civilian complaint or use-of-force report is filed, the litigation process can unearth details that did not surface during the internal investigation. When, for example, a man died of blunt force chest trauma two hours after being taken into Portland police custody, a critical question was how much force the involved deputies had used to bring him to the ground. The night of the man's death, the involved officer and deputy were videotaped at the Portland jail describing their confrontation. The audio portion of the tape was very scratchy, but Portland's internal affairs investigators did nothing to improve the sound. Only during litigation did plaintiff's counsel enhance the audio, at which point the involved officer's statements were found to contradict his statement to internal affairs.

Id. at 845. Although Professor Schwartz identifies limits to information-gathering through litigation (such as the gap in time between the events at issue and the revelation of relevant information, and the fact that lawsuits may succeed or fail for reasons unrelated to the merits of their claims), she posits that damages lawsuits have the potential to change the behavior of law enforcement far more than they currently do.

In addition to police departments' failure to gather information about suits against them, other institutional factors may limit policymakers' ability to implement reforms based on lessons learned in litigation, as Professor Rachel Harmon observes:

[F]ederal law cannot achieve much reform by imposing liability if state and local laws impose significant costs on the most effective reforms, creating countervailing economic and political incentives not to adopt them. This is the case now.

In a majority of states, for example, civil service laws heavily regulate recruiting, promoting, transferring, demoting, and terminating public employees, including police officers. . . . [T]hese laws empower employees to challenge any internal managerial action that affects them on both substantive and procedural grounds in a formal adversarial process. These challenges ensure frequent and costly legal battles when police departments demote, transfer, or fire any officer. . . .

A supervisor facing an officer who sometimes uses too much force faces two basic options: he can address the problem by transferring, retraining, demoting, or firing him, or he can leave him be. If the supervisor does nothing, the officer may someday engage in misconduct, which may cause cognizable injury to a victim. That victim may find a lawyer willing to sue, and the city may face some costs as a result, which may translate into some costs for the department. But if the supervisor transfers, demotes, or fires the officer, or even if he demands retraining, the same supervisor faces the practical certainty that the officer will appeal within the civil service system. . . .

Collective bargaining rights deter department-wide changes intended to prevent constitutional violations even more dramatically. . . . In the thirty-six states that require collective bargaining, police departments are required to bargain with police unions before imposing any new rule that could affect any term or condition of employment. . . . An agreement will presumably require compromise with the union, which typically will oppose policies that increase internal accountability for police officers.

Rachel A. Harmon, *The Problem of Policing*, 110 Mich. L. Rev. 761, 796-99 (2012).

To the extent damages are unreliable as a force of deterrence, are civil rights suits for money at all useful as impact litigation? There are several other respects in which they may be:

First, a damages case might result in law reform if it sets a meaningful precedent on appeal. For instance, prominent damages cases brought under constitutional provisions or federal civil rights statutes have shaped the scope and application of these sources of law. *See, e.g., Faragher v. City of Boca Raton*, 524 U.S. 775 (1998) (damages action under Title VII for employment discrimination based on sex; Court ruling helped define the scope of employer liability for sexual harassment); *Hudson v. McMillian*, 503 U.S. 1 (1992) (in prisoner's lawsuit seeking damages for assault by prison guards, Court held that Eighth Amendment prohibits excessive force against prisoners even where prisoner's injuries do not require medical treatment).

Second, if a damages case attracts significant media attention, it might increase scrutiny of problematic practices or change public opinion on an issue—first steps to legislative change in the future or a shift in societal norms. Professor Myriam Gilles argues that, through damages suits, "valuable information is unearthed and exposed," and "this sort of information and publicity . . . induces municipal policy-makers to take remedial actions." For instance, "the otherwise subterranean forces that are exposed in constitutional tort litigation against municipalities tend to draw a great deal of media attention, as evidenced by the 'above-the-fold' coverage of the New Jersey State Troopers in the recent racial profiling cases, and the NYPD in the Amadou Diallo case, to name but two prominent examples." The first incident to which Professor Gilles was referring was the 1998 police shooting of four black or Latino men riding together down the New Jersey Turnpike on their way to try out for basketball scholarships; the incident spurred a state-wide investigation into racial profiling in New Jersey. The second incident, which attracted national attention, was the shooting of an unarmed twenty-two-year-old West African man who was reaching for his wallet as New York City police officers questioned him in front of his home; the officers shot him forty-one times. Myriam E. Gilles, *In Defense of Making Government Pay: The Deterrent Effect of Constitutional Tort Remedies*, 35 Ga. L. Rev. 845, 859-61 & n.60 (2001). The Diallo family filed a wrongful death suit, which settled for $3 million; the police department abolished the unit whose officers shot Diallo. *See* Alan Feuer, *$3 Million Deal in Police Killing of Diallo in '99*, N.Y. Times, Jan. 7, 2004. Thus, "constitutional damage remedies, although denominated in dollars, clearly translate into the political currency that moves political actors." Gilles, *supra*, at 861.

Third, a suit for damages might garner enough attention from policymakers that they reform laws or policies even if the specific defendants would not have changed their own behavior in response to the lawsuit. Or if both the plaintiffs and the institutional defendant are more interested in policy reforms than in monetary compensation, a suit for damages might be settled for policy changes that could not have been imposed by a court or sought by the plaintiff directly. Consider, for instance, a set of influential damages cases involving protestors in the nation's capital. A May 1971 mass demonstration on the steps of the U.S. Capitol protesting U.S. military involvement in Vietnam (part of what became known as the "May Day" protests) ended in a mass arrest by U.S. Capitol Police and Washington, D.C., police. The resulting lawsuit for damages (along with expungement of convictions) on behalf of the arrested demonstrators yielded a substantial jury verdict. *See Dellums v. Powell*, 566 F.2d 167, 173-74 (D.C. Cir. 1977). Six years after the May Day arrests, a D.C. Circuit judge observed that police practices had changed in response: "A new police chief has had the benefit of reflection concerning what was done in the past and what the courts have said about those incidents" and "[t]he police department has manifested an attitude of low-key avoidance of confrontation." *Wash. Mobilization Comm. v. Cullinane*, 566 F.2d 107, 130 (D.C. Cir. 1977) (Leventhal, J., concurring in the denial of rehearing en banc). Another set of cases challenging a problematic mass arrest by D.C. police decades later spurred both formal policy change and legislative reform. In September 2002, during a demonstration against a World Bank meeting in Washington, police witnessed acts of vandalism, including the smashing of a window and overturning of trash cans and newspaper vending machines. A high-ranking police official ordered that hundreds of demonstrators who had gathered in Pershing Park be cordoned off by police and then arrested, even though no warning or dispersal order had been given, and the official could not be sure that the park contained only demonstrators who had violated the law. *See Barham v. Ramsey*, 434 F.3d 565, 568, 573-74 (D.C. Cir. 2006). Two cases seeking primarily damages were filed on behalf of groups of arrested demonstrators. (Requests for injunctive relief were included in both complaints, but in one case the request was not acted on, and in the other a preliminary injunction was denied as moot.) One of the cases was resolved by a settlement and consent decree under which the District paid hundreds of thousands of dollars to plaintiffs and also changed its policy regarding responses to demonstrations. *See Abbate v. Ramsey*, 355 F. Supp. 2d 377 (D.D.C. 2005). And, prompted in part by the Pershing Park incident, the D.C. Council passed a law to rein in police conduct at demonstrations by, for instance, restricting use of pepper spray and mass arrests. *See* First Amendment Assemblies Act, D.C. Code § 5-331.01 et seq.; D.C. Council Comm. on the Judiciary, Report on Bill No. 15-968 at 1 (Dec. 1, 2004) (opening with references to police responses to prior demonstrations, including "anti-globalization demonstrations . . . in 2002," and noting that the Council was enacting safeguards that were "first proposed in litigation following the 1971 'May Day' demonstrations against the Vietnam War").

Given the uncertainty surrounding various models for change through damages suits (including deterrence), why don't plaintiffs always seek injunctive relief along with damages? The answer is that the circumstances under which injunctive relief can be sought are narrower than those in which damages are available: Plaintiffs can seek damages whenever violations of their rights have caused them injury; injunctions can be imposed only where plaintiffs show that the injury complained of is ongoing or likely to befall them again. (We'll cover limitations on injunctive relief in detail in Chapter 11.)

What questions should impact litigators ask when building a civil rights case for damages? What factors beyond the legal merits can influence whether a damages case has the potential for impact beyond the parties themselves? How do the factors relevant to assessing potential impact vary based on the type of relief sought?

Do these various examples change your view of what impact litigation is, or should be? Can you think of circumstances in which impact litigation of one kind or another is not currently common but could be effective.

D. CRITIQUES OF IMPACT LITIGATION

Although civil rights enforcement through private civil actions has arguably produced a great deal of positive impact, several thoughtful critiques question whether impact litigation gets more credit than it deserves.

Derrick Bell, the first tenured African-American professor at Harvard Law School, famously explained the result in *Brown* in terms of "interest convergence":

> [T]he issue of school segregation and the harm it inflicted on black children did not first come to the Court's attention in the *Brown* litigation: blacks had been attacking the validity of these policies for 100 years. Yet, prior to *Brown*, black claims that segregated public schools were inferior had been met by orders requiring merely that facilities be made equal. What accounted, then, for the sudden shift in 1954 away from the separate but equal doctrine and towards a commitment to desegregation?
>
> I contend that the decision in *Brown* to break with the Court's long-held position on these issues cannot be understood without some consideration of the decision's value to whites, not simply those concerned about the immorality of racial inequality, but also those whites in policymaking positions able to see the economic and political advances at home and abroad that would follow abandonment of segregation. First, the decision helped to provide immediate credibility to America's struggle with Communist countries to win the hearts and minds of emerging third world peoples. . . . [T]he point was not lost on the news media. *Time* magazine, for example, predicted that the international impact of *Brown* would be scarcely less important than its effect on the education of black children: "In many countries, where U.S. prestige and leadership have been damaged by the fact of U.S. segregation, it will come as a timely reassertion of the basic American principle that 'all men are created equal.'"
>
> Second, *Brown* offered much needed reassurance to American blacks that the precepts of equality and freedom so heralded during World War II might yet be given meaning at home. Returning black veterans faced not only continuing discrimination, but also violent attacks in the South which rivalled those that took place at the conclusion of World War I. Their disillusionment and anger were poignantly expressed by the black actor, Paul Robeson, who in 1949 declared: "It is unthinkable . . . that American Negroes would go to war on behalf of those who have oppressed us for generations . . . against a country [the Soviet Union] which in one generation has raised our people to the full human dignity of mankind." It is not impossible to imagine that fear of the spread of such sentiment influenced subsequent racial decisions made by the courts.
>
> Finally, there were whites who realized that the South could make the transition from a rural, plantation society to the sunbelt with all its potential and profit only

when it ended its struggle to remain divided by state-sponsored segregation. Thus, segregation was viewed as a barrier to further industrialization in the South. . . .

Here, as in the abolition of slavery, there were whites for whom recognition of the racial equality principle was sufficient motivation. But, as with abolition, the number who would act on morality alone was insufficient to bring about the desired racial reform.

Derrick A. Bell, Jr., *Brown v. Board of Education and the Interest-Convergence Dilemma*, 93 Harv. L. Rev. 518, 523-25 (1980).

A complementary critique to Professor Bell's charge regarding the interests operating behind the scenes of *Brown* is Professor Michelle Alexander's concern that the interests that are *supposed* to drive impact litigation are in fact inadequately represented—and that, as a result, critical problems like the mass incarceration of people of color receive insufficient attention from civil rights litigators:

> The success of the brilliant legal crusade that led to *Brown v. Board of Education* has created a widespread perception that civil rights lawyers are the most important players in racial justice advocacy. . . . As public attention shifted from the streets to the courtroom, the extraordinary grassroots movement that made civil rights legislation possible faded from public view. The lawyers took over. . . .
>
> Instead of a moral crusade, the movement became an almost purely legal crusade. Civil rights advocates pursued their own agendas as unelected representatives of communities defined by race and displayed considerable skill navigating courtrooms and halls of power across America. The law became what the lawyers and lobbyists said it was, with little or no input from the people whose fate hung in the balance. . . .
>
> Lawyers have a tendency to identify and concentrate on problems they know how to solve—i.e., problems that can be solved through litigation. The mass incarceration of people of color is not that kind of problem.
>
> Widespread preoccupation with litigation, however, is not the only—or even the main—reason civil rights groups have shied away from challenging the new caste system. Challenging mass incarceration requires something civil rights advocates have long been reluctant to do: advocacy on behalf of criminals. . . . The "politics of respectability" has influenced civil rights litigation and advocacy, leading even the most powerful civil rights organizations to distance themselves from the most stigmatized elements of the community, especially lawbreakers. Advocates have found they are most successful when they draw attention to certain types of black people (those who are easily understood by mainstream whites as "good" and "respectable") and tell certain types of stories about them. Since the days when abolitionists struggled to eradicate slavery, racial justice advocates have gone to great lengths to identify black people who defy racial stereotypes, and they have exercised considerable message discipline, telling only those stories of racial injustice that will evoke sympathy among whites.
>
> A prime example is the Rosa Parks story. Rosa Parks was not the first person to refuse to give up her seat on a segregated bus in Montgomery, Alabama. Civil rights advocates considered and rejected two other black women as plaintiffs when planning a test case challenging segregation practices: Claudette Colvin and Mary Louise Smith. Both of them were arrested for refusing to give up their seats on Montgomery's segregated buses, just months before Rosa Parks refused to budge.

Colvin was fifteen years old when she defied segregation laws. Her case attracted national attention, but civil rights advocates declined to use her as a plaintiff because she got pregnant by an older man shortly after her arrest. Advocates worried that her "immoral" conduct would detract from or undermine their efforts to show that blacks were entitled to (and worthy of) equal treatment. Likewise, they decided not to use Mary Louise Smith as a plaintiff because her father was rumored to be an alcoholic. . . .

The time-tested strategy of using those who epitomize moral virtue as symbols in racial justice campaigns is far more difficult to employ in efforts to reform the criminal justice system.

Alexander, *supra*, at 225-28.

One of the deepest critiques of impact litigation is that of Professor Gerald Rosenberg. His analysis, which contrasts the view that courts can be effective agents to produce or spur social change (what he calls the "Dynamic Court" position) with the view that such change can arise from judicial action only in very narrow circumstances (what he calls the "Constrained Court" position) continues to pose vital questions about the value of seeking social change via the judicial process:

For courts, or any other institution, to effectively produce significant social reform, they must have the ability to develop appropriate policies and the power to implement them. This, in turn, requires a host of tools that courts, according to proponents of the Constrained Court view, lack. In particular, successful implementation requires enforcement powers. Court decisions, requiring people to act, are not self-executing. . . . In other words, for Court orders to be carried out, political elites, electorally accountable, must support them and act to implement them. . . . President Jackson recognized these limits . . . when he reputedly remarked about a decision with which he did not agree, "John Marshall has made his decision, now let him enforce it." More recently, the unwillingness of state authorities to follow court orders, and the need to send federal troops to Little Rock, Arkansas, to carry them out, makes the same point. Without elite support (the federal government in this case), the Court's orders would have been frustrated. . . .

A further obstacle for court effectiveness, assert believers in the Constrained Court view, is that significant social reform often requires large expenditures. Judges, in general prohibited from actively politicking and cutting deals, are not in a particularly powerful position to successfully order the other branches to expend additional funds. . . . While there may be exceptions where courts seize financial resources, they are rare precisely because courts are hesitant to issue such orders which violate separation of powers by in effect appropriating public funds. . . .

The claims of the Constrained Court view about the judiciary's lack of tools, and its dependence on others to implement its decisions, can be illustrated by one kind of significant social reform, the wholesale reshaping of bureaucracies. . . . [S]uccessful reshaping requires the acquiescence, if not the support, of administrators and staff. . . . And if administrators and staffs don't act voluntarily, there is little judges can do. While courts do have the power to cite recalcitrant bureaucrats for contempt, the use of such coercive power tends to make martyrs out of resisters and to strengthen the resolve of others to prevent change. . . . [Courts] lack the resources to gain adequate understanding of the intricacies of reform and the tools to [e]nsure compliance. . . .

Lacking powerful tools to force implementation, court decisions are often rendered useless given much opposition. Even if litigators seeking significant social reform win major victories in court, in implementation they often turn out to be worth very little.

Gerald Rosenberg, *The Hollow Hope* 15, 18-21 (1991). Professor Rosenberg illustrates these constraints by comparing the relative degrees of success of desegregation and abortion litigation:

While both had legal precedents on which to construct a winning legal argument, little else was similar. With civil rights, there was a great deal of white hostility to blacks, especially in the South. On the whole, political leaders, particularly Southerners, were either supportive of segregation or unwilling to confront it as an important issue. In addition, court decisions required individuals and institutions hostile to civil rights to implement the changes. Until Congress acted a decade later, these two constraints remained and none of the conditions necessary for change were present. After congressional and executive actions were taken, the constraints were overcome and conditions for change were created, including the creation of incentives, costs, and the context in which courts could be used as cover. Only then did change occur. In contrast, at the time of the abortion decisions there was much public and elite support for abortion. There was an active reform movement in the states, and Congress was quiet, with no indication of the opposition that many of its members would later provide.

Id. at 337. Professor Rosenberg also considers whether litigation could make a significant impact beyond the effect of judicial rulings themselves by changing societal norms and thus catalyzing reform through political means. His view of this avenue is no rosier:

Only a minority of Americans know what the courts have done on important issues. Fewer still combine that knowledge with the belief in the Supreme Court's constitutional role, a combination that would enable the Court, and the lower courts, to legitimate behavior. This makes courts a particularly poor tool for changing opinions or for mobilization. . . . Rally round the flag is one thing but rally round the brief (or opinion) is quite another! The evidence from the movements examined makes dubious any claim for important extra-judicial effects of court action.

Id. at 338.

Notes and Questions

1. Do you find any of these critiques persuasive? If so, do they change your perspective on impact litigation? If not, what are these commentators missing?

2. Which types of impact litigation are most seriously challenged by each critique?

3. What steps should impact litigators take to ensure that their strategies align with the goals of their clients and of the communities they are attempting to serve?

4. Is Professor Bell's critique of the *Brown* decision inconsistent with the strategy pursued by the NAACP? Should racial-justice advocates embrace interest

convergence where possible as greasing the wheels of progress? Spurn it as a corrupt bargain that will undermine advocates' ultimate goals? Something in between?

5. Relatedly, when if ever is "respectability politics" justified in impact litigation? What are the advantages and disadvantages of deploying that strategy? If the strategy is used, would naming it mitigate its disadvantages or merely sap its effectiveness?

6. Do Professor Rosenberg's concerns suggest that impact litigation is more appropriate in certain circumstances than others? That it ever justifies its costs? How do you imagine impact litigators and organizations like the ACLU and NAACP would respond to his critiques? In light of the challenges he identifies, why does impact litigation still occur at all?

7. For all the planning and strategy reflected in the various examples of impact litigation described in this chapter, some of the most significant cases in our nation's history have been initiated by individuals representing themselves rather than lawyers connected with a broader campaign. For instance, *Gideon v. Wainwright*, 372 U.S. 335 (1963), which held that the Constitution requires the government to provide attorneys for criminal defendants who cannot afford them, reached the Supreme Court because a criminal defendant who had (unsuccessfully) defended himself at trial on a breaking-and-entering charge "scribbled a note" from his prison cell and mailed it to the Supreme Court. David Cole, Gideon v. Wainwright *and* Strickland v. Washington: *Broken Promises, in Criminal Procedure Stories* 101 (Carol S. Steiker ed., 2006). Likewise, a pro se prisoner filed the case that led to the decision in *Johnson v. California*, 543 U.S. 499 (2005), holding that a policy of housing prisoners only with other prisoners of the same race was presumptively unconstitutional.

   How do these examples complicate the landscape of impact litigation? What lessons should attorneys at impact litigation organizations draw from them? Do they vindicate Professor Alexander's concern that lawyers' agendas don't always match those of the populations they are purporting to serve?

8. Which do you think are more important, the direct or the indirect effects of impact litigation? Why?

9. Some organizations, including the ACLU, are moving toward a model of what has been referred to as "integrated advocacy"—combining impact litigation, legislative policy work, and public education in a multifaceted approach to law reform. Does this development blunt the force of Professor Rosenberg's criticisms? Does the fact that law-reform organizations are hiring community organizers and investigative reporters suggest that they might be better equipped in the future to bridge the gap Professor Alexander identifies between lawyers and their clients? Does the trend away from a pure litigation focus vindicate the critiques we have read? Or does it merely formalize what Thurgood Marshall and his disciples in the impact litigation movement have been doing all along?

PART I

CAUSES OF ACTION TO ENFORCE THE CONSTITUTION

We begin our study by examining the contours of the causes of action plaintiffs can assert to seek redress for violations of their federal constitutional rights. Our focus on "causes of action" is more extensive than you'll find in many fields of law, because in many areas, the questions of whether and how the substance of the law may be enforced in court are not subjects of ambiguity or controversy. For instance, many statutes—like the Administrative Procedure Act, the Freedom of Information Act, and the Fair Credit Reporting Act—provide in express terms that private suits are available. And at common law, the concept of a "cause of action" is often not meaningfully distinct from the substantive right the common law protects: The "cause of action" for a breach of a contract or negligence is simply "breach of contract" or "negligence." That is, the court must evaluate whether the elements of the common law claim are met, but it need not conduct an independent analysis of whether the wronged party is entitled to come to court to seek relief on that claim.

By contrast, in civil litigation to enforce constitutional rights, the distinction between the substance of the claim and the cause of action is an important one, and the existence of the latter cannot be presumed. The substance of the right is provided by the constitutional provision the plaintiff is seeking to enforce: the First Amendment for freedom of speech; the Fourteenth Amendment for equal protection; and so on. But whether or not a constitutional violation occurred—in fact, generally *before* a court will even *inquire* whether a constitutional violation has occurred—the plaintiff must independently identify a valid "cause of action" of the types discussed in this part. *See* John F. Preis, *How the Federal Cause of Action Relates to Rights, Remedies, and Jurisdiction*, 67 Fla. L. Rev. 849, 856 (2015) (explaining how, with respect to civil rights litigation, "causes of action exist in one place and rights exist 'elsewhere'").

The possibility that a victim of unconstitutional conduct may be unable to vindicate the relevant constitutional right might seem surprising and troubling. *See Marbury v. Madison*, 5 U.S. 137, 163 (1803) ("The very essence of civil liberty certainly consists in the right of every individual to claim the protection of the laws, whenever he receives an injury. . . . The government of the United States has been emphatically termed a government of laws, and not of men. It will certainly cease to deserve this high appellation, if the laws furnish no remedy for the violation of a vested legal right."). And yet the possibility of non-enforcement is a fundamental reality of civil rights litigation. Indeed, one of the central themes of this book is how and why gaps have developed between rights and remedies in the field of civil rights.

(This theme recurs throughout the book: Part II will explore defenses and limitations on liability that can apply even where a valid cause of action for a constitutional violation exists. Part III will consider enforcement problems— both causes of action and their limitations—that arise in enforcing federal *statutory* civil rights protections, such as antidiscrimination laws affecting employment and education. And Part IV will address limitations on the remedies available for the enforcement of civil rights—again even where a cause of action for such enforcement exists.)

Our study of causes of action in this part is divided into two chapters, one for constitutional claims against state and local actors, and one covering such claims against federal actors.

The Rise of 42 U.S.C. § 1983

42 U.S.C. § 1983 reads:

> Every person who, under color of any statute, ordinance, regulation, custom, or usage, of any State or Territory or the District of Columbia, subjects, or causes to be subjected, any citizen of the United States or other person within the jurisdiction thereof to the deprivation of any rights, privileges, or immunities secured by the Constitution and laws, shall be liable to the party injured in an action at law, suit in equity, or other proper proceeding for redress . . . .

This statutory provision, enacted as part of the Ku Klux Klan Act of 1871 (the history of which is discussed below in our first principal case, *Monroe v. Pape*), is the most important tool for enforcing constitutional rights through civil litigation. (In criminal cases, a defendant's constitutional rights are enforced through various motions depending on the circumstances—for instance, motions to suppress evidence acquired in violation of the Fourth Amendment. Violations of civil rights can also be criminally prosecuted.)

The interpretation of § 1983 has heavily influenced how, how often, to what extent, by whom, and even *whether* constitutional (and to some extent, statutory) rights may be enforced. Although we'll cover several other statutes and doctrines that facilitate enforcement of civil rights, doctrines relating to 42 U.S.C. § 1983 account for at least half of the material in this book.

It is therefore useful at the outset to unpack the language of the statute and identify what this book will cover, as well as where you might seek answers to the questions this book doesn't cover.

"Every person who"

Which "person[s]" can be sued under § 1983 is hotly contested. Does "person" apply to individual government officials? To municipal governments like cities, counties, and school boards? To a state government? We'll explore who is a proper defendant under § 1983 and what defenses different types of defendants can raise.

"under color of any statute, ordinance, regulation, custom, or usage, of any State or Territory or the District of Columbia"

The meaning of "under color" is the first question we'll consider. In particular, does it cover a government official's unconstitutional action where that act was not endorsed by the government for whom that official works, or only official acts carried out pursuant to a government policy?

"subjects, or causes to be subjected"

The question of causation works mainly like it does in tort law; indeed, § 1983 claims are often referred to as "constitutional tort" claims. One important difference from tort-law causation concerns municipal defendants, to which a stricter standard of causation applies under § 1983. We will not cover traditional tort causation, but we will cover the special rule for municipal liability.

"any citizen of the United States or other person within the jurisdiction thereof"

This phrase implicates important questions about substantive constitutional law—such as to what extent the Constitution protects people present in the United States unlawfully and to what extent the Constitution protects individuals abroad. Those questions are left to courses on Constitutional Law.

"to the deprivation of any rights, privileges, or immunities secured by the Constitution"

The questions of what rights the U.S. Constitution protects and what those rights entail are left to courses on Constitutional Law.

"and laws"

We'll cover the complex subject of when § 1983 provides a remedy for violations of rights created by other federal statutes.

"shall be liable to the party injured in an action at law, suit in equity, or other proper proceeding for redress . . ."

Reflecting the time of the statute's drafting, "at law" refers to damages, and "in equity" refers mainly to injunctive relief, but the modern Federal Rules of Civil Procedure have established a uniform "civil action" that can seek either or both. Our study will consider the standards under § 1983 for obtaining compensatory and punitive damages, as well as doctrines limiting the availability and scope of injunctive relief.

One of the key themes in debates over the proper interpretation of § 1983 is the balance of power between state laws and institutions (including courts) on one hand and their federal counterparts on the other. The case for enforcing civil rights via federal courts applying federal laws like § 1983 is straightforward: State governments' historical role as the defenders and enforcers of slavery and later Jim Crow reveals them to be inherently less inclined or competent than the federal government to protect constitutional rights. It was the federal government that championed

Reconstruction, and that passed the Civil Rights Act of 1964, the Voting Rights Act of 1965, and the Fair Housing Act of 1968, among others. And federal judges are appointed by the president and so are not beholden to local interests or local voters who might vote out judges who make unpopular decisions. Thus (the argument goes), federal law and courts have a better track record and are more institutionally independent when it comes to protecting civil rights.

Skeptics of federal authority (either in this area specifically, or generally) have a variety of responses to this argument. The traditional and most general defense of state autonomy posits that states provide an important mechanism for local control, permitting policy decisions to be made at the level closest and most responsive to those whom those decisions will affect. *See, e.g.,* Steven G. Calabresi & Lucy D. Bickford, *Federalism and Subsidiarity: Perspectives from U.S. Constitutional Law*, 55 Nomos 123 (2012); James F. Blumstein, *Federalism and Civil Rights: Complementary and Competing Paradigms*, 47 Vand. L. Rev. 1251, 1252-53 (1994); Michael W. McConnell, *Federalism: Evaluating the Founders' Design*, 54 U. Chi. L. Rev. 1484, 1493 (1987).

There are arguments specific to the civil rights context as well. First, ceding too much power to the federal government at the expense of the states diminishes states' autonomy as "laboratories" to experiment with new policies, including policies of greater rights protection. *See* David F. Levi, Allison Eid, Joan Larsen, Goodwin Liu & Jeffrey Sutton, *51 Imperfect Solutions: State and Federal Judges Consider the Role of State Constitutions in Rights Innovation*, 103 Judicature 33 (2019). Today, some states offer broader civil rights protections than federal law does (as detailed at the end of this chapter in Section D). Second, the federal government does not have a monopoly on civil rights progressivism and has itself committed grave abuses of civil rights. Some states outlawed slavery in the pre-Civil War years, while the federal government was still enacting fugitive slave laws. And although the federal government can claim credit for many civil rights laws, the federal government was also responsible for expelling and decimating Native Americans tribes throughout much of U.S. history, and it interned Japanese-Americans during World War II. More recently, as Professor Charles F. Abernathy has observed in reference to increasingly punitive federal criminal justice policies in the late twentieth century, "[w]hen federal politicians are left with the choice of sensitively dealing with minority concerns or riding tall in the anti-crime saddle, riding tall is too often the winner, especially in an election year." Charles F. Abernathy, *Foreword: Federalism and Anti-Federalism as Civil Rights Tools*, 39 How. L.J. 615, 620 (1996).

The balance between state and federal authority is a significant consideration not only in the interpretation and application of § 1983, as this chapter illustrates, but also throughout most of the topics in this book.

The heart of this chapter is Section A, which considers the critical question whether § 1983's requirement that a defendant act "under color" of law is met when state or local law does not authorize the defendant's conduct. Section B considers another important interpretive question regarding the "under color" requirement: When can a private party be sued under § 1983? Section C considers the extent to which state laws or proceedings cabin plaintiffs' ability to invoke § 1983.

Section D provides a brief discussion of the role of parallel state-law causes of action in the enforcement of civil rights.

A. THE "UNDER COLOR" REQUIREMENT

The foundational case on the interpretation of § 1983 is *Monroe v. Pape*, a 1961 decision about the meaning of a critical phrase of the statute, "under color of any statute, ordinance, regulation, custom, or usage, of any State or Territory." *Monroe* is considered the catalyst for the widespread use of § 1983. One article counted just twenty-one cases decided under § 1983 in the first fifty years after enactment. Comment, *Civil Rights Act: Emergence of an Adequate Federal Civil Remedy?* 26 Ind. L.J. 361, 363 (1951). By contrast, an empirical study of one district court (the Central District of California, which includes Los Angeles) twenty years after *Monroe* concluded that 251 constitutional tort (probably mainly § 1983) cases were filed in that one district in a single year (fiscal year 1981). *See* Theodore Eisenberg & Stewart Schwab, *The Reality of Constitutional Tort Litigation*, 72 Cornell L. Rev. 641, 657, 670 (1987).

Why was *Monroe* so important? Prior to *Monroe*, § 1983 was already an accepted vehicle to seek injunctive relief against unconstitutional government policies. Indeed, it was cited (as "Act of April 20, 1871, Chapter 22, section 1") as a basis for relief in the original complaint filed in *Brown v. Board of Education*, Civ. No. T-315 (D. Kan. filed Feb. 26, 1951). Many constitutional wrongs, however, are not a matter of official policy. Sometimes officials violate the Constitution in circumstances where state or local law or policy is silent as to the legality of the conduct; sometimes officials' unconstitutional conduct is also unlawful under state or local law. Prior to *Monroe*, the Supreme Court had not addressed whether these types of violations— violations not undertaken pursuant to or authorized by state or local government policy—could be reached using § 1983.

In answering that question, *Monroe* relied heavily on two prior cases interpreting the statutory provision now codified at 18 U.S.C. § 242. That statute provides criminal penalties for the violation of a person's civil rights and, importantly, uses language nearly identical to that of § 1983 (emphasis added): "Whoever, *under color of any law, statute, ordinance, regulation, or custom*, willfully subjects, or causes to be subjected, any inhabitant of any State, Territory, or District to the deprivation of any rights, privileges, or immunities secured or protected by the Constitution and laws of the United States, or to different punishments, pains, or penalties, on account of such inhabitant being an alien, or by reason of his color, or race, than are prescribed for the punishment of citizens, shall be fined not more than $1,000, or imprisoned not more than one year, or both."

United States v. Classic, 313 U.S. 299 (1941), was a prosecution of Louisiana election officials who were alleged to have falsified the results of a primary election by altering and miscounting ballots. The main issue before the Court was whether the right to vote in a primary election was one of the "rights, privileges, or immunities secured or protected by the Constitution and laws of the United States" such that defendants could be charged as having deprived voters of their constitutional rights. Having answered that question in the affirmative, Justice Stone's opinion for the Court briefly explained (with no dissent on this point) how the defendants acted "under color of law":

> The alleged acts of appellees were committed in the course of their performance of duties under the Louisiana statute requiring them to count the ballots, to record the result of the count, and to certify the result of the election. Misuse of power, possessed by virtue of state law and made possible only because the wrongdoer is clothed with the authority of state law, is action taken "under color of" state law. Here the acts of appellees infringed the constitutional right and deprived the voters of the benefit of it within the meaning of [§ 242] . . . .

The Court revisited the "under color" language in *Screws v. United States*, 325 U.S. 91 (1945), in which the sheriff and two police officers of Baker County, Georgia, were prosecuted and convicted under what is now § 242 for beating a handcuffed African-American man to death with their fists and a blackjack after arresting him for stealing a tire. After rejecting a challenge to the constitutionality of § 242 and determining that the jury had been incorrectly instructed on the "willfulness" element (which required the convictions to be vacated), Justice Douglas's plurality opinion explained why the defendants *had* acted "under color" of law:

> They were officers of the law who made the arrest. By their own admissions they assaulted [the arrestee] in order to protect themselves and to keep their prisoner from escaping. It was their duty under Georgia law to make the arrest effective. Hence, their conduct comes within the statute.
>
> Some of the arguments which have been advanced in support of the contrary conclusion suggest that the question under [§ 242] is whether Congress has made it a federal offense for a state officer to violate the law of his State. But there is no warrant for treating the question in state law terms. The problem is not whether state law has been violated but whether an inhabitant of a State has been deprived of a federal right by one who acts under "color of any law." . . . The fact that it is also a violation of state law does not make it any the less a federal offense punishable as such. Nor does its punishment by federal authority encroach state authority or relieve the state from its responsibility for punishing state offenses. . . .
>
> *United States v. Classic* is . . . indistinguishable from this case so far as "under color of" state law is concerned. In each officers of the State were performing official duties; in each the power which they were authorized to exercise was misused. . . .
>
> It is said that we should abandon the holding of the *Classic* case. It is suggested that the present problem was not clearly in focus in that case and that its holding was ill-advised. A reading of the opinion makes plain that the question was squarely involved and squarely met. . . . It is clear that under "color" of law means under "pretense" of law. Thus acts of officers in the ambit of their personal pursuits are plainly excluded. Acts of officers who undertake to perform their official duties are included whether they hew to the line of their authority or overstep it. If, as suggested, the statute was designed to embrace only action which the State in fact authorized, the words "under color of any law" were hardly apt words to express the idea.

Dissenting on this point, Justice Roberts, joined by Justices Jackson and Frankfurter, invoked "policies inherent in our federal system and the undesirable consequences of federal prosecution for crimes which are obviously and predominantly state crimes no matter how much sophisticated argumentation may give them the appearance of federal crimes." The dissent argued:

> It has never been satisfactorily explained how a State can be said to deprive a person of liberty or property without due process of law when the foundation of the claim is that a minor official has disobeyed the authentic command of his State. . . .
>
> When due account is taken of the considerations that have heretofore controlled the political and legal relations between the States and the National Government, there is not the slightest warrant in the reason of things for torturing language plainly designed for nullifying a claim of acting under a State law that conflicts with the Constitution so as to apply to situations where State law is in conformity with the Constitution and local misconduct is in undisputed violation of that State law. In the absence of clear direction by Congress we should leave to the States the enforcement of their criminal law, and not relieve States of the responsibility for vindicating wrongdoing that is essentially local or weaken the habits of local law enforcement by tempting reliance on federal authority for an occasional unpleasant task of local enforcement.

Classic did not require a contrary result, the dissent argued, because "the focus of attention in the *Classic* case was not our present problem, but was the relation of primaries to the protection of the electoral process under the United States Constitution."

The interpretation in *Screws* and *Classic* of "under color" in 18 U.S.C. § 242 set the stage for interpretation of the similar "under color" language in § 242's civil counterpart, 42 U.S.C. § 1983.

Monroe v. Pape
365 U.S. 167 (1961)

■ *Mr. Justice* DOUGLAS *delivered the opinion of the Court.*

This case presents important questions concerning the construction of 42 U.S.C. § 1983, which reads as follows:

> "Every person who, under color of any statute, ordinance, regulation, custom or usage, of any State or Territory, subjects, or causes to be subjected, any citizen of the United States or other person within the jurisdiction thereof to the deprivation of any rights, privileges, or immunities secured by the Constitution and laws, shall be liable to the party injured in an action at law, suit in equity, or other proper proceeding for redress."

The complaint alleges that 13 Chicago police officers broke into petitioners' home in the early morning, routed them from bed, made them stand naked in the living room, and ransacked every room, emptying drawers and ripping mattress covers. It further alleges that Mr. Monroe was then taken to the police station and detained on "open" charges for 10 hours, while he was interrogated about a two-day-old murder, that he was not taken before a magistrate, though one was accessible, that he was not permitted to call his family or attorney, that he was subsequently released without criminal charges being preferred against him. It is alleged that the officers had no search warrant and no arrest warrant and that they acted "under color of the statutes, ordinances, regulations, customs and usages" of Illinois and of the City of Chicago. . . .

The City of Chicago moved to dismiss the complaint on the ground that it is not liable under the Civil Rights Acts nor for acts committed in performance of its governmental functions. All defendants moved to dismiss, alleging that the complaint alleged no cause of action under those Acts or under the Federal Constitution. The District Court dismissed the complaint. The Court of Appeals affirmed . . . .

Petitioners claim that the invasion of their home and the subsequent search without a warrant and the arrest and detention of Mr. Monroe without a warrant and without arraignment constituted a deprivation of their "rights, privileges, or immunities secured by the Constitution" within the meaning of § 1983. . . .

Section 1983 came onto the books as § 1 of the Ku Klux Act of April 20, 1871. It was one of the means whereby Congress exercised the power vested in it by § 5 of the Fourteenth Amendment to enforce the provisions of that Amendment. . . .

There can be no doubt . . . that Congress has the power to enforce provisions of the Fourteenth Amendment against those who carry a badge of authority of a State and represent it in some capacity, whether they act in accordance with their authority or misuse it. The question with which we now deal is the narrower one of whether Congress, in enacting § 1983, meant to give a remedy to parties deprived of constitutional rights, privileges and immunities by an official's abuse of his position. We conclude that it did so intend.

It is argued that "under color of" enumerated state authority excludes acts of an official or policeman who can show no authority under state law, state custom, or state usage to do what he did. In this case it is said that these policemen, in breaking into petitioners' apartment, violated the Constitution and laws of Illinois. It is pointed out that under Illinois law a simple remedy is offered for that violation and that, so far as it appears, the courts of Illinois are available to give petitioners that full redress which the common law affords for violence done to a person; and it is earnestly argued that no "statute, ordinance, regulation, custom or usage" of Illinois bars that redress. . . .

The [Ku Klux Klan Act]—in particular the section with which we are now concerned—had several purposes. There are threads of many thoughts running through the debates. One who reads them in their entirety sees that the present section had three main aims.

First, it might, of course, override certain kinds of [discriminatory] state laws. . . .

Second, it provided a remedy where state law was inadequate. That aspect of the legislation was summed up as follows by Senator Sherman of Ohio:

> "* * * it is said the reason is that any offense may be committed upon a negro by a white man, and a negro cannot testify in any case against a white man, so that the only way by which any conviction can be had in Kentucky in those cases is in the United States courts, because the United States courts enforce the United States laws by which negroes may testify."

But the purposes were much broader. The third aim was to provide a federal remedy where the state remedy, though adequate in theory, was not available in practice. The opposition to the measure complained that "It overrides the reserved powers of the States," just as they argued that the second section of the bill "absorb(ed) the entire jurisdiction of the State over their local and domestic affairs."

This Act of April 20, 1871, sometimes called "the third 'force bill,' " was passed by a Congress that had the Klan "particularly in mind." The debates are replete with references to the lawless conditions existing in the South in 1871. There was available to the Congress during these debates a report, nearly 600 pages in length, dealing with the activities of the Klan and the inability of the state governments to cope with it. This report was drawn on by many of the speakers. It was not the unavailability of state remedies but the failure of certain States to enforce the laws with an equal hand that furnished the powerful momentum behind this "force bill." Mr. Lowe of Kansas said:

> "While murder is stalking abroad in disguise, while whippings and lynchings and banishment have been visited upon unoffending American citizens, the local administrations have been found inadequate or unwilling to apply the proper corrective. . . . Immunity is given to crime, and the records of the public tribunals are searched in vain for any evidence of effective redress." . . .

While one main scourge of the evil—perhaps the leading one—was the Ku Klux Klan, the remedy created was not a remedy against it or its members but against those who representing a State in some capacity were unable or unwilling to enforce a state law. Senator Osborn of Florida put the problem in these terms:

> "That the State courts in the several States have been unable to enforce the criminal laws of their respective States or to suppress the disorders existing, and in fact that the preservation of life and property in many sections of the country is beyond the power of the State government, is a sufficient reason why Congress should, so far as they have authority under the Constitution, enact the laws necessary for the protection of citizens of the United States. . . ."

There was, it was said, no quarrel with the state laws on the books. It was their lack of enforcement that was the nub of the difficulty. Speaking of conditions in Virginia, Mr. Porter of that State said:

> "The outrages committed upon loyal men there are under the forms of law."

. . . Mr. Hoar of Massachusetts stated:

> "Now, it is an effectual denial by a State of the equal protection of the laws when any class of officers charged under the laws with their administration permanently and as a rule refuse to extend that protection. If every sheriff in South Carolina refuses to serve a writ for a colored man and those sheriffs are kept in office year after year by the people of South Carolina, and no verdict against them for their failure of duty can be obtained before a South Carolina jury, the State of South Carolina, through the class of officers who are its representatives to afford the equal protection of the laws to that class of citizens, has denied that protection. . . ."

Senator Pratt of Indiana spoke of the discrimination against Union sympathizers and Negroes in the actual enforcement of the laws:

"Plausibly and sophistically it is said the laws of North Carolina do not discriminate against them. . . .

"But it is a fact, asserted in the report, that of the hundreds of outrages committed upon loyal people through the agency of this Ku Klux organization not one has been punished. This defect in the administration of the laws does not extend to other cases. Vigorously enough are the laws enforced against Union people. They only fail in efficiency when a man of known Union sentiments, white or black, invokes their aid. Then Justice closes the door of her temples."

It was precisely that breadth of the remedy which the opposition emphasized. Mr. Kerr of Indiana referring to the section involved in the present litigation said: . . . "It is a covert attempt to transfer another large portion of jurisdiction from the State tribunals, to which it of right belongs, to those of the United States. . . ."

Although the legislation was enacted because of the conditions that existed in the South at that time, it is cast in general language and is as applicable to Illinois as it is to the States whose names were mentioned over and again in the debates. It is no answer that the State has a law which if enforced would give relief. The federal remedy is supplementary to the state remedy, and the latter need not be first sought and refused before the federal one is invoked. Hence the fact that Illinois by its constitution and laws outlaws unreasonable searches and seizures is no barrier to the present suit in the federal court.

We had before us in *United States v. Classic* 18 U.S.C. § 242, which provides a criminal punishment for anyone who "under color of any law, statute, ordinance, regulation, or custom" subjects any inhabitant of a State to the deprivation of "any rights, privileges, or immunities secured or protected by the Constitution or laws of the United States." . . . The right involved in the *Classic* case was the right of voters in a primary to have their votes counted. The laws of Louisiana required the defendants "to count the ballots, to record the result of the count, and to certify the result of the election." But according to the indictment they did not perform their duty. . . . [T]he Court ruled, "Misuse of power, possessed by virtue of state law and made possible only because the wrongdoer is clothed with the authority of state law, is action taken 'under color of' state law." There was a dissenting opinion; but the ruling as to the meaning of "under color of" state law was not questioned.

That view of the meaning of the words "under color of" state law, 18 U.S.C. § 242, was reaffirmed in *Screws v. United States*. The acts there complained of were committed by state officers in performance of their duties, viz., making an arrest effective. It was urged there, as it is here, that "under color of" state law should not be construed to duplicate in federal law what was an offense under state law. It was said there, as it is here, that the ruling in the *Classic* case as to the meaning of "under color of" state law was not in focus and was ill-advised. It was argued there, as it is here, that "under color of" state law included only action taken by officials pursuant to state law. We rejected that view. . . .

[Because § 242 was the model for the language of § 1983], it is beyond doubt that this phrase should be accorded the same construction in both statutes—in § 1983 and in 18 U.S.C. § 242....

We conclude that the meaning given "under color of" law in [*Classic* and *Screws*] was the correct one; and we adhere to it.

In the *Screws* case we dealt with a statute that imposed criminal penalties for acts "wilfully" done. We construed that word in its setting to mean the doing of an act with "a specific intent to deprive a person of a federal right." We do not think that gloss should be placed on § 1983 which we have here. The word "wilfully" does not appear in § 1983. Moreover, § 1983 provides a civil remedy, while in the *Screws* case we dealt with a criminal law challenged on the ground of vagueness. Section 1983 should be read against the background of tort liability that makes a man responsible for the natural consequences of his actions....

[The Court went on to rule that municipalities could not be liable under § 1983. Discussion of this issue is omitted here; it will be revisited in Chapter 5 when we cover municipal liability under § 1983.]

[The dismissal of the complaint as to the individual officers is] Reversed.

■ *Mr. Justice HARLAN, whom Mr. Justice STEWART joins, concurring....*

From my point of view, the policy of stare decisis, as it should be applied in matters of statutory construction and, to a lesser extent, the indications of congressional acceptance of this Court's earlier interpretation, require that it appear beyond doubt from the legislative history of the 1871 statute that *Classic* and *Screws* misapprehended the meaning of the controlling provision, before a departure from what was decided in those cases would be justified. Since I can find no such justifying indication in that legislative history, I join the opinion of the Court. However, what has been written on both sides of the matter makes some additional observations appropriate....

Since the [dissent's] suggested narrow construction of § 1983 presupposes that state measures were adequate to remedy unauthorized deprivations of constitutional rights and since the identical state relief could be obtained for state-authorized acts with the aid of Supreme Court review, this narrow construction would reduce the statute to having merely a jurisdictional function, shifting the load of federal supervision from the Supreme Court to the lower courts and providing a federal tribunal for fact findings in cases involving authorized action.... But the legislative debates do not disclose congressional concern about the burdens of litigation placed upon the victims of "authorized" constitutional violations contrasted to the victims of unauthorized violations. Neither did Congress indicate an interest in relieving the burden placed on this Court in reviewing such cases.

The statute becomes more than a jurisdictional provision only if one attributes to the enacting legislature the view that a deprivation of a constitutional right is significantly different from and more serious than a violation of a state right and therefore deserves a different remedy even though the same act may constitute both a state tort and the deprivation of a constitutional right. This view, by no means unrealistic as a common-sense matter,[5] is, I believe, more consistent with the flavor of the legislative history than is a view that the primary purpose of the statute was to grant a lower court forum for fact findings. For example, the tone is surely one of overflowing protection of constitutional rights, and there is not a hint of concern about the administrative burden on the Supreme Court. . . .

In my view, these considerations put in serious doubt the conclusion that § 1983 was limited to state-authorized unconstitutional acts, on the premise that state remedies respecting them were considered less adequate than those available for unauthorized acts.

I think this limited interpretation of § 1983 fares no better when viewed from the other possible premise for it, namely that state-approved constitutional deprivations were considered more offensive than those not so approved. For one thing, the enacting Congress was not unaware of the fact that there was a substantial overlap between the protections granted by state constitutional provisions and those granted by the Fourteenth Amendment. . . . Moreover, if indeed the legislature meant to distinguish between authorized and unauthorized acts and yet did not mean the statute to be inapplicable whenever there was a state constitutional provision which, reasonably interpreted, gave protection similar to that of a provision of the Fourteenth Amendment, would there not have been some explanation of this exception to the general rule? . . .

These difficulties in explaining the basis of a distinction between authorized and unauthorized deprivations of constitutional rights fortify my view that the legislative history does not bear the burden which stare decisis casts upon it. For this reason and for those stated in the opinion of the Court, I agree that we should not now depart from the holdings of the *Classic* and *Screws* cases.

▓ *Mr. Justice* FRANKFURTER, *dissenting except insofar as the Court holds that this action cannot be maintained against the City of Chicago.* . . .

[Prior to *Classic*], cases in this Court in which the "under color" provisions were invoked uniformly involved action taken either in strict pursuance of some

---

5. There will be many cases in which the relief provided by the state to the victim of a use of state power which the state either did not or could not constitutionally authorize will be far less than what Congress may have thought would be fair reimbursement for deprivation of a constitutional right. I will venture only a few examples. There may be no damage remedy for the loss of voting rights or for the harm from psychological coercion leading to a confession. And what is the dollar value of the right to go to unsegregated schools? Even the remedy for such an unauthorized search and seizure as Monroe was allegedly subjected to may be only the nominal amount of damages to physical property allowable in an action for trespass to land. It would indeed be the purest coincidence if the state remedies for violations of common-law rights by private citizens were fully appropriate to redress those injuries which only a state official can cause and against which the Constitution provides protection.

specific command of state law or within the scope of executive discretion in the administration of state laws. The same is true, with two exceptions, in the lower federal courts. . . .

A sharp change from this uniform application of seventy years was made in 1941, but without acknowledgment or indication of awareness of the revolutionary turnabout from what had been established practice. . . . This holding [in *Classic*] was summarily announced without exposition; it had been only passingly argued. . . . [In *Screws*,] the opinion of four of the six Justices who believed that the statute applied merely invoked *Classic* and stare decisis and did not reconsider the meaning which that case had uncritically assumed was to be attached to the language, "under color" of state authority. . . .

"The rule of stare decisis, though one tending to consistency and uniformity of decision, is not inflexible." . . . And with regard to the Civil Rights Acts there are reasons of particular urgency which authorize the Court—indeed, which make it the Court's responsibility—to reappraise in the hitherto skimpily considered context of § 1983 . . . . This is not an area of commercial law in which, presumably, individuals may have arranged their affairs in reliance on the expected stability of decision. . . . The issue in the present case concerns directly a basic problem of American federalism: the relation of the Nation to the States in the critically important sphere of municipal law administration. In this aspect, it has significance approximating constitutional dimension. . . .

[Section 1983], it has been noted, was patterned on the similar criminal provision of § 2, Act of April 9, 1866. The earlier Act had as its primary object the effective nullification of the Black Codes, those statutes of the Southern legislatures which had so burdened and disqualified the Negro as to make his emancipation appear illusory. The Act had been vetoed by President Johnson . . . .

Senator Trumbull, then Chairman of the Senate Judiciary Committee, in his remarks urging its passage over the veto, expressed the intendment of the second section as those who voted for it read it:

> "If an offense is committed against a colored person simply because he is colored, in a State where the law affords him the same protection as if he were white, this act neither has nor was intended to have anything to do with his case, because he has adequate remedies in the State courts; but if he is discriminated against under color of State laws because he is colored, then it becomes necessary to interfere for his protection." . . .

The original text of the present § 1983 contained words, left out in the Revised Statutes, which clarified the objective to which the provision was addressed:

> "That any person who, under color of any law, statute, ordinance, regulation, custom, or usage of any State, shall subject, or cause to be subjected, any person within the jurisdiction of the United States to the deprivation of any rights, privileges, or immunities secured by the Constitution of the United States, shall, *any such law, statute, ordinance, regulation, custom, or usage of the State to the contrary notwithstanding*, be liable to the party injured * * *." (emphasis added).

Representative Shellabarger, reporting the section, explained it to the House as "in its terms carefully confined to giving a civil action for such wrongs against citizenship as are done under color of State laws which abridge these rights." . . .

Insofar as the Court undertakes to demonstrate—as the bulk of its opinion seems to do—that § 1983 was meant to reach some instances of action not specifically authorized by the avowed, apparent, written law inscribed in the statute books of the States, the argument knocks at an open door. No one would or could, deny this, for by its express terms the statute comprehends deprivations of federal rights under color of any "statute, ordinance, regulation, custom, or usage" of a State. The question is, what class of cases other than those involving state statute law were meant to be reached. And, with respect to this question, the Court's conclusion is undermined by the very portions of the legislative debates which it cites. For surely the misconduct of individual municipal police officers, subject to the effective oversight of appropriate state administrative and judicial authorities, presents a situation which differs toto coelo from one in which "Immunity is given to crime, and the records of the public tribunals are searched in vain for any evidence of effective redress" . . . . These statements indicate that Congress—made keenly aware by the post-bellum conditions in the South that States through their authorities could sanction offenses against the individual by settled practice which established state law as truly as written codes—designed § 1983 to reach, as well, official conduct which, because engaged in "permanently and as a rule," or "systematically," came through acceptance by law-administering officers to constitute "custom, or usage" having the cast of law. They do not indicate an attempt to reach, nor does the statute by its terms include, instances of acts in defiance of state law and which no settled state practice, no systematic pattern of official action or inaction, no "custom, or usage, of any State," insulates from effective and adequate reparation by the State's authorities.

Rather, all the evidence converges to the conclusion that Congress by § 1983 created a civil liability enforceable in the federal courts only in instances of injury for which redress was barred in the state courts because some "statute, ordinance, regulation, custom, or usage" sanctioned the grievance complained of. This purpose, manifested even by the so-called "Radical" Reconstruction Congress in 1871, accords with the presuppositions of our federal system. The jurisdiction which Article III of the Constitution conferred on the national judiciary reflected the assumption that the state courts, not the federal courts, would remain the primary guardians of that fundamental security of person and property which the long evolution of the common law had secured to one individual as against other individuals. The Fourteenth Amendment did not alter this basic aspect of our federalism. . . .

My Brother Harlan's concurring opinion deserves separate consideration. . . . [I]t seems not unreasonable to reject the suggestion that state-sanctioned constitutional violations are no more offensive than violations not sanctioned by the majesty of state authority. Degrees of offensiveness, perhaps, lie largely in the eye of the person offended, but is it implausible to conclude that there is something more reprehensible, something more dangerous, in the action of the custodian of a public building who turns out a Negro pursuant to a local ordinance than in the action of the same custodian who turns out the same Negro, in violation of state law, to vent a personal bias? Or something more reprehensible about the public officer who beats a criminal suspect under orders from the Captain of Detectives, pursuant to a systematic and accepted custom of third-degree practice, than about the same officer who, losing his temper, breaks all local regulations and beats the same suspect? If it be admitted that there is a significant difference between the situation of the individual injured by another individual and who, although the latter is an agent of the State, can claim from the State's judicial or administrative processes the same protection and redress against him as would be available against any other individual, and the situation of one who, injured under the sanction of a state law which shields the offender, is left alone and helpless in the face of the asserted dignity of the State, then certainly, it was the latter of these two situations—that of the unprotected Southern Negroes and Unionists—about which Congress was concerned in 1871. . . .

Notes and Questions

1. What does "under color" mean according to the Court? What are the implications of *Monroe*'s holding for the officer whose conduct is unauthorized by state law?

2. In identifying the cause of the growth of civil rights litigation generally, it is hard to disentangle the influence of *Monroe* from other important legal trends during the mid-twentieth century, particularly the expansion of substantive constitutional rights and the newly authorized application ("Fourteenth Amendment incorporation") of many of those rights against state (not just federal) authorities:

   > [U]ntil incorporation, there simply were not many federal constitutional rights that could give rise to a cause of action (to say nothing of the pragmatic difficulties of bringing lawsuits during Jim Crow). Equal protection claims were notoriously difficult, the Privileges or Immunities Clause suffered narrow interpretation, and pre-incorporation Fourteenth Amendment due process did little for civil rights plaintiffs. In the First Amendment context, the right to free speech was incorporated in 1925, free assembly in 1937, free exercise in 1940, and establishment in 1947. Even then, many of these clauses did not enjoy robust interpretation until later decisions. . . . [T]he Fourth Amendment's warrant jurisprudence was not applied to states until three years after *Monroe* . . . . This left only a handful of federal rights that could be invoked by § 1983.

   Sina Kian, *The Path of the Constitution: The Original System of Remedies, How It Changed, and How the Court Responded*, 87 N.Y.U. L. Rev. 132, 187-88 (2012).

3. Consider the role that text, policy, legislative history, and precedent played in the majority, concurring, and dissenting opinions in *Monroe*. Which factor or factors were decisive? Which were irrelevant? How did the 1961 Court's emphasis

on particular interpretive techniques compare to what you would expect to see from the Court today?

4. One of the themes in the dissenting opinions in *Screws* and *Monroe* is that the Court never squarely considered the "under color" question in *Classic* and therefore improperly invoked stare decisis to drive its subsequent decisions when the question had never received a full airing. Is this a fair critique? Does the fact that the Court reached the same conclusion three times with increasing depth of analysis assuage the concern?

5. Who has the better of the legislative history debate—Justice Douglas or Justice Frankfurter? If you have a hard time deciding, does that recommend Justice Harlan's approach as the most intellectually honest? How does the use of legislative history in *Monroe* affect your view of its utility generally?

6. Consider the debate between Justices Harlan and Frankfurter over the special nature of constitutional violations committed "under color" of law. What makes such conduct especially bad—that the state *actually* approved of it or that it *appeared* to approve by its vesting of state authority in the malefactor? How do you suspect the Monroe family would have answered that question?

7. If Justice Frankfurter's view had prevailed, the Monroes, instead of suing the officers under § 1983, could have sued under Illinois tort law for trespass, battery, and other common law torts. What are the advantages, if any, of a federal remedy rooted in constitutional rather than tort law? Justice Harlan's footnote 5 offers one example. Can you think of others?

Note: § 1983 and the Defendant's State of Mind

The Court held in *Monroe* that § 1983 does not contain an intent requirement. The Court has subsequently reaffirmed this rule. *Parratt v. Taylor*, 451 U.S. 527, 534-35 (1981). Thus, the two elements a plaintiff must show are (1) that the defendant acted under color of state law, and (2) deprived a person of a right secured by the Constitution or laws of the United States. *Id.* at 535; *accord West v. Atkins*, 487 U.S. 42, 48 (1988).

As a result, the only state of mind that the plaintiff must prove is whatever state of mind is associated with the substantive constitutional claim at issue. For instance, a claim that relies on the defendant's unlawful motive—such as discrimination under the Equal Protection Clause or retaliation based on protected speech in violation of the First Amendment—requires a showing that the defendant possessed the requisite unlawful motive. By contrast, because a claim of unconstitutional prison conditions under the Eighth Amendment depends on a showing that prison officials exhibited "deliberate indifference," a plaintiff must show only that level of fault. And an unreasonable search claim may proceed notwithstanding the absence of unlawful motive because the existence of probable cause depends on the application of an objective standard.

B. THE "STATE ACTION" REQUIREMENT

Constitutional rights (with very few exceptions) do not reach the actions of private parties, only government actors. How does this rule—known as the "state action" requirement—interact with the Court's interpretation of "under color" in § 1983?

The rule limiting the reach of most constitutional rights to the conduct of governmental actors stems from a set of post-Civil War cases decided together and known as the *Civil Rights Cases*, 109 U.S. 3 (1883). The issue that unified these cases was whether the Civil Rights Act of 1875, which forbade race discrimination in public accommodations, was within Congress's constitutional power to enact. The two asserted bases for the law were Congress's power to enforce the Thirteenth Amendment (which prohibited slavery) and its power to enforce the Fourteenth Amendment (providing, among other things, for equal protection of the laws). The Supreme Court's decision in the *Civil Rights Cases*, finding neither basis sufficient for the law, was a major setback for civil rights. Effective legislation against discrimination in public accommodations would not be again enacted until the mid-twentieth century, when a Supreme Court with very different Justices would uphold it as an exercise of Congress's power to regulate interstate commerce.

We'll consider in Chapters 6 and 7 civil rights statutes reaching private discrimination. Constitutional Law classes cover the extent of congressional power to enact such legislation. For our purposes, the most significant holding of the *Civil Rights Cases* is that the Fourteenth Amendment reaches only "state action." Note that in this context, "state" really means "government," so "state action" is equally present in the actions of municipal officials as in those of employees of a state itself. Accordingly, to seek redress for violations of most constitutional rights—either rights found in the Fourteenth Amendment itself (like equal protection of the laws or due process) or rights found elsewhere that are applied to the states via Fourteenth Amendment (such as the First Amendment right to freedom of speech or the Fourth Amendment right against unreasonable searches and seizures)—a finding of state action is required.

The state action requirement informs the interpretation of § 1983 in an important respect. The question addressed in *Monroe v. Pape* was whether a state official could act "under color" of law when no governmental law or policy authorized—and even when state or local law or policy prohibited—the action in question. A different interpretive question regarding "under color" arises when plaintiffs ask courts to apply constitutional standards to conduct by individuals or entities who *are not government actors at all*. *Monroe* unquestionably involved state action because the defendants were local law enforcement officials, so the question of who is a government actor did not arise there. But the applicability of constitutional standards to nominally private actors is an important question, given governmental attempts (particularly in the first half of the twentieth century) to use private organizations to attempt end-runs around prohibitions on race discrimination and given the modern trend toward increasing privatization of important government functions like education and incarceration.

The Court has held that the question of who qualifies as a government actor for the purpose of the "under color" requirement is identical to the question of state action. *See, e.g., Rendell-Baker v. Kohn*, 457 U.S. 830, 837-38 (1982); *United States v. Price*, 383 U.S. 787, 794, n.7 (1966). Thus, the same "state action" showing that renders the defendant subject to the commands of the Fourteenth Amendment also simultaneously satisfies the § 1983 "under color" requirement.

One way to conceive of the result in *Monroe* is as reducing the "under color" question to *nothing but* the "state action" question. That is, given *Monroe*'s holding that a § 1983 defendant need not be acting according to a governmental policy or custom to be liable, a § 1983 plaintiff satisfies the "under color" requirement simply by demonstrating that the defendant's action is "state action"; nothing further is required.

For instance, *West v. Atkins*, 487 U.S. 42 (1988), considered whether a doctor who served as a part-time independent contractor for a state prison hospital acted "under color" of law when he treated a prisoner. Although the Court recited the *Monroe/Classic* definition of "under color" of law—that "the defendant in a § 1983 action . . . exercised power 'possessed by virtue of state law and made possible only because the wrongdoer is clothed with the authority of state law' "—the determinative question in *West* was the "state action" question: whether the physician's conduct in treating the prisoner "is fairly attributable to the State." The Court concluded that it was:

> Whether a physician is on the state payroll or is paid by contract, the dispositive issue concerns the relationship among the State, the physician, and the prisoner. Contracting out prison medical care does not relieve the State of its constitutional duty to provide adequate medical treatment to those in its custody, and it does not deprive the State's prisoners of the means to vindicate their Eighth Amendment rights. The State bore an affirmative obligation to provide adequate medical care to West; the State delegated that function to respondent Atkins; and respondent voluntarily assumed that obligation by contract.
>
> Nor does the fact that Doctor Atkins' employment contract did not require him to work exclusively for the prison make him any less a state actor than if he performed those duties as a full-time, permanent member of the state prison medical staff. It is the physician's function while working for the State, not the amount of time he spends in performance of those duties or the fact that he may be employed by others to perform similar duties, that determines whether he is acting under color of state law. In the State's employ, respondent worked as a physician at the prison hospital fully vested with state authority to fulfill essential aspects of the duty . . . to provide essential medical care to those the State had incarcerated. Doctor Atkins must be considered to be a state actor.

The state action doctrine, which is covered in many Constitutional Law classes, is primarily a substantive doctrine that defines the reach of constitutional guarantees. But state action functions as an enforcement doctrine, too: for any given substantive right (such as equal protection or freedom of speech), the state action doctrine defines the set of defendants against whom the right can be enforced. We therefore consider the subject here.

In most civil rights cases, the "state action" question is not a difficult one: Plaintiffs usually challenge conduct that is obviously governmental because it is undertaken by obviously governmental actors like a police officer, a municipal agency, a school board, or a public employer. State employees are normally state actors, the Court noted in *West*. (An interesting but limited exception to that principle is *Polk County v. Dodson*, 454 U.S. 312 (1981), which held that a public defender does not act under color of state law when representing a defendant in a criminal proceeding, because in that capacity the attorney is not subject to direction by the government, instead exercising independent professional judgment to serve the interests of the defendant—the government's adversary.)

What happens when plaintiffs seek to enforce constitutional norms against private parties? For such cases to succeed, they must fall within one of the several narrow and fact-intensive categories of cases in which courts have deemed private actors to be "state actors" subject to constitutional requirements. The jurisprudence in this field is meandering and not susceptible to easy generalizations. As the Court has explained:

> We have, for example, held that a challenged activity may be state action when it results from the State's exercise of "coercive power," when the State provides "significant encouragement, either overt or covert," or when a private actor operates as a "willful participant in joint activity with the State or its agents." We have treated a nominally private entity as a state actor when it is controlled by an "agency of the State," when it has been delegated a public function by the State, when it is "entwined with governmental policies," or when government is "entwined in [its] management or control."

Brentwood Acad. v. Tenn. Secondary Sch. Athletic Ass'n, 531 U.S. 288, 296 (2001). "Amidst such variety," the Court's observation that its "criteria lack rigid simplicity," *id.*, is surely an understatement.

Nonetheless, it is possible to group the cases into three categories based on the type of relationship (or asserted relationship) between the private party and the government. They are: first, cases in which a private actor acts like the government itself by performing a "public function"; second, cases in which a private actor employs a governmental mechanism to achieve a result that has the force of law; and third, cases in which the actions of private and public actors are otherwise "entwined." Note that this classification is about contexts, not rationales; it does not track the factors the court has considered in finding state action (which, as *Brentwood* noted, number more than three).

The "public function" doctrine saw several important early applications in the mid-twentieth century (in particular, application to voting and to privately owned towns), but the Supreme Court has narrowed the definition of "public function" in recent years, and so further applications have been limited. The government-mechanism cases, most of which are still good law, tend to involve private parties making use of the courts. Entwinement arguments rarely succeed, but a recent case shows that the theory remains viable.

1. PUBLIC FUNCTIONS

A private party can be a state actor when it performs a "public function." The criteria for identifying such functions have evolved over the years.

Perhaps the most important public function is the conduct of elections. In a set of decisions known as the "white primary" cases, the Supreme Court struck down a series of attempts to disenfranchise black voters in Texas through the use of nominally "private" primary elections in which only white voters could participate. Because of the dominance of the Democratic party throughout the South during the early part of the twentieth century, the winner of the Democratic primary was effectively guaranteed to win the general election; excluding African-Americans from that primary shut them out of the only election that mattered. Initially, the racially discriminatory nature of the Texas Democratic primary was decreed by state law, *see Nixon v. Herndon*, 273 U.S. 536, 539 (1927), or decided by a committee held to be an instrumentality of the state rather than the party, *Nixon v. Condon*, 286 U.S. 73, 84-85 (1932), so the question of state action was not at issue. To avoid the effect of the Supreme Court's two *Nixon* rulings invalidating these arrangements, the Democratic Party itself adopted a whites-only rule. The Court first held that the party's decision about its own membership was not state action, *see Grovey v. Townsend*, 295 U.S. 45, 55 (1935), but the Court reversed course the following decade in *Smith v. Allwright*, 321 U.S. 649, 663-64 (1944), which overruled *Grovey* and found state action:

> Primary elections are conducted by the party under state statutory authority. The county executive committee selects precinct election officials and the county, district or state executive committees, respectively, canvass the returns. These party committees or the state convention certify the party's candidates to the appropriate officers for inclusion on the official ballot for the general election. No name which has not been so certified may appear upon the ballot for the general election as a candidate of a political party. . . .
>
> The party takes its character as a state agency from the duties imposed upon it by state statutes; the duties do not become matters of private law because they are performed by a political party. . . . When primaries become a part of the machinery for choosing officials, state and national, as they have here, the same tests to determine the character of discrimination or abridgement should be applied to the primary as are applied to the general election. If the state requires a certain electoral procedure, prescribes a general election ballot made up of party nominees so chosen and limits the choice of the electorate in general elections for state offices, practically speaking, to those whose names appear on such a ballot, it endorses, adopts and enforces the discrimination against Negroes, practiced by a party entrusted by Texas law with the determination of the qualifications of participants in the primary. This is state action[.]

Finally, *Terry v. Adams*, 345 U.S. 461 (1953), held unconstitutional a scheme under which African-Americans were excluded from participating in candidate selection within a private political association at the county level, even though the process in question was not formally the party primary. Justice Black's opinion for himself and Justices Douglas and Burton described the arrangement as follows:

> The Jaybird Association or Party was organized in 1889. Its membership was then and always has been limited to white people; they are automatically members if their names appear on the official list of county voters. It has been run like other political parties with an executive committee named from the county's voting precincts. Expenses of the party are paid by the assessment of candidates for office in its primaries. Candidates for county offices submit their names to the Jaybird Committee in accordance with the normal practice followed by regular political parties all over the country. Advertisements and posters proclaim that these candidates are running subject to the action of the Jaybird primary. While there is no legal compulsion on successful Jaybird candidates to enter Democratic primaries they have nearly always done so and with few exceptions since 1889 have run and won without opposition in the Democratic primaries and the general elections that followed. Thus the party has been the dominant political group in the county since organization, having endorsed every county-wide official elected since 1889.
>
> It is apparent that Jaybird activities follow a plan purposefully designed to exclude Negroes from voting . . . .

The eight-Justice majority holding the system unconstitutional fractured into three opinions. Justice Black's opinion focused on the effect of the Jaybird primary in circumventing the Fifteenth Amendment without specifying how state action occurred; he found it "immaterial that the state does not control that part of this elective process which it leaves for the Jaybirds to manage." Justice Frankfurter's solo concurrence attributed the discrimination to Texas itself. Justice Clark's opinion for the largest bloc of Justices—himself, Chief Justice Vinson, and Justices Reed and Jackson—found that the Jaybird Party was a state actor, because "when a state structures its electoral apparatus in a form which devolves upon a political organization the uncontested choice of public officials, that organization itself, in whatever disguise, takes on those attributes of government which draw the Constitution's safeguards in play." Justice Minton alone dissented, arguing, "The State of Texas in its elections and primaries takes no cognizance of this Jaybird Association."

Another set of public function cases involved ownership or control of public spaces. The issue in *Marsh v. Alabama*, 326 U.S. 501 (1946), was whether the First Amendment protected a Jehovah's Witness who wished to distribute religious literature on the streets of Chickasaw, Alabama, a town that was entirely owned by the Gulf Shipbuilding Corporation, which prohibited such distribution. Other than private ownership, the town "has all the characteristics of any other American town," the Court observed. The company paid a sheriff's deputy to act as the town's policeman. Residents used company-owned streets and sidewalks to move from place to place. The Court, in an opinion by Justice Black, reversed the pamphleteer's conviction for criminal trespass under state law:

> Had the title to Chickasaw belonged not to a private but to a municipal corporation and had appellant been arrested for violating a municipal ordinance rather than a ruling by those appointed by the corporation to manage a company-town it would have been clear that appellant's conviction must be reversed. . . . Our question then narrows down to this: Can those people who live in or come to Chickasaw be denied freedom of press and religion simply because a single company has legal title to all the town? . . .

> We do not agree that the corporation's property interests settle the question. . . . Ownership does not always mean absolute dominion. The more an owner, for his advantage, opens up his property for use by the public in general, the more do his rights become circumscribed by the statutory and constitutional rights of those who use it. Thus, the owners of privately held bridges, ferries, turnpikes and railroads may not operate them as freely as a farmer does his farm. Since these facilities are built and operated primarily to benefit the public and since their operation is essentially a public function, it is subject to state regulation. And, though the issue is not directly analogous to the one before us we do want to point out by way of illustration that such regulation may not result in an operation of these facilities, even by privately owned companies, which unconstitutionally interferes with and discriminates against interstate commerce. Had the corporation here owned the segment of the four-lane highway which runs parallel to the "business block" and operated the same under a State franchise, doubtless no one would have seriously contended that the corporation's property interest in the highway gave it power to obstruct through traffic or to discriminate against interstate commerce.

Justice Jackson took no part; Justice Frankfurter concurred briefly. In dissent, Justice Reed objected (for himself, Chief Justice Stone, and Justice Burton) that "[t]he rights of the owner, which the Constitution protects as well as the right of free speech, are not outweighed by the interests of the trespasser, even though he trespasses in behalf of religion or free speech."

Evans v. Newton, 382 U.S. 296 (1966), extended the public-function rationale to a park in Macon, Georgia, that had been set aside in a U.S. Senator's will for use as "a park and pleasure ground" for white people only. After the city began permitting African-Americans to use the park, members of the park's board of managers sued to have the city removed as a trustee. The Georgia Supreme Court permitted the trustee substitution, but the U.S. Supreme Court, in an opinion by Justice Douglas, reversed:

> [The lesson of *Marsh* and *Terry*, among other cases, is that] when private individuals or groups are endowed by the State with powers or functions governmental in nature, they become agencies or instrumentalities of the State and subject to its constitutional limitations. . . .
>
> For years [the park] was an integral part of the City of Macon's activities. From the pleadings we assume it was swept, manicured, watered, patrolled, and maintained by the city as a public facility for whites only, as well as granted tax exemption. . . . The momentum it acquired as a public facility is certainly not dissipated ipso facto by the appointment of "private" trustees. . . .
>
> This conclusion is buttressed by the nature of the service rendered the community by a park . . . [which is] like a fire department or police department that traditionally serves the community. Mass recreation through the use of parks is plainly in the public domain . . . . Like the streets of the company town in *Marsh*, [and] the elective process of *Terry* . . . the predominant character and purpose of this park are municipal.

Justice White concurred in the judgment. Justice Black dissented, lamenting "the tremendous lopping off of power heretofore uniformly conceded by all to belong to the States." Justice Harlan, joined by Justice Stewart, dissented to argue that certiorari should be dismissed as improvidently granted because the record was not clear about the city's involvement with the park; he also disagreed with the majority on the merits because the park at issue "had its origin not in any significant governmental action or on any public land but rather in the personal social philosophy of Senator Bacon and on property owned by him."

Beginning in the 1970s and 1980s, the Supreme Court took a narrower view of the public-function doctrine than reflected in *Marsh*, *Evans*, and the white primary cases. For instance, in *Lloyd Corp. Ltd. v. Tanner*, 407 U.S. 551 (1972), the Court held, in an opinion by Justice Powell, that a private shopping center owner could prohibit handbilling on its property:

> [The handbillers argue] that the property of a large shopping center is "open to the public," serves the same purposes as a "business district" of a municipality, and therefore has been dedicated to certain types of public use. The argument is that such a center has sidewalks, streets, and parking areas which are functionally similar to facilities customarily provided by municipalities. . . .
>
> The argument reaches too far. The Constitution by no means requires such an attenuated doctrine of dedication of private property to public use. The closest decision in theory, *Marsh v. Alabama*, involved the assumption by a private enterprise of all of the attributes of a state-created municipality and the exercise by that enterprise of semiofficial municipal functions as a delegate of the State. In effect, the owner of the company town was performing the full spectrum of municipal powers and stood in the shoes of the State. In the instant case where is no comparable assumption or exercise of municipal functions or power.
>
> Nor does property lose its private character merely because the public is generally invited to use it for designated purposes. Few would argue that a free-standing store, with abutting parking space for customers, assumes significant public attributes merely because the public is invited to shop there. Nor is size alone the controlling factor. The essentially private character of a store and its privately owned abutting property does not change by virtue of being large or clustered with other stores in a modern shopping center.

Justice Marshall, for himself and Justices Douglas, Brennan, and Stewart, dissented, arguing that "the Lloyd Center is an integral part of the Portland community. . . . For many Portland citizens, Lloyd Center will so completely satisfy their wants that they will have no reason to go elsewhere for goods or services. If speech is to reach these people, it must reach them in Lloyd Center." Moreover, Justice Marshall objected, the Court's limitation on *Marsh* would come to distort the First Amendment in favor of those with the resources to buy mass-media ads: "As governments rely on private enterprise, public property decreases in favor of privately owned property. It becomes harder and harder for citizens to find means to communicate with other citizens. Only the wealthy may find effective communication possible unless we adhere to *Marsh v. Alabama*."

Lloyd Corp. identified an important limit on the reach of *Marsh* without providing a clear rule for identifying when a private actor becomes a state actor by virtue of its performance of a public function. The Court provided more guidance in *Jackson v. Metropolitan Edison Co.*, 419 U.S. 345 (1974). There, a customer of a private electricity company sued the company on a due process theory for turning off her electric service in error. The Court, per Justice Rehnquist, found no state action; the crucial consideration was whether the function the company performed was "exclusively" governmental:

> Petitioner . . . urges that state action is present because respondent provides an essential public service required to be supplied on a reasonably continuous basis by [state law], and hence performs a "public function." We have, of course, found state action present in the exercise by a private entity of powers traditionally exclusively reserved to the State. *See, e.g., Terry; Marsh; Evans.* If we were dealing with the exercise by Metropolitan of some power delegated to it by the State which is traditionally associated with sovereignty, such as eminent domain, our case would be quite a different one. But while the Pennsylvania statute imposes an obligation to furnish service on regulated utilities, it imposes no such obligation on the State. . . .
>
> Doctors, optometrists, lawyers, Metropolitan, and [a] grocery selling a quart of milk are all in regulated businesses, providing arguably essential goods and services, "affected with a public interest." We do not believe that such a status converts their every action, absent more, into that of the State.

Justice Douglas dissented, focusing on the utility's monopoly power and the importance of electricity to the modern home. Justices Brennan and Marshall each dissented as well.

Rendell-Baker v. Kohn, 457 U.S. 830 (1982), applied the approach in *Jackson* to reject application of the public-function doctrine to a private school that received nearly all of its funding from public sources for the purpose of educating special-needs or troubled students referred to it by state or municipal agencies. The plaintiffs in *Rendell-Baker* were former teachers who claimed that the school had violated their free speech and due process rights in firing them. Chief Justice Burger's opinion for the Court found that the school was not performing a public function:

> [T]he relevant question is not simply whether a private group is serving a "public function." We have held that the question is whether the function performed has been "traditionally the *exclusive* prerogative of the State." *Jackson* (emphasis added). There can be no doubt that the education of maladjusted high school students is a public function, but that is only the beginning of the inquiry. [State law] demonstrates that the State intends to provide services for such students at public expense. That legislative policy choice in no way makes these services the exclusive province of the State. Indeed, . . . until recently the State had not undertaken to provide education for students who could not be served by traditional public schools. That a private entity performs a function which serves the public does not make its acts state action.[7]

Justice White concurred briefly. In dissent, Justice Marshall, joined by Justice Brennan, did not disagree with the standard applied by the majority but nonetheless thought that the school's function was an important factor pointing toward a finding of state action: "The provision of education is one of the most

---

7. There is no evidence that the State has attempted to avoid its constitutional duties by a sham arrangement which attempts to disguise provision of public services as acts of private parties. *Cf. Evans* (private trustees appointed to manage previously public park for white persons only).

important tasks performed by government: it ranks at the very apex of the function of a State. . . . Clearly, if the State had decided to provide the service itself, its conduct would be measured against constitutional standards. The State should not be permitted to avoid constitutional requirements simply by delegating its statutory duty to a private entity."

The Court's most recent public-function case, *Manhattan Community Access Corp. v. Halleck*, 139 S. Ct. 1921 (2019), applied the restrictive criteria of *Jackson* and *Rendell-Baker* to a public-access television station:

> Under the Court's cases, a private entity may qualify as a state actor when it exercises "powers traditionally exclusively reserved to the State." *Jackson.* It is not enough that the federal, state, or local government exercised the function in the past, or still does. And it is not enough that the function serves the public good or the public interest in some way. Rather, to qualify as a traditional, exclusive public function within the meaning of our state-action precedents, the government must have traditionally *and* exclusively performed the function. *See Rendell-Baker*; *Jackson.*
>
> The Court has stressed that "very few" functions fall into that category. . . .
>
> The relevant function in this case is operation of public access channels on a cable system. That function has not traditionally and exclusively been performed by government.
>
> Since the 1970s, when public access channels became a regular feature on cable systems, a variety of private and public actors have operated public access channels, including: private cable operators; private nonprofit organizations; municipalities; and other public and private community organizations such as churches, schools, and libraries.

Despite this formulation of the public-function test—the Court's most stringent to date—footnote 1 of the opinion suggests that the theory of *West v. Atkins* may provide an alternative route to establish state action in a public-function setting without satisfying the "traditional" and "exclusive" criteria:

> [T]his Court has recognized that a private entity may, under certain circumstances, be deemed a state actor when the government has outsourced one of its constitutional obligations to a private entity. In *West v. Atkins*, for example, the State was constitutionally obligated to provide medical care to prison inmates. That scenario is not present here because the government has no such obligation to operate public access channels.

Dissenting, Justice Sotomayor, joined by Justices Ginsburg, Breyer, and Kagan, argued that the majority reached the wrong result because it misconstrued the facts. The public-access channel was owned by the City, according to the dissenters, so the private company was operating a public forum on behalf of the government owner. Accordingly, the dissenters argued that *West* should govern the outcome.

Notes and Questions

1. What activities has the Court identified as public functions whose performance by a private party constitutes state action? What activities has the Court ruled are not public functions?

2. How has the Court's approach to the definition of a public function changed from *Marsh* and *Terry* to *Jackson*, *Rendell-Baker*, and *Manhattan Community*? What is the current definition?

3. How would today's public-function standard apply to the facts in *Marsh*, *Terry*, and *Evans*? Would any of these cases come out differently today?

4. How if at all does the current doctrine discourage governments from delegating important functions to private actors to avoid constitutional limitations? Should it be the Court's responsibility to do so?

Applications

1. Privately run prisons. The Supreme Court has never decided whether private companies that run prisons for the government are state actors. *Cf. Richardson v. McKnight*, 521 U.S. 399, 413 (1997) (leaving question open). Given the increasing number of privately run prisons, the question whether these private companies must obey the Constitution has significant implications.

Most circuits that have considered the question have held that private prison operators are state actors, on a public-function rationale. *See Rosborough v. Mgmt. & Training Corp.*, 350 F.3d 459, 461 (5th Cir. 2003) ("Clearly, confinement of wrongdoers—though sometimes delegated to private entities—is a fundamentally governmental function."); *Skelton v. Pri-Cor, Inc.*, 963 F.2d 100, 102 (6th Cir. 1991) (relying on *Evans*, *Terry*, and *Marsh*); *accord Pollard v. The GEO Grp., Inc.*, 629 F.3d 843, 858 (9th Cir. 2010), *rev'd on other grounds sub nom. Minneci v. Pollard*, 565 U.S. 118 (2012).

The Fourth Circuit has disagreed. *See Holly v. Scott*, 434 F.3d 287, 293 (4th Cir. 2006) (finding public-function theory inapplicable under *Jackson*'s exclusivity requirement because "private operation of jails and prisons existed in the United States in the eighteenth and nineteenth centuries, and in England the practice dated back to the Middle Ages").

Which side of the debate is more faithful to the Court's public-function precedents? Is running a prison more or less a public function than maintaining a park? What sorts of incentives does the Fourth Circuit's approach create for the government in terms of privatizing prisons?

How could plaintiffs argue that the approach of footnote 1 of *Manhattan Community* supports a finding of state action notwithstanding the Fourth Circuit's historical analysis?

2. Charter schools. Another area in which private actors are involved in functions often performed by the government is public education. *Rendell-Baker* resolved whether a *private* school is a state actor, but what about a charter school that is legally a part of the *public* school system? This question has produced varying answers.

Most courts have treated charter schools as state actors because they are public schools under state law. For instance, federal courts in Minnesota, New York, Ohio, and Pennsylvania have held that charter schools in those states are state actors based on specific state laws defining charter schools as public. *See, e.g., ACLU of Minn. v. Tarek Ibn Ziyad Acad.*, 2009 WL 2215072, at *9-10 (D. Minn. July 21, 2009); *Matwijko v. Bd. of Trustees of Global Concepts Charter Sch.*, 2006 WL 2466868, at *3-*5 (W.D.N.Y. Aug. 24, 2006); *Riester v. Riverside Cmty. Sch.*, 257 F. Supp. 2d 968, 972-73 (S.D. Ohio 2002); *Irene B. v. Phila. Acad. Charter Sch.*, 2003 WL 24052009, at *10-11 (E.D. Pa. Jan. 29, 2003). The most thoroughly reasoned of these decisions also found that charter schools perform a public function: "[F]ree, public education, whether provided by public or private actors, is an historical, exclusive, and traditional state function." *Riester*, 257 F. Supp. 2d at 972; *see also Peltier v. Charter Day Sch., Inc.*, 384 F. Supp. 3d 579 (E.D.N.C. 2019) (finding a North Carolina charter school to be a state actor based on *Riester*'s public-function analysis in combination with the contours of North Carolina's regulation of charter schools).

The Tenth Circuit and some district courts have found the state-actor status of charter schools so obvious that they assumed it or decided it with little analysis. *See Brammer-Hoelter v. Twin Peaks Charter Acad.*, 602 F.3d 1175, 1188 (10th Cir. 2010); *Dupell v. Franklin Towne Charter Sch.*, 2016 WL 7042068, at *6 (D.N.J. Dec. 2, 2016); *Daugherty v. Vanguard Charter Sch. Acad.*, 116 F. Supp. 2d 897, 903 (W.D. Mich. 2000).

By contrast, the Ninth Circuit held that Arizona charter schools, despite the state's statutory classification of charter schools as public schools, are not state actors—at least for the purpose of their employment relationships. *See Caviness v. Horizon Community Learning Ctr., Inc.*, 590 F.3d 806, 813-18 (9th Cir. 2010). This decision may be limited to claims brought by teachers as opposed to students; the court noted (in accord with a few statements in Supreme Court opinions) that "a private entity may be designated a state actor for some purposes but still function as a private actor in other respects."

Caviness also rejected application of the public-function theory; the court viewed this result as dictated by *Rendell-Baker* and defined the relevant public function as the "provision of educational services," not (as in *Riester* and *Peltier*) the provision of *public* education. Along similar lines, the First Circuit held that a Maine school district's decision to engage a private school to provide the only publicly funded high school education in the district did not transform that school into a state actor on a public-function rationale: "Obviously, education is not and never has been a function reserved to the state. . . . [E]ven publicly funded education of last resort was not provided exclusively by government in Maine. Before public high schools became widespread, private grammar schools and academies received public funds and were the only secondary education available." *Logiodice v. Trs. of Me. Cent. Inst.*, 296 F.3d 22, 26-27 (1st Cir. 2002).

The prevailing approach of following the state's own classification of its charter schools has significant intuitive appeal and accords with principles of federalism. Is it clear from the Supreme Court's public-function cases whether the Court would endorse this approach? Which cases could be cited to support it?

What is the correct level of generality to define a public function? The more specifically it is defined (e.g., "providing free public education" rather than merely "education"), the easier it is to find "powers traditionally exclusively reserved to the

State." How do you expect the Supreme Court would approach this question? More generally, in considering what's "traditional," should any allowance be made for the fact that the functions of government in the United States have expanded over time? Or is that gap the whole point of the Court's test—to caution that a private party doesn't become a state actor simply by carrying out a function widely performed by a state *today*?

2. USAGE OF A GOVERNMENT MECHANISM

The hallmark of the cases in the government-mechanism category is the participation of a court in the deprivation of constitutional rights. As with the public-function doctrine, state action principles regarding the usage of a government mechanism are rooted in a case about race discrimination. The issue in *Shelley v. Kraemer*, 334 U.S. 1 (1948), was "the validity of court enforcement of private agreements, generally described as restrictive covenants, which have as their purpose the exclusion of persons of designated race or color from the ownership or occupancy of real property." As a result of these covenants, which were widespread across the nation and actively promoted by the federal government, it was unlawful to sell or rent affected properties to African-Americans; these clauses played a significant role in residential segregation by race in the United States. *See* Richard Rothstein, *The Color of Law: A Forgotten History of How Our Government Segregated America* 79-82, 216 (2017). Although courts have come to view it as an outlier, *Shelley*'s analysis, in Chief Justice Vinson's unanimous opinion for a shorthanded Court (Justices Reed, Jackson, and Rutledge not participating—all three recused themselves because their own homes contained racially restrictive covenants, *see* Rothstein, *supra*, at 91) is a key starting point for the theory behind the government-mechanism cases:

> These are cases in which the purposes of the agreements were secured only by judicial enforcement by state courts of the restrictive terms of the agreements. . . .
>
> We have no doubt that there has been state action in these cases in the full and complete sense of the phrase. The undisputed facts disclose that petitioners were willing purchasers of properties upon which they desired to establish homes. The owners of the properties were willing sellers; and contracts of sale were accordingly consummated. It is clear that but for the active intervention of the state courts, supported by the full panoply of state power, petitioners would have been free to occupy the properties in question without restraint.
>
> These are not cases, as has been suggested, in which the States have merely abstained from action, leaving private individuals free to impose such discriminations as they see fit. Rather, these are cases in which the States have made available to such individuals the full coercive power of government to deny to petitioners, on the grounds of race or color, the enjoyment of property rights in premises which petitioners are willing and financially able to acquire and which the grantors are willing to sell. The difference between judicial enforcement and nonenforcement of the restrictive covenants is the difference to petitioners between being denied rights of property available to other members of the community and being accorded full enjoyment of those rights on an equal footing.

The enforcement of the restrictive agreements by the state courts in these cases was directed pursuant to the common-law policy of the States as formulated by those courts in earlier decisions. . . . The judicial action in each case bears the clear and unmistakable imprimatur of the State. . . . State action, as that phrase is understood for the purposes of the Fourteenth Amendment, refers to exertions of state power in all forms.

Consider: What exactly is the theory of state action underlying *Shelley*? Whose action creates "state action" here?

As your answer to these questions might indicate, the theory of *Shelley* is potentially incredibly expansive, as "[s]tate action similar to that involved in *Shelley* can be found whenever a court does almost anything, from enjoining a trespass, to awarding damages for an assault, to enforcing a contract. And if all the state action doctrine means is that our private conduct is free from constitutional constraint as long as we do not want government protection against trespasses, torts, or breaches of contract, it does not mean much." David A. Sklansky, *The Private Police*, 46 UCLA L. Rev. 1165, 1263-64 (1999).

Shelley's logic points the way toward what foreign courts refer to as "horizontal" application of constitutional rights—that is, application of constitutional norms to relations between private parties (in contrast with the more familiar "vertical" applications to relations between private parties and the government). *See* Helen Hershkoff, *Horizontality and the "Spooky" Doctrines of American Law*, 59 Buff. L. Rev. 455, 464 (2011). Obviously, "horizontal" application is the core of what the Supreme Court rejected in the *Civil Rights Cases*; accordingly, both the Supreme Court and lower courts have generally refused to apply *Shelley*'s methodology to other circumstances. *See* Mark D. Rosen, *Was* Shelley v. Kraemer *Incorrectly Decided? Some New Answers*, 95 Cal. L. Rev. 451, 462, 466 (2007).

Yet *Shelley*'s approach has served as a (sometimes uncredited) model for other cases in which the involvement of the judiciary in approving or facilitating private conduct created "state action" subject to the Constitution. For instance, *New York Times Co. v. Sullivan*, 376 U.S. 254 (1964), famously held, based on the First Amendment, that an Alabama police chief had to clear an extremely high evidentiary bar to prevail in a libel suit over inaccuracies in a newspaper ad taken out by civil rights groups decrying racist tactics by law enforcement and others in response to civil rights activism. (Most courses on the First Amendment cover the substantive holding of this case.) The Court did not cite *Shelley*, but underlying the Court's partial constitutionalization of the common law of libel and defamation was the same theory of state action that animated *Shelley*, as articulated by Justice Brennan for the Court:

> We may dispose at the outset of . . . the proposition relied on by the [Alabama] Supreme Court [in ruling against the New York Times]—that "The Fourteenth Amendment is directed against State action and not private action." That proposition has no application to this case. Although this is a civil lawsuit between private parties, the Alabama courts have applied a state rule of law which petitioners claim to impose invalid restrictions on their constitutional freedoms of speech and press. It matters not that that law has been applied in a civil action and that it is common

law only, though supplemented by statute. The test is not the form in which state power has been applied but, whatever the form, whether such power has in fact been exercised.

The First Amendment framework of *New York Times* remains a critical protection for the press today. Thus, the principle of *Shelley*—that a private party's use of the courts in harming another private party can turn the act in question into "state action" subject to constitutional regulation—is alive and well in discrete contexts even if the theory itself has not been accepted more broadly.

Another application of *Shelley*'s approach (again, without citing *Shelley* as authority for it) concerns remedies available to creditors. *Lugar v. Edmondson Oil Co.*, 457 U.S. 922 (1982), was about a creditor's attempt to pursue a debt by "attaching" the assets of the debtor (i.e., sequestering them, though leaving the debtor in possession) prior to a judgment in the creditor's favor. Ultimately, the attachment was voided. The debtor subsequently sued the creditor, arguing that the creditor had acted jointly with the state to deprive him of his property without due process. Justice White's opinion for the Court found state action: "[A] private party's joint participation with state officials in the seizure of disputed property is sufficient to characterize that party as a 'state actor' for purposes of the Fourteenth Amendment. . . . Whatever may be true in other contexts, this is sufficient when the State has created a system whereby state officials will attach property on the ex parte application of one party to a private dispute." The four dissenters, Chief Justice Burger and Justices Powell, Rehnquist, and O'Connor, argued that the challenged conduct was essentially private. Justice Powell's dissent additionally criticized what he viewed as the unfairness of subjecting a private party to liability based on its use of a state procedure whose validity no court had questioned: "Respondent, who was represented by counsel, could have had no notion that his filing of a petition in state court, in the effort to secure payment of a private debt, made him a 'state actor' liable in damages for allegedly unconstitutional action by the Commonwealth of Virginia."

Finally, the Court held in *Edmonson v. Leesville Concrete Co.*, 500 U.S. 614 (1991), that the constitutional bar on striking potential jurors based on race—a rule originating in the context of criminal prosecutions—applies as well to private litigants in civil cases. Justice Kennedy's majority opinion relied on both *Lugar* and *Shelley*:

> Our precedents establish that, in determining whether a particular action or course of conduct is governmental in character, it is relevant to examine [among other factors] whether the injury caused is aggravated in a unique way by the incidents of governmental authority, *see Shelley*. . . .
>
> Although private use of state-sanctioned private remedies or procedures does not rise, by itself, to the level of state action, our cases have found state action when private parties make extensive use of state procedures with "the overt, significant assistance of state officials." *See Lugar*. It cannot be disputed that, without the overt, significant participation of the government, the peremptory challenge system, as well as the jury trial system of which it is a part, simply could not exist. As discussed above, peremptory challenges have no utility outside the jury system, a system which the government alone administers. . . .

Without the direct and indispensable participation of the judge, who beyond all question is a state actor, the peremptory challenge system would serve no purpose. By enforcing a discriminatory peremptory challenge, the court "has not only made itself a party to the [biased act], but has elected to place its power, property and prestige behind the [alleged] discrimination."

A traditional function of government is evident here. The peremptory challenge is used in selecting an entity that is a quintessential governmental body, having no attributes of a private actor. The jury exercises the power of the court and of the government that confers the court's jurisdiction. . . . Should either party to a cause invoke its Seventh Amendment right, the jury becomes the principal factfinder, charged with weighing the evidence, judging the credibility of witnesses, and reaching a verdict. The jury's factual determinations as a general rule are final. . . . These are traditional functions of government, not of a select, private group beyond the reach of the Constitution.

Justice O'Connor's dissent, joined by Chief Justice Rehnquist and Justice Scalia, viewed the government's responsibility as much more limited: "The decision to strike a juror is entirely up to the litigant, and the reasons for doing so are of no consequence to the judge. . . . In point of fact, the government has virtually no role in the use of peremptory challenges. . . . Whatever reason a private litigant may have for using a peremptory challenge, it is not the government's reason." Justice Scalia added a brief additional dissent.

As these cases illustrate, the rationale for finding state action when a private party uses a government mechanism has not remained constant. *Shelley* and *New York Times* relied simply on a court's involvement. By *Edmonson*, the Court—perhaps wary of the expansive implications of *Shelley*—found it necessary to rely on other aspects of the act at issue. Because the Court has decided few government-mechanism cases, and because their rationales have varied, it is difficult to predict when if ever the Court will find other court-enabled private activities to qualify as state action.

Consider the differences between the operation of the state action doctrine in *New York Times* and *Lugar*. In the former, the finding of state action triggers the application of constitutional *limits* to a civil plaintiff's cause of action. In the latter, the finding of state action exposes a civil plaintiff to subsequent *liability* for having attempted to use judicial process. Should this distinction in the consequences for the private party inform the Court's thinking about when state action should be recognized? How would the defendant in *Lugar* have known that its use of state attachment procedure could have resulted not just in a finding that attachment was inappropriate but also in its own subsequent liability?

What other private uses of judicial processes can you think of that might prompt findings of state action based on the use of a governmental mechanism? Does the logic of these cases lend itself to any government mechanisms other than courts?

3. ENTWINEMENT

Outside of the public-function and government-mechanism contexts, the Court has sometimes found that where private parties act in a manner that is "entwined" with government actors, the private parties become state actors.

One early example of this theory was *Burton v. Wilmington Parking Authority*, 365 U.S. 715 (1961). There the Court considered whether the privately owned Eagle Coffee Shoppe, which was sued for refusing service to an African-American, was a state actor because it was located in space it leased within a city parking garage. Justice Clark's opinion for the Court found that the multifaceted relationship between the restaurant and the municipal parking authority rendered Eagle a state actor because the land and building were publicly owned and maintained, and profits from Eagle's lease were "indispensable" to the success of the garage:

> Addition of all these activities, obligations and responsibilities of the Authority, the benefits mutually conferred, together with the obvious fact that the restaurant is operated as an integral part of a public building devoted to a public parking service, indicates that degree of state participation and involvement in discriminatory action which it was the design of the Fourteenth Amendment to condemn. . . . The State has so far insinuated itself into a position of interdependence with Eagle that it must be recognized as a joint participant in the challenged activity, which, on that account, cannot be considered to have been so "purely private" as to fall without the scope of the Fourteenth Amendment.

Justice Stewart concurred in the judgment based on his view that the Delaware statute Eagle had invoked to deny service to the plaintiff was itself discriminatory. The dissenters (Justices Frankfurter, Harlan, and Whittaker) would have sent the case back to the Delaware Supreme Court to clarify its holding.

Burton turned out to be the exception rather the rule; most subsequent cases have cabined the entwinement theory by ruling *out* bases for finding entwinement between a private actor and the government.

In *Moose Lodge No. 107 v. Irvis*, 407 U.S. 163 (1972), the Harrisburg, Pennsylvania, branch of a national fraternal organization refused restaurant service, on the basis of race, to an African-American guest of a white member of the organization. Justice Rehnquist's opinion for the Court rejected the argument that state action was present by virtue of the Pennsylvania Liquor Control Board's licensing of the privately-owned Moose Lodge to serve liquor:

> The only effect that the state licensing of Moose Lodge to serve liquor can be said to have on the right of any other Pennsylvanian to buy or be served liquor on premises other than those of Moose Lodge is that for some purposes club licenses are counted in the maximum number of licenses that may be issued in a given municipality. . . .
>
> [A]n applicant for a club license must make such physical alterations in its premises as the board may require, must file a list of the names and addresses of its members and employees, and must keep extensive financial records. The board is granted the right to inspect the licensed premises at any time when patrons, guests, or members are present.
>
> However detailed this type of regulation may be in some particulars, it cannot be said to in any way foster or encourage racial discrimination. Nor can it be said to make the State in any realistic sense a partner or even a joint venturer in the club's enterprise.

Justice Brennan (joined by Justice Marshall) dissented because, in his view, pervasive state regulation of liquor licensees, including Moose Lodge, "intertwine the

State with the operation of the Lodge bar in a 'significant way (and) lend (the State's) authority to the sordid business of racial discrimination.'" Justice Douglas also dissented.

The Court went further in rejecting state regulation as a basis for finding state action in *Jackson v. Metropolitan Edison Co.*, 419 U.S. 345 (1974), also discussed earlier in this section in connection with its public-function analysis. The question in *Jackson* was whether a private electricity company was a state actor for purposes of a customer's due process claim that her service had been terminated in error. Justice Rehnquist's majority opinion rejected the plaintiff's arguments that the state's "extensive" regulatory involvement with Metropolitan converted it into a state actor:

> The mere fact that a business is subject to state regulation does not by itself convert its action into that of the State for purposes of the Fourteenth Amendment. Nor does the fact that the regulation is extensive and detailed, as in the case of most public utilities, do so. . . .
>
> Petitioner first argues that "state action" is present because of the monopoly status allegedly conferred upon Metropolitan by the State of Pennsylvania. . . . [A]lthough certain monopoly aspects were presented in *Moose Lodge*, we found that the Lodge's action was not subject to the provisions of the Fourteenth Amendment. . . .
>
> In common with all corporations of the State, [Metropolitan] pays taxes to the State, and it is subject to a form of extensive regulation by the State in a way that most other business enterprises are not. But this was likewise true of the appellant club in *Moose Lodge* . . . .

Dissenting, Justice Douglas objected that Metropolitan was "a monopolist providing essential public services as a licensee of the State and within a framework of extensive state supervision and control." Justices Brennan and Marshall each dissented as well.

In *Blum v. Yaretsky*, 457 U.S. 991 (1982), the issue was whether nursing homes that received Medicaid funding from New York State were state actors when they sought to transfer patients to a lower level of care—decisions that triggered changes in the state's allocation of Medicaid money to those facilities. In an opinion by Justice Rehnquist, the Court held that the patients could not assert due process claims against New York State social-services officials:

> Respondents . . . do not challenge the adjustment of benefits [by the state], but the discharge or transfer of patients to lower levels of care without adequate notice or hearings. That the State responds to such actions by adjusting benefits does not render it responsible for those actions. The decisions about which respondents complain are made by physicians and nursing home administrators, all of whom are concededly private parties. . . .
>
> Respondents argue that state subsidization of the operating and capital costs of the facilities, payment of the medical expenses of more than 90% of the patients in the facilities, and the licensing of the facilities by the State, taken together convert the action of the homes into "state" action. But accepting all of these assertions as true, we are nonetheless unable to agree that the State is responsible for the decisions challenged by respondents. . . . That programs undertaken by the State result in substantial funding of the activities of a private entity is no more persuasive than

the fact of regulation of such an entity in demonstrating that the State is responsible for decisions made by the entity in the course of its business.

Justice White concurred briefly in the judgment. Justice Brennan, dissenting for himself and Justice Marshall, thought the majority was missing the larger picture of the state's involvement in the decisions at issue: "[N]ot only has the State established the system of treatment levels and utilization review in order to further its own fiscal goals, but that the State prescribes with as much precision as is possible the standards by which individual determinations are to be made."

Rendell-Baker v. Kohn, 457 U.S. 830 (1982), also discussed above in connection with public functions, dealt with "entwinement"-type arguments in considering whether state action was present when teachers were fired, allegedly unconstitutionally, by a private school that received most of its funding from the state and nearly all of its students based on state referrals of special-needs or at-risk students. Chief Justice Burger's majority opinion held state action lacking for reasons that tied together the principles of *Jackson* and *Blum* and also suggested that the state action analysis turned on the precise function that was the subject of the plaintiff's constitutional claim:

> [T]he Court of Appeals concluded that the fact that virtually all of the school's income was derived from government funding was the strongest factor to support a claim of state action. But in *Blum*, we held that the similar dependence of the nursing homes did not make the acts of the physicians and nursing home administrators acts of the State, and we conclude that the school's receipt of public funds does not make the discharge decisions acts of the State.
>
> The school, like the nursing homes, is not fundamentally different from many private corporations whose business depends primarily on contracts to build roads, bridges, dams, ships, or submarines for the government. Acts of such private contractors do not become acts of the government by reason of their significant or even total engagement in performing public contracts. . . .
>
> A second factor considered in *Blum* was the extensive regulation of the nursing homes by the State. . . . The Court relied on *Jackson*, where we held that state regulation, even if "extensive and detailed," did not make a utility's actions state action.
>
> Here the decisions to discharge the petitioners were not compelled or even influenced by any state regulation. Indeed, in contrast to the extensive regulation of the school generally, the various regulators showed relatively little interest in the school's personnel matters. The most intrusive personnel regulation promulgated by the various government agencies was the requirement that the Committee on Criminal Justice had the power to approve persons hired as vocational counselors. Such a regulation is not sufficient to make a decision to discharge, made by private management, state action.

Justice White concurred briefly in the judgment. In dissent, Justice Marshall, joined by Justice Brennan, would have found state action based on the combination of three factors: the school's "financial dependence on the State"; the fact that the "[t]he school is heavily regulated and closely supervised by the State," including in developing written hiring and firing rules; and "[t]he fact that the school is providing a substitute for public education," which is "one of the most important tasks performed by government."

Despite the Court's frequent reluctance to find state action by virtue of entwinement between the government and a private actor, the Court did so in *Brentwood Academy v. Tennessee Secondary School Athletic Ass'n*, 531 U.S. 288 (2001). A private nonprofit association of public and private schools governing Tennessee student athletics was sued by a member school, which claimed that the association's decision to penalize the school for writing a letter to incoming student athletes violated the First Amendment. Stressing that 84 percent of the association's members were public schools, Justice Souter's opinion for the majority held that it was a state actor:

> Interscholastic athletics obviously play an integral part in the public education of Tennessee, where nearly every public high school spends money on competitions among schools. Since a pickup system of interscholastic games would not do, these public teams need some mechanism to produce rules and regulate competition. The mechanism is an organization overwhelmingly composed of public school officials who select representatives (all of them public officials at the time in question here), who in turn adopt and enforce the rules that make the system work. Thus, by giving these jobs to the Association, the 290 public schools of Tennessee belonging to it can sensibly be seen as exercising their own authority to meet their own responsibilities. Unsurprisingly, then, the record indicates that half the council or board meetings documented here were held during official school hours, and that public schools have largely provided for the Association's financial support. . . . Unlike mere public buyers of contract services, whose payments for services rendered do not convert the service providers into public actors, *see Rendell-Baker*, the schools here obtain membership in the service organization and give up sources of their own income to their collective association. . . .
>
> [T]o the extent of 84% of its membership, the Association is an organization of public schools represented by their officials acting in their official capacity to provide an integral element of secondary public schooling. There would be no recognizable Association, legal or tangible, without the public school officials, who do not merely control but overwhelmingly perform all but the purely ministerial acts by which the Association exists and functions in practical terms. . . .
>
> To complement the entwinement of public school officials with the Association from the bottom up, the State of Tennessee has provided for entwinement from top down. State Board members are assigned ex officio to serve as members of the board of control and legislative council, and the Association's ministerial employees are treated as state employees to the extent of being eligible for membership in the state retirement system.

Justice Thomas's dissent, joined by Chief Justice Rehnquist and Justices Scalia and Kennedy, argued that the majority had impermissibly extended the concept of state action because the Association did not satisfy the public-function or government-involvement criteria for state action, and involved no "symbiotic relationship" of the sort in *Burton*.

Notes and Questions

1. Based on *Moose Lodge*, *Jackson*, *Blum*, and *Rendell-Baker*, identify the factors that the Court has said do not suffice to create a nexus that would allow for a finding of state action.

2. In light of the factors you have just identified, how do you explain *Burton* and *Brentwood*? *Burton*, of course, predates many of the cases limiting the concept of state action. Do you think *Burton* would come out the same way today? How do you account for *Brentwood*, which postdates the other major cases?

3. The Court has subsequently characterized *Burton* as finding state action based on a "symbiotic relationship" between the government and a private actor. What do you take to be the essence of that relationship that sufficed for a finding of state action? Or, put more concretely: What distinguishes the school in *Rendell-Baker* from the coffee shop in *Burton*?

4. Of the three types of relationships identified here as possible triggers for state action—public function, government mechanism, and entwinement—which has the clearest rules? Which is the most likely to lead to a finding of state action? The least?

5. One useful summary of the doctrine explains:

> [T]he current state action requirement is far more elaborate and elastic, depending on circumstances and the judges' disposition toward the particular constitutional claim, than the barebones approach announced in the *Civil Rights Cases*. There are plenty of established loopholes to the earlier understanding that the Fourteenth Amendment cannot apply to private parties—and all of them originated in and have developed in the context of the Court's race cases. . . . Where racism has operated in matters of voting (*Terry*), juries (*Edmonson*), and property rights (*Shelley*), the Court has been particularly willing to find state action. . . . *Edmonson* suggests that in cases involving racial discrimination, the state action doctrine entails a fair amount of flexibility, but is no clear signal as to how broadly the Court will apply its exceptions in other kinds of cases.

William N. Eskridge, Jr., *Some Effects of Identity-Based Social Movements on Constitutional Law in the Twentieth Century*, 100 Mich. L. Rev. 2062, 2330-32 (2002).

C. INTERACTION OF § 1983 WITH STATE LAW

In *Monroe*, the Court made a crucial decision not to foreclose the use of § 1983 when conduct forbidden by the Constitution is also forbidden (or at least unauthorized) by state law. But state law interacts with § 1983 in other important ways. Specifically, the Court has been called upon to decide:

- whether a plaintiff's failure to follow state administrative procedures forecloses resort to § 1983 (it generally doesn't);

- whether pending or completed state criminal proceedings obstruct a § 1983 claim raising related issues (they generally do); and
- whether, notwithstanding the lack of general exhaustion requirement for § 1983 and the applicability of § 1983 to actions unauthorized by state law, state procedures can defeat a § 1983 claim where they relate to the *substance* of the constitutional claim the plaintiff is asserting via § 1983 (they can).

These aspects of the relationship between § 1983 and state law are explored in turn.

1. EXHAUSTION AND § 1983

The principle that a plaintiff who has several alternative remedies available must try certain ones first (that is, "exhaust" those remedies) appears in a variety of contexts. Exhaustion requirements appear in a number of statutes, including several this book covers: the Federal Tort Claims Act, which provides a remedy for tortious conduct by federal employees (Chapter 2); Title VII of the Civil Rights Act of 1964, which prohibits employment discrimination (Chapter 6); and the Prison Litigation Reform Act (Chapter 12). More generally, exhaustion is a major principle of federal habeas corpus law and administrative law.

Does exhaustion apply to § 1983 actions?

Patsy v. Board of Regents
457 U.S. 496 (1982)

▪ *Justice MARSHALL delivered the opinion of the Court.*

This case presents the question whether exhaustion of state administrative remedies is a prerequisite to an action under 42 U.S.C. § 1983. Petitioner Georgia Patsy filed this action, alleging that her employer, Florida International University (FIU), had denied her employment opportunities solely on the basis of her race and sex. . . .

[W]e begin with a review of the legislative history to § 1 of the Civil Rights Act of 1871, the precursor to § 1983. Although we recognize that the 1871 Congress did not expressly contemplate the exhaustion question, we believe that the tenor of the debates over § 1 supports our conclusion that exhaustion of administrative remedies in § 1983 actions should not be judicially imposed.

The Civil Rights Act of 1871, along with the Fourteenth Amendment it was enacted to enforce, were crucial ingredients in the basic alteration of our federal system accomplished during the Reconstruction Era. During that time, the Federal Government was clearly established as a guarantor of the basic federal rights of individuals against incursions by state power. As we recognized, "[t]he very purpose of § 1983 was to interpose the federal courts between the States and the people, as guardians of the people's federal rights—to protect the people from unconstitutional action under color of state law, 'whether that action be executive, legislative, or judicial.'"

At least three recurring themes in the debates over § 1 cast serious doubt on the suggestion that requiring exhaustion of state administrative remedies would be consistent with the intent of the 1871 Congress. First, in passing § 1, Congress assigned to the federal courts a paramount role in protecting constitutional rights. . . . The 1871 Congress intended § 1 to "throw open the doors of the United States courts" to individuals who were threatened with, or who had suffered, the deprivation of constitutional rights, and to provide these individuals immediate access to the federal courts notwithstanding any provision of state law to the contrary. . . . [For instance,] Representative Elliott viewed the issue as whether "the Government of the United States [has] the right, under the Constitution, to protect a citizen in the exercise of his vested rights as an American citizen by . . . *the assertion of immediate jurisdiction through its courts*, without the appeal or agency of the State in which the citizen is domiciled."

A second theme in the debates further suggests that the 1871 Congress would not have wanted to impose an exhaustion requirement. A major factor motivating the expansion of federal jurisdiction through §§ 1 and 2 of the bill was the belief of the 1871 Congress that the state authorities had been unable or unwilling to protect the constitutional rights of individuals or to punish those who violated these rights. Of primary importance to the exhaustion question was the mistrust that the 1871 Congress held for the factfinding processes of state institutions. This perceived defect in the States' factfinding processes is particularly relevant to the question of exhaustion of administrative remedies: exhaustion rules are often applied in deference to the superior factfinding ability of the relevant administrative agency.

A third feature of the debates relevant to the exhaustion question is the fact that many legislators interpreted the bill to provide dual or concurrent forums in the state and federal system, enabling the plaintiff to choose the forum in which to seek relief. *Cf. Monroe v. Pape* ("The federal remedy is supplementary to the state remedy, and the latter need not be first sought and refused before the federal one is invoked"). . . .

We recognize, however, that drawing such a conclusion from this history alone is somewhat precarious: the 1871 Congress was not presented with the question of exhaustion of administrative remedies, nor was it aware of the potential role of state administrative agencies. Therefore, we do not rely exclusively on this legislative history. . . . Congress addressed the question of exhaustion under § 1983 when it recently enacted 42 U.S.C. § 1997e. The legislative history of § 1997e provides strong evidence of congressional intent on this issue.

The Civil Rights of Institutionalized Persons Act, 42 U.S.C. § 1997, was enacted primarily to ensure that the United States Attorney General has "legal standing to enforce existing constitutional rights and Federal statutory rights of institutionalized persons." In § 1997e, Congress also created a specific, limited exhaustion requirement for adult prisoners bringing actions pursuant to § 1983. Section 1997e and its legislative history demonstrate that Congress understood that exhaustion is not generally required in § 1983 actions, and that it decided to carve out only a narrow exception to this rule. A judicially imposed exhaustion requirement would be inconsistent with Congress' decision to adopt § 1997e and would usurp policy judgments that Congress has reserved for itself. . . .

Congress decided to adopt the limited exhaustion requirement of § 1997e in order to relieve the burden on the federal courts by diverting certain prisoner petitions back through state and local institutions, and also to encourage the States to develop appropriate grievance procedures. Implicit in this decision is Congress' conclusion that the no-exhaustion rule should be left standing with respect to other § 1983 suits.

A judicially imposed exhaustion requirement would also be inconsistent with the extraordinarily detailed exhaustion scheme embodied in § 1997e. Section 1997e carves out a narrow exception to the general no-exhaustion rule to govern certain prisoner claims, and establishes a procedure to ensure that the administrative remedies are adequate and effective. . . . This detailed scheme is inconsistent with discretion to impose, on an ad hoc basis, a judicially developed exhaustion rule in other cases. . . .

Respondent and the Court of Appeals argue that exhaustion of administrative remedies should be required because it would further various policies. They argue that an exhaustion requirement would lessen the perceived burden that § 1983 actions impose on federal courts; would further the goal of comity and improve federal-state relations by postponing federal-court review until after the state administrative agency had passed on the issue; and would enable the agency, which presumably has expertise in the area at issue, to enlighten the federal court's ultimate decision. . . .

[P]olicy considerations alone cannot justify judicially imposed exhaustion unless exhaustion is consistent with congressional intent. Furthermore, as the debates over incorporating the exhaustion requirement in § 1997e demonstrate, the relevant policy considerations do not invariably point in one direction, and there is vehement disagreement over the validity of the assumptions underlying many of them. The very difficulty of these policy considerations, and Congress' superior institutional competence to pursue this debate, suggest that legislative not judicial solutions are preferable.

Beyond the policy issues that must be resolved in deciding *whether* to require exhaustion, there are equally difficult questions concerning the design and scope of an exhaustion requirement. These questions include how to define those categories of § 1983 claims in which exhaustion might be desirable; how to unify and centralize the standards for judging the kinds of administrative procedures that should be exhausted; what tolling requirements and time limitations should be adopted; what is the res judicata and collateral estoppel effect of particular administrative determinations; what consequences should attach to the failure to comply with procedural requirements of administrative proceedings; and whether federal courts could grant necessary interim injunctive relief and hold the action pending exhaustion, or proceed to judgment without requiring exhaustion even though exhaustion might otherwise be required, where the relevant administrative agency is either powerless or not inclined to grant such interim relief. These and similar questions might be answered swiftly and surely by legislation, but would create costly, remedy-delaying, and court-burdening litigation if answered incrementally by the judiciary in the context of diverse constitutional claims relating to thousands of different state agencies. . . .

Based on the legislative histories of both § 1983 and § 1997e, we conclude that exhaustion of state administrative remedies should not be required as a prerequisite to bringing an action pursuant to § 1983. . . .

[Concurring opinions of White, J., and O'Connor, J., omitted.]

■ *Justice POWELL, with whom The Chief Justice joins . . . dissenting. . . .*

The requirement that a § 1983 plaintiff exhaust adequate state administrative remedies . . . rests on sound considerations. It does not defeat federal-court jurisdiction, it merely defers it. It permits the States to correct violations through their own procedures, and it encourages the establishment of such procedures. It is consistent with the principles of comity that apply whenever federal courts are asked to review state action or supersede state proceedings.

Moreover, and highly relevant to the effective functioning of the overburdened federal court system, the rule conserves and supplements scarce judicial resources. In 1961, the year that *Monroe v. Pape*, was decided, only 270 civil rights actions were begun in the federal district courts. In 1981, over 30,000 such suits were commenced. The result of this unprecedented increase in civil rights litigation is a heavy burden on the federal courts to the detriment of all federal-court litigants, including others who assert that their constitutional rights have been infringed. . . .

The Court seeks to support its no-exhaustion rule with indications of congressional intent. Finding nothing directly on point in the history of the Civil Rights Act itself, the Court places primary reliance on the recent Civil Rights of Institutionalized Persons Act. . . .

On the basis of the exhaustion provision in § 1997e . . . the Court contends that Congress has endorsed a *general* no-exhaustion rule. The irony in this reasoning should be obvious. A principal concern that prompted the Department of Justice to support, and the Congress to adopt, § 1997e was the vast increase in § 1983 suits brought by state prisoners in federal courts. . . . The burden on the system fairly can be described as enormous with few, if any, benefits that would not be available in meritorious cases if exhaustion of appropriate state administrative remedies were required prior to any federal-court litigation. It was primarily this problem that prompted enactment of § 1997e. . . .

Also revealing as to the limited purpose of § 1997e is Congress' consistent refusal to adopt legislation imposing a general no-exhaustion requirement. Thus, for example, in 1979, a bill was introduced into the Senate providing:

> "No court of the United States shall stay or dismiss any civil action brought under this Act on the ground that the party bringing such action failed to exhaust the remedies available in the courts or the administrative agencies of any State."
> S. 1983, 96th Cong., 1st Sess., § 5 (1979).

The bill was never reported out of committee.

The requirement that plaintiffs exhaust available and adequate administrative remedies—subject to well-developed exceptions—is firmly established in virtually every area of the law. This is dictated in § 1983 actions by common sense, as well as by comity and federalism, where adequate state administrative remedies are available. . . .

Notes and Questions

1. As between the majority and dissent in *Patsy*, which has the better argument regarding the implications of 42 U.S.C. § 1997e? Consider the comparative persuasiveness of arguments over the *enacted* § 1997e (on a question related to, but not the same as, the one before the Court in *Patsy*) and Justice Powell's argument based on an *unenacted* bill (confusingly, but perhaps not coincidentally, numbered Senate Bill 1983) regarding the precise issue before the Court. What criteria should determine which congressional inactions, if any, should be given significance and under what circumstances?

2. The Court's primary rationale for its holding in *Patsy* was congressional intent, both Reconstruction-era and modern. Another important and somewhat related consideration was institutional competence. Why was the majority reluctant to analyze policy considerations? Should it have done so? What do you make of the majority's inattention to the text of § 1983? Would the text have bolstered the majority's position or weakened it?

3. In *Felder v. Casey*, 487 U.S. 131 (1988), African-American Bobby Felder sought redress under § 1983 for a brutal beating by Milwaukee police officers—a beating Felder claimed was racially motivated. Wisconsin law barred actions against government agencies or officers unless the claimant notified the prospective defendant within 120 days of the alleged injury and provided an itemized statement of the relief sought. If the prospective defendant denied the claim, the claimant had to sue within six months of the denial. The Wisconsin Supreme Court held that Felder's attempt to sue the Milwaukee officers in state court was barred by these notice-of-claim rules.

The U.S. Supreme Court reversed. Writing for the Court, Justice Brennan explained that state procedures could not, consistent with the Supremacy Clause, be allowed to defeat the enforcement of a federal right. The Court found two problems with applying the notice-of-claim rule:

> First, . . . the notice requirement burdens the exercise of the federal right by forcing civil rights victims who seek redress in state courts to comply with a requirement that is entirely absent from civil rights litigation in federal courts. . . . Second, . . . the enforcement of such statutes in § 1983 actions brought in state court will frequently and predictably produce different outcomes in federal civil rights litigation based solely on whether that litigation takes place in state or federal court. States may not apply such an outcome-determinative law when entertaining substantive federal rights in their courts.

Thus, the Court concluded that the notice-of-claim procedure effectively obstructed the congressional design to make defendants answerable under federal law and amounted to an exhaustion requirement, which *Patsy* held was not required of § 1983 claims: "We think it plain that Congress never intended that those injured by governmental wrongdoers could be required, as a condition of recovery, to submit their claims to the government responsible for their injuries."

Justice O'Connor, joined by Chief Justice Rehnquist, dissented. She saw the notice-of-claim rule as beneficial because it promotes dispute resolution and enables the alleged wrongdoer to take corrective action. And a plaintiff should not be able to choose a state forum without abiding by its rules, she argued; a plaintiff who wishes to avoid state court rules could sue in federal court, where the *Patsy* no-exhaustion rule would apply.

What are some reasons you can imagine animating Felder's (or his lawyer's) decision to sue in state court? In light of those reasons, why shouldn't Felder have to take the state court system as he finds it, accepting its obstacles as well as its advantages?

How does our national conversation over police shootings of unarmed individuals shape your view of the opposing positions in *Felder*? Of the efficacy of notice-of-claim procedures specifically?

4. The Supreme Court has held that normal rules of preclusion apply when claims and issues raised in § 1983 cases have previously been litigated in state court. *See Migra v. Warren City Sch. Dist. Bd. of Educ.*, 465 U.S. 75 (1984); *Allen v. McCurry*, 449 U.S. 90 (1980). In so holding, the Court relied principally on the federal Full Faith and Credit Statute, 28 U.S.C. § 1738, which dates back to 1790, long before the passage of § 1983. *Allen*, 449 U.S. at 96 n.8.

Is the application of preclusion to § 1983 suits based on prior adjudications in state court consistent with *Patsy*? With *Felder*? How does the availability of preclusion affect the importance of *Patsy* to plaintiffs? What questions should a lawyer considering filing a § 1983 case be sure to ask the prospective client?

Note: Applying State Statutes of Limitations to § 1983 Claims

No limitations period appears in § 1983. Instead, 42 U.S.C. § 1988(a)—not to be confused with § 1988(b), which concerns the award of attorneys' fees and is covered in Chapter 10—provides that where the federal-law provisions governing civil rights enforcement "are deficient in the provisions necessary to furnish suitable remedies . . . the common law, as modified and changed by the constitution and statutes of the State wherein the court having jurisdiction of such civil or criminal cause is held, so far as the same is not inconsistent with the Constitution and laws of the United States, shall be extended to and govern the said courts in the trial and disposition of the cause."

In *Wilson v. Garcia*, 471 U.S. 261 (1985), the Court, speaking through Justice Stevens, interpreted § 1988(a) as requiring courts to select for § 1983 claims the "most analogous" state statute of limitations; the Court emphasized that a uniform rule for each state governing all § 1983 claims of whatever kind was necessary to avoid "obstruct[ing]" civil rights enforcement by "uncertainty in the applicable statute of limitation," which would cause "scarce resources [to] be dissipated by useless litigation on collateral matters." The Court approved a lower court's choice of the New Mexico statute of limitations for *personal injury* actions as the appropriate one to use for all § 1983 actions in New Mexico. The Court expressed confidence that this choice would not undermine enforcement of § 1983: "It is most unlikely that the period of limitations applicable to such claims ever was, or ever would be, fixed in a way that would discriminate against federal claims, or be inconsistent with federal law in any respect." The Court's approach in *Wilson* is not limited to New Mexico: "[A] State's personal injury statute of limitations should be applied to all § 1983 claims." *Owens v. Okure*, 488 U.S. 235, 240-41 (1989).

In a lone dissent in *Wilson*, Justice O'Connor argued that the result showed insufficient respect for state policy judgments about the appropriate limitations periods for different claims. She noted that § 1983 actions can resemble a variety of different types of claims depending on the constitutional right asserted—for instance, a school desegregation case is quite different than an excessive force case. Further, the Court's rule creates disuniformity where a § 1983 claim is joined with a state tort with a different limitations period. For example, she noted, under Pennsylvania law, "a § 1983 claim for violation of constitutional rights arising out of a breach of contract will be foreclosed in two years but its state law counterpart based on the identical breach will remain fresh and litigable at six years."

What type of uniformity does the majority seek to establish in applying state statutes of limitations? What type does Justice O'Connor prefer? Which type of uniformity is more important to maintain? Which more administrable?

Whatever its merits, the *Wilson* approach provides a straightforward rule for litigators. Even for states in which it can be tricky to figure out which limitations period applies to a personal injury suit based on state law alone, each federal court of appeals need only decide once for each state which limitations period to pick for § 1983 claims in that state, and henceforth (absent a change in the state's statute of limitations itself), the statute of limitations for § 1983 is established and easy for lawyers to ascertain.

2. COUSINS OF EXHAUSTION: ABSTENTION AND THE *HECK* BAR

Patsy held that non-incarcerated § 1983 litigants are not required to pursue alternative remedies on their way to federal court. (We'll return to the subject of exhaustion in the prison context in Chapter 12.) However, if the dispute is *already* being litigated elsewhere when the § 1983 case is filed, the relevant question is not *exhaustion* but *abstention*.

Abstention refers to a series of judicially created rules about circumstances when federal courts refrain from adjudicating disputes that would otherwise fall within their jurisdiction. A number of these rules pertain to the deference that federal courts give to state proceedings already in progress. The most significant example for purposes of civil rights litigation is the *Younger* doctrine that federal courts cannot enjoin state criminal prosecutions.

This doctrine takes its name from *Younger v. Harris*, 401 U.S. 37 (1971), in which a criminal defendant in state court claimed his prosecution violated his First Amendment rights and sued in federal court to enjoin it. The Supreme Court held that equitable principles foreclosed the requested injunction. Justice Black wrote for the Court:

> Since the beginning of this country's history Congress has, subject to few exceptions, manifested a desire to permit state courts to try state cases free from interference by federal courts. . . .
>
> The precise reasons for this longstanding public policy against federal court interference with state court proceedings have never been specifically identified but the primary sources of the policy are plain. One is the basic doctrine of equity jurisprudence that courts of equity should not act, and particularly should not act to restrain a criminal prosecution, when the moving party has an adequate remedy at law and will not suffer irreparable injury if denied equitable relief. The doctrine may originally have grown out of circumstances peculiar to the English judicial system and not applicable in this country, but its fundamental purpose of restraining equity jurisdiction within narrow limits is equally important under our Constitution, in order to prevent erosion of the role of the jury and avoid a duplication of legal proceedings and legal sanctions where a single suit would be adequate to protect the rights asserted. This underlying reason for restraining courts of equity from interfering with criminal prosecutions is reinforced by an even more vital consideration, the notion of "comity," that is, a proper respect for state functions, a recognition of the fact that the entire country is made up of a Union of separate state governments, and a continuance of the belief that the National Government will fare best if the States and their institutions are left free to perform their separate functions in their separate ways. This, perhaps for lack of a better and clearer way to describe it, is referred to by many as "Our Federalism," and one familiar with the profound debates that ushered our Federal Constitution into existence is bound to respect those who remain loyal to the ideals and dreams of "Our Federalism." The concept does not mean blind deference to "States' Rights" any more than it means centralization of control over every important issue in our National Government and its courts. The Framers rejected both these courses. What the concept does represent is a system in which there is sensitivity to the legitimate interests of both State and National Governments, and in which the National Government, anxious though it may be to vindicate and protect federal rights and federal interests, always endeavors to do so in ways that will not unduly interfere with the legitimate activities of the States. It should never be forgotten that this slogan, "Our Federalism," born in the early struggling days of our Union of States, occupies a highly important place in our Nation's history and its future. . . .
>
> Here a proceeding was already pending in the state court, affording Harris an opportunity to raise his constitutional claims.

Justice Douglas alone dissented, arguing, "The special circumstances when federal intervention in a state criminal proceeding is permissible . . . exist where for any reason the state statute being enforced is unconstitutional on its face."

Younger abstention has been extended to other types of proceedings also, including state civil and administrative proceedings. Under *Younger*, the pendency of certain types of proceedings in state court may obstruct a § 1983 suit, even though the plaintiff would not have been required to exhaust state remedies had the plaintiff reached federal court first.

(Several other types of abstention may bear on § 1983 suits as well. Because abstention is not a doctrine specific to civil rights litigation, and it is generally covered in a Federal Courts course, it will not be a subject of extended discussion here.)

Even state criminal proceedings that have *concluded* cast a shadow over related § 1983 litigation. Because Congress has codified the common law of habeas corpus into a strict and procedurally complex system of circumscribed review, the Court has thought it important not to permit challenges to criminal convictions using § 1983 instead of the federal habeas regime (which, unlike § 1983, requires exhaustion of state remedies). The next case shows that the Court's concern over conflict between § 1983 suits and habeas proceedings (also referred to as "collateral" review) extends beyond § 1983 actions seeking to overturn a conviction or obtain release from prison.

Heck v. Humphrey
512 U.S. 477 (1994)

■ *Justice* SCALIA *delivered the opinion of the Court....*

[An Indiana state court convicted Roy Heck of killing his wife. While his criminal appeal was pending, he filed this § 1983 suit against two prosecutors and an investigator whom he claimed knowingly destroyed evidence, among other violations. The complaint sought damages but did not challenge the conviction. The district court dismissed. The appeals court affirmed, reasoning that if Heck won, the state would be obliged to release him.] . . .

This case lies at the intersection of the two most fertile sources of federal-court prisoner litigation—the Civil Rights Act of 1871, 42 U.S.C. § 1983, and the federal habeas corpus statute, 28 U.S.C. § 2254. Both of these provide access to a federal forum for claims of unconstitutional treatment at the hands of state officials, but they differ in their scope and operation. In general, exhaustion of state remedies "is not a prerequisite to an action under § 1983," *Patsy* . . . . The federal habeas corpus statute, by contrast, requires that state prisoners first seek redress in a state forum.

Preiser v. Rodriguez, 411 U.S. 475 (1973) . . . held that habeas corpus is the exclusive remedy for a state prisoner who challenges the fact or duration of his confinement and seeks immediate or speedier release, even though such a claim may come within the literal terms of § 1983. We emphasize that *Preiser* did not create an exception to the "no exhaustion" rule of § 1983; it merely held that certain claims by state prisoners are not cognizable under that provision, and must be brought in habeas corpus proceedings, which do contain an exhaustion requirement.

This case is clearly not covered by the holding of *Preiser*, for petitioner seeks not immediate or speedier release, but monetary damages, as to which he could not "have sought and obtained fully effective relief through federal habeas corpus proceedings." . . .

[W]e see no need to abandon . . . our teaching that § 1983 contains no exhaustion requirement beyond what Congress has provided. The issue with respect to monetary damages challenging conviction is not, it seems to us, exhaustion; but rather, the same as the issue was with respect to injunctive relief challenging conviction in *Preiser*: whether the claim is cognizable under § 1983 at all. We conclude that it is not.

"We have repeatedly noted that 42 U.S.C. § 1983 creates a species of tort liability." . . . Thus, to determine whether there is any bar to the present suit, we look first to the common law of torts.

The common-law cause of action for malicious prosecution provides the closest analogy to claims of the type considered here because . . . it permits damages for confinement imposed pursuant to legal process. . . .

One element that must be alleged and proved in a malicious prosecution action is termination of the prior criminal proceeding in favor of the accused. This requirement "avoids parallel litigation over the issues of probable cause and guilt . . . and it precludes the possibility of the claimant [sic] succeeding in the tort action after having been convicted in the underlying criminal prosecution, in contravention of a strong judicial policy against the creation of two conflicting resolutions arising out of the same or identical transaction." Furthermore, "to permit a convicted criminal defendant to proceed with a malicious prosecution claim would permit a collateral attack on the conviction through the vehicle of a civil suit." This Court has long expressed similar concerns for finality and consistency and has generally declined to expand opportunities for collateral attack. We think the hoary principle that civil tort actions are not appropriate vehicles for challenging the validity of outstanding criminal judgments applies to § 1983 damages actions that necessarily require the plaintiff to prove the unlawfulness of his conviction or confinement, just as it has always applied to actions for malicious prosecution.

We hold that, in order to recover damages for allegedly unconstitutional conviction or imprisonment, or for other harm caused by actions whose unlawfulness would render a conviction or sentence invalid,[6] a § 1983 plaintiff must prove that the conviction or sentence has been reversed on direct appeal, expunged

---

6. An example of this latter category—a § 1983 action that does not seek damages directly attributable to conviction or confinement but whose successful prosecution would necessarily imply that the plaintiff's criminal conviction was wrongful—would be the following: A state defendant is convicted of . . . resisting arrest, defined as intentionally preventing a peace officer from effecting a lawful arrest. He then brings a § 1983 action against the arresting officer, seeking damages for violation of his Fourth Amendment right to be free from unreasonable seizures. In order to prevail in this § 1983 action, he would have to negate an element of the offense of which he has been convicted. Regardless of the state law concerning res judicata, the § 1983 action will not lie.

by executive order, declared invalid by a state tribunal authorized to make such determination, or called into question by a federal court's issuance of a writ of habeas corpus, 28 U.S.C. § 2254.

A claim for damages bearing that relationship to a conviction or sentence that has not been so invalidated is not cognizable under § 1983. Thus, when a state prisoner seeks damages in a § 1983 suit, the district court must consider whether a judgment in favor of the plaintiff would necessarily imply the invalidity of his conviction or sentence; if it would, the complaint must be dismissed unless the plaintiff can demonstrate that the conviction or sentence has already been invalidated. But if the district court determines that the plaintiff's action, even if successful, will not demonstrate the invalidity of any outstanding criminal judgment against the plaintiff, the action should be allowed to proceed, in the absence of some other bar to the suit. . . .

We do not engraft an exhaustion requirement upon § 1983, but rather deny the existence of a cause of action. Even a prisoner who has fully exhausted available state remedies has no cause of action under § 1983 unless and until the conviction or sentence is reversed, expunged, invalidated, or impugned by the grant of a writ of habeas corpus. . . . Just as a cause of action for malicious prosecution does not accrue until the criminal proceedings have terminated in the plaintiff's favor, so also a § 1983 cause of action for damages attributable to an unconstitutional conviction or sentence does not accrue until the conviction or sentence has been invalidated.[10]

Applying these principles to the present action, in which both courts below found that the damages claims challenged the legality of the conviction, we find that the dismissal of the action was correct. . . .

[Opinion of Thomas, J., concurring, omitted.]

▪ *Justice* SOUTER, *with whom Justice* BLACKMUN, *Justice* STEVENS, *and Justice* O'CONNOR *join, concurring in the judgment.* . . .

The Court's opinion can be read as saying nothing more than that now, after enactment of the habeas statute and because of it, prison inmates seeking § 1983 damages in federal court for unconstitutional conviction or confinement must

---

10. Justice Souter also adopts the common-law principle that one cannot use the device of a civil tort action to challenge the validity of an outstanding criminal conviction, but thinks it necessary to abandon that principle in those cases (of which no real-life example comes to mind) involving former state prisoners who, because they are no longer in custody, cannot bring postconviction challenges. We think the principle barring collateral attacks—a longstanding and deeply rooted feature of both the common law and our own jurisprudence—is not rendered inapplicable by the fortuity that a convicted criminal is no longer incarcerated. Justice Souter opines that disallowing a damages suit for a former state prisoner framed by Ku Klux Klan-dominated state officials is "hard indeed to reconcile . . . with the purpose of § 1983." But if, as Justice Souter appears to suggest, the goal of our interpretive enterprise under § 1983 were to provide a remedy for all conceivable invasions of federal rights that freedmen may have suffered at the hands of officials of the former States of the Confederacy, the entire landscape of our § 1983 jurisprudence would look very different. . . .

satisfy a requirement analogous to the malicious-prosecution tort's favorable-termination requirement.

That would be a sensible way to read the opinion, in part because the alternative would needlessly place at risk the rights of those outside the intersection of § 1983 and the habeas statute, individuals not "in custody" for habeas purposes. If these individuals (people who were merely fined, for example, or who have completed short terms of imprisonment, probation, or parole, or who discover (through no fault of their own) a constitutional violation after full expiration of their sentences), like state prisoners, were required to show the prior invalidation of their convictions or sentences in order to obtain § 1983 damages for unconstitutional conviction or imprisonment, the result would be to deny any federal forum for claiming a deprivation of federal rights to those who cannot first obtain a favorable state ruling. The reason, of course, is that individuals not "in custody" cannot invoke federal habeas jurisdiction, the only statutory mechanism besides § 1983 by which individuals may sue state officials in federal court for violating federal rights. That would be an untoward result. . . .

Consider the case of a former slave framed by Ku Klux Klan-controlled law-enforcement officers and convicted by a Klan-controlled state court of, for example, raping a white woman; and suppose that the unjustly convicted defendant did not (and could not) discover the proof of unconstitutionality until after his release from state custody. If it were correct to say that § 1983 independently requires a person not in custody to establish the prior invalidation of his conviction, it would have been equally right to tell the former slave that he could not seek federal relief even against the law-enforcement officers who framed him unless he first managed to convince the state courts that his conviction was unlawful. That would be a result hard indeed to reconcile either with the purpose of § 1983 or with the origins of what was "popularly known as the Ku Klux Act," the statute having been enacted in part out of concern that many state courts were "in league with those who were bent upon abrogation of federally protected rights." It would also be a result unjustified by the habeas statute or any other post-§ 1983 enactment. . . .

[W]hile the malicious-prosecution analogy provides a useful mechanism for implementing what statutory analysis requires, congressional policy as reflected in enacted statutes must ultimately be the guide. I would thus be clear that the proper resolution of this case (involving, of course, a state prisoner) is to construe § 1983 in light of the habeas statute and its explicit policy of exhaustion. I would not cast doubt on the ability of an individual unaffected by the habeas statute to take advantage of the broad reach of § 1983.

Notes and Questions

1. What rule emerges from *Heck*? How does Justice Souter's proposed approach differ from the majority's?

2. How does the majority justify its decision to borrow from tort law in defining the § 1983 cause of action here? Note that the Court has elsewhere held that a

§ 1983 violation has just two elements: (1) "the violation of a right secured by the Constitution and laws of the United States," and (2) "that the alleged deprivation was committed by a person acting under color of state law." *West v. Atkins*, 487 U.S. 42, 48 (1988). Where does the "favorable termination" requirement fit into this formulation?

3. Given the existence of the carefully calibrated habeas procedure for challenging convictions, it's easy to see why the Court would have feared end runs via § 1983 suits seeking a prisoner's release. But why must that restriction extend to actions seeking not release but damages based on a constitutional violation? The Court is concerned with the possibility for inconsistent adjudications—a prisoner could win his § 1983 constitutional lawsuit for damages yet lose his habeas suit for release under the more demanding standard applicable to such challenges. What's wrong with that? Our system allows for the possibility of inconsistent results in other areas where legal standards differ—for instance, a person can be acquitted of murder charges not proved beyond reasonable doubt yet held civilly liable for wrongful death on the same facts based on the "more likely than not" standard. (The O.J. Simpson case is a famous example of this tension.) Why isn't the same approach viable here? Is there something worse about keeping a person in prison after a federal court has awarded him damages for the constitutional violation that put him there? Something unseemly about a prisoner's collecting a damages award? Some other problem?

Applications

Consider the following three decisions in assessing *Heck*'s reach and its consequences.

1. The limits of *Heck*.   In *Wilkinson v. Dotson*, 544 U.S. 74 (2005), two Ohio prisoners brought § 1983 lawsuits to challenge Ohio's parole procedures on constitutional grounds after each prisoner was denied parole. Ohio defended based on the *Heck* bar. In an opinion by Justice Breyer, the Court held that the suit could proceed:

> [This Court's] cases, taken together, indicate that a state prisoner's § 1983 action is barred (absent prior invalidation)—no matter the relief sought (damages or equitable relief), no matter the target of the prisoner's suit (state conduct leading to conviction or internal prison proceedings)—if success in that action would necessarily demonstrate the invalidity of confinement or its duration. . . .
>
> Dotson and Johnson seek relief that will render invalid the state procedures used to deny parole eligibility (Dotson) and parole suitability (Johnson). Neither respondent seeks an injunction ordering his immediate or speedier release into the community. And . . . a favorable judgment will not "necessarily imply the invalidity of [their] conviction[s] or sentence[s]." *Heck*. Success for Dotson does not mean immediate release from confinement or a shorter stay in prison; it means at most new eligibility review, which at most will speed consideration of a new parole application. Success for Johnson means at most a new parole hearing at which Ohio parole authorities may, in their discretion, decline to shorten his prison term.

Because neither prisoner's claim would necessarily spell speedier release, neither lies at "the core of habeas corpus." . . .

Ohio points to language in *Heck* indicating that a prisoner's § 1983 damages action cannot lie where a favorable judgment would "necessarily imply the invalidity of his conviction or sentence." Ohio then argues that its parole proceedings are part of the prisoners' "sentence[s]"—indeed, an aspect of the "sentence[s]" that the § 1983 claims, if successful, will invalidate.

We do not find this argument persuasive. In context, *Heck* uses the word "sentence" to refer not to prison procedures, but to substantive determinations as to the length of confinement. . . . So understood, *Heck* is consistent with other cases permitting prisoners to bring § 1983 challenges to prison administrative decisions.

Justice Scalia, joined by Justice Thomas, concurred to note that a contrary result would distort habeas law.

In a solo dissent, Justice Kennedy argued that a challenge to prison parole procedures was cognizable in habeas and functionally indistinguishable from a habeas petition attacking the length of a sentence:

Everyone knows that when a prisoner succeeds in a habeas action and obtains a new sentencing hearing, the sentence may or may not be reduced. The sentence can end up being just the same, or perhaps longer. The prisoner's early release is by no means assured simply because the first sentence was found unlawful. Yet no one would say that an attack on judicial sentencing proceedings following conviction may be raised through an action under § 1983. The inconsistency in the Court's treatment of sentencing proceedings and parole proceedings is thus difficult to justify. . . .

If a parole determination is made in a proceeding flawed by errors of constitutional dimensions, as these respondents now allege, their continued confinement may well be the result of constitutional violation. Respondents thus raise a cognizable habeas claim of being "in custody in violation of the Constitution." In recognition of this elementary principle, this Court and the courts of appeals have adjudicated the merits of many parole challenges in federal habeas corpus proceedings. . . .

[The majority argues] that success on the claims will not necessarily entitle respondents to immediate release. This . . . proves far too much. If the Court's line of reasoning is sound, it would remove from the "core of habeas" any challenge to an unconstitutional sentencing procedure.

How much of a gap in the *Heck* framework, if any, does *Wilkinson* create? How clear is the line between *Heck*'s bar and *Wilkinson*'s exception?

2. *Heck's* **influence on timing of suit.** In *Wallace v. Kato*, 549 U.S. 384 (2007), a criminal defendant had been convicted but had his conviction overturned on appeal because his arrest was unconstitutional (and thus his post-arrest statements required to be suppressed); he then sued police under § 1983 for the original unconstitutional arrest. The question before the Supreme Court was whether Wallace's § 1983 suit was timely.

The Court began with the proposition that, by analogy to common law false arrest and false imprisonment claims, a suit for an unconstitutional arrest becomes ripe when the arrestee begins to be held pursuant to legal process—for instance, when he is arraigned on charges. At that point any wrongful detention would be attributable to *misuse of legal process*, not the original *arrest*. Thus, ordinarily, Wallace's unconstitutional arrest claim would have accrued (that is, become viable), and correspondingly his statute of limitations would have begun to run, when legal process was initiated against him even though he was not released from custody at that time.

Wallace argued that *Heck* required a different result. On his theory, his statute of limitations for the Fourth Amendment claim could not have started to run until after the conviction was overturned and the charges against him dropped; had he sued earlier, *Heck* would have barred the claim because a successful challenge to his arrest would have implied the invalidity of the criminal conviction.

The Supreme Court, per Justice Scalia, acknowledged that *Heck* can sometimes defer the accrual of a claim but held that it did not do so here:

> [T]he *Heck* rule for deferred accrual is called into play only when there exists "a conviction or sentence that has not been . . . invalidated," that is to say, an "outstanding criminal judgment." It delays what would otherwise be the accrual date of a tort action until the setting aside of an extant conviction which success in that tort action would impugn. . . . [Here, however, when Wallace's statute of limitations began to run] there was in existence no criminal conviction that the cause of action would impugn; indeed, there may not even have been an indictment.
>
> What petitioner seeks, in other words, is the adoption of a principle that goes well beyond *Heck*: that an action which would impugn *an anticipated future conviction* cannot be brought until that conviction occurs and is set aside. The impracticality of such a rule should be obvious. In an action for false arrest it would require the plaintiff (and if he brings suit promptly, the court) to speculate about whether a prosecution will be brought, whether it will result in conviction, and whether the pending civil action will impugn that verdict—all this at a time when it can hardly be known what evidence the prosecution has in its possession. And what if the plaintiff (or the court) guesses wrong, and the anticipated future conviction never occurs, because of acquittal or dismissal? Does that event (instead of the *Heck*-required setting aside of the extant conviction) trigger accrual of the cause of action? Or what if prosecution never occurs—what will the trigger be then?
>
> We are not disposed to embrace this bizarre extension of *Heck*. If a plaintiff files a false-arrest claim before he has been convicted (or files any other claim related to rulings that will likely be made in a pending or anticipated criminal trial), it is within the power of the district court, and in accord with common practice, to stay the civil action until the criminal case or the likelihood of a criminal case is ended. If the plaintiff is ultimately convicted, and if the stayed civil suit would impugn that conviction, *Heck* will require dismissal; otherwise, the civil action will proceed, absent some other bar to suit. . . .
>
> Petitioner has not brought to our attention, nor are we aware of, [state] cases providing tolling [of the statute of limitations] in even remotely comparable circumstances. . . . Nor would we be inclined to adopt a federal tolling rule to this effect. Under such a regime, it would not be known whether tolling is appropriate by reason of the *Heck* bar until it is established that the newly entered conviction would be impugned by the not-yet-filed, and thus utterly indeterminate, § 1983 claim. It would hardly be desirable to place the question of tolling *vel non* in this jurisprudential limbo, leaving it to be determined by those later events, and then pronouncing it retroactively.

Justice Stevens, joined by Justice Souter, concurred in the judgment based on an exception in habeas law that would have defeated Wallace's constitutional claim in a habeas attack on his conviction. Justice Breyer, joined by Justice Ginsburg, dissented, proposing that, in light of *Heck*, equitable tolling should be applied while the prosecution was pending and while any resulting conviction was in force. Otherwise, he argued, "large numbers of defendants will be sued immediately by all potential § 1983 plaintiffs with arguable *Heck* issues, no matter how meritless the claims; these suits may be endlessly stayed or dismissed and then, at some point in the future, some defendants will also be sued again."

In light of the practical problems Justice Breyer foresees, what justifies the majority's approach? What interests does it protect? Do you expect many recently arrested and newly charged defendants to file unconstitutional-arrest claims while their criminal cases are pending? Why or why not?

The Court subsequently distinguished *Wallace* in *McDonough v. Smith*, 139 S. Ct. 2149 (2019), which involved a constitutional claim for fabricating evidence in a criminal prosecution. A fabrication-of-evidence claim, the Court reasoned, was more like the claim in *Heck* than the claim in *Wallace*—unlike in *Wallace*, the claim "centers on evidence used to secure an indictment and at a criminal trial, so it does not require 'speculat[ion] about whether a prosecution will be brought,'" and like in *Heck* the claim "directly challenges . . . the prosecution itself." Accordingly, the Court held that the statute of limitations did not begin to run until the favorable termination of the criminal proceedings against the plaintiff. Three Justices would not have reached this question.

3. A problematic application?   A recent court of appeals decision illustrates the consequences and tenacity of the *Heck* bar. In *Griffin v. Baltimore Police Dep't*, 804 F.3d 692 (4th Cir. 2015), a man who had served more than thirty years in prison for murder sued the Baltimore Police Department and its officers for withholding material exculpatory evidence during his criminal trial, in violation of *Brady v. Maryland*, 373 U.S. 83 (1963). Although Griffin had sought habeas relief in the 1980s and 1990s, none of the withheld evidence came to light until 2011. In 2012, Griffin sought post-conviction relief in state court, as federal habeas law required him to do before he could bring a federal habeas petition. After the state court indicated it was prepared to order a new trial, Griffin accepted a deal from the state: In exchange for a consent motion to modify Griffin's sentence to time served without vacating the conviction, Griffin agreed not to pursue his pending petitions for post-conviction relief. That motion was granted, and Griffin was released. Accordingly, Griffin never sought federal habeas relief for his *Brady* claim.

The court of appeals held that *Heck* barred Griffin's subsequent § 1983 suit against the police, because victory for Griffin would "necessarily undermine the validity of Griffin's prior convictions." The court rejected Griffin's arguments that *Heck* should not apply because he had been released from custody before he could file a federal habeas petition on the *Brady* claim:

> The *Heck* bar is "not rendered inapplicable by the fortuity that a convicted criminal is no longer incarcerated." This rule prevents would-be § 1983 plaintiffs from

bringing suit even after they are released from custody and thus unable to challenge their conviction through a habeas petition. Were the rule otherwise, plaintiffs might simply wait to file their § 1983 actions until after their sentences were served, and thereby transform § 1983 into a new font of federal post-conviction review. . . .

[Griffin] points to [our decision in] *Wilson v. Johnson*, which recognizes an exception to the *Heck* bar in cases where a litigant "could not, as a practical matter, [have sought] habeas relief" while in custody. 535 F.3d 262, 268 (4th Cir. 2008). Griffin argues that he qualifies for this exception because he could not successfully pursue habeas relief while "deprived of the exculpatory evidence hidden by the police." There are several problems with his position.

In *Wilson*, this Court considered a § 1983 claim for damages alleging that the State of Virginia improperly extended Wilson's sentence by approximately three months. Wilson's case presented a potential problem identified by Justice Souter in *Heck*: because federal habeas suits may be filed only by individuals who are "in custody," petitioners with short sentences might find their claims moot before they could prosecute them. Without § 1983 as a backstop, these petitioners might lack access to federal courts altogether. After accepting Wilson's assertion that exhausting his claims prior to his release was impossible, we held that his action was cognizable under § 1983. Had we held otherwise, Wilson would have been entirely "left without access to a federal court." . . .

Griffin did not lack access to habeas relief while in custody. While Wilson had only a few months to make a habeas claim . . . Griffin had three decades. And Griffin actually did bring a federal habeas petition during his time in custody. Although his petition was denied, the fact that he was able to file it demonstrates that the concern animating *Wilson* . . . —that a citizen unconstitutionally punished might lack an opportunity for federal redress if kept in custody for only a short period of time—is absent in this case.

Griffin argues that he never had the opportunity to achieve meaningful habeas relief because evidence necessary to his case remained in the hands of the Baltimore Police Department. But likelihood of success is not the equivalent of opportunity to seek relief. . . .

Griffin's case is further undercut by the fact that he did eventually receive actual notice of possible official misconduct and still did not pursue additional federal habeas relief. . . . Griffin knew of possible police misconduct by, at the latest, August 4, 2011, the date of his evidentiary hearing in the Baltimore City Circuit Court. His custody did not terminate until over sixteen months later, on December 19, 2012.

Under the exhaustion requirement of federal habeas law, a federal habeas petition cannot be filed until state review proceedings have concluded. In light of that statutory bar, can you make sense of the court's conclusion that Griffin could have filed his petition between August 2011 and December 2012? Why does Griffin's failure to file a doomed federal petition during that time distinguish his situation from that in *Wilson*?

Does the existence of the *Wilson* exception answer Justice Souter's concerns about the reach of *Heck* (at least in the Fourth Circuit)? If you think not, is that because of the contours of the exception itself or how the court of appeals applied it in *Griffin*?

What incentives does *Griffin* create for prisoners who face the same circumstances Griffin did in 2012? If you were counsel to such a person today, how would you suggest proceeding? What choice would you expect the person to make?

3. The relevance of state remedies to § 1983 procedural due process claims

So far, we've seen the Supreme Court reject proposed rules that would subject § 1983 plaintiffs to broad limitations based on state law, either state substantive law (*Monroe*) or state procedures (*Patsy* and *Felder*). The relevance of state law and procedure to § 1983 claims is generally limited to a few discrete contexts: statutes of limitations, claims by incarcerated individuals, and claims that are (or were) the subject of state criminal proceedings.

There is a one type of constitutional claim, however, for which state remedies take on special relevance: procedural due process, which is a claim that a person has been deprived of a liberty or property interest without sufficient procedure. (Students who have not had Constitutional Law may wonder at the apparent redundancy of the phrase "*procedural* due process"; this awkward nomenclature is used to distinguish this doctrine from autonomy and privacy rights that fall under the heading of "*substantive* due process.") Procedural due process protections apply to a variety of contexts, including but not limited to deprivation of physical property, denial of public benefits such as welfare payments, and loss of child custody. What type of procedure is constitutionally adequate depends on the context. Sometimes procedures provided *after* people lose their liberty or property ("postdeprivation" procedures) are sufficient.

In keeping with our focus on enforcement doctrines rather than substantive constitutional law, we will not attempt comprehensive coverage of procedural due process, which may be covered in Constitutional Law or Civil Procedure. Our inquiry will be confined to the interaction between procedural due process and § 1983. *Monroe, Patsy*, and *Felder* all protect § 1983 plaintiffs from having their cases dismissed based on the content of state law or procedure. But a procedural due process claim squarely focuses on the adequacy of state procedures. In a § 1983 claim for a procedural due process violation, do considerations relevant to the constitutional merits override general § 1983 jurisprudence about how state procedures affect § 1983 actions? The Supreme Court has held that they do.

In *Parratt v. Taylor*, 451 U.S. 527 (1981), prison officials accidentally lost hobby materials that the plaintiff prisoner had ordered by mail. He sued for a deprivation of property without due process. The Court, per Justice Rehnquist, held that, although the plaintiff alleged a deprivation of property under color of state law, he failed to state a claim under § 1983 because he did not show that he had not received the process that he was "due." This question depended on state law: "[W]e must decide whether the tort remedies which the State of Nebraska provides as a means of redress for property deprivations satisfy the requirements of procedural due process." That Parratt received no process before the loss of the hobby materials was not dispositive:

> We have . . . recognized that postdeprivation remedies made available by the State can satisfy the Due Process Clause. In such cases, the normal predeprivation notice and opportunity to be heard is pretermitted if the State provides a postdeprivation remedy. . . . [Our] cases recognize that either the necessity of quick action by

the State or the impracticality of providing any meaningful predeprivation process, when coupled with the availability of some meaningful means by which to assess the propriety of the State's action at some time after the initial taking, can satisfy the requirements of procedural due process. . . .

[W]e have rejected the proposition that "at a meaningful time and in a meaningful manner" always requires the State to provide a hearing prior to the initial deprivation of property. This rejection is based in part on the impracticability in some cases of providing any preseizure hearing under a state-authorized procedure, and the assumption that at some time a full and meaningful hearing will be available.

Applying these principles, the Court held that the plaintiff had not stated a viable due process claim:

The justifications which we have found sufficient to uphold takings of property without any predeprivation process are applicable to a situation such as the present one involving a tortious loss of a prisoner's property as a result of a random and unauthorized act by a state employee. In such a case, the loss is not a result of some established state procedure and the State cannot predict precisely when the loss will occur. It is difficult to conceive of how the State could provide a meaningful hearing before the deprivation takes place. The loss of property, although attributable to the State as action under "color of law," is in almost all cases beyond the control of the State. Indeed, in most cases it is not only impracticable, but impossible, to provide a meaningful hearing before the deprivation. That does not mean, of course, that the State can take property without providing a meaningful postdeprivation hearing. The prior cases which have excused the prior-hearing requirement have rested in part on the availability of some meaningful opportunity subsequent to the initial taking for a determination of rights and liabilities. . . .

[Here,] the deprivation occurred as a result of the unauthorized failure of agents of the State to follow established state procedure. There is no contention that the procedures themselves are inadequate nor is there any contention that it was practicable for the State to provide a predeprivation hearing. Moreover, the State of Nebraska has provided respondent with the means by which he can receive redress for the deprivation. The State provides a remedy to persons who believe they have suffered a tortious loss at the hands of the State. Through this tort claims procedure the State hears and pays claims of prisoners housed in its penal institutions. This procedure was in existence at the time of the loss here in question but respondent did not use it. . . . The remedies provided could have fully compensated the respondent for the property loss he suffered, and we hold that they are sufficient to satisfy the requirements of due process. . . .

To accept respondent's argument that the conduct of the state officials in this case constituted a violation of the Fourteenth Amendment would almost necessarily result in turning every alleged injury which may have been inflicted by a state official acting under "color of law" into a violation of the Fourteenth Amendment cognizable under § 1983. It is hard to perceive any logical stopping place to such a line of reasoning. Presumably, under this rationale any party who is involved in nothing more than an automobile accident with a state official could allege a constitutional violation under § 1983. Such reasoning "would make of the Fourteenth Amendment a font of tort law to be superimposed upon whatever systems may already be administered by the States." We do not think that the drafters of the Fourteenth Amendment intended the Amendment to play such a role in our society.

Of the five additional opinions generated in the case, two merit mention. Concurring in the judgment only, Justice Powell would have held that the plaintiff failed to state a claim because *negligent* deprivations of property never give rise to a due process claim regardless of what procedures are available. Concurring in part and dissenting in part, Justice Marshall concluded that Nebraska procedures were inadequate because the plaintiff was not informed of them; according to Justice Marshall, "prison officials have an affirmative obligation to inform a prisoner who claims that he is aggrieved by official action about the remedies available under state law."

Distinguishing *Parratt* in *Logan v. Zimmerman Brush Co.*, 455 U.S. 422 (1982), the Court held that when a deprivation occurs as the result of a *misapplication* of an established state procedure, a due process claim is viable. There, a disabled employee pursued an employment discrimination claim against a private company under Illinois administrative procedures, which required the state Fair Employment Practices Commission to schedule a factfinding conference within 120 days. The Commission failed to do so, and the Illinois Supreme Court held that the employee's claim was therefore barred. The Supreme Court reversed, in an opinion by Justice Blackmun holding that the termination of the claim violated the employee's due process rights. In contrast to *Parratt*, the Court explained, here "it is the state system itself that destroys a complainant's property interest, by operation of law, whenever the Commission fails to convene a timely conference—whether the Commission's action is taken through negligence, maliciousness, or otherwise." Moreover, the Court reasoned, the only "postdeprivation process" available through state law—a state tort suit—would not restore the lost opportunity to bring a discrimination claim, because (among other reasons) it could not provide for reinstatement of the employee. Two concurrences argued that the employee had been deprived of equal protection as well as due process.

In *Hudson v. Palmer*, 468 U.S. 517 (1984), the Court considered, among other things, whether the rule of *Parratt*—that a due process claim for a § 1983 violation depended on the adequacy of state post-deprivation remedies—applied even when the alleged deprivation of liberty or property was *intentional* and not merely (as alleged in *Parratt*) negligent. The plaintiff in *Hudson* was a prisoner who claimed that a guard had intentionally destroyed his property during a shakedown of his cell. In an opinion by Chief Justice Burger, the Court (without dissent on this point) applied *Parratt* and held that the availability of state common law remedies defeated the due process claim. The factors supporting the holding in *Parratt* were equally present here, the Court reasoned:

> The underlying rationale of *Parratt* is that when deprivations of property are effected through random and unauthorized conduct of a state employee, predeprivation procedures are simply "impracticable" since the state cannot know when such deprivations will occur. We can discern no logical distinction between negligent and intentional deprivations of property insofar as the "practicability" of affording predeprivation process is concerned. The state can no more anticipate and control in advance the random and unauthorized intentional conduct of its employees than it can anticipate similar negligent conduct.

In *Daniels v. Williams*, 474 U.S. 327 (1986), a prison slip-and-fall case, the Court revisited whether negligent acts could violate due process and adopted Justice Powell's position from *Parratt* that they do not. As to the interpretation of § 1983, however, the Court reaffirmed that it "contains no state-of-mind requirement independent of that necessary to state a violation of the underlying constitutional right." Rather, "in any given § 1983 suit, the plaintiff must still prove a violation of the underlying constitutional right; and depending on the right, merely negligent conduct may not be enough to state a claim." Thus, the state-of-mind showing necessary to state a mind is entirely dependent on the substantive constitutional right at issue and is not a matter of § 1983 law. Justices Blackmun and Marshall each concurred in the judgment only. (In a decision announced the same day, *Davidson v. Cannon*, 474 U.S. 344 (1986), the Court applied *Daniels* to reject a negligence-based due process claim based on prison officials' failure to protect a prisoner from threatened violence by another prisoner. The Court's brief opinion did not discuss the contours of § 1983.)

Finally, *Zinermon v. Burch*, 494 U.S. 113 (1990), synthesized the teachings of the *Parratt* line of cases and reconciled them with *Monroe*. The plaintiff in *Zinermon* alleged that physicians and other staff at a Florida hospital deprived him of liberty without due process by admitting him as a "voluntary" mental patient when he was incompetent to give informed consent to his admission. The defendants argued that *Parratt* foreclosed the claim. In rejecting this argument, Justice Blackmun's opinion for the Court explained the significance of state procedures to different types of constitutional claims:

> [Under *Monroe*], overlapping state remedies are generally irrelevant to the question of the existence of a cause of action under § 1983. A plaintiff, for example, may bring a § 1983 action for an unlawful search and seizure despite the fact that the search and seizure violated the State's Constitution or statutes, and despite the fact that there are common-law remedies for trespass and conversion. As was noted in *Monroe*, in many cases there is "no quarrel with the state laws on the books," instead, the problem is the way those laws are or are not implemented by state officials.
>
> This general rule applies in a straightforward way to . . . [most constitutional claims]. As to these . . . types of claims, the constitutional violation actionable under § 1983 is complete when the wrongful action is taken. A plaintiff, under *Monroe v. Pape*, may invoke § 1983 regardless of any state-tort remedy that might be available to compensate him for the deprivation of these rights. . . .
>
> A § 1983 action may [also] be brought for a violation of procedural due process, but here the existence of state remedies is relevant in a special sense. In procedural due process claims, the deprivation by state action of a constitutionally protected interest in "life, liberty, or property" is not in itself unconstitutional; what is unconstitutional is the deprivation of such an interest without due process of law. The constitutional violation actionable under § 1983 is not complete when the deprivation occurs; it is not complete unless and until the State fails to provide due process. Therefore, to determine whether a constitutional violation has occurred, it is necessary to ask what process the State provided, and whether it was constitutionally adequate. This inquiry would examine the procedural safeguards built into the

statutory or administrative procedure of effecting the deprivation, and any remedies for erroneous deprivations provided by statute or tort law.

Accordingly, the Court had to decide what procedures were required before admitting a mental patient to a state hospital:

> To determine whether, as petitioners contend, the *Parratt* rule necessarily precludes § 1983 liability in this case, we must ask whether predeprivation procedural safeguards could address the risk of deprivations of the kind Burch alleges. . . . The risk is that some persons who come into Florida's mental health facilities will apparently be willing to sign forms authorizing admission and treatment, but will be incompetent to give the "express and informed consent" required for voluntary placement under [state law]. Indeed, the very nature of mental illness makes it foreseeable that a person needing mental health care will be unable to understand any proffered "explanation and disclosure of the subject matter" of the forms that person is asked to sign, and will be unable "to make a knowing and willful decision" whether to consent to admission. . . .
>
> We now consider whether predeprivation safeguards would have any value in guarding against the kind of deprivation Burch allegedly suffered. Petitioners urge that here, as in *Parratt* and *Hudson*, such procedures could have no value at all, because the State cannot prevent its officials from making random and unauthorized errors in the admission process. We disagree.
>
> The Florida statutes, of course, do not allow incompetent persons to be admitted as "voluntary" patients. But the statutes do not direct any member of the facility staff to determine whether a person is competent to give consent, nor to initiate the involuntary placement procedure for every incompetent patient. A patient who is willing to sign forms but incapable of informed consent certainly cannot be relied on to protest his "voluntary" admission and demand that the involuntary placement procedure be followed. The staff are the only persons in a position to take notice of any misuse of the voluntary admission process and to ensure that the proper procedure is followed.
>
> Florida chose to delegate to petitioners a broad power to admit patients . . . , i.e., to effect what, in the absence of informed consent, is a substantial deprivation of liberty. Because petitioners had state authority to deprive persons of liberty, the Constitution imposed on them the State's concomitant duty to see that no deprivation occur without adequate procedural protections.

The Court went on to reject the argument that the *Parratt* and *Hudson* cases applied to the type of "unauthorized" action that occurred here, and the Court reaffirmed the distinction between *Parratt-Hudson* and *Monroe*:

> [P]etitioners cannot characterize their conduct as "unauthorized" in the sense the term is used in *Parratt* and *Hudson*. The State delegated to them the power and authority to effect the very deprivation complained of here, Burch's confinement in a mental hospital, and also delegated to them the concomitant duty to initiate the procedural safeguards set up by state law to guard against unlawful confinement. In *Parratt* and *Hudson*, the state employees had no similar broad authority to deprive prisoners of their personal property, and no similar duty to initiate (for persons unable to protect their own interests) the procedural safeguards required before deprivations occur. The deprivation here is "unauthorized" only in the sense that it

was not an act sanctioned by state law, but, instead, was a "depriv[ation] of constitutional rights . . . by an official's abuse of his position." *Monroe*.[20]

Dissenting, Justice O'Connor (joined by Chief Justice Rehnquist and Justices Scalia and Kennedy) argued that *Parratt* and *Hudson* should apply:

> [F]or deprivations worked by such random and unauthorized departures from otherwise unimpugned and established state procedures the State provides the process due by making available adequate postdeprivation remedies. In *Parratt*, the Court addressed a deprivation which "occurred as a result of the unauthorized failure of agents of the State to follow established state procedure." The random nature of the state actor's unauthorized departure made it not "practicable for the State to provide a predeprivation hearing," and adequate postdeprivation remedies available through the State's tort system provided the process due under the Fourteenth Amendment. *Hudson* applied this reasoning to intentional deprivations by state actors and confirmed the distinction between deprivation pursuant to "an established state procedure" and that pursuant to "random and unauthorized action." In *Hudson*, the Court explained that the *Parratt* doctrine was applicable because "the state cannot possibly know in advance of a negligent deprivation of property," and that "[t]he controlling inquiry is solely whether the state is in a position to provide for predeprivation process."
>
> Application of *Parratt* and *Hudson* indicates that respondent has failed to state a claim allowing recovery under 42 U.S.C. § 1983. Petitioners' actions were unauthorized: they are alleged to have wrongly and without license departed from established state practices.

Further, the dissenters argued that *Zinermon* introduced confusion into procedural due process law: "[T]he Court marks out a vast terra incognita of unknowable duties and expansive liability of constitutional dimension."

Notes and Questions

1. Putting *Monroe* together with the *Parratt-Hudson* line of cases, when is a state remedy relevant to a § 1983 claim?

2. *Monroe* and *Parratt-Hudson* both pertain to actions of state or local officials that are "unauthorized" by state or local law. Do those cases use that term in the same way? If not, what is the difference? Does the fact that *Parratt* and *Hudson* pair that adjective with the word "random" (as in "random and unauthorized") help clarify the difference? If the difference comes down to the fact that *Parratt* and *Hudson* were about due process claims and *Monroe* was not, should *Zinermon* have come out the other way?

---

20. Contrary to the dissent's view of *Parratt* and *Hudson*, those cases do not stand for the proposition that in every case where a deprivation is caused by an "unauthorized . . . departure from established practices," state officials can escape § 1983 liability simply because the State provides tort remedies. This reading of *Parratt* and *Hudson* detaches those cases from their proper role as special applications of the settled principles expressed in [prior cases including] *Monroe*.

3. What is the relationship of *Parratt-Hudson* and *Patsy*? Functionally speaking, is exhaustion sometimes required, notwithstanding *Patsy*? How so? Is *Patsy* in jeopardy based on *Parratt-Hudson*? Why or why not?

D. PARALLEL STATE CAUSES OF ACTION

State law sometimes offers parallel means to enforce civil rights. Although covering the state-law civil rights landscape in every state is impractical here, it is worthwhile to identify the broad categories of parallel state enforcement mechanisms that exist so readers who will practice in this field know where to look to identify parallel state claims that might merit serious consideration for inclusion in a civil rights action.

First, although most constitutional law is federal constitutional law, the U.S. Constitution provides a floor, not a ceiling, for rights protection. State constitutions sometimes protect rights that the federal Constitution does not, such as a right to education. *See, e.g., Rose v. Council for Better Educ., Inc.,* 790 S.W.2d 186, 189 (Ky. 1989); *Abbott v. Burke,* 575 A.2d 359, 363 (N.J. 1990). As to rights recognized by both federal and state constitutions, the latter may protect the same rights to a greater degree. *See, e.g., Commonwealth v. Gonsalves,* 711 N.E.2d 108, 111 (Mass. 1999) (recognizing greater state constitutional protection against searches and seizures than exists under the Fourth Amendment); *York v. Wahkiakum Sch. Dist. No. 200,* 178 P.3d 995, 1006 (Wash. 2008) (refusing to recognize federal constitutional law's "special needs" exception to warrant requirement in the context of random student drug testing).

State constitutional rights may asserted through various mechanisms. Some states have statutes that parallel the federal § 1983. *See, e.g.,* Ark. Code § 16-123-105; Neb. Rev. Stat. § 20-148. Some states have more limited statutes aimed at interference with rights by threats, intimidation, or coercion. *See, e.g.,* Cal. Civ. Code § 52.1; Mass. Gen. Laws, ch. 12, §§ 11H-I; N.J. Stat. § 10:6-2; *cf.* Me. Rev. Stat. tit. 5, § 4682 (reaching interference with rights "by physical force or violence").

In other instances, state courts have interpreted their constitutions as providing freestanding causes of action to enforce certain state constitutional rights (some courts describe this result as holding that state constitutional provisions are "self-executing"). *See, e.g., Binette v. Sabo,* 710 A.2d 688, 693 (Conn. 1998); *Godfrey v. State,* 898 N.W.2d 844, 872 (Iowa 2017); *Widgeon v. Eastern Shore Hosp. Ctr.,* 479 A.2d 921, 930 (Md. 1984); *Dorwart v. Caraway,* 58 P.3d 128, 136 (Mont. 2002); *Brown v. State,* 674 N.E.2d 1129, 1138 (N.Y. 1996); *Zullo v. State,* 205 A.3d 466, 488 (Vt. 2019). These state-law causes of action frequently bear some resemblance to the *federal* cause of action (known as "*Bivens*" after the case that recognized it) that the Supreme Court has found available to enforce the *federal* Constitution against *federal* officers—which is the subject of the next chapter. A few state courts have refused to find a freestanding cause of action to enforce a state constitution. *See, e.g., City of Beaumont v. Bouillion,* 896 S.W.2d 143, 150 (Tex. 1995).

Second, state statutes may offer specific protections against discrimination that exceed those explicitly provided in the federal Constitution and statutes. For instance, state statutes may go beyond their federal counterparts by prohibiting discrimination based on categories that federal antidiscrimination law does not name, such as:

- sexual orientation, *see, e.g.,* Cal. Civ. Code §§ 51-52; Colo. Rev. Stat. § 24-34-402; D.C. Code § 2-1402.11; 775 Ill. Comp. Stat. 5/1-103 & 5/2-102; Iowa Code § 216.6; N.J. Stat. § 10:5-12(a); Or. Rev. Stat. § 659A.030; Rev. Code of Wash. 49.60.030;
- gender identity, *see, e.g.,* Cal. Gov't Code § 12940(a); D.C. Code § 2-1402.11; Iowa Code § 216.6; N.J. Stat. § 10:5-12(a);
- marital status, *see, e.g.,* Cal. Civ. Code §§ 51-52; D.C. Code § 2-1402.11; 775 Ill. Comp. Stat. 5/1-103 & 5/2-102; N.J. Stat. § 10:5-12(a); Or. Rev. Stat. § 659A.030; and
- genetic information, *see, e.g.,* Cal. Civ. Code §§ 51-52; D.C. Code § 2-1402.11; N.J. Stat. § 10:5-12(a).

(Note that this list is illustrative and not exhaustive as to either protected grounds or the jurisdictions that explicitly cover the grounds listed.)

Finally, outside of civil rights law entirely, traditional state tort law can sometimes offer remedies for conduct that violates a person's constitutional rights. For instance, if an officer enters your home without a warrant and no exception to the warrant requirement applies, that is generally a state-law trespass as well as a Fourth Amendment violation. Federal constitutional claims for excessive force, unconstitutional conditions of confinement through failure to provide medical treatment, and retaliatory discharge for the exercise of freedom of speech may all have state common law analogues depending on the circumstances and the state. For the three claims just listed, for instance, the relevant state-law torts could be, respectively, battery, negligence, and wrongful discharge in violation of public policy.

Why would civil rights litigators pursue these more generic claims alongside claims specifically aimed at the type of harm inflicted? Intuitively, constitutional claims for unreasonable search or cruel and unusual punishment may seem a better fit, in recognition that the wrong was of constitutional magnitude and perpetrated through an abuse of official authority. Put more concretely: An officer busting into your home isn't merely a trespass. Or, as Justice Harlan put it, explaining in his *Monroe v. Pape* concurrence what he surmised was the congressional intent behind § 1983, "a deprivation of a constitutional right is significantly different from and more serious than a violation of a state right and therefore deserves a different remedy even though the same act may constitute both a state tort and the deprivation of a constitutional right."

But there are important practical reasons to seek redress via state tort law where possible. The most important is that, as we'll see in Part II, § 1983 has been held to incorporate substantial defenses and limitations on liability. For instance, the Supreme Court has barred recovery under § 1983 against a municipality (such as a city, county, or school board) on a respondeat superior theory (Chapter 5). State tort plaintiffs, by contrast, usually *can* invoke such a theory, thus enabling plaintiffs to assert claims against institutional defendants where constitutional claims might be viable only against individual officials. Other reasons litigators sometimes invoke state tort laws alongside constitutional causes of action include the possibility that remedies might differ and the possibility that the substantive elements may be easier to prove. In some circumstances, of course, there is no tort-law analogue to a constitutional claim (discrimination, due process, and many types of First Amendment claims are all examples of constitutional violations that ordinary tort law usually does not reach). And sometimes strategic considerations might counsel against the inclusion of the state-law theories. But when parallel state-law theories are available, they are worth considering.

A caveat about state claims: Although notice-of-claim rules may not be used to bar § 1983 claims under *Felder v. Casey* (see Section C.1, above), a state is free to apply notice-of-claim rules to *state-law* causes of action, so a conscientious litigator should make sure to know and comply with any applicable rules of this type, which might require would-be plaintiffs to act sooner than the relevant statute of limitation runs.

CHAPTER 1 PROBLEMS

Problem 1A. Ft. Totten Institute (FTI) is a military boarding high school run by the 51st state, Douglass Commonwealth, and funded by grants from the U.S. military. According to school rules, violations of any law are also school disciplinary infractions.

One day, FTI student Barry O. Bahma is assaulted by two other FTI students off campus. He defends himself. Local police officer Jackson Andrews sees the fight and breaks it up. Bahma tells Andrews he was attacked and was defending himself. Andrews ignores him and issues disorderly conduct citations to all three boys. Disorderly conduct is a misdemeanor punishable by a $500 fine. An individual cited can just pay the fine or defend the charge in court. Self-defense is a defense to the charge.

Word of the fight quickly spreads around campus. All three boys are written up for school disciplinary infractions for breaking Douglass law.

FTI disciplinary offenses are investigated by Jay Polk Knox, who is a retired local detective and FTI alumnus and who works with the school on a volunteer basis. Knox is responsible for making a recommendation to FTI's president, who alone decides how to handle a disciplinary accusation after hearing from the investigator and the student. Bahma tells the president his story and says he'll be challenging the citation in state court based on self-defense. The president, eager to resolve the charge quickly, asks Knox whether he has viewed the incident footage from Officer Andrews's body-worn camera. Knox says he has, and that the footage corroborates the charge against Bahma. The president accepts Knox's representation and suspends Bahma from school for a month.

Although Bahma wasn't able to get the video before the FTI president ruled, Bahma obtains the Andrews body camera footage to use in defending against his disorderly conduct citation in state court. The footage clearly shows that Andrews saw Bahma defending himself from the other boys. Bahma's state court date has not yet been set.

1. Assume it is a due process violation for a public school official to lie to a decisionmaker as part of a disciplinary investigation. Can Bahma sue Knox under § 1983 for a due process violation? What obstacles does he face?

2. Now imagine that the Douglass state prosecutor offers Bahma a plea deal under which Bahma would plead guilty in exchange for a sentence of probation and no fine. What are the consequences for Bahma's § 1983 case if he takes the deal?

Problem 1B.   Under the law of the 51st state, Douglass Commonwealth, private security officers are individuals who are employed by private companies to perform security-related tasks after being trained by and receiving a license from a local police department. Private security officers have search and arrest powers, but only within the property that the company has assigned them to protect.

While Kinley McWilliam is shopping at a department store in Douglass Commonwealth, Howie Eisendwight, a private security officer who works for the store, confronts McWilliam and accuses her of shoplifting. McWilliam denies any wrongdoing, but Eisendwight orders McWilliam to turn out her pockets. When she does, a bag of cocaine falls to the floor. Eisendwight arrests McWilliam and turns her over to the police.

It turns out that the police already knew that McWilliam was involved in a drug-dealing operation. Coincidentally, they had obtained a warrant for her arrest and were actively looking for her when Eisendwight searched and arrested her.

McWilliam is charged with various drug crimes. She moves to suppress the evidence as the result of an unconstitutional search. The Douglass Commonwealth Superior Court denies the motion to suppress, ruling that the outstanding warrant and contemporaneous police search for McWilliam satisfied the "inevitable discovery doctrine," which permits illegally obtained evidence to be used if the government shows that the evidence would inevitably have been discovered by lawful means. McWilliam is convicted.

McWilliam files a civil suit against Eisendwight seeking damages for the search in the store. Leaving aside merits questions about the interpretation of the Fourth Amendment, what other obstacles does McWilliam face in seeking to hold Eisendwight liable? Can she overcome them?

Constitutional Claims Against Federal Officers

Section 1983 applies to deprivations of constitutional rights "under color of any statute, ordinance, regulation, custom, or usage, *of any State or Territory or the District of Columbia*" (emphasis added). What happens if the wrongdoer is acting "under color" of *federal* law? This chapter will answer that question. Although the same *defenses* can be invoked by local, state, and federal officials (as we'll see in Chapter 4), the *causes of action* are quite different.

A. THE CAUSES OF ACTION

Whereas § 1983 provides a single vehicle to seek both damages and injunctive relief for constitutional violations by state officials, different sources of authority are invoked to obtain different types of relief for constitutional violations by federal officials, and the Supreme Court has rendered the damages cause of action quite limited. This section introduces the basic mechanisms for seeking each type of relief; the following sections trace the complex evolution of the damages cause of action.

1. The *Bivens* cause of action for damages

Bivens v. Six Unknown Named Agents of the Federal Bureau of Narcotics
403 U.S. 388 (1971)

■ *Mr. Justice* Brennan *delivered the opinion of the Court....*

Petitioner's complaint alleged that ... respondents, agents of the Federal Bureau of Narcotics acting under claim of federal authority, entered his apartment and arrested him for alleged narcotics violations. The agents manacled petitioner in front of his wife and children, and threatened to arrest the entire family. They searched the apartment from stem to stern. Thereafter, petitioner was taken to the federal courthouse in Brooklyn, where he was interrogated, booked, and subjected to a visual strip search. [Plaintiff sued, claiming that police lacked a warrant and used excessive force. Plaintiff sought damages for Fourth Amendment violations. The district court dismissed for lack of a cause of action; the court of appeals affirmed.] ...

Respondents do not argue that petitioner should be entirely without remedy for an unconstitutional invasion of his rights by federal agents. In respondents' view, however, the rights that petitioner asserts—primarily rights of privacy—are creations of state and not of federal law. Accordingly, they argue, petitioner may obtain money damages to redress invasion of these rights only by an action in tort, under state law, in the state courts. In this scheme the Fourth Amendment would serve merely to limit the extent to which the agents could defend the state law tort suit by asserting that their actions were a valid exercise of federal power: if the agents were shown to have violated the Fourth Amendment, such a defense would be lost to them and they would stand before the state law merely as private individuals....

We think that respondents' thesis rests upon an unduly restrictive view of the Fourth Amendment's protection against unreasonable searches and seizures by federal agents, a view that has consistently been rejected by this Court. Respondents seek to treat the relationship between a citizen and a federal agent unconstitutionally exercising his authority as no different from the relationship between two private citizens. In so doing, they ignore the fact that power, once granted, does not disappear like a magic gift when it is wrongfully used. An agent acting—albeit unconstitutionally—in the name of the United States possesses a far greater capacity for harm than an individual trespasser exercising no authority other than his own. Accordingly, as our cases make clear, the Fourth Amendment operates as a limitation upon the exercise of federal power regardless of whether the State in whose jurisdiction that power is exercised would prohibit or penalize the identical act if engaged in by a private citizen. It guarantees to citizens of the United States the absolute right to be free from unreasonable searches and seizures carried out by virtue of federal authority. And "where federally protected rights have been invaded, it has been the rule from the beginning that courts will be alert to adjust their remedies so as to grant the necessary relief." . . .

A private citizen, asserting no authority other than his own, will not normally be liable in trespass if he demands, and is granted, admission to another's house. But one who demands admission under a claim of federal authority stands in a far different position. The mere invocation of federal power by a federal law enforcement official will normally render futile any attempt to resist an unlawful entry or arrest by resort to the local police; and a claim of authority to enter is likely to unlock the door as well. "In such cases there is no safety for the citizen, except in the protection of the judicial tribunals, for rights which have been invaded by the officers of the government, professing to act in its name. There remains to him but the alternative of resistance, which may amount to crime." Nor is it adequate to answer that state law may take into account the different status of one clothed with the authority of the Federal Government. For just as state law may not authorize federal agents to violate the Fourth Amendment, neither may state law undertake to limit the extent to which federal authority can be exercised. . . .

That damages may be obtained for injuries consequent upon a violation of the Fourth Amendment by federal officials should hardly seem a surprising proposition. Historically, damages have been regarded as the ordinary remedy for an invasion of personal interests in liberty. Of course, the Fourth Amendment does not in so many words provide for its enforcement by an award of money damages for the consequences of its violation. But "it is * * * well settled that where legal rights have been invaded, and a federal statute provides for a general right to sue for such invasion, federal courts may use any available remedy to make good the wrong done." The present case involves no special factors counseling hesitation in the absence of affirmative action by Congress. We are not dealing with a question of "federal fiscal policy". . . . Nor are we asked in this case to impose liability upon a congressional employee for actions contrary to no constitutional prohibition, but merely said to be in excess of the authority delegated to him by the Congress. Finally, we cannot accept respondents' formulation of the question as whether the availability of money damages is necessary to enforce the Fourth Amendment. For we have here no explicit congressional declaration that persons injured by a federal officer's violation of the Fourth Amendment may not recover money damages from the agents, but must instead be remitted to another remedy, equally effective in the view of Congress. The question is merely whether petitioner, if he can demonstrate an injury consequent upon the violation by federal agents of his Fourth Amendment rights, is entitled to redress his injury through a particular remedial mechanism normally available in the federal courts. "The very essence of civil liberty certainly consists in the right of every individual to claim the protection of the laws, whenever he receives an injury." *Marbury v. Madison.* Having concluded that petitioner's complaint states a cause of action under the Fourth Amendment, we hold that petitioner is entitled to recover money damages for any injuries he has suffered as a result of the agents' violation of the Amendment. . . .

▪ *Mr. Justice* HARLAN, *concurring in the judgment.* . . .

[I]t would be at least anomalous to conclude that the federal judiciary—while competent to choose among the range of traditional judicial remedies to implement statutory and common-law policies, and even to generate substantive rules governing primary behavior in furtherance of broadly formulated policies articulated by statute or Constitution—is powerless to accord a damages remedy to vindicate social policies which, by virtue of their inclusion in the Constitution, are aimed predominantly at restraining the Government as an instrument of the popular will. . . .

The major thrust of the Government's position is that, where Congress has not expressly authorized a particular remedy, a federal court should exercise its power to accord a traditional form of judicial relief at the behest of a litigant, who claims a constitutionally protected interest has been invaded, only where the remedy is "essential," or "indispensable for vindicating constitutional rights." . . .

These arguments for a more stringent test to govern the grant of damages in constitutional cases seem to be adequately answered by the point that the judiciary has a particular responsibility to assure the vindication of constitutional interests such as those embraced by the Fourth Amendment. To be sure, "it must be remembered that legislatures are ultimate guardians of the liberties and welfare of the people in quite as great a degree as the courts." But it must also be recognized that the Bill of Rights is particularly intended to vindicate the interests of the individual in the face of the popular will as expressed in legislative majorities; at the very least, it strikes me as no more appropriate to await express congressional authorization of traditional judicial relief with regard to these legal interests than with respect to interests protected by federal statutes.

The question then, is, as I see it, whether compensatory relief is "necessary" or "appropriate" to the vindication of the interest asserted. In resolving that question, it seems to me that the range of policy considerations we may take into account is at least as broad as the range of a legislature would consider with respect to an express statutory authorization of a traditional remedy. In this regard I agree with the Court that the appropriateness of according Bivens compensatory relief does not turn simply on the deterrent effect liability will have on federal official conduct. Damages as a traditional form of compensation for invasion of a legally protected interest may be entirely appropriate even if no substantial deterrent effects on future official lawlessness might be thought to result. Bivens, after all, has invoked judicial processes claiming entitlement to compensation for injuries resulting from allegedly lawless official behavior, if those injuries are properly compensable in money damages. I do not think a court of law—vested with the power to accord a remedy—should deny him his relief simply because he cannot show that future lawless conduct will thereby be deterred. . . .

[T]he limitations on state remedies for violation of common-law rights by private citizens argue in favor of a federal damages remedy. The injuries inflicted by officials acting under color of law, while no less compensable in damages than those inflicted by private parties, are substantially different in kind, as the

Court's opinion today discusses in detail. It seems to me entirely proper that these injuries be compensable according to uniform rules of federal law, especially in light of the very large element of federal law which must in any event control the scope of official defenses to liability. Certainly, there is very little to be gained from the standpoint of federalism by preserving different rules of liability for federal officers dependent on the State where the injury occurs.

Putting aside the desirability of leaving the problem of federal official liability to the vagaries of common-law actions, it is apparent that some form of damages is the only possible remedy for someone in Bivens' alleged position. It will be a rare case indeed in which an individual in Bivens' position will be able to obviate the harm by securing injunctive relief from any court. However desirable a direct remedy against the Government might be as a substitute for individual official liability, the sovereign still remains immune to suit. Finally, assuming Bivens' innocence of the crime charged, the "exclusionary rule" is simply irrelevant. For people in Bivens' shoes, it is damages or nothing. . . .

Judicial resources, I am well aware, are increasingly scarce these days. Nonetheless, when we automatically close the courthouse door solely on this basis, we implicitly express a value judgment on the comparative importance of classes of legally protected interests. And current limitations upon the effective functioning of the courts arising from budgetary inadequacies should not be permitted to stand in the way of the recognition of otherwise sound constitutional principles. . . .

[Opinions of Burger, C.J., and Blackmun, J., each dissenting, are omitted.]

■ *Mr. Justice* BLACK, *dissenting.* . . .

Although Congress has created . . . a federal cause of action against state officials acting under color of state law, it has never created such a cause of action against federal officials. If it wanted to do so, Congress could, of course, create a remedy against federal officials who violate the Fourth Amendment in the performance of their duties. But the point of this case and the fatal weakness in the Court's judgment is that neither Congress nor the State of New York has enacted legislation creating such a right of action. For us to do so is, in my judgment, an exercise of power that the Constitution does not give us.

Even if we had the legislative power to create a remedy, there are many reasons why we should decline to create a cause of action where none has existed since the formation of our Government. The courts of the United States as well as those of the States are choked with lawsuits. The number of cases on the docket of this Court have reached an unprecedented volume in recent years. A majority of these cases are brought by citizens with substantial complaints — persons who are physically or economically injured by torts or frauds or governmental infringement of their rights; persons who have been unjustly deprived of their liberty or their property; and persons who have not yet received the equal opportunity in education, employment, and pursuit of happiness that was the dream of our forefathers. Unfortunately, there have also been a growing number of frivolous lawsuits, particularly actions for damages against law enforcement officers whose conduct has been judicially sanctioned by state trial and appellate courts and in many instances even by this Court. . . . Of course, there are instances of legitimate grievances, but legislators might well desire to devote judicial resources to other problems of a more serious nature.

We sit at the top of a judicial system accused by some of nearing the point of collapse. Many criminal defendants do not receive speedy trials and neither society nor the accused are assured of justice when inordinate delays occur. Citizens must wait years to litigate their private civil suits. Substantial changes in correctional and parole systems demand the attention of the lawmakers and the judiciary. If I were a legislator I might well find these and other needs so pressing as to make me believe that the resources of lawyers and judges should be devoted to them rather than to civil damage actions against officers who generally strive to perform within constitutional bounds. There is also a real danger that such suits might deter officials from the proper and honest performance of their duties. . . .

The task of evaluating the pros and cons of creating judicial remedies for particular wrongs is a matter for Congress and the legislatures of the States. . . .

Notes and Questions

1. Consider the role of each of the following in the debates between the majority and dissenting Justices: text, legislative history, and policy. How do the Justices' approaches to each of these sources of authority compare to the analysis in *Monroe*?

2. Some of the arguments advanced in these opinions could be characterized as sweeping. Think about how far the Court might go in applying Justice Harlan's approach to filling gaps in the law, or how parsimonious the Court might be if it were guided by the policy arguments advanced by Justice Black. What limiting principles do the various Justices offer for their theories?

3. What clues does the Court provide as to the meaning of "special factors counseling hesitation"? What is the role of this concept in the holding? As we'll see, this concept has come to play a preeminent role in *Bivens* jurisprudence.

4. How important was it to the outcome that for Bivens, it was "damages or nothing"? Should it matter to the availability of a *Bivens* remedy whether an injunction is available? Whether state-law damages remedies are available?

   In this connection, consider Professor Akhil Amar's account of how enforcement of constitutional rights against federal officers worked prior to *Bivens*:

   > Plaintiff would sue defendant federal officer in trespass; defendant would claim federal empowerment that trumped the state law of trespass under the principles of the supremacy clause; and plaintiff, by way of reply, would play an even higher supremacy clause trump: Any federal empowerment was ultra vires and void because of Fourth Amendment limitations on federal power itself. If, but only

if, plaintiff could in fact prove that the Fourth Amendment had been violated, defendant's shield of federal power would dissolve, and he would stand as a naked tortfeasor.

Akhil Reed Amar, *Of Sovereignty and Federalism*, 96 Yale L.J. 1425, 1506-07 (1987). Is that so much worse than the *Bivens* regime? Why?

5. Justice Black argues that the existence of 42 U.S.C. § 1983 suggests Congress could have created a remedy against federal officials and chose not to. Is there a case to make that § 1983 *supports* the inference of a damages remedy? How are these arguments informed by the history of the enactment of § 1983?

In connection with these questions, consider the Court's observation in a sequel to *Bivens*, *Carlson v. Green*, 446 U.S. 14 (1980), a principal case in the next section, that "the 'constitutional design' would be stood on its head if federal officials did not face at least the same liability as state officials guilty of the same constitutional transgression."

The intuition that the Constitution should apply at least as vigorously to federal officials as to state and local ones has driven substantive constitutional interpretation as well as the scope of authorized remedies. For instance, in *Bolling v. Sharpe*, 347 U.S. 497 (1954)—which decided, on the same day as *Brown v. Board of Education*, that school segregation was unconstitutional in the District of Columbia—the Court explained that even though the Fourteenth Amendment (applicable to the states but not the federal government) includes an equal protection guarantee and the Fifth Amendment (applicable to the federal government also) does not, the latter must be interpreted to include equal protection as well: "In view of our decision that the Constitution prohibits the states from maintaining racially segregated public schools, it would be unthinkable that the same Constitution would impose a lesser duty on the Federal Government."

2. INJUNCTIVE RELIEF AGAINST FEDERAL OFFICIALS

Bivens recognized a cause of action against federal officials for damages. Does *Bivens* also authorize injunctive relief?

This question has caused some dispute in the lower courts. *Compare, e.g., Stuart v. Rech*, 603 F.3d 409, 412 (7th Cir. 2010) ("[T]he implied right of action authorized by *Bivens* is not affected by the particular relief sought."), *with Simmat v. U.S. Bureau of Prisons*, 413 F.3d 1225, 1231 (10th Cir. 2005) (suggesting that "[t]here is no such animal as a *Bivens* suit" for injunctive relief).

But a much older line of cases, dating back at least to *Ex parte Young*, 209 U.S. 123 (1908), reflects a practice of simply issuing injunctions for violations of the Constitution without identifying the "cause of action." In *Ex parte Young*, railroad shareholders sued the attorney general of Minnesota in federal court seeking to enjoin enforcement of a state statute setting railroad rates. The court issued the injunction, and the Supreme Court, on review of Attorney General Young's citation for contempt of the injunction, held that the court possessed the power to issue the injunction, as the Court's precedents "furnish ample justification for the assertion that individuals who, as officers of the state . . . threaten and are about to commence proceedings, either of a civil or criminal nature, to enforce against parties affected an unconstitutional act, violating the Federal Constitution, may be enjoined by a Federal court of equity."

Citing *Ex parte Young*, the Supreme Court has more recently made clear that federal courts possess inherent equitable power to enjoin violations of federal law by either federal or state officials:

> [W]e have long held that federal courts may in some circumstances grant injunctive relief against state officers who are violating, or planning to violate, federal law. *See, e.g., Ex parte Young.* But that has been true not only with respect to violations of federal law by state officials, but also with respect to violations of federal law by federal officials. . . . What our cases demonstrate is that, "in a proper case, relief may be given in a court of equity . . . to prevent an injurious act by a public officer." *Carroll v. Safford*, 3 How. 441, 463 (1845).
>
> The ability to sue to enjoin unconstitutional actions by state and federal officers is the creation of courts of equity, and reflects a long history of judicial review of illegal executive action, tracing back to England.

Armstrong v. Exceptional Child Center, Inc., 135 S. Ct. 1378, 1384 (2015). (You might note that, under *Armstrong*'s formulation, the inherent equitable power to enjoin *state* officials seems duplicative of the statutory authorization under § 1983. We'll consider in Chapter 8 the differences between these two sources of authority.)

Another cause of action sometimes employed to enjoin unconstitutional agency action is the Administrative Procedure Act. *See* 5 U.S.C. § 702 (providing judicial review for "[a] person suffering legal wrong because of agency action, or adversely affected or aggrieved by agency action" and reflecting the availability of injunctive relief by requiring that "any mandatory or injunctive decree shall specify the Federal officer or officers (by name or by title), and their successors in office, personally responsible for compliance").

As you read further in this chapter about the way *Bivens* has been interpreted and curtailed, it should become apparent why civil rights litigators today tend not to invoke *Bivens* when seeking an injunction against a federal official.

Figure 2.1 summarizes the causes of action used to seek damages and injunctive relief against federal and state officials.

Figure 2.1: Causes of action for constitutional claims, by type of official and remedy

		Against an official...	
	Use	**Acting under color of state (or local) law**	**Of the federal government**
If you seek...	**Damages:**	§ 1983	*Bivens*
	Injunction:	§ 1983 or inherent equitable power	inherent equitable power

B. THE FTCA AND EARLY *BIVENS* DEVELOPMENT

In the decade after *Bivens*, the Court applied the reasoning there to additional constitutional claims against federal officers. During this period, Congress appeared to signal its approval of the *Bivens* remedy through amendments to the Federal Tort Claims Act, which provides a parallel cause of action for *non-constitutional* tort claims. This statute merits attention both as a remedy that civil rights litigators sometimes assert in tandem with *Bivens* and as an interpretive guide to *Bivens* itself.

1. The Federal Tort Claims Act

Enacted in 1946 and subsequently amended over the years, the Federal Tort Claims Act (FTCA), 28 U.S.C. §§ 1346(b), 2671-2680, provides that, subject to certain exceptions, federal district courts may adjudicate claims against the United States for money damages

> for injury or loss of property, or personal injury or death caused by the negligent or wrongful act or omission of any employee of the Government while acting within the scope of his office or employment, under circumstances where the United States, if a private person, would be liable to the claimant in accordance with the law of the place where the act or omission occurred.

28 U.S.C. § 1346. Thus, the FTCA provides a cause of action for individuals injured by federal employees' conduct (within the scope of their employment) that would be tortious under local law. An FTCA claim is asserted against the United States itself, not the individual officer. The substance of the claim is derived from local law, so, for instance, a pedestrian struck by a federal employee driving in Boston in the course of the employee's duties would have to establish the elements of a Massachusetts common law negligence claim in order to prevail under the FTCA.

Numerous exceptions and limitations apply. Some of the main ones (this is not an exhaustive list) include:

- an exhaustion requirement that plaintiffs first present their claims to the appropriate federal agency, 28 U.S.C. § 2401;
- a bar against punitive damages or interest, 28 U.S.C. § 2674;
- the unavailability of a jury trial, 28 U.S.C. § 2402;
- the exclusion of claims "for injuries to [armed] service[members] where the injuries arise out of or are in the course of activity incident to service," *Feres v. United States*, 340 U.S. 135, 146 (1950);
- the exclusion of claims "based upon the exercise or performance or the failure to exercise or perform a discretionary function or duty on the part of a federal agency or an employee of the Government," 26 U.S.C. § 2680(a) (the "discretionary function exception"); and
- the exclusion of "[a]ny claim arising out of assault, battery, false imprisonment, false arrest, malicious prosecution, abuse of process, libel, slander, misrepresentation, deceit, or interference with contract rights" unless the tortious act was committed by an "investigative or law enforcement officer" empowered

to carry out searches, seizures, or arrests, 28 U.S.C. § 2680(h) (the "intentional tort exception").

Originally, the intentional tort exception was absolute. The current carve-out preserving intentional tort claims against law enforcement officials was enacted in 1974, after (and arguably in light of) *Bivens. See* Carlos M. Vázquez & Stephen I. Vladeck, *State Law, the Westfall Act, and the Nature of the* Bivens *Question*, 161 U. Pa. L. Rev. 509, 567 (2013). Civil rights litigators routinely consider bringing, and sometimes do bring, parallel FTCA claims alongside *Bivens* actions.

Another important aspect of the FTCA is its preclusion of state tort claims. In *Westfall v. Erwin*, 484 U.S. 292 (1988), the Supreme Court held that federal employees were not immune from state tort claims. Congress promptly amended the FTCA (via a law commonly known as the "Westfall Act" for the decision overruled) to provide that FTCA suits against the federal government are the exclusive remedy for torts committed by federal officials; thus, today federal employees are not subject to common law tort claims. 28 U.S.C. § 2679; *see Osborn v. Haley*, 549 U.S. 225, 229 (2007).

Of note, the exclusive-remedy provision of the FTCA specifically preserves a "civil action against an employee of the Government which is brought for a violation of the Constitution of the United States." *Id.* § 2679(b)(2)(A). The interplay between *Bivens* and the FTCA is addressed in several of the cases that follow.

2. Solidifying *Bivens*

The facts in *Davis v. Passman*, 442 U.S. 228 (1979), seem far removed from those in *Bivens*, but the same principle governed the outcome. Otto Passman was a Louisiana congressman who fired Shirley Davis as his deputy administrative assistant because, as Rep. Passman explained in writing, although she was "able, energetic and a very hard worker," he had concluded "that it was essential that the understudy to my Administrative Assistant be a man." Davis sued under the equal protection component of the Fifth Amendment's Due Process Clause, and one of the questions before the Supreme Court was whether she had a damages cause of action against Rep. Passman. Writing for the Court, Justice Brennan explained that she did:

> "Historically, damages have been regarded as the ordinary remedy for an invasion of personal interests in liberty." *Bivens.* Relief in damages would be judicially manageable, for the case presents a focused remedial issue without difficult questions of valuation or causation. Litigation under Title VII of the Civil Rights Act of 1964 has given federal courts great experience evaluating claims for backpay due to illegal sex discrimination. Moreover since respondent is no longer a Congressman, equitable relief in the form of reinstatement would be unavailing. And there are available no other alternative forms of judicial relief. For Davis, as for *Bivens*, "it is damages or nothing." . . .
>
> [T]he Court of Appeals appeared concerned that, if a damages remedy were made available to petitioner, the danger existed "of deluging federal courts with claims . . . ." We do not perceive the potential for such a deluge. . . . But perhaps the most fundamental answer to the concerns expressed by the Court of Appeals is that

provided by Mr. Justice Harlan concurring in *Bivens*: "... current limitations upon the effective functioning of the courts arising from budgetary inadequacies should not be permitted to stand in the way of the recognition of otherwise sound constitutional principles."

Chief Justice Burger and Justices Powell and Rehnquist each dissented, all focusing on separation of powers and the Constitution's Speech and Debate Clause, Art. I, § 6, cl. 1, which immunizes legislators for their legislative activities.

The following year, the Court provided its most expansive statement of the *Bivens* doctrine and addressed its relationship to the FTCA.

Carlson v. Green
446 U.S. 14 (1980)

■ *Mr. Justice BRENNAN delivered the opinion of the Court.*

Respondent brought this suit in the District Court for the Southern District of Indiana on behalf of the estate of her deceased son, Joseph Jones, Jr., alleging that he suffered personal injuries from which he died because the petitioners, federal prison officials, violated his due process, equal protection, and Eighth Amendment rights.[1] ...

Bivens established that the victims of a constitutional violation by a federal agent have a right to recover damages against the official in federal court despite the absence of any statute conferring such a right. Such a cause of action may be defeated in a particular case, however, in two situations. The first is when defendants demonstrate "special factors counselling hesitation in the absence of affirmative action by Congress." *Bivens*; *Davis*. The second is when defendants show that Congress has provided an alternative remedy which it explicitly declared to be a substitute for recovery directly under the Constitution and viewed as equally effective. *Bivens*; *Davis*.

Neither situation obtains in this case. First, the case involves no special factors counselling hesitation in the absence of affirmative action by Congress. Petitioners do not enjoy such independent status in our constitutional scheme as to suggest that judicially created remedies against them might be inappropriate. ...

Second, we have here no explicit congressional declaration that persons injured by federal officers' violations of the Eighth Amendment may not recover

---

1. More specifically, respondent alleged that petitioners, being fully apprised of the gross inadequacy of medical facilities and staff at the Federal Correction Center in Terre Haute, Ind., and of the seriousness of Jones' chronic asthmatic condition, nonetheless kept him in that facility against the advice of doctors, failed to give him competent medical attention for some eight hours after he had an asthmatic attack, administered contra-indicated drugs which made his attack more severe, attempted to use a respirator known to be inoperative which further impeded his breathing, and delayed for too long a time his transfer to an outside hospital. The complaint further alleges that Jones' death resulted from these acts and omissions, that petitioners were deliberately indifferent to Jones' serious medical needs, and that their indifference was in part attributable to racial prejudice.

money damages from the agents but must be remitted to another remedy, equally effective in the view of Congress. Petitioners point to nothing in the Federal Tort Claims Act (FTCA) or its legislative history to show that Congress meant to pre-empt a *Bivens* remedy or to create an equally effective remedy for constitutional violations. FTCA was enacted long before *Bivens* was decided, but when Congress amended FTCA in 1974 to create a cause of action against the United States for intentional torts committed by federal law enforcement officers, 28 U.S.C. § 2680(h), the congressional comments accompanying that amendment made it crystal clear that Congress views FTCA and *Bivens* as parallel, complementary causes of action:

> "[T]his provision should be viewed as a counterpart to the *Bivens* case[;] . . . it waives the defense of sovereign immunity so as to make the Government independently liable in damages for the same type of conduct that is alleged to have occurred in *Bivens* (and for which that case imposes liability upon the individual Government officials involved)." S. Rep. No. 93-588, p. 3 (1973).

In the absence of a contrary expression from Congress, § 2680(h) thus contemplates that victims of the kind of intentional wrongdoing alleged in this complaint shall have an action under FTCA against the United States as well as a *Bivens* action against the individual officials alleged to have infringed their constitutional rights.

This conclusion is buttressed by the significant fact that Congress follows the practice of explicitly stating when it means to make FTCA an exclusive remedy. Furthermore, Congress has not taken action on other bills that would expand the exclusivity of FTCA.

Four additional factors, each suggesting that the *Bivens* remedy is more effective than the FTCA remedy, also support our conclusion that Congress did not intend to limit respondent to an FTCA action. First, the *Bivens* remedy, in addition to compensating victims, serves a deterrent purpose.[6] Because the *Bivens* remedy is recoverable against individuals, it is a more effective deterrent than the FTCA remedy against the United States. It is almost axiomatic that the threat of damages has a deterrent effect, surely particularly so when the individual official faces personal financial liability.

Petitioners argue that FTCA liability is a more effective deterrent because the individual employees responsible for the Government's liability would risk loss of employment and because the Government would be forced to promulgate corrective policies. That argument suggests, however, that the superiors would not take the same actions when an employee is found personally liable for violation of a citizen's constitutional rights. The more reasonable assumption is that responsible superiors are motivated not only by concern for the public fisc but also by concern for the Government's integrity.

Second, our decisions, although not expressly addressing and deciding the question, indicate that punitive damages may be awarded in a *Bivens* suit.

---

6. Title 42 U.S.C. § 1983 serves similar purposes.

Punitive damages are "a particular remedial mechanism normally available in the federal courts," and are especially appropriate to redress the violation by a Government official of a citizen's constitutional rights. Moreover, punitive damages are available [under] § 1983 . . . and [we have previously suggested] that the "constitutional design" would be stood on its head if federal officials did not face at least the same liability as state officials guilty of the same constitutional transgression. But punitive damages in an FTCA suit are statutorily prohibited. Thus FTCA is that much less effective than a *Bivens* action as a deterrent to unconstitutional acts.

Third, a plaintiff cannot opt for a jury in an FTCA action, as he may in a *Bivens* suit. . . .

Fourth, an action under FTCA exists only if the State in which the alleged misconduct occurred would permit a cause of action for that misconduct to go forward. 28 U.S.C. § 1346(b) (United States liable "in accordance with the law of the place where the act or omission occurred"). Yet it is obvious that the liability of federal officials for violations of citizens' constitutional rights should be governed by uniform rules. The question whether respondent's action for violations by federal officials of federal constitutional rights should be left to the vagaries of the laws of the several States admits of only a negative answer in the absence of a contrary congressional resolution.

Plainly FTCA is not a sufficient protector of the citizens' constitutional rights, and without a clear congressional mandate we cannot hold that Congress relegated respondent exclusively to the FTCA remedy. . . .

[Opinions of Powell, J., concurring in judgment, and Burger, C.J., dissenting, omitted.]

■ *Mr. Justice* REHNQUIST, *dissenting.* . . .

The Court's opinion . . . lacks even an arguably principled basis for deciding in what circumstances an inferred constitutional damages remedy is appropriate and for defining the contours of such a remedy. And its "practical" conclusion is all the more anomalous in that Congress in 1974 amended the FTCA to permit private damages recoveries for intentional torts committed by federal law enforcement officers, thereby enabling persons injured by such officers' violations of their federal constitutional rights in many cases to obtain redress for their injuries.

In my view, it is "an exercise of power that the Constitution does not give us" for this Court to infer a private civil damages remedy from the Eighth Amendment or any other constitutional provision. *Bivens* (Black, J., dissenting). The creation of such remedies is a task that is more appropriately viewed as falling within the legislative sphere of authority. . . .

[I]t is obvious that when Congress has wished to authorize federal courts to grant damages relief, it has known how to do so and has done so expressly. For example, in 42 U.S.C. § 1983 Congress explicitly provided for federal courts to award damages against state officials who violate an individual's constitutional rights. With respect to federal officials, however, it has never provided for these types of damages awards. Rather, it chose a different route in 1974 by eliminating the immunity of federal officials under the FTCA. . . .

The Court not only fails to explain why the *Bivens* remedy is effective in the promotion of deterrence, but also does not provide any reason for believing that other sanctions on federal employees—such as a threat of deductions in pay, reprimand, suspension, or firing—will be ineffective in promoting the desired level of deterrence, or that Congress did not consider the marginal increase in deterrence here to be outweighed by other considerations. And while it may be generally true that the extent to which a sanction is imposed directly on a wrongdoer will have an impact on the effectiveness of a deterrent remedy, there are also a number of other factors that must be taken into account—such as the amount of damages necessary to offset the benefits of the objectionable conduct, the risk that the wrongdoer might escape liability, the clarity with which the objectionable conduct is defined, and the perceptions of the individual who is a potential wrongdoer. . . .

In addition, there are important policy considerations at stake here that Congress may decide outweigh the interest in deterrence promoted by personal liability of federal officials. Indeed, the fear of personal liability may "dampen the ardor of all but the most resolute, or the most irresponsible, in the unflinching discharge of their duties." And, as one commentator has observed: "Despite the small odds an employee will actually be held liable in a civil suit, morale within the federal services has suffered as employees have been dragged through drawn-out lawsuits, many of which are frivolous." . . .

Notes and Questions

1. The majority's point that "the *Bivens* remedy, in addition to compensating victims, serves a deterrent purpose" and corollary observation that "Title 42 U.S.C. § 1983 serves similar purposes" summarize what courts and scholars have recognized as the principal policy justifications for awarding damages for constitutional violations. How do the goals of compensation and deterrence map onto the legislative history of § 1983? The Court's rationale in creating *Bivens*? Can you think of rationales for civil rights litigation other than compensation and deterrence that courts ought to consider when shaping this area of law?

2. As an interpretive guide to *Bivens*, the FTCA seems to pull in two opposing directions. It both provides an alternative to *Bivens* and at the same time seems (via its legislative history) to endorse it as a parallel remedy. As between the majority and the dissent, which has the more persuasive account of the FTCA's implications for *Bivens*?

3. By 1980, the Court had held that *Bivens* actions are available for violations of the Fourth, Fifth, and Eighth Amendments. In these decisions, did the Court suggest there are any constitutional rights for which *Bivens* is *not* available?

4. Under the majority's approach in *Carlson*, how comprehensive must an alternative remedy be to foreclose the availability of *Bivens*? The Court would soon elaborate on its answer to that question.

C. THE DECLINE (AND FALL?) OF *BIVENS*

As explained in *Carlson*, the *Bivens* remedy was presumptively available for constitutional violations by federal officials, subject to just two exceptions—alternative remedies and "special factors." Although these concepts did little work in the first decade of *Bivens* jurisprudence, starting in the 1980s the Court began to infuse them with significant meaning, and by the 1990s and then even more in recent years, these exceptions expanded to the point that they practically swallow the rule of *Bivens* itself. At the core of this doctrinal shift is a fundamental question about the judiciary's proper role.

1. THE RISE OF "ALTERNATIVE REMEDIES" AND "SPECIAL FACTORS"

In *Bush v. Lucas*, 462 U.S. 367 (1983), a NASA aerospace engineer made public statements to the media criticizing the facility where he worked. He was demoted on the ground that his statements were false and misleading. The Federal Employee Appeals Authority upheld the demotion, but the Civil Service Commission's Appeals Review Board found that the demotion had violated Bush's First Amendment rights. NASA ultimately accepted the Board's recommendation that Bush be reinstated and receive back pay. While his administrative appeal from the demotion was pending, Bush filed a *Bivens* action for a violation of the First Amendment. The question before the Court was whether Bush had a cause of action.

The Court assumed for purposes of decision that Bush's First Amendment rights were violated and that the "civil service remedies were not as effective as an individual damages remedy and did not fully compensate him for the harm he suffered." Nonetheless, the Court held unanimously that his *Bivens* claim could not proceed. Writing for the Court, Justice Stevens did not retreat from *Carlson* but distinguished it, differentiating between the FTCA remedy asserted as an alternative there and the civil service protections available to Bush:

> [In *Carlson*,] there was no congressional determination foreclosing the damages claim and making the Federal Tort Claims Act exclusive. No statute expressly declared the FTCA remedy to be a substitute for a *Bivens* action; indeed, the legislative history of the 1974 amendments to the FTCA "made it crystal clear that Congress views FTCA and *Bivens* as parallel, complementary causes of action." . . .
>
> Federal civil servants are now protected by an elaborate, comprehensive scheme that encompasses substantive provisions forbidding arbitrary action by supervisors and procedures—administrative and judicial—by which improper action may be redressed. They apply to a multitude of personnel decisions that are made daily

by federal agencies. Constitutional challenges to agency action, such as the First Amendment claims raised by petitioner, are fully cognizable within this system. . . .

If the employee prevailed in the administrative process or upon judicial review, he was entitled to reinstatement with retroactive seniority. He also had a right to full back pay, including credit for periodic within-grade or step increases and general pay raises during the relevant period, allowances, differentials, and accumulated leave. Congress intended that these remedies would put the employee "in the same position he would have been in had the unjustified or erroneous personnel action not taken place."

Given the history of the development of civil service remedies and the comprehensive nature of the remedies currently available, it is clear that the question we confront today is quite different from the typical remedial issue confronted by a common-law court. The question is not what remedy the court should provide for a wrong that would otherwise go unredressed. It is whether an elaborate remedial system that has been constructed step by step, with careful attention to conflicting policy considerations, should be augmented by the creation of a new judicial remedy for the constitutional violation at issue. . . .

Congress is in a far better position than a court to evaluate the impact of a new species of litigation between federal employees on the efficiency of the civil service. Not only has Congress developed considerable familiarity with balancing governmental efficiency and the rights of employees, but it also may inform itself through factfinding procedures such as hearings that are not available to the courts.

Concurring, Justice Marshall (joined by Justice Blackmun) wrote "only to emphasize that in my view a different case would be presented if Congress had not created a comprehensive scheme that was specifically designed to provide full compensation to civil service employees who are discharged or disciplined in violation of their First Amendment rights, and that affords a remedy that is substantially as effective as a damage action."

In *Chappell v. Wallace*, 462 U.S. 296 (1983), five servicemembers in the U.S. Navy sued their vessel's commanding officer and seven other officers "alleg[ing] that because of [plaintiffs'] minority race [the officers] failed to assign them desirable duties, threatened them, gave them low performance evaluations, and imposed penalties of unusual severity." The Supreme Court unanimously held, in an opinion by Chief Justice Burger, that no *Bivens* action could be brought:

This Court's holding in *Bivens* authorized a suit for damages against federal officials whose actions violated an individual's constitutional rights, even though Congress had not expressly authorized such suits. The Court, in *Bivens* and its progeny, has expressly cautioned, however, that such a remedy will not be available when "special factors counselling hesitation" are present. . . .

The need for special regulations in relation to military discipline, and the consequent need and justification for a special and exclusive system of military justice, is too obvious to require extensive discussion; no military organization can function without strict discipline and regulation that would be unacceptable in a civilian setting. . . . The inescapable demands of military discipline and obedience to orders cannot be taught on battlefields; the habit of immediate compliance with military procedures and orders must be virtually reflex with no time for debate or reflection. The Court has often noted "the peculiar and special relationship of the soldier to his superiors," and has acknowledged that "the rights of men in the armed forces must perforce be conditioned to meet certain overriding demands of discipline and duty. . . ." This becomes imperative in combat, but conduct in combat inevitably reflects the training that precedes combat; for that reason, centuries of experience has developed a hierarchical structure of discipline and obedience to command, unique in its application to the military establishment and wholly different from civilian patterns. Civilian courts must, at the very least, hesitate long before entertaining a suit which asks the court to tamper with the established relationship between enlisted military personnel and their superior officers; that relationship is at the heart of the necessarily unique structure of the military establishment. . . .

Congress has exercised its plenary constitutional authority over the military, has enacted statutes regulating military life, and has established a comprehensive internal system of justice to regulate military life, taking into account the special patterns that define the military structure. The resulting system provides for the review and remedy of complaints and grievances such as those presented by respondents. Military personnel, for example, may avail themselves of the procedures and remedies created by Congress in Article 138 of the Uniform Code of Military Justice . . . .

Taken together, the unique disciplinary structure of the military establishment and Congress' activity in the field constitute "special factors" which dictate that it would be inappropriate to provide enlisted military personnel a *Bivens*-type remedy against their superior officers. *See Bush v. Lucas.*

Notes and Questions

1. What are the defining features of an "alternative remedy" according to the Court? Watch how this conception evolves throughout the rest of this chapter.

2. Are *Bush* and *Chappell* consistent with *Carlson*? If not, what has changed about the Court's thinking?

3. Is the FTCA a more or less comprehensive remedy than the civil service administrative regime at issue in *Bush*? What does the Court examine in deciding how comprehensive an alternative remedy is?

2. More aggressive applications of *Bivens*'s limits

The results in *Bush* and *Chappell* aren't too difficult to harmonize with the prior cases because the Court was being asked to insert the *Bivens* cause of action into areas of particular federal interest (the federal civil service and the military) that Congress had far more heavily regulated than the contexts at issue in *Bivens* itself, *Davis*, and *Carlson*.

The reasoning of the subsequent case *FDIC v. Meyer*, 510 U.S. 471 (1994), is much harder to reconcile with *Bivens*. In *Meyer*, the Court considered whether a bank officer who had been fired by a federal receiver, the Federal Savings and Loan Insurance Corporation (FSLIC), could use *Bivens* to bring due process claims against the FSLIC and the FSLIC official who fired him. The jury had awarded a $130,000 verdict against the FSLIC, but found in favor of the FSLIC official, Robert Pattullo, based on the defense of qualified immunity (which we'll study in Chapter 4). The court of appeals affirmed. FSLIC's successor entity, the Federal Deposit Insurance Corporation (FDIC), sought Supreme Court review. In a unanimous opinion by Justice Thomas, the Court reversed:

> In our most recent decisions, we have "responded cautiously to suggestions that *Bivens* remedies be extended into new contexts." In this case, Meyer seeks a significant extension of *Bivens*: He asks us to expand the category of defendants against whom *Bivens*-type actions may be brought to include not only federal *agents,* but federal *agencies* as well. . . .
>
> Meyer recognizes the absence of authority supporting his position, but argues that the "logic" of *Bivens* would support such a remedy. We disagree. In *Bivens,* the petitioner sued the agents of the Federal Bureau of Narcotics who allegedly violated his rights, not the Bureau itself. Here, Meyer brought precisely the claim that the logic of *Bivens* supports—a *Bivens* claim for damages against Pattullo, the FSLIC employee who terminated him.
>
> An additional problem with Meyer's "logic" argument is the fact that we implied a cause of action against federal officials in *Bivens* in part *because* a direct action against the Government was not available. In essence, Meyer asks us to imply a damages action based on a decision that presumed the *absence* of that very action. . . .
>
> It must be remembered that the purpose of *Bivens* is to deter *the officer.* *See Carlson.* If we were to imply a damages action directly against federal agencies, . . . there would be no reason for aggrieved parties to bring damages actions against individual officers. Under Meyer's regime, the deterrent effects of the *Bivens* remedy would be lost.
>
> Finally, a damages remedy against federal agencies would be inappropriate even if such a remedy were consistent with *Bivens.* Here, unlike in *Bivens,* there are "special factors counselling hesitation" in the creation of a damages remedy. *Bivens.* If we were to recognize a direct action for damages against federal agencies, we would be creating a potentially enormous financial burden for the Federal Government. Meyer disputes this reasoning and argues that the Federal Government already expends significant resources indemnifying its employees who are sued under *Bivens.* Meyer's argument implicitly suggests that the funds used for indemnification could be shifted to cover the direct liability of federal agencies. That may or may not be true, but decisions involving " 'federal fiscal policy' " are not ours to make. We leave it to Congress to weigh the implications of such a significant expansion of Government liability.

Considering *Chappell* and *Meyer* together, how has the Court defined "special factors counselling hesitation"? Do these cases define them in the same way? What other "special factors" might the Court recognize based on *Chappell* and *Meyer*?

Note the Court's reference to "indemnification"—an arrangement in which one party agrees to cover another's losses. As we'll explore in more detail (Chapter 4), government employers commonly indemnify their employees against legal liability—that is, agree in advance to pay judgments against them arising out of their performance of their duties—both to protect their employees and encourage people to work for the government.

What is the implication of plaintiff Meyer's indemnification argument for who pays *Bivens* judgments? The Court states, "If we were to imply a damages action directly against federal agencies, . . . there would be no reason for aggrieved parties to bring damages actions against individual officers. Under Meyer's regime, the deterrent effects of the *Bivens* remedy would be lost." If Meyer is right, what is the difference in terms of individual deterrence between liability for a government officer and liability for his agency? And are there any *Bivens* suits to which the "special factor" cited in the *Meyer* decision would *not* apply, functionally speaking?

The question whether imposing liability on entity defendants deters wrongdoing plays a central role in the next case.

Correctional Services Corp. v. Malesko
534 U.S. 61 (2001)

▪ *Chief Justice* REHNQUIST *delivered the opinion of the Court.*

We decide here whether the implied damages action first recognized in *Bivens v. Six Unknown Fed. Narcotics Agents*, should be extended to allow recovery against a private corporation operating a halfway house under contract with the Bureau of Prisons. We decline to so extend *Bivens*.

Petitioner Correctional Services Corporation (CSC), under contract with the federal Bureau of Prisons (BOP), operates Community Corrections Centers and other facilities that house federal prisoners and detainees. [Plaintiff John Malesko was an inmate with a heart condition who was housed in a CSC-run halfway house. Malesko's condition limited his ability to climb stairs. Malesko was assigned to fifth-floor living quarters and generally permitted to use the elevator, but one day a CSC employee forbade him to use it, and Malesko suffered a heart attack while climbing the stairs. Malesko filed a pro se action against CSC and unnamed CSC employees. By the time he was able to discover the identity of the unnamed employees and add them to the complaint, the statute of limitations had run. Accordingly, his claims were dismissed against all defendants except CSC.] . . .

Since *Carlson* we have consistently refused to extend *Bivens* liability to any new context or new category of defendants. . . .

[I]t is clear that the claim urged by respondent is fundamentally different from anything recognized in *Bivens* or subsequent cases. In 30 years of *Bivens* jurisprudence we have extended its holding only twice, to provide an otherwise nonexistent cause of action against individual officers alleged to have acted unconstitutionally, or to provide a cause of action for a plaintiff who lacked any alternative remedy for harms caused by an individual officer's unconstitutional conduct. Where such circumstances are not present, we have consistently rejected invitations to extend *Bivens*, often for reasons that foreclose its extension here.

The purpose of *Bivens* is to deter individual federal officers from committing constitutional violations. *Meyer* made clear that the threat of litigation and liability will adequately deter federal officers for *Bivens* purposes no matter that they . . . are indemnified by the employing agency or entity, or are acting pursuant to an entity's policy. *Meyer* also made clear that the threat of suit against an individual's employer was not the kind of deterrence contemplated by *Bivens*. This case is, in every meaningful sense, the same. For if a corporate defendant is available for suit, claimants will focus their collection efforts on it, and not the individual directly responsible for the alleged injury. On the logic of *Meyer*, inferring a constitutional tort remedy against a private entity like CSC is therefore foreclosed.

Respondent claims that even under *Meyer*'s deterrence rationale, implying a suit against private corporations acting under color of federal law is still necessary to advance the core deterrence purpose of *Bivens*. He argues that because corporations respond to market pressures and make decisions without regard to constitutional obligations, requiring payment for the constitutional harms they commit is the best way to discourage future harms. That may be so, but it has no relevance to *Bivens*, which is concerned solely with deterring the unconstitutional acts of individual officers. If deterring the conduct of a policymaking entity was the purpose of *Bivens*, then *Meyer* would have implied a damages remedy against the Federal Deposit Insurance Corporation; it was after all an agency policy that led to Meyer's constitutional deprivation. But *Bivens* from its inception has been based not on that premise, but on the deterrence of individual officers who commit unconstitutional acts.

There is no reason for us to consider extending *Bivens* beyond this core premise here. To begin with, no federal prisoners enjoy respondent's contemplated remedy. If a federal prisoner in a BOP facility alleges a constitutional deprivation, he may bring a *Bivens* claim against the offending individual officer, subject to the defense of qualified immunity. The prisoner may not bring a *Bivens* claim against the officer's employer, the United States, or the BOP. With respect to the alleged constitutional deprivation, his only remedy lies against the individual; a remedy *Meyer* found sufficient, and which respondent did not timely pursue. Whether it makes sense to impose asymmetrical liability costs on private prison facilities alone is a question for Congress, not us, to decide.

Nor are we confronted with a situation in which claimants in respondent's shoes lack effective remedies. Cf. *Bivens* (Harlan, J., concurring in judgment) ("For people in Bivens' shoes, it is damages or nothing"). It was conceded at oral argument that alternative remedies are at least as great, and in many respects greater, than anything that could be had under *Bivens*. For example, federal prisoners in private facilities enjoy a parallel tort remedy that is unavailable to prisoners housed in Government facilities. This case demonstrates as much, since respondent's complaint in the District Court arguably alleged no more than a quintessential claim of negligence. . . .

This also makes respondent's situation altogether different from *Bivens*, in which we found alternative state tort remedies to be "inconsistent or even hostile" to a remedy inferred from the Fourth Amendment. When a federal officer appears at the door and requests entry, one cannot always be expected to resist.

Yet lack of resistance alone might foreclose a cause of action in trespass or privacy. Therefore, we reasoned in *Bivens* that other than an implied constitutional tort remedy, "there remain[ed] . . . but the alternative of resistance, which may amount to a crime." Such logic does not apply to respondent, whose claim of negligence or deliberate indifference requires no resistance to official action . . . .

Inmates in respondent's position also have full access to remedial mechanisms established by the BOP, including suits in federal court for injunctive relief and grievances filed through the BOP's Administrative Remedy Program. . . .

[Concurring opinion of Scalia, J., joined by Thomas, J., is omitted.]

■ *Justice* STEVENS, *with whom Justice* SOUTER, *Justice* GINSBURG, *and Justice* BREYER *join, dissenting.* . . .

Meyer, which concluded that federal agencies are not suable under *Bivens*, does not lead to the outcome reached by the Court today. In that case, we did not discuss private corporate agents, nor suggest that such agents should be viewed differently from human ones. Rather, in *Meyer*, we drew a distinction between "federal agents" and "an agency of the Federal Government." . . .

[C]ommon sense, buttressed by all of the reasons that supported the holding in *Bivens*, leads to the conclusion that corporate agents should not be treated more favorably than human agents.

First, the Court argues that respondent enjoys alternative remedies against the corporate agent that distinguish this case from *Bivens*. In doing so, the Court characterizes *Bivens* and its progeny as cases in which plaintiffs lacked "any alternative remedy." In *Bivens*, however, even though the plaintiff's suit against the Federal Government under state tort law may have been barred by sovereign immunity, a suit against the officer himself under state tort law was theoretically possible. Moreover, as the Court recognized in *Carlson*, *Bivens* plaintiffs also have remedies available under the FTCA. Thus, the Court is incorrect to portray *Bivens* plaintiffs as lacking any other avenue of relief, and to imply as a result that respondent in this case had a substantially wider array of non-*Bivens* remedies at his disposal than do other *Bivens* plaintiffs. If alternative remedies provide a sufficient justification for closing the federal forum here, where the defendant is a private corporation, the claims against the individual defendants in *Carlson*, in light of the FTCA alternative, should have been rejected as well.[7]

It is ironic that the Court relies so heavily for its holding on this assumption that alternative effective remedies—primarily negligence actions in state court—are available to respondent. Like Justice Harlan, I think it "entirely proper that these injuries be compensable according to uniform rules of federal law, especially in light of the very large element of federal law which must in any event control the scope of official defenses to liability." *Bivens* (opinion

---

7. Although the Court lightly references administrative remedies that might be available to CSC-housed inmates, these are by no means the sort of comprehensive administrative remedies previously contemplated by the Court in *Bush* . . . .

concurring in judgment). And aside from undermining uniformity, the Court's reliance on state tort law will jeopardize the protection of the full scope of federal constitutional rights. State law might have comparable causes of action for tort claims like the Eighth Amendment violation alleged here, but other unconstitutional actions by prison employees, such as violations of the Equal Protection or Due Process Clauses, may find no parallel causes of action in state tort law. Even though respondent here may have been able to sue for some degree of relief under state law because his Eighth Amendment claim could have been pleaded as negligence, future plaintiffs with constitutional claims less like traditional torts will not necessarily be so situated.

Second, the Court claims that the deterrence goals of *Bivens* would not be served by permitting liability here. It cannot be seriously maintained, however, that tort remedies against corporate employers have less deterrent value than actions against their employees. As the Court has previously noted, the "organizational structure" of private prisons "is one subject to the ordinary competitive pressures that normally help private firms adjust their behavior in response to the incentives that tort suits provide—pressures not necessarily present in government departments." Thus, the private corporate entity at issue here is readily distinguishable from the federal agency in *Meyer*. Indeed, a tragic consequence of today's decision is the clear incentive it gives to corporate managers of privately operated custodial institutions to adopt cost-saving policies that jeopardize the constitutional rights of the tens of thousands of inmates in their custody.

The Court raises a concern with imposing "asymmetrical liability costs on private prison facilities," and further claims that because federal prisoners in Government-run institutions can only sue officers, it would be unfair to permit federal prisoners in private institutions to sue an "officer's employer." Permitting liability in the present case, however, would produce symmetry: both private and public prisoners would be unable to sue the principal (i.e., the Government), but would be able to sue the primary federal agent (i.e., the Government official or the corporation). Indeed, it is the Court's decision that creates asymmetry—between federal and state prisoners housed in private correctional facilities. Under 42 U.S.C. § 1983, a state prisoner may sue a private prison for deprivation of constitutional rights, yet the Court denies such a remedy to that prisoner's federal counterpart. . . .

It is apparent from the Court's critical discussion of the thoughtful opinions of Justice Harlan and his contemporaries, and from its erroneous statement of the question presented by this case as whether *Bivens* "should be extended" to allow recovery against a private corporation employed as a federal agent, that the driving force behind the Court's decision is a disagreement with the holding in *Bivens* itself. There are at least two reasons why it is improper for the Court to allow its decision in this case to be influenced by that predisposition. First, as is clear from the legislative materials cited in *Carlson*, Congress has effectively ratified the *Bivens* remedy; surely Congress has never sought to abolish it. Second, a rule that has been such a well-recognized part of our law for over 30 years should be accorded full respect by the Members of this Court, whether or not they would have endorsed that rule when it was first announced. For our primary duty is to apply and enforce settled law, not to revise that law to accord with our own notions of sound policy.

Notes and Questions

1. Are you more persuaded by the majority's or the dissent's account of how deterrence functions in the case of a non-individual defendant? Which view is more consistent with the assumptions underlying the common law tort principle of respondeat superior? Should that principle influence the Court's decision in the *Bivens* context, and if so, why? How do you account for the Court's unanimity in *Meyer*, which relied heavily on the same argument the majority does here?

2. The majority says little about whether Congress would have wanted a *Bivens* cause of action against a private prison corporation. In that connection, consider the structure of the FTCA, which subjects the United States, not individual officers, to liability. Does that law provide a clue about which parties Congress prefers to see as defendants? Should it matter?

3. Justice Stevens's dissent relies in part on an argument for symmetry between Malesko and state prisoners in privately run prisons. Although the majority view among lower courts is that private prisons are state actors, *see, e.g., Pollard v. The GEO Grp., Inc.*, 629 F.3d 843, 858 (9th Cir. 2010), *rev'd on other grounds sub nom. Minneci v. Pollard*, 565 U.S. 118 (2012); *Rosborough v. Mgmt. & Training Corp.*, 350 F.3d 459, 461 (5th Cir. 2003); *Skelton v. Pri-Cor, Inc.*, 963 F.2d 100, 102 (6th Cir. 1991); *contra Holly v. Scott*, 434 F.3d 287, 293 (4th Cir. 2006), the Supreme Court has never decided the issue. If the question of private prison corporations' amenability to suit under § 1983 for constitutional violations against state prisoners reaches the Supreme Court, how relevant should *Malesko* be to its determination—both doctrinally and in terms of policy?

4. *Meyer* quotes the following statement from *Schweiker v. Chilicky*, 487 U.S. 412 (1988), which rejected a *Bivens* cause of action for alleged due process violations in the denial of federal Social Security benefits: "Our more recent decisions have responded cautiously to suggestions that *Bivens* remedies be extended into new contexts." *Meyer* and *Malesko* count it as a mark against the plaintiffs that they seek to apply *Bivens* to a new "context." Is that what the Court appeared to be saying in *Schweiker*? If *Carlson* had been decided in 1990 instead of 1980, would the "context" argument have as much force? Does the "new context" inquiry imply there is something special about the specific constitutional rights asserted in *Bivens*, *Davis*, and *Carlson*? If not, what is the rationale for it?

* * *

The opinions in *Meyer* and *Malesko* both distinguish *Bivens* based on the nature of the defendant—individuals in *Bivens*, entities in *Meyer* and *Malesko*. Based on this rationale, what should the Court do with a *Bivens* claim against an individual employee of a private company running a federal prison? The next case answers, and in so doing, reveals further evolution in the Court's approach to alternative remedies.

Minneci v. Pollard

565 U.S. 118 (2012)

▪ *Justice* BREYER *delivered the opinion of the Court.* . . .

Richard Lee Pollard was a prisoner at a federal facility operated by a private company, the Wackenhut Corrections Corporation. In 2002 he filed a *pro se* complaint in federal court against several Wackenhut employees, who (now) include a security officer, a food-services supervisor, and several members of the medical staff. . . . [H]e claimed that these employees had deprived him of adequate medical care, had thereby violated the Eighth Amendment's prohibition against "cruel and unusual" punishment, and had caused him injury. He sought damages. . . .

[The Court has distilled the test for recognizing a *Bivens* remedy as follows:] "[T]he decision whether to recognize a *Bivens* remedy may require two steps. In the first place, there is the question whether any alternative, existing process for protecting the [constitutionally recognized] interest amounts to a convincing reason for the Judicial Branch to refrain from providing a new and freestanding remedy in damages. . . . But even in the absence of an alternative, a *Bivens* remedy is a subject of judgment: 'the federal courts must make the kind of remedial determination that is appropriate for a common-law tribunal, paying particular heed, however, to any special factors counselling hesitation before authorizing a new kind of federal litigation.'"

Since *Carlson,* the Court has had to decide in several different instances whether to imply a *Bivens* action. And in each instance it has decided against the existence of such an action. . . . [W]e conclude that Pollard cannot assert a *Bivens* claim.

That is primarily because Pollard's Eighth Amendment claim focuses upon a kind of conduct that typically falls within the scope of traditional state tort law. And in the case of a privately employed defendant, state tort law provides an "alternative, existing process" capable of protecting the constitutional interests at stake. The existence of that alternative here constitutes a "convincing reason for the Judicial Branch to refrain from providing a new and freestanding remedy in damages." Our reasoning is best understood if we set forth and explain why we reject Pollard's arguments to the contrary.

Pollard asks us to imply a *Bivens* action for four basic reasons—none of which we find convincing. First, Pollard argues that this Court has already decided in *Carlson* that a federal prisoner may bring an Eighth Amendment-based *Bivens* action against prison personnel; and we need do no more than simply apply *Carlson*'s holding here. *Carlson,* however, was a case in which a federal prisoner sought damages from personnel employed by the *government,* not personnel employed by a *private* firm. And for present purposes that fact—of employment status—makes a critical difference.

For one thing, the potential existence of an adequate "alternative, existing process" differs dramatically in the two sets of cases. Prisoners ordinarily *cannot* bring state-law tort actions against employees of the Federal Government.

See 28 U.S.C. §§ 2671, 2679(b)(1) (Westfall Act) (substituting United States as defendant in tort action against federal employee). But prisoners ordinarily *can* bring state-law tort actions against employees of a private firm.

For another thing, the Court specifically rejected Justice Stevens' somewhat similar suggestion in his dissenting opinion in *Malesko,* namely that a prisoner's suit against a private prison-management firm should fall within *Carlson*'s earlier holding because such a firm, like a federal employee, is a "federal agent." In rejecting the dissent's suggestion, the Court explained that the context in *Malesko* was "fundamentally different" from the contexts at issue in earlier cases, including *Carlson.* That difference, the Court said, reflected in part the nature of the defendant, *i.e.,* a corporate employer rather than an individual employee, and in part reflected the existence of alternative "effective" state tort remedies. This last-mentioned factor makes it difficult to square Pollard's argument with *Malesko*'s reasoning.

Second, Pollard argues that, because of the "vagaries" of state tort law, we should consider only whether *federal* law provides adequate alternative remedies. This argument flounders, however, on the fact that the Court rejected it in *Malesko*. State tort law, after all, can help to deter constitutional violations as well as to provide compensation to a violation's victim. . . .

Third, Pollard argues that state tort law does not provide remedies *adequate* to protect the constitutional interests at issue here. Pollard's claim, however, is a claim for physical or related emotional harm suffered as a result of aggravated instances of the kind of conduct that state tort law typically forbids. That claim arose in California, where state tort law provides for ordinary negligence actions, for actions based upon "want of ordinary care or skill," for actions for "negligent failure to diagnose or treat," and for actions based upon the failure of one with a custodial duty to care for another to protect that other from "'unreasonable risk of physical harm.'" California courts have specifically applied this law to jailers, including private operators of prisons.

Moreover, California's tort law basically reflects general principles of tort law present, as far as we can tell, in the law of every State. We have found specific authority indicating that state law imposes general tort duties of reasonable care (including medical care) on prison employees in every one of the eight States where privately managed secure federal facilities are currently located.

We note, as Pollard points out, that state tort law may sometimes prove less generous than would a *Bivens* action, say, by capping damages, or by forbidding recovery for emotional suffering unconnected with physical harm, or by imposing procedural obstacles, say, initially requiring the use of expert administrative panels in medical malpractice cases. But we cannot find in this fact sufficient basis to determine state law inadequate.

State-law remedies and a potential *Bivens* remedy need not be perfectly congruent. . . . Rather, in principle, the question is whether, in general, state tort law remedies provide roughly similar incentives for potential defendants to comply with the Eighth Amendment while also providing roughly similar compensation to victims of violations. The features of the two kinds of actions just mentioned suggest that, in practice, the answer to this question is "yes." And we have found nothing here to convince us to the contrary.

Fourth, Pollard argues that there "may" be similar kinds of Eighth Amendment claims that state tort law does not cover. But Pollard does not convincingly show that there are such cases. . . .

For these reasons, where, as here, a federal prisoner seeks damages from privately employed personnel working at a privately operated federal prison, where the conduct allegedly amounts to a violation of the Eighth Amendment, and where that conduct is of a kind that typically falls within the scope of traditional state tort law (such as the conduct involving improper medical care at issue here), the prisoner must seek a remedy under state tort law. We cannot imply a *Bivens* remedy in such a case. . . .

■ *Justice* SCALIA, *with whom Justice* THOMAS *joins, concurring.*

I join the opinion of the Court because I agree that a narrow interpretation of the rationale of *Bivens* would not cause the holding of that case to apply to the circumstances of this case. Even if the narrowest rationale of *Bivens* did apply here, however, I would decline to extend its holding. *Bivens* is "a relic of the heady days in which this Court assumed common-law powers to create causes of action" by constitutional implication. We have abandoned that power. . . . I would limit *Bivens* and its two follow-on cases (*Davis* and *Carlson*) to the precise circumstances that they involved.

■ *Justice* GINSBURG, *dissenting.*

Were Pollard incarcerated in a federal- or state-operated facility, he would have a federal remedy for the Eighth Amendment violations he alleges. For the reasons stated in the dissenting opinion I joined in *Correctional Services Corp. v. Malesko* (opinion of Stevens, J.), I would not deny the same character of relief to Pollard, a prisoner placed by federal contract in a privately operated prison. Pollard may have suffered "aggravated instances" of conduct state tort law forbids, but that same aggravated conduct, when it is engaged in by official actors, also offends the Federal Constitution. Rather than remitting Pollard to the "vagaries" of state tort law, *Carlson,* I would hold his injuries, sustained while serving a federal sentence, "compensable according to uniform rules of federal law," *Bivens* (Harlan, J., concurring in judgment).

Indeed, there is stronger cause for providing a federal remedy in this case than there was in *Malesko.* There, the question presented was whether a *Bivens* action lies against a private corporation that manages a facility housing federal prisoners. Suing a corporate employer, the majority observed in *Malesko,* would not serve to deter individual officers from conduct transgressing constitutional limitations on their authority. Individual deterrence, the Court reminded, was the consideration central to the *Bivens* decision. Noting the availability of state tort remedies, the majority in *Malesko* declined to "exten[d] *Bivens* beyond [that decision's] core premise," *i.e.,* deterring individual officers. Pollard's case, in contrast, involves *Bivens'* core concern: His suit seeking damages directly from individual officers would have precisely the deterrent effect the Court found absent in *Malesko.* . . .

Notes and Questions

1. How has the Court's understanding of "alternative remedies" that foreclose a *Bivens* claim evolved since *Bush*?

2. In Justice Ginsburg's telling, *Minneci* betrays the promise of *Malesko* by rejecting a *Bivens* claim against an individual officer even though the individual/entity distinction was the reason the Court rejected the claim against the entity in *Malesko*. What is the majority's answer to this charge? Does the majority think the reasoning in *Malesko* was flawed?

3. How do you reconcile the Court's opinion in *Minneci* with its refusal in early *Bivens* cases to subject plaintiffs to the "vagaries" of state tort law? With its conclusion in *Carlson* that the FTCA did not provide a sufficient alternative remedy? After *Minneci*, what remedial schemes are *insufficient* to foreclose a *Bivens* action?

4. In light of your answers to the previous two questions, what is the functional difference between the approaches of the majority and concurring opinions? Is the Court just playing a shell game with *Bivens* plaintiffs?

5. What effect are *Minneci* and *Malesko* likely to have on the cost-competitiveness of privately run versus government-run federal prisons?

3. REFORMULATION OF THE *BIVENS* INQUIRY

The Court's retreat from *Bivens* has continued. Its latest word on the subject (albeit with only six Justices participating) establishes further barriers to *Bivens* claims outside of contexts previously recognized.

Ziglar v. Abbasi
137 S. Ct. 1843 (2017)

■ *Justice* KENNEDY *delivered the opinion of the Court . . . .*

In the weeks following the September 11, 2001, terrorist attacks—the worst in American history—the Federal Bureau of Investigation (FBI) received more than 96,000 tips from members of the public. Some tips were based on well-grounded suspicion of terrorist activity, but many others may have been based on fear of Arabs and Muslims. FBI agents "questioned more than 1,000 people with suspected links to the [September 11] attacks in particular or to terrorism in general." . . .

[M]ore than 700 individuals were arrested and detained on immigration charges. If . . . the FBI designated an alien as "of interest" to the investigation, or if it had doubts about the proper designation in a particular case, the alien was detained subject to a "hold-until-cleared policy." The aliens were held without bail.

Respondents were among some 84 aliens who were subject to the hold-until-cleared policy and detained at the Metropolitan Detention Center (MDC) in Brooklyn, New York. They were held in the Administrative Maximum Special Housing Unit (or Unit) of the MDC. The complaint includes these allegations: Conditions in the Unit were harsh. Pursuant to official Bureau of Prisons policy, detainees were held in "'tiny cells for over 23 hours a day.'" Lights in the cells were left on 24 hours. Detainees had little opportunity for exercise or recreation. They were forbidden to keep anything in their cells, even basic hygiene products such as soap or a toothbrush. When removed from the cells for any reason, they were shackled and escorted by four guards. They were denied access to most forms of communication with the outside world. And they were strip searched often—any time they were moved, as well as at random in their cells.

Some of the harsh conditions in the Unit were not imposed pursuant to official policy. According to the complaint, prison guards engaged in a pattern of "physical and verbal abuse." Guards allegedly slammed detainees into walls; twisted their arms, wrists, and fingers; broke their bones; referred to them as terrorists; threatened them with violence; subjected them to humiliating sexual comments; and insulted their religion.

Respondents are six men of Arab or South Asian descent. Five are Muslims. Each was illegally in this country, arrested during the course of the September 11 investigation, and detained in the Administrative Maximum Special Housing Unit for periods ranging from three to eight months. After being released respondents were removed from the United States.

[Respondents sued several high-level federal officials, including former Attorney General John Ashcroft, former FBI Director Robert Mueller, and the former head of the Immigration and Nationalization Service James Ziglar (the "Executive Officials"), and the warden and associate warden of the MDC, for unconstitutional conditions of confinement, discrimination, and searches and seizures.] . . .

Bivens, *Davis*, and *Carlson* . . . represent the only instances in which the Court has approved of an implied damages remedy under the Constitution itself. . . .

[I]t is a significant step under separation-of-powers principles for a court to determine that it has the authority, under the judicial power, to create and enforce a cause of action for damages against federal officials in order to remedy a constitutional violation. When determining whether traditional equitable powers suffice to give necessary constitutional protection—or whether, in addition, a damages remedy is necessary—there are a number of economic and governmental concerns to consider. Claims against federal officials often create substantial costs, in the form of defense and indemnification. Congress, then, has a substantial responsibility to determine whether, and the extent to which, monetary and other liabilities should be imposed upon individual officers and employees of the Federal Government. In addition, the time and administrative costs attendant upon intrusions resulting from the discovery and trial process are significant factors to be considered. In an analogous context, Congress, it is fair to assume, weighed those concerns in deciding not to substitute the Government as defendant in suits seeking damages for constitutional violations. *See* 28 U.S.C. § 2679(b)(2)(A) (providing that certain provisions of the Federal Tort Claims Act do not apply to any claim against a federal employee "which is brought for a violation of the Constitution"). . . .

[I]t is possible that the analysis in the Court's three *Bivens* cases might have been different if they were decided today. To be sure, no congressional enactment has disapproved of these decisions. And it must be understood that this opinion is not intended to cast doubt on the continued force, or even the necessity, of *Bivens* in the search-and-seizure context in which it arose. *Bivens* does vindicate the Constitution by allowing some redress for injuries, and it provides instruction and guidance to federal law enforcement officers going forward. The settled law of *Bivens* in this common and recurrent sphere of law enforcement, and the undoubted reliance upon it as a fixed principle in the law, are powerful reasons to retain it in that sphere.

Given the notable change in the Court's approach to recognizing implied causes of action, however, the Court has made clear that expanding the *Bivens* remedy is now a "disfavored" judicial activity. This is in accord with the Court's observation that it has "consistently refused to extend *Bivens* to any new context or new category of defendants." *Malesko*. Indeed, the Court has refused to do so for the past 30 years. . . .

When a party seeks to assert an implied cause of action under the Constitution itself . . . separation-of-powers principles are or should be central to the analysis. The question is "who should decide" whether to provide for a damages remedy, Congress or the courts? *Bush*.

The answer most often will be Congress. When an issue " 'involves a host of considerations that must be weighed and appraised,' " it should be committed to " 'those who write the laws' " rather than " 'those who interpret them.' " *Ibid.* . . . As a result, the Court has urged "caution" before "extending *Bivens* remedies into any new context." *Malesko*. The Court's precedents now make clear that a *Bivens* remedy will not be available if there are " 'special factors counselling hesitation in the absence of affirmative action by Congress.' " *Carlson*.

This Court has not defined the phrase "special factors counselling hesitation." The necessary inference, though, is that the inquiry must concentrate on whether the Judiciary is well suited, absent congressional action or instruction, to consider and weigh the costs and benefits of allowing a damages action to proceed. Thus, to be a "special factor counselling hesitation," a factor must cause a court to hesitate before answering that question in the affirmative. . . .

The proper test for determining whether a case presents a new *Bivens* context is as follows. If the case is different in a meaningful way from previous *Bivens* cases decided by this Court, then the context is new. Without endeavoring to create an exhaustive list of differences that are meaningful enough to make a given context a new one, some examples might prove instructive. A case might differ in a meaningful way because of the rank of the officers involved; the constitutional right at issue; the generality or specificity of the official action; the extent of judicial guidance as to how an officer should respond to the problem or emergency to be confronted; the statutory or other legal mandate under which the officer was operating; the risk of disruptive intrusion by the Judiciary into the functioning of other branches; or the presence of potential special factors that previous *Bivens* cases did not consider.

In the present suit, respondents' detention policy claims challenge the confinement conditions imposed on illegal aliens pursuant to a high-level executive policy created in the wake of a major terrorist attack on American soil. Those claims bear little resemblance to the three *Bivens* claims the Court has approved in the past: a claim against FBI agents for handcuffing a man in his own home without a warrant; a claim against a Congressman for firing his female secretary; and a claim against prison officials for failure to treat an inmate's asthma. The Court of Appeals therefore should have held that this was a new *Bivens* context. Had it done so, it would have recognized that a special factors analysis was required before allowing this damages suit to proceed.

After considering the special factors necessarily implicated by the detention policy claims, the Court now holds that those factors show that whether a damages action should be allowed is a decision for the Congress to make, not the courts.

With respect to the claims against the Executive Officials, it must be noted that a *Bivens* action is not "a proper vehicle for altering an entity's policy." *Malesko*. Furthermore, a *Bivens* claim is brought against the individual official for his or her own acts, not the acts of others. "The purpose of *Bivens* is to deter the officer." *Meyer*. . . .

Even if the action is confined to the conduct of a particular Executive Officer in a discrete instance, these claims would call into question the formulation and implementation of a general policy. This, in turn, would necessarily require inquiry and discovery into the whole course of the discussions and deliberations that led to the policies and governmental acts being challenged. These consequences counsel against allowing a *Bivens* action against the Executive Officials, for the burden and demand of litigation might well prevent them—or, to be more precise, future officials like them—from devoting the time and effort required for the proper discharge of their duties.

A closely related problem, as just noted, is that the discovery and litigation process would either border upon or directly implicate the discussion and deliberations that led to the formation of the policy in question. Allowing a damages suit in this context, or in a like context in other circumstances, would require courts to interfere in an intrusive way with sensitive functions of the Executive Branch. . . .

In addition to this special factor, which applies to the claims against the Executive Officials, there are three other special factors that apply as well to the detention policy claims against all of the petitioners. First, respondents' detention policy claims challenge more than standard "law enforcement operations." They challenge as well major elements of the Government's whole response to the September 11 attacks, thus of necessity requiring an inquiry into sensitive issues of national security. Were this inquiry to be allowed in a private suit for damages, the *Bivens* action would assume dimensions far greater than those present in *Bivens* itself, or in either of its two follow-on cases, or indeed in any putative *Bivens* case yet to come before the Court.

National-security policy is the prerogative of the Congress and President. . . . [Therefore] "courts traditionally have been reluctant to intrude upon the authority of the Executive in military and national security affairs" unless "Congress specifically has provided otherwise." . . .

Furthermore, in any inquiry respecting the likely or probable intent of Congress, the silence of Congress is relevant; and here that silence is telling. In the almost 16 years since September 11, the Federal Government's responses to that terrorist attack have been well documented. . . . Nevertheless, "[a]t no point did Congress choose to extend to any person the kind of remedies that respondents seek in this lawsuit."

This silence is notable because it is likely that high-level policies will attract the attention of Congress. Thus, when Congress fails to provide a damages remedy in circumstances like these, it is much more difficult to believe that "congressional inaction" was "inadvertent."

It is of central importance, too, that this is not a case like *Bivens* or *Davis* in which "it is damages or nothing." . . . Respondents . . . challenge large-scale policy decisions concerning the conditions of confinement imposed on hundreds of prisoners. To address those kinds of decisions, detainees may seek injunctive relief. And in addition to that, we have left open the question whether they might be able to challenge their confinement conditions via a petition for a writ of habeas corpus. . . .

There is a persisting concern, of course, that absent a *Bivens* remedy there will be insufficient deterrence to prevent officers from violating the Constitution. In circumstances like those presented here, however, the stakes on both sides of the argument are far higher than in past cases the Court has considered. If *Bivens* liability were to be imposed, high officers who face personal liability for damages might refrain from taking urgent and lawful action in a time of crisis. And, as already noted, the costs and difficulties of later litigation might intrude upon and interfere with the proper exercise of their office.

On the other side of the balance, the very fact that some executive actions have the sweeping potential to affect the liberty of so many is a reason to consider proper means to impose restraint and to provide some redress from injury. There is therefore a balance to be struck, in situations like this one, between deterring constitutional violations and freeing high officials to make the lawful decisions necessary to protect the Nation in times of great peril. The proper balance is one for the Congress, not the Judiciary, to undertake. For all of these reasons, the Court of Appeals erred by allowing respondents' detention policy claims to proceed under *Bivens*.

One of respondents' claims under *Bivens* requires a different analysis: the prisoner abuse claim against the MDC's warden, Dennis Hasty. The allegation is that Warden Hasty violated the Fifth Amendment by allowing prison guards to abuse respondents. . . .

[T]he first question a court must ask in a case like this one is whether the claim arises in a new *Bivens* context, i.e., whether "the case is different in a meaningful way from previous *Bivens* cases decided by this Court."

It is true that this case has significant parallels to one of the Court's previous *Bivens* cases, *Carlson*. There, the Court did allow a *Bivens* claim for prisoner mistreatment—specifically, for failure to provide medical care. And the allegations of injury here are just as compelling as those at issue in *Carlson*. This is especially true given that the complaint alleges serious violations of Bureau of Prisons policy.

Yet even a modest extension is still an extension. And this case does seek to extend *Carlson* to a new context. As noted above, a case can present a new context for *Bivens* purposes if it implicates a different constitutional right; if judicial precedents provide a less meaningful guide for official conduct; or if there are potential special factors that were not considered in previous *Bivens* cases.

The constitutional right is different here, since *Carlson* was predicated on the Eighth Amendment and this claim is predicated on the Fifth. And the judicial guidance available to this warden, with respect to his supervisory duties, was less developed. . . .

Furthermore, legislative action suggesting that Congress does not want a damages remedy is itself a factor counseling hesitation. Some 15 years after *Carlson* was decided, Congress passed the Prison Litigation Reform Act of 1995, which made comprehensive changes to the way prisoner abuse claims must be brought in federal court. . . .

The differences between this claim and the one in *Carlson* are perhaps small, at least in practical terms. Given this Court's expressed caution about extending the *Bivens* remedy, however, the new-context inquiry is easily satisfied. Some differences, of course, will be so trivial that they will not suffice to create a new *Bivens* context. But here the differences identified above are at the very least meaningful ones. Thus, before allowing this claim to proceed under *Bivens*, the Court of Appeals should have performed a special factors analysis. It should have analyzed whether there were alternative remedies available or other "sound reasons to think Congress might doubt the efficacy or necessity of a damages remedy" in a suit like this one.

[In the only part of Justice Kennedy's opinion not to command a majority, a plurality of the Court concluded that a remand on this claim was appropriate so that the lower courts could perform the "special factors" analysis.] . . .

If the facts alleged in the complaint are true, then what happened to respondents in the days following September 11 was tragic. Nothing in this opinion should be read to condone the treatment to which they contend they were subjected. The question before the Court, however, is not whether petitioners' alleged conduct was proper. . . .

Instead, the question with respect to the *Bivens* claims is whether to allow an action for money damages in the absence of congressional authorization. . . .

Justice SOTOMAYOR, *Justice* KAGAN, *and Justice* GORSUCH *took no part in the consideration or decision of these cases.*

[*Opinion of Thomas, J., concurring in part and concurring in the judgment, omitted.*]

■ *Justice* BREYER, *with whom Justice* GINSBURG *joins, dissenting.* . . .

The context here is not "new," or "fundamentally different" than our previous *Bivens* cases. First, the plaintiffs are civilians, not members of the military. They are not citizens, but the Constitution protects noncitizens against serious mistreatment, as it protects citizens. Some or all of the plaintiffs here may have been illegally present in the United States. But that fact cannot justify physical mistreatment. Nor does anyone claim that that fact deprives them of a *Bivens* right available to other persons, citizens and noncitizens alike.

Second, the defendants are Government officials. They are not members of the military or private persons. Two are prison wardens. Three others are high-ranking Department of Justice officials. Prison wardens have been defendants in *Bivens* actions, as have other high-level Government officials. One of the defendants in *Carlson* was the Director of the Bureau of Prisons; the defendant in *Davis* was a Member of Congress. . . .

Third, from a *Bivens* perspective, the injuries that the plaintiffs claim they suffered are familiar ones. They focus upon the conditions of confinement. The plaintiffs say that they were unnecessarily shackled, confined in small unhygienic cells, subjected to continuous lighting (presumably preventing sleep), unnecessarily and frequently strip searched, slammed against walls, injured physically, and subject to verbal abuse. They allege that they suffered these harms because of their race or religion, the defendants having either turned a blind eye to what was happening or themselves introduced policies that they knew would lead to these harms even though the defendants knew the plaintiffs had no connections to terrorism.

These claimed harms are similar to, or even worse than, the harms the plaintiffs suffered in *Bivens* (unreasonable search and seizure in violation of the Fourth Amendment), *Davis* (unlawful discrimination in violation of the Fifth Amendment), and *Carlson* (deliberate indifference to medical need in violation of the Eighth Amendment). Indeed, we have said that, "[i]f a federal prisoner in a [Bureau of Prisons] facility alleges a constitutional deprivation, he may bring a *Bivens* claim against the offending individual officer, subject to the defense of qualified immunity." *Malesko*. . . .

It is true that the plaintiffs bring their "deliberate indifference" claim against Warden Hasty under the Fifth Amendment's Due Process Clause, not the Eighth Amendment's Cruel and Unusual Punishment Clause, as in *Carlson*. But that is because the latter applies to convicted criminals while the former applies to pretrial and immigration detainees. Where the harm is the same, where this Court has held that both the Fifth and Eighth Amendments give rise to *Bivens*' remedies, and where the only difference in constitutional scope consists of a circumstance (the absence of a conviction) that makes the violation here worse, it cannot be maintained that the difference between the use of the two Amendments is "fundamental." . . .

Because the context here is not new, I would allow the plaintiffs' constitutional claims to proceed. . . .

Neither a prospective injunction nor a writ of habeas corpus . . . will normally provide plaintiffs with redress for harms they have already suffered. And here plaintiffs make a strong claim that neither was available to them—at least not for a considerable time. Some of the plaintiffs allege that for two or three months they were subject to a "communications blackout"; that the prison "staff did not permit them visitors, legal or social telephone calls, or mail"; that their families and attorneys did not know where they were being held; that they could not receive visits from their attorneys; that subsequently their lawyers could call them only once a week; and that some or all of the defendants "interfered with the detainees' effective access to legal counsel." These claims make it virtually impossible to say that here there is an "elaborate, comprehensive" alternative remedial scheme similar to schemes that, in the past, we have found block the application of *Bivens* to new contexts. *Bush*. If these allegations are proved, then in this suit, it is "damages or nothing." *Bivens* (Harlan, J., concurring in judgment). . . .

I can find no "special factors [that] counse[l] hesitation before authorizing" this *Bivens* action. . . .

The Court . . . finds the "silence" of Congress "notable" in that Congress, though likely aware of the "high-level policies" involved in this suit, did not "choose to extend to any person the kind of remedies" that the plaintiffs here "seek." . . .

[But t]he Court initially saw that silence as indicating an absence of congressional hostility to the Court's exercise of its traditional remedy-inferring powers. See *Bivens*; *Davis*. Congress' subsequent silence contains strong signs that it accepted *Bivens* actions as part of the law. After all, Congress rejected a proposal that would have eliminated *Bivens* by substituting the U.S. Government as a defendant in suits against federal officers that raised constitutional claims. Later, Congress expressly immunized federal employees acting in the course of their official duties from tort claims except those premised on violations of the Constitution. 28 U.S.C. § 2679(b)(2)(A). We stated that it is consequently "crystal clear that Congress views [the Federal Tort Claims Act] and *Bivens* as [providing] parallel, complementary causes of action." *Carlson*. . . .

In my view, the Court's strongest argument is that *Bivens* should not apply to policy-related actions taken in times of national-security need, for example, during war or national-security emergency. As the Court correctly points out, the Constitution grants primary power to protect the Nation's security to the Executive and Legislative Branches, not to the Judiciary. But the Constitution also delegates to the Judiciary the duty to protect an individual's fundamental constitutional rights. Hence when protection of those rights and a determination of security needs conflict, the Court has a role to play. . . .

[A] *Bivens* action comes accompanied by many legal safeguards designed to prevent the courts from interfering with Executive and Legislative Branch activity reasonably believed to be necessary to protect national security. . . . The Constitution itself takes account of public necessity. Thus, for example, the Fourth Amendment does not forbid all Government searches and seizures; it forbids only those that are "unreasonable." Ordinarily, it requires that a police officer obtain a search warrant before entering an apartment, but should the officer observe a woman being dragged against her will into that apartment, he should, and will, act at once. The Fourth Amendment makes allowances for such "exigent circumstances." Similarly, the Fifth Amendment bars only conditions of confinement that are not "reasonably related to a legitimate governmental objective." What is unreasonable and illegitimate in time of peace may be reasonable and legitimate in time of war. . . .

[C]ourts can, and should, tailor discovery orders so that they do not unnecessarily or improperly interfere with the official's work. . . . It can "structure . . . limited discovery by examining written responses to interrogatories and requests to admit before authorizing depositions, and by deferring discovery directed to high-level officials until discovery of front-line officials has been completed and has demonstrated the need for discovery higher up the ranks." . . .

Given these safeguards against undue interference by the Judiciary in times of war or national-security emergency, the Court's abolition, or limitation of, *Bivens* actions goes too far. If you are cold, put on a sweater, perhaps an overcoat, perhaps also turn up the heat, but do not set fire to the house.

At the same time, there may well be a particular need for *Bivens* remedies when security-related Government actions are at issue. History tells us of far too many instances where the Executive or Legislative Branch took actions during time of war that, on later examination, turned out unnecessarily and unreasonably to have deprived American citizens of basic constitutional rights. We have read about the Alien and Sedition Acts, the thousands of civilians imprisoned during the Civil War, and the suppression of civil liberties during World War I. The pages of the U.S. Reports themselves recite this Court's refusal to set aside the Government's World War II action removing more than 70,000 American citizens of Japanese origin from their west coast homes and interning them in camps—an action that at least some officials knew at the time was unnecessary. . . .

Notes and Questions

1. What constitutes a "new context" for *Bivens*, according to the Court? How does the "new context" question relate to the rationales that drove the original result in *Bivens*? What reasons does the Court give for its approach to the "new context" question?

2. List all the "special factors" the Court has recognized as precluding *Bivens*. Does *Abbasi* suggest this is an exhaustive list?

3. How has the test for recognition of a *Bivens* remedy, and in particular the questions of "context" and "special factors," evolved from *Carlson* to *Abbasi*? What rationale does the Court give for this evolution?

4. In what ways has the Court changed its view of how the FTCA, and specifically 28 U.S.C. § 2679(b)(2)(A), reflects Congress's opinion of *Bivens*?

5. Consider the alternative-remedies analysis in the majority opinion. The Court cites both injunctive relief and habeas corpus as possible alternatives to damages here. As we'll learn later (Chapter 11), obtaining injunctive relief after a constitutional violation has ended can be quite difficult, as it requires proof that the unlawful conduct is very likely to be repeated, and suing *during* the confinement would have been difficult here because, as Justice Breyer points out in dissent, the detainees faced impediments to communicating with attorneys. As for habeas, the majority does not guarantee that it is available; it merely notes that the question is "open." Is the majority's reliance on these possible alternatives a faithful application of, an extension of, or a repudiation of the alternative-remedies analysis in *Minneci*?

6. Which rationales underlying the original *Bivens* decision, if any, still enjoy the support of a majority of the Court? Why doesn't the majority just overrule *Bivens* already? What reasons does the majority give for refusing to do so, and how do those reasons square with the rest of the Court's *Bivens* jurisprudence over the past quarter-century?

7. The majority rejects a role for *Bivens* in shaping policy choices but continues to recognize the role of *Bivens* in deterring misconduct by government officials. Is there tension between those positions? Consider how the arguments over the proper role of *Bivens* in redressing *unauthorized* instances of misconduct (as opposed to unlawful *policies*) mirror those in *Monroe* over the proper role of § 1983. In light of the respective lineups of the Justices in *Abbasi* and *Monroe*, are there identifiably "liberal" and "conservative" approaches to this question?

Note: *Bivens* in Practice

The pragmatic importance of *Bivens* in providing a remedy for constitutional violations by federal officials is hotly debated. An influential analysis in 1999 by Judge Pillard found:

Although [*Bivens*] appears to provide a mechanism for remedying constitutional violations, its application has rarely led to damages recoveries. Government figures reflect that, out of approximately 12,000 *Bivens* claims filed between 1971 and 1985, *Bivens* plaintiffs actually obtained a judgment that was not reversed on appeal in only four cases. While similar figures have not been systematically kept since 1985, recoveries from both settlements and litigated judgments continue to be extraordinarily rare. According to one estimate, plaintiffs obtain a judgment awarding them damages in a fraction of one percent of *Bivens* cases and obtain a monetary settlement in less than one percent of such cases.

Cornelia T.L. Pillard, *Taking Fiction Seriously: The Strange Results of Public Officials' Individual Liability Under* Bivens, 88 Geo. L.J. 65, 66 (1999).

Professor Alexander Reinert's more recent study, however, concluded:

Bivens cases are much more successful than has been assumed by the legal community, and . . . in some respects they are nearly as successful as other kinds of challenges to governmental misconduct. Depending on the procedural posture, presence of counsel, and type of case, success rates for *Bivens* suits range from 16% to more than 40%, which is at least an order of magnitude greater than has previously been estimated.

Alexander A. Reinert, *Measuring the Success of* Bivens *Litigation and Its Consequences for the Individual Liability Model*, 62 Stan. L. Rev. 809, 813 (2010).

Does the difficulty in winning a *Bivens* suit affect your view of the wisdom of the decision? Of the importance of *Bivens*? In what ways might the *Bivens* cause of action exert influence that cannot easily be captured by statistics regarding the success of cases?

Applications

It didn't take long for *Abbasi* to generate further debate. The Fifth and Ninth Circuits soon interpreted *Abbasi* quite differently in two cases in which U.S. Border Patrol officers shot unarmed Mexican minors playing near the border on Mexican soil.

In the Fifth Circuit case, Sergio Adrián Hernández Güereca, a 15-year-old Mexican national, was playing with friends in the dry cement culvert that separates El Paso, Texas, from Ciudad Juarez, Mexico. On the U.S. side of the culvert is a fence. According to the complaint, Hernández and his friends were playing a game in which they ran up to the fence, touched it, and ran back down into the culvert. Border Patrol Agent Jesus Mesa, Jr., arrived and detained one of Hernández's friends in U.S. territory and Hernández ran across the international boundary back into Mexican territory. Mesa then fired at least two shots across the border at Hernández, killing him. Hernández was unarmed and unthreatening at the time. Hernández's parents sued Mesa for damages under *Bivens*, alleging Fourth and Fifth Amendment violations. After a trip up to the Supreme Court, which rejected a defense we'll study later in Chapter 4 (qualified immunity), the en banc Fifth Circuit held, 13-2, that a *Bivens* claim was unavailable. *Hernandez v. Mesa*, 885 F.3d 811 (5th Cir. 2018) (en banc). Judge Jones's opinion for the en banc majority reasoned as follows:

Because Hernandez was a Mexican citizen with no ties to this country, and his death occurred on Mexican soil, the very existence of any "constitutional" right benefitting him raises novel and disputed issues. There has been no direct judicial guidance concerning the extraterritorial scope of the Constitution and its potential application to foreign citizens on foreign soil. . . .

[Plaintiffs'] unprecedented claims embody not merely a "modest extension"—which *Abbasi* describes as a "new" *Bivens* context—but a virtual repudiation of the Court's holding. *Abbasi* is grounded in the conclusion that *Bivens* claims are now a distinctly "disfavored" remedy and are subject to strict limitations arising from the constitutional imperative of the separation of powers. The newness of this "new context" should alone require dismissal of the plaintiffs' damage claims. Nevertheless, we turn next to the "special factors" analysis assuming arguendo that some type of constitutional claims could be conjured here. . . .

To begin with, this extension of *Bivens* threatens the political branches' supervision of national security. . . . [T]he threat of *Bivens* liability could undermine the Border Patrol's ability to perform duties essential to national security. . . . Although members of the Border Patrol like Agent Mesa may conduct activities analogous to domestic law enforcement, this case involved shots fired across the border within the scope of Agent Mesa's employment. . . .

Implying a private right of action for damages in this transnational context increases the likelihood that Border Patrol agents will "hesitate in making split second decisions." Considering the "systemwide" impact of this *Bivens* extension, there are "sound reasons to think Congress might doubt [its] efficacy." *Abbasi.*

Extending *Bivens* in this context also risks interference with foreign affairs and diplomacy more generally. This case is hardly sui generis: the United States government is always responsible to foreign sovereigns when federal officials injure foreign citizens on foreign soil. These are often delicate diplomatic matters, and, as such, they "are rarely proper subjects for judicial intervention." . . .

[T]he absence of a federal remedy does not mean the absence of deterrence. . . . For cross-border shootings like this one . . . criminal investigations and prosecutions are already a deterrent. While it is true that numerous federal agencies investigated Agent Mesa's conduct and decided not to bring charges, the DOJ is currently prosecuting another Border Patrol agent in Arizona for the cross-border murder of a Mexican citizen. *See United States v. Swartz*, No. 15-CR-1723 (D. Ariz. Sept. 23, 2015). . . .

Finally, the extraterritorial aspect of this case is itself a special factor that underlies and aggravates the separation-of-powers issues already discussed. . . . The Supreme Court "has never created or even favorably mentioned a non-statutory right of action for damages on account of conduct that occurred outside the borders of the United States."

In dissent, Judge Prado (joined by Judge Graves) argued that the plaintiffs were raising an ordinary excessive force claim, capable of being adjudicated under established constitutional standards without affecting national security policy or foreign relations:

If recognizing a *Bivens* remedy in this context implicates border security or the Border Patrol's operations, so too would any suit against a Border Patrol agent for unconstitutional actions taken in the course and scope of his or her employment.

Yet, as the majority recognizes, Border Patrol agents are unquestionably subject to *Bivens* suits when they commit constitutional violations on U.S. soil. It makes little sense to argue that a suit against a Border Patrol agent who shoots and kills someone standing a few feet beyond the U.S. border implicates border and national security issues, but at the same time contend that those concerns are not implicated when the same agent shoots someone standing a few feet inside the border.

The Ninth Circuit panel in *Rodriguez v. Swartz*, 899 F.3d 719 (9th Cir. 2018)—a civil suit against the same border patrol officer whose federal prosecution the *Hernandez* court cited as an example of deterrence beyond the *Bivens* remedy—took an approach more like Judge Prado's than the Fifth Circuit en banc majority's. The facts of *Rodriguez* were similar to those of *Hernandez*:

> Lonnie Swartz was on duty as a U.S. Border Patrol agent on the American side of our border with Mexico. J.A., a sixteen-year-old boy, was peacefully walking down the Calle Internacional, a street in Nogales, Mexico, that runs parallel to the border. Without warning or provocation, Swartz shot J.A. dead. Swartz fired somewhere between 14 and 30 bullets across the border at J.A., and he hit the boy, mostly in the back, with about 10 bullets. J.A. was not committing a crime. He did not throw rocks or engage in any violence or threatening behavior against anyone or anything. And he did not otherwise pose a threat to Swartz or anyone else. He was just walking down a street in Mexico.

Judge Kleinfeld wrote for a 2-1 panel majority that J.A.'s mother's *Bivens* action against the officer was cognizable:

> *Abbasi* went out of its way to emphasize that the Court did "not intend[ ] to cast doubt on the continued force, or even the necessity, of *Bivens* in the search-and-seizure context in which it arose." . . .
>
> [I]n the right case, we may extend *Bivens* into a new context. After all, if *Bivens* could not be expanded so that it applied in a new context, there would be no need for "caution" or treating expansion as a "disfavored judicial activity," or considering whether there was an adequate alternative remedy or special factors. Determining that the context was new would be the end of the inquiry, not the beginning. . . .
>
> Swartz and the United States have suggested several possible alternative remedies. But even though an alternative remedy need not be "perfectly congruent" with *Bivens* or "perfectly comprehensive," it still must be "adequate." None of the suggested alternatives is adequate. . . .
>
> [T]he FTCA . . . specifically provides that the United States cannot be sued for claims "arising in a foreign country." . . . J.A. suffered his deadly injury in Mexico, so Rodriguez cannot sue the United States under the FTCA. . . .
>
> The United States suggests that Rodriguez could sue Swartz for wrongful death under Arizona tort law. But . . . it appears that the Westfall Act would bar such a claim. . . .
>
> The United States indicted and tried Swartz for murdering J.A. Though a jury acquitted him of murder, the government has indicated that it will retry him for manslaughter. If he is convicted, federal law will require him to pay restitution to J.A.'s estate. The United States argues that such restitution is an adequate remedy.
>
> But restitution is not an adequate remedy for several reasons. First, even if a federal agent commits a crime in the course of his employment, the government

has discretion whether to charge him. A criminal charge is the government's remedy, not the victim's. Second, Swartz can be convicted of a crime only if his guilt is proven "beyond a reasonable doubt." By contrast, a *Bivens* claim requires the jury to find only that it is "more likely than not" that Swartz used objectively unreasonable force. So even if Swartz is acquitted of all criminal charges, he could still be liable for money damages. Third, criminal charges were potentially available in *Bivens* itself, yet that availability did not bar a damages cause of action. . . .

[W]e cannot extend *Bivens* if a "special factor" counsels hesitation. . . . The special factors analysis is almost always performed at a high level of specificity, not at the abstract level. For example, *Ziglar v. Abbasi* looked at specific claims about detention policies in the aftermath of the September 11 attacks, not at seizures and prison policies generally. . . .

[T]his case involves the unjustifiable and intentional killing of someone who was simply walking down a street in Mexico and who did not direct any activity toward the United States. Our discussion is limited to those facts. . . .

Rodriguez does not challenge any government policy whatsoever. And neither the United States nor Swartz argues that he followed government policy. . . . Rodriguez also sued a rank-and-file officer, not the head of the Border Patrol or any other policymaking official. This case is therefore like the ones that *Abbasi* distinguished—those involving "standard law enforcement operations" and "individual instances of . . . law enforcement overreach." The standards governing Swartz's conduct are the same here as they would be in any other excessive force case. . . .

We recognize that Border Patrol agents protect the United States from unlawful entries and terrorist threats. Those activities help guarantee our national security. But no one suggests that national security involves shooting people who are just walking down a street in Mexico. Moreover, holding Swartz liable for this constitutional violation would not meaningfully deter Border Patrol agents from performing their duties. . . . It cannot harm national security to hold Swartz civilly liable any more than it would to hold him criminally liable, and the government is currently trying to do the latter. Thus, national security is not a special factor here.

The United States argues that we should not extend *Bivens* here because the cross-border nature of the shooting implicates foreign policy. . . . But the United States has not explained how any policy is implicated or could be complicated by applying *Bivens* to this shooting. . . . There is no American foreign policy embracing shootings like the one pleaded here.

Judge Milan Smith dissented, disagreeing with both the majority's application of *Abbasi* and its approach to that decision generally. Regarding the latter, Judge Smith objected, "The majority fails to accord any meaningful significance to the conclusion that this case presents a new context for a *Bivens* claim. By the majority's reckoning, the fact that a *Bivens* claim presents a new context means only that a court must perform the second half of the *Bivens* analysis—the special-factors inquiry—and nothing more. This approach clearly flouts the Supreme Court's instructions." Judge Smith would have held, following *Hernandez*, that the newness of the context alone defeated the *Bivens* claim. Further, he argued, the case is "brimming" with special factors counseling hesitation: foreign relations, border security, and extraterritoriality. Additionally, Judge Smith did not believe the absence of any other federal remedy was inadvertent; instead, the foreign-country exception to the FTCA implied that Congress would not have wanted a *Bivens* claim to be available.

As between *Rodriguez* and *Hernandez*, which is a better interpretation of *Abbasi*? More faithful to underlying rationale of *Bivens*? Is the Fifth Circuit's treatment of the "new context" inquiry a faithful application or an extension of how that concept is used in *Abbasi*?

Petitions for certiorari were filed in both cases. In May 2019, the Supreme Court granted the petition in *Hernandez* to review the *Bivens* question. How do you predict the Supreme Court will rule?

CHAPTER 2 PROBLEMS

Problem 2A.   Return to Problem 1A at the end of Chapter 1. Change the scenario in two ways: *First*, assume that once Bahma indicates to the state prosecutor he is going to fight the disorderly conduct charge in court, the prosecutor simply drops the charge (so, no future state court date, no plea deal). *Second*, assume that the investigator Jay Polk Knox, instead of being a retired local detective who volunteers for the school, is an active-duty U.S. military officer who is detailed to FTI because of the school's military affiliation. The scenario is otherwise the same. Can Bahma sue Knox for the due process violation?

Problem 2B.   Due to a quirk of federal-local relations in the District of Columbia, the entity responsible for overseeing evictions in the District of Columbia is the United States Marshals Service (USMS). When marshals are overseeing an eviction, USMS policy calls for the assigned marshal to arrive with a crew of movers hired by the landlord, knock on the door of the tenant to be evicted, explain what is happening, and provide a law enforcement presence while the movers remove the tenant's possessions.

While overseeing an otherwise routine D.C. eviction at the home of tenant Madison James, federal Marshal Jefferson Thomas thinks that James looks suspicious and that she is probably a drug dealer. Based only on his hunch, Thomas ransacks James's home and causes $3,000 in damage. Thomas finds no evidence of drug dealing, but he does find a copy of the *Anarchist Cookbook*, a book that contains instructions on bomb-making and credit card fraud, among other things. Thomas confiscates the book. The eviction crew then removes James's possessions in accordance with the eviction notice.

James files a *Bivens* action for damages against Thomas and the U.S. Marshals Service. She asserts that Thomas violated the First Amendment by confiscating her book without an opportunity to challenge that decision, in violation of *A Quantity of Books v. Kansas*, 378 U.S. 205 (1964), concerning the seizure of allegedly pornographic material. James also claims that Thomas violated her Fourth Amendment rights by unreasonably searching her property without a warrant.

James files her action in the U.S. District Court for the District of Columbia. The U.S. Court of Appeals for the D.C. Circuit has recognized a *Bivens* cause of action for the violation of First Amendment rights in the context of police breaking up a protest. *See Dellums v. Powell*, 566 F.2d 167 (D.C. Cir. 1977). Several other circuits have held likewise. The Supreme Court has never decided the question.

Can James seek damages under *Bivens* against Thomas for the Fourth Amendment violation? For the First Amendment violation? Against the USMS for either violation?

Problem 2C. Woodson Wildrow is a presidential candidate of a racist political party, the Know-Everythings. The party platform includes prohibiting all immigration to the United States by non-white people. Wildrow is elected president. On his first day in office, he signs an executive order (the "EO") banning immigration by anyone who is not white.

Ibrahim Lincoln is a dark-skinned Sudanese refugee who obtained a visa to enter the United States before Wildrow promulgated the ban. Lincoln flies to the United States. When he lands, U.S. customs agent Harding G. Warren denies Lincoln entry based on the EO and sends him back to Sudan on the next plane.

Congress is outraged by the EO. It passes, over President Wildrow's veto, the Immigration Non-Discrimination Act (INDA), which adds a new chapter to federal immigration law consisting of these three sections:

> "The race or color of anyone attempting to immigrate to the United States may not be used as a substantial factor in the decision to deny the prospective immigrant entry, except during a war declared by Congress." 8 U.S.C. § 91.
>
> "In any agency proceeding regarding the denial of entry to any prospective immigrant to the United States, the prospective immigrant may assert a violation of § 91 to defeat the denial of entry. If the assertion of § 91 is rejected, the prospective immigrant may petition for review in the U.S. Court of Appeals for the D.C. Circuit." 8 U.S.C. § 92.
>
> "In any action or proceeding to enforce a provision of this chapter, the court, in its discretion, may allow the prevailing party, other than the United States, a reasonable attorney's fee as part of the costs." 8 U.S.C. § 93.

With the EO now repealed, Lincoln once again flies to the United States. This time he is admitted.

Once in the United States, Lincoln sues Agent Warren under *Bivens* for denying him entry (the first time) based on race, in violation of the equal protection component of the Due Process Clause of the Fifth Amendment. Lincoln seeks damages for the cost of his return plane flight and for his anxiety at being forced to return to Sudan. The law does not provide Agent Warren with a just-following-orders defense.

Agent Warren argues that there's no *Bivens* cause of action. Will this argument succeed?

PART II

CONSTITUTIONAL TORT CLAIMS—LIMITATIONS AND DEFENSES

Part I introduced the basic tools of constitutional enforcement for civil rights litigators: the causes of action. This part examines the many doctrines—some constitutional, some statutory, and some developed by the courts alone—that blunt these tools for the enforcement of constitutional rights by limiting the defendants that can be sued and the circumstances under which claims can succeed.

These various obstacles are arranged in this part by type of defendant: states (Chapter 3), individual officers (Chapter 4), and municipal defendants such as cities, counties, and school boards (Chapter 5). That order reflects the historical sequence in which their defenses were recognized by the Supreme Court. Our coverage of individual officers will touch on the issue of private contractors performing government functions, but note that in general, because of the state action limitation discussed in Chapter 1, constitutional civil rights actions generally lie only against governmental and not private actors. (Part III of the book, which covers statutory as opposed to constitutional civil rights claims, will introduce tools to enforce civil rights against private as well as governmental defendants.) A final introductory point: As we'll see, the defenses available to individual officers (Chapter 4) apply to federal as well as state and local officers, so plaintiffs suing federal agents must contend with these as well as the limitations on *Bivens*.

Sovereign Immunity and Suits Against States

Although it is formally a defense, sovereign immunity is in some respects foundational to the development of civil rights litigation. Many of the tools that civil rights litigators use were developed as responses to, as work-arounds for, or in the shadow of the powerful doctrine of sovereign immunity, which protects a state and its agencies from suit. (For that reason, some instructors may assign this chapter first.)

Originally, sovereign immunity referred to the principle of English law that the sovereign (for most of English history, the King) could not be sued without his consent. Although U.S. law has borrowed much from English common law, you might expect we would have quickly discarded this monarchist doctrine as inconsistent with the rule of law. Indeed, in what is generally considered the Supreme Court's first blockbuster case, the Court rejected sovereign immunity. But that result did not hold for long.

The first section of this chapter summarizes the history and background of the Eleventh Amendment and discusses the scope of sovereign immunity generally. The remainder of the chapter concerns the implications of sovereign immunity for civil rights enforcement. If states themselves cannot be sued, what recourse is available when state officials violate someone's rights?

A. THE DEVELOPMENT AND REACH OF SOVEREIGN IMMUNITY

1. THE PASSAGE OF THE ELEVENTH AMENDMENT

In *Chisholm v. Georgia*, 2 U.S. 419 (1793), Georgia was sued for having failed to pay for Revolutionary War supplies it had ordered from a South Carolina merchant. By a 4-1 margin, the Court held that it had jurisdiction over the suit, with each Justice writing his own opinion (in the manner of the day). Dean John Manning summarizes the major themes running through the various opinions:

> First, two opinions emphasized that because sovereign immunity originated in the feudal notion that the Crown was a sovereign who was above his or her subjects, its premises did not apply to a republican system of government in which sovereignty resides with the people. Second, several Justices reasoned that even if sovereign immunity survived a republican form of government, the states necessarily ceded a measure of their sovereignty to the nation when they assented to the Constitution. . . . Third, certain majority opinions invoked other heads of Article III jurisdiction to establish the basic point that the states did not join the union with their background immunity intact. In particular, Article III created jurisdiction in controversies "between two or more States," a meaningless provision unless a state could subject another state to suit in federal court. . . .
>
> Justice Iredell's dissent . . . emphasized that section 14 of the Judiciary Act of 1789 authorized such courts merely to issue writs "'agreeable to the principles and usages of law.'" For him, the crucial point was that Congress had instructed the federal courts (including the Supreme Court) to look to existing law in determining the availability of compulsory process against the states. In the absence of any state or federal statute specifically addressing that question, Justice Iredell reasoned that section 14 necessarily incorporated the common law of the states—a body of law that, in his view, had not materially deviated from the common law pertaining to the sovereign immunity of the English Crown. That tradition excluded an unconsented common law action to recover a debt from a state.

John F. Manning, *The Eleventh Amendment and the Reading of Precise Constitutional Texts*, 113 Yale L.J. 1663, 1676-80 (2004).

Judge William Fletcher narrates what happened next:

> The reaction to *Chisholm* was immediate and hostile. The Georgia House of Representatives passed a bill declaring that any persons attempting to levy a judgment in the case "are hereby declared to be guilty of felony, and shall suffer death, without the benefit of clergy, by being hanged." Other states were alarmed by the decision, not only because of the symbolic affront to their sovereignty, but also because of their considerable indebtedness in the postwar period. . . .
>
> One day after the Court announced its decision in *Chisholm*, a constitutional amendment was proposed in the House of Representatives:
>
>> That no state shall be liable to be made a party defendant in any of the judicial courts, established, or which shall be established under the authority of the United States, at the suit of any person or persons whether a citizen or citizens, or a foreigner or foreigners, of any body politic or corporate, whether within or without the United States.
>
> The next day another amendment was proposed in the House:
>
>> The Judicial power of the United States shall not extend to any suits in law or equity, commenced or prosecuted against one of the United States by citizens of another state, or by citizens or subjects of any foreign state.

Both resolutions were tabled, and Congress adjourned less than a month later without taking action. In January, 1794, during the next session, the text of what would become the eleventh amendment was proposed in both the House and the Senate:

> The Judicial power of the United States shall not be construed to extend to any suit[] in law or equity, commenced or prosecuted against one of the United States by citizens of another state, or by citizens or subjects of any foreign state.

William A. Fletcher, *A Historical Interpretation of the Eleventh Amendment: A Narrow Construction of an Affirmative Grant of Jurisdiction Rather Than a Prohibition Against Jurisdiction*, 35 Stan. L. Rev. 1033, 1058-59 (1983). The amendment was passed in March 1794 and was ratified by the required twelve states by February 1795.

What does the Eleventh Amendment mean? The words seem only to apply to the narrow circumstances of *Chisholm* itself: a suit invoking "[t]he Judicial power of the United States"—that is, a suit in federal court—and "commenced or prosecuted against *one* of the United States by citizens of *another* state" or of a foreign country (emphasis added). In concrete terms, then, according to the text of the Eleventh Amendment, a South Carolinian can't sue Georgia in federal court, but a Georgian can. And the Eleventh Amendment poses no bar to suits in state courts.

Early on, these propositions were not tested, because the Eleventh Amendment was easily evaded through formalistic pleading choices. For instance, in *Osborn v. Bank of the United States*, 22 U.S. 738, 857 (1824), Chief Justice Marshall reasoned that "in all cases where jurisdiction depends on the party, it is the party named in the record. Consequently, the 11th amendment, which restrains the jurisdiction granted by the constitution over suits against States, is, of necessity, limited to those suits in which a State is a party on the record."

But after the Civil War (as after the Revolutionary War), post-war debt fueled litigation against states that tested their amenability to suit. In interpreting the Eleventh Amendment, the Court made some interpretive choices that appear surprising in light of the text.

2. WHICH PLAINTIFFS ARE RESTRICTED BY SOVEREIGN IMMUNITY?

The Eleventh Amendment's text applies to a suit "commenced or prosecuted against *one* of the United States by citizens of *another* state" (emphasis added). But in *Hans v. Louisiana*, 134 U.S. 1 (1890), the Court held unanimously that the Eleventh Amendment barred a citizen of Louisiana from suing Louisiana to recover on state bonds. Justice Bradley's opinion for the Court explained:

> *Chisholm v. Georgia* . . . created such a shock of surprise throughout the country that, at the first meeting of congress thereafter, the eleventh amendment to the constitution was almost unanimously proposed, and was in due course adopted by the legislatures of the states. This amendment, expressing the will of the ultimate

sovereignty of the whole country, superior to all legislatures and all courts, actually reversed the decision of the supreme court. . . .

This view of the force and meaning of the amendment is important. It shows that, on this question of the suability of the states by individuals, the highest authority of this country was in accord rather with the minority than with the majority of the court in the decision of the case of *Chisholm v. Georgia*; and this fact lends additional interest to the able opinion of Mr. Justice Iredell on that occasion. The other justices were more swayed by a close observance of the letter of the constitution, without regard to former experience and usage; and because the letter said that the judicial power shall extend to controversies "between a state and citizens of another state"; and "between a state and foreign states, citizens or subjects," they felt constrained to see in this language a power to enable the individual citizens of one state, or of a foreign state, to sue another state of the Union in the federal courts. Justice Iredell, on the contrary, contended that it was not the intention to create new and unheard of remedies, by subjecting sovereign states to actions at the suit of individuals . . . .

The eighty-first number of the Federalist, written by Hamilton, has the following profound remarks: ". . . It is inherent in the nature of sovereignty not to be amenable to the suit of an individual without its consent. This is the general sense and the general practice of mankind; and the exemption, as one of the attributes of sovereignty, is now enjoyed by the government of every state in the Union. Unless, therefore, there is a surrender of this immunity in the plan of the convention, it will remain with the states, and the danger intimated must be merely ideal. . . ."

[L]ooking at the subject as Hamilton did, and as Mr. Justice Iredell did, in the light of history and experience and the established order of things, [their views] were clearly right, as the people of the United States in their sovereign capacity subsequently decided. *[The Court quotes at length the views of James Madison and John Marshall to similar effect.]* . . .

The letter is appealed to now, as it was then, as a ground for sustaining a suit brought by an individual against a state. The reason against it is as strong in this case as it was in that. It is an attempt to strain the constitution and the law to a construction never imagined or dreamed of. Can we suppose that, when the eleventh amendment was adopted, it was understood to be left open for citizens of a state to sue their own state in the federal courts, while the idea of suits by citizens of other states, or of foreign states, was indignantly repelled? Suppose that congress, when proposing the eleventh amendment, had appended to it a proviso that nothing therein contained should prevent a state from being sued by its own citizens in cases arising under the constitution or laws of the United States, can we imagine that it would have been adopted by the states? The supposition that it would is almost an absurdity on its face.

The truth is that the cognizance of suits and actions unknown to the law, and forbidden by the law, was not contemplated by the constitution when establishing the judicial power of the United States. . . .

It is not necessary that we should enter upon an examination of the reason or expediency of the rule which exempts a sovereign state from prosecution in a court of justice at the suit of individuals. This is fully discussed by writers on public law. It is enough for us to declare its existence. The legislative department of a state represents its polity and its will, and is called upon by the highest demands of natural and political law to preserve justice and judgment, and to hold inviolate the public obligations. Any departure from this rule, except for reasons most cogent, (of which the legislature, and not the courts, is the judge), never fails in the end to incur the odium of the world, and to bring lasting injury upon the state itself. But to deprive the legislature of the power of judging what the honor and safety of the state may require, even at the expense of a temporary failure to discharge the public debts, would be attended with greater evils than such failure can cause.

Thus, in short, the Supreme Court read the Eleventh Amendment as reaffirming a proposition it believed inherent in the original Constitution itself: the immunity of the sovereign from suit without its consent.

Consider what tools of interpretation *Hans* uses. As among text, policy, and history, which is given the greatest weight? What weight is given to the others? Why?

Although *Hans* remains good law, the broad reading of the Eleventh Amendment remains controversial. Judge Fletcher, for instance, makes this case for a much narrower interpretation:

A close reading of the several versions of the amendment proposed in Congress [quoted in the excerpt from Judge Fletcher's analysis above] suggests that the eleventh amendment had a more modest purpose than to forbid private citizens' suits against the states. . . . [T]he second and third proposals are strikingly different [from the first]. Instead of providing that "no state shall be liable to be made a party defendant [in federal court]," as did the first proposal, they provide, in words echoing article III, that "the judicial power shall not extend" and "the judicial power . . . shall not be construed to extend" to certain private citizens' suits against the states. This difference suggests that the amendment was intended to modify article III directly by repealing one of its affirmative grants. Further, instead of addressing the amendment to all citizens regardless of their citizenship, as did the first proposal, the second and third proposals address only out-of-state and foreign citizens, paralleling article III's affirmative authorization of federal court jurisdiction in suits "between a state and citizens of another state" and between a state and "foreign . . . Citizens or Subjects." The narrowness of the amendment's coverage and its congruence with the affirmative authorization in article III of state-citizen diversity jurisdiction suggest strongly that rather than intending to create a general state sovereign immunity protection from all suits by private citizens, as the first proposal would have done, the drafters of the second and third proposals intended only to limit the scope of that part of article III's jurisdictional grant—the state-citizen diversity clause—that had led to *Chisholm*.

The eleventh amendment's failure to mention in-state citizens suggests that its drafters did not intend it to reach federal question suits, for if they intended the amendment to forbid them, their drafting was extraordinarily inept. . . . Further, the amendment mentions only suits in law and equity. Admiralty was at that time an extremely important part of the federal courts' jurisdiction, and it is therefore unlikely that the failure to mention admiralty was inadvertent. This suggests that the adopters did not intend to forbid suits in admiralty, just as their failure to mention in-state citizens suggests that they did not intend to forbid federal question suits. . . .

The most plausible interpretation of the eleventh amendment thus appears to be that it was designed simply and narrowly to overturn the result the Supreme Court had reached in *Chisholm v. Georgia*. Under this interpretation, the adopters of the amendment were following the traditions of common law lawyers in solving only the problem in front of them by requiring a limiting construction of the state-citizen diversity clause. They declined to say whether the states could be made liable to a private citizen under a federal cause of action, just as Justice Iredell had declined to answer that question in his dissenting opinion in *Chisholm*.

Fletcher, *supra*, at 1060-63.

The construction of sovereign immunity in *Hans*, though expansive, did not undermine the well-established distinction between states and municipalities, nor extend immunity to the latter. Indeed, on the same day as the decision in *Hans*, Justice Brewer's unanimous opinion for the Court in *Lincoln County v. Luning*, 133 U.S. 529 (1890), made short work of the argument for *municipal* sovereign immunity:

> This is an action on bonds and coupons. . . . [I]t is claimed that, because the county is an integral part of the state, it could not, under the eleventh amendment of the federal constitution, be sued in the circuit court. . . .
>
> [T]he records of this court, for the last 30 years, are full of suits against counties; and it would seem as though by general consent the jurisdiction of the federal courts in such suits had become established. But, irrespective of this general acquiescence, the jurisdiction of the circuit courts is beyond question. The eleventh amendment limits the jurisdiction only as to suits against a state. . . . [W]hile the county is territorially a part of the state, yet politically it is also a corporation created by, and with such powers as are given to it by, the state. In this respect, it is a part of the state only in that remote sense in which any city, town, or other municipal corporation may be said to be a part of the state.

3. IN WHICH VENUES DOES SOVEREIGN IMMUNITY APPLY?

The phrase "citizens of another state" is not the only part of the Eleventh Amendment that does not capture the full scope of the immunity the Court has recognized. The Supreme Court has also found that the implications of the Eleventh Amendment reach beyond merely "[t]he Judicial power of the United States."

In *Alden v. Maine*, 527 U.S. 706 (1999), the Court considered whether Maine could be sued in its *own* courts by state employees for violations of federal wage and hour law. The Court held, per Justice Kennedy, that sovereign immunity barred the suit. He began by discussing the relationship between the Eleventh Amendment and sovereign immunity:

> The Eleventh Amendment makes explicit reference to the States' immunity from suits "commenced or prosecuted against one of the United States by Citizens of another State, or by Citizens or Subjects of any Foreign State." We have, as a result, sometimes referred to the States' immunity from suit as "Eleventh Amendment immunity." The phrase is convenient shorthand but something of a misnomer, for the sovereign immunity of the States neither derives from, nor is limited by, the terms of the Eleventh Amendment. Rather, as the Constitution's structure, its history, and the authoritative interpretations by this Court make clear, the States'

immunity from suit is a fundamental aspect of the sovereignty which the States enjoyed before the ratification of the Constitution, and which they retain today (either literally or by virtue of their admission into the Union upon an equal footing with the other States) except as altered by the plan of the Convention or certain constitutional Amendments.

The focus on history over text naturally followed from the Court's understanding of the significance of the Eleventh Amendment:

> The Court has been consistent in interpreting the adoption of the Eleventh Amendment as conclusive evidence "that the decision in *Chisholm* was contrary to the well-understood meaning of the Constitution," and that the views expressed by Hamilton, Madison, and Marshall during the ratification debates, and by Justice Iredell in his dissenting opinion in *Chisholm*, reflect the original understanding of the Constitution. *See, e.g., Hans.* In accordance with this understanding, we have recognized a "presumption that no anomalous and unheard-of proceedings or suits were intended to be raised up by the Constitution—anomalous and unheard of when the constitution was adopted." *Hans.* As a consequence, we have looked to "history and experience, and the established order of things," rather than "[a]dhering to the mere letter" of the Eleventh Amendment, *id.*, in determining the scope of the States' constitutional immunity from suit. . . .
>
> The Eleventh Amendment confirmed, rather than established, sovereign immunity as a constitutional principle; it follows that the scope of the States' immunity from suit is demarcated not by the text of the Amendment alone but by fundamental postulates implicit in the constitutional design.

The immunity of states in their own courts was one such "fundamental postulate":

> While the constitutional principle of sovereign immunity does pose a bar to federal jurisdiction over suits against nonconsenting States, this is not the only structural basis of sovereign immunity implicit in the constitutional design. Rather, "[t]here is also the postulate that States of the Union, still possessing attributes of sovereignty, shall be immune from suits, without their consent, save where there has been 'a surrender of this immunity in the plan of the convention.'" (quoting The Federalist No. 81). This separate and distinct structural principle is not directly related to the scope of the judicial power established by Article III, but inheres in the system of federalism established by the Constitution.

Dissenting, Justice Souter, joined by Justices Stevens, Ginsburg, and Breyer, objected that in the course of "confront[ing] the fact that the state forum renders the Eleventh Amendment beside the point," the Court "has responded by discerning [that] . . . a State's sovereign immunity from all individual suits is a 'fundamental aspect' of state sovereignty. . . . [I]f the Court's current reasoning is correct, the Eleventh Amendment itself was unnecessary."

Alden was about a state sued in its *own* courts. The Supreme Court subsequently extended the same reasoning to protect a state from suit in *another* state's courts. *Franchise Tax Bd. v. Hyatt*, 139 S. Ct. 1485 (2019).

How does *Alden*'s account of the significance of the Eleventh Amendment compare to that of *Hans*? Does *Alden* merely clarify *Hans*, or extend it? If the "fundamental aspect of sovereignty" view is a correct historical understanding of the constitutional design, how did four out of five Justices (including one of the authors of the Federalist Papers, Chief Justice John Jay) miss it in *Chisholm*? And why did it take more than 200 years after the enactment of the Eleventh Amendment for the Court to articulate it?

B. SOVEREIGN IMMUNITY'S LIMITS

We now turn from the history and background of sovereign immunity to a study of its implications for civil rights enforcement. How and to what extent, in light of sovereign immunity, can states ever be held accountable for, or enjoined from, violating civil rights?

If the story of the previous section is that of a Court maximizing the reach of sovereign immunity, the story of this one is that of a Court engaging in jurisprudential gymnastics to create work-arounds for sovereign immunity's broad sweep so that some checks against unlawful action can, functionally, still exist.

1. *EX PARTE YOUNG*

One of the Court's key work-arounds for sovereign immunity involves suits seeking injunctions against states' unconstitutional conduct.

In *Ex parte Young*, 209 U.S. 123 (1908), railroad shareholders sued the attorney general of Minnesota, Edward Young, in federal court to enjoin enforcement of a state statute setting railroad rates. The court issued the injunction. Young tried to enforce the statute anyway, and the court held him in contempt.

At the Supreme Court, Young asserted that the contempt citation was invalid because the federal court had lacked jurisdiction to issue an injunction to prevent a violation of the federal Constitution and because Young was entitled to sovereign immunity. The Court rejected both claims in an opinion by Justice Peckham:

> We have . . . upon this record, the case of an unconstitutional act of the state legislature and an intention by the attorney general of the state to endeavor to enforce its provisions, to the injury of the company, in compelling it, at great expense, to defend legal proceedings of a complicated and unusual character, and involving questions of vast importance to all employees and officers of the company, as well as to the company itself. The question that arises is whether there is a remedy that the parties interested may resort to, by going into a Federal court of equity, in a case involving a violation of the Federal Constitution, and obtaining a judicial investigation of the problem, and, pending its solution, obtain freedom from suits, civil or criminal, by a temporary injunction, and, if the question be finally decided favorably to the contention of the company, a permanent injunction restraining all such actions or proceedings. . . .

[Our precedents] furnish ample justification for the assertion that individuals who, as officers of the state, are clothed with some duty in regard to the enforcement of the laws of the state, and who threaten and are about to commence proceedings, either of a civil or criminal nature, to enforce against parties affected an unconstitutional act, violating the Federal Constitution, may be enjoined by a Federal court of equity from such action. . . .

It is . . . argued that the only proceeding which the attorney general could take to enforce the statute, so far as his office is concerned, was one by mandamus, which would be commenced by the state, in its sovereign and governmental character, and that the right to bring such action is a necessary attribute of a sovereign government. It is contended that the complainants do not complain and they care nothing about any action which Mr. Young might take or bring as an ordinary individual, but that he was complained of as an officer, to whose discretion is confided the use of the name of the state of Minnesota so far as litigation is concerned, and that when or how he shall use it is a matter resting in his discretion and cannot be controlled by any court.

The answer to all this is the same as made in every case where an official claims to be acting under the authority of the state. The act to be enforced is alleged to be unconstitutional; and if it be so, the use of the name of the state to enforce an unconstitutional act to the injury of complainants is a proceeding without the authority of, and one which does not affect, the state in its sovereign or governmental capacity. It is simply an illegal act upon the part of a state official in attempting, by the use of the name of the state, to enforce a legislative enactment which is void because unconstitutional. If the act which the state attorney general seeks to enforce be a violation of the Federal Constitution, the officer, in proceeding under such enactment, comes into conflict with the superior authority of that Constitution, and he is in that case stripped of his official or representative character and is subjected in his person to the consequences of his individual conduct. The state has no power to impart to him any immunity from responsibility to the supreme authority of the United States. It would be an injury to complainant to harass it with a multiplicity of suits or litigation generally in an endeavor to enforce penalties under an unconstitutional enactment, and to prevent it ought to be within the jurisdiction of a court of equity.

Justice Harlan dissented alone:

[T]he suit instituted . . . was, as to the defendant Young, one against him as, and only because he was, attorney general of Minnesota. No relief was sought against him individually, but only in his capacity as attorney general. . . . It would therefore seem clear that within the true meaning of the 11th Amendment the suit brought in the Federal court was one, in legal effect, against the state,—as much so as if the state had been formally named on the record as a party,—and therefore it was a suit to which, under the Amendment, so far as the state or its attorney general was concerned, the judicial power of the United States did not and could not extend. If this proposition be sound it will follow,—indeed, it is conceded that if, so far as relief is sought against the attorney general of Minnesota, this be a suit against the state,—then, the order of the Federal court enjoining that officer from taking any action, suit, step, or proceeding to compel the railway company to obey the Minnesota statute was beyond the jurisdiction of that court and wholly void; in which case, that officer was at liberty to proceed in the discharge of his official duties as defined by the laws of the state, and the order adjudging him to be in contempt . . . was a nullity.

The fact that the Federal circuit court had . . . preliminarily (but not finally) held the statutes of Minnesota and the orders of its railroad and warehouse commission in question to be in violation of the Constitution of the United States, was no reason why that court should have laid violent hands upon the attorney general of Minnesota . . . .

This principle, if firmly established, would work a radical change in our governmental system. It would inaugurate a new era in the American judicial system and in the relations of the national and state governments. It would enable the subordinate Federal courts to supervise and control the official action of the states as if they were "dependencies" or provinces. It would place the states of the Union in a condition of inferiority never dreamed of when the Constitution was adopted or when the 11th Amendment was made a part of the supreme law of the land.

Ex parte Young is significant in part because it solidified federal courts' inherent equitable power to enjoin constitutional violations, as discussed in Chapter 2, Section A. But it is most famous for its holding on sovereign immunity, the so-called "*Ex parte Young* fiction." The fiction is, of course, that a state official who acts unconstitutionally is, by virtue of so doing, *no longer a state official* and therefore suable like any individual.

Notes and Questions

1. What is the rule of *Ex parte Young*? In light of this rule, what differentiates a suit barred by sovereign immunity from one that may proceed?

2. Consider the "fiction" that is at the heart of the Court's opinion. Do you find support for the "fiction" in text, in history, in policy? Consider the consequences if Justice Harlan's view prevailed. His position has functional, intuitive appeal in its characterization of Young's status, and it's also consistent with *Hans*. Why did the Court overwhelmingly reject it?

3. How do you reconcile *Ex parte Young* with *Hans*? Or are they about different issues?

4. How do you reconcile *Ex parte Young* with *Monroe v. Pape* (Chapter 1)? Would the *Monroe* Court have characterized *Young* as acting "under color"? If so, how can a person simultaneously be acting "under color" of state law yet also be "stripped of his official or representative character"? Or is this area of law becoming so metaphysical as to defy attempts to harmonize it?

2. THE MODERN SYNTHESIS OF *HANS* AND *EX PARTE YOUNG*

Ex parte Young arose out of a suit for injunctive relief. Should the "fiction" apply in a suit seeking compensation for past wrongs? The next case considers that question.

Edelman v. Jordan
415 U.S. 651 (1974)

■ *Mr. Justice* REHNQUIST *delivered the opinion of the Court.*

[Respondent John Jordan filed a class action against Illinois and Cook County officials alleging that these officials' administration of a federal welfare program, Aid to the Aged, Blind, or Disabled (AABD), denied plaintiffs benefits in violation of the Fourteenth Amendment. The complaint sought, among other things, an injunction requiring defendants "to award to the entire class of plaintiffs all AABD benefits wrongfully withheld." The district court issued the requested injunction and the court of appeals affirmed over the Illinois officials' objection that the Eleventh Amendment barred awarding retroactive benefits. Joel Edelman, Director of the Illinois Department of Public Aid, sought certiorari.]

While the [Eleventh] Amendment by its terms does not bar suits against a State by its own citizens, this Court has consistently held that an unconsenting State is immune from suits brought in federal courts by her own citizens as well as by citizens of another State. *Hans.* It is also well established that even though a State is not named a party to the action, the suit may nonetheless be barred by the Eleventh Amendment. . . . The rule has evolved that a suit by private parties seeking to impose a liability which must be paid from public funds in the state treasury is barred by the Eleventh Amendment.

The Court of Appeals in this case, while recognizing that the *Hans* line of cases permitted the State to raise the Eleventh Amendment as a defense to suit by its own citizens, nevertheless concluded that the Amendment did not bar the award of retroactive payments of the statutory benefits found to have been wrongfully withheld. The Court of Appeals held that the above-cited cases, when read in light of this Court's landmark decision in *Ex parte Young*, do not preclude the grant of such a monetary award in the nature of equitable restitution.

Petitioner concedes that *Ex parte Young* is no bar to that part of the District Court's judgment that prospectively enjoined petitioner's predecessors from failing to process applications within the time limits established by the federal regulations. Petitioner argues, however, that *Ex parte Young* does not extend so far as to permit a suit which seeks the award of an accrued monetary liability which must be met from the general revenues of a State, absent consent or waiver by the State of its Eleventh Amendment immunity, and that therefore the award of retroactive benefits by the District Court was improper. . . .

[T]he relief awarded in *Ex parte Young* was prospective only; the Attorney General of Minnesota was enjoined to conform his future conduct of that office to the requirement of the Fourteenth Amendment. Such relief is analogous to that awarded by the District Court in the prospective portion of its order under review in this case.

But the retroactive position of the District Court's order here, which requires the payment of a very substantial amount of money which that court held should have been paid, but was not, stands on quite a different footing. These funds will obviously not be paid out of the pocket of petitioner Edelman. . . . The funds to satisfy the award in this case must inevitably come from the general revenues of the State of Illinois, and thus the award resembles far more closely the monetary award against the State itself, than it does the prospective injunctive relief awarded in *Ex parte Young*. . . .

We do not read *Ex parte Young* or subsequent holdings of this Court to indicate that any form of relief may be awarded against a state officer, no matter how closely it may in practice resemble a money judgment payable out of the state treasury, so long as the relief may be labeled "equitable" in nature. The Court's opinion in *Ex parte Young* hewed to no such line.

As in most areas of the law, the difference between the type of relief barred by the Eleventh Amendment and that permitted under *Ex parte Young* will not in many instances be that between day and night. The injunction issued in *Ex parte Young* was not totally without effect on the State's revenues, since the state law which the Attorney General was enjoined from enforcing provided substantial monetary penalties against railroads which did not conform to its provisions. Later cases from this Court have authorized equitable relief which has probably had greater impact on state treasuries than did that awarded in *Ex parte Young*. . . . But the fiscal consequences to state treasuries in these cases were the necessary result of compliance with decrees which by their terms were prospective in nature. State officials, in order to shape their official conduct to the mandate of the Court's decrees, would more likely have to spend money from the state treasury than if they had been left free to pursue their previous course of conduct. Such an ancillary effect on the state treasury is a permissible and often an inevitable consequence of the principle announced in *Ex parte Young*.

But that portion of the District Court's decree which petitioner challenges on Eleventh Amendment grounds goes much further than any of the cases cited. It requires payment of state funds, not as a necessary consequence of compliance in the future with a substantive federal-question determination, but as a form of compensation to those whose applications were processed on the slower time schedule at a time when petitioner was under no court-imposed obligation to conform to a different standard. While the Court of Appeals described this retroactive award of monetary relief as a form of "equitable restitution," it is in practical effect indistinguishable in many aspects from an award of damages against the State. It will to a virtual certainty be paid from state funds, and not from the pockets of the individual state officials who were the defendants in the action. It is measured in terms of a monetary loss resulting from a past breach of a legal duty on the part of the defendant state officials. . . .

The Court of Appeals held in the alternative that even if the Eleventh Amendment be deemed a bar to the retroactive relief awarded respondent in this case, the State of Illinois had waived its Eleventh Amendment immunity and consented to the bringing of such a suit by participating in the federal AABD program . . . and agreeing to administer federal and state funds in compliance with federal law. Constructive consent is not a doctrine commonly associated with the surrender of constitutional rights, and we see no place for it here. In deciding whether a State has waived its constitutional protection under the Eleventh Amendment, we will find waiver only where stated "by the most express language or by such overwhelming implications from the text as (will) leave no room for any other reasonable construction."

The mere fact that a State participates in a program through which the Federal Government provides assistance for the operation by the State of a system of public aid is not sufficient to establish consent on the part of the State to be sued in the federal courts. And while this Court has . . . authorized suits by one private party against another in order to effectuate a statutory purpose, it has never done so in the context of the Eleventh Amendment and a state defendant. . . .

■ *Mr. Justice* DOUGLAS, *dissenting.* . . .

As the complaint in the instant case alleges violations by officials of Illinois of the Equal Protection Clause of the Fourteenth Amendment, it seems that the case is governed by *Ex parte Young* so far as injunctive relief is concerned. The main thrust of the argument is that the instant case asks for relief which if granted would affect the treasury of the State.

Most welfare decisions by federal courts have a financial impact on the States. Under the existing federal-state cooperative system, a state desiring to participate, submits a "state plan" to HEW for approval; once HEW approves the plan the State is locked into the cooperative scheme until it withdraws. . . . [T]he distinction [between retroactive and prospective relief] is not relevant or material because the result in every welfare case coming here is to increase or reduce the financial responsibility of the participating State. In no case when the responsibility of the State is increased to meet the lawful demand of the beneficiary, is there any levy on state funds. Whether the decree is prospective only or requires payments for the weeks or months wrongfully skipped over by the state officials, the nature of the impact on the state treasury is precisely the same. . . .

■ *Mr. Justice* BRENNAN, *dissenting.*

This suit is brought by Illinois citizens against Illinois officials. In that circumstance, Illinois may not invoke the Eleventh Amendment, since that Amendment bars only federal court suits against States by citizens of other States. Rather, the question is whether Illinois may avail itself of the nonconstitutional but ancient doctrine of sovereign immunity as a bar to respondent's claim for retroactive AABD payments. In my view Illinois may not assert sovereign immunity [because] the States surrendered that immunity in Hamilton's words, "in the plan of the Convention," that formed the Union, at least insofar as the States granted Congress specifically enumerated powers. Congressional authority to enact the Social Security Act, of which AABD is a part, is to be found in Art. I, § 8, cl. 1, one of the enumerated powers granted Congress by the States in the Constitution. I remain of the opinion that "because of its surrender, no immunity exists that can be the subject of a congressional declaration or a voluntary waiver," and thus have no occasion to inquire whether or not Congress authorized an action for AABD retroactive benefits, or whether or not Illinois voluntarily waived the immunity by its continued participation in the program....

■ *Mr. Justice MARSHALL, with whom Mr. Justice BLACKMUN joins, dissenting.*

The Social Security Act's categorical assistance programs, including the Aid to the Aged, Blind, or Disabled (AABD) program involved here, are fundamentally different from most federal legislation. Unlike the Fair Labor Standards Act [for instance]...the Social Security Act does not impose federal standards and liability upon all who engage in certain regulated activities, including often-unwilling state agencies. Instead, the Act seeks to induce state participation in the federal welfare programs by offering federal matching funds in exchange for the State's voluntary assumption of the Act's requirements. I find this basic distinction crucial: it leads me to conclude that by participation in the programs, the States waive whatever immunity they might otherwise have from federal court orders requiring retroactive payment of welfare benefits.

In its contacts with the Social Security Act's assistance programs in recent years, the Court has frequently described the Act as a "scheme of cooperative federalism." While this phrase captures a number of the unique characteristics of these programs, for present purposes it serves to emphasize that the States' decision to participate in the programs is a voluntary one. In deciding to participate, however, the States necessarily give up their freedom to operate assistance programs for the needy as they see fit, and bind themselves to conform their programs to the requirements of the federal statute and regulations....

Illinois elected to participate in the AABD program, and received and expended substantial federal funds in the years at issue. It thereby obligated itself to comply with federal law....

Benefits under the categorical assistance programs "are a matter of statutory entitlement for persons qualified to receive them." Retroactive payment of benefits secures for recipients this entitlement which was withheld in violation of federal law. Equally important, the courts' power to order retroactive payments is an essential remedy to insure future state compliance with federal requirements. No other remedy can effectively deter States from the strong temptation to cut welfare budgets by circumventing the stringent requirements of federal law....

Absent any remedy which may act with retroactive effect, state welfare officials have everything to gain and nothing to lose by failing to comply with the congressional mandate that assistance be paid with reasonable promptness to all eligible individuals. This is not idle speculation without basis in practical experience. In this very case, for example, Illinois officials have knowingly violated since 1968 federal regulations on the strength of an argument as to its invalidity which even the majority deems unworthy of discussion. Without a retroactive-payment remedy, we are indeed faced with "the spectre of a state, perhaps calculatingly, defying federal law and thereby depriving welfare recipients of the financial assistance Congress thought it was giving them." Like the Court of Appeals, I cannot believe that Congress could possibly have intended any such result....

Notes and Questions

1. Consider the line that the Court has drawn between when sovereign immunity applies and when it does not. What is the essence of that distinction?

2. How does *Edelman* distinguish *Ex parte Young*? Is there a basis in history? Text? A relevant difference between the status of Edelman and Young as state officials? If not, how do you explain the Court's ruling?

3. Justice Rehnquist admits the line drawn in *Edelman* will not always be clear. Can you think of particularly difficult applications? What if the relief rejected in *Edelman* were characterized as a "prospective" injunction to ensure *future* remediation of *past* deficiencies in payment? Different result? If not, how do you reconcile that answer with the acknowledged susceptibility of state officials to suits seeking desegregation decrees, which are about remediating past discrimination?

4. Consider the three different theories advanced by the various dissenting opinions. What are the differences among them?

5. Both Justice Brennan and Justice Marshall argue that Illinois has waived immunity, but in different ways. Whose position is broader? How do their positions square with previous sovereign immunity cases, particularly *Hans*?

6. Justice Marshall raises the possibility that the Court's ruling provides an incentive for states to flout their obligations under federal benefit programs. How does the majority answer this concern?

7. The Justices all agree that sovereign immunity can be waived. According to the majority, what rules govern whether a waiver has occurred? States are sophisticated actors, with plenty of lawyers and policymakers to advise the relevant decisionmakers about when to participate in a federal program. What justifies the Court's presumption against finding a waiver?

3. WAIVER AND ABROGATION

As the opinions in *Edelman* reflect, "waiver" means voluntary relinquishment. The majority there refused to find waiver absent "the most express language or by such overwhelming implications from the text as will leave no room for any other reasonable construction." This type of requirement is known as a "clear statement rule."

You might wonder when a state would ever voluntarily relinquish its immunity. One circumstance in which this occurs is when Congress clearly conditions the receipt of federal funds on a waiver of sovereign immunity. Two important civil rights statutes we'll study in Chapter 7—Title VI of the Civil Rights Act of 1964 and Title IX of the Education Amendments of 1972—are examples.

States can also lose their sovereign immunity involuntarily—in the narrow circumstances in which Congress is authorized to "abrogate" (i.e., to annul or invalidate) it. The next case discusses one such circumstance: when Congress acts pursuant to its constitutional power to enforce the Fourteenth Amendment.

The Fourteenth Amendment, whose first section prevents states from denying individuals equal protection of the laws and due process of law, goes on to authorize Congress to "enforce by appropriate legislation, the provisions of this article." U.S. Const., amend. XIV, § 5. Constitutional Law courses covering congressional powers generally explore the scope of the § 5 enforcement power, including the extent of legislation authorized by that section. We will not cover that question here. The question relevant to our study, i.e., to the *enforcement* of the civil rights laws (rather than Congress's authority to *enact* them), is what happens to state sovereign immunity when Congress *does* legislate pursuant to its power under § 5 of the Fourteenth Amendment. The next case answers.

Fitzpatrick v. Bitzer
427 U.S. 445 (1976)

■ *Mr. Justice* REHNQUIST *delivered the opinion of the Court.*

In the 1972 Amendments to Title VII of the Civil Rights Act of 1964, Congress, acting under § 5 of the Fourteenth Amendment, authorized federal courts to award money damages in favor of a private individual against a state government found to have subjected that person to employment discrimination on the basis of "race, color, religion, sex, or national origin." The principal question presented by these cases is whether, as against the shield of sovereign immunity afforded the State by the Eleventh Amendment, *Edelman v. Jordan*, Congress has the power to authorize Federal courts to enter such an award against the State as a means of enforcing the substantive guarantees of the Fourteenth Amendment. . . .

[Plaintiffs sued Connecticut officials on behalf of all present and retired male state employees; the plaintiffs claimed that the state's retirement benefit plan discriminated on the basis of sex.] Title VII, which originally did not include state and local governments, had in the interim been amended to bring the States within its purview. . . .

In *Edelman* this Court held that monetary relief awarded by the District Court to welfare plaintiffs, by reason of wrongful denial of benefits which had occurred previous to the entry of the District Court's determination of their wrongfulness, violated the Eleventh Amendment. . . .

All parties in the instant litigation agree . . . that the suit for retroactive benefits by the petitioners is in fact indistinguishable from that sought to be maintained in *Edelman*, since what is sought here is a damages award payable to a private party from the state treasury.

Our analysis begins where *Edelman* ended, for in this Title VII case the "threshold fact of congressional authorization," to sue the State as employer is clearly present. [Unlike a prior case involving] congressional authorization . . . based on the power of Congress under the Commerce Clause[,] here . . . the Eleventh Amendment defense is asserted in the context of legislation passed pursuant to Congress' authority under § 5 of the Fourteenth Amendment.

As ratified by the States after the Civil War, that Amendment quite clearly contemplates limitations on their authority. . . . The substantive provisions are by express terms directed at the States. Impressed upon them by those provisions are duties with respect to their treatment of private individuals. Standing behind the imperatives is Congress' power to "enforce" them "by appropriate legislation."

[*Justice Rehnquist goes on to analyze and quote from the 1880 case* Ex parte Virginia. *The Court there wrote that the Civil War Amendments*] "were intended to be, what they really are, limitations of the power of the States and enlargements of the power of Congress." [As specific to the Fourteenth Amendment:] "[T]he Constitution now expressly gives authority for congressional interference and compulsion in the cases embraced within the Fourteenth Amendment. It is but a limited authority, true, extending only to a single class of cases; but within its limits it is complete." . . .

There can be no doubt that [this Court's cases have] sanctioned intrusions by Congress, acting under the Civil War Amendments, into the judicial, executive, and legislative spheres of autonomy previously reserved to the States. The legislation considered in each case was grounded on the expansion of Congress' powers with the corresponding diminution of state sovereignty found to be intended by the Framers and made part of the Constitution upon the States' ratification of those Amendments, a phenomenon aptly described as a "carv(ing) out" in *Ex parte Virginia*.

It is true that none of these previous cases presented the question of the relationship between the Eleventh Amendment and the enforcement power granted to Congress under § 5 of the Fourteenth Amendment. But we think that the Eleventh Amendment, and the principle of state sovereignty which it embodies, *see Hans v. Louisiana*, are necessarily limited by the enforcement provisions of § 5 of the Fourteenth Amendment. In that section Congress is expressly granted authority to enforce "by appropriate legislation" the substantive provisions of the Fourteenth Amendment, which themselves embody significant limitations on state authority. When Congress acts pursuant to § 5, not only is it exercising legislative authority that is plenary within the terms of the constitutional grant, it is exercising that authority under one section of a constitutional Amendment whose other sections by their own terms embody limitations on state authority. We think that Congress may, in determining what is "appropriate legislation" for the purpose of enforcing the provisions of the Fourteenth Amendment, provide for private suits against States or state officials which are constitutionally impermissible in other contexts.

[*Opinions of Brennan, J., and Stevens, J., each concurring in judgment, are omitted.*]

Note: *Seminole Tribe* and the Limits of *Fitzpatrick*

Fitzpatrick holds that Congress can abrogate sovereign immunity using its Fourteenth Amendment powers. Can it do the same via its other enumerated powers? Generally not, the Court has held. The Court's treatment of congressional prerogatives under the Fourteenth Amendment has proved the exception rather than the rule.

In *Seminole Tribe v. Florida*, 517 U.S. 44 (1996), the Court held that Congress could not use its Article I powers to abrogate state sovereign immunity even if it stated clearly its intent to do so. The Court distinguished *Fitzpatrick* on the ground that the Fourteenth Amendment, "adopted well after the adoption of the Eleventh Amendment and the ratification of the Constitution, operated to alter the pre-existing balance between state and federal power achieved by Article III and the Eleventh Amendment. . . . *Fitzpatrick* cannot be read to justify limitation of the principle embodied in the Eleventh Amendment through appeal to antecedent provisions of the Constitution." Justices Souter's wide-ranging dissent, joined by Justices Stevens, Ginsburg, and Breyer, criticized the majority for expanding the "invented" Eleventh Amendment of *Hans* in a manner that he concluded was ahistorical as well as (obviously) atextual.

Notes and Questions

1. In light of the line drawn by *Edelman*, what is the practical significance of a finding that Congress has abrogated state sovereign immunity? What remedies are available even absent abrogation (or waiver)? What remedy would be *unavailable* absent abrogation (or waiver)?

2. The Court has applied the "clear statement rule" to abrogation as well as to waiver. *See, e.g., Dellmuth v. Muth*, 491 U.S. 223, 230 (1989). Is this rule, which amounts to a presumption in favor of sovereign immunity, equally justified for both abrogation and waiver? If not, in which context is the argument stronger for requiring a clear statement? Why?

3. *Fitzpatrick*'s unanimity on the subject of sovereign immunity is rare, certainly in the modern era. Why was this such an uncontroversial case for a Court that two years earlier required a clear statement before it would find an intent to dispense with sovereign immunity? Was such a clear statement evident in the Fourteenth Amendment itself? As we'll see, the more conservative Justices continue to be as protective of state prerogatives as ever. What made this case different?

4. The *Seminole Tribe* majority's analysis appears to boil down to a recency rule: The Fourteenth Amendment, having postdated the Eleventh, permits its abrogation by Congress; Article I, having *pre*dated the Eleventh Amendment, does not. How important should the date of the Eleventh Amendment be, in light of the Court's repeated resort to principles of sovereign immunity inherent in the Constitution? Could a congressional power to abrogate state sovereign immunity have inhered in the original constitutional design alongside sovereign immunity itself?

4. APPLYING *EDELMAN* AND *FITZPATRICK*

As *Edelman* noted, "the difference between the type of relief barred by the Eleventh Amendment and that permitted under *Ex parte Young* will not in many instances be that between day and night." Consider the following applications of the distinction, which reveal the complexity of both the prospective/retrospective line and the clear statement rule. The first is a pure application of *Edelman*. The second implicates both *Edelman* and *Fitzpatrick*.

(a) **Expensive injunctions.** Just a few years after *Edelman*, the Court affirmed an injunction costing the State of Michigan over $5 million in the school desegregation case *Milliken v. Bradley*, 433 U.S. 267 (1977) ("*Milliken II*"). After an earlier remedial order was vacated in the Court's first decision in the case ("*Milliken I*," which we'll study in Chapter 12), the case returned to the Court presenting, among other issues, whether Michigan could be required to shoulder half the costs of the court-ordered remedy where it was found to have contributed to maintaining a segregated school system in Detroit. On that question, Chief Justice Burger's opinion for the Court explained why sovereign immunity did not shield Michigan:

> Petitioners ... contend that the District Court's order, even if otherwise proper, violates the Eleventh Amendment. In their view, the requirement that the state defendants pay one-half the additional costs attributable to the four educational components is, "in practical effect, indistinguishable from an award of money damages against the state based upon the asserted prior misconduct of state officials." Arguing from this premise, petitioners conclude that the "award" in this case is barred under this Court's holding in *Edelman v. Jordan*. . . .
>
> The decree to share the future costs of educational components in this case fits squarely within the prospective-compliance exception reaffirmed by *Edelman*. That exception, which had its genesis in *Ex parte Young*, permits federal courts to enjoin state officials to conform their conduct to requirements of federal law, notwithstanding a direct and substantial impact on the state treasury. The order challenged here does no more than that. The decree requires state officials, held responsible for unconstitutional conduct, in findings which are not challenged, to eliminate a de jure segregated school system. . . . The educational components, which the District Court ordered into effect prospectively, are plainly designed to wipe out continuing conditions of inequality produced by the inherently unequal dual school system long maintained by Detroit.
>
> These programs were not, and as a practical matter could not be, intended to wipe the slate clean by one bold stroke, as could a retroactive award of money in *Edelman*. Rather, by the nature of the antecedent violation, which on this record caused significant deficiencies in communications skills—reading and speaking— the victims of Detroit's de jure segregated system will continue to experience the effects of segregation until such future time as the remedial programs can help dissipate the continuing effects of past misconduct. Reading and speech deficiencies cannot be eliminated by judicial fiat; they will require time, patience, and the skills of specially trained teachers. That the programs are also "compensatory" in nature does not change the fact that they are part of a plan that operates prospectively to bring about the delayed benefits of a unitary school system. We therefore hold that such prospective relief is not barred by the Eleventh Amendment.

No Justice dissented in *Milliken II*.

Eighteen years later, in another desegregation case, Justice Thomas opined in a solo concurrence that requiring the State of Missouri to pay half the costs of a remedial order for improvements to the Kansas City school district implicated sovereign immunity:

> [It] come[s] perilously close to abrogating the State's Eleventh Amendment immunity from federal money damages awards. *See Edelman v. Jordan.* Although we held in *Milliken II* that such remedies did not run afoul of the Eleventh Amendment, it is difficult to see how they constitute purely prospective relief rather than retrospective compensation. Of course, the state treasury inevitably must fund a State's compliance with injunctions commanding prospective relief, but that does not require a State to supply money to comply with orders that have a backward-looking, compensatory purpose.

Missouri v. Jenkins, 515 U.S. 70, 132 n.5 (1995) (Thomas, J., concurring).

(b) Attorneys' fees and "ancillarity." *Hutto v. Finney*, 437 U.S. 678 (1978), required another thorny application of *Edelman*. That case involved long-running prison litigation resulting in multiple remedial orders by the district court for conditions that it found to violate the Eighth Amendment's prohibition on cruel and unusual punishment. (We'll return to *Hutto* in our study of institutional reform litigation in Chapter 12.) After a series of remedial orders, appeals, and further hearings, the court found that the State of Arkansas had failed to remedy the unconstitutional conditions and had acted in bad faith. The court awarded plaintiffs $20,000 in attorneys' fees for the state's bad faith and separately awarded $2,500 in attorneys' fees on appeal. Among the issues before the Court in *Hutto* were whether these awards were barred by sovereign immunity. Justice Stevens's majority opinion held that they were not. Turning first to the bad faith fees, the Court reasoned:

> Aware that the difference between retroactive and prospective relief "will not in many instances be that between day and night," the Court emphasized in *Edelman* that the distinction did not immunize the States from their obligation to obey costly federal-court orders. The cost of compliance is "ancillary" to the prospective order enforcing federal law.[15] The line between retroactive and prospective relief cannot be so rigid that it defeats the effective enforcement of prospective relief.
>
> The present case requires application of that principle. In exercising their prospective powers under *Ex parte Young* and *Edelman v. Jordan*, federal courts are not reduced to issuing injunctions against state officers and hoping for compliance. Once issued, an injunction may be enforced. Many of the court's most effective enforcement weapons involve financial penalties. A criminal contempt prosecution for "resistance to [the court's] lawful . . . order" may result in a jail term or a fine. Civil contempt proceedings may yield a conditional jail term or fine. Civil contempt may also be punished by a remedial fine, which compensates the party who won the injunction for the effects of his opponent's noncompliance. If a state agency

---

15. "Ancillary" costs may be very large indeed. Last Term, for example, this Court rejected an Eleventh Amendment defense and approved an injunction ordering a State to pay almost $6 million to help defray the costs of desegregating the Detroit school system. *Milliken II*.

refuses to adhere to a court order, a financial penalty may be the most effective means of insuring compliance. The principles of federalism that inform Eleventh Amendment doctrine surely do not require federal courts to enforce their decrees only by sending high state officials to jail. The less intrusive power to impose a fine is properly treated as ancillary to the federal court's power to impose injunctive relief.

In this case, the award of attorney's fees for bad faith served the same purpose as a remedial fine imposed for civil contempt. It vindicated the District Court's authority over a recalcitrant litigant. . . . We see no reason to distinguish this award from any other penalty imposed to enforce a prospective injunction. Hence the substantive protections of the Eleventh Amendment do not prevent an award of attorney's fees against the Department's officers in their official capacities.

Regarding attorneys' fees for the appeal, the Court's analysis invoked a different theory:

[The appellate fee award is founded] on the provisions of the Civil Rights Attorney's Fees Awards Act of 1976. The Act declares that, in suits under 42 U.S.C. § 1983 and certain other statutes, federal courts may award prevailing parties reasonable attorney's fees "as part of the costs."

As this Court made clear in *Fitzpatrick v. Bitzer*, Congress has plenary power to set aside the States' immunity from retroactive relief in order to enforce the Fourteenth Amendment. When it passed the Act, Congress undoubtedly intended to exercise that power and to authorize fee awards payable by the States when their officials are sued in their official capacities. The Act itself could not be broader. It applies to "any" action brought to enforce certain civil rights laws. It contains no hint of an exception for States defending injunction actions; indeed, the Act primarily applies to laws passed specifically to restrain state action. *See, e.g.,* 42 U.S.C. § 1983.

The legislative history is equally plain . . . .

The Attorney General does not quarrel with the rule established in *Fitzpatrick v. Bitzer*. Rather, he argues that these plain indications of legislative intent are not enough. In his view, Congress must enact express statutory language making the States liable if it wishes to abrogate their immunity. . . .

The Act imposes attorney's fees "as part of the costs." Costs have traditionally been awarded without regard for the States' Eleventh Amendment immunity. The practice of awarding costs against the States goes back to 1849 in this Court. The Court has never viewed the Eleventh Amendment as barring such awards, even in suits between States and individual litigants.[24] . . .

Just as a federal court may treat a State like any other litigant when it assesses costs, so also many Congress amend its definition of taxable costs and have the amended class of costs apply to the States, as it does to all other litigants, without expressly stating that it intends to abrogate the States' Eleventh Amendment immunity. For it would be absurd to require an express reference to state litigants

---

24. While the decisions allowing the award of costs against States antedate the line drawn between retroactive and prospective relief in *Edelman*, such awards do not seriously strain that distinction. Unlike ordinary "retroactive" relief such as damages or restitution, an award of costs does not compensate the plaintiff for the injury that first brought him into court. Instead, the award reimburses him for a portion of the expenses he incurred in seeking prospective relief. . . .

whenever a filing fee, or a new item, such as an expert witness' fee, is added to the category of taxable costs.

Justice Brennan concurred briefly to discuss the role of recent precedents in the result. In a partial dissent, Justice Powell, joined in full by Chief Justice Burger and in part by Justices White and Rehnquist, objected to the majority's treatment of the appellate fees:

> In this case, as in *Edelman*, "the threshold fact of congressional authorization to sue a class of defendants which literally includes States is wholly absent." Absent such authorization, grounded in statutory language sufficiently clear to alert every voting Member of Congress of the constitutional implications of particular legislation, we undermine the values of federalism served by the Eleventh Amendment by inferring from congressional silence an intent to "place new or even enormous fiscal burdens on the States." . . .
>
> I am unwilling to ignore otherwise applicable principles simply because the statute in question imposes substantial monetary liability as an element of "costs." Counsel fees traditionally have not been part of the routine litigation expenses assessed against parties in American courts. Quite unlike those routine expenses, an award of counsel fees may involve substantial sums and is not a charge intimately related to the mechanics of the litigation. . . .
>
> Moreover, counsel-fee awards cannot be viewed as having the kind of "ancillary effect on the state treasury," *Edelman*, that avoids the need for an explicit waiver of Eleventh Amendment protections. As with damages and restitutory relief, an award of counsel fees could impose a substantial burden on the State to make unbudgeted disbursements to satisfy an obligation stemming from past (as opposed to post-litigation) activities. It stretches the rationale of *Edelman* beyond recognition to characterize such awards as "the necessary result of compliance with decrees which by their terms [are] prospective in nature." In the case of a purely prospective decree, budgeting can take account of the expenditures entailed in compliance, and the State retains some flexibility in implementing the decree, which may reduce the impact on the state fisc. In some situations fiscal considerations may induce the State to curtail the activity triggering the constitutional obligation. Here, in contrast, the State must satisfy a potentially substantial liability without the measure of flexibility that would be available with respect to prospective relief.

In a separate dissent, Justice Rehnquist, joined by Justice White as to the fees issues, argued that the majority erred as to the bad-faith fees as well as the appellate fees, because "[a] State's jealous defense of its authority to operate its own correctional system cannot casually be equated with contempt of court."

When the Court again confronted the issue of fees and sovereign immunity, it revisited the holding in *Hutto*. In the desegregation decision *Missouri v. Jenkins*, 491 U.S. 274 (1989), a forerunner of the 1995 decision discussed in the previous note, a lower court awarded attorneys' fees to the plaintiffs' counsel and enhanced that fee to compensate the attorneys for delays in payment. The Court, in an opinion by Justice Brennan, again addressed the propriety of fee awards against a state in light of the Eleventh Amendment:

> In *Hutto*, the lower courts had awarded attorney's fees against the State of Arkansas, in part pursuant to § 1988, in connection with litigation over the conditions of

confinement in that State's prisons. The State contended that any such award was subject to the Eleventh Amendment's constraints on actions for damages payable from a State's treasury. We relied, in rejecting that contention, on the distinction drawn in our earlier cases between "retroactive monetary relief" and "prospective injunctive relief." *See Edelman; Ex parte Young.* Attorney's fees, we held, belonged to the latter category, because they constituted reimbursement of "expenses incurred in litigation seeking only prospective relief," rather than "retroactive liability for pre-litigation conduct." *Hutto.* We explained: "Unlike ordinary 'retroactive' relief such as damages or restitution, an award of costs does not compensate the plaintiff for the injury that first brought him into court. Instead, the award reimburses him for a portion of the expenses he incurred in seeking prospective relief." Section 1988, we noted, fit easily into the longstanding practice of awarding "costs" against States, for the statute imposed the award of attorney's fees "as part of the costs."

After *Hutto,* therefore, it must be accepted as settled that an award of attorney's fees ancillary to prospective relief is not subject to the strictures of the Eleventh Amendment. . . .

Missouri contends, however, that the principle enunciated in *Hutto* has been undermined by subsequent decisions of this Court that require Congress to "express its intention to abrogate the Eleventh Amendment in unmistakable language in the statute itself." The flaw in this argument lies in its misreading of the holding of *Hutto.* It is true that in *Hutto* we noted that Congress could, in the exercise of its enforcement power under § 5 of the Fourteenth Amendment, set aside the States' immunity from retroactive damages, and that Congress intended to do so in enacting § 1988. But we also made clear that the application of § 1988 to the States did not depend on congressional abrogation of the States' immunity. We did so in rejecting precisely the "clear statement" argument that Missouri now suggests has undermined *Hutto.* Arkansas had argued that § 1988 did not plainly abrogate the States' immunity. . . . We responded as follows: ". . . The Act imposes attorney's fees 'as part of the costs.' Costs have traditionally been awarded without regard for the States' Eleventh Amendment immunity."

The holding of *Hutto,* therefore, was not just that Congress had spoken sufficiently clearly to overcome Eleventh Amendment immunity in enacting § 1988, but rather that the Eleventh Amendment did not apply to an award of attorney's fees ancillary to a grant of prospective relief. . . .

We reaffirm our holding in *Hutto v. Finney* that the Eleventh Amendment has no application to an award of attorney's fees, ancillary to a grant of prospective relief, against a State.

The Court went on to hold that entitlement to attorneys' fees includes the possibility of enhancement for delay. Justice O'Connor, joined by Chief Justice Rehnquist and Justice Scalia, dissented from that holding. She characterized *Hutto* in this manner: "In *Hutto* the Court was able to avoid deciding whether § 1988 met the 'clear statement' rule only because attorney's fees (without any enhancement) are not considered retroactive in nature."

Notes and Questions

1. What do these cases reveal about the nature of the prospective/retrospective distinction? To what extent and in what respects can a "prospective" remedy be

"compensatory" or "backward-looking" without running afoul of the Eleventh Amendment? How would Justice Thomas answer that question?

2. Given the Court's concern with protecting state treasuries, how do you explain its willingness to countenance a very expensive injunction in *Milliken II*? Does that result suggest that the *Edelman* majority drew an ill-advised distinction, or that it serves values other than or in addition to protecting a state's bottom line? What are those values? Could the Court have drawn other lines to serve them?

3. *Hutto* considered two different types of fee awards against a state and found sovereign immunity inapplicable to each type for different reasons. What is the difference between the two theories? How can the holding regarding the appellate fees be squared with the "clear statement rule" normally applied to both waiver and abrogation of sovereign immunity? Does it help the Court's reasoning on that point that costs, according to footnote 24, are ancillary (the Court uses the term "incidental") to awards of prospective relief? Should the Court have applied the same theory to both types of fees?

4. Does *Jenkins* merely apply *Hutto* or reinterpret it? Do the majority and dissent disagree about the meaning of *Hutto*?

5. Which case provides the better basis for holding that fee awards against states are exempt from sovereign immunity—*Edelman* or *Fitzpatrick*? If the former, why does it matter to the *Jenkins* Court that § 1988 designated attorneys' fees as awardable "as part of the costs"? If the latter, why does it matter whether attorneys' fees are retroactive?

6. In light of these applications of *Edelman* to expensive injunctions and to attorneys' fees, what does the concept of "prospective" relief mean? Would it be accurate simply to replace the terms "retrospective" and "prospective" with, respectively, "damages" and "non-damages"?

C. DAMAGES AGAINST STATE OFFICIALS UNDER § 1983

So far, we've encountered three important exceptions to the sovereign immunity defense: first, suits for prospective relief (or relief ancillary to it) that name a state official rather than the state, *see Ex parte Young*; second, suits under statutes through which a state has waived its immunity, as described in *Edelman* (although the statute at issue there was not such a statute, the Court held); and third, suits under statutes enacted pursuant to Congress's power to enforce the Fourteenth Amendment, *see Fitzpatrick*. Can any of these exceptions be used as a tool to obtain *damages* under § 1983 for a constitutional violation by a state?

Edelman rejects the use of the first (*Ex parte Young*) theory to obtain damages from a state official. The second exception identified—waiver—generally occurs, as noted in the previous section, when a state accepts federal funds conditioned on a waiver of immunity, and that circumstance does not describe § 1983. But the third exception we have seen—abrogation by a statute that enforces the Fourteenth Amendment—looks more promising, as § 1983 would appear to be such a statute.

In the next case, the Court considered whether a § 1983 suit could be used to obtain damages from a state. Formally, sovereign immunity was *not* available, because the case was filed in state court; recall that prior to the Court's 1999 decision in *Alden v. Maine* (discussed in Section A), sovereign immunity had not been held to bar such a suit. Nonetheless, the Court's statutory interpretation of § 1983—drawing heavily on principles of sovereign immunity—addressed whether § 1983 can be used, in either state or federal court, to sue a state directly for damages.

Will v. Michigan Department of State Police
491 U.S. 58 (1989)

■ *Justice WHITE delivered the opinion of the Court.*

This case presents the question whether a State, or an official of the State while acting in his or her official capacity, is a "person" within the meaning of 42 U.S.C. § 1983.

Petitioner Ray Will filed suit . . . alleging various violations of the United States and Michigan Constitutions as grounds for a claim under § 1983. He alleged that he had been denied a promotion to a data systems analyst position with the Department of State Police for an improper reason, that is, because his brother had been a student activist and the subject of a "red squad" file maintained by respondent. Named as defendants were the Department of State Police and the Director of State Police in his official capacity, also a respondent here. . . .

Petitioner filed the present § 1983 actions in Michigan state court, which places the question whether a State is a person under § 1983 squarely before us since the Eleventh Amendment does not apply in state courts. . . .

We observe initially that if a State is a "person" within the meaning of § 1983, the section is to be read as saying that "every person, including a State, who, under color of any statute, ordinance, regulation, custom, or usage, of any State or Territory or the District of Columbia, subjects. . . ." That would be a decidedly awkward way of expressing an intent to subject the States to liability. At the very least, reading the statute in this way is not so clearly indicated that it provides reason to depart from the often-expressed understanding that "'in common usage, the term "person" does not include the sovereign, [and] statutes employing the [word] are ordinarily construed to exclude it.'" . . .

The language of § 1983 also falls far short of satisfying the ordinary rule of statutory construction that if Congress intends to alter the "usual constitutional balance between the States and the Federal Government," it must make its intention to do so "unmistakably clear in the language of the statute." . . . "In traditionally sensitive areas, such as legislation affecting the federal balance, the requirement of clear statement assures that the legislature has in fact faced, and intended to bring into issue, the critical matters involved in the judicial decision." . . .

"One important assumption underlying the Court's decisions in this area is that members of the 42d Congress were familiar with common-law principles, including defenses previously recognized in ordinary tort litigation, and that they likely intended these common-law principles to obtain, absent specific provisions to the contrary." The doctrine of sovereign immunity was a familiar doctrine at common law. . . . We cannot conclude that § 1983 was intended to disregard the well-established immunity of a State from being sued without its consent.

The legislative history of § 1983 does not suggest a different conclusion. Petitioner contends that the congressional debates on § 1 of the 1871 Act indicate that § 1983 was intended to extend to the full reach of the Fourteenth Amendment and thereby to provide a remedy " 'against all forms of official violation of federally protected rights.' " He refers us to various parts of the vigorous debates accompanying the passage of § 1983 and revealing that it was the failure of the States to take appropriate action that was undoubtedly the motivating force behind § 1983. The inference must be drawn, it is urged, that Congress must have intended to subject the States themselves to liability. But the intent of Congress to provide a remedy for unconstitutional state action does not without more include the sovereign States among those persons against whom § 1983 actions would lie. Construing § 1983 as a remedy for "official violation of federally protected rights" does no more than confirm that the section is directed against state action—action "under color of" state law. It does not suggest that the State itself was a person that Congress intended to be subject to liability.

Although there were sharp and heated debates, the discussion of § 1 of the bill, which contained the present § 1983, was not extended. And although in other respects the impact on state sovereignty was much talked about, no one suggested that § 1 would subject the States themselves to a damages suit under federal law. There was complaint that § 1 would subject state officers to damages liability, but no suggestion that it would also expose the States themselves. We find nothing substantial in the legislative history that leads us to believe that Congress intended that the word "person" in § 1983 included the States of the Union. And surely nothing in the debates rises to the clearly expressed legislative intent necessary to permit that construction.

Likewise, the Act of Feb. 25, 1871, § 2 (the "Dictionary Act"),[8] . . . does not counsel a contrary conclusion here. . . . [W]e disagree with Justice Brennan that at the time the Dictionary Act was passed "the phrase 'bodies politic and corporate' was understood to include the States." Rather, an examination of authorities of the era suggests that the phrase was used to mean corporations, both private and public (municipal), and not to include the States. In our view, the Dictionary Act, like § 1983 itself and its legislative history, fails to evidence a clear congressional intent that States be held liable.

---

8. The Dictionary Act provided that "in all acts hereafter passed . . . the word 'person' may extend and be applied to bodies politic and corporate . . . unless the context shows that such words were intended to be used in a more limited sense." Act of Feb. 25, 1871, § 2.

Petitioner asserts, alternatively, that state officials should be considered "persons" under § 1983 even though acting in their official capacities. In this case, petitioner named as defendant not only the Michigan Department of State Police but also the Director of State Police in his official capacity.

Obviously, state officials literally are persons. But a suit against a state official in his or her official capacity is not a suit against the official but rather is a suit against the official's office. As such, it is no different from a suit against the State itself. We see no reason to adopt a different rule in the present context, particularly when such a rule would allow petitioner to circumvent congressional intent by a mere pleading device.[10]

We hold that neither a State nor its officials acting in their official capacities are "persons" under § 1983. The judgment of the Michigan Supreme Court is affirmed.

■ *Justice* BRENNAN, *with whom Justice* MARSHALL, *Justice* BLACKMUN, *and Justice* STEVENS *join, dissenting.*

Because this case was brought in state court, the Court concedes, the Eleventh Amendment is inapplicable here. Like the guest who would not leave, however, the Eleventh Amendment lurks everywhere in today's decision and, in truth, determines its outcome. . . .

[T]his case is not decided on the basis of our ordinary method of statutory construction; instead, the Court disposes of it by means of various rules of statutory interpretation that it summons to its aid each time the question looks close. . . .

Where the Eleventh Amendment applies, the Court has devised a clear-statement principle more robust than its requirement of clarity in any other situation. . . . Since this case was brought in state court, however, this strict drafting requirement has no application here. The Eleventh Amendment can hardly be "a consideration" in a suit to which it does not apply. . . .

Although § 1983 itself does not define the term "person," we are not without a statutory definition of this word. "Any analysis of the meaning of the word 'person' in § 1983 . . . must begin . . . with the Dictionary Act." Passed just two months before § 1983, and designed to "suppl[y] rules of construction for all legislation," the Dictionary Act provided:

> "That in all acts hereafter passed . . . the word 'person' may extend and be applied
> to bodies politic and corporate . . . unless the context shows that such words were
> intended to be used in a more limited sense. . . ." Act of Feb. 25, 1871, § 2.

---

10. Of course a state official in his or her official capacity, when sued for injunctive relief, would be a person under § 1983 because "official-capacity actions for prospective relief are not treated as actions against the State." *Kentucky v. Graham*, 473 U.S. 159, 167, n. 14 (1985); *Ex parte Young*. This distinction is "commonplace in sovereign immunity doctrine," L. Tribe, American Constitutional Law § 3-27, p. 190, n.3 (2d ed. 1988), and would not have been foreign to the 19th-century Congress that enacted § 1983. . . .

. . . Both before and after the time when the Dictionary Act and § 1983 were passed, the phrase "bodies politic and corporate" was understood to include the States. *[Justice Brennan here cites treatises from 1866 and 1901 and several cases ranging from 1793 to 1915, including one of the opinions supporting the result in* Chisholm *and Justice Iredell's dissent in that case.]* . . .

Thus, the question before us is whether the presumption that the word "person" in § 1 of the Civil Rights Act of 1871 included bodies politic and corporate—and hence the States—is overcome by anything in the statute's language and history. Certainly nothing in the statutory language overrides this presumption. The statute is explicitly directed at action taken "under color of" state law, and thus supports rather than refutes the idea that the "persons" mentioned in the statute include the States. Indeed, for almost a century—until *Monroe v. Pape*—it was unclear whether the statute applied at all to action not authorized by the State, and the enduring significance of the first cases construing the Fourteenth Amendment, pursuant to which § 1 was passed, lies in their conclusion that the prohibitions of this Amendment do not reach private action. In such a setting, one cannot reasonably deny the significance of § 1983's explicit focus on state action.

Unimpressed by such arguments, the Court simply asserts that reading "States" where the statute mentions "person" would be "decidedly awkward." The Court does not describe the awkwardness that it perceives, but I take it that its objection is that the under-color-of-law requirement would be redundant if States were included in the statute because States necessarily act under color of state law. But § 1983 extends as well to natural persons, who do not necessarily so act; in order to ensure that they would be liable only when they did so, the statute needed the under-color-of-law requirement. The only way to remove the redundancy that the Court sees would have been to eliminate the catchall phrase "person" altogether, and separately describe each category of possible defendants and the circumstances under which they might be liable. I cannot think of a situation not involving the Eleventh Amendment, however, in which we have imposed such an unforgiving drafting requirement on Congress. . . .

[W]e too easily forget, I think, the circumstances existing in this country when the early civil rights statutes were passed. "[V]iewed against the events and passions of the time," *United States v. Price*, 383 U.S. 787, 803 (1966) [(applying 18 U.S.C. § 242, the statute at issue in *Classic* and *Screws*, along with a related statute, to the prosecution of eighteen individuals accused of murdering three civil rights workers in Philadelphia, Mississippi)], I have little doubt that § 1 of the Civil Rights Act of 1871 included States as "persons." . . .

Congress [was] in the midst of altering the " 'balance between the States and the Federal Government.' " It was fighting to save the Union, and in doing so, it transformed our federal system. It is difficult, therefore, to believe that this same Congress did not intend to include States among those who might be liable under § 1983 for the very deprivations that were threatening this Nation at that time. . . .

■ *Justice STEVENS, dissenting.*

Legal doctrines often flourish long after their raison d'être has perished. The doctrine of sovereign immunity rests on the fictional premise that the "King can do no wrong." Even though the plot to assassinate James I in 1605, the execution of Charles I in 1649, and the Colonists' reaction to George III's stamp tax made rather clear the fictional character of the doctrine's underpinnings, British subjects found a gracious means of compelling the King to obey the law rather than simply repudiating the doctrine itself. They held his advisers and his agents responsible. . . .

If prospective relief can be awarded against state officials under § 1983 and the State is the real party in interest in such suits, the State must be a "person" which can be held liable under § 1983. No other conclusion is available. . . .

Notes and Questions

1. Begin by identifying the holding in *Will*. What statutory term did the Court interpret, and what did the majority conclude that term means?

2. The majority disclaims reliance on the Eleventh Amendment, which at the time of this decision did not apply in state court. The dissenters nonetheless claim that "[l]ike the guest who would not leave . . . the Eleventh Amendment lurks everywhere in today's decision." What role if any does the Court's prior Eleventh Amendment/sovereign immunity jurisprudence play in the majority's statutory interpretation?

3. As noted in Section A.3 of this chapter, the Court went on to reject, in *Alden v. Maine*, the proposition that sovereign immunity was inapplicable in state court. Does that development weaken the persuasiveness of the principal dissent in *Will*, which mainly charged that the majority applied sovereign-immunity principles where they did not belong?

4. Under *Will*, a state official is a "person" when sued for injunctive relief but is not a "person" when sued for damages. Where does the Court find the basis for that distinction? Is it grounded in text? In history? Or is it just an expedient to align the interpretation of § 1983 with *Edelman*? Justice Stevens was the only member of the Court to criticize this oddity.

5. After *Will*, how, if at all, can an individual obtain compensation for the violation of the person's constitutional rights by the state?

* * *

Will's interpretation of § 1983 seemed to leave little room for an individual to obtain damages for constitutional violations by the state or its officials. The Supreme Court was soon asked to decide whether *Will* created complete immunity in this regard. It unanimously answered in the negative by returning to the same distinction on which it based the *Ex parte Young* exception to sovereign immunity: the difference between a state and the individuals it employs.

Hafer v. Melo
502 U.S. 21 (1991)

■ *Justice O'Connor delivered the opinion of the Court.*

In *Will v. Michigan Dept. of State Police*, we held that state officials "acting in their official capacities" are outside the class of "persons" subject to liability under 42 U.S.C. § 1983. Petitioner takes this language to mean that § 1983 does not authorize suits against state officers for damages arising from official acts. We reject this reading of *Will* and hold that state officials sued in their individual capacities are "persons" for purposes of § 1983.

[Petitioner Barbara Hafer was elected as Pennsylvania's auditor general. She then fired about two dozen employees, some allegedly on the ground that they had supported her opponent in the election. The employees sued her under § 1983 (among other claims) and sought (among other relief) damages against her in her "individual" capacity.] . . .

[T]he District Court dismissed all claims. In relevant part, the court held that the § 1983 claims against Hafer were barred because, under *Will*, she could not be held liable for employment decisions made in her official capacity as auditor general.

The Court of Appeals for the Third Circuit reversed this portion of the District Court's decision. . . . While Hafer's power to hire and fire derived from her position as auditor general, it said, a suit for damages based on the exercise of this authority could be brought against Hafer in her personal capacity. Because Hafer acted under color of state law, respondents could maintain a § 1983 individual-capacity suit against her. . . .

[O]fficial-capacity suits " 'generally represent only another way of pleading an action against an entity of which an officer is an agent.' " Suits against state officials in their official capacity therefore should be treated as suits against the State. Indeed, when officials sued in this capacity in federal court die or leave office, their successors automatically assume their roles in the litigation. . . . For the same reason, the only immunities available to the defendant in an official-capacity action are those that the governmental entity possesses.

Personal-capacity suits, on the other hand, seek to impose individual liability upon a government officer for actions taken under color of state law. Thus, "[o]n the merits, to establish personal liability in a § 1983 action, it is enough to show that the official, acting under color of state law, caused the deprivation of a federal right." . . .

Our decision in *Will v. Michigan Dept. of State Police* turned in part on these differences between personal- and official-capacity actions. The principal issue in *Will* was whether States are "persons" subject to suit under § 1983. . . .

Will itself makes clear that the distinction between official-capacity suits and personal-capacity suits is more than "a mere pleading device." State officers sued for damages in their official capacity are not "persons" for purposes of the suit because they assume the identity of the government that employs them. By contrast, officers sued in their personal capacity come to court as individuals.

A government official in the role of personal-capacity defendant thus fits comfortably within the statutory term "person."

Hafer seeks to overcome the distinction between official- and personal-capacity suits by arguing that § 1983 liability turns not on the capacity in which state officials are sued, but on the capacity in which they acted when injuring the plaintiff. Under *Will*, she asserts, state officials may not be held liable in their personal capacity for actions they take in their official capacity. Although one Court of Appeals has endorsed this view, we find it both unpersuasive as an interpretation of § 1983 and foreclosed by our prior decisions.

Through § 1983, Congress sought "to give a remedy to parties deprived of constitutional rights, privileges and immunities by an official's abuse of his position." *Monroe v. Pape*. Accordingly, it authorized suits to redress deprivations of civil rights by persons acting "under color of any [state] statute, ordinance, regulation, custom, or usage." 42 U.S.C. § 1983. The requirement of action under color of state law means that Hafer may be liable for discharging respondents precisely because of her authority as auditor general. We cannot accept the novel proposition that this same official authority insulates Hafer from suit.

In an effort to limit the scope of her argument, Hafer distinguishes between two categories of acts taken under color of state law: those outside the official's authority or not essential to the operation of state government, and those both within the official's authority and necessary to the performance of governmental functions. Only the former group, she asserts, can subject state officials to personal liability under § 1983; the latter group (including the employment decisions at issue in this case) should be considered acts of the State that cannot give rise to a personal-capacity action.

The distinction Hafer urges finds no support in the broad language of § 1983. To the contrary, it ignores our holding that Congress enacted § 1983 " 'to enforce provisions of the Fourteenth Amendment against those who carry a badge of authority of a State and represent it in some capacity, whether they act in accordance with their authority or misuse it.' " Because of that intent, we have held that in § 1983 actions the statutory requirement of action "under color of" state law is just as broad as the Fourteenth Amendment's "state action" requirement. . . .

Hafer further asks us to read *Will*'s language concerning suits against state officials as establishing the limits of liability under the Eleventh Amendment. She asserts that imposing personal liability on officeholders may infringe on state sovereignty by rendering government less effective; thus, she argues, the Eleventh Amendment forbids personal-capacity suits against state officials in federal court.

Most certainly, *Will*'s holding does not rest directly on the Eleventh Amendment. . . . We considered the Eleventh Amendment in *Will* only because the fact that Congress did not intend to override state immunity when it enacted § 1983 was relevant to statutory construction: "Given that a principal purpose behind the enactment of § 1983 was to provide a federal forum for civil rights claims," Congress' failure to authorize suits against States in federal courts suggested that it also did not intend to authorize such claims in state courts. . . .

[And under *Ex parte Young* and its progeny] the Eleventh Amendment does not erect a barrier against suits to impose "individual and personal liability" on state officials under § 1983. . . .

We hold that state officials, sued in their individual capacities, are "persons" within the meaning of § 1983. The Eleventh Amendment does not bar such suits, nor are state officers absolutely immune from personal liability under § 1983 solely by virtue of the "official" nature of their acts.

Justice THOMAS *took no part in the consideration or decision of this case.*

Notes and Questions

1. This chapter covers a lot of historical and theoretical ground, but the takeaway can be boiled down to a few basic rules. What are those rules? Was there a simpler way to reach them in light of the principles of federalism and sovereignty the Court is applying? If so, at what point did the Court fall down the rabbit hole?

2. Consider *Hafer* and *Will* together. Without *Hafer*, what would have been left of § 1983 suits for damages in light of *Will*? Did *Will* therefore make *Hafer* inevitable? Had the Court reached the opposite conclusion in *Will* and never reached the question in *Hafer*, how if at all would § 1983 litigation be different?

3. The Court assures us that the official/individual capacity distinction is not a mere "pleading device." If not, what is it? Has the Court suggested it will second-guess a plaintiff's designation of a defendant as being sued "in an individual capacity"?

4. Consider how often civil rights plaintiffs, particularly incarcerated individuals, lack attorneys. A cynical view of the Court's sovereign immunity jurisprudence is that it functions mainly as a trap for uncounseled litigants who don't know how to plead their way around sovereign immunity. How might the Court respond to that charge?

5. *Edelman* took a functional approach to assessing the risk to state treasuries, stating bluntly that the state official Joel Edelman was never going to pay the judgment against him. Why did the Court take a different approach in *Hafer*? Was Barbara Hafer likely to pay if plaintiffs obtained a judgment against her? Can the two cases stand together? In light of *Hafer*, how successful was *Edelman* ultimately at defending state treasuries?

Note: Exceptions to the *Hafer* Rule

In light of *Hafer*, would the *Edelman* plaintiffs have succeeded if only they had specified that they were suing the relevant Illinois officials in their "personal" capacities? Probably not, explains Professor John Jeffries, who has flagged a small set of exceptions to *Hafer*'s rule authorizing damages against state officials named in their individual capacities. He identifies three considerations as relevant in determining when courts will decide that a suit, though pleaded against an individual-capacity defendant, is in fact one against a state: First, in some cases, it is simply "too hard to pretend that the [state official] was in any way responsible for the problem or that the money [at issue] would come from anywhere but the state treasury." Second, where a "suit sound[s] in contract rather than tort," individual liability is less likely, because "[t]raditional rules of agency declare that while a servant is liable for a tort committed in the master's business, the servant is not responsible for the master's contracts." Third, "[i]n statutory cases, somewhat more often than in constitutional cases, courts occasionally follow *Edelman* in refusing to allow . . . suing state officers. . . . Most examples involve alleged underpayment of Medicare or Medicaid reimbursements." Professor Jeffries summarizes:

> Like *Edelman* itself, the cases are analytically irreconcilable with the broad current of Section 1983 decisions. The reasons given in the occasional case where the Eleventh Amendment bars relief against a state officer apply equally well in the vast number of cases where it does not. As an approximation, one might say that *Edelman* is more likely to be followed in statutory rather than constitutional cases, in cases where the underlying claim is more like contract than tort, and in cases where the fiction that any resulting judgment will be paid by the officer personally is impossible to maintain. In most recent cases disallowing officer suits, all three factors are present. Outside that (not very crisply defined) context, the alternative of suing a state officer under Section 1983 is freely available.

John C. Jeffries, Jr., *In Praise of the Eleventh Amendment and Section 1983*, 84 Va. L. Rev. 47, 66-68 (1998).

The question of who actually pays when an individual official is successfully sued for damages under § 1983 is an important consideration not just for questions about sovereign immunity but also in assessing the doctrines governing the liability of individual officers—the subject of the next chapter.

Note: Injunctive Relief and Individual-Capacity Defendants

Ex parte Young, Edelman, and *Hafer* explain what happens if a plaintiff sues a state official in an official capacity and what happens if a plaintiff seeks *damages* against a state official in an individual capacity. What would happen if a plaintiff sought an *injunction* against an official in an *individual* capacity? The answer is a subject of dispute.

Some courts have held that an injunction against an official in an individual capacity is simply unavailable, because a government official is capable of harming the plaintiff only in an official capacity. *See, e.g., Feit v. Ward*, 886 F.2d 848, 858 (7th Cir. 1989); *Frank v. Relin*, 1 F.3d 1317, 1327 (2d Cir. 1993); *Hatfill v. Gonzales*, 519 F. Supp. 2d 13, 19-24 (D.D.C. 2007). This position, although it appears to be the majority rule, seems problematic. First, it is in serious tension with *Hafer*, which held that an individual-capacity defendant is susceptible to liability for conduct taken as a government official because the actions at issue were taken "under color" of law within the meaning of § 1983, regardless of the capacity in which the defendant is named: "The requirement of action under color of state law means that Hafer may be liable for discharging respondents precisely because of her authority as auditor general. We cannot accept the novel proposition that this same official authority insulates Hafer from suit." Although *Hafer* was a case about damages, nothing in *Hafer*'s discussion or logic suggests that its invocation of the "under color" principle holds only for damages suits. Second, the Supreme Court in *Ex parte Young* itself described its exception to sovereign immunity by stating that the official is subject to suit "in his person," and the modern Court has characterized *Ex parte Young* as recognizing an "exception . . . for certain suits seeking declaratory and injunctive relief against state officers *in their individual capacities." Idaho v. Coeur d'Alene Tribe*, 521 U.S. 261, 269 (1997) (emphasis added). The reason officers are usually named in their "official capacity" when plaintiffs seek injunctive relief is not because that is the capacity in which they are acting when harming the plaintiff, but because that capacity produces a more robust injunction that will not terminate when the current officeholder leaves office. *See* Fed. R. Civ. P. 25(d) ("An action does not abate when a public officer who is a party in an official capacity dies, resigns, or otherwise ceases to hold office while the action is pending. The officer's successor is automatically substituted as a party.").

Accordingly, the more persuasive view is that individual-capacity injunctions are available; they simply do not bind the official's successor. *See, e.g., Redondo-Borges v. U.S. Dep't of Hous. & Urban Dev.*, 421 F.3d 1, 7 (1st Cir. 2005); *MCI Telecomm. Corp. v. Bell Atl. Pa.*, 271 F.3d 491, 506 (3d Cir. 2001); *Common Cause/Ga. v. Billups*, 2005 WL 8160541, at *4-5 (N.D. Ga. Oct. 19, 2005).

One possible scenario in which plaintiffs might desire such an injunction is where the defendant is a *municipal* employee. An official-capacity suit would be subject to defenses that a personal-capacity suit would not be, because the official-capacity suit would be treated as a suit against the municipal entity, thereby bringing into play limits on municipal liability (see Chapter 5) not applicable to individual defendants.

Figure 3.1 summarizes the consequences of suing officials in their various capacities.

Figure 3.1: Picking the right "capacity" in which to name state officials

Result		Against a state official in the official's . . .	
		Official capacity	**Individual capacity**
If you seek...	**Damages:**	Barred. Same as naming state. *(Edelman)*	Available. An individual isn't the state. *(Hafer)*
	Injunction:	Available via *Ex parte Young.* Binds future office holders.	Split of authority: *either* it's available but doesn't run with the office, *or* unavailable.

Note that a plaintiff can name a defendant in both the official and individual capacity to seek both damages and an injunction.

CHAPTER 3 PROBLEMS

Problem 3A.   The 51st state, Douglass Commonwealth, participates in a cooperative federal-state program, the Veteran Assistance Program (VAP). Under VAP, states receive money to provide assistance to disabled military veterans and agree to distribute the money according to the criteria in the federal VAP statute. The statute says nothing about sovereign immunity. When Douglass finds itself in a budget crunch, it begins paying VAP beneficiaries only 95 percent of the benefits to which they are entitled under federal law.

Three VAP beneficiaries file a class action in federal court against the chairwoman of the Douglass Office of Veteran Affairs, Nedy Jonefken, seeking injunctive relief only. The plaintiffs obtain an injunction against Jonefken requiring payment of 100 percent of benefits on a prospective basis immediately. She complies for six months.

Then a budget impasse in Congress shuts down the federal government. VAP lapses during that time and is left unfunded for two months. When Congress resolves the impasse, it reauthorizes VAP going forward (but not retroactively during the time it lapsed). All the states that participated in the program previously join it once again. But three months later, Douglass again faces financial difficulties. Again, it cuts VAP payments to 95 percent of the statutory entitlement.

The same three beneficiaries who previously sued now come to your law office seeking your help in filing another class action. The plaintiffs want to seek both a court order requiring full benefits in the future *and* damages for unpaid benefits since VAP reauthorization.

You agree to represent the plaintiffs. In what capacity do you name the defendant? What relief do you seek? Do you expect to be able to obtain unpaid benefits? Why or why not?

Problem 3B.   A criminal defense attorney you know asks you to help him with a civil rights case arising in the Town of Bellevue, in the 51st state, Douglass Commonwealth. You trust that he knows his constitutional law, but he isn't an expert in civil litigation. The complaint is reprinted below. Assume it asserts valid constitutional claims. What would you recommend that he change to maximize the chances of success?

IN THE U.S. DISTRICT COURT FOR THE DISTRICT OF DOUGLASS

Lynn JONSONDON	)	
v.	)	*COMPLAINT FOR DAMAGES AND*
Nick RICHARDSON; Com. of DOUGLASS	)	*INJUNCTIVE RELIEF*

Lynn Jonsondon, by and through her attorneys, alleges as follows:

1. This court has jurisdiction because there is a federal question. 28 U.S.C. § 1331. Venue is proper because all the events occurred in this district. *Id.* § 1391(e).

2. On May 21, 2019, Lynn Jonsondon was driving on South Capitol St., in Bellevue, Douglass Com., obeying all laws and displaying a bumper sticker with the letter "A" inscribed over a circle.

3. This symbol represents the political philosophy of Anarchism.

4. Nick Richardson, a Douglass state trooper, pulled Jonsondon over.

5. Richardson had no basis to believe Jonsondon had violated any law.

6. Officer Richardson identified no reason for the stop. He asked Jonsondon about her bumper sticker and whether she was going to "blow up the White House."

7. Jonsondon said she was not and asked if she could leave.

8. Officer Richardson said no, because "you anarchist types need to respect the law." He continued to detain her while inquiring further about her political beliefs.

9. After twenty minutes, Officer Richardson told her she could leave.

10. Officer Richardson never cited Jonsondon for any violation of law.

11. This is the third time this month Jonsondon has been stopped by a Douglass officer who asked about her bumper sticker but identified no violation of law.

12. On information and behalf, Douglass has a policy of harassing drivers who espouse Anarchist political beliefs.

CLAIM I: VIOLATION OF U.S. CONSTITUTION, AMENDMENT I

13. By detaining Plaintiff because of her speech, Defendants violated Plaintiff's First Amendment right to freedom of speech.

CLAIM II: VIOLATION OF U.S. CONSTITUTION, AMENDMENT IV

14. By detaining Plaintiff without any suspicion, Defendants violated Plaintiff's Fourth Amendment right to be free from unreasonable searches and seizures.

PRAYER FOR RELIEF

Wherefore, Plaintiff prays this Court to grant her the following relief:

(a) damages against Defendants in an amount to be Defendants by a jury;

(b) an injunction preventing all further detention of Plaintiff by Defendants or their officers, agents, or employees, for Plaintiff's speech;

(c) reasonable attorneys' fees and costs; and

(d) any other relief this Court deems just and proper.

Individual Defenses: Absolute Immunity, Qualified Immunity, and the Limits on Supervisory Liability

In Chapter 3, we learned that damages suits against states are unavailable under § 1983, *Will*, but that "personal capacity" suits against state (and local) officials are available, *Hafer*. As a result of this framework, the limitations on and defenses to individual liability have become among the most influential doctrines governing when constitutional claims can be brought for money damages. Government officials sued under § 1983 (and *Bivens*) generally may assert one of two types of immunity: absolute immunity and qualified immunity. Either defense, if successful, defeats the plaintiff's claim. The showings required for each type will be explored in detail in this chapter.

The Supreme Court summarized the rationale for immunity jurisprudence as follows:

> To the extent that the threat of liability encourages [government] officials to carry out their duties in a lawful and appropriate manner, and to pay their victims when they do not, it accomplishes exactly what it should. By its nature, however, the threat of liability can create perverse incentives that operate to inhibit officials in the proper performance of their duties. . . . When officials are threatened with personal liability for acts taken pursuant to their official duties, they may well be induced to act with an excess of caution or otherwise to skew their decisions in ways that result in less than full fidelity to the objective and independent criteria that ought to guide their conduct. In this way, exposing government officials to the same legal hazards faced by other citizens may detract from the rule of law instead of contributing to it.

Forrester v. White, 484 U.S. 219 (1988). As you read the cases that follow and identify the key aspects of each doctrine (who may claim each type of immunity, when it may be claimed, and how if at all the plaintiff may overcome it), consider too whether the contours of the various immunity doctrines are justified by these interests, and whether these interests, in turn, outweigh the interests of those whose rights have been violated.

By way of introduction, we'll read the case that incorporated both qualified and absolute judicial immunity into § 1983. We'll then consider each type of immunity in turn in greater detail—first absolute immunity (Section A), then qualified immunity (Section B). The chapter concludes by covering a third important constraint on individual liability: the limits on liability for *supervisory* government officials (Section C).

Pierson v. Ray
386 U.S. 547 (1967)

▪ *Mr. Chief Justice* WARREN *delivered the opinion of Court.*

These cases present issues involving the liability of local police officers and judges under 42 U.S.C. § 1983. Petitioners . . . were members of a group of 15 white and Negro Episcopal clergymen who [as part of their "prayer pilgrimage" in 1961 from New Orleans to Detroit to visit church institutions and other places in the North and South to promote racial equality and integration] attempted to use segregated facilities at an interstate bus terminal in Jackson, Mississippi, in 1961. They were arrested by respondents Ray, Griffith, and Nichols, policemen of the City of Jackson, and charged with violating § 2087.5 of the Mississippi Code, which makes guilty of a misdemeanor anyone who congregates with others in a public place under circumstances such that a breach of the peace may be occasioned thereby, and refuses to move on when ordered to do so by a police officer. Petitioners waived a jury trial and were convicted of the offense by respondent Spencer, a municipal police justice. [One petitioner won on appeal and the cases against the rest of the petitioners were dropped.]

Having been vindicated . . . petitioners brought this action for damages [under § 1983]. A jury returned verdicts for respondents on both counts. On appeal, the Court of Appeals for the Fifth Circuit held that respondent Spencer was immune from liability under both § 1983 and the common law of Mississippi for acts committed within his judicial jurisdiction. As to the police officers, the court noted that § 2087.5 of the Mississippi Code was held unconstitutional as applied to similar facts in *Thomas v. Mississippi*, 380 U.S. 524 (1965). Although *Thomas* was decided years after the arrest involved in this trial, the court held that the policemen would be liable in a suit under § 1983 for an unconstitutional arrest even if they acted in good faith and with probable cause in making an arrest under a state statute not yet held invalid. The court believed that this stern result was required by *Monroe v. Pape*. . . . [T]he Court of Appeals reversed and remanded for a new trial on the § 1983 claim against the police officers [based on trial error.] . . .

We find no difficulty in agreeing with the Court of Appeals that Judge Spencer is immune from liability for damages for his role in these convictions. The record is barren of any proof or specific allegation that Judge Spencer played any role in these arrests and convictions other than to adjudge petitioners guilty when their cases came before his court. Few doctrines were more solidly established at common law than the immunity of judges from liability for damages for acts committed within their judicial jurisdiction....

This immunity applies even when the judge is accused of acting maliciously and corruptly, and it "is not for the protection or benefit of a malicious or corrupt judge, but for the benefit of the public, whose interest it is that the judges should be at liberty to exercise their functions with independence and without fear of consequences." It is a judge's duty to decide all cases within his jurisdiction that are brought before him, including controversial cases that arouse the most intense feelings in the litigants. His errors may be corrected on appeal, but he should not have to fear that unsatisfied litigants may hound him with litigation charging malice or corruption. Imposing such a burden on judges would contribute not to principled and fearless decisionmaking but to intimidation.

We do not believe that this settled principle of law was abolished by § 1983, which makes liable "every person" who under color of law deprives another person of his civil rights. The legislative record gives no clear indication that Congress meant to abolish wholesale all common-law immunities. Accordingly, this Court held in *Tenney v. Brandhove*, 341 U.S. 367 (1951), that the immunity of legislators for acts within the legislative role was not abolished. The immunity of judges for acts within the judicial role is equally well established, and we presume that Congress would have specifically so provided had it wished to abolish the doctrine.

The common law has never granted police officers an absolute and unqualified immunity, and the officers in this case do not claim that they are entitled to one. Their claim is rather that they should not be liable if they acted in good faith and with probable cause in making an arrest under a statute that they believed to be valid. Under the prevailing view in this country a peace officer who arrests someone with probable cause is not liable for false arrest simply because the innocence of the suspect is later proved. Restatement, Second, Torts § 121 (1965). A policeman's lot is not so unhappy that he must choose between being charged with dereliction of duty if he does not arrest when he has probable cause, and being mulcted in damages if he does. Although the matter is not entirely free from doubt, the same consideration would seem to require excusing him from liability for acting under a statute that he reasonably believed to be valid but that was later held unconstitutional on its face or as applied.

The Court of Appeals [thought its result required by] *Monroe v. Pape*. *Monroe v. Pape* presented no question of immunity, however, and none was decided.... [We said in *Monroe* that] § 1983 "should be read against the background of tort liability that makes a man responsible for the natural consequences of his actions." Part of the background of tort liability, in the case of police officers making an arrest, is the defense of good faith and probable cause.

We hold that the defense of good faith and probable cause, which the Court of Appeals found available to the officers in the common-law action for false arrest and imprisonment, is also available to them in the action under § 1983. This holding does not, however, mean that the count based thereon should be dismissed. The Court of Appeals ordered dismissal of the common-law count on the theory that the police officers were not required to predict our decision in *Thomas v. Mississippi*. We agree that a police officer is not charged with predicting the future course of constitutional law. But the petitioners in this case did not simply argue that they were arrested under a statute later held unconstitutional. They claimed and attempted to prove that the police officers arrested them solely for attempting to use the "White Only" waiting room [and not for breach of the peace]. . . .

[The Court went on to hold that a new trial on that theory was required because the jury's verdict was "influenced by irrelevant and prejudicial evidence."]

■ *Mr. Justice* DOUGLAS, *dissenting.*

I do not think that all judges, under all circumstances, no matter how outrageous their conduct are immune from suit under 42 U.S.C. § 1983. The Court's ruling is not justified by the admitted need for a vigorous and independent judiciary, is not commanded by the common-law doctrine of judicial immunity, and does not follow inexorably from our prior decisions.

The statute, which came on the books as § 1 of the Ku Klux Klan Act of April 20, 1871, provides that "every person" who under color of state law or custom "subjects, or causes to be subjected, any citizen . . . to the deprivation of any rights, privileges, or immunities secured by the Constitution and laws, shall be liable to the party injured in an action at law, suit in equity, or other proper proceeding for redress." To most, "every person" would mean every person, not every person except judges. . . .

The congressional purpose seems to me to be clear. A condition of lawlessness existed in certain of the States, under which people were being denied their civil rights. Congress intended to provide a remedy for the wrongs being perpetrated. And its members were not unaware that certain members of the judiciary were implicated in the state of affairs which the statute was intended to rectify. . . .

It is said that, at the time of the statute's enactment, the doctrine of judicial immunity was well settled and that Congress cannot be presumed to have intended to abrogate the doctrine since it did not clearly evince such a purpose. This view is beset by many difficulties. It assumes that Congress could and should specify in advance all the possible circumstances to which a remedial statute might apply and state which cases are within the scope of a statute. . . .

Congress of course acts in the context of existing common-law rules, and in construing a statute a court considers the "common law before the making of the Act." But Congress enacts a statute to remedy the inadequacies of the pre-existing law, including the common law. It cannot be presumed that the common law is the perfection of reason, is superior to statutory law and that the legislature always changes law for the worse. Nor should the canon of construction "statutes in derogation of the common law are to be strictly construed" be applied so as to weaken a remedial statute whose purpose is to remedy the defects of the preexisting law. . . .

This is not to say that a judge who makes an honest mistake should be subjected to civil liability. It is necessary to exempt judges from liability for the consequences of their honest mistakes. The judicial function involves an informed exercise of judgment. It is often necessary to choose between differing versions of fact, to reconcile opposing interests, and to decide closely contested issues. Decisions must often be made in the heat of trial. A vigorous and independent mind is needed to perform such delicate tasks. It would be unfair to require a judge to exercise his independent judgment and then to punish him for having exercised it in a manner which, in retrospect, was erroneous. Imposing liability for mistaken, though honest judicial acts, would curb the independent mind and spirit needed to perform judicial functions. Thus, a judge who sustains a conviction on what he forthrightly considers adequate evidence should not be subjected to liability when an appellate court decides that the evidence was not adequate. Nor should a judge who allows a conviction under what is later held an unconstitutional statute.

But that is far different from saying that a judge shall be immune from the consequences of any of his judicial actions, and that he shall not be liable for the knowing and intentional deprivation of a person's civil rights. What about the judge who conspires with local law enforcement officers to "railroad" a dissenter? What about the judge who knowingly turns a trial into a "kangaroo" court? Or one who intentionally flouts the Constitution in order to obtain a conviction? Congress, I think, concluded that the evils of allowing intentional, knowing deprivations of civil rights to go unredressed far outweighed the speculative inhibiting effects which might attend an inquiry into a judicial deprivation of civil rights. . . .

Notes and Questions

1. Which type of immunity did each type of defendant get? How is each type of immunity defined?

2. As we have seen, text frequently played a less prominent role than legislative history in early cases interpreting § 1983. So it may not have surprised you that the majority did not find the text conclusive. But what of legislative history? What is the majority's answer to Justice Douglas on that point?

3. *Pierson* is about civil rights advocates suing a judge for constitutional violations under a law aimed in part at protecting constitutional rights against biased judges. That context seems ideal for a rejection of judicial immunity under § 1983. Does it surprise you that the Court, which was if anything more

liberal in 1967 than when it decided *Monroe* in 1961, was nearly unanimous on the issue of judicial immunity and unanimous on the issue of the officers' "good faith and probable cause" defense (later known as qualified immunity)? The Court seems to have found the policy arguments in favor of these defenses persuasive. What is special about the circumstances of judges and police that they should be able to claim these defenses? Is the ruling in *Pierson* justified by the rapid expansion in substantive constitutional rights during the decade that preceded it?

4. The Court's point that an officer should not be expected to predict the course of constitutional law has a lot of intuitive appeal. Which is fairer, to require such prescience on the part of the officer or to let a constitutional violation go unremedied? If neither is attractive, is there another way to address this problem?

5. Justice Douglas is neither satisfied with the majority's application of judicial immunity nor comfortable leaving judges defenseless. What rule would he apply? How does that rule square with his reading of the text and legislative history of § 1983?

* * *

With this relatively brief opinion (relying on a snippet of the prior *Tenney* case, which pertained to legislative immunity only), the Court launched two of the most significant defenses in civil rights litigation. We now examine each in greater detail.

A. ABSOLUTE IMMUNITY

Our study of absolute immunity begins with the two groups of officials that most often claim it: judges and prosecutors. We conclude with a brief look at absolute immunity for legislators.

Note that other applications of absolute immunity exist also. One is for the President for acts done within the scope of the office. *See Nixon v. Fitzgerald*, 457 U.S. 731, 756 (1982) (immunity from damages); *Franklin v. Massachusetts*, 505 U.S. 788, 802-03 (1992) (quoting principle from *Mississippi v. Johnson*, 71 U.S. 475 (1866), that "in general 'this court has no jurisdiction of a bill to enjoin the president in the performance of his official duties'"). Another is for trial and grand-jury witnesses in defending against claims concerning their testimony. *See Rehberg v. Paulk*, 566 U.S. 356, 369 (2012).

1. JUDICIAL IMMUNITY

We pick up the development of judicial immunity where *Pierson* left off. The next case considers in more detail the prerequisites for application of judicial immunity.

Stump v. Sparkman
435 U.S. 349 (1978)

■ *Mr. Justice* WHITE *delivered the opinion of the Court....*

On July 9, 1971, Ora Spitler McFarlin, the mother of respondent Linda Kay Spitler Sparkman, presented to Judge Harold D. Stump of the Circuit Court of DeKalb County, Ind., a document captioned "Petition To Have Tubal Ligation Performed On Minor and Indemnity Agreement." . . . In this petition Mrs. McFarlin stated under oath that her daughter was 15 years of age and was "somewhat retarded," although she attended public school and had been promoted each year with her class. The petition further stated that Linda had been associating with "older youth or young men" and had stayed out overnight with them on several occasions. As a result of this behavior and Linda's mental capabilities, it was stated that it would be in the daughter's best interest if she underwent a tubal ligation in order "to prevent unfortunate circumstances. . . ." . . . The petition was approved by Judge Stump on the same day. He affixed his signature as "Judge, DeKalb Circuit Court," to the statement that he did "hereby approve the above Petition. . . ."

On July 15, 1971, Linda Spitler entered the DeKalb Memorial Hospital, having been told that she was to have her appendix removed. The following day a tubal ligation was performed upon her. She was released several days later, unaware of the true nature of her surgery.

Approximately two years after the operation, Linda Spitler was married to respondent Leo Sparkman. Her inability to become pregnant led her to discover that she had been sterilized during the 1971 operation. [They sued various defendants on various theories, including a constitutional claim against Judge Stump.] . . .

The governing principle of law is well established and is not questioned by the parties. As early as 1872, the Court recognized that it was "a general principle of the highest importance to the proper administration of justice that a judicial officer, in exercising the authority vested in him, [should] be free to act upon his own convictions, without apprehension of personal consequences to himself." *Bradley v. Fisher.* For that reason the Court held that "judges of courts of superior or general jurisdiction are not liable to civil actions for their judicial acts, even when such acts are in excess of their jurisdiction, and are alleged to have been done maliciously or corruptly." Later we held that this doctrine of judicial immunity was applicable in suits under 42 U.S.C. § 1983, for the legislative record gave no indication that Congress intended to abolish this long-established principle. *Pierson.* . . .

[T]he necessary inquiry in determining whether a defendant judge is immune from suit is whether at the time he took the challenged action he had jurisdiction over the subject matter before him. Because "some of the most difficult and embarrassing questions which a judicial officer is called upon to consider and determine relate to his jurisdiction . . . ," *Bradley*, the scope of the judge's jurisdiction must be construed broadly where the issue is the immunity of the judge. A judge will not be deprived of immunity because the action he took was in error, was done maliciously, or was in excess of his authority; rather, he will be subject to liability only when he has acted in the "clear absence of all jurisdiction."[7]

We cannot agree that there was a "clear absence of all jurisdiction" in the DeKalb County Circuit Court to consider the petition presented by Mrs. McFarlin. As an Indiana Circuit Court Judge, Judge Stump had "original exclusive jurisdiction in all cases at law and in equity whatsoever . . . ," jurisdiction over the settlement of estates and over guardianships, appellate jurisdiction as conferred by law, and jurisdiction over "all other causes, matters and proceedings where exclusive jurisdiction thereof is not conferred by law upon some other court, board or officer." Ind. Code § 33-4-4-3. This is indeed a broad jurisdictional grant; yet the Court of Appeals concluded that Judge Stump did not have jurisdiction over the petition authorizing Linda Sparkman's sterilization.

In so doing, the Court of Appeals noted that the Indiana statutes provided for the sterilization of institutionalized persons under certain circumstances, but otherwise contained no express authority for judicial approval of tubal ligations. It is true that the statutory grant of general jurisdiction to the Indiana circuit courts does not itemize types of cases those courts may hear and hence does not expressly mention sterilization petitions presented by the parents of a minor. But in our view, it is more significant that there was no Indiana statute and no case law in 1971 prohibiting a circuit court, a court of general jurisdiction, from considering a petition of the type presented to Judge Stump. The statutory authority for the sterilization of institutionalized persons in the custody of the State does not warrant the inference that a court of general jurisdiction has no power to act on a petition for sterilization of a minor in the custody of her parents. . . . [N]either by statute nor by case law has the broad jurisdiction granted to the circuit courts of Indiana been circumscribed to foreclose consideration of a petition for authorization of a minor's sterilization. . . .

We conclude that the Court of Appeals, employing an unduly restrictive view of the scope of Judge Stump's jurisdiction, erred in holding that he was not entitled to judicial immunity. Because the court over which Judge Stump presides is one of general jurisdiction, neither the procedural errors he may have committed nor the lack of a specific statute authorizing his approval of the petition in question rendered him liable in damages for the consequences of his actions.

---

7. In *Bradley*, the Court illustrated the distinction between lack of jurisdiction and excess of jurisdiction with the following examples: if a probate judge, with jurisdiction over only wills and estates, should try a criminal case, he would be acting in the clear absence of jurisdiction and would not be immune from liability for his action; on the other hand, if a judge of a criminal court should convict a defendant of a nonexistent crime, he would merely be acting in excess of his jurisdiction and would be immune.

The respondents argue that even if Judge Stump had jurisdiction to consider the petition presented to him by Mrs. McFarlin, he is still not entitled to judicial immunity because his approval of the petition did not constitute a "judicial" act. It is only for acts performed in his "judicial" capacity that a judge is absolutely immune, they say. We do not disagree with this statement of the law, but we cannot characterize the approval of the petition as a nonjudicial act....

The relevant cases demonstrate that the factors determining whether an act by a judge is a "judicial" one relate to the nature of the act itself, i. e., whether it is a function normally performed by a judge, and to the expectations of the parties, i. e., whether they dealt with the judge in his judicial capacity. Here, both factors indicate that Judge Stump's approval of the sterilization petition was a judicial act. State judges with general jurisdiction not infrequently are called upon in their official capacity to approve petitions relating to the affairs of minors, as for example, a petition to settle a minor's claim. Furthermore, as even respondents have admitted, at the time he approved the petition presented to him by Mrs. McFarlin, Judge Stump was "acting as a county circuit court judge." We may infer from the record that it was only because Judge Stump served in that position that Mrs. McFarlin, on the advice of counsel, submitted the petition to him for his approval. Because Judge Stump performed the type of act normally performed only by judges and because he did so in his capacity as a Circuit Court Judge, we find no merit to respondents' argument that the informality with which he proceeded rendered his action nonjudicial and deprived him of his absolute immunity.[12]

Both the Court of Appeals and the respondents seem to suggest that, because of the tragic consequences of Judge Stump's actions, he should not be immune.... Disagreement with the action taken by the judge, however, does not justify depriving that judge of his immunity. Despite the unfairness to litigants that sometimes results, the doctrine of judicial immunity is thought to be in the best interests of "the proper administration of justice . . . [, for it allows] a judicial officer, in exercising the authority vested in him [to] be free to act upon his own convictions, without apprehension of personal consequences to himself." *Bradley v. Fisher.* The fact that the issue before the judge is a controversial one is all the more reason that he should be able to act without fear of suit....

Mr. Justice BRENNAN *took no part in the consideration or decision of this case.*

---

12. Mr. Justice Stewart's dissent suggests that Judge Stump's approval of Mrs. McFarlin's petition was not a judicial act because of the absence of what it considers the "normal attributes of a judicial proceeding." These attributes are said to include a "case," with litigants and the opportunity to appeal, in which there is "principled decisionmaking." But under Indiana law, Judge Stump had jurisdiction to act as he did; the proceeding instituted by the petition placed before him was sufficiently a "case" under Indiana law to warrant the exercise of his jurisdiction, whether or not he then proceeded to act erroneously. That there were not two contending litigants did not make Judge Stump's act any less judicial. Courts and judges often act ex parte. They issue search warrants in this manner, for example, often without any "case" having been instituted, without any "case" ever being instituted, and without the issuance of the warrant being subject to appeal. Yet it would not destroy a judge's immunity if it is alleged and offer of proof is made that in issuing a warrant he acted erroneously and without principle.

■ *Mr. Justice* STEWART, *with whom Mr. Justice* MARSHALL *and Mr. Justice* POWELL *join, dissenting. . . .*

[T]he scope of judicial immunity is limited to liability for "judicial acts," and I think that what Judge Stump did on July 9, 1971, was beyond the pale of anything that could sensibly be called a judicial act. . . .

The Court finds two reasons for holding that Judge Stump's approval of the sterilization petition was a judicial act. First, the Court says, it was "a function normally performed by a judge." Second, the Court says, the act was performed in Judge Stump's "judicial capacity." With all respect, I think that the first of these grounds is factually untrue and that the second is legally unsound.

When the Court says that what Judge Stump did was an act "normally performed by a judge," it is not clear to me whether the Court means that a judge "normally" is asked to approve a mother's decision to have her child given surgical treatment generally, or that a judge "normally" is asked to approve a mother's wish to have her daughter sterilized. But whichever way the Court's statement is to be taken, it is factually inaccurate. In Indiana, as elsewhere in our country, a parent is authorized to arrange for and consent to medical and surgical treatment of his minor child. Ind. Code Ann. § 16-8-4-2. And when a parent decides to call a physician to care for his sick child or arranges to have a surgeon remove his child's tonsils, he does not, "normally" or otherwise, need to seek the approval of a judge. On the other hand, Indiana did in 1971 have statutory procedures for the sterilization of certain people who were institutionalized. But these statutes provided for administrative proceedings before a board established by the superintendent of each public hospital. Only if after notice and an evidentiary hearing, an order of sterilization was entered in these proceedings could there be review in a circuit court. See Ind. Code Ann. §§ 16-13-13-1 through 16-13-13-4.

In sum, what Judge Stump did on July 9, 1971, was in no way an act "normally performed by a judge." Indeed, there is no reason to believe that such an act has ever been performed by any other Indiana judge, either before or since.

When the Court says that Judge Stump was acting in "his judicial capacity" in approving Mrs. McFarlin's petition, it is not clear to me whether the Court means that Mrs. McFarlin submitted the petition to him only because he was a judge, or that, in approving it, he said that he was acting as a judge. But however the Court's test is to be understood, it is, I think, demonstrably unsound.

It can safely be assumed that the Court is correct in concluding that Mrs. McFarlin came to Judge Stump with her petition because he was a County Circuit Court Judge. But false illusions as to a judge's power can hardly convert a judge's response to those illusions into a judicial act. In short, a judge's approval of a mother's petition to lock her daughter in the attic would hardly be a judicial act simply because the mother had submitted her petition to the judge in his official capacity.

If, on the other hand, the Court's test depends upon the fact that Judge Stump said he was acting in his judicial capacity, it is equally invalid. It is true that Judge Stump affixed his signature to the approval of the petition as "Judge, DeKalb

Circuit Court." But the conduct of a judge surely does not become a judicial act merely on his own say-so. A judge is not free, like a loose cannon, to inflict indiscriminate damage whenever he announces that he is acting in his judicial capacity. . . .

There was no "case," controversial or otherwise. There were no litigants. There was and could be no appeal. And there was not even the pretext of principled decision-making. The total absence of any of these normal attributes of a judicial proceeding convinces me that the conduct complained of in this case was not a judicial act. . . .

■ *Mr. Justice POWELL, dissenting.* . . .

Bradley v. Fisher, which established the absolute judicial immunity at issue in this case, recognized that the immunity was designed to further the public interest in an independent judiciary, sometimes at the expense of legitimate individual grievances. *Accord, Pierson v. Ray.* The *Bradley* Court accepted those costs to aggrieved individuals because the judicial system itself provided other means for protecting individual rights: "Against the consequences of [judges'] erroneous or irregular action, from whatever motives proceeding, the law has provided for private parties numerous remedies, and to those remedies they must, in such cases, resort."

Underlying the *Bradley* immunity, then, is the notion that private rights can be sacrificed in some degree to the achievement of the greater public good deriving from a completely independent judiciary, because there exist alternative forums and methods for vindicating those rights.

But where a judicial officer acts in a manner that precludes all resort to appellate or other judicial remedies that otherwise would be available, the underlying assumption of the *Bradley* doctrine is inoperative. In this case, as Mr. Justice Stewart points out, Judge Stump's unjudicial conduct insured that "[t]here was and could be no appeal." The complete absence of normal judicial process foreclosed resort to any of the "numerous remedies" that "the law has provided for private parties." *Bradley.* . . .

Notes and Questions

1. Many government officials make difficult decisions that presumably should be made neutrally, "without apprehension of personal consequences" such as legal liability. Governors make life-or-death clemency decisions. Police officers make split-second life-or-death decisions whether to use deadly force. These officials have qualified immunity, which (as we'll see) is a type of immunity that is powerful yet can sometimes be overcome by plaintiffs. What is it about judges that requires a higher, absolute immunity? *Cf. Forrester v. White*, 484 U.S. 219, 226 (1988) ("One can reasonably wonder whether judges, who have been primarily responsible for developing the law of official immunities, are not inevitably more sensitive to the ill effects that vexatious lawsuits can have on the judicial function than they are to similar dangers in other contexts.").

2. If you disagree with the outcome here, is the problem the judicial immunity rule itself? Or the Court's judgment that this outcome was necessary to preserve it?

3. Why aren't the dissenters' criteria of formality and appealability a sufficient basis to distinguish this case from those that could be characterized as within the "heartland" of judicial immunity? Using the majority's response in footnote 12 as a jumping-off point, can you think of circumstances in which judges act without formality or appealability and also come within the policy rationale of *Bradley*?

Note: The Outer Bounds of Judicial Immunity

Judicial immunity is absolute when it applies—i.e., there are no degrees of absolute immunity. When the judge is immune, there can be no liability. However, *Stump* points to two circumstances in which judges do not have immunity: when acting in the clear absence of jurisdiction and when not performing judicial acts.

Consider a few applications of these limits. *Forrester v. White*, 484 U.S. 219 (1988), asked "whether a state-court judge has absolute immunity from a suit for damages under 42 U.S.C. § 1983 for his decision to dismiss a subordinate court employee . . . on account of her sex, in violation of the Equal Protection Clause of the Fourteenth Amendment." In an opinion by Justice O'Connor, the Court unanimously denied absolute immunity:

> The decided cases . . . suggest an intelligible distinction between judicial acts and the administrative, legislative, or executive functions that judges may on occasion be assigned by law to perform. . . .
>
> In the case before us, we think it clear that Judge White was acting in an administrative capacity when he demoted and discharged Forrester. Those acts—like many others involved in supervising court employees and overseeing the efficient operation of a court—may have been quite important in providing the necessary conditions of a sound adjudicative system. The decisions at issue, however, were not themselves judicial or adjudicative. As Judge Posner pointed out below, a judge who hires or fires a probation officer cannot meaningfully be distinguished from a district attorney who hires and fires assistant district attorneys, or indeed from any other Executive Branch official who is responsible for making such employment decisions. Such decisions, like personnel decisions made by judges, are often crucial to the efficient operation of public institutions (some of which are at least as important as the courts), yet no one suggests that they give rise to absolute immunity from liability in damages under § 1983. . . .
>
> Absolute immunity, however, is "strong medicine, justified only when the danger of [officials' being] deflect[ed from the effective performance of their duties] is very great." (Posner, J., dissenting). The danger here is not great enough. . . . To conclude that, because a judge acts within the scope of his authority, such employment decisions are brought within the court's "jurisdiction," or converted into "judicial acts," would lift form above substance.

In *Archie v. Lanier*, 95 F.3d 438 (6th Cir. 1996), several women sued Judge David Lanier under § 1983 for allegedly using his position to sexually harass and assault them. For instance, the lead plaintiff alleged that she applied for a secretarial position and during the interview, Lanier "threatened her with granting her parents custody of Archie's daughter if she did not comply with his sexual requests, after which statement he physically and sexually assaulted her." A court employee and a litigant in a pending case also alleged that Lanier raped them. The Sixth Circuit affirmed the district court's denial of absolute immunity:

> Whether Lanier's actions were "judicial acts" must be answered by looking at "the 'nature' and 'function' of the act, not the 'act itself.'" That is to say, "we look to the particular act's relation to a general function normally performed by a judge" to determine whether the action complained of was indeed a judicial act. Ultimately, it is the "nature" of the function performed, rather than the identity of the person who performed it, that informs a court's immunity analysis. . . .
>
> [T]he analytical key "in attempting to draw the line" between functions for which judicial immunity attaches and those for which it does not is the determination whether the questioned activities are "truly judicial acts" or "acts that simply happen to have been done by judges." It is the nature of the function involved that determines whether an act is "truly" judicial.
>
> And, this court has held that "'[a]ny time an action taken by a judge is not an adjudication between parties, it is less likely that the act [will be found to be] a judicial one.'"
>
> The burden is on Lanier to show that the actions plaintiffs challenge justify the invocation of such immunity. This he has failed to do. . . . We hold that stalking and sexually assaulting a person, no matter the circumstances, do not constitute "judicial acts." The fact that, regrettably, Lanier happened to be a judge when he committed these reprehensible acts is not relevant to the question of whether he is entitled to immunity. Clearly he is not.

These decisions seem hard to quarrel with. But what if a judge makes a *judicial decision* for reasons motivated by a person's sex, such as ruling in a litigant's favor as a quid pro quo for a sexual favor, or ruling against a party based on the party's race? Same result, under *Forrester* and *Archie*? If not, is the test for a "judicial act" is miscalibrated? Are there other avenues for recourse for litigants subjected to such blatantly improper decision making? Do these alternatives make judicial immunity more tolerable in such circumstances?

Consider too, the following passage from *Forrester*: "Absolute immunity . . . is strong medicine, justified only when the danger of officials' being deflected from the effective performance of their duties is very great. The danger here is not great enough" (citation, internal quotation marks, and source's alteration marks omitted). Does this analysis suggest absolute immunity doctrine should rely more on case-by-case adjudication to balance the interests in every circumstance? Or would such an approach defeat the entire point of absolute immunity?

Note: Injunctions Against Judges

In *Pulliam v. Allen*, 466 U.S. 522 (1984), the Court ruled that judges were not immune from suits for injunctive relief. But twelve years later, in the omnibus Federal Courts Improvement Act of 1996, Congress amended § 1983 to add the following proviso:

[I]n any action brought against a judicial officer for an act or omission taken in such officer's judicial capacity, injunctive relief shall not be granted unless a declaratory decree was violated or declaratory relief was unavailable.

What is the practical effect of this rule? What purpose does it serve?

2. Prosecutorial immunity

As *Pierson* reflects, judges have absolute immunity (i.e., they cannot be held liable) and police officers have what the Court has come to call qualified immunity (i.e., they can assert a defense that is not absolute). Should prosecutors be treated like judges or police in terms of what immunity they may assert? The next case answers.

Imbler v. Pachtman
424 U.S. 409 (1976)

■ *Mr. Justice* Powell *delivered the opinion of the Court....*

[In January 1961, two men attempted to rob a store run by Morris Hasson. One shot and killed him. Imbler was charged with the murder.] The primary identification witness was Alfred Costello, a passerby on the night of the crime, who testified that he had a clear view both as the gunman emerged from the market and again a few moments later when the fleeing gunman after losing his hat turned to fire a shot at Costello and to shed his coat before continuing on. Costello positively identified Imbler as the gunman....

Imbler's defense was an alibi. He claimed to have spent the night of the Hasson killing bar-hopping.... This testimony was corroborated by Mayes ... who also claimed to have accompanied Imbler on the earlier rounds of the bars. The jury found Imbler guilty and fixed punishment at death. On appeal the Supreme Court of California affirmed unanimously over numerous contentions of error.

Shortly thereafter Deputy District Attorney Richard Pachtman, who had been the prosecutor at Imbler's trial and who is the respondent before this Court, wrote to the Governor of California describing evidence turned up after trial by himself and an investigator for the state correctional authority. In substance, the evidence consisted of newly discovered corroborating witnesses for Imbler's alibi, as well as new revelations about prime witness Costello's background which indicated that he was less trustworthy than he had represented originally to Pachtman and in his testimony. Pachtman noted that leads to some of this information had been available to Imbler's counsel prior to trial but apparently had not been developed, that Costello had testified convincingly and withstood intense cross-examination, and that none of the new evidence was conclusive of Imbler's innocence. He explained that he wrote from a belief that "a prosecuting attorney had a duty to be fair and see that all true facts whether helpful to the case or not, should be presented."[5]

---

5. The record does not indicate what specific action was taken in response to Pachtman's letter. We do note that the letter was dated August 17, 1962, and that Imbler's execution, scheduled for September 12, 1962, subsequently was stayed.

[Imbler filed a state habeas corpus petition and argued that the prosecution had knowingly used false testimony at trial. He lost. The following year, his death sentence was overturned on unrelated grounds. Rather than resentence him, the State stipulated to a life sentence. Imbler then sought federal habeas relief. The federal court found eight instances of misconduct at Imbler's trial — six that amounted to the culpable use of misleading or false testimony by the prosecution and two suppressions of evidence favorable to Imbler by the police or by a police fingerprint expert. The district court granted relief, the court of appeals affirmed, and Imbler was released.]

Imbler filed a civil rights action, under 42 U.S.C. § 1983 and related statutes, against respondent Pachtman, the police fingerprint expert, and various other officers of the Los Angeles police force. He alleged that a conspiracy among them unlawfully to charge and convict him had caused him loss of liberty and other grievous injury. . . .

The Courts of Appeals . . . are virtually unanimous that a prosecutor enjoys absolute immunity from § 1983 suits for damages when he acts within the scope of his prosecutorial duties. These courts sometimes have described the prosecutor's immunity as a form of "quasi-judicial" immunity and referred to it as derivative of the immunity of judges recognized in *Pierson v. Ray*. Petitioner focuses upon the "quasi-judicial" characterization, and contends that it illustrates a fundamental illogic. . . . He argues that the prosecutor, as a member of the executive branch, cannot claim the immunity reserved for the judiciary, but only a qualified immunity akin to that accorded other executive officials in this Court's previous cases. Petitioner takes an overly simplistic approach to the issue of prosecutorial liability. . . .

The common-law immunity of a prosecutor is based upon the same considerations that underlie the common-law immunities of judges and grand jurors acting within the scope of their duties. These include concern that harassment by unfounded litigation would cause a deflection of the prosecutor's energies from his public duties, and the possibility that he would shade his decisions instead of exercising the independence of judgment required by his public trust. . . .

If a prosecutor had only a qualified immunity, the threat of § 1983 suits would undermine performance of his duties no less than would the threat of common-law suits for malicious prosecution. A prosecutor is duty bound to exercise his best judgment both in deciding which suits to bring and in conducting them in court. The public trust of the prosecutor's office would suffer if he were constrained in making every decision by the consequences in terms of his own potential liability in a suit for damages. Such suits could be expected with some frequency, for a defendant often will transform his resentment at being prosecuted into the ascription of improper and malicious actions to the State's advocate. *Cf. Bradley; Pierson*. Further, if the prosecutor could be made to answer in court each time such a person charged him with wrongdoing, his energy and attention would be diverted from the pressing duty of enforcing the criminal law.

Moreover, suits that survived the pleadings would pose substantial danger of liability even to the honest prosecutor. The prosecutor's possible knowledge of a witness' falsehoods, the materiality of evidence not revealed to the defense, the propriety of a closing argument, and ultimately in every case the likelihood that prosecutorial misconduct so infected a trial as to deny due process, are typical of issues with which judges struggle in actions for post-trial relief, sometimes to differing conclusions.[22] The presentation of such issues in a § 1983 action often would require a virtual retrial of the criminal offense in a new forum, and the resolution of some technical issues by the lay jury. It is fair to say, we think, that the honest prosecutor would face greater difficulty in meeting the standards of qualified immunity than other executive or administrative officials. Frequently acting under serious constraints of time and even information, a prosecutor inevitably makes many decisions that could engender colorable claims of constitutional deprivation. Defending these decisions, often years after they were made, could impose unique and intolerable burdens upon a prosecutor responsible annually for hundreds of indictments and trials.

The affording of only a qualified immunity to the prosecutor also could have an adverse effect upon the functioning of the criminal justice system. Attaining the system's goal of accurately determining guilt or innocence requires that both the prosecution and the defense have wide discretion in the conduct of the trial and the presentation of evidence. The veracity of witnesses in criminal cases frequently is subject to doubt before and after they testify, as is illustrated by the history of this case. If prosecutors were hampered in exercising their judgment as to the use of such witnesses by concern about resulting personal liability, the triers of fact in criminal cases often would be denied relevant evidence.

The ultimate fairness of the operation of the system itself could be weakened by subjecting prosecutors to § 1983 liability. Various post-trial procedures are available to determine whether an accused has received a fair trial. These procedures include the remedial powers of the trial judge, appellate review, and state and federal post-conviction collateral remedies. In all of these the attention of the reviewing judge or tribunal is focused primarily on whether there was a fair trial under law. This focus should not be blurred by even the subconscious knowledge that a post-trial decision in favor of the accused might result in the prosecutor's being called upon to respond in damages for his error or mistaken judgment.[25]

We conclude that the considerations outlined above dictate the same absolute immunity under § 1983 that the prosecutor enjoys at common law. To be

---

22. This is illustrated by the history of the disagreement as to the culpability of the prosecutor's conduct in this case. We express no opinion as to which of the courts was correct.

25. The possibility of personal liability also could dampen the prosecutor's exercise of his duty to bring to the attention of the court or of proper officials all significant evidence suggestive of innocence or mitigation. At trial this duty is enforced by the requirements of due process, but after a conviction the prosecutor also is bound by the ethics of his office to inform the appropriate authority of after-acquired or other information that casts doubt upon the correctness of the conviction. Indeed, the record in this case suggests that respondent's recognition of this duty led to the post-conviction hearing which in turn resulted ultimately in the District Court's granting of the writ of habeas corpus.

sure, this immunity does leave the genuinely wronged defendant without civil redress against a prosecutor whose malicious or dishonest action deprives him of liberty. But the alternative of qualifying a prosecutor's immunity would disserve the broader public interest. It would prevent the vigorous and fearless performance of the prosecutor's duty that is essential to the proper functioning of the criminal justice system. Moreover, it often would prejudice defendants in criminal cases by skewing post-conviction judicial decisions that should be made with the sole purpose of insuring justice. . . .

We emphasize that the immunity of prosecutors from liability in suits under § 1983 does not leave the public powerless to deter misconduct or to punish that which occurs. This Court has never suggested that the policy considerations which compel civil immunity for certain governmental officials also place them beyond the reach of the criminal law. Even judges, cloaked with absolute civil immunity for centuries, could be punished criminally for willful deprivations of constitutional rights on the strength of 18 U.S.C. § 242, the criminal analog of § 1983. The prosecutor would fare no better for his willful acts. Moreover, a prosecutor stands perhaps unique, among officials whose acts could deprive persons of constitutional rights, in his amenability to professional discipline by an association of his peers. These checks undermine the argument that the imposition of civil liability is the only way to insure that prosecutors are mindful of the constitutional rights of persons accused of crime.

It remains to delineate the boundaries of our holding. . . . [T]he Court of Appeals emphasized that each of respondent's challenged activities was an "integral part of the judicial process." The purpose of the Court of Appeals' focus upon the functional nature of the activities rather than respondent's status was to distinguish and leave standing those cases, in its Circuit and in some others, which hold that a prosecutor engaged in certain investigative activities enjoys, not the absolute immunity associated with the judicial process, but only a good-faith defense comparable to the policeman's. We agree with the Court of Appeals that respondent's activities were intimately associated with the judicial phase of the criminal process, and thus were functions to which the reasons for absolute immunity apply with full force. We have no occasion to consider whether like or similar reasons require immunity for those aspects of the prosecutor's responsibility that cast him in the role of an administrator or investigative officer rather than that of advocate.

We hold only that in initiating a prosecution and in presenting the State's case, the prosecutor is immune from a civil suit for damages under § 1983.[34] . . .

Mr. Justice STEVENS *took no part in the consideration or decision of this case.*

---

34. Mr. Justice White, concurring in the judgment, would distinguish between willful use by a prosecutor of perjured testimony and willful suppression by a prosecutor of exculpatory information. In the former case, Mr. Justice White agrees that absolute immunity is appropriate. He thinks, however, that only a qualified immunity is appropriate where information relevant to the defense is "unconstitutionally withheld . . . from the court."

We do not accept the distinction urged by Mr. Justice White for several reasons. As a matter of principle, we perceive no less an infringement of a defendant's rights by the knowing use of

■ *Mr. Justice* WHITE, *with whom Mr. Justice* BRENNAN *and Mr. Justice* MARSHALL *join, concurring in the judgment.*

I concur in the judgment of the Court and in much of its reasoning. I agree with the Court that the gravamen of the complaint in this case is that the prosecutor knowingly used perjured testimony; and that a prosecutor is absolutely immune from suit for money damages under 42 U.S.C. § 1983 for presentation of testimony later determined to have been false, where the presentation of such testimony is alleged to have been unconstitutional solely because the prosecutor did not believe it or should not have believed it to be true. . . . I disagree with any implication that absolute immunity for prosecutors extends to suits based on claims of unconstitutional suppression of evidence because I believe such a rule would threaten to injure the judicial process and to interfere with Congress' purpose in enacting 42 U.S.C. § 1983, without any support in statutory language or history. . . .

The absolute immunity extended to prosecutors . . . is designed to encourage them to bring information to the court which will resolve the criminal case. That is its single justification. Lest they withhold valuable but questionable evidence or refrain from making valuable but questionable arguments, prosecutors are protected from liability for submitting before the court information later determined to have been false to their knowledge. It would stand this immunity rule on its head, however, to apply it to a suit based on a claim that the prosecutor unconstitutionally withheld information from the court. Immunity from a suit based upon a claim that the prosecutor suppressed or withheld evidence would discourage precisely the disclosure of evidence sought to be encouraged by the rule granting prosecutors immunity from defamation suits. Denial of immunity for unconstitutional withholding of evidence would encourage such disclosure. A prosecutor seeking to protect himself from liability for failure to disclose evidence may be induced to disclose more than is required. But, this will hardly injure the judicial process. Indeed, it will help it. Accordingly, lower courts have held that unconstitutional suppression of exculpatory evidence is beyond the scope of "duties constituting an integral part of the judicial process" and have refused to extend absolute immunity to suits based on such claims.

---

perjured testimony than by the deliberate withholding of exculpatory information. . . . Moreover, the distinction is not susceptible of practical application. A claim of using perjured testimony simply may be reframed and asserted as a claim of suppression of the evidence upon which the knowledge of perjury rested. . . . Denying absolute immunity from suppression claims could thus eviscerate, in many situations, the absolute immunity from claims of using perjured testimony.

We further think Mr. Justice White's suggestion, that absolute immunity should be accorded only when the prosecutor makes a "full disclosure" of all facts casting doubt upon the State's testimony, would place upon the prosecutor a duty exceeding the disclosure requirements of *Brady* and its progeny. It also would weaken the adversary system at the same time it interfered seriously with the legitimate exercise of prosecutorial discretion.

Equally important, unlike constitutional violations committed in the courtroom improper summations, introduction of hearsay evidence in violation of the Confrontation Clause, knowing presentation of false testimony which truly are an "integral part of the judicial process," the judicial process has no way to prevent or correct the constitutional violation of suppressing evidence. The judicial process will by definition be ignorant of the violation when it occurs; and it is reasonable to suspect that most such violations never surface. It is all the more important, then, to deter such violations by permitting damage actions under 42 U.S.C. § 1983 to be maintained in instances where violations do surface.

The stakes are high. . . . It is apparent that the injury to a defendant which can be caused by an unconstitutional suppression of exculpatory evidence is substantial, particularly if the evidence is never uncovered. It is virtually impossible to identify any injury to the judicial process resulting from a rule permitting suits for such unconstitutional conduct, and it is very easy to identify an injury to the process resulting from a rule which do not permit such suits. Where the reason for the rule extending absolute immunity to prosecutors disappears, it would truly be "monstrous to deny recovery."

[Justice White reviews the complaint's allegations of withholding of evidence and concludes that they fail for reasons other than immunity.][9] . . .

Thus, the only constitutional violation adequately alleged against the prosecutor is that he knew in his mind that testimony presented by him was false; and from a suit based on such a violation, without more, the prosecutor is absolutely immune. For this reason, I concur in the judgment reached by the majority in this case.

---

9. The majority points out that the knowing use of perjured testimony is as reprehensible as the deliberate suppression of exculpatory evidence. This is beside the point. The reason for permitting suits against prosecutors for suppressing evidence is not that suppression is especially reprehensible but that the only effect on the process of permitting such suits will be a beneficial one [because] more information will be disclosed to the court; whereas one of the effects of permitting suits for knowing use of perjured testimony will be detrimental to the process—prosecutors may withhold questionable but valuable testimony from the court.

The majority argues that any "claim of using perjured testimony simply may be reframed and asserted as a claim of suppression." Our treatment of the allegations in this case conclusively refutes the argument. It is relatively easy to allege that a government witness testified falsely and that the prosecutor did not believe the witness; and, if the prosecutor's subjective belief is a sufficient basis for liability, the case would almost certainly have to go to trial. If such suits were permitted, this case would have to go to trial. It is another matter entirely to allege specific objective facts known to the prosecutor of sufficient importance to justify a conclusion that he violated a constitutional duty to disclose. It is no coincidence that petitioner failed to make any such allegations in this case. More to the point and quite apart from the relative difficulty of pleading a violation of *Brady v. Maryland*, a rule permitting suits based on withholding of specific facts unlike suits based on the prosecutor's disbelief of a witness' testimony will have no detrimental effect on the process. Risk of being sued for suppression will impel the prosecutor to err if at all on the side of overdisclosure. Risk of being sued for disbelieving a witness will impel the prosecutor to err on the side of withholding questionable evidence. The majority does not appear to respond to this point. Any suggestion that the distinction between suits based on suppression of facts helpful to the defense and suits based on other kinds of constitutional violations cannot be understood by district judges who would have to apply the rule is mystifying. The distinction is a simple one.

Notes and Questions

1. Compare the immunity applicable to prosecutors (absolute) to that applicable to police officers (qualified). Which group has more power over the lives of individuals? Which group is more in need of deterrence? For which group are there more opportunities beyond § 1983 to correct mistakes?

2. How convincing is the majority's discussion of alternative means to correct and deter prosecutorial malfeasance in light of Justice White's point that *Brady* violations are difficult to detect because their very nature consists of concealment? How does the majority respond to Justice White's proposed distinction and his argument that denying absolute immunity for withholding evidence will not deter any prosecutorial conduct we should want to encourage?

3. Justice Holmes (and others before him) famously opined that "hard cases make bad law." Does that maxim help explain the result here? How might the majority's approach have differed if Pachtman hadn't himself come forward with the exculpatory evidence? On the other hand, isn't it always true that any rule punishing wrongdoing risks chilling the self-reporting of misconduct? Is that problem worse for prosecutors than for other government officials?

4. Although (as noted) the president has absolute immunity, a state governor does not, the Court held in *Scheuer v. Rhodes*, 416 U.S. 232 (1974). That case arose out of the 1970 Kent State shootings, in which four unarmed students were killed by Ohio National Guard troops at a college protest over U.S. military actions in Southeast Asia. The families of several victims sued the governor and adjutant general of Ohio, officers of the Ohio National Guard, and the president of Kent State University. Chief Justice Burger's opinion for the Court allowed these defendants to claim only qualified immunity:

   > § 1983 would be drained of meaning were we to hold that the acts of a governor or other high executive officer have "the quality of a supreme and unchangeable edict, overriding all conflicting rights of property and unreviewable through the judicial power of the federal government."

   Why should high officials like a governor and an adjutant general (the commander of the state militia) receive a lower level of immunity than a prosecutor, who is subordinate to other executive officials? Does the answer lie in the nature of their tasks? The frequency with which they could be sued? Something else? Or do Justices simply have more sympathy for lawyers than for other officials?

   In addition to governors, the Court has denied absolute immunity to other high-ranking officials. *See Mitchell v. Forsyth*, 472 U.S. 511, 520-24 (1985) (cabinet officers and individuals performing national security investigations); *Harlow v. Fitzgerald*, 457 U.S. 800, 808-13 (1982) (presidential aides).

* * *

Following *Imbler*, the Court has had to determine when a prosecutor is performing a function "intimately associated with the judicial phase of the criminal process" so as to acquire absolute immunity. In 2009, the Court summarized its holdings:

> In the years since *Imbler*, we have held that absolute immunity applies when a prosecutor prepares to initiate a judicial proceeding, or appears in court to present evidence in support of a search warrant application. We have held that absolute immunity does not apply when a prosecutor gives advice to police during a criminal investigation, when the prosecutor makes statements to the press, or when a prosecutor acts as a complaining witness in support of a warrant application.

Van de Kamp v. Goldstein, 555 U.S. 335 (2009) (citing various parts of *Burns v. Reed*, 500 U.S. 478 (1991); *Kalina v. Fletcher*, 522 U.S. 118, 127, 130 (1997); and *Buckley v. Fitzsimmons*, 509 U.S. 259 (1993)). Having drawn these lines regarding when a prosecutor acts as a prosecutor versus an advisor, witness, or public speaker, the Court next faced a question about when a prosecutor acts as an *administrator*.

Van de Kamp v. Goldstein
555 U.S. 335 (2009)

■ *Justice* BREYER *delivered the opinion of the Court.* . . .

In 1998, respondent Thomas Goldstein (then a prisoner) filed a habeas corpus action in the Federal District Court for the Central District of California. He claimed that in 1980 he was convicted of murder; that his conviction depended in critical part upon the testimony of Edward Floyd Fink, a jailhouse informant; that Fink's testimony was unreliable, indeed false; that Fink had previously received reduced sentences for providing prosecutors with favorable testimony in other cases; that at least some prosecutors in the Los Angeles County District Attorney's Office knew about the favorable treatment; that the office had not provided Goldstein's attorney with that information; and that, among other things, the prosecution's failure to provide Goldstein's attorney with this potential impeachment information had led to his erroneous conviction. [The court granted the writ, the court of appeals affirmed, and Goldstein was released, having served twenty-four years in prison.]

Upon his release Goldstein filed this § 1983 action against petitioners, the former Los Angeles County district attorney and chief deputy district attorney. Goldstein's complaint (which for present purposes we take as accurate) asserts in relevant part that the prosecution's failure to communicate to his attorney the facts about Fink's earlier testimony-related rewards violated the prosecution's constitutional duty to "insure communication of all relevant information on each case [including agreements made with informants] to every lawyer who deals with it." Moreover, it alleges that this failure resulted from the failure of petitioners (the office's chief supervisory attorneys) adequately to train and to supervise the prosecutors who worked for them as well as their failure to establish an information system about informants. . . .

Goldstein claims that the district attorney and his chief assistant violated their constitutional obligation to provide his attorney with impeachment-related information, *see Giglio v. United States*, 405 U.S. 150 (1972) [(applying

Brady obligation to information that could be used to impeach prosecution witness)] because, as the Court of Appeals wrote, they failed "to adequately train and supervise deputy district attorneys on that subject," and because, as Goldstein's complaint adds, they "failed to create any system for the Deputy District Attorneys handling criminal cases to access information pertaining to the benefits provided to jailhouse informants and other impeachment information." We agree with Goldstein that, in making these claims, he attacks the office's administrative procedures. We are also willing to assume with Goldstein, but purely for argument's sake, that *Giglio* imposes certain obligations as to training, supervision, or information-system management.

Even so, we conclude that prosecutors involved in such supervision or training or information-system management enjoy absolute immunity from the kind of legal claims at issue here. Those claims focus upon a certain kind of administrative obligation—a kind that itself is directly connected with the conduct of a trial. Here, unlike with other claims related to administrative decisions, an individual prosecutor's error in the plaintiff's specific criminal trial constitutes an essential element of the plaintiff's claim. The administrative obligations at issue here are thus unlike administrative duties concerning, for example, workplace hiring, payroll administration, the maintenance of physical facilities, and the like. Moreover, the types of activities on which Goldstein's claims focus necessarily require legal knowledge and the exercise of related discretion, e.g., in determining what information should be included in the training or the supervision or the information-system management. And in that sense also Goldstein's claims are unlike claims of, say, unlawful discrimination in hiring employees. Given these features of the case before us, we believe absolute immunity must follow. . . .

[I]n terms of *Imbler*'s functional concerns, a suit charging that a supervisor made a mistake directly related to a particular trial, on the one hand, and a suit charging that a supervisor trained and supervised inadequately, on the other, would seem very much alike.

That is true, in part, for the practical reason that it will often prove difficult to draw a line between general office supervision or office training (say, related to *Giglio*) and specific supervision or training related to a particular case. To permit claims based upon the former is almost inevitably to permit the bringing of claims that include the latter. It is also true because one cannot easily distinguish, for immunity purposes, between claims based upon training or supervisory failures related to *Giglio* and similar claims related to other constitutional matters (obligations under *Brady*, for example). And that being so, every consideration that *Imbler* mentions militates in favor of immunity.

As we have said, the type of "faulty training" claim at issue here rests in necessary part upon a consequent error by an individual prosecutor in the midst of trial, namely, the plaintiff's trial. If, as *Imbler* says, the threat of damages liability for such an error could lead a trial prosecutor to take account of that risk when making trial-related decisions, so, too, could the threat of more widespread liability throughout the office (ultimately traceable to that trial error) lead both that prosecutor and other office prosecutors as well to take account of such a risk. . . .

Moreover, because better training or supervision might prevent most, if not all, prosecutorial errors at trial, permission to bring such a suit here would grant permission to criminal defendants to bring claims in other similar instances, in effect claiming damages for (trial-related) training or supervisory failings. Further, given the complexity of the constitutional issues, inadequate training and supervision suits could, as in *Imbler*, "pose substantial danger of liability even to the honest prosecutor." Finally, as *Imbler* pointed out, defending prosecutorial decisions, often years after they were made, could impose "unique and intolerable burdens upon a prosecutor responsible annually for hundreds of indictments and trials." . . .

At the same time, to permit this suit to go forward would create practical anomalies. A trial prosecutor would remain immune, even for intentionally failing to turn over, say *Giglio* material; but her supervisor might be liable for negligent training or supervision. Small prosecution offices where supervisors can personally participate in all of the cases would likewise remain immune from prosecution; but large offices, making use of more general officewide supervision and training, would not. Most important, the ease with which a plaintiff could restyle a complaint charging a trial failure so that it becomes a complaint charging a failure of training or supervision would eviscerate *Imbler*. . . .

Goldstein argues that the creation of an information management system is a more purely administrative task, less closely related to the "judicial phase of the criminal process," than are supervisory or training tasks. He adds that technically qualified individuals other than prosecutors could create such a system and that they could do so prior to the initiation of criminal proceedings.

In our view, however, these differences do not require a different outcome. The critical element of any information system is the information it contains. Deciding what to include and what not to include in an information system is little different from making similar decisions in respect to training. Again, determining the criteria for inclusion or exclusion requires knowledge of the law.

Moreover, the absence of an information system is relevant here if, and only if, a proper system would have included information about the informant Fink. Thus, were this claim allowed, a court would have to review the office's legal judgments, not simply about whether to have an information system but also about what kind of system is appropriate, and whether an appropriate system would have included *Giglio*-related information about one particular kind of trial informant. Such decisions—whether made prior to or during a particular trial—are "intimately associated with the judicial phase of the criminal process." *Imbler*. And, for the reasons set out above, all *Imbler*'s functional considerations (and the anomalies we mentioned earlier) apply here as well. . . .

Notes and Questions

1. What would Justice White, based on his concurrence in *Imbler*, have had to say about this result? What beneficial prosecutorial activities does the *Van de Kamp* decision avoid deterring?

2. Why is the Court troubled by the possibility that the trial attorney who intentionally failed to disclose *Brady* material could receive absolute immunity while that attorney's supervisor receives only qualified immunity? Aren't such disparities inevitable when taking a functional approach? If the Court's real concern is that the line prosecutor is immune for intentional misconduct, why shouldn't the Court revisit *Imbler* rather than rule against Goldstein?

3. Both in *Imbler* and *Van de Kamp*, the Court feared that creating avenues to avoid absolute immunity would enable clever plaintiffs to reframe their grievances in a manner that avoids the absolute immunity defense. What changes would be needed to transform a failure-to-disclose claim into a plausibly pleaded failure-to-train claim? How many such cases would be brought? Why shouldn't courts be open to viewing such reframings not as mere strategic ploys but an appropriate means to promote the goals of absolute immunity by avoiding prosecutorial liability for trial decisions?

4. Looking at the absolute immunity cases we've studied, do you think the Court has struck the right balance between the compensation and deterrence objectives of § 1983 and the goals of protecting the independence of crucial actors in the justice system? If not, what rule would you propose?

3. Legislative immunity

The policy rationale for absolute legislative immunity is similar to the one underlying immunity for judges and prosecutors, but immunity for legislators has a quasi-constitutional pedigree, as Justice Frankfurter explained in his opinion for the Court in *Tenney v. Brandhove*, 341 U.S. 367 (1951):

> Freedom of speech and action in the legislature was taken as a matter of course by those who severed the Colonies from the Crown and founded our Nation. It was deemed so essential for representatives of the people that it was written into the Articles of Confederation and later into the Constitution. Article V of the Articles of Confederation is quite close to the English Bill of Rights: "Freedom of speech and debate in Congress shall not be impeached or questioned in any court or place out of Congress * * *." Article I, § 6, of the Constitution provides: "* * * for any Speech or Debate in either House, (the Senators and Representatives) shall not be questioned in any other Place."

Accordingly, the Court recognized absolute legislative immunity from § 1983 claims as a matter of constitutional avoidance:

> Did Congress by the general language of its 1871 statute mean to overturn the tradition of legislative freedom achieved in England by Civil War and carefully preserved

in the formation of State and National Governments here? Did it mean to subject legislators to civil liability for acts done within the sphere of legislative activity? Let us assume, merely for the moment, that Congress has constitutional power to limit the freedom of State legislators acting within their traditional sphere. That would be a big assumption. But we would have to make an ever rasher assumption to find that Congress thought it had exercised the power. . . . We cannot believe that Congress . . . would impinge on a tradition so well grounded in history and reason by covert inclusion in the general language before us.

The Court in *Tenney* went on to apply the "tradition" of absolute legislative immunity to the work of a state investigative committee, which the plaintiff accused of having held a hearing to intimidate him out of exercising his free speech rights:

Investigations . . . are an established part of representative government. Legislative committees have been charged with losing sight of their duty of disinterestedness. In times of political passion, dishonest or vindictive motives are readily attributed to legislative conduct and as readily believed. Courts are not the place for such controversies. Self-discipline and the voters must be the ultimate reliance for discouraging or correcting such abuses.

Justice Black concurred to note that a witness could, notwithstanding legislators' immunity from damages suits, still raise the unconstitutionality of the committee's action in defending against contempt charges arising out of the committee's questioning. In a solo dissent, Justice Douglas "agree[d] with the opinion of the Court as a statement of general principles governing the liability of legislative committees and members of the legislatures," but argued that these principles should not be absolute and should yield in the face of constitutional violations.

The next case considers the breadth of legislative immunity. Given the doctrine's grounding in Article I of the Constitution, does legislative immunity extend to local legislators (whose authority is not traceable to the Constitution)? To executive branch officials (who don't engage in "Speech" or "Debate" in the legislature)?

Bogan v. Scott-Harris
523 U.S. 44 (1998)

■ *Justice* THOMAS *delivered the opinion of the Court.*

[Respondent Janet Scott-Harris was administrator of the Department of Health and Human Services (DHHS) for the City of Fall River, Massachusetts. She received a complaint accusing an employee of repeatedly using racial slurs to colleagues. Scott-Harris initiated the process of firing the employee, but the employee used her political connections, including with petitioner Marilyn Roderick, vice president of the city council, to obtain a suspension in lieu of termination. Petitioner Daniel Bogan, the mayor of Fall River, then reduced the punishment further. In conjunction with the city budget process, the council passed an ordinance eliminating DHHS, of which Scott-Harris was the sole employee. Roderick voted with the 6-2 majority in favor. Bogan signed the ordinance into law. Scott-Harris sued Bogan, Roderick, and other defendants; she alleged that eliminating her position was motivated by racial animus and a desire to retaliate for the employment action she had tried to take. The jury returned a verdict in favor of Scott-Harris on the First Amendment claim against Bogan, Roderick, and the City.]

The United States Court of Appeals for the First Circuit set aside the verdict against the city but affirmed the judgments against Roderick and Bogan. Although the court concluded that petitioners have "absolute immunity from civil liability for damages arising out of their performance of legitimate legislative activities," it held that their challenged conduct was not "legislative." Relying on the jury's finding that "constitutionally sheltered speech was a substantial or motivating factor" underlying petitioners' conduct, the court reasoned that the conduct was administrative, rather than legislative, because Roderick and Bogan "relied on facts relating to a particular individual [respondent] in the decisionmaking calculus." . . .

The principle that legislators are absolutely immune from liability for their legislative activities has long been recognized in Anglo-American law. This privilege "has taproots in the Parliamentary struggles of the Sixteenth and Seventeenth Centuries" and was "taken as a matter of course by those who severed the Colonies from the Crown and founded our Nation." *Tenney*. The Federal Constitution, the Constitutions of many of the newly independent States, and the common law thus protected legislators from liability for their legislative activities.

Recognizing this venerable tradition, we have held that state and regional legislators are entitled to absolute immunity from liability under § 1983 for their legislative activities. . . . Because the common law accorded local legislators the same absolute immunity it accorded legislators at other levels of government, and because the rationales for such immunity are fully applicable to local legislators, we now hold that local legislators are likewise absolutely immune from suit under § 1983 for their legislative activities.

The common law at the time § 1983 was enacted deemed local legislators to be absolutely immune from suit for their legislative activities. New York's highest court, for example, held that municipal aldermen were immune from suit for their discretionary decisions. The court explained that when a local legislator exercises discretionary powers, he "is exempt from all responsibility by action for the motives which influence him, and the manner in which such duties are performed. If corrupt, he may be impeached or indicted, but the law will not tolerate an action to redress the individual wrong which may have been done." These principles, according to the court, were "too familiar and well settled to require illustration or authority."

Shortly after § 1983 was enacted, the Mississippi Supreme Court reached a similar conclusion, holding that town aldermen could not be held liable under state law for their role in the adoption of an allegedly unlawful ordinance. . . .

Treatises of that era confirm that this was the pervasive view. . . .

Absolute immunity for local legislators under § 1983 finds support not only in history, but also in reason. The rationales for according absolute immunity to federal, state, and regional legislators apply with equal force to local legislators. Regardless of the level of government, the exercise of legislative discretion should not be inhibited by judicial interference or distorted by the fear of personal liability. Furthermore, the time and energy required to defend against a lawsuit are of particular concern at the local level, where the part-time citizen-legislator remains commonplace. And the threat of liability may significantly deter service in local government, where prestige and pecuniary rewards may pale in comparison to the threat of civil liability. . . .

[O]f course, the ultimate check on legislative abuse—the electoral process—applies with equal force at the local level, where legislators are often more closely responsible to the electorate. . . .

Absolute legislative immunity attaches to all actions taken "in the sphere of legitimate legislative activity." *Tenney*. The Court of Appeals held that petitioners' conduct in this case was not legislative because their actions were specifically targeted at respondent. . . .

Whether an act is legislative turns on the nature of the act, rather than on the motive or intent of the official performing it. The privilege of absolute immunity "would be of little value if [legislators] could be subjected to the cost and inconvenience and distractions of a trial upon a conclusion of the pleader, or to the hazard of a judgment against them based upon a jury's speculation as to motives." *Tenney*. Furthermore, it simply is "not consonant with our scheme of government for a court to inquire into the motives of legislators." We therefore held that the defendant in *Tenney* had acted in a legislative capacity even though he allegedly singled out the plaintiff for investigation in order "to intimidate and silence plaintiff and deter and prevent him from effectively exercising his constitutional rights."

This leaves us with the question whether, stripped of all considerations of intent and motive, petitioners' actions were legislative. We have little trouble concluding that they were. Most evidently, petitioner Roderick's acts of voting for an ordinance were, in form, quintessentially legislative. Petitioner Bogan's introduction of a budget and signing into law an ordinance also were formally legislative, even though he was an executive official. We have recognized that officials outside the legislative branch are entitled to legislative immunity when they perform legislative functions; Bogan's actions were legislative because they were integral steps in the legislative process.

Respondent, however, asks us to look beyond petitioners' formal actions to consider whether the ordinance was legislative in substance. We need not determine whether the formally legislative character of petitioners' actions is alone sufficient to entitle petitioners to legislative immunity, because here the ordinance, in substance, bore all the hallmarks of traditional legislation. The ordinance reflected a discretionary, policymaking decision implicating the budgetary priorities of the city and the services the city provides to its constituents.

Moreover, it involved the termination of a position, which, unlike the hiring or firing of a particular employee, may have prospective implications that reach well beyond the particular occupant of the office. And the city council, in eliminating DHHS, certainly governed "in a field where legislators traditionally have power to act." *Tenney*. Thus, petitioners' activities were undoubtedly legislative....

Notes and Questions

1. What limits, if any, does the Court impose on what types of legislators may claim absolute immunity or for what types of actions they may claim it? Putting the discussion in *Bogan* together with the result in *Van de Kamp* (which also concerned a claim of an "administrative" function), how easy do you suspect it will be for a plaintiff to argue that a legislator's act falls outside the scope of absolute immunity?

2. Comparing the rationales for absolute immunity in the contexts of judges, prosecutors, and legislators, which is most persuasive? Which is least persuasive? How does the susceptibility of each type of actor to other forms of accountability shape your view?

3. *Tenney* and *Bogan* both suggest that the voters have an obvious check against legislative abuse: the ballot box. Consider your own behavior as a voter. How strongly do you weigh a legislator's individual acts of retaliation such as that alleged in *Bogan* in considering whether to vote to reelect a candidate for legislative office? How does that compare to the weight you assign factors like policy positions and political party affiliation?

B. QUALIFIED IMMUNITY

Government officials who lack absolute immunity are entitled to claim qualified immunity, which, as we'll see, has become less and less "qualified" over the years. This powerful defense against suits for damages shapes civil rights litigation to a significant degree by providing defendants an opportunity to assert, early and often, an immunity from suit even if their conduct violated the Constitution. Procedural aspects of the qualified immunity doctrine play an important role in determining when and whether courts will decide if the conduct challenged in a civil rights action was unconstitutional or whether that question will be avoided. Some private actors, too, who are reachable under § 1983 because they qualify as "state actors" (see Chapter 1, Section B), can also assert the qualified immunity defense.

This section first introduces the policy rationales for qualified immunity and traces the development of the qualified immunity rule and its scope. We then consider, in turn, three aspects of the doctrine (the showing needed to overcome immunity, the role of defendant's subjective knowledge and intent, and the procedural aspects of qualified immunity) that explain its influence on civil rights litigation and on courts' interpretation of the Constitution itself. The penultimate subsection explores the availability of qualified immunity for non-governmental actors. We conclude by covering critiques of the doctrine and their implications for the premises underlying qualified immunity.

1. RATIONALE, REACH, AND STANDARD

The Court's 1967 decision in *Pierson v. Ray* was the first to apply the defense that would become known as qualified immunity. During the fifteen years following *Pierson*'s recognition of what it called the "good faith and probable cause" defense for officers, the Supreme Court's decisions applying the doctrine elaborated on its justification, expanded its reach, and transformed its content.

In *Scheuer v. Rhodes*, 416 U.S. 232 (1974), a civil rights suit seeking redress for the shootings of student protestors at Kent State University in 1970, the Court, in a unanimous opinion by Chief Justice Burger, explained the rationale for qualified immunity in these terms:

> [O]fficial immunity apparently rested, in its genesis, on two mutually dependent rationales: (1) the injustice, particularly in the absence of bad faith, of subjecting to liability an officer who is required, by the legal obligations of his position, to exercise discretion; (2) the danger that the threat of such liability would deter his willingness to execute his office with the decisiveness and the judgment required by the public good. . . .
>
> [In considering the development of this doctrine at common law,] one policy consideration seems to pervade the analysis: the public interest requires decisions and action to enforce laws for the protection of the public. Mr. Justice Jackson expressed this general proposition succinctly, stating "it is not a tort for government to govern." Public officials, whether governors, mayors or police, legislators or judges, who fail to make decisions when they are needed or who do not act to implement decisions when they are made do not fully and faithfully perform the duties of their offices. Implicit in the idea that officials have some immunity—absolute or qualified—for their acts, is a recognition that they may err. The concept of immunity assumes this and goes on to assume that it is better to risk some error and possible injury from such error than not to decide or act at all.

Whereas these justifications for the doctrine have endured, *Scheuer*'s formulation of the standard proved to have less staying power. The *Scheuer* Court envisioned a sliding scale that applied a different level of protection to different officers depending on the amount of discretion they exercised:

> When a court evaluates police conduct relating to an arrest its guideline is "good faith and probable cause." In the case of higher officers of the executive branch, however, the inquiry is far more complex since the range of decisions and choices—whether the formulation of policy, of legislation, of budgets, or of day-to-day decisions—is virtually infinite. . . . [S]ince the options which a chief executive and his principal subordinates must consider are far broader and far more subtle than those made by officials with less responsibility, the range of discretion must be comparably broad. . . .

> [I]n varying scope, a qualified immunity is available to officers of the executive branch of government, the variation being dependent upon the scope of discretion and responsibilities of the office and all the circumstances as they reasonably appeared at the time of the action on which liability is sought to be based. It is the existence of reasonable grounds for the belief formed at the time and in light of all the circumstances, coupled with good-faith belief, that affords a basis for qualified immunity of executive officers for acts performed in the course of official conduct.

After *Scheuer*, what was the test for qualified immunity?

Another significant, but also short-lived, aspect of *Scheuer* was the Court's view concerning when in the lifespan of a case qualified immunity claims become susceptible to resolution:

> If the immunity is qualified, not absolute, the scope of that immunity will necessarily be related to facts as yet not established either by affidavits, admissions, or a trial record. Final resolution of this question must take into account the functions and responsibilities of these particular defendants in their capacities as officers of the state government . . . .

Based on this passage, when in the litigation process would you expect the qualified immunity defense to be adjudicated?

The Court both expanded the reach of qualified immunity and refined the test for applying it in *Wood v. Strickland*, 420 U.S. 308 (1975). There, two Arkansas high school students claimed their due process rights were violated when they were expelled for spiking the punch at the meeting of a school extracurricular organization. Although *Pierson* and *Scheuer* concerned law enforcement, Justice White's opinion for the Court had no trouble concluding that qualified immunity was available to school board members as well:

> Liability for damages for every action which is found subsequently to have been violative of a student's constitutional rights and to have caused compensable injury would unfairly impose upon the school decisionmaker the burden of mistakes made in good faith in the course of exercising his discretion within the scope of his official duties. School board members, among other duties, must judge whether there have been violations of school regulations and, if so, the appropriate sanctions for the violations. Denying any measure of immunity in these circumstances "would contribute not to principled and fearless decision-making but to intimidation." *Pierson.* The imposition of monetary costs for mistakes which were not unreasonable in the light of all the circumstances would undoubtedly deter even the most conscientious school decisionmaker from exercising his judgment independently, forcefully, and in a manner best serving the long-term interest of the school and the students. The most capable candidates for school board positions might be deterred from seeking office if heavy burdens upon their private resources from monetary liability were a likely prospect during their tenure.

The Court also made explicit an important limitation on the scope of qualified immunity by stating that "immunity from damages does not ordinarily bar equitable relief as well."

The Court applied the following qualified immunity standard to school officials' conduct:

> [A] school board member is not immune from liability for damages under § 1983 if he knew or reasonably should have known that the action he took within his sphere of official responsibility would violate the constitutional rights of the student affected, or if he took the action with the malicious intention to cause a deprivation of constitutional rights or other injury to the student.

The Court characterized this standard as consisting of both a "subjective" and an "objective" component. In a partial dissent, Justice Powell, joined by Chief Justice Burger and Justices Blackmun and Rehnquist, took issue with the "objective" component, whose inclusion he believed represented a significant change:

> This harsh standard, requiring knowledge of what is characterized as "settled, indisputable law," leaves little substance to the doctrine of qualified immunity. The Court's decision appears to rest on an unwarranted assumption as to what lay school officials know or can know about the law and constitutional rights. These officials will now act at the peril of some judge or jury subsequently finding that a good-faith belief as to the applicable law was mistaken and hence actionable.

The standard applied in *Wood*, like that in *Scheuer*, would not last long, but the confinement of immunity to claims for damages and the extension of qualified immunity to officials other than state law enforcement have stuck.

Butz v. Economou, 438 U.S. 478 (1978), further extended the reach of the doctrine by holding that federal officers enjoy the same qualified immunity as—but no more than—the immunity applicable to constitutional claims against state officers:

> [I]n the absence of congressional direction to the contrary, there is no basis for according to federal officials a higher degree of immunity from liability when sued for a constitutional infringement as authorized by *Bivens* than is accorded state officials when sued for the identical violation under § 1983. The constitutional injuries made actionable by § 1983 are of no greater magnitude than those for which federal officials may be responsible. The pressures and uncertainties facing decisionmakers in state government are little if at all different from those affecting federal officials. We see no sense in holding a state governor liable but immunizing the head of a federal department; in holding the administrator of a federal hospital immune where the superintendent of a state hospital would be liable; in protecting the warden of a federal prison where the warden of a state prison would be vulnerable; or in distinguishing between state and federal police participating in the same investigation. Surely, federal officials should enjoy no greater zone of protection when they violate federal constitutional rules than do state officers.

Justice Rehnquist, joined by Chief Justice Burger and Justices Stewart and Stevens, dissented, arguing mainly on the basis of history that absolute immunity was the more appropriate rule. Despite the Court's recent retrenchment regarding the scope of *Bivens* (Chapter 2), the Court has continued to apply the same qualified immunity standard (and, indeed, all the defenses and limits pertaining to individual liability) to both *Bivens* and § 1983 actions. After *Wood* and *Butz*, any government official, whether federal, state, or local, who is sued for constitutional violations and who is not entitled to absolute immunity can invoke qualified immunity.

Meanwhile, the Court had become dissatisfied with the qualified immunity test it had developed and decided to modify it substantially, setting the doctrine on its present course.

Harlow v. Fitzgerald
457 U.S. 800 (1982)

■ *Justice* POWELL *delivered the opinion of the Court.* . . .

In this suit for civil damages petitioners Bryce Harlow and Alexander Butterfield are alleged to have participated in a conspiracy to violate the constitutional and statutory rights of the respondent A. Ernest Fitzgerald. Respondent avers that petitioners entered the conspiracy in their capacities as senior White House aides to former President Richard M. Nixon. . . .

[In 1968, respondent Fitzgerald, an Air Force management analyst, testified before a congressional subcommittee about cost overruns and unexpected technical difficulties concerning the development of a particular airplane. In January 1970, a year after President Nixon assumed office, Fitzgerald was dismissed from his job during a departmental reorganization. Fitzgerald sued various administration officials, claiming his termination was unconstitutional retaliation for his testimony. After motion practice and extensive discovery, three defendants remained: two White House aides (Harlow and Butterfield) and former President Nixon (whose case the Supreme Court decided separately).]

Together with their codefendant Richard Nixon, petitioners Harlow and Butterfield moved for summary judgment on February 12, 1980. . . . The court found that genuine issues of disputed fact remained for resolution at trial. . . .

The resolution of immunity questions inherently requires a balance between the evils inevitable in any available alternative. In situations of abuse of office, an action for damages may offer the only realistic avenue for vindication of constitutional guarantees. *See Bivens.* It is this recognition that has required the denial of absolute immunity to most public officers. At the same time, however, it cannot be disputed seriously that claims frequently run against the innocent as well as the guilty—at a cost not only to the defendant officials, but to society as a whole. These social costs include the expenses of litigation, the diversion of official energy from pressing public issues, and the deterrence of able citizens from acceptance of public office. Finally, there is the danger that fear of being sued will "dampen the ardor of all but the most resolute, or the most irresponsible [public officials], in the unflinching discharge of their duties."

In identifying qualified immunity as the best attainable accommodation of competing values [in prior cases] we relied on the assumption that this standard would permit "[i]nsubstantial lawsuits [to] be quickly terminated." Yet petitioners advance persuasive arguments that the dismissal of insubstantial lawsuits without trial—a factor presupposed in the balance of competing interests struck by our prior cases—requires an adjustment of the "good faith" standard established by our decisions.

Qualified or "good faith" immunity is an affirmative defense that must be pleaded by a defendant official. Decisions of this Court have established that the "good faith" defense has both an "objective" and a "subjective" aspect. The objective element involves a presumptive knowledge of and respect for "basic, unquestioned constitutional rights." *Wood v. Strickland*. The subjective component refers to "permissible intentions." *Ibid.* Characteristically the Court has defined these elements by identifying the circumstances in which qualified immunity would not be available. Referring both to the objective and subjective elements, we have held that qualified immunity would be defeated if an official "knew or reasonably should have known that the action he took within his sphere of official responsibility would violate the constitutional rights of the [plaintiff], or if he took the action with the malicious intention to cause a deprivation of constitutional rights or other injury. . . ." *Ibid.*

The subjective element of the good-faith defense frequently has proved incompatible with our admonition . . . that insubstantial claims should not proceed to trial. Rule 56 of the Federal Rules of Civil Procedure provides that disputed questions of fact ordinarily may not be decided on motions for summary judgment. And an official's subjective good faith has been considered to be a question of fact that some courts have regarded as inherently requiring resolution by a jury.

In the context of [our] attempted balancing of competing values, it now is clear that substantial costs attend the litigation of the subjective good faith of government officials. Not only are there the general costs of subjecting officials to the risks of trial—distraction of officials from their governmental duties, inhibition of discretionary action, and deterrence of able people from public service. There are special costs to "subjective" inquiries of this kind. Immunity generally is available only to officials performing discretionary functions. In contrast with the thought processes accompanying "ministerial" tasks, the judgments surrounding discretionary action almost inevitably are influenced by the decisionmaker's experiences, values, and emotions. These variables explain in part why questions of subjective intent so rarely can be decided by summary judgment. Yet they also frame a background in which there often is no clear end to the relevant evidence. Judicial inquiry into subjective motivation therefore may entail broad-ranging discovery and the deposing of numerous persons, including an official's professional colleagues. Inquiries of this kind can be peculiarly disruptive of effective government.

Consistently with the balance at which we aimed in [prior cases], we conclude today that bare allegations of malice should not suffice to subject government officials either to the costs of trial or to the burdens of broad-reaching discovery. We therefore hold that government officials performing discretionary functions generally are shielded from liability for civil damages insofar as their conduct does not violate clearly established statutory or constitutional rights of which a reasonable person would have known.

Reliance on the objective reasonableness of an official's conduct, as measured by reference to clearly established law, should avoid excessive disruption of government and permit the resolution of many insubstantial claims on summary judgment. On summary judgment, the judge appropriately may determine, not only the currently applicable law, but whether that law was clearly established at the time an action occurred. If the law at that time was not clearly established, an official could not reasonably be expected to anticipate subsequent legal developments, nor could he fairly be said to "know" that the law forbade conduct not previously identified as unlawful. Until this threshold immunity question is resolved, discovery should not be allowed. If the law was clearly established, the immunity defense ordinarily should fail, since a reasonably competent public official should know the law governing his conduct....

By defining the limits of qualified immunity essentially in objective terms, we provide no license to lawless conduct. The public interest in deterrence of unlawful conduct and in compensation of victims remains protected by a test that focuses on the objective legal reasonableness of an official's acts. Where an official could be expected to know that certain conduct would violate statutory or constitutional rights, he should be made to hesitate; and a person who suffers injury caused by such conduct may have a cause of action. But where an official's duties legitimately require action in which clearly established rights are not implicated, the public interest may be better served by action taken "with independence and without fear of consequences." *Pierson v. Ray.* ...

■ Justice BRENNAN, *with whom Justice* MARSHALL *and Justice* BLACKMUN *join, concurring.*

I agree with the substantive standard announced by the Court today.... I write separately only to note that given this standard, it seems inescapable to me that some measure of discovery may sometimes be required to determine exactly what a public-official defendant did "know" at the time of his actions....

[Separate concurring statement of Brennan, White, Marshall, and Blackmun, JJ.; concurring statement by Rehnquist, J.; and dissenting opinion of Burger, C.J., omitted. None concerned the standard for qualified immunity.]

Notes and Questions

1. According to *Scheuer* and *Harlow*, what interests does qualified immunity serve? What are the doctrine's costs? Has the Court struck the right balance between these competing considerations?

2. What part of the test for qualified immunity did *Harlow* change and why?

3. Were there any interests the Court overlooked in *Harlow* that would have counseled in favor of retaining the subjective component of the standard? Is ignorance of the law worse than malice?

4. Does Harlow's modification of the doctrine benefit civil rights plaintiffs or defendants? In what ways?

5. In this malleable area of law, we find several about-faces and false trails.

   a. Recall that *Scheuer* envisioned qualified immunity as an issue for trial. Now the Court seems to want to shield defendants even from discovery. Does this shift reflect a broader change in the Court's understanding of the purpose of qualified immunity, or just a practical concern about the implementation of the old standard?

   b. After the haggling over the standard in *Wood*, why do you think the Justices all agreed to the modification in *Harlow*? In particular, how do you account for the views of the dissenters in *Wood*, who in *Harlow* agreed to jettison the only part of the test they wanted in *Wood* while retaining only the part of the test to which they objected?

   c. Do the majority and Justice Brennan completely agree about the objective nature of the standard? As we'll see, the standard evolved to eliminate any avenue for discovery along the lines suggested in Justice Brennan's concurrence.

   d. After *Harlow*, the Court let *Scheuer's* suggestion of a variable approach to the standard for immunity recede into history. The modern qualified immunity inquiry as articulated in *Harlow* is applied the same way regardless of the scope of the defendant officer's discretion.

6. As noted, one of the defendants whom the plaintiff sued for his termination was President Nixon. In a companion case to *Harlow*, *Nixon v. Fitzgerald*, 457 U.S. 731 (1982), the Court held that the president enjoys absolute immunity for acts within the scope of his office.

Note: Allocation of the "Burden" in Qualified Immunity Analysis

The Supreme Court has held that "[s]ince qualified immunity is a defense, the burden of pleading it rests with the defendant." *Gomez v. Toledo*, 446 U.S. 635, 640 (1980).

But in an oft-quoted gloss on the qualified immunity standard, the Supreme Court stated in *Malley v. Briggs*, 475 U.S. 335, 341 (1986), that qualified immunity protects "all but the plainly incompetent or those who knowingly violate the law." Where does that characterization suggest the burden ought to lie? Does *Malley* accurately summarize *Harlow*, or does this formulation represent yet another strengthening of immunity?

In contrast to the burden of *pleading* immunity, which *Gomez* addressed, the burden of *showing whether it applies once invoked* has been the subject of dispute. As Professor Alexander Reinert catalogues, some circuits place the burden on the defendant, others allocate it to the plaintiff, and still others employ a burden-shifting approach. *See* Alexander A. Reinert, *Qualified Immunity at Trial*, 93 Notre

Dame L. Rev. 2065, 2071 (2018). In practice, although the defendant has the burden to raise the defense, per *Gomez*, once it is asserted, the plaintiff must work hard to overcome it. As the Court has applied the *Harlow* standard increasingly strictly over the past few decades, plaintiffs have, in a functional sense, come to bear the burden of defeating qualified immunity whenever the defendants invoke it.

2. DEFINING "CLEARLY ESTABLISHED LAW"

Although *Harlow*'s structure for qualified immunity analysis has remained constant since 1982, the Court's application of that analysis has become increasingly defendant-friendly over the years. The main driver of this trend is the Court's articulation of what it means for the law to be "clearly established"—a question that the Court began to address in the next main case, *Anderson v. Creighton*. *Anderson* also provided an important clarification about the application of the qualified immunity standard where the constitutional right at issue is measured by a government actor's "reasonableness." And *Anderson* reveals important assumptions on the Justices' part about how often law enforcement officers are protected by "indemnification"—an arrangement in which one party agrees to cover another's losses. As we'll see when we revisit the concept of indemnification in Section B.6, the question whether government employers commonly indemnify their employees against legal liability has important implications for whether qualified immunity is needed to perform its putative functions.

Anderson v. Creighton
483 U.S. 635 (1987)

▧ *Justice SCALIA delivered the opinion of the Court. . . .*

Petitioner Russell Anderson is an agent of the Federal Bureau of Investigation. On November 11, 1983, Anderson and other state and federal law enforcement officers conducted a warrantless search of the home of respondents, the Creighton family. The search was conducted because Anderson believed that Vadaain Dixon, a man suspected of a bank robbery committed earlier that day, might be found there. He was not. [The Creightons sued Anderson.] . . .

When government officials abuse their offices, "action[s] for damages may offer the only realistic avenue for vindication of constitutional guarantees." *Harlow v. Fitzgerald*. On the other hand, permitting damages suits against government officials can entail substantial social costs, including the risk that fear of personal monetary liability and harassing litigation will unduly inhibit officials in the discharge of their duties. Our cases have accommodated these conflicting concerns by generally providing government officials performing discretionary functions with a qualified immunity, shielding them from civil damages liability as long as their actions could reasonably have been thought consistent with the rights they are alleged to have violated. Somewhat more concretely, whether an official protected by qualified immunity may be held personally liable for an allegedly unlawful official action generally turns on the "objective legal reasonableness" of the action, assessed in light of the legal rules that were "clearly established" at the time it was taken, *Harlow*.

The operation of this standard, however, depends substantially upon the level of generality at which the relevant "legal rule" is to be identified. For example, the right to due process of law is quite clearly established by the Due Process Clause, and thus there is a sense in which any action that violates that Clause (no matter how unclear it may be that the particular action is a violation) violates a clearly established right. Much the same could be said of any other constitutional or statutory violation. But if the test of "clearly established law" were to be applied at this level of generality, it would bear no relationship to the "objective legal reasonableness" that is the touchstone of *Harlow*. Plaintiffs would be able to convert the rule of qualified immunity that our cases plainly establish into a rule of virtually unqualified liability simply by alleging violation of extremely abstract rights. *Harlow* would be transformed from a guarantee of immunity into a rule of pleading. Such an approach, in sum, would destroy "the balance that our cases strike between the interests in vindication of citizens' constitutional rights and in public officials' effective performance of their duties," by making it impossible for officials "reasonably [to] anticipate when their conduct may give rise to liability for damages." It should not be surprising, therefore, that our cases establish that the right the official is alleged to have violated must have been "clearly established" in a more particularized, and hence more relevant, sense: The contours of the right must be sufficiently clear that a reasonable official would understand that what he is doing violates that right. This is not to say that an official action is protected by qualified immunity unless the very action in question has previously been held unlawful, but it is to say that in the light of pre-existing law the unlawfulness must be apparent.

Anderson contends that the Court of Appeals misapplied these principles. We agree. The Court of Appeals' brief discussion of qualified immunity consisted of little more than an assertion that a general right Anderson was alleged to have violated—the right to be free from warrantless searches of one's home unless the searching officers have probable cause and there are exigent circumstances—was clearly established. The Court of Appeals specifically refused to consider the argument that it was not clearly established that the circumstances with which Anderson was confronted did not constitute probable cause and exigent circumstances. The previous discussion should make clear that this refusal was erroneous. It simply does not follow immediately from the conclusion that it was firmly established that warrantless searches not supported by probable cause and exigent circumstances violate the Fourth Amendment that Anderson's search was objectively legally unreasonable. We have recognized that it is inevitable that law enforcement officials will in some cases reasonably but mistakenly conclude that probable cause is present, and we have indicated that in such cases those officials—like other officials who act in ways they reasonably believe to be lawful—should not be held personally liable. The same is true of their conclusions regarding exigent circumstances.

It follows from what we have said that the determination whether it was objectively legally reasonable to conclude that a given search was supported by probable cause or exigent circumstances will often require examination of the information possessed by the searching officials. But contrary to the Creightons' assertion, this does not reintroduce into qualified immunity analysis the inquiry into officials' subjective intent that Harlow sought to minimize. The relevant question in this case, for example, is the objective (albeit fact-specific) question whether a reasonable officer could have believed Anderson's warrantless search to be lawful, in light of clearly established law and the information the searching officers possessed. Anderson's subjective beliefs about the search are irrelevant.

The principles of qualified immunity that we reaffirm today require that Anderson be permitted to argue that he is entitled to summary judgment on the ground that, in light of the clearly established principles governing warrantless searches, he could, as a matter of law, reasonably have believed that the search of the Creightons' home was lawful.[3] . . .

[T]he Creightons argue that it is inappropriate to give officials alleged to have violated the Fourth Amendment—and thus necessarily to have unreasonably searched or seized—the protection of a qualified immunity intended only to protect reasonable official action. It is not possible, that is, to say that one "reasonably" acted unreasonably. The short answer to this argument is that it is foreclosed by the fact that we have previously extended qualified immunity to officials who were alleged to have violated the Fourth Amendment. Even if that were not so, however, we would still find the argument unpersuasive. Its surface appeal is attributable to the circumstance that the Fourth Amendment's guarantees have been expressed in terms of "unreasonable" searches and seizures. Had an equally serviceable term, such as "undue" searches and seizures been employed, what might be termed the "reasonably unreasonable" argument against application of Harlow to the Fourth Amendment would not be available—just as it would be available against application of Harlow to the Fifth Amendment if the term "reasonable process of law" had been employed there. The fact is that, regardless of the terminology used, the precise content of most of the Constitution's civil-liberties guarantees rests upon an assessment of what accommodation between governmental need and individual freedom is reasonable, so that the Creightons' objection, if it has any substance, applies to the application of Harlow generally. We have frequently observed, and our many cases on the point amply demonstrate,

---

3. The Creightons argue that the qualified immunity doctrine need not be expanded to apply to the circumstances of this case, because the Federal Government and various state governments have established programs through which they reimburse officials for expenses and liability incurred in suits challenging actions they have taken in their official capacities. Because our holding today does not extend official qualified immunity beyond the bounds articulated in Harlow and our subsequent cases, an argument as to why we should not do so is beside the point. Moreover, even assuming that conscientious officials care only about their personal liability and not the liability of the government they serve, the Creightons do not and could not reasonably contend that the programs to which they refer make reimbursement sufficiently certain and generally available to justify reconsideration of the balance struck in Harlow . . . .

the difficulty of determining whether particular searches or seizures comport with the Fourth Amendment. Law enforcement officers whose judgments in making these difficult determinations are objectively legally reasonable should no more be held personally liable in damages than should officials making analogous determinations in other areas of law. . . .

■ *Justice* STEVENS, *with whom Justice* BRENNAN *and Justice* MARSHALL *join, dissenting*. . . .

In this Court, Anderson has not argued that any relevant rule of law—whether the probable-cause requirement or the exigent-circumstances exception to the warrant requirement—was not "clearly established" in November 1983. Rather, he argues that a competent officer might have concluded that the particular set of facts he faced did constitute "probable cause" and "exigent circumstances," and that his own reasonable belief that the conduct engaged in was within the law suffices to establish immunity. But the factual predicate for Anderson's argument is not found in the Creightons' complaint, but rather in the affidavits that he has filed in support of his motion for summary judgment. Obviously, the respondents must be given an opportunity to have discovery to test the accuracy and completeness of the factual basis for the immunity claim. . . .

[Additionally,] this Court has decided to apply a double standard of reasonableness in damages actions against federal agents who are alleged to have violated an innocent citizen's Fourth Amendment rights. By double standard I mean a standard that affords a law enforcement official two layers of insulation from liability or other adverse consequence, such as suppression of evidence. . . . [T]he Court seems prepared and even anxious in this case to remove any requirement that the officer must obey the Fourth Amendment when entering a private home. I remain convinced that in a suit for damages as well as in a hearing on a motion to suppress evidence, "an official search and seizure cannot be both 'unreasonable' and 'reasonable' at the same time." . . .

Unquestionably, there is, and always has been, some uncertainty in the application of the probable-cause standard to particular cases. It is nevertheless a standard that has survived the test of time both in England and in America. . . . Indeed, it is worth emphasizing that the probable-cause standard itself recognizes the fair leeway that law enforcement officers must have in carrying out their dangerous work. The concept of probable cause leaves room for mistakes, provided always that they are mistakes that could have been made by a reasonable officer. I find nothing in this Court's new standard that provides the officer with any more guidance . . . .

[U]ntil now the Court has not found intolerable the use of a probable-cause standard to protect the police officer from exposure to liability simply because his reasonable conduct is subsequently shown to have been mistaken. Today, however, the Court counts the law enforcement interest twice and the individual's privacy interest only once.

The Court's double-counting approach reflects understandable sympathy for the plight of the officer and an overriding interest in unfettered law enforcement. It ascribes a far lesser importance to the privacy interest of innocent citizens than did the Framers of the Fourth Amendment. The importance of that interest and the possible magnitude of its invasion are both illustrated by the facts of this case.[21]

The home of an innocent family was invaded by several officers without a warrant, without the owner's consent, with a substantial show of force, and with blunt expressions of disrespect for the law and for the rights of the family members. . . . I see no reason why the family's interest in the security of its own home should be accorded a lesser weight than the Government's interest in carrying out an invasion that was unlawful. Arguably, if the Government considers it important not to discourage such conduct, it should provide indemnity to its officers. Preferably, however, it should furnish the kind of training for its law enforcement agents that would entirely eliminate the necessity for the Court to distinguish between the conduct that a competent officer considers reasonable and the conduct that the Constitution deems reasonable. . . .

---

21. The Court of Appeals described the search of respondents' home in some detail. Its opinion reads, in part, as follows [taking the facts in the light most favorable to the Creightons]:

". . . On the night of November 11, 1983, Sarisse and Robert Creighton and their three young daughters were spending a quiet evening at their home when a spotlight suddenly flashed through their front window. Mr. Creighton opened the door and was confronted by several uniformed and plain clothes officers, many of them brandishing shotguns. All of the officers were white; the Creightons are black. . . . [O]ne of the officers told him to 'keep his hands in sight' while the other officers rushed through the door. When Mr. Creighton asked if they had a search warrant, one of the officers told him, 'We don't have a search warrant [and] don't need [one]; you watch too much TV.'

"Mr. Creighton asked the officers to put their guns away because his children were frightened, but the officers refused. Mrs. Creighton awoke to the shrieking of her children, and was confronted by an officer who pointed a shotgun at her. She allegedly observed the officers yelling at her three daughters to 'sit their damn asses down and stop screaming.' . . .

"One of the officers asked Mr. Creighton if he had a red and silver car. As Mr. Creighton led the officers downstairs to his garage, where his maroon Oldsmobile was parked, one of the officers punched him in the face, knocking him to the ground, and causing him to bleed from the mouth and the forehead. . . . The officer claims that Mr. Creighton attempted to grab his shotgun, even though Mr. Creighton was not a suspect in any crime and had no contraband in his home or on his person. Shaunda, the Creighton's ten-year-old daughter, witnessed the assault and screamed for her mother to come help. She claims that one of the officers then hit her. . . .

"During the melee, family members and friends began arriving at the Creighton's home. Mrs. Creighton claims that she was embarrassed in front of her family and friends by the invasion of their home and their rough treatment as if they were suspects in a major crime. . . . The officers did not discover the allegedly unspecified 'fugitive' at the Creightons' home or any evidence whatsoever that he had been there or that the Creightons were involved in any type of criminal activity. Nonetheless, the officers then arrested and handcuffed Mr. Creighton for obstruction of justice and brought him to the police station where he was jailed overnight, then released without being charged."

Notes and Questions

1. *Anderson* has come to be known for two important principles: the Court's requirement that qualified immunity be analyzed at the appropriate "level of generality" and what the dissent describes as the "double standard of reasonableness." Which do you think has been more important to the development of an increasingly officer-protective standard for qualified immunity, and why?

2. There's a surface appeal to both sides of the "double counting" debate because each rests on a intuitively reasonable assumption—for the majority, the notion that qualified immunity protects reasonable mistakes no matter what the underlying constitutional standard; for the dissent, the proposition that "reasonableness" is already built into the Fourth Amendment standard and so no further examination of "reasonableness" is necessary or appropriate. Is one of these premises more justifiable than the other? Is it a question of whether the Court prefers consistency in Fourth Amendment doctrine as opposed to consistency in qualified immunity doctrine? Or does the choice just depend on the Justices' ideological leanings?

3. Figure 4.1 illustrates the majority's logic in *Anderson* regarding reasonableness: Because the solid and dashed lines represent different distinctions (the former, between constitutional conduct and unconstitutional conduct; the latter, between clearly established constitutional violations and conduct that is not a clearly established violation), they should not be collapsed into a single line in Fourth Amendment cases just because of the happenstance that the substantive constitutional standard and the qualified immunity standard both use the word "reasonable." Rather, according to the *Anderson* majority, the goal of qualified immunity is to provide an extra layer of protection from liability for officers who make a reasonable mistake as to the constitutionality of their conduct—no matter what right they are alleged to have violated.

Figure 4.1: How qualified immunity provides an extra layer of protection for defendants

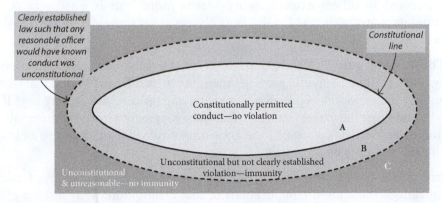

A: An action that is constitutionally permissible
B: An unconstitutional action for which officer receives qualified immunity
C: An unconstitutional action for which officer lacks qualified immunity

Immunity is denied only if the defendant's conduct falls not just outside the solid interior border (the line drawn by the Constitution itself) but also outside the dashed outer border (the extra layer of protection provided by qualified immunity). Thus, an act falling between the two lines (represented by point "B") is unconstitutional, yet the defendant is immune from suit for damages.

How would the dissenters redraw the diagram to support their view? Does illustrating these positions persuade you to one position or the other?

4. In what turned into a reprise of the *Anderson* debate over the "double standard of reasonableness," the Court in *Saucier v. Katz*, 533 U.S. 194 (2001), considered whether Fourth Amendment excessive force claims—which, like search and seizure claims, are evaluated based on the officer's reasonableness—are subject to the same qualified immunity analysis as other types of claims. Relying on *Anderson*, the Court answered that question in the affirmative:

> Qualified immunity operates in this case . . . just as it does in others, to protect officers from the sometimes "hazy border between excessive and acceptable force," and to ensure that before they are subjected to suit, officers are on notice their conduct is unlawful. . . .
>
> The deference owed officers facing suits for alleged excessive force is not different in some qualitative respect from the probable-cause inquiry in *Anderson*. Officers can have reasonable, but mistaken, beliefs as to the facts establishing the existence of probable cause or exigent circumstances, for example, and in those situations courts will not hold that they have violated the Constitution. Yet, even if a court were to hold that the officer violated the Fourth Amendment by conducting an unreasonable, warrantless search, *Anderson* still operates to grant officers immunity for reasonable mistakes as to the legality of their actions. The same analysis is applicable in excessive force cases, where in addition to the deference officers receive on the underlying constitutional claim, qualified immunity can apply in the event the mistaken belief was reasonable.

Concurring in the judgment only, Justice Ginsburg, joined by Justices Stevens and Breyer, disagreed with the majority on the standard, objecting that "[t]he two-part test today's decision imposes holds large potential to confuse."

5. Why are the facts in *Anderson* so much more important to the dissent than to the majority? As we continue our study of qualified immunity, notice which side of the debate—the more officer-protective side or the side more interested in officer accountability—leans more heavily on the facts. Do you detect any patterns? Do the facts always assist one side? What role does race play?

6. The dissent argues, "[I]f the Government considers it important not to discourage such conduct, it should provide indemnity to its officers." Would that wholly answer the majority's concerns about protecting officers? If not, why not? If so, why shouldn't the Court just leave the policy judgment regarding indemnification to each federal, state, or local government rather than imposing a blanket rule of immunity on all of them?

7. In footnote 3, the majority makes an assumption about the availability of indemnification. What are the implications of that assumption? Why did the plaintiffs argue that this question is an important one? If the Court is empirically wrong that indemnification is rare, should qualified immunity be reconsidered? (Spoiler alert: As we'll see in Section B.6, below, a recent empirical study contradicts the Court's assumption in footnote 3.)

8. The analysis in *Anderson* shows how the question of whether the conduct was constitutional and the question whether any violation was "clearly established" are distinct from each other. Some courts have, further, broken down the "clearly established" inquiry into two subparts: first, whether the rule of constitutional law to be applied is itself "clearly established" (rather than, for instance, a rule that is ambiguous, novel, or debatable), and second, whether the specific conduct at issue clearly violates that rule. *See, e.g., Jennings v. Jones*, 499 F.3d 2, 10 (1st Cir. 2007). Analytically, this bifurcation makes sense, as is it possible for an official to receive qualified immunity *either* because the rule of law was unclear *or* because the law, however clear, did not clearly apply to the specific conduct challenged.

However, most courts, including the Supreme Court, have in recent years characterized the "clearly established" inquiry as a unitary one, as in this recent formulation: "An officer cannot be said to have violated a clearly established right unless the right's contours were sufficiently definite that any reasonable official in the defendant's shoes would have understood that he was violating it." *Kisela v. Hughes*, 138 S. Ct. 1148, 1153 (2018) (per curiam) (citation and internal quotation marks omitted). Note that this statement encompasses both the clarity question ("unless the right's contours were sufficiently definite") and the question of the law's applicability to the conduct at issue ("that any reasonable official in the defendant's shoes would have understood that he was violating it").

It is important to recognize *both* how courts frame the "clearly established" question *and* how it may be applied to shield the defendant in either of two ways—based on lack of clarity in the law or based on doubts about the law's application to the circumstance at issue.

9. What is the Court's precise holding on the "level of generality" issue in *Anderson*? What guidance does the Court provide regarding how to define a right at the "more particularized" level the Court requires? This is a question with which courts continue to struggle, as we'll see.

10. What is the dissent's answer to the majority's "level of generality" holding? Does the dissent articulate a contrary rule? If so, what is it? If not, what do you think it should be? What are the choices? Or is the debate less about the rule than its application?

* * *

The level-of-generality issue has continued to vex and divide jurists at all levels of the federal judiciary. At the Supreme Court level, the Court has revisited the issue repeatedly. In the next case, *Hope v. Pelzer*, the Court cautioned against insisting that plaintiffs identify prior cases with similar facts, and also suggested that some violations are so obvious that even general descriptions of a right can suffice to overcome qualified immunity. Following *Hope*, however, the Court has repeatedly sent a contrary message to lower courts by reversing decisions that denied immunity based on too general a description of the right at issue and adding modifiers and glosses to *Harlow* and *Anderson* suggesting that the standard, though retaining its structure, has become stricter in application.

After reading *Hope* and a more recent, contrasting case from the Court, we'll examine lower courts' struggle with the level-of-generality question.

Hope v. Pelzer
536 U.S. 730 (2002)

▪ *Justice* STEVENS *delivered the opinion of the Court.* . . .

In 1995, Alabama was the only State that followed the practice of chaining inmates to one another in work squads. It was also the only State that handcuffed prisoners to "hitching posts" if they either refused to work or otherwise disrupted work squads.[1] . . .

On June 7, 1995, Hope . . . took a nap during the morning bus ride to the chain gang's worksite, and when it arrived he was less than prompt in responding to an order to get off the bus. An exchange of vulgar remarks led to a wrestling match with a guard. Four other guards intervened, subdued Hope, handcuffed him, placed him in leg irons and transported him back to the prison where he was put on the hitching post. The guards made him take off his shirt, and he remained shirtless all day while the sun burned his skin. He remained attached to the post for approximately seven hours. During this 7-hour period, he was given water only once or twice and was given no bathroom breaks. At one point, a guard taunted Hope about his thirst. According to Hope's affidavit: "[The guard] first gave water to some dogs, then brought the water cooler closer to me, removed its lid, and kicked the cooler over, spilling the water onto the ground."

[Hope sued three prison guards under § 1983, and the district court granted qualified immunity.] The United States Court of Appeals for the Eleventh Circuit affirmed. . . . [A]pplying Circuit precedent concerning qualified immunity, the court stated that " 'the federal law by which the government official's conduct should be evaluated must be preexisting, obvious and mandatory,' " and established, not by " 'abstractions,' " but by cases that are " 'materially similar' " to the facts in the case in front of us. . . .

" '[T]he unnecessary and wanton infliction of pain . . . constitutes cruel and unusual punishment forbidden by the Eighth Amendment.' " We have said that "[a]mong 'unnecessary and wanton' inflictions of pain are those that are 'totally without penological justification.' " In making this determination in the context of prison conditions, we must ascertain whether the officials involved acted with "deliberate indifference" to the inmates' health or safety. We may infer the existence of this subjective state of mind from the fact that the risk of harm is obvious.

As the facts are alleged by Hope, the Eighth Amendment violation is obvious. Any safety concerns had long since abated by the time petitioner was handcuffed to the hitching post because Hope had already been subdued, handcuffed, placed in leg irons, and transported back to the prison. He was

---

1. . . . . [T]he hitching post is a horizontal bar " 'made of sturdy, nonflexible material,' " placed between 45 and 57 inches from the ground. Inmates are handcuffed to the hitching post in a standing position and remain standing the entire time they are placed on the post. Most inmates are shackled to the hitching post with their two hands relatively close together and at face level.

separated from his work squad and not given the opportunity to return to work. Despite the clear lack of an emergency situation, the respondents knowingly subjected him to a substantial risk of physical harm, to unnecessary pain caused by the handcuffs and the restricted position of confinement for a 7-hour period, to unnecessary exposure to the heat of the sun, to prolonged thirst and taunting, and to a deprivation of bathroom breaks that created a risk of particular discomfort and humiliation. The use of the hitching post under these circumstances violated the "basic concept underlying the Eighth Amendment[, which] is nothing less than the dignity of man." This punitive treatment amounts to gratuitous infliction of "wanton and unnecessary" pain that our precedent clearly prohibits.

Despite their participation in this constitutionally impermissible conduct, respondents may nevertheless be shielded from liability for civil damages if their actions did not violate "clearly established statutory or constitutional rights of which a reasonable person would have known." *Harlow*. In assessing whether the Eighth Amendment violation here met the *Harlow* test, the Court of Appeals required that the facts of previous cases be "'materially similar' to Hope's situation." This rigid gloss on the qualified immunity standard . . . is not consistent with our cases.

As we have explained, qualified immunity operates "to ensure that before they are subjected to suit, officers are on notice their conduct is unlawful." For a constitutional right to be clearly established, its contours "must be sufficiently clear that a reasonable official would understand that what he is doing violates that right. This is not to say that an official action is protected by qualified immunity unless the very action in question has previously been held unlawful, but it is to say that in the light of pre-existing law the unlawfulness must be apparent." *Anderson*. . . .

[O]fficials can still be on notice that their conduct violates established law even in novel factual circumstances. Indeed, [we have previously] expressly rejected a requirement that previous cases be "fundamentally similar." Although earlier cases involving "fundamentally similar" facts can provide especially strong support for a conclusion that the law is clearly established, they are not necessary to such a finding. The same is true of cases with "materially similar" facts. Accordingly, . . . the salient question that the Court of Appeals ought to have asked is whether the state of the law in 1995 gave respondents fair warning that their alleged treatment of Hope was unconstitutional. It is to this question that we now turn.

The use of the hitching post as alleged by Hope "unnecessar[ily] and wanton[ly] inflicted pain," and thus was a clear violation of the Eighth Amendment. Arguably, the violation was so obvious that our own Eighth Amendment cases gave respondents fair warning that their conduct violated the Constitution. Regardless, in light of binding Eleventh Circuit precedent, an Alabama Department of Corrections (ADOC) regulation, and a DOJ report informing the ADOC of the constitutional infirmity in its use of the hitching post, we readily conclude that the respondents' conduct violated "clearly established statutory or constitutional rights of which a reasonable person would have known." *Harlow*.

Cases decided by the Court of Appeals for the Fifth Circuit before 1981 are binding precedent in the Eleventh Circuit today. In one of those cases, decided in 1974, the Court of Appeals reviewed a District Court decision finding a number of constitutional violations in the administration of Mississippi's prisons. *Gates v. Collier*, 501 F.2d 1291. That opinion squarely held that several of those "forms of corporal punishment run afoul of the Eighth Amendment [and] offend contemporary concepts of decency, human dignity, and precepts of civilization which we profess to possess." Among those forms of punishment were "handcuffing inmates to the fence and to cells for long periods of time, . . . and forcing inmates to stand, sit or lie on crates, stumps, or otherwise maintain awkward positions for prolonged periods." The fact that *Gates* found several forms of punishment impermissible does not, as respondents suggest, lessen the force of its holding with respect to handcuffing inmates to cells or fences for long periods of time. Nor, for the purpose of providing fair notice to reasonable officers administering punishment for past misconduct, is there any reason to draw a constitutional distinction between a practice of handcuffing an inmate to a fence for prolonged periods and handcuffing him to a hitching post for seven hours. The Court of Appeals' conclusion to the contrary exposes the danger of a rigid, overreliance on factual similarity. . . . In light of *Gates*, the unlawfulness of the alleged conduct should have been apparent to the respondents.

The reasoning, though not the holding, in a case decided by the Eleventh Circuit in 1987 sent the same message to reasonable officers in that Circuit. In *Ort v. White*, 813 F.2d 318, the Court of Appeals held that an officer's temporary denials of drinking water to an inmate who repeatedly refused to do his share of the work assigned to a farm squad "should not be viewed as punishment in the strict sense, but instead as necessary coercive measures undertaken to obtain compliance with a reasonable prison rule, i.e., the requirement that all inmates perform their assigned farm squad duties." "The officer's clear motive was to encourage Ort to comply with the rules and to do the work required of him, after which he would receive the water like everyone else." The court cautioned, however, that a constitutional violation might have been present "if later, once back at the prison, officials had decided to deny [Ort] water as punishment for his refusal to work." So too would a violation have occurred if the method of coercion reached a point of severity such that the recalcitrant prisoner's health was at risk. Although the facts of the case are not identical, *Ort*'s premise is that "physical abuse directed at [a] prisoner after he terminate[s] his resistance to authority would constitute an actionable eighth amendment violation." This premise has clear applicability in this case. Hope was not restrained at the worksite until he was willing to return to work. Rather, he was removed back to the prison and placed under conditions that threatened his health. *Ort* therefore gave fair warning to respondents that their conduct crossed the line of what is constitutionally permissible.

Relevant to the question whether *Ort* provided fair warning to respondents that their conduct violated the Constitution is a regulation promulgated by

ADOC in 1993. The regulation authorizes the use of the hitching post when an inmate refuses to work or is otherwise disruptive to a work squad.... The regulation also states that an inmate "will be allowed to join his assigned squad" whenever he tells an officer "that he is ready to go to work."... If regularly observed, a requirement that would effectively give the inmate the keys to the handcuffs that attached him to the hitching post would have made this case more analogous to the practice upheld in *Ort*, rather than the kind of punishment *Ort* described as impermissible....

Respondents violated clearly established law. Our conclusion that "a reasonable person would have known," of the violation is buttressed by the fact that the DOJ specifically advised the ADOC of the unconstitutionality of its practices before the incidents in this case took place.... Although there is nothing in the record indicating that the DOJ's views were communicated to respondents, this exchange lends support to the view that reasonable officials in the ADOC should have realized that the use of the hitching post under the circumstances alleged by Hope violated the Eighth Amendment prohibition against cruel and unusual punishment.

The obvious cruelty inherent in this practice should have provided respondents with some notice that their alleged conduct violated Hope's constitutional protection against cruel and unusual punishment. Hope was treated in a way antithetical to human dignity—he was hitched to a post for an extended period of time in a position that was painful, and under circumstances that were both degrading and dangerous. This wanton treatment was not done of necessity, but as punishment for prior conduct. Even if there might once have been a question regarding the constitutionality of this practice, the Eleventh Circuit precedent of *Gates* and *Ort*, as well as the DOJ report condemning the practice, put a reasonable officer on notice that the use of the hitching post under the circumstances alleged by Hope was unlawful. The "fair and clear warning," that these cases provided was sufficient to preclude the defense of qualified immunity at the summary judgment stage.

In response to Justice Thomas' thoughtful dissent, we [observe that] ... in applying the objective immunity test of what a reasonable officer would understand, the significance of federal judicial precedent is a function in part of the Judiciary's structure. The unreported District Court opinions cited by the officers are distinguishable on their own terms.[12] But regardless, they would be no match for the Circuit precedents in *Gates*, which held that "handcuffing inmates to the fence and to cells for long periods of time" was unconstitutional, and *Ort*, which suggested that it would be unconstitutional to inflict gratuitous pain on an inmate (by refusing him water) when punishment was unnecessary to enforce on-the-spot discipline....

The judgment of the Court of Appeals is reversed.

---

12. In three of the decisions, the inmates were given the choice between working or being restrained. In others, the inmates were offered regular water and bathroom [or] ... the inmate was restrained for approximately 45 minutes.

■ *Justice* Thomas, *with whom* The Chief Justice *and Justice* Scalia *join, dissenting*. . . .

In evaluating whether it was clearly established in 1995 that respondents' conduct violated the Eighth Amendment, the Court of Appeals properly noted that "[i]t is important to analyze the facts in [the prior cases relied upon by petitioner where courts found Eighth Amendment violations], and determine if they are materially similar to the facts in the case in front of us." The right not to suffer from "cruel and unusual punishments," U.S. Const., Amdt. 8, is an extremely abstract and general right. In the vast majority of cases, the text of the Eighth Amendment does not, in and of itself, give a government official sufficient notice of the clearly established Eighth Amendment law applicable to a particular situation. Rather, one must look to case law to see whether "the right the official is alleged to have violated [has] been 'clearly established' in a more particularized, and hence more relevant, sense: The contours of the right must be sufficiently clear that a reasonable official would understand that what he is doing violates that right." *Anderson v. Creighton.*

In conducting this inquiry, it is crucial to look at precedent applying the relevant legal rule in similar factual circumstances. Such cases give government officials the best indication of what conduct is unlawful in a given situation. If, for instance, "various courts have agreed that certain conduct [constitutes an Eighth Amendment violation] under facts not distinguishable in a fair way from the facts presented in the case at hand," *Saucier*, then a plaintiff would have a compelling argument that a defendant is not entitled to qualified immunity.

That is not to say, of course, that conduct can be "clearly established" as unlawful only if a court has already passed on the legality of that behavior under materially similar circumstances. Certain actions so obviously run afoul of the law that an assertion of qualified immunity may be overcome even though court decisions have yet to address "materially similar" conduct. Or, as the Court puts it, "officials can still be on notice that their conduct violates established law even in novel factual circumstances." . . .

[T]he relevant question is whether it should have been clear to [the guards] in 1995 that attaching petitioner to a restraining bar violated the Eighth Amendment. As the Court notes, at that time Alabama was the only State that used this particular disciplinary method when prisoners refused to work or disrupted work squads. Previous litigation over Alabama's use of the restraining bar, however, did nothing to warn reasonable Alabama prison guards that attaching a prisoner to a restraining bar was unlawful, let alone that the illegality of such conduct was clearly established. In fact, the outcome of those cases effectively forecloses petitioner's claim that it should have been clear to respondents in 1995 that handcuffing petitioner to a restraining bar violated the Eighth Amendment.

For example, a year before the conduct at issue in this case took place, the United States District Court for the Northern District of Alabama rejected the Eighth Amendment claim of an Alabama prisoner who was attached to a restraining bar for five hours after he refused to work and scuffled with guards.

The District Court reasoned that attaching the prisoner to a restraining bar "was a measured response to a potentially volatile situation and a clear warning to other inmates that refusal to work would result in immediate discipline subjecting the offending inmate to similar conditions experienced by work detail inmates rather than a return to inside the institution." The District Court therefore concluded that there was a "substantial penological justification" for attaching the plaintiff to the restraining bar. . . .

Federal District Courts in five other Alabama cases decided before 1995 similarly rejected claims that handcuffing a prisoner to a restraining bar or other stationary object violated the Eighth Amendment. By contrast, petitioner is unable to point to any Alabama decision issued before respondents affixed him to the restraining bar holding that a prison guard engaging in such conduct violated the Eighth Amendment. . . .

[I]f the application of this Court's general Eighth Amendment jurisprudence to the use of a restraining bar was as "obvious" as the Court claims, one wonders how Federal District Courts in Alabama could have repeatedly arrived at the opposite conclusion, and how respondents, in turn, were to realize that these courts had failed to grasp the "obvious."

The Department of Justice report referenced by the Court does nothing to demonstrate that it should have been clear to respondents that attaching petitioner to a restraining bar violated his Eighth Amendment rights. To begin with, the Court concedes that there is no indication the Justice Department's recommendation that the ADOC stop using the restraining bar was ever communicated to respondents, prison guards in the small town of Capshaw, Alabama. In any event, an extraordinarily well-informed prison guard in 1995, who had read both the Justice Department's report and Federal District Court decisions addressing the use of the restraining bar, could have concluded only that there was a dispute as to whether handcuffing a prisoner to a restraining bar constituted an Eighth Amendment violation, not that such a practice was clearly unconstitutional.

The ADOC regulation relied upon by the Court not only fails to provide support for its holding today; the regulation weighs in respondents' favor because it expressly authorized prison guards to affix prisoners to a restraining bar when they were "disruptive to the work squad." . . .

Finally, the "binding Eleventh Circuit precedent" relied upon by the Court, was plainly insufficient to give respondents fair warning that their alleged conduct ran afoul of petitioner's Eighth Amendment rights. The Court of Appeals held in *Ort v. White*, 813 F.2d 318 (C.A.11 1987), that a prison guard did not violate an inmate's Eighth Amendment rights by denying him water when he refused to work, and the Court admits that this holding provides no support for petitioner. . . .

To be sure, the Court correctly notes that the Court of Appeals in *Ort* suggested that it "might have reached a different decision" had the prison officer denied the inmate water after he had returned to the prison instead of while he was out with the work squad. But the suggestion in dicta . . . does not come close to clearly establishing the unconstitutionality of attaching a disruptive inmate to a restraining bar after he is removed from his work squad and back within prison walls.

Admittedly, the other case upon which the Court relies, *Gates v. Collier*, 501 F.2d 1291 (C.A.5 1974), is more on point.... It is not reasonable, however, to read *Gates* as establishing a bright-line rule forbidding the attachment of prisoners to a restraining bar. For example, in referring to the fact that prisoners were handcuffed to a fence and cells "for long periods of time," the Court of Appeals did not indicate whether it considered a "long period of time" to be 1 hour, 5 hours, or 25 hours....

In the face of recent Federal District Court decisions specifically rejecting prisoners' claims that Alabama prison guards violated their Eighth Amendment rights by attaching them to a restraining bar as well as a state regulation authorizing such conduct, it seems contrary to the purpose of qualified immunity to hold that one vague sentence plucked out of a 21-year-old Court of Appeals opinion provided clear notice to respondents in 1995 that their conduct was unlawful....

Notes and Questions

1. After dispensing with the requirement of a "materially similar" precedent, the Court identifies two different theories under which a plaintiff can overcome qualified immunity. How are they different? To what extent must the plaintiff rely on specific precedents for each? To what extent do the two theories overlap?

2. Can *Hope* and *Anderson* be harmonized?

3. Considerations of fairness support both the plaintiff's and defendants' arguments regarding the implications of prior precedent. Which is more unfair where a constitutional violation has occurred but no "materially similar" case has been decided: to deny a plaintiff recovery or to deny defendants immunity?

4. There is intuitive appeal to the majority's position that even novel conduct can be so obviously unconstitutional that qualified immunity will be inappropriate. As the Court later put it (albeit in granting immunity): "The unconstitutionality of outrageous conduct obviously will be unconstitutional, this being the reason . . . that the easiest cases don't even arise." *Safford Unified Sch. Dist. No. 1 v. Redding*, 557 U.S. 364, 377 (2009) (citation and internal quotation marks and alteration omitted). The dissenters in *Hope* do not disagree. So what is the substance of the disagreement between the majority and the dissent?

5. How reasonable are the majority's assumptions about what a "reasonable officer" should know? Does anyone think that Alabama prison guards would have known that pre-1981 Fifth Circuit precedent binds the Eleventh Circuit and therefore would have made sure to read *Gates*? Or that they would be familiar with dicta from *Ort*? For that matter, are governmental officials who are not lawyers likely to read court decisions at all? Recall that Justice Powell, dissenting from the pre-*Harlow* decision *Wood v. Strickland*, criticized the Court's "unwarranted assumption as to what lay . . . officials know or can know about

the law and constitutional rights." Do you think maintaining such knowledge should be part of their job? If not, whose job is it to make sure police know all the constitutional limits that apply to them?

6. If you find the Court's assumptions about lay officials' knowledge far-fetched, does that suggest the guards did not in fact have "fair warning"? Or is the standard itself problematic?

7. What is the majority's answer to Justice Thomas's point that if the violation here was so "obvious," then Alabama district courts wouldn't have missed it? As you may know, federal district court decisions are not treated as binding precedent, even in the district court that issued these decisions. When if ever should non-binding district court case law bear on the question whether a right is "clearly established"?

8. More generally, how should a division of opinion among jurists affect the qualified immunity analysis? In *Wilson v. Layne*, 526 U.S. 603 (1999), the Court unanimously held that it was unconstitutional for the police to permit a member of the press to accompany them when executing an arrest warrant at a private home (a "media ride-along"). But the Court granted qualified immunity to the officers sued for engaging in such a practice. It reasoned, in part:

> Between the time of the events of this case and today's decision, a split among the Federal Circuits in fact developed on the question whether media ride-alongs that enter homes subject the police to money damages. If judges thus disagree on a constitutional question, it is unfair to subject police to money damages for picking the losing side of the controversy.

That judges didn't know the right answer makes it difficult to imagine that police officers could. How far does this principle extend? Does disagreement by any judge about the constitutionality of a particular practice automatically justify qualified immunity? How many judges must believe that a practice is constitutional for the law to be unclear? What are the implications of this argument for a case in which a three-judge panel of a court of appeals splits 2-1 on whether particular conduct is constitutional? Should qualified immunity in such a case be automatic? Why or why not?

9. According to the majority, can dicta from prior cases "clearly establish" a right?

10. Are the majority's uses of the ADOC policy and the DOJ report consistent with the standard for qualified immunity? Can either of these sources "clearly establish" the law for the purpose of qualified immunity? If not, of what legitimate use are they? Or is the majority shoring up an otherwise weak case for showing that the law was "clearly established"?

* * *

The *Hope* case (aptly named from the perspective of a civil rights plaintiff) represented the high-water mark for plaintiffs in the modern era of qualified immunity jurisprudence. The following case is typical of the Court's approach to the level-of-generality issue in the years since *Hope*.

Mullenix v. Luna
136 S. Ct. 305 (2015)

■ PER CURIAM.

[When a Tulia, Texas, police officer attempted to arrest Israel Leija, Jr., in his car one night in March 2010, Leija sped off, leading officers on an 18-minute car chase at speeds between 85 and 110 miles per hour. During the chase, Leija called the Tulia Police dispatcher and threatened to shoot at officers if they did not abandon their pursuit. The dispatcher relayed the threats to the pursuing officers and reported that Leija might be intoxicated. Meanwhile, other officers set up tire spikes at three locations to try to stop Leija's car. Texas State Trooper Chadrin Mullenix proposed to his fellow officers by radio that he try to disable Leija's car by shooting at it from the overpass above the first set of spikes. He had not been trained on this tactic or attempted it before. One of the officers chasing Leija responded approvingly to Mullenix, and Mullenix took up a shooting position on the overpass. But Mullenix's supervisor, Sergeant Byrd, told him to "stand by" and "see if the spikes work first." About three minutes later, Leija's car approached the spikes. Before it reached them, Mullenix fired six shots. The car continued forward, hit the spike strip, and rolled over twice. It was later determined that Mullenix's shots had killed Leija. Representatives of Leija's estate and of his minor child sued Mullenix under § 1983 for unconstitutionally excessive force. Mullenix claimed qualified immunity, which the district court denied. The court of appeals affirmed.] . . .

The doctrine of qualified immunity shields officials from civil liability so long as their conduct " 'does not violate clearly established statutory or constitutional rights of which a reasonable person would have known.' " A clearly established right is one that is "sufficiently clear that every reasonable official would have understood that what he is doing violates that right." "We do not require a case directly on point, but existing precedent must have placed the statutory or constitutional question beyond debate." Put simply, qualified immunity protects "all but the plainly incompetent or those who knowingly violate the law."

"We have repeatedly told courts . . . not to define clearly established law at a high level of generality." The dispositive question is "whether the violative nature of particular conduct is clearly established." This inquiry " 'must be undertaken in light of the specific context of the case, not as a broad general proposition.' " Such specificity is especially important in the Fourth Amendment context, where the Court has recognized that "[i]t is sometimes difficult for an officer to determine how the relevant legal doctrine, here excessive force, will apply to the factual situation the officer confronts."

In this case, the Fifth Circuit held that Mullenix violated the clearly established rule that a police officer may not " 'use deadly force against a fleeing felon who does not pose a sufficient threat of harm to the officer or others.' " Yet this Court has previously considered—and rejected—almost that exact formulation of the qualified immunity question in the Fourth Amendment context. In *Brosseau v. Haugen*, 543 U.S. 194, 198 (2004) (per curiam), which also involved the shooting of a suspect fleeing by car, the Ninth Circuit denied qualified immunity on the ground that the officer had violated the clearly established rule . . . that "deadly force is only permissible where the officer has probable cause to believe that the suspect poses a threat of serious physical harm, either to the officer or to others." This Court summarily reversed, holding that use of the "general" test for excessive force was "mistaken." The correct inquiry, the Court explained, was whether it was clearly established that the Fourth Amendment prohibited the officer's conduct in the " 'situation [she] confronted': whether to shoot a disturbed felon, set on avoiding capture through vehicular flight, when persons in the immediate area are at risk from that flight." The Court considered three court of appeals cases discussed by the parties, noted that "this area is one in which the result depends very much on the facts of each case," and concluded that the officer was entitled to qualified immunity because "[n]one of [the cases] *squarely governs* the case here." (emphasis added).

Anderson v. Creighton is also instructive on the required degree of specificity. There, the lower court had denied qualified immunity based on the clearly established "right to be free from warrantless searches of one's home unless the searching officers have probable cause and there are exigent circumstances." This Court faulted that formulation for failing to address the actual question at issue: whether "the circumstances with which Anderson was confronted . . . constitute[d] probable cause and exigent circumstances." Without answering that question, the Court explained, the conclusion that Anderson's search was objectively unreasonable did not "follow immediately" from—and thus was not clearly established by—the principle that warrantless searches not supported by probable cause and exigent circumstances violate the Fourth Amendment. . . .

Far from clarifying the issue, excessive force cases involving car chases reveal the hazy legal backdrop against which Mullenix acted. In *Brosseau* itself, the Court held that an officer did not violate clearly established law when she shot a fleeing suspect out of fear that he endangered "other officers on foot who [she] believed were in the immediate area," "the occupied vehicles in [his] path," and "any other citizens who *might* be in the area." (emphasis added). The threat Leija posed was at least as immediate as that presented by a suspect who had just begun to drive off and was headed only in the general direction of officers and bystanders. By the time Mullenix fired, Leija had led police on a 25-mile chase at extremely high speeds, was reportedly intoxicated, had twice threatened to shoot officers, and was racing towards an officer's location. . . .

Given Leija's conduct, we cannot say that only someone "plainly incompetent" or who "knowingly violate[s] the law" would have perceived a sufficient threat and acted as Mullenix did.

The dissent focuses on the availability of spike strips as an alternative means of terminating the chase. . . . Spike strips, however, present dangers of their own, not only to drivers who encounter them at speeds between 85 and 110 miles per hour, but also to officers manning them. . . . The dissent can cite no case from this Court denying qualified immunity because officers entitled to terminate a high-speed chase selected one dangerous alternative over another.

Even so, the dissent argues, there was no governmental interest that justified acting before Leija's car hit the spikes. Mullenix explained, however, that he feared Leija might attempt to shoot at or run over the officers manning the spike strips. Mullenix also feared that even if Leija hit the spike strips, he might still be able to continue driving in the direction of other officers. . . . Mullenix hoped his actions would stop the car in a manner that avoided the risks to other officers and other drivers that relying on spike strips would entail. . . . Ultimately, whatever can be said of the wisdom of Mullenix's choice, this Court's precedents do not place the conclusion that he acted unreasonably in these circumstances "beyond debate."

More fundamentally, the dissent repeats the Fifth Circuit's error. It defines the qualified immunity inquiry at a high level of generality—whether any governmental interest justified choosing one tactic over another—and then fails to consider that question in "the specific context of the case." *Brosseau*. As in *Anderson*, the conclusion that Mullenix's reasons were insufficient to justify his actions simply does not "follow immediately" from the general proposition that force must be justified.

Cases decided by the lower courts since *Brosseau* likewise have not clearly established that deadly force is inappropriate in response to conduct like Leija's. The Fifth Circuit here principally relied on its own decision in *Lytle v. Bexar County*, 560 F.3d 404 (2009), denying qualified immunity to a police officer who had fired at a fleeing car and killed one of its passengers. That holding turned on the court's assumption, for purposes of summary judgment, that the car was moving away from the officer and had already traveled some distance at the moment the officer fired. The court held that a reasonable jury could conclude that a receding car "did not pose a sufficient threat of harm such that the use of deadly force was reasonable." . . . Without implying that *Lytle* was either correct or incorrect, it suffices to say that *Lytle* does not clearly dictate the conclusion that Mullenix was unjustified in perceiving grave danger and responding accordingly, given that Leija was speeding towards a confrontation with officers he had threatened to kill. . . .

[Q]ualified immunity protects actions in the " 'hazy border between excessive and acceptable force.' " *Brosseau*.

Because the constitutional rule applied by the Fifth Circuit was not " 'beyond debate,' " we grant Mullenix's petition for certiorari and reverse the Fifth Circuit's determination that Mullenix is not entitled to qualified immunity.

[Opinion of Scalia, J., concurring in the judgment, omitted.]

■ *Justice* SOTOMAYOR, *dissenting.* . . .

This Court has rejected the idea that "an official action is protected by qualified immunity unless the very action in question has previously been held unlawful." Instead, the crux of the qualified immunity test is whether officers have "fair notice" that they are acting unconstitutionally. *Hope*. . . .

This Court's precedents clearly establish that the Fourth Amendment is violated unless the "'governmental interests'" in effectuating a particular kind of seizure outweigh the "'nature and quality of the intrusion on the individual's Fourth Amendment interests.'" There must be a "governmental interes[t]" not only in effectuating a seizure, but also in "how [the seizure] is carried out." Balancing a particular governmental interest in the use of deadly force against the intrusion occasioned by the use of that force is inherently a fact-specific inquiry, not susceptible to bright lines. But it is clearly established that the government must have some interest in using deadly force over other kinds of force.

Here, then, the clearly established legal question—the question a reasonable officer would have asked—is whether, under all the circumstances as known to Mullenix, there was a governmental interest in shooting at the car rather than waiting for it to run over spike strips.

The majority does not point to any such interest here. . . .

The majority first suggests that Mullenix did not wait for the results of the spikes, as his superior advised, because of his concern for the officers manning the strips. But Leija was going to come upon those officers whether or not Mullenix's shooting tactic was successful: Mullenix took his shot when Leija was between 25 and 30 yards away from the spike strip, traveling at 85 miles per hour. . . .

The majority notes that spike strips are fallible. But Mullenix had no information to suggest that shooting to disable a car had a higher success rate, much less that doing so with no training and at night was more likely to succeed. . . .

[T]he majority's exhortation that the right at stake not be defined at "a high level of generality" is a red herring. The majority adduces various facts that the Fifth Circuit supposedly ignored in its qualified immunity analysis, including that Leija was "a reportedly intoxicated fugitive, set on avoiding capture through high-speed vehicular flight, who twice during his flight had threatened to shoot police officers, and who was moments away from encountering an officer at Cemetery Road." But not one of those facts goes to the governmental interest in shooting over awaiting the spike strips. . . .

The majority also glosses over the facts that Mullenix had time to ask Byrd for permission to fire upon Leija and that Byrd—Mullenix's superior officer—told Mullenix to "stand by." There was no reason to believe that Byrd did not have all the same information Mullenix did, including the knowledge that an officer was stationed beneath the overpass. . . .

By sanctioning a "shoot first, think later" approach to policing, the Court renders the protections of the Fourth Amendment hollow. . . .

Notes and Questions

1. The analysis in *Mullenix* begins by restating the principles governing qualified immunity analysis, quoted from various cases since *Harlow* but mostly cases decided after *Hope*. The Court uses phrases like "sufficiently clear that every

reasonable official would have understood that what he is doing violates that right" and "placed the . . . constitutional question beyond debate." Do these formulations suggest the Court is applying a new standard? The same standard more strictly? What do you make of the majority's failure to discuss *Hope*?

2. One possible way to reconcile *Hope* with *Mullenix* (and the case it discusses extensively, *Brosseau*) is to explain the latter in terms of the need for a split-second decision in a dangerous situation. In several other cases in the past fifteen years, the Court has, by large majorities, granted immunity to officers in cases involving either high-speed chases or shootings of armed individuals. *See, e.g., Kisela v. Hughes*, 138 S. Ct. 1148 (2018) (per curiam) (7-2 vote); *White v. Pauly*, 137 S. Ct. 548 (2017) (per curiam) (unanimous); *Plumhoff v. Rickard*, 572 U.S. 765 (2014) (unanimous). Should the Court handle the qualified immunity inquiry differently in "split-second" cases as opposed to other cases? Should a different standard apply? If so, what should that be? What criteria should the Court use to determine when a special "split-second" standard applies?

3. Is the crux of Justice Sotomayor's dissent about the standard or its application to these facts?

4. Consider the implications of *Mullenix* for the plaintiff's task in overcoming qualified immunity. In light of the lessons the majority draws from *Anderson* and *Brosseau* concerning the level-of-generality question, what must a plaintiff be able to show? How often will the plaintiff succeed?

5. Figure 4.2 illustrates the trend of the Court's qualified immunity cases toward an ever-more-specific level of generality. Note that the two theories espoused in *Hope* represent two different levels of generality—the "fair warning" standard suggests precedent is required but need not resemble the facts of the case before the court; by contrast, a plaintiff could win under the "obviousness" standard without citing any prior precedent at all. But as the chart shows, the cases since *Hope* all fall toward the very bottom of the chart; to the extent the Court has discussed the "obviousness" theory, it has suggested this route to defeating immunity should apply rarely.

Note: Sources of "Clearly Established" Law

Which precedent determines whether the law is "clearly established"? Is Supreme Court precedent required? Binding precedent from the circuit in which the case is litigated? The Supreme Court has explained that a plaintiff can defeat qualified immunity by showing either "controlling authority" (i.e., from the circuit in question or the Supreme Court) or a "robust consensus of cases of persuasive authority." *District of Columbia v. Wesby*, 138 S. Ct. 577, 590 (2018) (citation and internal quotation marks omitted); *accord Plumhoff v. Rickard*, 572 U.S. 765, 780 (2014); *Ashcroft v. al-Kidd*, 563 U.S. 731, 742 (2011).

Figure 4.2: *The spectrum of levels-of-generality required in qualified immunity cases, plotted over time*

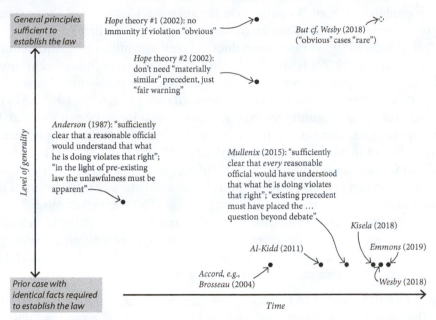

The vertical axis represents level of generality, with the top pole representing the most general definition of the right and the bottom pole the most specific. The horizontal axis is time. Over the past few decades, the Court's qualified immunity cases have trended toward requiring rights to be defined at lower levels of generality (i.e., with increasing specificity). This trend contrasts with the two theories articulated in the Hope *case (the "fair warning" standard and the "obviousness" exception), each represented by its own point.*

Applications

The lower courts have struggled to apply the "clearly established" test consistently. Professor John Jeffries has characterized it as "a mare's nest of complexity and confusion." John C. Jeffries, Jr., *What's Wrong with Qualified Immunity?* 62 Fla. L. Rev. 851, 852 (2010). *Accord* Karen M. Blum, *Section 1983 Litigation: The Maze, the Mud, and the Madness*, 23 Wm. & Mary Bill Rts. J. 913, 962-64 (2015) ("[S]o much of the law surrounding Section 1983 litigation remains uncertain, unpredictable, and seemingly dependent upon the 'judicial experience and common sense' of the particular judge hearing the case." (quoting *Ashcroft v. Iqbal*, 556 U.S. 662, 679 (2009); footnotes omitted)).

One appellate judge has lamented that "courts of appeals are divided—intractably—over precisely what degree of factual similarity must exist" for the law to be "clearly established." *Zadeh v. Robinson*, 902 F.3d 483, 498 (5th Cir. 2018) (Willett, J., concurring dubitante). Leading scholars of federal jurisdiction have identified the same problem. *See* Richard Fallon, Jr., et al., *Hart & Wechsler's The Federal Courts and the Federal System* 1047-50 (7th ed. 2015). As Dean Chemerinsky has explained, "[t]here is an obvious tension between *Hope v. Pelzer*, declaring that there need not be a case on point . . . and the subsequent cases, finding qualified immunity based on the lack of a case on point." Erwin Chemerinsky, *Federal Jurisdiction*, § 8.6.3, at 595 (7th ed. 2016).

Consider these examples of lower courts' efforts to apply the standard:

1. New technologies.   Can constitutional limits on the use of new weaponry be "clearly established" even if courts have not previously considered those specific weapons? Some courts have answered that question in the affirmative, explaining that "novel technology, without more, does not entitle an officer to qualified immunity." *Edrei v. Maguire*, 892 F.3d 525, 542 (2d Cir. 2018) (denying qualified immunity to officers who employed long-range acoustic device despite absence of cases about that specific weapon); *accord Phillips v. Community Ins. Corp.*, 678 F.3d 513, 528 (7th Cir. 2012) (denying immunity for excessive force claim for using a device akin to a bean-bag shotgun, even though no prior case held the use of that weapon unconstitutional). But in *Mattos v. Agarano*, 661 F.3d 433, 452 (9th Cir. 2011) (en banc), the Ninth Circuit granted immunity to an officer who deployed a Taser on a non-threatening victim of a domestic dispute, because "there was no Supreme Court decision or decision of our court addressing the use of a Taser in dart mode."

If the answer to the constitutional question must truly be "beyond debate" to defeat immunity, shouldn't the involvement of a new type of weapon always trigger qualified immunity—at least for the first officer using it unconstitutionally? Then again, wouldn't that approach conflict with *Hope*?

2. Intra-circuit variation in levels of generality required.   Two sets of decisions from the Sixth Circuit are instructive about the difficulty of ensuring consistent application.

First, in *Baynes v. Cleland*, 799 F.3d 600, 614-15 (6th Cir. 2015), the Sixth Circuit rejected qualified immunity for an officer sued for handcuffing a suspect too tightly, even though no case addressed the specific circumstances presented—the plaintiff complained only once, and the police-car ride during which he was handcuffed was only twenty minutes long. Circuit precedent holding that "excessively forceful or unduly tight handcuffing is a constitutional violation" established the law with the necessary specificity, the court ruled. Citing *Hope*, the court opined that "[r]equiring any more particularity than this would contravene the Supreme Court's explicit rulings that neither a 'materially similar,' 'fundamentally similar,' or 'case directly on point'—let alone a factually identical case—is required." But in *Latits v. Philips*, 878 F.3d 541, 546, 552-53 (6th Cir. 2017), the same court took a different approach to the level-of-generality question. In that case, officers chased a motorist and forced him to stop, but he attempted to drive off again, and one of the officers shot him. Circuit precedent had, according to the court, "clearly established that shooting a driver while positioned to the side of his fleeing car violates the Fourth Amendment, absent some indication suggesting that the driver poses more than a fleeting threat." But the court granted qualified immunity because prior circuit cases concerned drivers who "attempted to *initiate* flight" rather than someone who fled, was stopped, then attempted to flee *again*. The court characterized this as an "important factual distinction" but did not explain why it was important, particularly in light of the court's conclusion that the driver did not present an immediate danger.

Second, and perhaps even more revealing, two different panels of the Sixth Circuit reached different conclusions regarding qualified immunity on the same facts in a single case. Two Nashville police officers pursued Alexander Baxter in response to a report of a residential burglary. Baxter fled from one home into the basement of another, where the officers, with the help of a police dog, found him. One of the officers secured the dog, and Baxter sat motionless on the ground with his hands in the air for five to ten seconds. Then, without warning, the officer once again released his dog, and it bit Baxter in his armpit; Baxter required emergency medical treatment as a result. Baxter sued for excessive force, and the district court denied qualified immunity. Relying on a prior case holding that an officer clearly violated the Fourth Amendment when he used a police dog without warning against an unarmed residential burglary suspect who was found lying on the ground with his arms at his side, the Sixth Circuit affirmed the denial of qualified immunity. *Baxter v. Harris*, 2016 WL 11517046 (6th Cir. Aug. 30, 2016) (mem. order). After discovery, the officers sought summary judgment, again asserting qualified immunity. The district court denied the motion, but a new Sixth Circuit panel reversed. Even though the appeals court did not disagree with the district court's finding that Baxter's evidence "entirely corroborate[d]" the facts in the complaint, the new panel reversed the denial of immunity, explaining: "Baxter does not point us to any case law suggesting that raising his hands, on its own, is enough to put Harris on notice that a canine apprehension was unlawful in these circumstances." *Baxter v. Bracey*, 751 Fed. App'x 869, 872 (6th Cir. 2018), *pet. for cert. filed*, Apr. 8, 2019.

Consider these cases together with *Anderson*, *Hope*, and *Mullenix* (including its discussion of *Brosseau*). Do they paint a unified picture of what it means for a right to be "clearly established"? Or is the qualified immunity standard essentially a battleground on which different wings of the Court and different appellate panels continue to fight over the proper balance between accountability and immunity, with the facts of each individual case tipping the scales in one direction or another? *See* Alan K. Chen, *The Intractability of Qualified Immunity*, 93 Notre Dame L. Rev. 1937, 1951 (2018).

Do apparent inconsistencies in application of the qualified immunity standard suggest that further clarification from the Court is needed? Or is the standard inherently too malleable to be applied consistently, given that different judges will have different perspectives on any given set of facts? Is the "clearly established" standard any worse in this regard than other vague legal concepts like the "reasonableness" standard that defines key elements in tort law as well as substantive Fourth Amendment law? Why do courts seem to have so much trouble applying it consistently?

3. Subjectivity in Qualified Immunity After *Harlow*

Harlow's revision of the qualified immunity standard purported to limit the doctrine to its "objective" prong, jettisoning its "subjective" aspect. This shift reduced, but did not eliminate, inquiry into characteristics and circumstances specific to the defendant. Several "subjective" questions remain relevant.

First, consider the defendant's subjective knowledge of the law at the time of the challenged conduct. Although the Court has never followed up on Justice Brennan's suggestion in his *Harlow* concurrence that courts should consider whether the specific defendant *actually knew* the relevant legal principles, the qualified immunity standard does take account of what legal principles a reasonable officer *could* have known *in the circumstances of* the defendant. Thus, decisions that postdate the challenged conduct cannot "clearly establish" the law for the purpose of evaluating that conduct. This principle goes all the way back to *Pierson v. Ray* ("[A] police officer is not charged with predicting the future course of constitutional law.").

One appellate decision takes this point further. On September 5, 2008, a federal officer recommended searches of certain passengers' cabins on a cruise ship in the Caribbean, and on September 6, other federal officers conducted those searches. In the U.S. District Court of the Virgin Islands (which is in the Third Circuit), the passengers sued all these officers for Fourth Amendment violations. The plaintiffs relied on a Third Circuit decision called *Whitted*, decided September 4, 2008, holding that a cabin search on a cruise ship requires reasonable suspicion. When the case of the September 2008 searches reached the Third Circuit, it held that the officers were entitled to qualified immunity because a ruling issued one or two days before the challenged conduct does not "clearly establish" the law:

> When such a ruling is made . . . it is beyond belief that within two days the government could determine what was "reasonable suspicion" and what new policy was required to conform to the ruling, much less communicate that new policy to the [its] officers. . . . [W]e conclude that the *Whitted* standard was not clearly established . . . on September 5 or 6. Within one or two days, neither [the officer who recommended the search] nor the [searching] officers could reasonably be expected to have learned of this development in our Fourth Amendment jurisprudence. At that time, it would not have been beyond debate that, absent reasonable suspicion, the Fourth Amendment prohibited the search of the travelers' cabins. For purposes of qualified immunity, a legal principle does not become "clearly established" the day we announce a decision, or even one or two days later.

Bryan v. United States, 913 F.3d 356, 363 (3d Cir. 2019).

The *Pierson* principle regarding law that postdates the challenged conduct is uncontroversial; the reasoning in *Bryan* seems more problematic. How long should it take for a decision to become "clearly established"? The *Bryan* panel refused to say, explaining that it was only deciding the case before it. How could that line be drawn? A fixed amount of time would be easy to administer but arbitrary (why a week and not a month?); a more nuanced test involving a multi-factor standard would be hard to apply consistently. Would a plaintiff be entitled to discovery about when the officers actually learned of the law? When they had the opportunity to learn it? Would such discovery be consistent with *Harlow*?

Second, consider the defendant's knowledge of the facts relevant to the constitutionality of the conduct. Are the facts known to the specific officer relevant to the qualified immunity analysis? *Hernandez v. Mesa*, 137 S. Ct. 2003 (2017) (per curiam), explains that they are. That case "involve[d] a tragic cross-border incident in which a United States Border Patrol agent standing on United States soil shot and killed a Mexican national standing on Mexican soil." The victim, Sergio Adrián Hernández Güereca, was a 15-year-old boy who (accepting the complaint's allegations as true) had been playing with his friends at the border and posed no threat to anyone. In his parents' subsequent *Bivens* suit for damages based on various constitutional violations, an important substantive question was whether the Constitution protected Sergio, a Mexican who was shot while in Mexico. The district court dismissed the case and the Fifth Circuit affirmed, holding (among other things) that the officer was entitled to qualified immunity because the question whether the Constitution protected a Mexican citizen with no significant connection to the United States was unsettled. The Court vacated and remanded in light of *Ziglar v. Abbasi* for determination whether a *Bivens* claim existed (see Chapter 2)—a decision that might obviate the need to address the thorny extraterritoriality question. But the Court also held that qualified immunity had been granted in error based on after-acquired facts:

> In [applying qualified immunity], the en banc Court of Appeals relied on the fact that Hernández was "an alien who had no significant voluntary connection to . . . the United States." It is undisputed, however, that Hernández's nationality and the extent of his ties to the United States were unknown to Mesa at the time of the shooting. The en banc Court of Appeals therefore erred in granting qualified immunity based on those facts.
>
> The "dispositive inquiry in determining whether a right is clearly established is whether it would be clear to a reasonable officer that his conduct was unlawful in the situation he confronted." *Saucier v. Katz.* The qualified immunity analysis thus is limited to "the facts that were knowable to the defendant officers" at the time they engaged in the conduct in question. Facts an officer learns after the incident ends—whether those facts would support granting immunity or denying it—are not relevant.

No Justice disagreed with the holding on qualified immunity.

Third, consider the defendant's subjective intent in engaging in the challenged conduct. *Harlow* held that the defendant's bad faith was irrelevant to the issue of qualified immunity. But the merits of some constitutional claims *require* a showing of impermissible motive. For instance, if it is alleged that a city denied a restaurant a liquor license because the owner was a woman, an equal protection claim requires the plaintiff to show that her sex was the reason for the denial rather than some permissible reason. Can a defendant's motive be considered if it is relevant to the merits of the constitutional violation itself?

The Court answered yes in *Crawford-El v. Britton*, 523 U.S. 574 (1998). The plaintiff there was a litigious prisoner in the Washington, D.C., correctional system. Because of overcrowding at the District's prison, he was transferred, first to Washington State, then to a series of facilities elsewhere. His belongings were transferred separately. When the D.C. Department of Corrections received his belongings from Washington State, defendant, a D.C. correctional officer, had plaintiff's brother-in-law pick them up, rather than shipping them directly to plaintiff's next destination. As a result, plaintiff did not recover the belongings for several months. He sued the correctional officer, alleging that her diversion of his property was intended to retaliate against him for exercising his First Amendment rights. When the case reached the court of appeals, it held that in an unconstitutional-motive case, a plaintiff must establish motive by clear and convincing evidence. The Supreme Court, in an opinion by Justice Stevens, reversed:

> The [D.C. Circuit's] heightened burden of proof applies . . . to the wide array of different federal law claims for which an official's motive is a necessary element, such as claims of race and gender discrimination in violation of the Equal Protection Clause, cruel and unusual punishment in violation of the Eighth Amendment, and termination of employment based on political affiliation in violation of the First Amendment, as well as retaliation for the exercise of free speech or other constitutional rights. A bare majority of the Court of Appeals regarded this sweeping rule as a necessary corollary to our opinion in *Harlow*. . . .
>
> Our holding that "bare allegations of malice" cannot overcome the qualified immunity defense did not implicate the elements of the plaintiff's initial burden of proving a constitutional violation. . . . [A]n essential element of some constitutional claims is a charge that the defendant's conduct was improperly motivated. For example, Fitzgerald's constitutional claims against President Nixon and his aides were based on the theory that they had retaliated against him for speaking out on a matter of public concern. . . . Thus, although evidence of improper motive is irrelevant on the issue of qualified immunity, it may be an essential component of the plaintiff's affirmative case. Our holding in *Harlow*, which related only to the scope of an affirmative defense, provides no support for making any change in the nature of the plaintiff's burden of proving a constitutional violation.
>
> Nevertheless, the en banc court's ruling makes just such a change in the plaintiff's cause of action. The court's clear and convincing evidence requirement applies to the plaintiff's showing of improper intent (a pure issue of fact), not to the separate qualified immunity question whether the official's alleged conduct violated clearly established law, which is an "essentially legal question." Indeed, the court's heightened proof standard logically should govern even if the official never asserts an immunity defense. Such a rule is not required by the holding in *Harlow*. . . .
>
> There are several reasons why we believe that here, unlike *Harlow*, the proper balance does not justify a judicial revision of the law to bar claims that depend on proof of an official's motive. Initially, there is an important distinction between the "bare allegations of malice" that would have provided the basis for rebutting a qualified immunity defense under *Wood v. Strickland* and the allegations of intent that are essential elements of certain constitutional claims. Under *Wood*, the mere allegation of intent to cause any "other injury," not just a deprivation of constitutional rights, would have permitted an open-ended inquiry into subjective motivation. When intent is an element of a constitutional violation, however, the primary focus is not on any possible animus directed at the plaintiff; rather, it is more specific, such as an intent to disadvantage all members of a class that includes the plaintiff, or to deter public comment on a specific issue of public importance. . . .
>
> Moreover, existing law already prevents this more narrow element of unconstitutional motive from automatically carrying a plaintiff to trial. The immunity standard in *Harlow* itself eliminates all motive-based claims in which the official's conduct did not violate clearly established law. . . . Furthermore, various procedural mechanisms already enable trial judges to weed out baseless claims that feature a subjective element . . . .

The unprecedented change made by the Court of Appeals in this case . . . lacks any common-law pedigree and alters the cause of action itself in a way that undermines the very purpose of § 1983—to provide a remedy for the violation of federal rights.[16]

Justice Kennedy concurred briefly. In dissent, Chief Justice Rehnquist, joined by Justice O'Connor, argued that the policy rationale of *Harlow* requires additional protection for officers from motive-based claims:

It is not enough to say that because (1) the law in this area is "clearly established," and (2) this type of claim always turns on a defendant official's subjective intent, that (3) qualified immunity is therefore never available. Such logic apparently approves the "protracted and complex," course of litigation in this case, runs afoul of *Harlow*'s concern that insubstantial claims be prevented from going to trial, and ensures that officials will be subject to the "peculiarly disruptive" inquiry into their subjective intent that the *Harlow* rule was designed to prevent. Such a rule would also allow plaintiffs to strip defendants of *Harlow*'s protections by a simple act of pleading— any minimally competent attorney (or pro se litigant) can convert any adverse decision into a motive-based tort, and thereby subject government officials to some measure of intrusion into their subjective worlds.

Such a result is quite inconsistent with the logic and underlying principles of *Harlow*. In order to preserve the protections that *Harlow* conferred, it is necessary to construct a qualified immunity test in this context that is also based exclusively on objective factors, and prevents plaintiffs from engaging in "peculiarly disruptive" subjective investigations until after the immunity inquiry has been resolved in their favor. The test I propose accomplishes this goal. Under this test, when a plaintiff alleges that an official's action was taken with an unconstitutional or otherwise unlawful motive, the defendant will be entitled to immunity and immediate dismissal of the suit if he can offer a lawful reason for his action and the plaintiff cannot establish, through objective evidence, that the offered reason is actually a pretext.

Justice Scalia's dissent, joined by Justice Thomas, went further:

The § 1983 that the Court created in 1961 bears scant resemblance to what Congress enacted almost a century earlier. I refer, of course, to the holding of *Monroe v. Pape*, which converted an 1871 statute covering constitutional violations committed "under color of any statute, ordinance, regulation, custom, or usage of any State," into a statute covering constitutional violations committed without the authority of any statute, ordinance, regulation, custom, or usage of any State, and indeed even constitutional violations committed in stark violation of state civil or criminal law. . . . *Monroe* changed a statute that had generated only 21 cases in the first 50 years of its existence into one that pours into the federal courts tens of thousands of suits each year, and engages this Court in a losing struggle to prevent the Constitution from degenerating into a general tort law. (The present suit,

---

16. Ironically, the heightened standard of proof directly limits the availability of the remedy in cases involving the specific evil at which the Civil Rights Act of 1871 (the predecessor of § 1983) was originally aimed—race discrimination. *See Monroe v. Pape.*

involving the constitutional violation of misdirecting a package, is a good enough example.) . . .

We find ourselves engaged, therefore, in the essentially legislative activity of crafting a sensible scheme of qualified immunities for the statute we have invented—rather than applying the common law embodied in the statute that Congress wrote. My preference is, in undiluted form, . . . extending the "objective reasonableness" test of *Harlow v. Fitzgerald* to qualified immunity insofar as it relates to intent-based constitutional torts. . . .

[Under the] test I favor . . . once the trial court finds that the asserted grounds for the official action were objectively valid (e.g., the person fired for alleged incompetence was indeed incompetent), it would not admit any proof that something other than those reasonable grounds was the genuine motive (e.g., the incompetent person fired was a Republican). This is of course a more severe restriction upon "intent-based" constitutional torts [than proposed by the Chief Justice]; I am less put off by that consequence than some may be, since I believe that no "intent-based" constitutional tort would have been actionable under the § 1983 that Congress enacted.

Does the dissenters' willingness to rewrite the rules for particular types of claims reflect fidelity to *Harlow* or hostility toward those types of claims (or toward the Court's § 1983 jurisprudence generally)? Do the dissenters explain how their respective rules would preserve meritorious claims of race discrimination—which, as the majority notes, is a type of motive-based constitutional claim? If this case were about a prison guard who assaulted a prisoner because of his race rather than a guard who misdirected a prisoner's possessions because of his speech, would the dissenters view the issue differently?

Are you persuaded by the majority's reconciliation of its rule with *Harlow*? You might find that the rule of *Anderson*—in which the Court rejected an attempt to modify the qualified immunity standard when the underlying constitutional standard was one of reasonableness—provides a helpful framework for understanding *Crawford-El*. Return to Figure 4.1 on page 213 and consider the implications of the positions taken in *Crawford-El* by the court of appeals, Chief Justice Rehnquist, and Justice Scalia: If heightened proof of motive is required or if motive-based claims may not be asserted once an objectively valid reason for the challenged action is identified, the solid line (representing the constitutional boundary) would effectively move further out toward the immunity line. One way to understand *Crawford-El* is as a kind of corollary to *Anderson*: In both cases, the Court preserves the integrity of each line (the constitutional line and the immunity line) for its own purpose, independent of the other. Put more concretely, if it is impermissible to tamper with the test for immunity based on the standard for particular constitutional claims (*Anderson*), it is equally inappropriate to tamper with the standard for particular constitutional claims because of content of the test for immunity (*Crawford-El*).

Chief Justice Rehnquist thought *Anderson*, far from complementing *Crawford-El*, conflicted with it. A footnote in his dissent warned that the majority's result "threatens to 'Balkanize' the rule of qualified immunity," and cited *Anderson* for the proposition that "[a]n immunity that has as many variants as there are modes of official action and types of rights would not give conscientious officials that assurance of protection that it is the object of the doctrine to provide." Which account is more persuasive?

4. Procedural aspects of qualified immunity

The substantive result when qualified immunity is applied is clear: Lawsuits seeking damages for constitutional violations are defeated. Perhaps less facially apparent—but no less important—is the role of qualified immunity *procedures* in determining both how easily officers may be held accountable for misconduct and how easily the relevant constitutional principles become "clearly established" so that future plaintiffs may overcome the immunity defense. Two procedural aspects of qualified immunity are particularly influential: first, how early in the litigation qualified immunity must be resolved and by whom; and second, whether courts may avoid ruling on whether the plaintiffs' constitutional rights were violated if the court concludes that, whatever the answer to the constitutional question, the right was not "clearly established."

Regarding the first issue (the "who" and "when" of qualified immunity), *Hunter v. Bryant*, 502 U.S. 224 (1991), provided important guidance about the role of jury and the stage of the case at which the Court expected the qualified immunity question to be resolved. The facts were bizarre: In May 1985, plaintiff James Bryant delivered a handwritten letter to an office of the University of Southern California. The letter discussed a plot by a person called "Mr. Image" to assassinate President Reagan during his upcoming trip to Germany. Secret Service agents Hunter and Jordan investigated. University employees identified Bryant as the man who delivered the letter and said he'd made remarks about assassination. The agents visited Bryant's home. He admitted writing the letter but refused to identify "Mr. Image" and answered questions in a rambling fashion. Bryant was arrested for threatening the president. Charges were ultimately dropped. Bryant sued various government defendants on a range of theories.

The district court whittled the case down to Bryant's Fourth Amendment claim against Agents Hunter and Jordan for his warrantless arrest. The agents moved for summary judgment on qualified immunity grounds; the district court denied the motion. The Ninth Circuit affirmed, but the Supreme Court reversed, holding that the court of appeals erred in permitting the qualified immunity question to go to a jury:

> The Court of Appeals' confusion is evident from its statement that "[w]hether a reasonable officer could have believed he had probable cause is a question for the trier of fact, and summary judgment . . . based on lack of probable cause is proper only if there is only one reasonable conclusion a jury could reach." This statement of law is wrong for two reasons. First, it routinely places the question of immunity in the hands of the jury. Immunity ordinarily should be decided by the court long before trial. Second, the court should ask whether the agents acted reasonably under settled law in the circumstances, not whether another reasonable, or more reasonable, interpretation of the events can be constructed five years after the fact.

The Court concluded that qualified immunity was required, because even if the agents were mistaken in their belief that they had probable cause, that belief was reasonable as matter of law. Justice Scalia briefly concurred, and Justices Kennedy and Stevens each dissented; only Justice Stevens thought that the Ninth Circuit's approach and application of that approach were correct.

Another procedural aspect of qualified immunity governing when the question will be decided is defendants' ability to appeal denials of immunity on an interlocutory basis (i.e., before the case is over). The default rule governing what questions are appealable is the "final judgment rule" embodied in 28 U.S.C. § 1291, which vests courts of appeals with jurisdiction over appeals from "final decisions" of district courts. The rule of finality embodies a policy judgment that piecemeal appeals are generally inefficient; accordingly, parties must wait until the end of a case to seek review of most asserted errors. Parties need not wait, however, to appeal those few rulings that "finally determine claims of right separable from, and collateral to, rights asserted in the action, too important to be denied review and too independent of the cause itself to require that appellate consideration be deferred until the whole case is adjudicated." *Cohen v. Beneficial Industrial Loan Corp.*, 337 U.S. 541, 546 (1949). Thus, although a party whose motion to dismiss or for summary judgment fails usually lacks immediate recourse to an appellate court, the "collateral order" rule allows certain types of decisions to be appealed right away.

The question in *Mitchell v. Forsyth*, 472 U.S. 511 (1985), was whether qualified immunity falls into the narrow category of immediately-appealable "collateral orders." That case was a suit for damages stemming from a warrantless wiretap authorized by John Mitchell, who was President Nixon's Attorney General. Mitchell claimed both absolute and qualified immunity. After rejecting the position that an attorney general is entitled to absolute immunity for non-prosecutorial functions, Justice White's majority opinion held that Mitchell was entitled to an interlocutory appeal from the district court's denial of qualified immunity:

> A major characteristic of the denial or granting of a claim appealable under [the] "collateral order" doctrine is that "unless it can be reviewed before [the proceedings terminate], it can never be reviewed at all." When a district court has denied a defendant's claim of right not to stand trial, on double jeopardy grounds, for example, we have consistently held the court's decision appealable, for such a right cannot be effectively vindicated after the trial has occurred. Thus, the denial of a substantial claim of absolute immunity is an order appealable before final judgment, for the essence of absolute immunity is its possessor's entitlement not to have to answer for his conduct in a civil damages action.
>
> At the heart of the issue before us is the question whether qualified immunity shares this essential attribute of absolute immunity—whether qualified immunity is in fact an entitlement not to stand trial under certain circumstances. The conception animating the qualified immunity doctrine as set forth in *Harlow v. Fitzgerald*, is that "where an official's duties legitimately require action in which clearly established rights are not implicated, the public interest may be better served by action taken 'with independence and without fear of consequences.'" . . . [T]he "consequences" with which we were concerned in *Harlow* are not limited to liability for money damages; they also include "the general costs of subjecting officials to the risks of trial—distraction of officials from their governmental duties, inhibition of discretionary action, and deterrence of able people from public service." *Harlow*. Indeed, *Harlow* emphasizes that even such pretrial matters as discovery are to be avoided if possible, as "[i]nquiries of this kind can be peculiarly disruptive of effective government." . . .

Harlow thus recognized an entitlement not to stand trial or face the other burdens of litigation, conditioned on the resolution of the essentially legal question whether the conduct of which the plaintiff complains violated clearly established law. The entitlement is an *immunity from suit* rather than a mere defense to liability; and like an absolute immunity, it is effectively lost if a case is erroneously permitted to go to trial. Accordingly, the reasoning that underlies the immediate appealability of an order denying absolute immunity indicates to us that the denial of qualified immunity should be similarly appealable: in each case, the district court's decision is effectively unreviewable on appeal from a final judgment.

The Court went on to hold that Mitchell was immune because the Supreme Court decision demonstrating that his conduct was unconstitutional was issued a year after the challenged action. Justices Powell and Rehnquist did not participate in the decision. Chief Justice Burger and Justices O'Connor and Stevens each wrote concurring opinions; none disagreed with the majority regarding interlocutory appeal.

Justice Brennan, joined by Justice Marshall, dissented on that issue:

[I]f one's right to summary judgment under Federal Rule of Civil Procedure 56 were characterized as a right not to stand trial where the opposing party has failed to create a genuine issue of material fact, denials of summary judgment motions would be immediately appealable. . . . Similar results would follow with a host of constitutional (e.g., right to jury trial, right to due process), statutory (e.g., venue, necessary parties), or other rights; if the right be characterized as a right not to stand trial except in certain circumstances, it follows ineluctably that the right cannot be vindicated on final judgment. . . .

The Court claims that subjecting officials to trial may lead to "'distraction of officials from their governmental duties, inhibition of discretionary action, and deterrence of able people from public service.'" Even if I agreed with the Court that in the post-*Harlow* environment these evils were all real, I could not possibly agree that they justify the Court's conclusion. These same ill results would flow from an adverse decision on any dispositive preliminary issue in a lawsuit against an official defendant—whether based on a statute of limitations, collateral estoppel, lack of jurisdiction, or the like. . . . Yet I hardly think the Court is prepared to hold that a government official suffering an adverse ruling on any of these issues would be entitled to an immediate appeal.

[T]he right to interlocutory appeal recognized today is generally available to (and can be expected to be widely pursued by) virtually any governmental official who is sued in his personal capacity, regardless of the merits of his claim to qualified immunity or the strength of the claim against him. As a result, I fear that today's decision will give government officials a potent weapon to use against plaintiffs, delaying litigation endlessly with interlocutory appeals.

Mitchell did, as Justice Brennan predicted, open the door to the widespread pursuit of appeals from qualified immunity denials. (Whether the attendant delays in case resolution are justified by the values served by these appeals remains a matter of debate.)

But the Supreme Court recognized an important exception to the interlocutory-appeal right in *Johnson v. Jones*, 515 U.S. 304 (1995). The plaintiff there, a diabetic, claimed that five officers found him while he was having an insulin seizure, mistook him for drunk, and arrested him using excessive force instead of attending to his medical needs; the plaintiff suffered broken ribs as a result. Three of the officers moved for summary judgment on the ground that, whatever their two comrades had done, the evidence did not implicate the three movants in the plaintiff's injuries. The district court denied summary judgment, holding that circumstantial evidence in the record supported the claims against these three officers as well as the other two. The three officers took an interlocutory appeal from the denial of qualified immunity at summary judgment, but the court of appeals dismissed the appeal for lack of jurisdiction, holding that an "evidence insufficiency" or "we didn't do it" contention was not the type of ruling covered by *Mitchell*. The Supreme Court's unanimous opinion by Justice Breyer affirmed:

> The dispute underlying the *Mitchell* appeal involved the application of "clearly established" law to a given (for appellate purposes undisputed) set of facts. And, the Court, in its opinion, explicitly limited its holding to appeals challenging, not a district court's determination about what factual issues are "genuine," but the purely legal issue what law was "clearly established." . . .
>
> [T]he issue here at stake—the existence, or nonexistence, of a triable issue of fact—is the kind of issue that trial judges, not appellate judges, confront almost daily. Institutionally speaking, appellate judges enjoy no comparative expertise in such matters. And, to that extent, interlocutory appeals are less likely to bring important error-correcting benefits here than where purely legal matters are at issue, as in *Mitchell*. . . .
>
> [T]he close connection between this kind of issue and the factual matter that will likely surface at trial means that the appellate court, in the many instances in which it upholds a district court's decision denying summary judgment, may well be faced with approximately the same factual issue again, after trial, with just enough change (brought about by the trial testimony) to require it, once again, to canvass the record. That is to say, an interlocutory appeal concerning this kind of issue in a sense makes unwise use of appellate courts' time, by forcing them to decide in the context of a less developed record, an issue very similar to one they may well decide anyway later, on a record that will permit a better decision. . . .
>
> We recognize that, whether a district court's denial of summary judgment amounts to (a) a determination about pre-existing "clearly established" law, or (b) a determination about "genuine" issues of fact for trial, it still forces public officials to trial. And, to that extent, it threatens to undercut the very policy (protecting public officials from lawsuits) that (the *Mitchell* Court held) militates in favor of immediate appeals. Nonetheless, the countervailing considerations that we have mentioned . . . are too strong to permit the extension of *Mitchell* to encompass appeals from orders of the sort before us.

Notes and Questions

1. What is the difference between the type of case in which an interlocutory appeal is allowed and the type in which it is forbidden?

2. All three of these cases—*Hunter*, *Mitchell*, and *Johnson*—are about how quickly the qualified immunity question should be determined and the proper scope

of factual adjudication in that determination. Do they speak with a single voice on these questions? If the Court is so interested in getting qualified immunity issues out of the hands of the jury (*Hunter*), why did it reject certain types of interlocutory appeals (*Johnson*)? Why doesn't the "immunity from suit" characterization (*Mitchell*) require the resolution of all appeals, no matter how fact-based, forthwith (*Johnson*)? Can you reconcile these cases?

3. Why is early termination of § 1983 officer suits such an important goal, in the view of the *Hunter* and *Mitchell* majorities? Which of the underlying purposes of qualified immunity, if any, does it serve?

4. What are the effects of these three cases on parties' incentives to settle?

* * *

We now turn to the issue of the *sequence* of decision for the two questions encompassed within a qualified immunity determination. In opposing a qualified immunity defense, a civil rights plaintiff must establish two separate but related propositions: first, that a constitutional right was violated; and second, that the right in question (considered at the appropriate level of generality) was "clearly established." In what order should courts resolve these two questions? In what circumstances can or should they avoid answering both?

The court gave a clear (but not, it turns out, the final) answer to these questions in *Saucier v. Katz*, 533 U.S. 194 (2001). There, a protestor at a speech by Vice President Gore sued police who removed him from the speech using (allegedly) excessive force. Although the bulk of the Court's decision concerned whether the reasonableness inquiry for excessive force merges with the reasonableness inquiry for qualified immunity (applying *Anderson*, the Court held that is does not, see Section B.2), Justice Kennedy's opinion for the Court also laid out the proper procedure for adjudicating qualified immunity questions:

> In a suit against an officer for an alleged violation of a constitutional right, the requisites of a qualified immunity defense must be considered in proper sequence. . . .
>
> A court required to rule upon the qualified immunity issue must consider . . . this threshold question: Taken in the light most favorable to the party asserting the injury, do the facts alleged show the officer's conduct violated a constitutional right? This must be the initial inquiry. In the course of determining whether a constitutional right was violated on the premises alleged, a court might find it necessary to set forth principles which will become the basis for a holding that a right is clearly established. This is the process for the law's elaboration from case to case, and it is one reason for our insisting upon turning to the existence or nonexistence of a constitutional right as the first inquiry. The law might be deprived of this explanation were a court simply to skip ahead to the question whether the law clearly established that the officer's conduct was unlawful in the circumstances of the case.
>
> If no constitutional right would have been violated were the allegations established, there is no necessity for further inquiries concerning qualified immunity. On the other hand, if a violation could be made out on a favorable view of the parties' submissions, the next, sequential step is to ask whether the right was clearly established.

The benefit of facilitating "the law's elaboration from case" is significant. The absence of a ruling on the constitutional merits not only leaves officers and the public at large without guidance as to their rights, but also sets up the possibility that a particular type of conduct could be unconstitutional yet never redressable: If no court addresses the constitutional merits, the violation will never become "clearly established" so as to defeat qualified immunity. The constitutional violation could recur and qualified immunity would apply every time.

Nonetheless, the two-step process of *Saucier*, which came to be known as the "order of battle," drew widespread criticism. One of the most influential objections was that the order of battle promoted unnecessary constitutional decisionmaking: If the end result of the case was to grant immunity, why decide the constitutional question at all?

Several longstanding traditions counsel against unnecessary decisionmaking, particularly in the area of constitutional law. One relevant tradition, famously espoused by Justice Brandeis and still invoked in the modern era, urges that the Court "not pass upon a constitutional question although properly presented by the record, if there is also present some other ground upon which the case may be disposed of." *Ashwander v. Tenn. Valley Auth.*, 297 U.S. 288, 347 (1936) (Brandeis, J., concurring); *see, e.g., Slack v. McDaniel*, 529 U.S. 473, 485 (2000); *City of Mesquite v. Aladdin's Castle, Inc.*, 455 U.S. 283, 294-95 (1982). Another tradition is the Court's unwillingness to issue "advisory opinions," i.e., opinions that deal in "abstractions" rather than concrete controversies. *See Muskrat v. United States*, 219 U.S. 346, 354 (1911) (tracing this tradition to Chief Justice Jay's refusal to answer an abstract question of law posed by the Washington Administration). Many jurists objected to the "order of battle" because it required deciding a constitutional question that could be avoided.

Eight years after *Saucier*, the Court reconsidered the order-of-battle requirement.

Pearson v. Callahan
555 U.S. 223 (2009)

▓ *Justice ALITO delivered the opinion of the Court.* . . .

[An informant for a Utah law enforcement task force told police that plaintiff Afton Callahan had arranged to sell the informant drugs that evening. After the informant was admitted into Callahan's home, and the transaction occurred, the informant gave a pre-arranged signal to police, who entered without a warrant and arrested Callahan. The criminal case against Callahan was thrown out because of the warrantless entry. Callahan then sued under § 1983. The district court held that the officers violated the Fourth Amendment but granted qualified immunity because they could reasonably have relied on the "consent-once-removed" doctrine, which permits officers to enter a home without a warrant when consent to enter has been granted to an undercover officer or informant who has observed contraband in plain view. The Tenth Circuit reversed, holding that the constitutional violation was clearly established because that circuit had not broadened the "consent-once-removed" doctrine to informants as well as undercover officers.]

Our decisions prior to *Saucier* had held that "the better approach to resolving cases in which the defense of qualified immunity is raised is to determine first whether the plaintiff has alleged a deprivation of a constitutional right at all." *Saucier* made that suggestion a mandate. For the first time, we held that whether "the facts alleged show the officer's conduct violated a constitutional right . . . must be the initial inquiry" in every qualified immunity case. Only after completing this first step, we said, may a court turn to "the next, sequential step," namely, "whether the right was clearly established."

This two-step procedure, the *Saucier* Court reasoned, is necessary to support the Constitution's "elaboration from case to case" and to prevent constitutional stagnation. "The law might be deprived of this explanation were a court simply to skip ahead to the question whether the law clearly established that the officer's conduct was unlawful in the circumstances of the case." . . .

Although "[w]e approach the reconsideration of [our] decisions . . . with the utmost caution," "[s]tare decisis is not an inexorable command." Revisiting precedent is particularly appropriate where, as here, a departure would not upset expectations, the precedent consists of a judge-made rule that was recently adopted to improve the operation of the courts, and experience has pointed up the precedent's shortcomings. . . .

Nor does this matter implicate "the general presumption that legislative changes should be left to Congress." We recognize that "considerations of stare decisis weigh heavily in the area of statutory construction, where Congress is free to change this Court's interpretation of its legislation." But the *Saucier* rule is judge made and implicates an important matter involving internal Judicial Branch operations. Any change should come from this Court, not Congress. . . .

Lower court judges, who have had the task of applying the *Saucier* rule on a regular basis for the past eight years, have not been reticent in their criticism of *Saucier*'s "rigid order of battle." Members of this Court have also voiced criticism of the *Saucier* rule.

Where a decision has "been questioned by Members of the Court in later decisions and [has] defied consistent application by the lower courts," these factors weigh in favor of reconsideration. Collectively, the factors we have noted make our present reevaluation of the *Saucier* two-step protocol appropriate.

On reconsidering the procedure required in *Saucier*, we conclude that, while the sequence set forth there is often appropriate, it should no longer be regarded as mandatory. The judges of the district courts and the courts of appeals should be permitted to exercise their sound discretion in deciding which of the two prongs of the qualified immunity analysis should be addressed first in light of the circumstances in the particular case at hand.

Although we now hold that the *Saucier* protocol should not be regarded as mandatory in all cases, we continue to recognize that it is often beneficial. For one thing, there are cases in which there would be little if any conservation of judicial resources to be had by beginning and ending with a discussion of the "clearly established" prong. "[I]t often may be difficult to decide whether a right is clearly established without deciding precisely what the existing constitutional right happens to be." *Lyons v. Xenia*, 417 F.3d 565, 581 (C.A.6 2005) (Sutton, J., concurring). In some cases, a discussion of why the relevant facts do not violate clearly established law may make it apparent that in fact the relevant facts do not make out a constitutional violation at all. In addition, the *Saucier* Court was certainly correct in noting that the two-step procedure promotes the development of constitutional precedent and is especially valuable with respect to questions that do not frequently arise in cases in which a qualified immunity defense is unavailable.

At the same time, however, the rigid *Saucier* procedure comes with a price. The procedure sometimes results in a substantial expenditure of scarce judicial resources on difficult questions that have no effect on the outcome of the case. There are cases in which it is plain that a constitutional right is not clearly established but far from obvious whether in fact there is such a right. District courts and courts of appeals with heavy caseloads are often understandably unenthusiastic about what may seem to be an essentially academic exercise.

Unnecessary litigation of constitutional issues also wastes the parties' resources. . . . *Saucier*'s two-step protocol "disserve[s] the purpose of qualified immunity" when it "forces the parties to endure additional burdens of suit—such as the costs of litigating constitutional questions and delays attributable to resolving them—when the suit otherwise could be disposed of more readily." Brief for National Association of Criminal Defense Lawyers as Amicus Curiae 30.

Although the first prong of the *Saucier* procedure is intended to further the development of constitutional precedent, opinions following that procedure often fail to make a meaningful contribution to such development. For one thing, there are cases in which the constitutional question is so factbound that the decision provides little guidance for future cases. . . .

A constitutional decision resting on an uncertain interpretation of state law is also of doubtful precedential importance. . . .

When qualified immunity is asserted at the pleading stage, the precise factual basis for the plaintiff's claim or claims may be hard to identify. . . .

There are circumstances in which the first step of the *Saucier* procedure may create a risk of bad decisionmaking. The lower courts sometimes encounter cases in which the briefing of constitutional questions is woefully inadequate.

Although the *Saucier* rule prescribes the sequence in which the issues must be discussed by a court in its opinion, the rule does not—and obviously cannot—specify the sequence in which judges reach their conclusions in their own internal thought processes. Thus, there will be cases in which a court will rather quickly and easily decide that there was no violation of clearly established law before turning to the more difficult question whether the relevant facts make out a constitutional question at all. In such situations, there is a risk that a court may not devote as much care as it would in other circumstances to the decision of the constitutional issue.

Rigid adherence to the *Saucier* rule may make it hard for affected parties to obtain appellate review of constitutional decisions that may have a serious prospective effect on their operations. Where a court holds that a defendant committed a constitutional violation but that the violation was not clearly established, the defendant may face a difficult situation. As the winning party, the defendant's right to appeal the adverse holding on the constitutional question may be contested.[2] In cases like *Bunting*, the "prevailing" defendant faces an unenviable choice: "compl[y] with the lower court's advisory dictum without opportunity to seek appellate [or certiorari] review," or "def[y] the views of the lower court, adher[e] to practices that have been declared illegal, and thus invit[e] new suits" and potential "punitive damages."

Adherence to *Saucier*'s two-step protocol departs from the general rule of constitutional avoidance and runs counter to the "older, wiser judicial counsel 'not to pass on questions of constitutionality . . . unless such adjudication is unavoidable.'" *See Ashwander v. TVA*, 297 U.S. 288, 347 (1936) (Brandeis, J., concurring). . . .

[Granting] flexibility properly reflects our respect for the lower federal courts that bear the brunt of adjudicating these cases. Because the two-step *Saucier* procedure is often, but not always, advantageous, the judges of the district courts and the courts of appeals are in the best position to determine the order of decisionmaking that will best facilitate the fair and efficient disposition of each case.

Any misgivings concerning our decision to withdraw from the mandate set forth in *Saucier* are unwarranted. Our decision does not prevent the lower courts from following the *Saucier* procedure; it simply recognizes that those courts should have the discretion to decide whether that procedure is worthwhile in particular cases. Moreover, the development of constitutional law is by no means entirely dependent on cases in which the defendant may seek qualified immunity. Most of the constitutional issues that are presented in § 1983 damages actions and *Bivens* cases also arise in cases in which that defense is not available, such as criminal cases and § 1983 cases against a municipality, as well as § 1983 cases against individuals where injunctive relief is sought instead of or in addition to damages. . . .

---

2. In *Bunting [v. Mellen]*, the Court of Appeals followed the *Saucier* two-step protocol and first held that the Virginia Military Institute's use of the word "God" in a "supper roll call" ceremony violated the Establishment Clause, but then granted the defendants qualified immunity because the law was not clearly established at the relevant time. *Mellen v. Bunting*, 327 F.3d 355, 365-376 (C.A.4 2003), *cert. denied*, 541 U.S. 1019 (2004). Although they had a judgment in their favor below, the defendants asked this Court to review the adverse constitutional ruling. Dissenting from the denial of certiorari, Justice Scalia, joined by Chief Justice Rehnquist, criticized "a perceived procedural tangle of the Court's own making." The "tangle" arose from the Court's "'settled refusal' to entertain an appeal by a party on an issue as to which he prevailed" below, a practice that insulates from review adverse merits decisions that are "locked inside" favorable qualified immunity rulings.

[The Court then exercised its discretion to reach only the "clearly established" question in Callahan's case without addressing the constitutional merits. The Court noted that the federal courts of appeals had widely accepted the "consent-once-removed" doctrine prior to the conduct at issue here, and the Seventh Circuit had applied it where the consent was, as here, given to an informant rather than an undercover officer, even though the Tenth Circuit now disagreed with that application. Therefore, the Court determined that the claimed right at issue was not "clearly established" and so reversed the denial of qualified immunity.]

Notes and Questions

1. Figures 4.3 and 4.4 illustrate how *Saucier* and *Pearson* differ. Notice which outcomes are possible under each regime.

2. To a defender of *Saucier*, the Court's treatment of the merits in *Pearson* itself is perhaps the best illustration of the flaws of the new flexible approach. The Court recognized a circuit split but avoided resolving it by skipping to the "clearly established" inquiry. The Court thus left the law where it found it—unsettled. Do the benefits of the new rule justify this result—and many others like it?

3. A supporter of *Pearson* might observe that civil actions raising constitutional claims for damages are not the only means to obtain rulings on constitutional questions. Criminal cases may involve constitutional claims raised via motions to suppress evidence or other challenges; civil cases may seek injunctive relief (to which qualified immunity is no defense) or may proceed against municipalities (which, as we'll learn in Chapter 5, lack qualified immunity).

   Each of these mechanisms has its own limitations, however: There are exceptions to the exclusionary rule in criminal cases; many plaintiffs lack standing to seek injunctive relief (see Chapter 11); and special limitations apply to municipal

Figure 4.3: *Qualified immunity order of battle under* Saucier—*three possible paths*

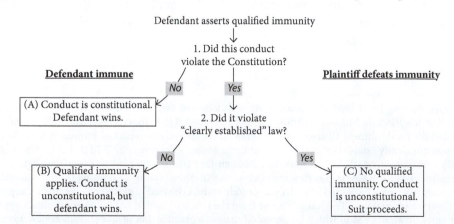

The Saucier *"order of battle" required a strict sequence of decision for qualified immunity motions. As a result, the court would always answer the constitutional question presented.*

Figure 4.4: *Qualified immunity decisionmaking after* Pearson—*four possible paths*

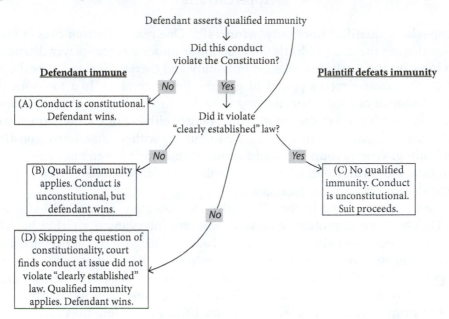

The paths identified in Saucier *are still available, but after* Pearson, *courts also have a new option to resolve qualified immunity questions: avoid the constitutional question, skip to the "clearly established" inquiry, and answer that in the negative (outcome "D"). The result is a grant of immunity based on the absence of "clearly established" law, with no decision establishing the law for the future.*

liability for constitutional violations (see Chapter 5). Should the Court have considered the likelihood that constitutional law will actually be developed in these alternative contexts before abandoning the order of battle? Or does allowing courts the discretion to reach the constitutional question provide sufficient safeguard against stagnation in constitutional law?

4. Is the Court correct that litigating the merits and immunity at the same time imposes a significant burden on the parties? How many extra briefs does the *Saucier* approach require?

5. In *Wilson v. Layne*, 526 U.S. 603 (1999), the Court recognized a constitutional violation where police permitted a member of the press to accompany them when executing an arrest warrant at a private home, but the Court held that the law had not been clearly established, and so qualified immunity applied. In a solo dissent, Justice Stevens objected that "the Court today authorizes one free violation" of the constitutional rule it recognized. What are the implications of this criticism for decisions in which a court skips the merits question entirely? Is there a limit to the number of "free violations"?

6. Which is better for civil rights plaintiffs, *Saucier* or *Pearson*? In light of the "free violation" concern, it might seem the former. Why might plaintiffs prefer the latter? Civil rights organizations were not of one mind on this issue: The ACLU filed an amicus brief urging the Court to retain *Saucier*, while the National Association of Criminal Defense Lawyers urged the Court to abandon it.

Applications

1. Appeals by qualified immunity "winners."   One reason *Pearson* cites in favor of abandoning the order of battle is the conundrum for a repeat-player defendant who loses on the merits but wins on immunity and therefore cannot appeal even though the adverse merits precedent governs future conduct. In a footnote, the Court discusses one such case, *Bunting v. Mellen*, in which it had recently denied review. *Pearson*'s grant of discretion reduces the likelihood of such situations arising, because defendants can now receive immunity without an adverse constitutional ruling. When a court *does* find a constitutional violation en route to granting immunity, should the Court relax its usual rule against appealing from a victory and permit the winning party to seek review?

The Court answered in the affirmative in *Camreta v. Greene*, 563 U.S. 692 (2011). There, child protective services workers interviewed a girl at her elementary school about allegations of sexual abuse. The girl's mother sued, claiming the interview violated the Fourth Amendment. The court of appeals agreed but granted qualified immunity. The winning government defendants sought Supreme Court review. Justice Kagan's opinion for the majority held that the grant of immunity did not prevent the Court from reviewing the case, because even though the defendants had won and would not have to pay damages, they still had a personal stake in appealing:

> [W]hen immunized officials seek to challenge a ruling that their conduct violated the Constitution . . . the judgment may have prospective effect on the parties. The court in such a case says: "Although this official is immune from damages today, what he did violates the Constitution and he or anyone else who does that thing again will be personally liable." If the official regularly engages in that conduct as part of his job (as Camreta does), he suffers injury caused by the adverse constitutional ruling. So long as it continues in effect, he must either change the way he performs his duties or risk a meritorious damages action. Only by overturning the ruling on appeal can the official gain clearance to engage in the conduct in the future. . . . And conversely, if the person who initially brought the suit may again be subject to the challenged conduct, she has a stake in preserving the court's holding. Only if the ruling remains good law will she have ongoing protection from the practice.

The majority also held that this situation justified an exception to the Court's usual prudential rule of refusing to consider cases where review is sought by the prevailing party:

> The constitutional determinations that prevailing parties ask us to consider in these cases are not mere dicta or "statements in opinions." They are rulings that have a significant future effect on the conduct of public officials—both the prevailing parties and their co-workers—and the policies of the government units to which they belong. And more: they are rulings self-consciously designed to produce this effect, by establishing controlling law and preventing invocations of immunity in later cases. And still more: they are rulings designed this way with this Court's permission, to promote clarity—and observance—of constitutional rules. . . .

In . . . qualified immunity cases, a court can enter judgment without ever ruling on the (perhaps difficult) constitutional claim the plaintiff has raised. Small wonder, then, that a court might leave that issue for another day.

But we have long recognized that this day may never come—that our regular policy of avoidance sometimes does not fit the qualified immunity situation because it threatens to leave standards of official conduct permanently in limbo. . . .

For this reason, we have permitted lower courts to avoid avoidance—that is, to determine whether a right exists before examining whether it was clearly established. . . . In general, courts should think hard, and then think hard again, before turning small cases into large ones. But it remains true that following the two-step sequence—defining constitutional rights and only then conferring immunity—is sometimes beneficial to clarify the legal standards governing public officials. . . .

Given its purpose and effect, such a decision is reviewable in this Court at the behest of an immunized official. No mere dictum, a constitutional ruling preparatory to a grant of immunity creates law that governs the official's behavior. . . . [I]f our usual bar on review applied, it would undermine the very purpose served by the two-step process, "which is to clarify constitutional rights without undue delay." *Bunting* (Scalia, J., dissenting from denial of certiorari).

The Court cautioned that it was leaving open whether an *appeals court* could entertain an appeal from a *district court* decision ruling against the defendant on the merits but granting immunity. That situation could be different, the majority explained, because district court opinions, unlike appellate decisions, are not binding precedent. The Court went on to conclude that a separate jurisdictional problem barred adjudication in *Camreta*: The case had become moot because S.G. had moved to another state and therefore had no personal stake in protection against unconstitutional interrogation by her old school district.

Concurring, Justice Scalia indicated a willingness to reconsider the *Pearson* rule:

I join the Court's opinion, which reasonably applies our precedents, strange though they may be. The alternative solution, as Justice Kennedy suggests, is to end the extraordinary practice of ruling upon constitutional questions unnecessarily when the defendant possesses qualified immunity. *See Saucier v. Katz.* The parties have not asked us to adopt that approach, but I would be willing to consider it in an appropriate case.

Concurring in the judgment, Justice Sotomayor, joined by Justice Breyer, would have gone no further than to hold the case moot.

In dissent, Justice Kennedy, joined by Justice Thomas, agreed with the majority's identification of the problem but argued that it chose the wrong solution:

Under today's decision, it appears that the Court's ability to review merits determinations in qualified immunity cases is contingent on the defendant who has been sued. A defendant who has left the government's employ or otherwise lacks an interest in disputing the merits will be unable to obtain further review. . . .

When an officer is sued for taking an extraordinary action, such as using excessive force during a high-speed car chase, there is little possibility that a constitutional decision on the merits will again influence that officer's conduct. The officer . . . would have no interest in litigating the merits in the court of appeals and, under the Court's rule, would seem unable to obtain review of a merits ruling by petitioning for certiorari. . . . Once again, the decision today allows plaintiffs to obtain binding constitutional determinations on the merits that lie beyond this Court's jurisdiction to review. The Court thus fails to solve the problem it identifies. . . .

The Court's analysis appears to rest on the premise that the reasoning of the decision below in itself causes Camreta injury. . . .

An inert rule of law does not cause particular, concrete injury; only the specific threat of its enforcement can do so. . . . Without an adverse judgment from which to appeal, Camreta has in effect filed a new declaratory judgment action in this Court against the Court of Appeals. This is no more consistent with Article III than filing a declaratory judgment action against this Court for its issuance of an adverse precedent or against Congress in response to its enactment of an unconstitutional law.

If today's decision proves to be more than an isolated anomaly, the Court might find it necessary to reconsider its special permission that the Courts of Appeals may issue unnecessary merits determinations in qualified immunity cases with binding precedential effect.

Thus, the ink had hardly dried on the Court's unanimous solution to the "order of battle" question in *Pearson* when *Camreta* arose and reflected new objections to that solution. Of the seven Justices who took a position on the main issue in *Camreta*, three appeared ready to reconsider the *Pearson* rule in light of principles that did not appear to be on the Court's radar in *Saucier* or *Pearson*. Thus, in the course of a decade, three Justices (Scalia, Kennedy, and Thomas) moved from the position that courts must address the merits first (*Saucier*) to allowing courts discretion to choose whether to address the merits (*Pearson*) to suggesting that perhaps courts should never address the merits unless they also determine that the law is "clearly established" (the concurrence and dissent in *Camreta*). Does the Justices' vacillation about the appropriate rule reflect some deeper problem with the way the procedural jurisprudence of qualified immunity has evolved? Or does this particular question just lack a fully satisfactory answer?

The dissent argues with some force that a judicial decision in these circumstances would be wholly advisory and that defendants' certiorari petition effectively asked for a declaratory judgment against the court of appeals. What is the majority's answer, and how persuasive is it? Does it matter that individual law enforcement officers are almost always, in practice, represented by counsel for the governmental body that employs them?

The majority permits defendants to seek review from merits rulings against them even when they nonetheless receive immunity. The dissent would disallow such review but also (it suggests) the underlying type of ruling from which such review is sought (i.e., a ruling recognizing a violation but granting immunity). Is anyone satisfied with the result in *Bunting*—where the appeals court could render a merits decision en route to granting immunity but the defendant could not seek review? Why not? Isn't that the most straightforward application of the prohibition against advisory opinions in light of the *Pearson* framework?

2. Strategic behavior in the courts of appeals. Professor Jack Beerman warned that the Court's failure to provide guidance in *Pearson* regarding when courts should reach the constitutional merits would create problems:

> Leaving to the standardless, unreviewable discretion of courts the decision whether to reach the constitutional merits before determining whether a right is clearly established . . . invites strategic behavior by courts and litigants who, in each case, are left to determine whether it would be beneficial to reach the merits or to try to influence whether the merits are reached. Judges who believe strongly in the doctrine of constitutional avoidance will be in a quandary as they watch their colleagues shape constitutional law through merits decisions in qualified immunity cases. . . . [I]t seems inconsistent with fundamental principles of judicial behavior to leave the determination of whether to make an "unnecessary" decision of constitutional law to the unconstrained discretion of individual judges.

Jack M. Beermann, *Qualified Immunity and Constitutional Avoidance*, 2009 Sup. Ct. Rev. 139, 143.

Through empirical analysis of post-*Pearson* qualified immunity decisions, Professors Aaron Nielson and Christopher Walker have confirmed Professor Beerman's hypothesis that *Pearson* opens the door to judicial behavior that could be characterized as "strategic." For instance:

> In contrast to D[emocrat-appointed] judges, R[epublican-appointed] judges were much more likely (27.4% to 18.0%) to decide not to exercise their *Pearson* discretion and just hold that the right was not clearly established—thus making no new constitutional law. This is consistent with the theory that R[epublican-appointed] judges in the aggregate would be less likely to use *Pearson* discretion because the constitutional question is unnecessary to the judgment.

Aaron L. Nielson & Christopher J. Walker, *The New Qualified Immunity*, 89 S. Cal. L. Rev. 1, 45-46 (2015). In a follow-up study, the authors considered how the composition of three-judge panels affected the decision whether to reach a constitutional question. Examining the differences between panels consisting entirely of judges appointed by Democrats (3D panels) and panels consisting entirely of judges appointed by Republicans (3R panels), the authors found that

> the panel effects are pronounced and statistically significant—suggesting that the unified panels are more aggressive in finding no constitutional violations (for 3R panels) and in recognizing new constitutional rights (for 3D panels), and that mixed panels lead to more normal patterns in the use of *Pearson* discretion.

Aaron L. Nielson & Christopher J. Walker, *Strategic Immunity*, 66 Emory L.J. 55, 117 (2016).

Is "strategic behavior" a significant drawback of *Pearson*? Answering this question requires defining "strategic" and making normative judgments about whether such behavior is a bug of our system or a feature. Isn't "strategic" behavior in this context just another way to describe "giving effect to one's views," and isn't that, in turn, merely the act of judging? Moreover, aren't judges' baseline views why presidents nominate them to begin with? Don't judges act "strategically"—i.e., give effect to their views—no matter what the baseline rule?

On the other hand, there's a difference between acknowledging tendencies and encouraging them. If we are serious about the idea of the rule of law and neutral principles that don't vary from judge to judge and circuit to circuit, shouldn't we circumscribe the opportunities for "strategic" behavior as much as possible? One way to do that, Professors Nielson and Walker suggest, is to require judges to justify in writing their exercise of discretion under *Pearson*. Nielson & Walker, *Strategic Immunity*, 66 Emory L.J. at 119. Will that help? Or will judges just be equally strategic about their reasons for exercising discretion?

3. The Supreme Court's own exercise of discretion.   In the years since *Pearson*, the Supreme Court has decided numerous qualified immunity cases in summary fashion, reversing a lower court's denial of immunity without deciding whether the conduct at issue was constitutional. *See, e.g., City of Escondido v. Emmons*, 139 S. Ct. 500 (2019) (per curiam); *Kisela v. Hughes*, 138 S. Ct. 1148 (2018) (per curiam); *White v. Pauly*, 137 S. Ct. 548 (2017) (per curiam); *Mullenix v. Luna*, 136 S. Ct. 305 (2015) (per curiam); *Taylor v. Barkes*, 135 S. Ct. 2042 (2015) (per curiam); *Carroll v. Carman*, 574 U.S. 13 (2014) (per curiam); *Stanton v. Sims*, 571 U.S. 3 (2013) (per curiam).

Although the Supreme Court's own rules state that it does not generally take cases solely to correct errors by courts of appeals, that is what seems to be happening here. Indeed, these cases accomplish little else—they do not clarify substantive constitutional law and (as in *Pearson* itself) they sometimes leave asserted circuit splits on the merits unresolved. Remarking on this practice, two Justices have criticized "a disturbing trend regarding the use of this Court's resources": that the Court "ha[s] not hesitated to summarily reverse courts for wrongly denying officers the protection of qualified immunity in cases involving the use of force" while "we rarely intervene where courts wrongly afford officers the benefit of qualified immunity in these same cases." *Salazar-Limon v. City of Houston*, 137 S. Ct. 1277, 1282-83 (2017) (Sotomayor, J., joined by Ginsburg, J., dissenting from denial of certiorari).

Does the summary-reversal trend identified here affect how you evaluate *Pearson*? If you think these summary reversals are problematic, is the problem *Pearson*? The practice of summary reversal generally? Qualified immunity generally? Some combination of these?

5.   QUALIFIED IMMUNITY AND PRIVATE ACTORS

Recall from Chapter 1 that sometimes private actors may be sued under § 1983 because they are classified as "state actors" and therefore act "under color" of law. Does the same immunity that applies to government officials apply to private actors as well? The answer varies based on the activity in which the private actor is engaged.

In *Wyatt v. Cole*, 504 U.S. 158 (1992), one rancher (Wyatt) sued another (Cole) after Cole used a Mississippi replevin statute to obtain a state court order that the county sheriff seize two dozen cattle, a tractor, and other personal property from Wyatt. The state statute was held to violate due process, and Cole was held to be a state actor suable under § 1983. (If this seems like a curious result, return to the discussion of *Lugar v. Edmondson Oil Co.*, 457 U.S. 922 (1982), in Chapter 1, Section B.) The question before the Court was whether Cole could claim qualified immunity. Justice O'Connor's opinion for the Court held that he could not:

> [A]s our precedents make clear, the reasons for recognizing such an immunity were based not simply on the existence of a good faith defense at common law, but on the special policy concerns involved in suing government officials. . . .
>
> Qualified immunity strikes a balance between compensating those who have been injured by official conduct and protecting government's ability to perform its traditional functions. Accordingly, we have recognized qualified immunity for government officials where it was necessary to preserve their ability to serve the public good or to ensure that talented candidates were not deterred by the threat of damages suits from entering public service. In short, the qualified immunity recognized in *Harlow* acts to safeguard government, and thereby to protect the public at large, not to benefit its agents.
>
> These rationales are not transferable to private parties. . . . Unlike school board members, or police officers, or Presidential aides, private parties hold no office requiring them to exercise discretion; nor are they principally concerned with enhancing the public good. Accordingly, extending *Harlow* qualified immunity to private parties would have no bearing on whether public officials are able to act forcefully and decisively in their jobs or on whether qualified applicants enter public service. Moreover, unlike with government officials performing discretionary functions, the public interest will not be unduly impaired if private individuals are required to proceed to trial to resolve their legal disputes. In short, the nexus between private parties and the historic purposes of qualified immunity is simply too attenuated to justify such an extension of our doctrine of immunity.

Justice Kennedy, joined by Justice Scalia, concurred to assert that the focus of the analysis should be history, not policy. Dissenting, Chief Justice Rehnquist, joined by Justices Souter and Thomas, argued that both history and policy supported the extension of immunity.

Wyatt involved a context far from the ones presented by most § 1983 claims against private parties. *Wyatt*'s significance lies in its application to private parties performing more traditional government functions, as in the next two cases about private prison guards and attorneys performing contract work for the government.

Richardson v. McKnight
521 U.S. 399 (1997)

▪ *Justice* BREYER *delivered the opinion of the Court.* . . .

[An individual incarcerated at a privately-run prison in Tennessee sued two prison guards for excessive force—specifically, subjecting him to extremely tight physical restraints. The guards asserted qualified immunity. The district court denied immunity and the appeals court affirmed.] . . .

History does not reveal a "firmly rooted" tradition of immunity applicable to privately employed prison guards. Correctional services in the United States have undergone various transformations. Government-employed prison guards may have enjoyed a kind of immunity defense arising out of their status as public employees at common law. But correctional functions have never been exclusively public. Private individuals operated local jails in the 18th century, and private contractors were heavily involved in prison management during the 19th century.

During that time, some States, including southern States like Tennessee, leased their entire prison systems to private individuals or companies. . . . [W]e have found evidence that the common law provided mistreated prisoners in prison leasing States with remedies against mistreatment by those private lessors. Yet, we have found no evidence that the law gave purely private companies or their employees any special immunity from such suits. . . .

Whether the immunity doctrine's purposes warrant immunity for private prison guards presents a closer question. *Wyatt*, consistent with earlier precedent, described the doctrine's purposes as protecting "government's ability to perform its traditional functions" by providing immunity where "necessary to preserve" the ability of government officials "to serve the public good or to ensure that talented candidates were not deterred by the threat of damages suits from entering public service." Earlier precedent described immunity as protecting the public from unwarranted timidity on the part of public officials . . . .

The guards argue that those purposes support immunity whether their employer is private or public. Since private prison guards perform the same work as state prison guards, they say, they must require immunity to a similar degree. . . . [But] a purely functional approach bristles with difficulty, particularly since, in many areas, government and private industry may engage in fundamentally similar activities, ranging from electricity production, to waste disposal, to even mail delivery.

Petitioners' argument also overlook certain important differences that, from an immunity perspective, are critical. First, the most important special government immunity-producing concern—unwarranted timidity—is less likely present, or at least is not special, when a private company subject to competitive market pressures operates a prison. Competitive pressures mean not only that a firm whose guards are too aggressive will face damages that raise costs, thereby threatening its replacement, but also that a firm whose guards are too timid will face threats of replacement by other firms with records that demonstrate their ability to do both a safer and a more effective job.

These ordinary marketplace pressures are present here. The private prison guards before us work for a large, multistate private prison management firm. The firm is systematically organized to perform a major administrative task for profit. . . . It must buy insurance sufficient to compensate victims of civil rights torts. And, since the firm's first contract expires after three years, its performance is disciplined, not only by state review, but also by pressure from potentially competing firms who can try to take its place. . . .

[Moreover], lawsuits may well "'distrac[t]'" these employees "'from their . . . duties,'" but the risk of "distraction" alone cannot be sufficient grounds for an immunity. Our qualified immunity cases do not contemplate the complete elimination of lawsuit-based distractions. . . . Given a continual and conceded need for deterring constitutional violations and our sense that the firm's tasks are not enormously different in respect to their importance from various other publicly important tasks carried out by private firms, we are not persuaded that the threat of distracting workers from their duties is enough virtually by itself to justify providing an immunity. . . .

[W]e have answered the immunity question narrowly, in the context in which it arose. That context is one in which a private firm, systematically organized to assume a major lengthy administrative task (managing an institution) with limited direct supervision by the government, undertakes that task for profit and potentially in competition with other firms. The case does not involve a private individual briefly associated with a government body, serving as an adjunct to government in an essential governmental activity, or acting under close official supervision. . . .

■ *Justice* SCALIA, *with whom* THE CHIEF JUSTICE, *Justice* KENNEDY, *and Justice* THOMAS *join, dissenting.* . . .

I agree with the Court . . . that we must look to history to resolve this case. I do not agree with the Court, however, that the petitioners' claim to immunity is defeated if they cannot provide an actual case, antedating or contemporaneous with the enactment of § 1983, in which immunity was successfully asserted by a private prison guard. It is only the absence of such a case, and not any explicit rejection of immunity by any common-law court, that the Court relies upon. The opinion observes that private jailers existed in the 19th century, and that they were successfully sued by prisoners. But one could just as easily show that government-employed jailers were successfully sued at common law, often with no mention of possible immunity. Indeed, as far as my research has disclosed, there may be more case-law support for immunity in the private-jailer context than in the government-jailer context. . . .

The parties concede that petitioners perform a prototypically governmental function (enforcement of state-imposed deprivation of liberty), and one that gives rise to qualified immunity. . . .

Private individuals have regularly been accorded immunity when they perform a governmental function that qualifies. We have long recognized the absolute immunity of grand jurors, noting that like prosecutors and judges they must "exercise a discretionary judgment on the basis of evidence presented to them." *Imbler.* "It is the functional comparability of [grand jurors'] judgments to those of the judge that has resulted in [their] being referred to as 'quasi-judicial' officers, and their immunities being termed 'quasi-judicial' as well." *Ibid.* Likewise, witnesses who testify in court proceedings have enjoyed immunity, regardless of whether they were government employees. . . . I think it highly unlikely that we would deny prosecutorial immunity to those private attorneys increasingly employed by various jurisdictions in this country to conduct high-visibility criminal prosecutions. There is no more reason for treating private prison guards differently.

Later in its opinion, the Court seeks to establish that there are policy reasons for denying to private prison guards the immunity accorded to public ones. As I have indicated above, I believe that history and not judicially analyzed policy governs this matter—but even on its own terms the Court's attempted policy distinction is unconvincing. The Court . . . says that "unwarranted timidity" on the part of private guards is less likely to be a concern, since their companies are subject to market pressures that encourage them to be effective in the performance of their duties. If a private firm does not maintain a proper level of order, the Court reasons, it will be replaced by another one—so there is no need for qualified immunity to facilitate the maintenance of order.

This is wrong for several reasons. First of all, it is fanciful to speak of the consequences of "market" pressures in a regime where public officials are the only purchaser, and other people's money the medium of payment. Ultimately, one prison-management firm will be selected to replace another prison-management firm only if a decision is made by some political official not to renew the contract. This is a government decision, not a market choice. . . . Secondly and more importantly, however, if one assumes a political regime that is bent on emulating the market in its purchase of prison services, it is almost certainly the case that, short of mismanagement so severe as to provoke a prison riot, price (not discipline) will be the predominating factor in such a regime's selection of a contractor. A contractor's price must depend upon its costs; lawsuits increase costs; and "fearless" maintenance of discipline increases lawsuits. . . . [T]he more cautious the prison guards, the fewer the lawsuits, the higher the profits. In sum, it seems that "market-competitive" private prison managers have even greater need than civil-service prison managers for immunity as an incentive to discipline. . . .

Filarsky v. Delia
566 U.S. 377 (2012)

▪ *Chief Justice ROBERTS delivered the opinion of the Court. . . .*

[The City of Rialto, California, was investigating whether its firefighter Nicholas Delia had improperly continued to take sick leave in order to do home improvement projects after his illness had ended. The City required Delia to appear for an investigatory interview conducted by private attorney Steve Filarsky, an experienced employment lawyer who had previously represented the City in several investigations. Delia claimed he had building materials for a home improvement job but hadn't done any work. At Filarsky's urging, the Fire Chief ordered Delia to produce the building materials over his objection that it would violate his Fourth Amendment rights. City officials then followed Delia to his home and he and his attorney brought out four rolls of insulation. Delia sued the City, its Fire Department, and a number of individuals including Filarsky. The district court granted qualified immunity to all individual defendants but the court of appeals reversed as to Filarsky, holding that because he was a private attorney, he could not claim qualified immunity.] . . .

At common law, government actors were afforded certain protections from liability, based on the reasoning that "the public good can best be secured by allowing officers charged with the duty of deciding upon the rights of others, to act upon their own free, unbiased convictions, uninfluenced by any apprehensions." . . .

In determining whether [the distinction between city employees and a private individual retained by the city] is valid, we look to the "general principles of tort immunities and defenses" applicable at common law, and the reasons we have afforded protection from suit under § 1983. *Imbler*.

Under our precedent, the inquiry begins with the common law as it existed when Congress passed § 1983 in 1871. Understanding the protections the common law afforded to those exercising government power in 1871 requires an appreciation of the nature of government at that time. In the mid-nineteenth century, government was smaller in both size and reach. It had fewer responsibilities, and operated primarily at the local level. Local governments faced tight budget constraints, and generally had neither the need nor the ability to maintain an established bureaucracy staffed by professionals. . . .

[T]o a significant extent, government was "administered by members of society who temporarily or occasionally discharge[d] public functions." . . .

Private citizens were actively involved in government work, especially where the work most directly touched the lives of the people. It was not unusual, for example, to see the owner of the local general store step behind a window in his shop to don his postman's hat. Nor would it have been a surprise to find, on a trip to the docks, the local ferryman collecting harbor fees as public wharfmaster. . . .

This mixture of public responsibility and private pursuits extended even to the highest levels of government. Until the position became full-time in 1853, for example, the Attorney General of the United States was expected to and did maintain an active private law practice. . . .

Given all this, it should come as no surprise that the common law did not draw a distinction between public servants and private individuals engaged in public service in according protection to those carrying out government responsibilities. Government actors involved in adjudicative activities, for example, were protected by an absolute immunity from suit. This immunity applied equally to "the highest judge in the State or nation" and "the lowest officer who sits as a court and tries petty causes," including those who served as judges on a part-time or episodic basis. Justices of the peace, for example, often maintained active private law practices (or even had nonlegal livelihoods), and generally served in a judicial capacity only part-time. In fact, justices of the peace were not even paid a salary by the government, but instead received compensation through fees payable by the parties that came before them. Yet the common law extended the same immunity "to a justice of the peace as to any other judicial officer."

The common law also extended certain protections to individuals engaged in law enforcement activities, such as sheriffs and constables. . . . The protections provided by the common law did not turn on whether someone we today would call a police officer worked for the government full-time or instead for both public and private employers. . . .

Nothing about the reasons we have given for recognizing immunity under § 1983 counsels against carrying forward the common law rule. . . .

We have called the government interest in avoiding "unwarranted timidity" on the part of those engaged in the public's business "the most important special government immunity-producing concern." Ensuring that those who serve the government do so "with the decisiveness and the judgment required by the public good," *Scheuer*, is of vital importance regardless whether the individual sued as a state actor works full-time or on some other basis.

Affording immunity not only to public employees but also to others acting on behalf of the government similarly serves to " 'ensure that talented candidates [are] not deterred by the threat of damages suits from entering public service.' " *Richardson* (quoting *Wyatt*). The government's need to attract talented individuals is not limited to full-time public employees. Indeed, it is often when there is a particular need for specialized knowledge or expertise that the government must look outside its permanent work force to secure the services of private individuals. This case is a good example: Filarsky had 29 years of specialized experience as an attorney in labor, employment, and personnel matters, with particular expertise in conducting internal affairs investigations. The City of Rialto certainly had no permanent employee with anything approaching those qualifications. To the extent such private individuals do not depend on the government for their livelihood, they have freedom to select other work—work that will not expose them to liability for government actions. This makes it more likely that the most talented candidates will decline public engagements if they do not receive the same immunity enjoyed by their public employee counterparts. . . .

Our decisions in *Wyatt* and *Richardson* are not to the contrary. . . . *Wyatt* involved no government agents, no government interests, and no government need for immunity. . . .

Richardson was a self-consciously "narrow[]" decision. The Court made clear that its holding was not meant to foreclose all claims of immunity by private individuals. Instead, the Court emphasized that the particular circumstances of that case— "a private firm, systematically organized to assume a major lengthy administrative task (managing an institution) with limited direct supervision by the government, undertak[ing] that task for profit and potentially in competition with other firms"— combined sufficiently to mitigate the concerns underlying recognition of governmental immunity under § 1983. Nothing of the sort is involved here, or in the typical case of an individual hired by the government to assist in carrying out its work.

A straightforward application of the rule set out above is sufficient to resolve this case. Though not a public employee, Filarsky was retained by the City to assist in conducting an official investigation into potential wrongdoing. There is no dispute that government employees performing such work are entitled to seek the protection of qualified immunity. The Court of Appeals rejected Filarsky's claim to the protection . . . solely because he was not a permanent, full-time employee of the City. The common law, however, did not draw such distinctions, and we see no justification for doing so under § 1983. . . .

[Concurring opinions of Ginsburg, J., and Sotomayor, J., omitted.]

Notes and Questions

1. What factors does the Court analyze in deciding cases about private parties' assertion of qualified immunity? What role do text and legislative intent play?

2. The dissenters in *Richardson* argue for a functional approach and against the apparent anomaly of two different immunity standards for workers doing the same job. How does that position compare to the Court's approach to the *Bivens* question in *Minneci v. Pollard* (Chapter 2), which also considered whether private prison guards should be subject to the same standards as their government-employee counterparts?

3. How persuasive is the Court's resort to the history (or the absence of it) in light of the avowedly policy-based approach of *Harlow*? What justifies consulting different sources of law for the development of qualified immunity depending on whether the actors at issue are public or private?

4. Is *Filarsky* convincing in distinguishing *Richardson*? In light of *Filarsky*, should *Richardson* have been overruled? Is the latter likely to be extended to additional circumstances? Is this an(other) instance of the Justices identifying with lawyers and affording them extra protection? *Cf. Imbler v. Pachtman* (Section A.2).

5. Which decision reflects a more realistic account of market forces, *Richardson* or *Filarsky*? Won't attorney Filarsky, like Richardson's company, try to do a good and vigorous job regardless of the protection of qualified immunity, in order to keep the government's business? Or is all of this beside the point, as the *Richardson* dissenters suggest, because government contracts don't operate like a normal market anyway?

6. *Richardson* assumes without deciding that private prison guards may be sued as state actors under § 1983. Although the majority view among lower courts is that private prisons are state actors, *see, e.g., Pollard v. The GEO Grp., Inc.*, 629 F.3d 843, 858 (9th Cir. 2010), *rev'd on other grounds sub nom. Minneci v. Pollard*, 565 U.S. 118 (2012); *Rosborough v. Mgmt. & Training Corp.*, 350 F.3d 459, 461 (5th Cir. 2003); *Skelton v. Pri-Cor, Inc.*, 963 F.2d 100, 102 (6th Cir. 1991); *contra Holly v. Scott*, 434 F.3d 287, 293 (4th Cir. 2006), the Supreme Court has never decided the issue.

6. CRITIQUES OF QUALIFIED IMMUNITY

In recent years, qualified immunity has come under serious attack, not only from outside the Court but also—despite the Court's robust summary-reversal docket, noted in Section B.4—from some of the Justices as well. Criticism of the doctrine has focused on several sets of issues:

First, as noted in Section B.2, the level-of-generality question regarding what counts as "clearly established" law has led to inconsistent application of the doctrine.

Second, recent empirical research has called into doubt one of the Court's key rationales for qualified immunity: protecting public officials from personal liability to avoid deterring them from performing their public functions. Recall that the Court opined more than thirty years ago that plaintiffs "could not reasonably contend that [indemnification programs] make reimbursement sufficiently certain and generally available to justify reconsideration of the balance struck in *Harlow*." *Anderson v. Creighton*, 483 U.S. 635, 641 n.3 (1987). But Professor Joanna Schwartz analyzed litigation payments and indemnification practices across the country, and her findings were dramatic:

> Police officers are virtually always indemnified. Between 2006 and 2011, in forty-four of the country's largest jurisdictions, officers financially contributed to settlements and judgments in just .41% of the approximately 9225 civil rights damages actions resolved in plaintiffs' favor, and their contributions amounted to just .02% of the over $730 million spent by cities, counties, and states in these cases. Officers did not pay a dime of the over $3.9 million awarded in punitive damages. And officers in the thirty-seven small and mid-sized jurisdictions in my study never contributed to settlements or judgments in lawsuits brought against them. Governments satisfied settlements and judgments in police misconduct cases even when indemnification was prohibited by statute or policy. And governments satisfied settlements and judgments in full even when officers were disciplined or terminated by the department or criminally prosecuted for their conduct.

As Professor Schwartz went on to observe:

> My findings of widespread indemnification undermine assumptions of financial responsibility relied upon in civil rights doctrine. Although the Court's stringent qualified immunity standard rests in part on the concern that individual officers will be overdeterred by the threat of financial liability, actual practice suggests that these officers have nothing reasonably to fear, at least where payouts are concerned.

Joanna C. Schwartz, *Police Indemnification*, 89 N.Y.U. L. Rev. 885, 890 (2014).

A related study by Professor Schwartz and Professors James Pfander and Alexander Reinert found that, like state and local officers sued under § 1983, *Bivens* defendants rarely pay damages personally. *See* Pfander, Reinert & Schwartz, *The Myth of Personal Liability: Who Pays When* Bivens *Claims Succeed*, 72 Stan. L. Rev. ____ (forthcoming 2020).

Third (and perhaps most obvious, in light of the applications we have studied), qualified immunity hinders enforcement of constitutional rights and the development of constitutional law. *See, e.g.,* Judge Lynn Adelman, *The Supreme Court's Quiet Assault on Civil Rights*, Dissent (Fall 2017); Erwin Chemerinsky, *Closing the Courthouse Doors*, 41 Hum. Rts. 5, 5 (2014); David Rudovsky, *The Qualified Immunity Doctrine in the Supreme Court: Judicial Activism and the Restriction of Constitutional Rights*, 138 U. Pa. L. Rev. 23, 55 (1989). And dismissal rates alone may tell only part of the story, as many plaintiffs' lawyers consider the possibility of a successful qualified immunity defense when deciding whether to file a case in the first place. *See* Alexander A. Reinert, *Does Qualified Immunity Matter?* 8 U. St. Thomas L.J. 477, 492-93 (2011).

Finally, and perhaps most influential in recent years, scholars have persuasively argued that the Court's original historical account of the "defense of good faith and probable cause" in *Pierson v. Ray* was flawed. As Professor William Baude has documented, "lawsuits against officials for constitutional violations did not generally permit a good-faith defense during the early years of the Republic," and the "'strict rule of personal official liability, even though its harshness to officials was quite clear,' was a fixture of the founding era." William Baude, *Is Qualified Immunity Unlawful?* 106 Cal. L. Rev. 45, 55-56 (2018) (quoting David E. Engdahl, *Immunity and Accountability for Positive Governmental Wrongs*, 44 U. Colo. L. Rev. 1, 19 (1972)); *see also* James E. Pfander & Jonathan L. Hunt, *Public Wrongs and Private Bills: Indemnification and Government Accountability in the Early Republic*, 85 N.Y.U. L. Rev. 1862, 1863-64 (2010).

In the face of these criticisms, qualified immunity has its (partial) defenders. For instance, Professors Aaron Nielson and Christopher Walker posit that qualified immunity is useful as a course-correction to *Monroe v. Pape* (Chapter 1), which permitted damages suits against state and local officials under § 1983 even where they are also violating state law. If *Monroe* was wrongly decided, as Justice Scalia argued in *Crawford-El* (earlier in this chapter, Section B.3), "then perhaps qualified immunity simply moves the law closer to where it should have been all along." Aaron L. Nielson & Christopher J. Walker, *A Qualified Defense of Qualified Immunity*, 93 Notre Dame L. Rev. 1853, 1869 (2018). Professors Nielson and Walker also defend qualified immunity on the basis that it ensures officers are held liable only where they have fair notice that their conduct is unlawful—a basic value underlying due process. *Id.* at 1872-73.

Professor John Jeffries offers a more fundamental defense of qualified immunity, arguing that it not only serves its function of "easing the ordinary, workaday business of government" but also "has deep structural advantages for American constitutionalism":

> [L]imiting money damages for constitutional violations fosters the development of constitutional law. Most obviously, the right-remedy gap in constitutional torts facilitates constitutional change by reducing the costs of innovation. The growth and development of American constitutionalism are thereby enhanced. More importantly, the fault-based regime for damages liability biases constitutional remedies in favor of the future. Limitations on damages, together with modern expansions in injunctive relief, shift constitutional adjudication from reparation toward reform. Resources are directed away from cash compensation for past injury and toward the prevention of future harm. The result is a rolling redistribution of wealth from older to younger, as the societal investment in constitutional law is channeled toward future progress and away from backward-looking relief.

John C. Jeffries, Jr., *The Right-Remedy Gap in Constitutional Law*, 109 Yale L.J. 87, 90 (1999). (Like Professors Nielsen and Walker, who offer only a "qualified" defense of qualified immunity, Professor Jeffries does not defend the doctrine unreservedly; he has, for instance, criticized the doctrine's application as muddled, largely because of the confusion associated with the level-of-generality inquiry. *See* John C. Jeffries, Jr., *What's Wrong with Qualified Immunity?* 62 Fla. L. Rev. 851, 854 (2010).)

The Court itself has sent mixed signals about the doctrine in recent years. On one hand, the Court has, as we have seen, continued to raise the bar for overcoming qualified immunity. It has also sent a strong message about the importance of qualified immunity through repeated summary reversals and by ruling in favor of qualified immunity in nearly every case it has heard on the issue in recent years. *See* Kit Kinports, *The Supreme Court's Quiet Expansion of Qualified Immunity*, 100 Minn. L. Rev. Headnotes 62, 63-64 (2016).

On the other hand, Justice Thomas recently unleashed this broadside against the Court's current qualified immunity jurisprudence:

> The Civil Rights Act of 1871 . . . established causes of action for plaintiffs to seek money damages from Government officers who violated federal law. Although the Act made no mention of defenses or immunities, "we have read it in harmony with general principles of tort immunities and defenses rather than in derogation of them." We have done so because "[c]ertain immunities were so well established in 1871 . . . that 'we presume that Congress would have specifically so provided had it wished to abolish' them." Immunity is thus available under the statute if it was "historically accorded the relevant official" in an analogous situation "at common law," unless the statute provides some reason to think that Congress did not preserve the defense. . . .
>
> [Qualified immunity doctrine] started off by applying common-law rules. In *Pierson*, we held that police officers are not absolutely immune from a § 1983 claim arising from an arrest made pursuant to an unconstitutional statute because the common law never granted arresting officers that sort of immunity. Rather, we concluded that police officers could assert "the defense of good faith and probable cause" against the claim for an unconstitutional arrest because that defense was available against the analogous torts of "false arrest and imprisonment" at common law.
>
> In further elaborating the doctrine of qualified immunity for executive officials, however, we have diverged from the historical inquiry mandated by the statute. In the decisions following *Pierson*, we have "completely reformulated qualified immunity along principles not at all embodied in the common law." *Anderson* (discussing *Harlow*). Instead of asking whether the common law in 1871 would have accorded immunity to an officer for a tort analogous to the plaintiff's claim under § 1983, we instead grant immunity to any officer whose conduct "does not violate clearly established statutory or constitutional rights of which a reasonable person would have known." We apply this "clearly established" standard "across the board" and without regard to "the precise nature of the various officials' duties or the precise character of the particular rights alleged to have been violated." *Anderson*. We have not attempted to locate that standard in the common law as it existed in 1871, however, and some evidence supports the conclusion that common-law immunity as it existed in 1871 looked quite different from our current doctrine. *See generally* Baude, *Is Qualified Immunity Unlawful?* 106 Cal. L. Rev. (forthcoming 2018).
>
> Because our analysis is no longer grounded in the common-law backdrop against which Congress enacted the 1871 Act, we are no longer engaged in "interpret [ing] the intent of Congress in enacting" the Act. Our qualified immunity precedents instead represent precisely the sort of "freewheeling policy choice[s]" that we have previously disclaimed the power to make. We have acknowledged, in fact, that the "clearly established" standard is designed to "protec[t] the balance between vindication of constitutional rights and government officials' effective performance of their duties." The Constitution assigns this kind of balancing to Congress, not the Courts. . . .
>
> Until we shift the focus of our inquiry to whether immunity existed at common law, we will continue to substitute our own policy preferences for the mandates of Congress. In an appropriate case, we should reconsider our qualified immunity jurisprudence.

Ziglar v. Abbasi, 137 S. Ct. 1843, 1870-72 (2017) (Thomas, J., concurring in part and concurring in the judgment).

One of the Court's most recent cases on qualified immunity reflects *both* contradictory trends in qualified immunity thinking. Even as the majority is as insistent as ever on strict application of the principles of *Anderson* and *Mullenix*—and enforces them via a summary reversal—a powerful dissent reveals that Justice Thomas is not the only member of the Court who seems ready to reconsider qualified immunity.

Kisela v. Hughes
138 S. Ct. 1148 (2018)

▪ PER CURIAM. . . .

[A 911 caller reported that a woman was hacking a tree with a kitchen knife. Three officers, including Kisela, responded to the location.]

[They] spotted a woman, later identified as Sharon Chadwick, standing next to a car in the driveway of a nearby house. A chain-link fence with a locked gate separated Chadwick from the officers. The officers then saw another woman, Hughes, emerge from the house carrying a large knife at her side. Hughes matched the description of the woman who had been seen hacking a tree. Hughes walked toward Chadwick and stopped no more than six feet from her.

All three officers drew their guns. At least twice they told Hughes to drop the knife. Viewing the record in the light most favorable to Hughes, Chadwick said "take it easy" to both Hughes and the officers. Hughes appeared calm, but she did not acknowledge the officers' presence or drop the knife. The top bar of the chain-link fence blocked Kisela's line of fire, so he dropped to the ground and shot Hughes four times through the fence. . . .

[E]ven assuming a Fourth Amendment violation occurred—a proposition that is not at all evident—on these facts Kisela was at least entitled to qualified immunity. . . .

This Court has "'repeatedly told courts—and the Ninth Circuit in particular—not to define clearly established law at a high level of generality.'"

"[S]pecificity is especially important in the Fourth Amendment context, where the Court has recognized that it is sometimes difficult for an officer to determine how the relevant legal doctrine, here excessive force, will apply to the factual situation the officer confronts." . . .

[I]t does not suffice for a court simply to state that an officer may not use unreasonable and excessive force, deny qualified immunity, and then remit the case for a trial on the question of reasonableness. An officer "cannot be said to have violated a clearly established right unless the right's contours were sufficiently definite that any reasonable official in the defendant's shoes would have understood that he was violating it." That is a necessary part of the qualified-immunity standard, and it is a part of the standard that the Court of Appeals here failed to implement in a correct way.

Kisela says he shot Hughes because, although the officers themselves were in no apparent danger, he believed she was a threat to Chadwick. Kisela had mere seconds to assess the potential danger to Chadwick. He was confronted with a woman who had just been seen hacking a tree with a large kitchen knife and whose behavior was erratic enough to cause a concerned bystander to call 911. . . . Kisela was separated from Hughes and Chadwick by a chain-link fence; Hughes had moved to within a few feet of Chadwick; and she failed to acknowledge at least two commands to drop the knife. Those commands were loud enough that Chadwick, who was standing next to Hughes, heard them. This is far from an obvious case in which any competent officer would have known that shooting Hughes to protect Chadwick would violate the Fourth Amendment. . . .

■ *Justice* SOTOMAYOR, *with whom Justice* GINSBURG *joins, dissenting.*

Officer Andrew Kisela shot Amy Hughes while she was speaking with her roommate, Sharon Chadwick, outside of their home. The record, properly construed at this stage, shows that at the time of the shooting: Hughes stood stationary about six feet away from Chadwick, appeared "composed and content," and held a kitchen knife down at her side with the blade facing away from Chadwick. Hughes was nowhere near the officers, had committed no illegal act, was suspected of no crime, and did not raise the knife in the direction of Chadwick or anyone else. Faced with these facts, the two other responding officers held their fire, and one testified that he "wanted to continue trying verbal command[s] and see if that would work." But not Kisela. He thought it necessary to use deadly force, and so, without giving a warning that he would open fire, he shot Hughes four times, leaving her seriously injured.

If this account of Kisela's conduct sounds unreasonable, that is because it was. . . . Viewing the facts in the light most favorable to Hughes, as the Court must at summary judgment, a jury could find that Kisela violated Hughes' clearly established Fourth Amendment rights by needlessly resorting to lethal force. . . .

Because Kisela plainly lacked any legitimate interest justifying the use of deadly force against a woman who posed no objective threat of harm to officers or others, had committed no crime, and appeared calm and collected during the police encounter, he was not entitled to qualified immunity. . . .

This unwarranted summary reversal is symptomatic of "a disturbing trend regarding the use of this Court's resources" in qualified-immunity cases. . . . [T]his Court routinely displays an unflinching willingness "to summarily reverse courts for wrongly denying officers the protection of qualified immunity" but "rarely intervene[s] where courts wrongly afford officers the benefit of qualified immunity in these same cases." Such a one-sided approach to qualified immunity transforms the doctrine into an absolute shield for law enforcement officers, gutting the deterrent effect of the Fourth Amendment.

The majority today exacerbates that troubling asymmetry. Its decision is not just wrong on the law; it also sends an alarming signal to law enforcement officers and the public. It tells officers that they can shoot first and think later, and it tells the public that palpably unreasonable conduct will go unpunished. Because there is nothing right or just under the law about this, I respectfully dissent.

Notes and Questions

1. Of the various critiques leveled against qualified immunity, which appear to resonate most with members of the Court? Which if any do you find persuasive?

2. How serious a challenge do Professor Schwartz's findings about indemnification pose to the assumptions behind qualified immunity? If she is right, which justifications for the doctrine remain valid?

3. If qualified immunity reform is desirable, which branch of government should undertake that task—Congress or the courts? Are both branches' institutional authority equivalent with respect to this project? Does it matter that the Supreme Court has repeatedly revised § 1983 law generally, and qualified immunity jurisprudence in particular, with virtually no participation from Congress and without feeling particularly constrained by stare decisis? *See* Scott Michelman, *The Branch Best Qualified To Abolish Immunity*, 93 Notre Dame L. Rev. 1999, 2007-11 (2018) (arguing that in light of the Court's unique role in shaping qualified immunity, combined with constitutional tort litigation's "close nexus with constitutional law itself," the Court should take the lead in reforming or abolishing qualified immunity). How can the argument for judicial reform be reconciled with what the Supreme Court has said recently in related contexts about separation of powers (e.g., the majority opinion in *Ziglar v. Abbasi*, Chapter 2)? Must it be?

4. If qualified immunity reform is to occur, how should the doctrine be changed? Should it be abolished altogether, leaving officers with no defense other than the constitutionality of their conduct? Or is there some intermediate position? What principles, values, and sources of law should drive this decision?

C. LIMITS ON SUPERVISORY LIABILITY

In addition to the absolute and qualified immunity defenses, a third limitation on liability, although not formally a "defense" or an "immunity," influences who can be liable for constitutional violations and under what circumstances. This limitation is the restriction on liability for supervisors of officials who have violated a person's constitutional rights.

Before 2009, the courts of appeals agreed that supervisors could be liable for their subordinates' constitutional violations under certain conditions but did not agree as to precisely what those conditions were. All agreed that merely being a supervisor of someone who committed a violation was insufficient: that is, courts did not permit respondeat superior liability. But some degree of fault on the part of the supervisor could render that person liable. Some circuits required "deliberate indifference" for supervisory liability; others permitted liability based on "knowledge and acquiescence" in unconstitutional conduct. *See* Kit Kinports, *The Buck Does Not Stop Here: Supervisory Liability in Section 1983 Cases*, 1997 U. Ill. L. Rev. 147, 154-55.

The Supreme Court addressed supervisory liability in the next case, which will be familiar to most students from Civil Procedure as a landmark case on the Rule 8 pleading standard. Regarding supervisory liability, lower courts are still debating how broadly the Court's holding reached.

Ashcroft v. Iqbal
556 U.S. 662 (2009)

■ *Justice* KENNEDY *delivered the opinion of the Court.*

Respondent Javaid Iqbal is a citizen of Pakistan and a Muslim. In the wake of the September 11, 2001, terrorist attacks he was arrested in the United States on criminal charges and detained by federal officials. Respondent claims he was deprived of various constitutional protections while in federal custody. To redress the alleged deprivations, respondent filed a complaint against numerous federal officials, including John Ashcroft, the former Attorney General of the United States, and Robert Mueller, the Director of the Federal Bureau of Investigation (FBI). Ashcroft and Mueller are the petitioners in the case now before us. As to these two petitioners, the complaint alleges that they adopted an unconstitutional policy that subjected respondent to harsh conditions of confinement on account of his race, religion, or national origin. . . .

[After the 9/11 attacks, the FBI and other entities within the Department of Justice investigated more than a 1,000 people and detained hundreds.]

Respondent was one of the detainees. According to his complaint, in November 2001, [federal agents] arrested him on charges of fraud in relation to identification documents and conspiracy to defraud the United States. Pending trial for those crimes, respondent was housed at the Metropolitan Detention Center (MDC) in Brooklyn, New York. Respondent was designated a person "of high interest" to the September 11 investigation and in January 2002 was placed in a section of the MDC known as the Administrative Maximum Special Housing Unit (ADMAX SHU). As the facility's name indicates, the ADMAX SHU incorporates the maximum security conditions allowable under Federal Bureau of Prison regulations. ADMAX SHU detainees were kept in lockdown 23 hours a day, spending the remaining hour outside their cells in handcuffs and leg irons accompanied by a four-officer escort.

Respondent pleaded guilty to the criminal charges, served a term of imprisonment, and was removed to his native Pakistan. He then filed a *Bivens* action . . . against 34 current and former federal officials and 19 "John Doe" federal corrections officers. The defendants range from the correctional officers who had day-to-day contact with respondent during the term of his confinement, to the wardens of the MDC facility, all the way to petitioners—officials who were at the highest level of the federal law enforcement hierarchy.

[Allegations against defendants other than Ashcroft and Mueller included that various defendants beat and kicked plaintiff while he was in custody, strip searched him repeatedly, and refused to allow him and other Muslim detainees to pray.] . . .

[As to Ashcroft and Mueller, t]he complaint contends that petitioners designated respondent a person of high interest on account of his race, religion, or national origin, in contravention of the First and Fifth Amendments to the Constitution. The complaint alleges that "the [FBI], under the direction of Defendant Mueller, arrested and detained thousands of Arab Muslim men . . . as part of its investigation of the events of September 11." It further alleges that "[t]he policy of holding post-September-11th detainees in highly restrictive conditions of confinement until they were 'cleared' by the FBI was approved by Defendants Ashcroft and Mueller in discussions in the weeks after September 11, 2001." Lastly, the complaint posits that petitioners "each knew of, condoned, and willfully and maliciously agreed to subject" respondent to harsh conditions of confinement "as a matter of policy, solely on account of [his] religion, race, and/or national origin and for no legitimate penological interest." The pleading names Ashcroft as the "principal architect" of the policy, and identifies Mueller as "instrumental in [its] adoption, promulgation, and implementation." . . .

Because vicarious liability is inapplicable to *Bivens* and § 1983 suits, a plaintiff must plead that each Government-official defendant, through the official's own individual actions, has violated the Constitution.

The factors necessary to establish a *Bivens* violation will vary with the constitutional provision at issue. Where the claim is invidious discrimination in contravention of the First and Fifth Amendments, our decisions make clear that the plaintiff must plead and prove that the defendant acted with discriminatory purpose. Under extant precedent purposeful discrimination requires more than "intent as volition or intent as awareness of consequences." . . . It follows that, to state a claim based on a violation of a clearly established right, respondent must plead sufficient factual matter to show that petitioners adopted and implemented the detention policies at issue not for a neutral, investigative reason but for the purpose of discriminating on account of race, religion, or national origin.

Respondent disagrees. He argues that, under a theory of "supervisory liability," petitioners can be liable for "knowledge and acquiescence in their subordinates' use of discriminatory criteria to make classification decisions among detainees." That is to say, respondent believes a supervisor's mere knowledge of his subordinate's discriminatory purpose amounts to the supervisor's violating the Constitution. We reject this argument. Respondent's conception of "supervisory liability" is inconsistent with his accurate stipulation that petitioners may not be held accountable for the misdeeds of their agents. In a § 1983 suit or a *Bivens* action—where masters do not answer for the torts of their servants—the term "supervisory liability" is a misnomer. Absent vicarious liability, each Government official, his or her title notwithstanding, is only liable for his or her own misconduct. In the context of determining whether there is a violation of clearly established right to overcome qualified immunity, purpose rather than knowledge is required to impose *Bivens* liability on the subordinate for unconstitutional discrimination; the same holds true for an official charged with violations arising from his or her superintendent responsibilities. . . .

Under Federal Rule of Civil Procedure 8(a)(2), a pleading must contain a "short and plain statement of the claim showing that the pleader is entitled to relief." . . . [T]he pleading standard Rule 8 announces does not require "detailed factual allegations," but it demands more than an unadorned, the-defendant-unlawfully-harmed-me accusation. A pleading that offers "labels and conclusions" or "a formulaic recitation of the elements of a cause of action will not do." Nor does a complaint suffice if it tenders "naked assertion[s]" devoid of "further factual enhancement." . . . [W]e conclude that respondent's complaint has not "nudged [his] claims" of invidious discrimination "across the line from conceivable to plausible." . . .

Respondent pleads that petitioners "knew of, condoned, and willfully and maliciously agreed to subject [him]" to harsh conditions of confinement "as a matter of policy, solely on account of [his] religion, race, and/or national origin and for no legitimate penological interest." The complaint alleges that Ashcroft was the "principal architect" of this invidious policy, and that Mueller was "instrumental" in adopting and executing it. These bare assertions . . . amount to nothing more than a "formulaic recitation of the elements" of a constitutional discrimination claim . . . .

[The Court found these assertions too conclusory and also held that the claim of discrimination was not "plausible" because there was an "obvious alternative explanation" for the arrests: that the nation's top law enforcement officials, in light of the fact that "the September 11 attacks were perpetrated by 19 Arab Muslim hijackers who counted themselves members in good standing of al Qaeda, an Islamic fundamentalist group" led "by another Arab Muslim—Osama bin Laden—and composed in large part of his Arab Muslim disciples," possessed a "nondiscriminatory intent to detain aliens who were illegally present in the United States and who had potential connections to those who committed terrorist acts." The Court observed that its holding was limited to Ashcroft and Mueller, not any other defendants.]

▪ Justice SOUTER, with whom Justice STEVENS, Justice GINSBURG, and Justice BREYER join, dissenting.

This case . . . comes to us with the explicit concession of petitioners Ashcroft and Mueller that an officer may be subject to *Bivens* liability as a supervisor on grounds other than respondeat superior. The Court apparently rejects this concession and, although it has no bearing on the majority's resolution of this case, does away with supervisory liability under *Bivens*. . . . I respectfully dissent from both the rejection of supervisory liability as a cognizable claim in the face of petitioners' concession, and from the holding that the complaint fails to satisfy Rule 8(a)(2) of the Federal Rules of Civil Procedure. . . .

According to the majority, because Iqbal concededly cannot recover on a theory of respondeat superior, it follows that he cannot recover under any theory of supervisory liability. The majority says that in a *Bivens* action, "where masters do not answer for the torts of their servants," "the term 'supervisory liability' is a misnomer," and that "[a]bsent vicarious liability, each Government official, his or her title notwithstanding, is only liable for his or her own misconduct." Lest there be any mistake, in these words the majority is not narrowing the scope of supervisory liability; it is eliminating *Bivens* supervisory liability entirely. The nature of a supervisory liability theory is that the supervisor may be liable, under certain conditions, for the wrongdoing of his subordinates, and it is this very principle that the majority rejects. *Ante*, at 1952 ("[P]etitioners cannot be held liable unless they themselves acted on account of a constitutionally protected characteristic").

[The majority's] cursory analysis . . . rests on the assumption that only two outcomes are possible here: respondeat superior liability, in which "an employer is subject to liability for torts committed by employees while acting within the scope of their employment," Restatement (Third) of Agency § 2.04 (2005), or no supervisory liability at all. The dichotomy is false. Even if an employer is not liable for the actions of his employee solely because the employee was acting within the scope of employment, there still might be conditions to render a supervisor liable for the conduct of his subordinate.

In fact, there is quite a spectrum of possible tests for supervisory liability: it could be imposed where a supervisor has actual knowledge of a subordinate's constitutional violation and acquiesces; or where supervisors " 'know about the conduct and facilitate it, approve it, condone it, or turn a blind eye for fear of what they might see' "; or where the supervisor has no actual knowledge of the violation but was reckless in his supervision of the subordinate; or where the supervisor was grossly negligent. *[Justice Souter cites lower-court cases espousing each of these standards.]* I am unsure what the general test for supervisory liability should be, and in the absence of briefing and argument I am in no position to choose or devise one.

Neither is the majority, but what is most remarkable about its foray into supervisory liability is that its conclusion has no bearing on its resolution of the case. The majority says that all of the allegations in the complaint that Ashcroft and Mueller authorized, condoned, or even were aware of their subordinates' discriminatory conduct are "conclusory" and therefore are "not entitled to be assumed true." . . . [O]n the majority's understanding of Rule 8(a)(2) pleading standards, even if the majority accepted Ashcroft and Mueller's concession and asked whether the complaint sufficiently alleges knowledge and deliberate indifference, it presumably would still conclude that the complaint fails to plead sufficient facts and must be dismissed. . . .

[Dissenting opinion of Breyer, J., omitted.]

Notes and Questions

1. Under the majority's conception of supervisory liability, what would Iqbal have had to plead to state a valid claim against Ashcroft and Mueller? How likely is it that he could have credibly done so without discovery?

2. Is Justice Souter correct that the majority has done away with supervisory liability under *Bivens* (and therefore, § 1983) entirely? If not, what is left of it?

3. Justice Souter identifies a series of possible supervisory liability rules that he characterizes as falling between the poles of respondeat superior and the abolition of supervisory liability. Which would be most effective from the perspective of deterrence? Of administrability? Of fairness to government officials? Does the majority opinion leave any room for them to continue to apply? When?

Applications

Notwithstanding Justice Souter's interpretation of the majority opinion in *Iqbal*, most courts have *not* held that it abolished supervisory liability. *See generally* Karen M. Blum, *Section 1983 Litigation: The Maze, the Mud, and the Madness*, 23 Wm. & Mary Bill Rts. J. 913, 922 (2015); Alexander A. Reinert, *National Security and the Shadows of Judicial "Common Sense,"* 96 Iowa L. Rev. Bull. 1, 5 (2010).

A useful discussion of the post-*Iqbal* landscape appears in *Barkes v. First Correctional Medical, Inc.*, 766 F.3d 307 (3d Cir. 2014), in which the family of a prisoner who committed suicide at a Delaware prison sued prison officials for failing to take adequate care to prevent the suicide in light of the prisoner's psychiatric history and previous attempted suicide. The Third Circuit held both that the defendants were not entitled to qualified immunity and that the Delaware Department of Corrections Commissioner and the prison warden could be subject to supervisory liability for failing to supervise prison staff if their failure reflected deliberate indifference (which is the standard for the merits of the Eighth Amendment claim).

Over a dissent, the court of appeals analyzed the effect of *Iqbal* on supervisory liability as follows:

> In rejecting Iqbal's claim, the Supreme Court first recognized that "[t]he factors necessary to establish a *Bivens* violation will vary with the constitutional provision at issue." The claim presented in *Iqbal*—discrimination in violation of the First and Fifth Amendments—requires that the plaintiff prove that the defendant acted with a discriminatory purpose, and "purposeful discrimination requires more than 'intent as volition or intent as awareness of consequences.' " . . . [I]t necessarily followed that Ashcroft and Mueller could be held liable only if they had "adopted and implemented the detention policies at issue . . . for the purpose of discriminating on account of race, religion, or national origin." . . . [Thus,] the Court expressly tied the level of intent necessary for superintendent liability to the underlying constitutional tort.
>
> This aspect of *Iqbal* has bedeviled the Courts of Appeals to have considered it, producing varied interpretations of its effect on supervisory liability. The dissenters in *Iqbal* believed the majority to be abolishing supervisory liability in its entirety, and at least [the Fifth Circuit] Court of Appeals impliedly confirmed this view,

albeit without much in the way of discussion. The Ninth Circuit, on the other hand, has suggested that under *Iqbal* the United States Attorney General could be liable for knowingly "fail[ing] to act in the light of even unauthorized abuses" . . . .

Most courts have gravitated to the center, recognizing that because the state of mind necessary to establish a § 1983 or *Bivens* claim varies with the constitutional provision at issue, so too does the state of mind necessary to trigger liability in a supervisory capacity. The Tenth Circuit, for example, held that, after *Iqbal*, § 1983 liability may attach to "a defendant-supervisor who creates, promulgates, implements, or in some other way possesses responsibility for the continued operation of a policy the enforcement (by the defendant-supervisor or her subordinates) of which 'subjects, or causes to be subjected,'" the plaintiff to a constitutional deprivation, if the supervisor "acted with the state of mind required to establish the alleged constitutional deprivation." *Dodds v. Richardson*, 614 F.3d 1185, 1199 (10th Cir. 2010). The Court of Appeals in *Dodds* reasoned that such a standard "complies with *Iqbal*'s requirement that § 1983 liability only be imposed upon those defendants whose own individual actions cause a constitutional deprivation because it requires plaintiffs [to] prove each defendant took some act with the constitutionally applicable state of mind that caused the alleged constitutional violation." *[The Third Circuit cited or discussed decisions of the First, Seventh, Eighth, and Ninth Circuits to similar effect.]* . . .

We do not read *Iqbal* to have abolished supervisory liability in its entirety. Rather, we agree with those courts that have held that, under *Iqbal*, the level of intent necessary to establish supervisory liability will vary with the underlying constitutional tort alleged. In this case, the underlying tort is the denial of adequate medical care in violation of the Eighth Amendment's prohibition on cruel and unusual punishment, and the accompanying mental state is subjective deliberate indifference. . . . [Prior to *Iqbal*, we permitted a claim that] a state official, by virtue of his or her own deliberate indifference to known deficiencies in a government policy or procedure, has allowed to develop an environment in which there is an unreasonable risk that a constitutional injury will occur, and that such an injury does occur. Liability in such a situation is, as *Iqbal* requires, imposed not vicariously but based on the supervisor's own misconduct, because to exhibit deliberate indifference to such a situation is a culpable mental state under the Eighth Amendment.

Dissenting, Judge Hardiman argued: "Since *Iqbal*, supervisory liability claims must spring from 'actions' or 'misconduct'; the mere fact that the supervisor occupied a position of authority is insufficient. Accordingly, the overwhelming weight of authority requires plaintiffs to establish the supervisor's *personal involvement* in his subordinates' misfeasance" (emphasis added).

The defendants sought Supreme Court review, arguing that the Court should clarify the rules for supervisory liability. The Supreme Court summarily reversed, holding that there was no violation of a "clearly established" Eighth Amendment right. *Taylor v. Barkes*, 135 S. Ct. 2042 (2015) (per curiam). The Court did not address supervisory liability.

Is the Third Circuit's interpretation of *Iqbal* more persuasive than Justice Souter's?

CHAPTER 4 PROBLEMS

Problem 4A. Harry William Henrison comes to your law office seeking help. He has just been released from the local jail, where he served a year-long sentence. From the day he entered last year until the day he left, a guard who had a grudge against him prevented him from going outside to exercise and allowed him out of his cell to exercise for only one hour per month.

The following are excerpts from the decision in *Martin v. Anburen*, which was handed down a year before Henrison began serving his sentence, and which is binding in your jurisdiction:

> Plaintiff is a prison inmate. After verbal dispute with prison guards thirteen months ago, prison authorities denied him all exercise outside his cell. He claimed this restriction was cruel and unusual punishment and sought injunctive relief to remove these restrictions, which the district court granted. . . .
>
> Many courts have recognized that "some form of regular outdoor exercise is extremely important to the psychological and physical well being of inmates." *Bailey v. Shillinger*, 828 F.2d 651, 653 (10th Cir. 1987) (citing *Spain v. Procunier*, 600 F.2d 189, 199 (9th Cir. 1979)); *accord Williams v. Greifinger*, 97 F.3d 699, 703-05 (2d Cir. 1996) (discussing contours of right to out-of-cell exercise); *Mitchell v. Rice*, 954 F.2d 187, 191 (4th Cir. 1992) ("Generally a prisoner should be permitted some regular out-of-cell exercise."); *Davenport v. DeRobertis*, 844 F.2d 1310, 1313 (7th Cir. 1988) (upholding district court finding that allowing inmates in segregation unit only one hour of out-of-cell exercise a week violated Eighth Amendment). Particularly relevant here is *Housley v. Dodson*, 41 F.3d 597, 599 (10th Cir. 1994), where the court concluded that an inmate who alleged he had received only thirty minutes of out-of-cell exercise in three months stated an Eighth Amendment claim.
>
> We agree with these holdings and conclude that the district court did not err in enjoining the restriction at issue.

Henrison wants to seek damages against the guard who kept him inside. Evaluate the strength of the qualified immunity defense that the guard would likely raise if you brought a § 1983 claim for damages against him.

(Source Note: The facts of Martin v. Anburen *are based on, and some of the text is quoted from,* Perkins v. Kan. Dep't of Corr., *165 F.3d 803 (10th Cir. 1999).)*

Problem 4B. The City of Georgetown, in Douglass Commonwealth, has a history of contracting out government functions. Shortly after it was founded as a Maryland town in 1751, Georgetown began paying private local attorneys to sit as part-time judges. Georgetown was later incorporated into a federal territory, the District of Columbia, which had no such practice. When most of the territory within the District of Columbia was recognized as the new state of Douglass Commonwealth and Georgetown once again became a city, Georgetown again hired independent contractors as municipal judges.

Lyssa S. Ugrant, a recent law school graduate, begins a yearlong clerkship for Georgetown municipal judge Cannon James Bew, an independent contractor.

When Ugrant learns during her clerkship year that she has passed the Douglass bar, she wants to get sworn in immediately, because clerks who are bar members get paid more. Most applicants must wait months for the statewide swearing-in, but state law gives judges the authority to swear in their own clerks. Under state law, a bar application is considered an "ex parte petition" to the court, which is "granted" when the applicant is sworn in.

Ugrant and her co-clerks, who are all male, arrive at Judge Bew's courtroom for a swearing-in ceremony. Also present is Georgetown Chief Judge Monroe James, a city employee who hires and oversees all the independent-contractor judges. Ugrant, like her co-clerks, is dressed in suit pants and a suit jacket. Judge Bew arrives, looks at his clerks and says, "Miss Ugrant, I will not swear you in looking like that." Shocked, Ugrant replies, "Your Honor, I am professionally dressed, like my colleagues." Judge Bew replies, "A lady lawyer should dress like a lady. If you want me to swear you in, put on a skirt and come back." Ugrant protests to Chief Judge James, who replies, "It is each judge's prerogative to determine whom to swear in." Ugrant is angry, but, not wanting to lose her chance at early bar admission and her raise, goes home and returns in a skirt. When Ugrant returns, Judge Bew says, "Turn around so I can get a look." Shocked, Ugrant exclaims, "Your Honor!" Bew insists, "If you want to be admitted today, turn around!" Ugrant looks pleadingly at James, who only shrugs. Chagrined, Ugrant turns around. Bew then swears in Ugrant and her colleagues.

Ugrant then quits and sues Judges Bew and James, in their individual capacities, seeking damages under § 1983 for violating her right to equal protection of the laws. There is no precedent anywhere in the country regarding discrimination in bar swearings-in. Aside from arguing the merits of the equal protection claim, what other defenses can Bew and James raise? Will they succeed?

Problem 4C. A law in your state directs the state Division of Occupational Licensing to create and maintain a state Controlled Substance Database of all prescriptions for controlled substances filled at pharmacies in the state. Pharmacists are required to report patients' controlled-substance prescription records to the database.

To investigate a recent theft of medicines from ambulances belonging to a local fire department, police officer Clint William uses the database to obtain, without a warrant, the records of all 480 employees of the fire department. One of the employees is Herbert Bushwalk. As a result of the search, Officer William learns that Bushwalk is taking prescription opioids for back pain. William reports that information to Bushwalk's supervisor. Although the medication was lawfully prescribed by his physician, the fire department is concerned about possible on-the-job impairment. Bushwalk is suspended from his job.

Bushwalk sues William for violating his rights under the Fourth Amendment when he searched the database without a warrant. William claims qualified immunity.

Evaluate William's defense based on the following three binding legal principles/sources, which all predate Officer William's database query:

1. A search occurs for purposes of the Fourth Amendment when a law enforcement officer invades a person's "reasonable expectation of privacy." *Katz v. United States*, 389 U.S. 347 (1967).

2. "[A] search conducted without a judicial warrant is per se unreasonable under the Fourth Amendment," *Arizona v. Gant*, 556 U.S. 332, 338 (2009), subject to exceptions not relevant here.

3. In *Gro v. Ercleveland*, a decision from the court of appeals with jurisdiction over your state, a state hospital administrator, Ercleveland, suspected the plaintiff, Gro, of forging prescriptions. Without a warrant, Ercleveland queried the Controlled Substance Database for Gro's prescription records. Ercleveland turned the records over to police. Charges for fraudulently altering a prescription were filed against Gro but later dismissed. Gro sued Ercleveland for violating her rights under the Fourth Amendment prohibition on unreasonable searches and the Fourteenth Amendment due process right to informational privacy. The district court dismissed the case, and the appeals court affirmed based on qualified immunity. It wrote:

> Because privacy regarding matters of health is closely intertwined with the activities afforded protection by the Supreme Court, we have held that there is a constitutional right to privacy that protects an individual from the disclosure of information concerning a person's health. We have previously applied this right in the context of an employer's search of an employee's medical records, and in the context of a government official's disclosure of a person's HIV status.
>
> We have no difficulty concluding that, whether under the Fourth or Fourteenth Amendment, protection of a right to privacy in a person's prescription drug records, which contain intimate facts of a personal nature, is sufficiently similar to other areas already protected within the ambit of privacy. Information contained in prescription records may reveal facts about a person's illnesses, whether a woman is taking fertility medication, and more. Thus, it seems clear that a person has a reasonable expectation of privacy in her prescription drug records.
>
> However, we had not previously announced that protection before today. Moreover, whether a warrant is required to conduct an investigatory search of prescription records is an issue that has not been settled, and is an issue we need not decide in the present case. Because the privacy right in prescription drug records was not clearly established when Ercleveland acted, he is entitled to qualified immunity. The judgment is affirmed.

(Source Note: The facts of the hypothetical are based on Pyle v. Woods, *874 F.3d 1257 (10th Cir. 2017). The facts of* Gro v. Ercleveland *are based on, and some of the text is quoted from,* Douglas v. Dobbs, *419 F.3d 1097 (10th Cir. 2005).)*

Problem 4D.   Consider the following complaint and the case that follows. Is defendant Penny Pincher entitled to qualified immunity? (Allegations relevant to defendant Tenleytown will be revisited in connection with municipal liability, in Chapter 5.)

IN THE U.S. DISTRICT COURT FOR THE DISTRICT OF DOUGLASS

Marcia CLEARWATER	)	
v.	)	*COMPLAINT FOR DAMAGES*
CITY OF TENLEYTOWN;	)	
Penny PINCHER		

Marcia Clearwater, by and through her attorneys, alleges as follows:

PARTIES

1. Plaintiff Marcia Clearwater was Sanitation Inspector of the City of Tenleytown for twenty years, until she was fired on February 1, 2020.
2. Defendant City of Tenleytown is a municipality in Douglass Commonwealth. It is governed by a seven-member City Council and by a City Manager.
3. Defendant Penny Pincher is the City Manager for Tenleytown. She is sued in her individual capacity.

JURISDICTION AND VENUE

4. This court has jurisdiction because there is a federal question. 28 U.S.C. § 1331. Venue is proper because all the events occurred in this district. *Id.* § 1391(e).

FACTUAL ALLEGATIONS

5. The Tenleytown City Council hired Penny Pincher as City Manager in 2016.
6. Pincher previously worked for the City of Anacostia, which fired Pincher after she was held liable in a lawsuit for violating two civil servants' First Amendment rights by firing them for their political beliefs.
7. Before that, Pincher worked for the Brookland School Board. There, she invited local clergy to kindergarten classes each morning to lead a prayer. A court struck down the clergy program under the First Amendment.
8. As Sanitation Inspector, part of Clearwater's job was to oversee the team of engineers hired by the City to do a yearly inspection of the City's water treatment plant.

9. Prior to 2018, the City contracted with the firm of Reservoir Dire, which specializes in water treatment, to perform the annual inspections.

10. In 2018, Pincher decided to hire the plumbing firm Twist & Shout (T&S), instead of Reservoir Dire, for the inspection.

11. The first inspection by T&S occurred in October 2018. T&S spent only thirty minutes. In Clearwater's experience, Reservoir Dire's inspections usually lasted three hours.

12. Clearwater spoke to Pincher and expressed concerns about the quality of the inspection performed by T&S. Pincher ignored her.

13. At the October 2019 inspection, again performed by T&S, Clearwater had to point out to the T&S inspectors the basic features of the treatment system.

14. In January 2020, Tenleytown began receiving complaints that City tap water smelled odd. Clearwater believed such a smell could indicate untreated water.

15. Clearwater told Pincher about the complaints and reiterated her professional judgment that the T&S inspectors were inadequate. Again, Pincher rebuffed her.

16. On January 25, 2020, Pincher received an email from a reporter at the *Tenleytown Tribune* asking about the smell of the Tenleytown water and resident safety.

17. Pincher forwarded the email to Clearwater and instructed her to return the reporter's call and explain the City's position: The public has nothing to worry about.

18. Clearwater had never been asked to speak to the press in her role as Sanitation Inspector. Uncomfortable lying to the public, Clearwater did not call the reporter.

19. On January 27, when Pincher found out that Clearwater hadn't called the reporter, Pincher drew up papers to have Clearwater fired. The stated ground was "Insubordination: failure to follow order regarding reporter."

20. In firing Clearwater, Pincher followed the usual process in Tenleytown: Pincher created a Notice of Personnel Action (NOPA) and submitted it to the Council, which approved it along with all pending NOPAs at its next meeting, on motion of the Chair, Lee G. Slater.

21. The Council approved the Clearwater NOPA on February 1, 2020.

22. Pincher is responsible for hiring and firing all Tenleytown department heads, without interference from the Council, so Pincher is the final policymaker for the City.

23. In the alternative, the City ratified the firing when it approved the NOPA.

24. The City failed to investigate Pincher before hiring her, with the result that the City hired a Manager whose career as a public official reflected repeated disregard for the First Amendment, as demonstrated by Pincher's experiences in Anacostia and Brookland.

CLAIM FOR RELIEF: U.S. CONST., AMEND. I / 42 U.S.C. § 1983

25. By firing Clearwater in retaliation for her speech on a matter of public concern, defendants Tenleytown and Pincher violated Clearwater's rights under the First Amendment and are therefore liable under 42 U.S.C. § 1983.

PRAYER FOR RELIEF

WHEREFORE, plaintiff respectfully requests judgment against defendants as follows:

(a) Compensatory damages in an amount to be determined at trial;

(b) Punitive damages against Defendant Pincher in an amount to be determined at trial;

(c) Attorneys' fees and costs associated with this action;

(d) Any further relief this Court deems just and proper.

Plaintiff demands a trial by jury.

Teddyroose v. Elt, 912 F.3d 1390 (Douglass Com. Cir. 2019)

Sergeant Teddyroose was a police officer who alleges that Police Chief Elt fired him after Teddyroose refused to rewrite a police report about a particular incident involving a fellow officer. Teddyroose and Officer John Andrewson had arrested a suspect, Ty Lerjohn. Lerjohn called Andrewson an obscene name. Andrewson struck the still-handcuffed Lerjohn in the face. Lerjohn filed a civilian complaint against Andrewson for excessive force. Teddyroose filed his report, which corroborated Lerjohn's complaint. The next day, Chief Elt summoned Teddyroose to his office and demanded that he rewrite the report to say that Lerjohn and Andrewson had been fighting when Andrewson struck his blow. Teddyroose refused and was fired. He sued under 42 U.S.C. § 1983, alleging First Amendment retaliation. Elt moved to dismiss based on qualified immunity. The district court granted the motion, holding that Teddyroose failed to allege a constitutional violation. We hold that the district court's constitutional analysis was erroneous but nonetheless affirm based on the absence of clearly established law.

We exercise our discretion to turn first to the merits. *Pearson v. Callahan.* The First Amendment limits the ability of a public employer to leverage the employment relationship to restrict freedom of speech employees enjoy as private citizens. However, not all speech by an employee is automatically entitled to First Amendment protection. To be protected from adverse employment actions for his speech, an employee must have spoken (1) "as a citizen" rather than as part of his job responsibilities, (2) on a matter of public concern, and (3) in circumstances in which the government's interest in the efficiency of its workplace does not outweigh the employee's interest.

Elements (2) are (3) are easily met here. The performance of police in the course of their duties is obviously a matter of public concern because of the importance of their work to public safety. And the government has no interest in disseminating false information.

The question whether Teddyroose spoke "as a citizen" is closer. As a rule of thumb, activities required of an employee as part of his employment duties are not performed "as a citizen" if they are not the kind of activity engaged in by citizens who do not work for the government. For this purpose, there is no difference between compelled speech and compelled silence, for the First Amendment protects the decision of both what to say and what *not* to say. Further, it is a state crime to file a false report with the police. Thus, retracting a truthful statement to law enforcement officials and substituting one that is false would expose the speaker—whether he be a police officer or a civilian—to criminal liability.

This court's prior decision in *Hoo v. Erherbert* provides an instructive contrast. There, the head of the lottery unit of a state's revenue division contended that he was fired for refusing to testify dishonestly before the state's Gaming Board by presenting proposed changes to a lottery game in a positive light. We rejected Hoo's claim, because he was directed to present his office's views, not his own. Although the plaintiff understood the order to mean that he should "lie" to the Board, there is no evidence anyone ordered him to misrepresent either the facts or his personal views.

In the present case, Teddyroose had a strong First Amendment interest in refusing to make a dishonest report. Teddyroose's refusal to falsely exculpate Andrewson has a civilian analogue. A citizen has a First Amendment right to decide what not to say, and, accordingly, to reject governmental efforts to require him to make statements he believes are false. Thus, a citizen who has truthfully reported a crime has the indisputable right to reject pressure from the police to have him rescind his accusation and falsely exculpate the accused. And a civilian who acceded to such pressure would subject himself to criminal liability, as would a police officer. Of course a police officer has a duty not to substitute a falsehood for the truth, but he plainly has that duty as a citizen as well.

Elt argues that Teddyroose's refusal was part of his job because Elt ordered him to write the new report. If Teddyroose has a First Amendment right not to write the report, Elt warns, employees could refuse to write any document required by their employer, and insubordination would become commonplace. We reject this contention because it ignores the context of Teddyroose's refusals. Teddyroose was pressured to withdraw the truthful report he had filed and to submit one that was false. Therefore, his refusals to accede to those demands constituted speech activity that was significantly different from the mere filing of his initial report.

In sum, the First Amendment protects the right of a citizen to refuse to retract a report to the police that he believes is true, and to refuse to make a statement that he believes is false.

However, the plaintiff points to no prior case remotely similar to this one, and because one of the elements of the First Amendment test is a close call, the constitutional violation here was not so "obvious" that general principles should have put Elt on notice he was violating his employee's rights. *Cf. Hope v. Pelzer.* Therefore, we affirm the dismissal of the complaint because the right asserted was not clearly established.

(Source Note: The facts of Teddyroose v. Elt *are based on, and some of the text is quoted from,* Jackler v. Byrne, *658 F.3d 225 (2d Cir. 2011).)*

Municipal Liability

As we have seen, states and individuals have powerful defenses to liability. What about municipalities—cities, towns, counties, school boards, and so forth—sued for their employees' constitutional violations? Municipalities' susceptibility to civil rights enforcement has evolved over time. As we learned in Chapter 3, they do not share in a state's sovereign immunity. However, the Court initially ruled that municipalities were not proper defendants under § 1983 at all. That view persisted in theory even as courts were in fact granting relief in desegregation lawsuits against a type of municipal defendant: school boards. The Court then reversed course and allowed suits against municipalities, but only subject to complex restrictions that differ both from sovereign immunity and from the individual immunities we studied in the previous chapter.

Section A introduces the basis for municipal liability and the special standard that governs it—the requirement that the municipality's policy or custom cause the constitutional violation. Sections B and C explore various ways to meet that standard.

A. THE BASIC RULES FOR MUNICIPAL LIABILITY

Monroe v. Pape (Chapter 1) is principally known today for its interpretation of the critical statutory phrase "under color." Equally important at the time, however, was its holding that municipalities could *not* be held liable under § 1983. On this point, the Court reasoned as follows:

> When the bill that became the Act of April 20, 1871, was being debated in the Senate, Senator Sherman of Ohio proposed an amendment which would have made "the inhabitants of the county, city, or parish" in which certain acts of violence occurred liable "to pay full compensation" to the person damaged or his widow or legal representative. . . .

[The House of Representatives objected to this proposal, because, as Representative Poland explained,] "the House had solemnly decided that in their judgment Congress had no constitutional power to impose any obligation upon county and town organizations, the mere instrumentality for the administration of state law." The question of constitutional power of Congress to impose civil liability on municipalities was vigorously debated with powerful arguments advanced in the affirmative. . . .

The response of the Congress to the proposal to make municipalities liable for certain actions being brought within federal purview by the Act of April 20, 1871, was so antagonistic that we cannot believe that the word "person" was used in this particular Act to include them. Accordingly we hold that the motion to dismiss the complaint against the City of Chicago was properly granted.

In 1978, the Court reconsidered the question of municipal liability under § 1983.

Monell v. Department of Social Services
436 U.S. 658 (1978)

▨ *Mr. Justice* BRENNAN *delivered the opinion of the Court.*

Petitioners, a class of female employees of the Department of Social Services and of the Board of Education of the city of New York, commenced this action under 42 U.S.C. § 1983 in July 1971. The gravamen of the complaint was that the Board and the Department had as a matter of official policy compelled pregnant employees to take unpaid leaves of absence before such leaves were required for medical reasons. The suit sought injunctive relief and backpay for periods of unlawful forced leave. Named as defendants in the action were the Department and its Commissioner, the Board and its Chancellor, and the city of New York and its Mayor. In each case, the individual defendants were sued solely in their official capacities.

[The district court] held moot petitioners' claims for injunctive and declaratory relief since the City of New York and the Board, after the filing of the complaint, had changed their policies. . . . No one now challenges this conclusion. . . . [The district court dismissed the claim for backpay based on *Monroe v. Pape*, and the court of appeals affirmed.] . . .

In *Monroe*, we held that "Congress did not undertake to bring municipal corporations within the ambit of [§ 1983]." The sole basis for this conclusion was an inference drawn from Congress' rejection of the "Sherman amendment" to the bill which became the Civil Rights Act of 1871, the precursor of § 1983. . . . [The House's rationale for rejecting the Sherman amendment,] we thought, showed that Congress doubted its "constitutional power . . . to impose civil liability on municipalities," and that such doubt would have extended to any type of civil liability.

A fresh analysis of the debate on the Civil Rights Act of 1871, and particularly of the case law which each side mustered in its support, shows, however, that *Monroe* incorrectly equated the "obligation" [that the Sherman amendment would have imposed on municipalities] with "civil liability." . . .

The main features of the conference committee draft of the Sherman amendment were these: First, a cause of action was given to persons injured by

> "any persons riotously and tumultuously assembled together . . . with intent to deprive any person of any right conferred upon him by the Constitution and laws of the United States, or to deter him or punish him for exercising such right, or by reason of his race, color, or previous condition of servitude . . . ."

Second, the bill provided that the action would be against the county, city, or parish in which the riot had occurred. . . . Third, . . . the conference substitute made the government defendant liable on the judgment if it was not satisfied against individual defendants who had committed the violence. . . .

In the ensuing debate on the first conference report, which was the first debate of any kind on the Sherman amendment, Senator Sherman explained that the purpose of his amendment was to enlist the aid of persons of property in the enforcement of the civil rights laws by making their property "responsible" for Ku Klux Klan damage. . . .

The first conference substitute passed the Senate but was rejected by the House. . . .

House opponents of the Sherman amendment—whose views are particularly important since only the House voted down the amendment—. . . argued that the local units of government upon which the amendment fastened liability were not obligated to keep the peace at state law and further that the Federal Government could not constitutionally require local governments to create police forces, whether this requirement was levied directly, or indirectly by imposing damages for breach of the peace on municipalities. [Representative Blair described the proposal as] "altogether without a precedent in this country. . . . That amendment claims the power in the General Government to . . . lay such obligations as it may please upon the municipalities, which are the creations of the States alone. . . ."

[Then-recent cases provided] support for Blair's view that the Sherman amendment, by putting municipalities to the Hobson's choice of keeping the peace or paying civil damages, attempted to impose obligations on municipalities by indirection that could not be imposed directly, thereby threatening to "destroy the government of the States."

If municipal liability under § 1 of the Civil Rights Act of 1871 created a similar Hobson's choice, we might conclude, as *Monroe* did, that Congress could not have intended municipalities to be among the "persons" to which that section applied. But this is not the case.

First, opponents expressly distinguished between imposing an obligation to keep the peace and merely imposing civil liability for damages on a municipality that was obligated by state law to keep the peace, but which had not in violation of the Fourteenth Amendment. Representative Poland, for example, reasoning from Contract Clause precedents, indicated that Congress could constitutionally confer jurisdiction on the federal courts to entertain suits seeking to hold municipalities liable for using their authorized powers in violation of the Constitution—which is as far as § 1 of the Civil Rights Act went:

> "I presume . . . that where a State had imposed a duty [to keep the peace] upon [a] municipality . . . an action would be allowed to be maintained against them in the courts of the United States under the ordinary restrictions as to jurisdiction. But the enforcing [of] a liability, existing by their own contract, or by a State law, in the courts, is a very widely different thing from devolving a new duty or liability upon them by the national Government, which has no power either to create or destroy them, and no power or control over them whatever."

Second, . . . [i]t must be remembered that [at the time, the Supreme Court] vigorously enforced the Contract Clause against municipalities—an enforcement effort which included various forms of "positive" relief, such as ordering that taxes be levied and collected to discharge federal-court judgments, once a constitutional infraction was found. Thus, federal judicial enforcement of the Constitution's express limits on state power, since it was done so frequently, must . . . have been permissible. . . .

From the foregoing discussion, it is readily apparent that nothing said in debate on the Sherman amendment would have prevented holding a municipality liable under § 1 of the Civil Rights Act for its own violations of the Fourteenth Amendment. The question remains, however, whether the general language describing those to be liable under § 1—"any person"—covers more than natural persons. An examination of the debate on § 1 and application of appropriate rules of construction show unequivocally that § 1 was intended to cover legal as well as natural persons. . . .

In both Houses, statements of the supporters of § 1 corroborated that Congress, in enacting § 1, intended to give a broad remedy for violations of federally protected civil rights. Moreover, since municipalities through their official acts could, equally with natural persons, create the harms intended to be remedied by § 1, and, further, since Congress intended § 1 to be broadly construed, there is no reason to suppose that municipal corporations would have been excluded from the sweep of § 1. One need not rely on this inference alone, however, for the debates show that Members of Congress understood "persons" to include municipal corporations.

Representative Bingham, for example, in discussing § 1 of the bill, explained that he had drafted § 1 of the Fourteenth Amendment with the case of *Barron v. Mayor of Baltimore*, 7 Pet. 243 (1833), especially in mind. "In [that] case the city had taken private property for public use, without Compensation . . . , and there was no redress for the wrong . . . ." Bingham's further remarks clearly indicate his view that such takings by cities, as had occurred in *Barron*, would be redressable under § 1 of the bill. . . . Given this purpose, it beggars reason to suppose that Congress would have exempted municipalities from suit, insisting instead that compensation for a taking come from an officer in his individual capacity rather than from the government unit that had the benefit of the property taken.

In addition, by 1871, it was well understood that corporations should be treated as natural persons for virtually all purposes of constitutional and statutory analysis. . . .

That the "usual" meaning of the word "person" would extend to municipal corporations is also evidenced by an Act of Congress which had been passed only months before the Civil Rights Act was passed. This Act provided that

> "in all acts hereafter passed . . . the word 'person' may extend and be applied to bodies politic and corporate . . . unless the context shows that such words were intended to be used in a more limited sense."

Municipal corporations in 1871 were included within the phrase "bodies politic and corporate" and, accordingly, the "plain meaning" of § 1 is that local government bodies were to be included within the ambit of the persons who could be sued under § 1 of the Civil Rights Act. Indeed, a Circuit Judge, writing in 1873 in what is apparently the first reported case under § 1, read the Dictionary Act in precisely this way in a case involving a corporate plaintiff and a municipal defendant.

Our analysis of the legislative history of the Civil Rights Act of 1871 compels the conclusion that Congress did intend municipalities and other local government units to be included among those persons to whom § 1983 applies. Local governing bodies,[55] therefore, can be sued directly under § 1983 for monetary, declaratory, or injunctive relief where, as here, the action that is alleged to be unconstitutional implements or executes a policy statement, ordinance, regulation, or decision officially adopted and promulgated by that body's officers. . . .

On the other hand, the language of § 1983, read against the background of the same legislative history, compels the conclusion that Congress did not intend municipalities to be held liable unless action pursuant to official municipal policy of some nature caused a constitutional tort. In particular, we conclude that a municipality cannot be held liable solely because it employs a tortfeasor—or, in other words, a municipality cannot be held liable under § 1983 on a respondeat superior theory.

We begin with the language of § 1983 as originally passed:

> "*[A]ny person who*, under color of any law, statute, ordinance, regulation, custom, or usage of any State, *shall subject, or cause to be subjected*, any person . . . to the deprivation of any rights, privileges, or immunities secured by the Constitution of the United States, shall, any such law, statute, ordinance, regulation, custom, or usage of the State to the contrary notwithstanding, be liable to the party injured in any action at law, suit in equity, or other proper proceeding for redress . . . ." (emphasis added).

---

55. Since official-capacity suits generally represent only another way of pleading an action against an entity of which an officer is an agent—at least where Eleventh Amendment considerations do not control analysis—our holding today that local governments can be sued under § 1983 necessarily decides that local government officials sued in their official capacities are "persons" under § 1983 in those cases in which, as here, a local government would be suable in its own name.

The italicized language plainly imposes liability on a government that, under color of some official policy, "causes" an employee to violate another's constitutional rights. At the same time, that language cannot be easily read to impose liability vicariously on governing bodies solely on the basis of the existence of an employer-employee relationship with a tortfeasor. Indeed, the fact that Congress did specifically provide that A's tort became B's liability if B "caused" A to subject another to a tort suggests that Congress did not intend § 1983 liability to attach where such causation was absent.

The primary constitutional justification for the Sherman amendment was that it was a necessary and proper remedy for the failure of localities to protect citizens. . . . [Some] proponents of the amendment apparently viewed it as a form of vicarious liability for the unlawful acts of the citizens of the locality. And whether intended or not, the amendment as drafted did impose a species of vicarious liability on municipalities since it could be construed to impose liability even if a municipality did not know of an impending or ensuing riot or did not have the wherewithal to do anything about it. Indeed, the amendment held a municipality liable even if it had done everything in its power to curb the riot. . . . Strictly speaking, of course, the fact that Congress refused to impose vicarious liability for the wrongs of a few private citizens does not conclusively establish that it would similarly have refused to impose vicarious liability for the torts of a municipality's employees. Nonetheless, when Congress' rejection of the only form of vicarious liability presented to it is combined with the absence of any language in § 1983 which can easily be construed to create respondeat superior liability, the inference that Congress did not intend to impose such liability is quite strong.

Equally important, creation of a federal law of respondeat superior would have raised all the constitutional problems associated with the obligation to keep the peace, an obligation Congress chose not to impose. . . . To this day, there is disagreement about the basis for imposing liability on an employer for the torts of an employee when the sole nexus between the employer and the tort is the fact of the employer-employee relationship. Nonetheless, two justifications tend to stand out. First is the common-sense notion that no matter how blameless an employer appears to be in an individual case, accidents might nonetheless be reduced if employers had to bear the cost of accidents. Second is the argument that the cost of accidents should be spread to the community as a whole on an insurance theory.

[But both of these justifications were advanced in support of the Sherman amendment. They were] obviously insufficient to sustain the amendment against perceived constitutional difficulties and there is no reason to suppose that a more general liability imposed for a similar reason would have been thought less constitutionally objectionable. . . .

We conclude, therefore, that a local government may not be sued under § 1983 for an injury inflicted solely by its employees or agents. Instead, it is when execution of a government's policy or custom, whether made by its lawmakers or by those whose edicts or acts may fairly be said to represent official policy, inflicts the injury that the government as an entity is responsible under § 1983. Since this case unquestionably involves official policy as the moving force of the constitutional violation found by the District Court, we must reverse the judgment below. In so doing, we have no occasion to address, and do not address, what the full contours of municipal liability under § 1983 may be. . . .

Although we have stated that stare decisis has more force in statutory analysis than in constitutional adjudication because, in the former situation, Congress can correct our mistakes through legislation, we have never applied stare decisis mechanically to prohibit overruling our earlier decisions determining the meaning of statutes. Nor is this a case where we should "place on the shoulders of Congress the burden of the Court's own error."

First, *Monroe v. Pape*, insofar as it completely immunizes municipalities from suit under § 1983, was a departure from prior practice [including five cases from 1873 to 1955], in each of which municipalities were defendants in § 1983 suits. Moreover, the constitutional defect that led to the rejection of the Sherman amendment would not have distinguished between municipalities and school boards, each of which is an instrumentality of state administration. For this reason, our cases—decided both before and after *Monroe*—holding school boards liable in § 1983 actions are inconsistent with *Monroe*. . . . Thus, while we have reaffirmed *Monroe* without further examination on three occasions, it can scarcely be said that *Monroe* is so consistent with the warp and woof of civil rights law as to be beyond question.

Second, the principle of blanket immunity established in *Monroe* cannot be cabined short of school boards. Yet such an extension would itself be inconsistent with recent expressions of congressional intent. In the wake of our decisions, Congress not only has shown no hostility to federal-court decisions against school boards, but it has indeed rejected efforts to strip the federal courts of jurisdiction over school boards. Moreover, recognizing that school boards are often defendants in school desegregation suits, which have almost without exception been § 1983 suits, Congress has twice passed legislation authorizing grants to school boards to assist them in complying with federal-court decrees. . . .

Third, municipalities can assert no reliance claim which can support an absolute immunity. As Mr. Justice Frankfurter said in *Monroe*, "[t]his is not an area of commercial law in which, presumably, individuals may have arranged their affairs in reliance on the expected stability of decision." (dissenting in part). Indeed, municipalities simply cannot "arrange their affairs" on an assumption that they can violate constitutional rights indefinitely since injunctive suits against local officials under § 1983 would prohibit any such arrangement. And it scarcely need be mentioned that nothing in *Monroe* encourages municipalities to violate constitutional rights or even suggests that such violations are anything other than completely wrong.

Finally, . . . there can be no doubt that § 1 of the Civil Rights Act was intended to provide a remedy, to be broadly construed, against all forms of official violation of federally protected rights. Therefore, absent a clear statement in the legislative history supporting the conclusion that § 1 was not to apply to the official

acts of a municipal corporation—which simply is not present—there is no justification for excluding municipalities from the "persons" covered by § 1....

■ *Mr. Justice POWELL, concurring....*

The Court correctly rejects a view of the legislative history that would produce
the anomalous result of immunizing local government units from monetary liability for action directly causing a constitutional deprivation, even though such
actions may be fully consistent with, and thus not remediable under, state law.
No conduct of government comes more clearly within the "under color of" state
law language of § 1983. It is most unlikely that Congress intended public officials acting under the command or the specific authorization of the government
employer to be exclusively liable for resulting constitutional injury....

[*Monroe* and its progeny on municipal liability are] difficult to reconcile on a
principled basis with a parallel series of cases in which the Court has assumed sub
silentio that some local government entities could be sued under § 1983. If now,
after full consideration of the question, we continued to adhere to *Monroe*, grave
doubt would be cast upon the Court's exercise of § 1983 jurisdiction over school
boards. Since "the principle of blanket immunity established in *Monroe* cannot
be cabined short of school boards," the conflict is squarely presented.... And, as
the Court points out, Congress has focused specifically on this Court's school
board decisions in several statutes. Thus the exercise of § 1983 jurisdiction over
school boards, while perhaps not premised on considered holdings, has been
longstanding. Indeed, it predated *Monroe*....

■ *Mr. Justice STEVENS, concurring in part.*

Since [the respondeat superior portions] of the opinion of the Court are merely
advisory and are not necessary to explain the Court's decision, I join only [the
portions holding that municipalities are "persons" and reversing the judgment.]

■ *Mr. Justice REHNQUIST, with whom THE CHIEF JUSTICE joins, dissenting.*

Seventeen years ago, in *Monroe v. Pape*, this Court held that the 42d Congress
did not intend to subject a municipal corporation to liability as a "person" within
the meaning of 42 U.S.C. § 1983. Since then, the Congress has remained silent,
but this Court has reaffirmed that holding on at least three separate occasions.
Today, the Court abandons this long and consistent line of precedents, offering
in justification only an elaborate canvass of the same legislative history which
was before the Court in 1961. Because I cannot agree that this Court is "free
to disregard these precedents," which have been "considered maturely and
recently" by this Court, I am compelled to dissent.

As this Court has repeatedly recognized, considerations of stare decisis are
at their strongest when this Court confronts its previous constructions of legislation. In all cases, private parties shape their conduct according to this Court's
settled construction of the law, but the Congress is at liberty to correct our mistakes of statutory construction, unlike our constitutional interpretations, whenever it sees fit....

Only the most compelling circumstances can justify this Court's abandonment of such firmly established statutory precedents. . . .

The Court does not demonstrate that any exception to this general rule is properly applicable here. The Court's first assertion, that *Monroe* "was a departure from prior practice," is patently erroneous. [In none of the pre-*Monroe* cases the Court cites] was the question now before us raised by any of the litigants or addressed by this Court. . . .

Nor is there any indication that any later Congress has ever approved suit against any municipal corporation under § 1983. Of all its recent enactments, only the Civil Rights Attorney's Fees Awards Act of 1976, explicitly deals with the Civil Rights Act of 1871. . . . There is plainly no language in the 1976 Act which would enlarge the parties suable under those substantive sections; it simply provides that parties who are already suable may be made liable for attorney's fees. . . .

The Court's assertion that municipalities have no right to act "on an assumption that they can violate constitutional rights indefinitely," is simply beside the point. Since *Monroe*, municipalities have had the right to expect that they would not be held liable retroactively for their officers' failure to predict this Court's recognition of new constitutional rights. No doubt innumerable municipal insurance policies and indemnity ordinances have been founded on this assumption, which is wholly justifiable under established principles of stare decisis. To obliterate those legitimate expectations without more compelling justifications than those advanced by the Court is a significant departure from our prior practice. . . .

Monroe may not be overruled unless it has been demonstrated "beyond doubt from the legislative history of the 1871 statute that [*Monroe*] misapprehended the meaning of the controlling provision." *Monroe* (Harlan, J., concurring). The Court must show not only that Congress, in rejecting the Sherman amendment, concluded that municipal liability was not unconstitutional, but also that, in enacting § 1, it intended to impose that liability. I am satisfied that no such showing has been made. . . .

At the time § 1983 was enacted the only federal case to consider the status of corporations under the Fourteenth Amendment had concluded, with impeccable logic, that a corporation was neither a "citizen" nor a "person." *Insurance Co. v. New Orleans*, 13 Fed. Cas. 67 (CC La. 1870).

Furthermore . . . no state court had ever held that municipal corporations were always liable in tort in precisely the same manner as other persons. . . .

The Court is probably correct that the rejection of the Sherman amendment does not lead ineluctably to the conclusion that Congress intended municipalities to be immune from liability under all circumstances. . . . The meaning of § 1 of the Act of 1871 has been subjected in this case to a more searching and careful analysis than it was in *Monroe*, and it may well be that on the basis of this closer analysis of the legislative debates a conclusion contrary to the *Monroe* holding could have been reached when that case was decided 17 years ago. But the rejection of the Sherman amendment remains instructive in that here alone did the legislative debates squarely focus on the liability of municipal corporations, and that liability was rejected. Any inference which might be drawn from the Dictionary Act or from general expressions of benevolence in the debate on § 1 that the word "person" was intended to include municipal corporations falls far short of showing "beyond doubt" that this Court in *Monroe* "misapprehended the meaning of the controlling provision." . . .

The decision in *Monroe v. Pape* was the fountainhead of the torrent of civil rights litigation of the last 17 years. Using § 1983 as a vehicle, the courts have articulated new and previously unforeseeable interpretations of the Fourteenth Amendment. At the same time, the doctrine of municipal immunity enunciated in *Monroe* has protected municipalities and their limited treasuries from the consequences of their officials' failure to predict the course of this Court's constitutional jurisprudence. None of the Members of this Court can foresee the practical consequences of today's removal of that protection. Only the Congress, which has the benefit of the advice of every segment of this diverse Nation, is equipped to consider the results of such a drastic change in the law. It seems all but inevitable that it will find it necessary to do so after today's decision.

Notes and Questions

1. Consider first the practical effect of the *Monell* lawsuit. When did New York change its policy and why? What does that teach you about the practice of impact litigation?

2. What is the rule for municipal liability that emerged from *Monell*? What must a plaintiff show for a municipality to be liable for a constitutional violation?

3. Are you more persuaded by *Monell*'s or *Monroe*'s analysis of the meaning of the Sherman amendment? Should that legislative history have been the Court's primary consideration in reconsidering *Monell*? Notwithstanding its starring role in the majority opinion, do you think the Sherman amendment drove the decisionmaking here? What other factors seem to have contributed? What other rationales would have supported the result?

4. The majority divines from the legislative history *both* that "person" includes "municipality" *and* that only a municipal "policy or custom" can subject a municipality to liability. Are the majority's analyses reaching each of these conclusions compatible with one another? Why or why not?

5. Consider the textual basis for the Court's argument against respondeat superior. How is the Court's reasoning to be reconciled with the Court's embrace of tort-law principles in *Monroe*, where the Court wrote that "Section 1983 should be read against the background of tort liability"?

6. Consider the "reliance" argument in favor of stare decisis. Is it fair of the majority to devalue a municipality's reliance on *Monroe* because it should not have expected to be allowed to violate the Constitution? What other reliance interests might be at risk if such a principle were extended to other contexts?

7. Notice that the individual defendants here were sued in their official capacities. The effect of this designation, as the Court explains in footnote 55, is the same as naming the municipality itself, because "official-capacity suits generally represent only another way of pleading an action against an entity of which an officer is an agent." The same rule holds for *state* officials, as we saw in Chapter 3—subject to the crucial *Ex parte Young* exception permitting an injunction in an official-capacity suit against a state official even though such relief would not be available against the state itself. By contrast, municipal liability doctrine has no *Ex parte Young* exception. Thus, under *Monell*, there is no functional difference between naming a municipal official in an official capacity and naming the municipality itself.

* * *

If municipalities are "persons" who can be sued under § 1983, does it logically follow that they may assert the same defenses as other "persons"—such as the defense of qualified immunity? The next case answers.

Owen v. City of Independence
445 U.S. 622 (1980)

■ *Mr. Justice* BRENNAN *delivered the opinion of the Court.*

[The Independence, Missouri, Chief of Police sued the City and several of its officials after he was fired without prior notice, a hearing, or an appeal. Chief Owen claimed that his due process rights were violated both by the firing and by city officials' making public allegations of misconduct against him. The court of appeals granted the City qualified immunity, holding that the unconstitutionality of the conduct at issue was not established until two Supreme Court decisions issued two months after plaintiff's firing.] . . .

[N]otwithstanding § 1983's expansive language and the absence of any express incorporation of common-law immunities, we have, on several occasions, found that a tradition of immunity was so firmly rooted in the common law and was supported by such strong policy reasons that "Congress would have specifically so provided had it wished to abolish the doctrine." *Pierson v. Ray*. . . . Where the immunity claimed by the defendant was well established at common law at the time § 1983 was enacted, and where its rationale was compatible with the purposes of the Civil Rights Act, we have construed the statute to incorporate that immunity. . . .

As *Monell* recounted, by 1871 municipalities—like private corporations—were treated as natural persons for virtually all purposes of constitutional and statutory analysis. In particular, they were routinely sued in both federal and state courts. Local governmental units were regularly held to answer in damages for a wide range of statutory and constitutional violations, as well as for common-law actions for breach of contract. And although, as we discuss below, a municipality was not subject to suit for all manner of tortious conduct, it is clear that at the time § 1983 was enacted, local governmental bodies did not enjoy the sort of "good-faith" qualified immunity extended to them by the Court of Appeals. . . .

[I]n the hundreds of cases from that era awarding damages against municipal governments for wrongs committed by them, one searches in vain for much mention of a qualified immunity based on the good faith of municipal officers. . . .

That municipal corporations were commonly held liable for damages in tort was also recognized by the 42d Congress. *See Monell.* For example, Senator Stevenson, in opposing the Sherman amendment's creation of a municipal liability for the riotous acts of its inhabitants, stated the prevailing law: "Numberless cases are to be found where a statutory liability has been created against municipal corporations for injuries resulting from a neglect of corporate duty." Nowhere in the debates, however, is there a suggestion that the common law excused a city from liability on account of the good faith of its authorized agents, much less an indication of a congressional intent to incorporate such an immunity into the Civil Rights Act. . . .

To be sure, there were two doctrines that afforded municipal corporations some measure of protection from tort liability. The first sought to distinguish between a municipality's "governmental" and "proprietary" functions; as to the former, the city was held immune, whereas in its exercise of the latter, the city was held to the same standards of liability as any private corporation. The second doctrine immunized a municipality for its "discretionary" or "legislative" activities, but not for those which were "ministerial" in nature. A brief examination of the application and the rationale underlying each of these doctrines demonstrates that Congress could not have intended them to limit a municipality's liability under § 1983.

The governmental-proprietary distinction owed its existence to the dual nature of the municipal corporation. On the one hand, the municipality was a corporate body, capable of performing the same "proprietary" functions as any private corporation, and liable for its torts in the same manner and to the same extent, as well. On the other hand, the municipality was an arm of the State, and when acting in that "governmental" or "public" capacity, it shared the immunity traditionally accorded the sovereign. . . .

That the municipality's common-law immunity for "governmental" functions derives from the principle of sovereign immunity . . . explains why that doctrine could not have served as the basis for the qualified privilege respondent city claims under § 1983. . . . [T]he municipality's "governmental" immunity is obviously abrogated by the sovereign's enactment of a statute making it amenable to suit. Section 1983 was just such a statute. By including municipalities within the class of "persons" subject to liability for violations of the Federal Constitution and laws, Congress—the supreme sovereign on matters of federal law—abolished whatever vestige of the State's sovereign immunity the municipality possessed.

The second common-law distinction between municipal functions—that protecting the city from suits challenging "discretionary" decisions—was grounded not on the principle of sovereign immunity, but on a concern for separation of powers. A large part of the municipality's responsibilities involved broad discretionary decisions on issues of public policy. . . . For a court or jury, in the guise of a tort suit, to review the reasonableness of the city's judgment on these matters would be an infringement upon the powers properly vested in a coordinate and coequal branch of government. . . . [C]ourts therefore refused to entertain suits against the city "either for the non-exercise of, or for the manner in which in good faith it exercises, discretionary powers of a public or legislative character." . . .

Once again, an understanding of the rationale underlying the common-law immunity for "discretionary" functions explains why that doctrine cannot serve as the foundation for a good-faith immunity under § 1983. That common-law doctrine merely prevented courts from substituting their own judgment on matters within the lawful discretion of the municipality. But a municipality has no "discretion" to violate the Federal Constitution; its dictates are absolute and imperative. . . .

In sum, we can discern no "tradition so well grounded in history and reason" that would warrant the conclusion that in enacting § 1 of the Civil Rights Act, the 42d Congress sub silentio extended to municipalities a qualified immunity based on the good faith of their officers. . . .

Our rejection of a construction of § 1983 that would accord municipalities a qualified immunity for their good-faith constitutional violations is compelled both by the legislative purpose in enacting the statute and by considerations of public policy. The central aim of the Civil Rights Act was to provide protection to those persons wronged by the " '[m]isuse of power, possessed by virtue of state law and made possible only because the wrongdoer is clothed with the authority of state law.' " *Monroe.* . . .

How "uniquely amiss" it would be, therefore, if the government itself . . . were permitted to disavow liability for the injury it has begotten. A damages remedy against the offending party is a vital component of any scheme for vindicating cherished constitutional guarantees, and the importance of assuring its efficacy is only accentuated when the wrongdoer is the institution that has been established to protect the very rights it has transgressed. Yet owing to the qualified immunity enjoyed by most government officials, many victims of municipal malfeasance would be left remediless if the city were also allowed to assert a good-faith defense. Unless countervailing considerations counsel otherwise, the injustice of such a result should not be tolerated.

Moreover, § 1983 was intended not only to provide compensation to the victims of past abuses, but to serve as a deterrent against future constitutional deprivations, as well. The knowledge that a municipality will be liable for all of its injurious conduct, whether committed in good faith or not, should create an incentive for officials who may harbor doubts about the lawfulness of their intended actions to err on the side of protecting citizens' constitutional rights. Furthermore, the threat that damages might be levied against the city may encourage those in a policymaking position to institute internal rules and programs designed to minimize the likelihood of unintentional infringements on constitutional rights. Such procedures are particularly beneficial in preventing those "systemic" injuries that result not so much from the conduct of any single individual, but from the interactive behavior of several government officials, each of whom may be acting in good faith. . . .

[One rationale for qualified immunity is that it is unfair to impose liability on an official who is forced to act in some discretionary manner by the nature of his position. But i]t hardly seems unjust to require a municipal defendant which has violated a citizen's constitutional rights to compensate him for the injury suffered thereby. Indeed, Congress enacted § 1983 precisely to provide a remedy for such abuses of official power. *Monroe.* Elemental notions of fairness dictate that one who causes a loss should bear the loss. . . .

After all, it is the public at large which enjoys the benefits of the government's activities, and it is the public at large which is ultimately responsible for its administration. Thus, even where some constitutional development could not have been foreseen by municipal officials, it is fairer to allocate any resulting financial loss to the inevitable costs of government borne by all the taxpayers, than to allow its impact to be felt solely by those whose rights, albeit newly recognized, have been violated. . . .

[A second rationale for official immunity is that the threat of liability would deter good governance by making officials excessively timid. T]he inhibiting effect is significantly reduced, if not eliminated, however, when the threat of personal liability is removed. First, as an empirical matter, it is questionable whether the hazard of municipal loss will deter a public officer from the conscientious exercise of his duties; city officials routinely make decisions that either require a large expenditure of municipal funds or involve a substantial risk of depleting the public fisc. More important, though, is the realization that consideration of the municipality's liability for constitutional violations is quite properly the concern of its elected or appointed officials. Indeed, a decisionmaker would be derelict in his duties if, at some point, he did not consider whether his decision comports with constitutional mandates and did not weigh the risk that a violation might result in an award of damages from the public treasury. As one commentator aptly put it: "Whatever other concerns should shape a particular official's actions, certainly one of them should be the constitutional rights of individuals who will be affected by his actions. To criticize section 1983 liability because it leads decisionmakers to avoid the infringement of constitutional rights is to criticize one of the statute's raisons d'être." . . .

We believe that today's decision, together with prior precedents in this area, properly allocates these costs among the three principals in the scenario of the § 1983 cause of action: the victim of the constitutional deprivation; the officer whose conduct caused the injury; and the public, as represented by the municipal entity. The innocent individual who is harmed by an abuse of governmental authority is assured that he will be compensated for his injury. The offending official, so long as he conducts himself in good faith, may go about his business secure in the knowledge that a qualified immunity will protect him from personal liability for damages that are more appropriately chargeable to the populace as a whole. And the public will be forced to bear only the costs of injury inflicted by the "execution of a government's policy or custom, whether made by its lawmakers or by those whose edicts or acts may fairly be said to represent official policy." *Monell.* . . .

■ *Mr. Justice* POWELL, *with whom* THE CHIEF JUSTICE, *Mr. Justice* STEWART, *and Mr. Justice* REHNQUIST *join, dissenting.*

The Court today holds that the city of Independence may be liable in damages for violating a constitutional right that was unknown when the events in this case occurred. . . . This strict liability approach inexplicably departs from this Court's prior decisions under § 1983 and runs counter to the concerns of the 42d Congress when it enacted the statute. The Court's ruling also ignores the vast weight of common-law precedent as well as the current state law of municipal immunity. For these reasons, and because this decision will hamper local governments unnecessarily, I dissent. . . .

Until two years ago, municipal corporations enjoyed absolute immunity from § 1983 claims. *Monroe.* But *Monell* held that local governments are "persons" within the meaning of the statute, and thus are liable in damages for constitutional violations inflicted by municipal policies. . . . After today's decision, municipalities will have gone in two short years from absolute immunity under § 1983 to strict liability. As a policy matter, I believe that strict municipal liability unreasonably subjects local governments to damages judgments for actions that were reasonable when performed. It converts municipal governance into a hazardous slalom through constitutional obstacles that often are unknown and unknowable. . . .

The Court today abandons any attempt to harmonize § 1983 with traditional tort law. It points out that municipal immunity may be abrogated by legislation. Thus, according to the Court, Congress "abolished" municipal immunity when it included municipalities "within the class of 'persons' subject to liability" under § 1983.

This reasoning flies in the face of our prior decisions under this statute. We have held repeatedly that "immunities 'well grounded in history and reason' [were not] abrogated 'by covert inclusion in the general language' of § 1983." The peculiar nature of the Court's position emerges when the status of executive officers under § 1983 is compared with that of local governments. . . . [T]his Court has refused to find an abrogation of traditional [individual] immunity in a statute that does not mention immunities. Yet the Court now views the enactment of § 1983 as a direct abolition of traditional municipal immunities. Unless the Court is overruling its previous immunity decisions, the silence in § 1983 must mean that the 42d Congress mutely accepted the immunity of executive officers, but silently rejected common-law municipal immunity. I find this interpretation of the statute singularly implausible.

Important public policies support the extension of qualified immunity to local governments. . . . The allocation of public resources and the operational policies of the government itself are activities that lie peculiarly within the competence of executive and legislative bodies. When charting those policies, a local official should not have to gauge his employer's possible liability under § 1983 if he incorrectly—though reasonably and in good faith—forecasts the course of constitutional law. Excessive judicial intrusion into such decisions can only distort municipal decisionmaking and discredit the courts. . . .

In addition, basic fairness requires a qualified immunity for municipalities. . . . Constitutional law is what the courts say it is, and—as demonstrated by today's decision and its precursor, *Monell*—even the most prescient lawyer would hesitate to give a firm opinion on matters not plainly settled. Municipalities, often acting in the utmost good faith, may not know or anticipate when their action or inaction will be deemed a constitutional violation. . . .

[M]any local governments lack the resources to withstand substantial unanticipated liability under § 1983. Even enthusiastic proponents of municipal liability have conceded that ruinous judgments under the statute could imperil local governments. By simplistically applying the theorems of welfare economics and ignoring the reality of municipal finance, the Court imposes strict liability on the level of government least able to bear it. . . .

The Court's decision . . . runs counter to the common law in the 19th century, which recognized substantial tort immunity for municipal actions. Nineteenth-century courts generally held that municipal corporations were not liable for acts undertaken in their "governmental," as opposed to their "proprietary," capacity. Most States now use other criteria for determining when a local government should be liable for damages. Still, the governmental/proprietary distinction retains significance because it was so widely accepted when § 1983 was enacted. It is inconceivable that a Congress thoroughly versed in current legal doctrines, *see Monell*, would have intended through silence to create the strict liability regime now imagined by this Court. . . .

Notes and Questions

1. Putting *Monell* and *Owen* together, what is the rule for when municipalities are liable for constitutional violations under § 1983? How does this set of rules differ from those governing the liability of individual officials under *Monroe v. Pape* (Chapter 1) and *Harlow v. Fitzgerald* (Chapter 4)?

2. Which set of limitations on liability—those applicable to individual defendants or those applicable to municipal defendants—is more difficult for plaintiffs to overcome? Is that answer the same in all situations? Would plaintiffs be better off if the Court applied the same rules to both municipal and individual defendants? If so, which regime (*Monell/Owen* or *Monroe/Harlow*) should plaintiffs prefer? Or is it advantageous to plaintiffs, when considering which set of limitations on liability to attempt to overcome, to be able to pick their poison?

3. Doesn't *Owen* repudiate all the policy arguments that the *Monell* Court made just two years earlier to justify imposing the policy/custom limitation on municipal liability? How does the Court explain the change? Or is *Monell* itself so internally contradictory that it's difficult to be faithful to all of it?

4. Do *Monell* and *Owen* affect your view of *Will v. Mich. Dep't of State Police* (Chapter 3), holding that Congress could not have intended to abrogate state sovereign immunity absent a clear statement? Can you reconcile the Court's approach to the word "person" in the municipal liability context with its approach to the same word in *Will*, particularly now that the Court in *Owen* has explicitly drawn the connection between municipalities and sovereign immunity?

5. Justice Powell complains vividly that the Court's decision "converts municipal governance into a hazardous slalom through constitutional obstacles that often are unknown and unknowable." Perhaps the upcoming winter Olympics (held that year in Lake Placid, New York, a few weeks after the argument in *Owen*) influenced his choice of metaphor, but is a municipal official's plight really as bad as all that? Is it more hazardous than, for instance, the circumstances of state officials, whose unlawful conduct (as we learned in Chapter 3) could subject the state to an expensive injunction and liability for attorneys' fees? Or for that matter, municipalities' liability under ordinary tort law for the common law torts of their employees by virtue of respondeat superior?

6. How does the Court explain the divergent treatment of individuals and municipalities when it comes to qualified immunity? Are you persuaded?

Note: *Monell* and Injunctive Relief

Does *Monell*'s policy/custom requirement apply regardless of the type of relief sought? In *Los Angeles County v. Humphries*, 562 U.S. 29 (2010), a California couple was accused of child abuse but later exonerated. However, pursuant to California law, their names were added to a Child Abuse Central Index, where their names would remain available to various state agencies for at least ten years. The statute had no procedures for allowing individuals to challenge their inclusion in the Index, and neither California nor Los Angeles County had created such procedures. The couple sued the County and other defendants under § 1983 for violating their due process rights by failing to create a mechanism through which they could contest inclusion in the Index. The couple sought damages, an injunction, and declaratory relief. The case reached the Supreme Court on the limited issue of whether non-monetary, prospective relief could be granted against the County in the absence of a municipal policy or custom. The Supreme Court unanimously held that it could not. Writing for the Court, Justice Breyer explained:

> The language of § 1983 read in light of *Monell*'s understanding of the legislative history explains why claims for prospective relief, like claims for money damages, fall within the scope of the "policy or custom" requirement. Nothing in the text of § 1983 suggests that the causation requirement contained in the statute should change with the form of relief sought. In fact, the text suggests the opposite when it provides that a person who meets § 1983's elements "shall be liable . . . in an action at law, suit in equity, or other proper proceeding for redress." Thus, as *Monell* explicitly stated, "[l]ocal governing bodies . . . can be sued directly under § 1983 for monetary,

declaratory, or injunctive relief where, as here, the action that is alleged to be unconstitutional implements or executes" a policy or custom (emphasis added). . . .

Monell's logic also argues against any such relief-based bifurcation. . . . For whether an action or omission is a municipality's "own" has to do with the nature of the action or omission, not with the nature of the relief that is later sought in court. . . .

Finally, respondents [argue] that applying *Monell*'s requirement to prospective relief claims will leave some set of ongoing constitutional violations beyond redress. Despite the fact that four Circuits apply *Monell*'s requirement to prospective relief, however, respondents have not presented us with any actual or hypothetical example that provides serious cause for concern.

For these reasons, we hold that *Monell*'s "policy or custom" requirement applies in § 1983 cases irrespective of whether the relief sought is monetary or prospective.

Is the Court's focus on the text of § 1983 consistent with its approach to that statute in prior cases? Would a consideration of the policy concerns underlying *Monell* have yielded a different result?

Note that the original defendants in this case included the County sheriff and two County detectives. Could the couple have obtained the prospective relief they needed without suing the County at all? Recall the observation at the end of Chapter 3, Section C, that plaintiffs may sometimes find it advantageous to seek an injunction against a municipal official *in an individual capacity* to avoid naming the municipality, although courts are divided regarding whether to permit such suits. Does *Humphries* affect your view on whether such suits should be allowed? The Court didn't seem to take seriously the possibility that *Humphries* would bar a suit where suing a municipality is necessary to obtain relief. Should it have? If not, does this case have any practical effect?

B. ACTIONS BY POLICYMAKERS

When is a constitutional violation attributable to a municipal policy? That question was easy in *Monell*, where the policy took the form of a specific rule. The municipal liability inquiry becomes harder when that level of formality is absent. Can the actions of municipal officers give rise to municipal liability? If so, which ones?

The Court began to answer that question in *City of Oklahoma City v. Tuttle*, 471 U.S. 808 (1985), and *Pembaur v. City of Cincinnati*, 475 U.S. 469 (1986).

In *Tuttle*, a man was shot and killed by an Oklahoma City police officer, who thought (wrongly) that the man was reaching for a gun. The victim's widow sued both the officer and the City for excessive force. The plaintiff's theory was that the City was liable for the shooting because its training of the officer had been inadequate. The jury returned a verdict for the officer based on qualified immunity but held the City liable for the shooting. The jury had been instructed that it could infer inadequate training from the nature of the violation itself. The appeals court affirmed. The Supreme Court reversed. The case produced no majority opinion on the municipal liability question, as the Justices fractured on the precise rationale for reversal. (As a result, the contours of a failure-to-train claim were not clarified until *City of Canton v. Harris*, 489 U.S. 378 (1989), a principal case in Section C.) Seven Justices did, however, agree in *Tuttle* on an important principle: The unconstitutional actions of a line officer could not, on their own, satisfy the *Monell* requirement of a municipal "policy." The plurality opinion of Justice Rehnquist, joined by Chief Justice Burger and Justices White and O'Connor, argued that reversal was required because the jury had been instructed in such a manner that it "could . . . have imposed liability on the city based solely upon proof that it employed a non-policymaking officer who violated the Constitution." Justice Brennan's concurrence in the judgment, joined by Justices Marshall and Blackmun, agreed that "the scope of § 1983 liability does not permit such liability to be imposed merely on evidence of the wrongful actions of a single city employee not authorized to make city policy." Justice Powell did not participate. Justice Stevens dissented alone, arguing that the "policy" requirement of *Monell* was "dicta of the least persuasive kind," having been both unnecessary to the holding and not responsive to any argument advanced by either party.

If a line officer's misconduct cannot, in isolation, subject a municipality to liability, what about the actions of a high-ranking official? The Court turned to this question in *Pembaur*. Dr. Pembaur was indicted for fraud. Subpoenas were issued for two of his employees. Cincinnati and Hamilton County police officers went to Dr. Pembaur's medical clinic because they thought the employees were there. Dr. Pembaur refused them entry. The officers sought advice by calling the County prosecutor, who told them to "go in and get" the witnesses. The officers broke down the door with an axe. The witnesses were not there. Dr. Pembaur sued the officers, the City of Cincinnati, and Hamilton County for violating his Fourth Amendment rights. (Incidentally, Dr. Pembaur was acquitted of the fraud charges but convicted for obstructing the officers when they tried to enter his clinic.) The district court dismissed claims against the County because no "policy" had been shown, and the court of appeals affirmed. The Supreme Court reversed. Justice Brennan wrote for the majority:

> The "official policy" requirement was intended to distinguish acts of the municipality from acts of employees of the municipality, and thereby make clear that municipal liability is limited to action for which the municipality is actually responsible. *Monell* reasoned that recovery from a municipality is limited to acts that are, properly speaking, acts "of the municipality"—that is, acts which the municipality has officially sanctioned or ordered.
>
> With this understanding, it is plain that municipal liability may be imposed for a single decision by municipal policymakers under appropriate circumstances. No one has ever doubted, for instance, that a municipality may be liable under § 1983 for a single decision by its properly constituted legislative body—whether or not that body had taken similar action in the past or intended to do so in the future—because even a single decision by such a body unquestionably constitutes an act of official government policy. But the power to establish policy is no more the exclusive province of the legislature at the local level than at the state or national level. *Monell*'s language makes clear that it expressly envisioned other officials "whose acts or edicts may fairly be said to represent official policy," *Monell*, and whose decisions therefore may give rise to municipal liability under § 1983. . . .
>
> To be sure, "official policy" often refers to formal rules or understandings . . . that are intended to, and do, establish fixed plans of action to be followed under similar circumstances consistently and over time. . . . However, . . . a government frequently chooses a course of action tailored to a particular situation and not intended to

control decisions in later situations. If the decision to adopt that particular course of action is properly made by that government's authorized decisionmakers, it surely represents an act of official government "policy" as that term is commonly understood. More importantly, where action is directed by those who establish governmental policy, the municipality is equally responsible whether that action is to be taken only once or to be taken repeatedly.

Speaking for only a plurality, Justice Brennan continued:

The fact that a particular official — even a policymaking official — has discretion in the exercise of particular functions does not, without more, give rise to municipal liability based on an exercise of that discretion. The official must also be responsible for establishing final government policy respecting such activity before the municipality can be held liable.[12]

Authority to make municipal policy may be granted directly by a legislative enactment or may be delegated by an official who possesses such authority, and of course, whether an official had final policymaking authority is a question of state law. . . . We hold that municipal liability under § 1983 attaches where — and only where — a deliberate choice to follow a course of action is made from among various alternatives by the official or officials responsible for establishing final policy with respect to the subject matter in question.

Justice Brennan regained his majority for his application of these principles:

Unsure of the proper course of action to follow, [the officers at the clinic] sought instructions from their supervisors. The instructions they received were to follow the orders of the County Prosecutor. The Prosecutor made a considered decision based on his understanding of the law and commanded the officers forcibly to enter petitioner's clinic. That decision directly caused the violation of petitioner's Fourth Amendment rights. . . .

Respondent suggests that the County Prosecutor was merely rendering "legal advice" when he ordered the Deputy Sheriffs to "go in and get" the witnesses. . . .

However . . . Ohio Rev. Code Ann. § 309.09(A) provides that county officers may "require . . . instructions from [the County Prosecutor] in matters connected with their official duties." Pursuant to standard office procedure, the Sheriff's Office referred this matter to the Prosecutor and then followed his instructions. . . . In ordering the Deputy Sheriffs to enter petitioner's clinic the County Prosecutor was acting as the final decisionmaker for the county, and the county may therefore be held liable under § 1983.

Concurring in part and in the judgment, Justice Stevens argued that the Court should simply apply respondeat superior:

This is not a hard case. If there is any difficulty, it arises from the problem of obtaining a consensus on the meaning of the word "policy" — a word that does not appear

---

12. Thus, for example, the County Sheriff may have discretion to hire and fire employees without also being the county official responsible for establishing county employment policy. If this were the case, the Sheriff's decisions respecting employment would not give rise to municipal liability, although similar decisions with respect to law enforcement practices, over which the Sheriff is the official policymaker, would give rise to municipal liability. . . .

in the text of 42 U.S.C. § 1983, the statutory provision that we are supposed to be construing. The difficulty is thus a consequence of this Court's lawmaking efforts rather than the work of the Congress of the United States. . . .

The legislative history indicating that Congress did not intend to impose civil liability on municipalities for the conduct of third parties, merely confirms the view that it did intend to impose liability for the governments' own illegal acts — including those acts performed by their agents in the course of their employment. . . . [B]oth the broad remedial purpose of the statute and the fact that it embodied contemporaneous common-law doctrine, including respondeat superior, require a conclusion that Congress intended that a governmental entity be liable for the constitutional deprivations committed by its agents in the course of their duties. . . .

To the extent that . . . "policy" concerns are relevant, . . . primary responsibility for protecting the constitutional rights of the residents of Hamilton County from the officers of Hamilton County should rest on the shoulders of the county itself, rather than on the several agents who were trying to perform their jobs. . . . The county has the resources and the authority that can best avoid future constitutional violations and provide a fair remedy for those that have occurred in the past.

Justices White and O'Connor also concurred briefly. Justice Powell, joined by Chief Justice Burger and Justice Rehnquist, dissented:

[N]o official county policy could have been created solely by an off-hand telephone response from a busy County Prosecutor. . . .

In my view, the question whether official policy — in any normal sense of the term — has been made in a particular case is not answered by explaining who has final authority to make policy. The question here is not "could the County Prosecutor make policy?" but rather, "did he make policy?" . . .

Today's decision finds that policy is established because a policymaking official made a decision on the telephone that was within the scope of his authority. The Court ignores the fact that no business organization or governmental unit makes binding policy decisions so cavalierly. . . .

In my view, proper resolution of the question whether official policy has been formed should focus on two factors: (i) the nature of the decision reached or the action taken, and (ii) the process by which the decision was reached or the action was taken. . . .

Applying these factors to the instant case demonstrates that no official policy was formulated. . . . The Court's result today rests on the implicit conclusion that the Prosecutor's response — "go in and get them" — altered the prior case-by-case approach of the Department and formed a new rule to apply in all similar cases. Nothing about the Prosecutor's response to the inquiry over the phone, nor the circumstances surrounding the response, indicates that such a rule of general applicability was formed.

Similarly, nothing about the way the decision was reached indicates that official policy was formed. The prosecutor, without time for thoughtful consideration or consultation, simply gave an off-the-cuff answer to a single question. There was no process at all.

Notes and Questions

1. Why was there such broad agreement on the result in *Tuttle*? What's wrong with a presumption that an egregious and fatal constitutional violation reflected a failure to train on the municipality's part?

2. Identify the three different approaches to municipal liability reflected in the opinions of Justices Brennan, Stevens, and Powell in *Pembaur*. Which is easiest to apply? Which is hardest? Should the Court take administrability into account?

3. In the years between the confrontation at the clinic and the resolution of Dr. Pembaur's case, the Supreme Court had held that, absent exigent circumstances, officers cannot enter a person's property without a warrant in search of a third party. Because that holding postdated the alleged constitutional violation, the district court granted the officers qualified immunity. Dr. Pembaur did not appeal this holding. How should the disposition of officer suits affect the Court's approach to the municipal liability question, if at all? Does it matter that there will be constitutional violations for which no one will be held accountable?

4. No Justice joined Justice Stevens in either *Tuttle* or *Pembaur*. Why is the rest of the Court so averse to respondeat superior for constitutional claims against municipalities, given that they face that rule all the time under ordinary tort law? Is it clear Congress wouldn't have wanted that result? Why?

5. In *Pembaur*, no Justice denied that a single isolated incident could sometimes give rise to municipal liability. Is that result faithful to the requirement of showing a "policy" or "custom"? Is a single isolated act a "policy" or "custom" in an ordinary sense? How does the Court address this objection?

* * *

Tuttle ruled out municipal liability based on a *line officer's* single action. *Pembaur* permitted municipal liability based on the single action of a *final policymaker*. The former holding was simple; the latter gave rise to further questions. Who qualifies as a final policymaker? In what way must that person have been involved in the constitutional violation to subject the municipality to liability? The next case addresses these questions, laying out the rules governing municipal liability claims predicated on the actions of a policymaker (as distinct from claims based on the type of formal policy present in *Monell* or claims based on municipal *inaction*, which are discussed in the next section).

City of St. Louis v. Praprotnik
485 U.S. 112 (1988)

▪ *Justice O'CONNOR announced the judgment of the Court and delivered an opinion in which THE CHIEF JUSTICE, Justice WHITE, and Justice SCALIA join.* . . .

[Respondent James H. Praprotnik was an architect working for the city of St. Louis in its Community Development Agency (CDA). Praprotnik was suspended or evaluated unfavorably several times but successfully appealed these personnel actions to city authorities, included a successful 1980 appeal to the city's Civil Service Commission. CDA's director, Frank Hamsher, then transferred Praprotnik to the city's Heritage and Urban Design Commission (Heritage). Praprotnik objected to the transfer before the Civil Service Commission, without success. He then filed suit in federal court. Meanwhile, at Heritage, Praprotnik became involved in disputes with the head of Heritage, Robert Killen. Again Praprotnik suffered an adverse personnel action, again he appealed, and he obtained partial relief. Ultimately, Praprotnik was laid off based on funding concerns. He amended his federal lawsuit to include a claim that the layoff was carried out for pretextual reasons in violation of due process and the First Amendment. The jury returned a verdict finding no individual city official liable but holding St. Louis liable. The court of appeals affirmed part of the judgment against the city.] . . .

In *Monell* itself, it was undisputed that there had been an official policy requiring city employees to take actions that were unconstitutional under this Court's decisions. . . .

In the years since *Monell* was decided, the Court has considered several cases involving isolated acts by government officials and employees. We have assumed that an unconstitutional governmental policy could be inferred from a single decision taken by the highest officials responsible for setting policy in that area of the government's business. At the other end of the spectrum, we have held that an unjustified shooting by a police officer cannot, without more, be thought to result from official policy.

Two Terms ago, in *Pembaur*, we undertook to define more precisely when a decision on a single occasion may be enough to establish an unconstitutional municipal policy. Although the Court was unable to settle on a general formulation, Justice Brennan's opinion articulated several guiding principles. First, a majority of the Court agreed that municipalities may be held liable under § 1983 only for acts for which the municipality itself is actually responsible, "that is, acts which the municipality has officially sanctioned or ordered." Second, only those municipal officials who have "final policymaking authority" may by their actions subject the government to § 1983 liability.

Third, whether a particular official has "final policymaking authority" is a question of state law. Fourth, the challenged action must have been taken pursuant to a policy adopted by the official or officials responsible under state law for making policy in that area of the city's business. . . . Today, we set out again to clarify the issue that we last addressed in *Pembaur*.

We begin by reiterating that the identification of policymaking officials is a question of state law. "Authority to make municipal policy may be granted directly by a legislative enactment or may be delegated by an official who possesses such authority, and of course, whether an official had final policymaking authority is a question of state law." *Pembaur*.[1] . . .

---

1. Unlike Justice Brennan, we would not replace this standard with a new approach in which state law becomes merely an "appropriate starting point" for an "assessment of a municipality's actual power structure." Municipalities cannot be expected to predict how courts or juries will assess their

Without attempting to canvass the numberless factual scenarios that may come to light in litigation, we can be confident that state law (which may include valid local ordinances and regulations) will always direct a court to some official or body that has the responsibility for making law or setting policy in any given area of a local government's business.[2]

We are not, of course, predicting that state law will always speak with perfect clarity. We have no reason to suppose, however, that federal courts will face greater difficulties here than those that they routinely address in other contexts. We are also aware that there will be cases in which policymaking responsibility is shared among more than one official or body. In the case before us, for example, it appears that the Mayor and Aldermen are authorized to adopt such ordinances relating to personnel administration as are compatible with the City Charter. See St. Louis City Charter, Art. XVIII, § 7(b). The Civil Service Commission, for its part, is required to "prescribe . . . rules for the administration and enforcement of the provisions of this article, and of any ordinance adopted in pursuance thereof, and not inconsistent therewith." § 7(a). Assuming that applicable law does not make the decisions of the Commission reviewable by the Mayor and Aldermen, or vice versa, one would have to conclude that policy decisions made either by the Mayor and Aldermen or by the Commission would be attributable to the city itself. In any event, however, a federal court would not be justified in assuming that municipal policymaking authority lies somewhere other than where the applicable law purports to put it. And certainly there can be no justification for giving a jury the discretion to determine which officials are high enough in the government that their actions can be said to represent a decision of the government itself.

As the plurality in *Pembaur* recognized, special difficulties can arise when it is contended that a municipal policymaker has delegated his policymaking authority to another official. If the mere exercise of discretion by an employee could give rise to a constitutional violation, the result would be indistinguishable

---

"actual power structures," and this uncertainty could easily lead to results that would be hard in practice to distinguish from the results of a regime governed by the doctrine of respondeat superior. It is one thing to charge a municipality with responsibility for the decisions of officials invested by law, or by a "custom or usage" having the force of law, with policymaking authority. It would be something else, and something inevitably more capricious, to hold a municipality responsible for every decision that is perceived as "final" through the lens of a particular factfinder's evaluation of the city's "actual power structure."

2. Justice Stevens, who believes that *Monell* incorrectly rejected the doctrine of respondeat superior, suggests a new theory that reflects his perceptions of the congressional purposes underlying § 1983. This theory would apparently ignore state law, and distinguish between "high" officials and "low" officials on the basis of an independent evaluation of the extent to which a particular official's actions have "the potential of controlling governmental decisionmaking," or are "perceived as the actions of the city itself." . . . [W]e think the legal test is too imprecise to hold much promise of consistent adjudication or principled analysis. We can see no reason, except perhaps a desire to come as close as possible to respondeat superior without expressly adopting that doctrine, that could justify introducing such unpredictability into a body of law that is already so difficult. . . .

from respondeat superior liability. If, however, a city's lawful policymakers could insulate the government from liability simply by delegating their policymaking authority to others, § 1983 could not serve its intended purpose. It may not be possible to draw an elegant line that will resolve this conundrum, but certain principles should provide useful guidance.

First, whatever analysis is used to identify municipal policymakers, egregious attempts by local governments to insulate themselves from liability for unconstitutional policies are precluded by a separate doctrine. Relying on the language of § 1983, the Court has long recognized that a plaintiff may be able to prove the existence of a widespread practice that, although not authorized by written law or express municipal policy, is "so permanent and well settled as to constitute a 'custom or usage' with the force of law." That principle, which has not been affected by *Monell* or subsequent cases, ensures that most deliberate municipal evasions of the Constitution will be sharply limited.

Second, as the *Pembaur* plurality recognized, the authority to make municipal policy is necessarily the authority to make final policy. When an official's discretionary decisions are constrained by policies not of that official's making, those policies, rather than the subordinate's departures from them, are the act of the municipality. Similarly, when a subordinate's decision is subject to review by the municipality's authorized policymakers, they have retained the authority to measure the official's conduct for conformance with their policies. If the authorized policymakers approve a subordinate's decision and the basis for it, their ratification would be chargeable to the municipality because their decision is final. . . .

The city cannot be held liable under § 1983 unless respondent proved the existence of an unconstitutional municipal policy. Respondent does not contend that anyone in city government ever promulgated, or even articulated, such a policy. Nor did he attempt to prove that such retaliation was ever directed against anyone other than himself. . . . The Mayor and Aldermen enacted no ordinance designed to retaliate against respondent or against similarly situated employees. On the contrary, the city established an independent Civil Service Commission and empowered it to review and correct improper personnel actions. Respondent does not deny that his repeated appeals from adverse personnel decisions repeatedly brought him at least partial relief, and the Civil Service Commission never so much as hinted that retaliatory transfers or layoffs were permissible. Respondent points to no evidence indicating that the Commission delegated to anyone its final authority to interpret and enforce [its employment policies].

The Court of Appeals concluded that "appointing authorities," like Hamsher and Killen, who had the authority to initiate transfers and layoffs, were municipal "policymakers." The court based this conclusion on its findings (1) that the decisions of these employees were not individually reviewed for "substantive propriety" by higher supervisory officials; and (2) that the Civil Service Commission decided appeals from such decisions, if at all, in a circumscribed manner that gave substantial deference to the original decisionmaker. We find these propositions insufficient to support the conclusion that Hamsher and

Killen were authorized to establish employment policy for the city with respect to transfers and layoffs. To the contrary, the City Charter expressly states that the Civil Service Commission has the power and the duty:

> "To consider and determine any matter involved in the administration and enforcement of this [Civil Service] article and the rules and ordinances adopted in accordance therewith that may be referred to it for decision by the director [of personnel], or on appeal by any appointing authority, employee, or taxpayer of the city, from any act of the director or of any appointing authority. The decision of the commission in all such matters shall be final, subject, however, to any right of action under any law of the state or of the United States." St. Louis City Charter, Art. XVIII, § 7(d).

This case therefore resembles the hypothetical example in *Pembaur*: "[I]f [city] employment policy was set by the [Mayor and Aldermen and by the Civil Service Commission], only [those] bod[ies'] decisions would provide a basis for [city] liability. This would be true even if the [Mayor and Aldermen and the Commission] left the [appointing authorities] discretion to hire and fire employees and [they] exercised that discretion in an unconstitutional manner. . . ." A majority of the Court of Appeals panel determined that the Civil Service Commission's review of individual employment actions gave too much deference to the decisions of appointing authorities like Hamsher and Killen. Simply going along with discretionary decisions made by one's subordinates, however, is not a delegation to them of the authority to make policy. It is equally consistent with a presumption that the subordinates are faithfully attempting to comply with the policies that are supposed to guide them. It would be a different matter if a particular decision by a subordinate was cast in the form of a policy statement and expressly approved by the supervising policymaker. It would also be a different matter if a series of decisions by a subordinate official manifested a "custom or usage" of which the supervisor must have been aware. In both those cases, the supervisor could realistically be deemed to have adopted a policy that happened to have been formulated or initiated by a lower-ranking official. But the mere failure to investigate the basis of a subordinate's discretionary decisions does not amount to a delegation of policymaking authority, especially where (as here) the wrongfulness of the subordinate's decision arises from a retaliatory motive or other unstated rationale. In such circumstances, the purposes of § 1983 would not be served by treating a subordinate employee's decision as if it were a reflection of municipal policy.

Justice Brennan's opinion, concurring in the judgment, finds implications in our discussion that we do not think necessary or correct. We nowhere say or imply, for example, that "a municipal charter's precatory admonition against discrimination or any other employment practice not based on merit and fitness effectively insulates the municipality from any liability based on acts inconsistent with that policy." . . . Refusals to carry out stated policies could obviously help to show that a municipality's actual policies were different from the ones that had been announced. . . .

Nor do we believe that we have left a "gaping hole" in § 1983 that needs to be filled with the vague concept of "de facto final policymaking authority."

Except perhaps as a step towards overruling *Monell* and adopting the doctrine of respondeat superior, ad hoc searches for officials possessing such "de facto" authority would serve primarily to foster needless unpredictability in the application of § 1983.

We cannot accept either the Court of Appeals' broad definition of municipal policymakers or respondent's suggestion that a jury should be entitled to define for itself which officials' decisions should expose a municipality to liability. Respondent has suggested that the record will support an inference that policymaking authority was in fact delegated to individuals who took retaliatory action against him and who were not exonerated by the jury. . . . [Reviewing that claim] is best left to the Court of Appeals. . . . Accordingly, the decision of the Court of Appeals is reversed, and the case is remanded for further proceedings consistent with this opinion.

Justice KENNEDY *took no part in the consideration or decision of this case.*

■ *Justice* BRENNAN, *with whom Justice* MARSHALL *and Justice* BLACKMUN *join, concurring in the judgment. . . .*

I believe that the commendable desire of today's plurality to "define more precisely when a decision on a single occasion may be enough" to subject a municipality to § 1983 liability, has led it to embrace a theory of municipal liability that is both unduly narrow and unrealistic, and one that ultimately would permit municipalities to insulate themselves from liability for the acts of all but a small minority of actual city policymakers. . . .

In my view, *Pembaur* controls this case. As an "appointing authority," Hamsher was empowered under the City Charter to initiate lateral transfers such as the one challenged here, subject to the approval of both the Director of Personnel and the appointing authority of the transferee agency. The Charter, however, nowhere confers upon agency heads any authority to establish city policy, final or otherwise, with respect to such transfers. . . . At most, then, the record demonstrates that Hamsher had the authority to determine how best to effectuate a policy announced by his superiors, rather than the power to establish that policy. . . . Hamsher had discretionary authority to transfer CDA employees laterally; that he may have used this authority to punish respondent for the exercise of his First Amendment rights does not, without more, render the city liable for respondent's resulting constitutional injury. . . .

These determinations, it seems to me, are sufficient to dispose of this case, and I therefore think it unnecessary to decide, as the plurality does, who the actual policymakers in St. Louis are. I question more than the mere necessity of these determinations, however, for I believe that in the course of passing on issues not before us, the plurality announces legal principles that are inconsistent with our earlier cases and unduly restrict the reach of § 1983 in cases involving municipalities.

The plurality begins its assessment of St. Louis' power structure by asserting that the identification of policymaking officials is a question of state law, by which it means that the question is neither one of federal law nor of fact, at least "not . . . in the usual sense." Instead, the plurality explains, courts are to identify municipal policymakers by referring exclusively to applicable state statutory law. Not surprisingly, the plurality cites no authority for this startling proposition, nor could it, for we have never suggested that municipal liability should be determined in so formulaic and unrealistic a fashion. In any case in which the policymaking authority of a municipal tortfeasor is in doubt, state law will naturally be the appropriate starting point, but ultimately the factfinder must determine where such policymaking authority actually resides, and not simply "where the applicable law purports to put it." As the plurality itself acknowledges, local governing bodies may take myriad forms. We in no way slight the dignity of municipalities by recognizing that in not a few of them real and apparent authority may diverge, and that in still others state statutory law will simply fail to disclose where such authority ultimately rests. Indeed, in upholding the Court of Appeals' determination in *Pembaur* that the County Prosecutor was a policymaking official with respect to county law enforcement practices, a majority of this Court relied on testimony which revealed that the County Sheriff's office routinely forwarded certain matters to the Prosecutor and followed his instructions in those areas. While the majority splintered into three separate camps on the ultimate theory of municipal liability, and the case generated five opinions in all, not a single Member of the Court suggested that reliance on such extra-statutory evidence of the county's actual allocation of policymaking authority was in any way improper. Thus . . . juries can and must find the predicate facts necessary to a determination whether a given official possesses final policymaking authority. While the jury instructions in this case were regrettably vague, the plurality's solution tosses the baby out with the bath water. The identification of municipal policymakers is an essentially factual determination "in the usual sense," and is therefore rightly entrusted to a properly instructed jury.

Nor does the "custom or usage" doctrine adequately compensate for the inherent inflexibility of a rule that leaves the identification of policymakers exclusively to state statutory law. That doctrine, under which municipalities and States can be held liable for unconstitutional practices so well settled and permanent that they have the force of law, has little if any bearing on the question whether a city has delegated de facto final policymaking authority to a given official. A city practice of delegating final policymaking authority to a subordinate or mid-level official would not be unconstitutional in and of itself, and an isolated unconstitutional act by an official entrusted with such authority would obviously not amount to a municipal "custom or usage." Under *Pembaur*, of course, such an isolated act should give rise to municipal liability. Yet a case such as this would fall through the gaping hole the plurality's construction leaves in § 1983, because state statutory law would not identify the municipal actor as a policymaking official, and a single constitutional deprivation, by definition, is not a well-settled and permanent municipal practice carrying the force of law.

For these same reasons, I cannot subscribe to the plurality's narrow and overly rigid view of when a municipal official's policymaking authority is "final."

Attempting to place a gloss on *Pembaur*'s finality requirement, the plurality suggests that whenever the decisions of an official are subject to some form of review—however limited—that official's decisions are nonfinal. Under the plurality's theory, therefore, even where an official wields policymaking authority with respect to a challenged decision, the city would not be liable for that official's policy decision unless reviewing officials affirmatively approved both the "decision and the basis for it." Reviewing officials, however, may as a matter of practice never invoke their plenary oversight authority, or their review powers may be highly circumscribed. Under such circumstances, the subordinate's decision is in effect the final municipal pronouncement on the subject. Certainly a § 1983 plaintiff is entitled to place such considerations before the jury, for the law is concerned not with the niceties of legislative draftsmanship but with the realities of municipal decisionmaking, and any assessment of a municipality's actual power structure is necessarily a factual and practical one. . . .

Under the plurality's analysis . . . even the hollowest promise of review is sufficient to divest all city officials save the mayor and governing legislative body of final policymaking authority. While clarity and ease of application may commend such a rule, we have remained steadfast in our conviction that Congress intended to hold municipalities accountable for those constitutional injuries inflicted not only by their lawmakers, but also "by those whose edicts or acts may fairly be said to represent official policy." *Monell.* Because the plurality's mechanical "finality" test is fundamentally at odds with the pragmatic and factual inquiry contemplated by *Monell*, I cannot join what I perceive to be its unwarranted abandonment of the traditional factfinding process in § 1983 actions involving municipalities. . . .

▣ *Justice STEVENS, dissenting. . . .*

Both *Pembaur* and the plurality and concurring opinions today acknowledge that a high official who has ultimate control over a certain area of city government can bind the city through his unconstitutional actions even though those actions are not in the form of formal rules or regulations. Although the Court has explained its holdings by reference to the nonstatutory term "policy," it plainly has not embraced the standard understanding of that word as covering a rule of general applicability. Instead it has used that term to include isolated acts not intended to be binding over a class of situations. But when one remembers that the real question in cases such as this is not "what constitutes city policy?" but rather "when should a city be liable for the acts of its agents?", the inclusion of single acts by high officials makes sense, for those acts bind a municipality in a way that the misdeeds of low officials do not.

Every act of a high official constitutes a kind of "statement" about how similar decisions will be carried out; the assumption is that the same decision would have been made, and would again be made, across a class of cases. Lower officials do not control others in the same way. Since their actions do not dictate the responses of various subordinates, those actions lack the potential of controlling governmental decisionmaking; they are not perceived as the actions of the city itself. If a County police officer had broken down Dr. Pembaur's door on the officer's own initiative, this would have been seen as the action of an overanxious officer, and would not have sent a message to other officers that similar actions would be countenanced. One reason for this is that the County Prosecutor himself could step forward and say "that was wrong"; when the County Prosecutor authorized the action himself, only a self-correction would accomplish the same task, and until such time his action would have countywide ramifications. Here, the Mayor, those working for him, and the agency heads are high-ranking officials; accordingly, we must assume that their actions have citywide ramifications, both through their similar response to a like class of situations, and through the response of subordinates who follow their lead. . . .

Notes and Questions

1. How many paths to municipal liability does the plurality identify? What are they? How clearly marked is each?

2. Which test is most administrable—the plurality's, Justice Brennan's, or Justice Stevens's?

3. The plurality suggests that a municipality can be liable for actions by a municipal official who has been delegated final decisionmaking authority by the final policymaker. Although the plurality refers to the "special difficulties" with such a claim, it does not rule it out, and it remands for further proceedings regarding the plaintiff's contention that "the record will support an inference that policymaking authority was in fact delegated to individuals who took retaliatory action against him and who were not exonerated by the jury." The *Pembaur* plurality likewise stated, "Authority to make municipal policy may be granted directly by a legislative enactment or may be delegated by an official who possesses such authority." Courts of appeals widely recognize the viability of a delegation theory. *See, e.g., Miller v. Calhoun Cty.*, 408 F.3d 803, 814 (6th Cir. 2005); *Holloman ex rel. Holloman v. Harland*, 370 F.3d 1252, 1291 (11th Cir. 2004); *Riddick v. Sch. Bd. of City of Portsmouth*, 238 F.3d 518, 523 (4th Cir. 2000).

   How well can this theory coexist with the *Praprotnik* plurality's evident interest in removing decisions about municipal liability from the hands of the jury? That question has sparked debate. *Compare, e.g., Barone v. City of Springfield*, 902 F.3d 1091, 1109 (9th Cir. 2018) (holding delegation is question of fact that can defeat summary judgment), *and Kujawski v. Bd. of Comm'rs*, 183 F.3d 734, 739 (7th Cir. 1999) (same), *with Milligan-Hitt v. Bd. of Trustees*, 523 F.3d 1219, 1223-24 (10th Cir. 2008) (reversing jury verdict for plaintiff on delegated-authority theory because "final policymaking authority is a question of law, which should not have gone to the jury").

4. In addition to questions about whether a delegation of authority has occurred, what other factual issues might arise based on the plurality's various theories of municipal liability? Won't a jury inevitably be involved in deciding some of these questions? If not, why not?

5. Justice Brennan is highly critical of the plurality's approach, which he contends facilitates the avoidance of liability. Figure 5.1 illustrates the various routes to municipal liability via the actions of a final policymaker and also the "gaping hole" Justice Brennan sees in liability for certain types of decisions. How well founded is Justice Brennan's concern? *Cf.* Fred Smith, *Local Sovereign Immunity*, 116 Colum. L. Rev. 409, 412 (2016) (arguing that "the local inoculation from legal accountability for federal constitutional violations is a consequential, de facto form of 'local sovereign immunity'").

6. If you were counsel to a municipality seeking to minimize its exposure under § 1983, how would you structure the municipality's operations and decision-making processes? If you were a state seeking to protect your municipalities from liability, what laws might you pass? Are you persuaded by the plurality's assurance that it has not opened the door to manipulation?

7. How do the text, legislative history, and rationale of § 1983 support the Justices' various theories of municipal liability? From what source(s) of authority are these theories derived?

8. *McMillian v. Monroe County*, 520 U.S. 781 (1997), highlights the consequences of a formalistic rather than functional approach to identifying a final policymaker. After Walter McMillian's murder conviction was overturned and he was released following six years on death row, McMillian brought a § 1983 action against Monroe County, Alabama, and County Sheriff Tom Tate for suppressing exculpatory evidence and intimidating a witness into making false statements. The Court held that Monroe County could not be

Figure 5.1: Paths to municipal liability—or nonliability—involving the action of a final policymaker

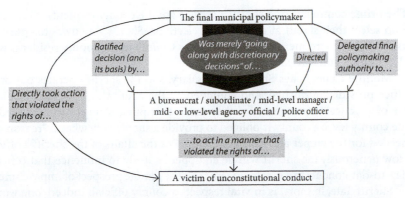

This chart illustrates several ways for a "final policymaker" to be involved in a constitutional violation by a municipality. Pembaur *and* Praprotnik *recognized several paths to municipal liability via involvement of a final policymaker (the four thin arrows to the sides of the diagram). But Justice Brennan accused the* Praprotnik *plurality of creating a "gaping hole...in § 1983," because actions falling into the category defined by the* Praprotnik *plurality as not creating municipal liability (the thick black arrow through the shaded oval in the center) are far more typical of how municipalities actually operate. (Note that this chart illustrates only municipal liability theories that rely on actions of a final policymaker. Explicit municipal policies, customs, and municipal failures-to-act are separate theories.)*

liable based on the actions of Sheriff Tate because Alabama sheriffs are policymakers for the State, not for the County. Chief Justice Rehnquist explained for the majority:

> Alabama's Constitution, adopted in 1901, states that "[t]he executive department shall consist of a governor, lieutenant governor, attorney-general, state auditor, secretary of state, state treasurer, superintendent of education, commissioner of agriculture and industries, and a sheriff for each county." Ala. Const. of 1901, Art. V, § 112. . . .
>
> [The Alabama Supreme Court] has held unequivocally that sheriffs are state officers, and that tort claims brought against sheriffs based on their official acts therefore constitute suits against the State, not suits against the sheriff's county. Thus, Alabama counties are not liable under a theory of respondeat superior for a sheriff's official acts that are tortious. . . .
>
> [Petitioner argues that under our approach,] sheriffs will be characterized differently in different States. But while it might be easier to decide cases arising under § 1983 and *Monell* if we insisted on a uniform, national characterization for all sheriffs, such a blunderbuss approach would ignore a crucial axiom of our government: the States have wide authority to set up their state and local governments as they wish. . . .
>
> [McMillian argues] that state and local governments will manipulate the titles of local officials in a blatant effort to shield the local governments from liability. But such efforts are already foreclosed by our decision in *Praprotnik* (plurality opinion) ("[E]gregious attempts by local governments to insulate themselves from liability for unconstitutional policies are precluded" by allowing plaintiffs to prove that "a widespread practice" has been established by " 'custom or usage' with the force of law"). And there is certainly no evidence of such manipulation here; indeed, the Alabama provisions that cut most strongly against petitioner's position predate our decision in *Monell* by some time.

In dissent, Justice Ginsburg, joined by Justices Stevens, Souter, and Breyer, argued:

> The prime controllers of a sheriff's service are the county residents, the people who select their sheriff at quadrennial elections. Sheriff Tate owes his position as chief law enforcement officer of Monroe County to the county residents who elected him, and who can unseat him. . . .
>
> Monroe County pays Sheriff Tate's salary, and the sheriff operates out of an office provided, furnished, and equipped by the county. . . . These obligations are of practical importance, for they mean that purse strings can be pulled at the county level; a county is obliged to provide a sheriff only what is "reasonably needed for the proper and efficient conduct of the affairs of the sheriff's office." How generously the sheriff will be equipped is likely to influence that officer's day-to-day conduct to a greater extent than the remote prospect of impeachment.
>
> Sheriff Tate, in short, is in vital respects a county official. Indeed, one would be hard pressed to think of a single official who more completely represents the exercise of significant power within a county. . . .
>
> The Court's Alabama-specific approach, however, assures that today's immediate holding is of limited reach.

What is the heart of the dispute between the majority and the dissent—the proper rule or its application to Alabama sheriffs?

Both the majority and the dissent seem confident that the *McMillian* decision will not encourage manipulation by states seeking to spare their countries from § 1983 liability. But given the importance of federalism to the Court's reasoning, why couldn't this decision be applied to a state that, in response to *McMillian*, changed its statutes or constitution to classify sheriffs as state officials?

C. MUNICIPAL INACTION

At first glance, the notion that a municipality could be liable under *Monell* for a failure to act might seem unlikely. After all, if the actual *actions* of most municipal officials don't create municipal liability, how could liability arise when no municipal official has done anything at all? The next case explains, giving rise to a line of cases about municipal liability for inactions, including failures to train or supervise employees (covered in Section C.1) and failure to screen potential hires (covered in Section C.2).

1. FAILURE TO TRAIN (OR SUPERVISE)

City of Canton v. Harris
489 U.S. 378 (1989)

■ *Justice* WHITE *delivered the opinion of the Court.*

In this case, we are asked to determine if a municipality can ever be liable under 42 U.S.C. § 1983 for constitutional violations resulting from its failure to train municipal employees. We hold that, under certain circumstances, such liability is permitted by the statute.

In April 1978, respondent Geraldine Harris was arrested by officers of the Canton Police Department. Mrs. Harris was brought to the police station in a patrol wagon.

When she arrived at the station, Mrs. Harris was found sitting on the floor of the wagon. She was asked if she needed medical attention, and responded with an incoherent remark. After she was brought inside the station for processing, Mrs. Harris slumped to the floor on two occasions. Eventually, the police officers left Mrs. Harris lying on the floor to prevent her from falling again. No medical attention was ever summoned for Mrs. Harris. After about an hour, Mrs. Harris was released from custody, and taken by an ambulance (provided by her family) to a nearby hospital. There, Mrs. Harris was diagnosed as suffering from several emotional ailments; she was hospitalized for one week and received subsequent outpatient treatment for an additional year. . . .

[The City of Canton] urges us to adopt the rule that a municipality can be found liable under § 1983 only where "the policy in question [is] itself unconstitutional." Whether such a rule is a valid construction of § 1983 is a question the Court has left unresolved . . . . There can be little doubt that on its face the city's policy regarding medical treatment for detainees is constitutional. The policy states that the city jailer "shall . . . have [a person needing medical care] taken to a hospital for medical treatment, with permission of his supervisor. . . ." It is difficult to see what constitutional guarantees are violated by such a policy.

Nor, without more, would a city automatically be liable under § 1983 if one of its employees happened to apply the policy in an unconstitutional manner, for liability would then rest on respondeat superior. The claim in this case, however, is that if a concededly valid policy is unconstitutionally applied by a municipal employee, the city is liable if the employee has not been adequately trained and the constitutional wrong has been caused by that failure to train. For reasons explained below, we conclude, as have all the Courts of Appeals that have addressed this issue, that there are limited circumstances in which an allegation of a "failure to train" can be the basis for liability under § 1983. Thus, we reject petitioner's contention that only unconstitutional policies are actionable under the statute. . . .

We hold today that the inadequacy of police training may serve as the basis for § 1983 liability only where the failure to train amounts to deliberate indifference to the rights of persons with whom the police come into contact.[8] This rule is most consistent with our admonition . . . that a municipality can be liable under § 1983 only where its policies are the "moving force [behind] the constitutional violation." Only where a municipality's failure to train its employees in a relevant respect evidences a "deliberate indifference" to the rights of its inhabitants can such a shortcoming be properly thought of as a city "policy or custom" that is actionable under § 1983. As Justice Brennan's opinion in *Pembaur* put it: "[M]unicipal liability under § 1983 attaches where—and only where—a deliberate choice to follow a course of action is made from among various alternatives" by city policymakers. Only where a failure to train reflects a "deliberate" or "conscious" choice by a municipality—a "policy" as defined by our prior cases—can a city be liable for such a failure under § 1983.

---

8. The "deliberate indifference" standard we adopt for § 1983 "failure to train" claims does not turn upon the degree of fault (if any) that a plaintiff must show to make out an underlying claim of a constitutional violation. For example, this Court has never determined what degree of culpability must be shown before the particular constitutional deprivation asserted in this case—a denial of the due process right to medical care while in detention—is established. Indeed, [we have] reserved decision on the question whether something less than the Eighth Amendment's "deliberate indifference" test may be applicable in claims by detainees asserting violations of their due process right to medical care while in custody. We need not resolve here the question . . . [because] petitioner has conceded that, as the case comes to us, we must assume that respondent's constitutional right to receive medical care was denied by city employees . . . .

Monell's rule that a city is not liable under § 1983 unless a municipal policy causes a constitutional deprivation will not be satisfied by merely alleging that the existing training program for a class of employees, such as police officers, represents a policy for which the city is responsible. That much may be true.

The issue in a case like this one, however, is whether that training program is adequate; and if it is not, the question becomes whether such inadequate training can justifiably be said to represent "city policy." It may seem contrary to common sense to assert that a municipality will actually have a policy of not taking reasonable steps to train its employees. But it may happen that in light of the duties assigned to specific officers or employees the need for more or different training is so obvious, and the inadequacy so likely to result in the violation of constitutional rights, that the policymakers of the city can reasonably be said to have been deliberately indifferent to the need.[10] In that event, the failure to provide proper training may fairly be said to represent a policy for which the city is responsible, and for which the city may be held liable if it actually causes injury.

It could also be that the police, in exercising their discretion, so often violate constitutional rights that the need for further training must have been plainly obvious to the city policymakers, who, nevertheless, are "deliberately indifferent" to the need.

In resolving the issue of a city's liability, the focus must be on adequacy of the training program in relation to the tasks the particular officers must perform. That a particular officer may be unsatisfactorily trained will not alone suffice to fasten liability on the city, for the officer's shortcomings may have resulted from factors other than a faulty training program. It may be, for example, that an otherwise sound program has occasionally been negligently administered. Neither will it suffice to prove that an injury or accident could have been avoided if an officer had had better or more training, sufficient to equip him to avoid the particular injury-causing conduct. Such a claim could be made about almost any encounter resulting in injury, yet not condemn the adequacy of the program to enable officers to respond properly to the usual and recurring situations with which they must deal. And plainly, adequately trained officers occasionally make mistakes; the fact that they do says little about the training program or the legal basis for holding the city liable.

Moreover, for liability to attach in this circumstance the identified deficiency in a city's training program must be closely related to the ultimate injury. Thus in the case at hand, respondent must still prove that the deficiency in training actually caused the police officers' indifference to her medical needs. Would the

---

10. For example, city policymakers know to a moral certainty that their police officers will be required to arrest fleeing felons. The city has armed its officers with firearms, in part to allow them to accomplish this task. Thus, the need to train officers in the constitutional limitations on the use of deadly force, can be said to be "so obvious," that failure to do so could properly be characterized as "deliberate indifference" to constitutional rights.

injury have been avoided had the employee been trained under a program that was not deficient in the identified respect? Predicting how a hypothetically well-trained officer would have acted under the circumstances may not be an easy task for the factfinder, particularly since matters of judgment may be involved, and since officers who are well trained are not free from error and perhaps might react very much like the untrained officer in similar circumstances. But judge and jury, doing their respective jobs, will be adequate to the task.

To adopt lesser standards of fault and causation would open municipalities to unprecedented liability under § 1983. In virtually every instance where a person has had his or her constitutional rights violated by a city employee, a § 1983 plaintiff will be able to point to something the city "could have done" to prevent the unfortunate incident. Thus, permitting cases against cities for their "failure to train" employees to go forward under § 1983 on a lesser standard of fault would result in de facto respondeat superior liability on municipalities—a result we rejected in *Monell*. It would also engage the federal courts in an endless exercise of second-guessing municipal employee-training programs. This is an exercise we believe the federal courts are ill suited to undertake, as well as one that would implicate serious questions of federalism.

Consequently, while claims such as respondent's—alleging that the city's failure to provide training to municipal employees resulted in the constitutional deprivation she suffered—are cognizable under § 1983, they can only yield liability against a municipality where that city's failure to train reflects deliberate indifference to the constitutional rights of its inhabitants. . . .

[T]he standard of proof the District Court ultimately imposed on respondent . . . was a lesser one than the one we adopt today. Whether respondent should have an opportunity to prove her case under the "deliberate indifference" rule we have adopted is a matter for the Court of Appeals to deal with on remand. . . .

[Opinions of Brennan, J., concurring, and O'Connor, J., concurring in part and dissenting in part, omitted. Neither disagreed with the standards set forth in the majority opinion.]

Notes and Questions

1. What is the standard the Court has set for municipal liability for inactions?

2. Why shouldn't the absence of training of a particular type, combined with a constitutional violation that the training could have prevented, give rise to an inference of deliberative indifference? What more does the Court require? Why?

3. The question presented here—when if ever is a municipality liable for a failure to train its officers?—could have been answered in a variety of ways. At one end of the spectrum (setting aside respondeat superior, which the Court has never embraced), the Court could have held that any violation that can be traced back to an inadequacy in training is a basis for municipal liability. At the other end,

it could have held that a failure to act is never a basis for holding municipalities liable. In staking out a middle position, what sources of authority did the Court draw on? What justifies the standard the Court announced?

4. What principles guide the Court's jurisprudence in this area, other than a desire to avoid the "extremes" of no municipal liability on one hand and respondeat superior on the other?

5. What guidance does the Court provide regarding when the need for training is sufficiently obvious?

6. If you were a lawyer for a municipality, what steps would you take in response to this decision to minimize liability going forward?

* * *

How many constitutional violations must a municipality's employees commit before the municipality's failure to train qualifies as "deliberate indifference" to a likely future violation? *Canton*'s footnote 10 suggests that the answer may in certain circumstances be "none." The next case, taking a stricter view of the limits of the failure-to-train theory, characterizes footnote 10 as describing an exceptional circumstance; usually, the majority instructs, a pattern of violations will be required.

Connick v. Thompson
563 U.S. 51 (2011)

▪ *Justice THOMAS delivered the opinion of the Court.*

The Orleans Parish District Attorney's Office now concedes that, in prosecuting respondent John Thompson for attempted armed robbery, prosecutors failed to disclose evidence that should have been turned over to the defense under *Brady v. Maryland*. Thompson was convicted. Because of that conviction Thompson elected not to testify in his own defense in his later trial for murder, and he was again convicted. Thompson spent 18 years in prison, including 14 years on death row. One month before Thompson's scheduled execution, his investigator discovered the undisclosed evidence from his armed robbery trial. [The withheld evidence was a crime-lab report that tested a swatch of fabric with a sample of the robber's blood, which was type B. Thompson has blood type O. A former assistant district attorney then revealed that one of the prosecutors on Thompson's robbery case confessed that he had intentionally suppressed the blood evidence report.] The reviewing court determined that the evidence was exculpatory, and both of Thompson's convictions were vacated.

After his release from prison, Thompson sued petitioner Harry Connick, in his official capacity as the Orleans Parish District Attorney, for damages under 42 U.S.C. § 1983. Thompson alleged that Connick had failed to train his prosecutors adequately about their duty to produce exculpatory evidence and that the lack of training had caused the nondisclosure in Thompson's robbery case.

The jury awarded Thompson $14 million, and the [court of appeals affirmed]. We granted certiorari to decide whether a district attorney's office may be held liable under § 1983 for failure to train based on a single *Brady* violation. We hold that it cannot. . . .

" '[D]eliberate indifference' is a stringent standard of fault, requiring proof that a municipal actor disregarded a known or obvious consequence of his action." Thus, when city policymakers are on actual or constructive notice that a particular omission in their training program causes city employees to violate citizens' constitutional rights, the city may be deemed deliberately indifferent if the policymakers choose to retain that program. . . . A less stringent standard of fault for a failure-to-train claim "would result in de facto respondeat superior liability on municipalities . . . ."

A pattern of similar constitutional violations by untrained employees is "ordinarily necessary" to demonstrate deliberate indifference for purposes of failure to train. Policymakers' "continued adherence to an approach that they know or should know has failed to prevent tortious conduct by employees may establish the conscious disregard for the consequences of their action—the 'deliberate indifference'—necessary to trigger municipal liability." Without notice that a course of training is deficient in a particular respect, decisionmakers can hardly be said to have deliberately chosen a training program that will cause violations of constitutional rights.

Although Thompson does not contend that he proved a pattern of similar *Brady* violations, he points out that, during the ten years preceding his armed robbery trial, Louisiana courts had overturned four convictions because of *Brady* violations by prosecutors in Connick's office. Those four reversals could not have put Connick on notice that the office's *Brady* training was inadequate with respect to the sort of *Brady* violation at issue here. None of those cases involved failure to disclose blood evidence, a crime lab report, or physical or scientific evidence of any kind. . . .

In *Canton*, the Court left open the possibility that, "in a narrow range of circumstances," a pattern of similar violations might not be necessary to show deliberate indifference. The Court posed the hypothetical example of a city that arms its police force with firearms and deploys the armed officers into the public to capture fleeing felons without training the officers in the constitutional limitation on the use of deadly force. Given the known frequency with which police attempt to arrest fleeing felons and the "predictability that an officer lacking specific tools to handle that situation will violate citizens' rights," the Court theorized that a city's decision not to train the officers about constitutional limits on the use of deadly force could reflect the city's deliberate indifference to the "highly predictable consequence," namely, violations of constitutional rights. The Court sought not to foreclose the possibility, however rare, that the unconstitutional consequences of failing to train could be so patently obvious that a city could be liable under § 1983 without proof of a pre-existing pattern of violations.

Failure to train prosecutors in their *Brady* obligations does not fall within the narrow range of *Canton*'s hypothesized single-incident liability. The obvious need for specific legal training that was present in the *Canton* scenario is absent here. Armed police must sometimes make split-second decisions with life-or-death consequences. There is no reason to assume that police academy applicants are familiar with the constitutional constraints on the use of deadly force. And, in the absence of training, there is no way for novice officers to obtain the legal knowledge they require. Under those circumstances there is an obvious need for some form of training. In stark contrast, legal "[t]raining is what differentiates attorneys from average public employees."

Attorneys are trained in the law and equipped with the tools to interpret and apply legal principles, understand constitutional limits, and exercise legal judgment. Before they may enter the profession and receive a law license, all attorneys must graduate from law school or pass a substantive examination; attorneys in the vast majority of jurisdictions must do both. These threshold requirements are designed to ensure that all new attorneys have learned how to find, understand, and apply legal rules. . . .

Attorneys who practice with other attorneys, such as in district attorney's offices, also train on the job as they learn from more experienced attorneys. . . .

In light of this regime of legal training and professional responsibility, recurring constitutional violations are not the "obvious consequence" of failing to provide prosecutors with formal in-house training about how to obey the law. . . . A district attorney is entitled to rely on prosecutors' professional training and ethical obligations in the absence of specific reason, such as a pattern of violations, to believe that those tools are insufficient to prevent future constitutional violations in "the usual and recurring situations with which [the prosecutors] must deal." *Canton*. A licensed attorney making legal judgments, in his capacity as a prosecutor, about *Brady* material simply does not present the same "highly predictable" constitutional danger as *Canton*'s untrained officer.

A second significant difference between this case and the example in *Canton* is the nuance of the allegedly necessary training. The *Canton* hypothetical assumes that the armed police officers have no knowledge at all of the constitutional limits on the use of deadly force. But it is undisputed here that the prosecutors in Connick's office were familiar with the general *Brady* rule. Thompson's complaint therefore cannot rely on the utter lack of an ability to cope with constitutional situations that underlies the *Canton* hypothetical, but rather must assert that prosecutors were not trained about particular *Brady* evidence or the specific scenario related to the violation in his case. That sort of nuance simply cannot support an inference of deliberate indifference here. . . .

It does not follow that, because *Brady* has gray areas and some *Brady* decisions are difficult, prosecutors will so obviously make wrong decisions that failing to train them amounts to "a decision by the city itself to violate the Constitution." To prove deliberate indifference, Thompson needed to show that Connick was on notice that, absent additional specified training, it was "highly predictable" that the prosecutors in his office would be confounded by those gray areas and make incorrect *Brady* decisions as a result. In fact, Thompson had to show that it was so predictable that failing to train the prosecutors amounted to conscious disregard for defendants' *Brady* rights. He did not do so. . . .

■ *Justice* SCALIA, *with whom Justice* ALITO *joins, concurring.* . . .

Thompson's failure-to-train theory at trial was not based on a pervasive culture of indifference to *Brady*, but rather on the inevitability of mistakes over enough iterations of criminal trials. . . .

That theory of deliberate indifference would repeal the law of *Monell* in favor of the Law of Large Numbers. *Brady* mistakes are inevitable. So are all species of error routinely confronted by prosecutors: authorizing a bad warrant; losing a *Batson* claim; crossing the line in closing argument; or eliciting hearsay that violates the Confrontation Clause. Nevertheless, we do not have "de facto respondeat superior liability," *Canton*, for each such violation under the rubric of failure-to-train simply because the municipality does not have a professional educational program covering the specific violation in sufficient depth. Were Thompson's theory the law, there would have been no need for *Canton*'s footnote to confine its hypothetical to the extreme circumstance of arming police officers with guns without telling them about the constitutional limitations upon shooting fleeing felons . . . .

■ *Justice* GINSBURG, *with whom Justice* BREYER, *Justice* SOTOMAYOR, *and Justice* KAGAN *join, dissenting.* . . .

As the trial record in the § 1983 action reveals, the conceded, long-concealed prosecutorial transgressions were neither isolated nor atypical.

From the top down, the evidence showed, members of the District Attorney's Office, including the District Attorney himself, misperceived *Brady*'s compass and therefore inadequately attended to their disclosure obligations. Throughout the pretrial and trial proceedings against Thompson, the team of four engaged in prosecuting him for armed robbery and murder hid from the defense and the court exculpatory information Thompson requested and had a constitutional right to receive. The prosecutors did so despite multiple opportunities, spanning nearly two decades, to set the record straight. Based on the prosecutors' conduct relating to Thompson's trials, a fact trier could reasonably conclude that inattention to *Brady* was standard operating procedure at the District Attorney's Office.

What happened here, the Court's opinion obscures, was no momentary oversight, no single incident of a lone officer's misconduct. Instead, the evidence demonstrated that misperception and disregard of *Brady*'s disclosure requirements were pervasive in Orleans Parish. That evidence, I would hold, established persistent, deliberately indifferent conduct for which the District Attorney's Office bears responsibility under § 1983. . . .

Brady violations, as this case illustrates, are not easily detected. But for a chance discovery made by a defense team investigator weeks before Thompson's scheduled execution, the evidence that led to his exoneration might have remained under wraps. The prosecutorial concealment Thompson encountered, however, is bound to be repeated unless municipal agencies bear responsibility—made tangible by § 1983 liability—for adequately conveying what *Brady* requires and for monitoring staff compliance. Failure to train, this Court has said, can give rise to municipal liability under § 1983 "where the failure . . . amounts to deliberate indifference to the rights of persons with whom the [untrained employees] come into contact." *Canton*. That standard is well met in this case. . . .

Connick admitted to the jury that his earlier understanding of *Brady*, conveyed in prior sworn testimony, had been too narrow. Even at trial Connick persisted in misstating *Brady*'s requirements. For example, Connick urged that there could be no *Brady* violation arising out of "the inadvertent conduct of [an] assistant under pressure with a lot of case load." The court, however, correctly instructed the jury that, in determining whether there has been a *Brady* violation, the "good or bad faith of the prosecution does not matter."

The testimony of other leaders in the District Attorney's Office revealed similar misunderstandings. Those misunderstandings, the jury could find, were in large part responsible for the gross disregard of *Brady* rights Thompson experienced. [ADA] Dubelier [who tried Thompson's murder case] admitted that he never reviewed police files, but simply relied on the police to flag any potential *Brady* information. The court, however, instructed the jury that an individual prosecutor has a "duty . . . to learn of any favorable evidence known to others acting on the government's behalf in the case, including the police." [ADA] Williams [who tried both Thompson's murder and robbery cases] was asked whether "*Brady* material includes documents in the possession of the district attorney that could be used to impeach a witness, to show that he's lying"; he responded simply, and mistakenly, "No." . . .

In 1985, Connick acknowledged, many of his prosecutors "were coming fresh out of law school," and the Office's "[h]uge turnover" allowed attorneys with little experience to advance quickly to supervisory positions. By 1985, Dubelier and Williams were two of the highest ranking attorneys in the Office, yet neither man had even five years of experience as a prosecutor. . . .

Dubelier and Williams told the jury that they did not recall any *Brady* training in the Office.

Connick testified that he relied on supervisors, including Dubelier and Williams, to ensure prosecutors were familiar with their *Brady* obligations. Yet Connick did not inquire whether the supervisors themselves understood the importance of teaching newer prosecutors about *Brady*. . . .

[I]n 1985 trial attorneys "sometimes . . . went to Mr. Connick" with *Brady* questions, "and he would tell them" how to proceed. But Connick acknowledged that he had "stopped reading law books . . . and looking at opinions" when he was first elected District Attorney in 1974. . . .

Louisiana did not require continuing legal education at the time of Thompson's trials. Primary responsibility for keeping prosecutors au courant with developments in the law, therefore, resided in the District Attorney's Office. . . .

In *Canton*, this Court spoke of circumstances in which the need for training may be "so obvious," and the lack of training "so likely" to result in constitutional violations, that policymakers who do not provide for the requisite training "can reasonably be said to have been deliberately indifferent to the need" for such training. This case, I am convinced, belongs in the category *Canton* marked out. . . .

Based on the evidence presented, the jury could conclude that *Brady* errors by untrained prosecutors would frequently cause deprivations of defendants' constitutional rights. The jury learned of several *Brady* oversights in Thompson's trials and heard testimony that Connick's Office had one of the worst *Brady* records in the country. . . .

Unquestionably, a municipality that leaves police officers untrained in constitutional limits on the use of deadly weapons places lives in jeopardy. *Canton*. But as this case so vividly shows, a municipality that empowers prosecutors to press for a death sentence without ensuring that those prosecutors know and honor *Brady* rights may be no less "deliberately indifferent" to the risk to innocent lives. . . .

The Court nevertheless holds *Canton*'s example inapposite. It maintains that professional obligations, ethics rules, and training—including on-the-job training—set attorneys apart from other municipal employees, including rookie police officers. . . . But the jury heard and rejected [Connick's] argument to that effect. . . .

On what basis can one be confident that law schools acquaint students with prosecutors' unique obligation under *Brady*? . . . Dubelier's alma mater, like most other law faculties, does not make criminal procedure a required course. . . .

The majority further suggests that a prior pattern of similar violations is necessary to show deliberate indifference to defendants' *Brady* rights. The text of § 1983 contains no such limitation. Nor is there any reason to imply such a limitation. A district attorney's deliberate indifference might be shown in several ways short of a prior pattern. This case is one such instance. . . .

I would uphold the jury's verdict awarding damages to Thompson for the gross, deliberately indifferent, and long-continuing violation of his fair trial right.

Notes and Questions

1. Given the strict standard for municipal liability, why didn't the plaintiff just sue the DA in his individual capacity? (Chapter 4, Section A has the answer.) How does the answer to that question bear on your evaluation of the decision in *Connick*? Of related doctrines?

2. How does the importance of factual questions to the dispute between the majority and the dissent shape the meaning of this case? On what bases can future plaintiffs try to narrow the significance of *Connick*?

3. The majority and the dissent debate the application of *Canton* footnote 10 and how easily deliberate indifference can be shown absent a pattern of prior

violations. But wasn't there just such a pattern here? The dissent notes that the jury "heard testimony that Connick's Office had one of the worst *Brady* records in the country," and even the majority acknowledged that "[a]lthough Thompson does not contend that he proved a pattern of similar *Brady* violations, he points out that, during the ten years preceding his armed robbery trial, Louisiana courts had overturned four convictions because of *Brady* violations by prosecutors in Connick's office." Why did the majority nonetheless conclude that no relevant pattern existed? Should Thompson have argued that he did show a pattern?

4. After *Connick*, how frequently do you expect arguments based on *Canton* footnote 10 to succeed? In what types of situations could *Canton* footnote 10 still apply?

5. Courts have long recognized that *Brady* violations can be committed by police officers as well as attorneys. *See, e.g., Barbee v. Warden*, 331 F.2d 842, 846 (4th Cir. 1964). Would this case have come out differently if the problem was that Orleans Parish had failed to train its *police officers* in their responsibilities under *Brady*? From a policy standpoint, should that distinction matter to whether a *Brady* violation can be redressed through a civil damages action? Why or why not?

6. Based on your own experience as a law student and as a legal intern, how reasonable do you think the majority's assumptions are about what a new lawyer knows about *Brady* coming out of law school?

Note: Failure to Supervise

A number of lower courts have held that a "failure to supervise," which is evaluated using the same standards as failure-to-train claims, also gives rise to municipal liability under § 1983.

Not all failure-to-supervise claims fit the same model. For instance, sometimes a failure to supervise, like a failure to train, consists of a failure to take appropriate measures to avoid a known risk posed by the activity of a whole category of municipal officer. In *Cash v. County of Erie*, 654 F.3d 324 (2d Cir. 2011), the court found that the evidence at trial had been sufficient to establish that a county sheriff had been deliberately indifferent to the need to supervise male guards interacting with female prisoners in the county jail in order to prevent sexual assaults. This context, like a failure-to-train claim, involves a failure to provide needed oversight of municipal personnel generally.

By contrast, some failure-to-supervise claims posit failures of supervision and discipline regarding *particular officers* whom municipal authorities should have known required oversight because of their responsibilities and/or warning signs about their behavior. A case of this kind is *S.M. v. Lincoln County*, 874 F.3d 581 (8th Cir. 2017), in which the court upheld a verdict against a municipality for its sheriff's failure to supervise a particular drug court officer who sexually assaulted underage drug court participants in his capacity as their monitor in the drug court program. The sheriff both failed to supervise the monitor generally and ignored specific troubling behavior, including the monitor's decision to visit drug court participants alone (a violation of policy) and the fact that the monitor "spent a disproportionate amount of time supervising female participants who were 'attractive, young, and new to the Drug Court program and kind of naive.'"

Which version of the failure-to-supervise theory is easier to plead plausibly prior to discovery? Which type of claim will give rise to a need for broader discovery?

2. FAILURE TO SCREEN

Another kind of municipal "failure to" claim sometimes asserted is the failure to screen municipal hires. In analyzing this theory, the Court took as its starting point the original "failure to" theory (failure to train) but found important differences between the two contexts. At the same time, a few Justices began to wonder whether municipal liability doctrine had taken a wrong turn.

Board of County Commissioners of Bryan County v. Brown
520 U.S. 397 (1997)

■ *Justice O'CONNOR delivered the opinion of the Court. . . .*

[Respondent Jill Brown and her husband were driving in their truck late at night when they encountered a police checkpoint. They turned away from the checkpoint; the police pursued them; a chase ensued; the Browns ultimately halted.]

After he got out of the squad car, Deputy Sheriff Morrison pointed his gun toward the Browns' vehicle and ordered the Browns to raise their hands. Reserve Deputy Burns, who was unarmed, rounded the corner of the vehicle on the passenger's side. Burns twice ordered respondent from the vehicle. When she did not exit, he used an "arm bar" technique, grabbing respondent's arm at the wrist and elbow, pulling her from the vehicle, and spinning her to the ground. Respondent's knees were severely injured, and she later underwent corrective surgery. Ultimately, she may need knee replacements.

Respondent sought compensation for her injuries under 42 U.S.C. § 1983 and state law from Burns, Bryan County Sheriff B.J. Moore, and the county itself. Respondent claimed, among other things, that Bryan County was liable for Burns' alleged use of excessive force based on Sheriff Moore's decision to hire Burns, the son of his nephew. Specifically, respondent claimed that Sheriff Moore had failed to adequately review Burns' background. Burns had a record of driving infractions and had pleaded guilty to various driving-related and other misdemeanors, including assault and battery, resisting arrest, and public drunkenness. . . . At trial, Sheriff Moore testified that he had obtained Burns' driving record and a report on Burns from the National Crime Information Center, but had not closely reviewed either. . . .

Counsel for Bryan County stipulated that Sheriff Moore "was the policy maker for Bryan County regarding the Sheriff's Department." . . .

[The jury concluded that the force used was excessive] and that the "hiring policy" . . . of Bryan County "in the case of Stacy Burns as instituted by its policymaker, B.J. Moore," were each "so inadequate as to amount to deliberate indifference to the constitutional needs of the Plaintiff." [The court of appeals affirmed the judgment for Brown.] . . .

The parties join issue on whether, under *Monell* and subsequent cases, a single hiring decision by a county sheriff can be a "policy" that triggers municipal liability. . . .

[I]t is not enough for a § 1983 plaintiff merely to identify conduct properly attributable to the municipality. The plaintiff must also demonstrate that, through its deliberate conduct, the municipality was the "moving force" behind the injury alleged. That is, a plaintiff must show that the municipal action was taken with the requisite degree of culpability and must demonstrate a direct causal link between the municipal action and the deprivation of federal rights. . . .

Sheriff Moore's hiring decision was itself legal, and Sheriff Moore did not authorize Burns to use excessive force. Respondent's claim, rather, is that a single facially lawful hiring decision can launch a series of events that ultimately cause a violation of federal rights. Where a plaintiff claims that the municipality has not directly inflicted an injury, but nonetheless has caused an employee to do so, rigorous standards of culpability and causation must be applied to ensure that the municipality is not held liable solely for the actions of its employee. *See Canton.*

In relying heavily on *Pembaur*, respondent blurs the distinction between § 1983 cases that present no difficult questions of fault and causation and those that do. . . . In *Pembaur*, it was not disputed that the prosecutor had specifically directed the action resulting in the deprivation of petitioner's rights. The conclusion that the decision was that of a final municipal decisionmaker and was therefore properly attributable to the municipality established municipal liability. No questions of fault or causation arose.

Claims not involving an allegation that the municipal action itself violated federal law, or directed or authorized the deprivation of federal rights, present much more difficult problems of proof. . . .

Respondent does not claim that she can identify any pattern of injuries linked to Sheriff Moore's hiring practices. . . . Where a claim of municipal liability rests on a single decision, not itself representing a violation of federal law and not directing such a violation, the danger that a municipality will be held liable without fault is high. Because the decision necessarily governs a single case, there can be no notice to the municipal decisionmaker, based on previous violations of federally protected rights, that his approach is inadequate. Nor will it be readily apparent that the municipality's action caused the injury in question, because the plaintiff can point to no other incident tending to make it more likely that the plaintiff's own injury flows from the municipality's action, rather than from some other intervening cause.

In *Canton*, we did not foreclose the possibility that evidence of a single violation of federal rights, accompanied by a showing that a municipality has

failed to train its employees to handle recurring situations presenting an obvious potential for such a violation, could trigger municipal liability. . . . The proffered analogy between failure-to-train cases and inadequate screening cases is
not persuasive. In leaving open in *Canton* the possibility that a plaintiff might
succeed in carrying a failure-to-train claim without showing a pattern of constitutional violations, we simply hypothesized that, in a narrow range of circumstances, a violation of federal rights may be a highly predictable consequence of
a failure to equip law enforcement officers with specific tools to handle recurring situations. The likelihood that the situation will recur and the predictability
that an officer lacking specific tools to handle that situation will violate citizens'
rights could justify a finding that policymakers' decision not to train the officer
reflected "deliberate indifference" to the obvious consequence of the policymakers' choice—namely, a violation of a specific constitutional or statutory right.
The high degree of predictability may also support an inference of causation—
that the municipality's indifference led directly to the very consequence that was
so predictable.

Where a plaintiff presents a § 1983 claim premised upon the inadequacy of
an official's review of a prospective applicant's record, however, there is a particular danger that a municipality will be held liable for an injury not directly
caused by a deliberate action attributable to the municipality itself. Every injury
suffered at the hands of a municipal employee can be traced to a hiring decision
in a "but-for" sense: But for the municipality's decision to hire the employee, the
plaintiff would not have suffered the injury. To prevent municipal liability for a
hiring decision from collapsing into respondeat superior liability, a court must
carefully test the link between the policymaker's inadequate decision and the
particular injury alleged.

In attempting to import the reasoning of *Canton* into the hiring context,
respondent ignores the fact that predicting the consequence of a single hiring
decision, even one based on an inadequate assessment of a record, is far more
difficult than predicting what might flow from the failure to train a single law
enforcement officer as to a specific skill necessary to the discharge of his duties.
As our decision in *Canton* makes clear, "deliberate indifference" is a stringent
standard of fault, requiring proof that a municipal actor disregarded a known
or obvious consequence of his action. Unlike the risk from a particular glar-
ing omission in a training regimen, the risk from a single instance of inadequate screening of an applicant's background is not "obvious" in the abstract;
rather, it depends upon the background of the applicant. A lack of scrutiny may
increase the likelihood that an unfit officer will be hired, and that the unfit officer will, when placed in a particular position to affect the rights of citizens, act
improperly. But that is only a generalized showing of risk. The fact that inadequate scrutiny of an applicant's background would make a violation of rights
more likely cannot alone give rise to an inference that a policymaker's failure to
scrutinize the record of a particular applicant produced a specific constitutional
violation. . . .

We assume that a jury could properly find in this case that Sheriff Moore's assessment of Burns' background was inadequate. . . . But this showing of an instance of inadequate screening is not enough to establish "deliberate indifference." In layman's terms, inadequate screening of an applicant's record may reflect "indifference" to the applicant's background. For purposes of a legal inquiry into municipal liability under § 1983, however, that is not the relevant "indifference." A plaintiff must demonstrate that a municipal decision reflects deliberate indifference to the risk that a violation of a particular constitutional or statutory right will follow the decision. Only where adequate scrutiny of an applicant's background would lead a reasonable policymaker to conclude that the plainly obvious consequence of the decision to hire the applicant would be the deprivation of a third party's federally protected right can the official's failure to adequately scrutinize the applicant's background constitute "deliberate indifference." . . .

[A] finding of culpability simply cannot depend on the mere probability that any officer inadequately screened will inflict any constitutional injury. Rather, it must depend on a finding that this officer was highly likely to inflict the particular injury suffered by the plaintiff. The connection between the background of the particular applicant and the specific constitutional violation alleged must be strong. . . .

Even assuming without deciding that proof of a single instance of inadequate screening could ever trigger municipal liability, the evidence in this case was insufficient to support a finding that, in hiring Burns, Sheriff Moore disregarded a known or obvious risk of injury. To test the link between Sheriff Moore's hiring decision and respondent's injury, we must ask whether a full review of Burns' record reveals that Sheriff Moore should have concluded that Burns' use of excessive force would be a plainly obvious consequence of the hiring decision.[1] . . .

Burns' record reflected various misdemeanor infractions. Respondent claims that the record demonstrated such a strong propensity for violence that Burns' application of excessive force was highly likely. The primary charges on which respondent relies, however, are those arising from a fight on a college campus where Burns was a student. In connection with this single incident, Burns was charged with assault and battery, resisting arrest, and public drunkenness.

---

1. In suggesting that our decision complicates this Court's § 1983 municipal liability jurisprudence by altering the understanding of culpability, Justice Souter and Justice Breyer misunderstand our approach. We do not suggest that a plaintiff in an inadequate screening case must show a higher degree of culpability than the "deliberate indifference" required in *Canton v. Harris*; we need not do so, because, as discussed below, respondent has not made a showing of deliberate indifference here. . . . Ensuring that lower courts link the background of the officer to the constitutional violation alleged does not complicate our municipal liability jurisprudence with degrees of "obviousness," but seeks to ensure that a plaintiff in an inadequate screening case establishes a policymaker's deliberate indifference—that is, conscious disregard for the known and obvious consequences of his actions.

In January 1990, when he pleaded guilty to those charges, Burns also pleaded guilty to various driving-related offenses, including nine moving violations and a charge of driving with a suspended license. In addition, Burns had previously pleaded guilty to being in actual physical control of a vehicle while intoxicated.

The fact that Burns had pleaded guilty to traffic offenses and other misdemeanors may well have made him an extremely poor candidate for reserve deputy. Had Sheriff Moore fully reviewed Burns' record, he might have come to precisely that conclusion. But unless he would necessarily have reached that decision because Burns' use of excessive force would have been a plainly obvious consequence of the hiring decision, Sheriff Moore's inadequate scrutiny of Burns' record cannot constitute "deliberate indifference" to respondent's federally protected right to be free from a use of excessive force....

Because there was insufficient evidence on which a jury could base a finding that Sheriff Moore's decision to hire Burns reflected conscious disregard of an obvious risk that a use of excessive force would follow, the District Court erred in submitting respondent's inadequate screening claim to the jury....

■ *Justice SOUTER, with whom Justice STEVENS and Justice BREYER join, dissenting.*

In *Pembaur v. Cincinnati*, we held a municipality liable under 42 U.S.C. § 1983 for harm caused by the single act of a policymaking officer in a matter within his authority but not covered by a policy previously identified. The central question presented here is whether that rule applies to a single act that itself neither violates nor commands a violation of federal law. The answer is yes if the single act amounts to deliberate indifference to a substantial risk that a violation of federal law will result. With significant qualifications, the Court assumes so, too, in theory, but it raises such skeptical hurdles to reaching any such conclusion in practice that it virtually guarantees its disposition of this case: it holds as a matter of law that the sheriff's act could not be thought to reflect deliberate indifference to the risk that his subordinate would violate the Constitution by using excessive force. I respectfully dissent as much from the level of the Court's skepticism as from its reversal of the judgment....

[The Court] suggests that the trial court insufficiently appreciated the specificity of the risk to which such indifference must be deliberate in order to be actionable; it expresses deep skepticism that such appreciation of risk could ever reasonably be attributed to the policymaker who has performed only a single unsatisfactory, but not facially unconstitutional, act; and it finds the record insufficient to make any such showing in this case. The Court is serially mistaken. This case presents no occasion to correct or refine the District Court's jury instructions on the degree of risk required for deliberate indifference; the Court's skepticism converts a newly demanding formulation of the standard of fault into a virtually categorical impossibility of showing it in a case like this; and the record in this case is perfectly sufficient to support the jury's verdict even on the Court's formulation of the high degree of risk that must be shown....

While we speculated in *Canton* that "[i]t could ... be that the police, in exercising their discretion, so often violate constitutional rights that the need for further training must have been plainly obvious to the city policymakers, who, nevertheless, are 'deliberately indifferent' to the need," we did not purport to be defining the fault of deliberate indifference universally as the failure to act in relation to a "plainly obvious consequence" of harm. Nor did we, in addressing the requisite risk that constitutional violations will occur, suggest that the deliberate indifference necessary to establish municipal liability must be, as the Court says today, indifference to the particular constitutional violation that in fact occurred.

The Court's formulation that deliberate indifference exists only when the risk of the subsequent, particular constitutional violation is a plainly obvious consequence of the hiring decision, while derived from *Canton*, is thus without doubt a new standard. . . .

■ *Justice* BREYER, *with whom Justice* STEVENS *and Justice* GINSBURG *join, dissenting.*

In *Monell*, this Court said that municipalities cannot be held liable for constitutional torts under 42 U.S.C. § 1983 "on a respondeat superior theory," but they can be held liable "when execution of" a municipality's "policy or custom . . . inflicts the injury." That statement has produced a highly complex body of interpretive law. Today's decision exemplifies the law's complexity. . . . It . . . elaborates this Court's requirement that a consequence be "so likely" to occur that a policymaker could "reasonably be said to have been deliberately indifferent" with respect to it, *Canton*, with an admonition that the unconstitutional consequence must be "plainly obvious." The majority fears that a contrary view of prior precedent would undermine *Monell's* basic distinction. That concern, however, rather than leading us to spin ever finer distinctions as we try to apply *Monell's* basic distinction between liability that rests upon policy and liability that is vicarious, suggests that we should reexamine the legal soundness of that basic distinction itself.

I believe that the legal prerequisites for reexamination of an interpretation of an important statute are present here. The soundness of the original principle is doubtful. The original principle has generated a body of interpretive law that is so complex that the law has become difficult to apply. Factual and legal changes have divorced the law from the distinction's apparent original purposes. And there may be only a handful of individuals or groups that have significantly relied upon perpetuation of the original distinction. If all this is so, later law has made the original distinction, not simply wrong, but obsolete and a potential source of confusion. . . .

First, consider *Monell's* original reasoning. The *Monell* "no vicarious liability" principle rested upon a historical analysis of § 1983 and upon § 1983's literal language—language that imposes liability upon (but only upon) any "person." . . . Essentially, the history on which *Monell* relied consists almost exclusively of the fact that the Congress that enacted § 1983 rejected an amendment (called the Sherman amendment) that would have made municipalities vicariously liable for the marauding acts of private citizens. That fact, as Justice Stevens and others have pointed out, does not argue against vicarious liability for the act of municipal employees—particularly since municipalities, at the time, were vicariously liable for many of the acts of their employees. . . .

Second, *Monell*'s basic effort to distinguish between vicarious liability and liability derived from "policy or custom" has produced a body of law that is neither readily understandable nor easy to apply. Today's case provides a good example. . . .

Consider some of the other distinctions that this Court has had to make as it has sought to distinguish liability based upon policymaking from liability that is "vicarious." It has proved necessary, for example, to distinguish further, between an exercise of policymaking authority and an exercise of delegated discretionary policy-implementing authority. Without some such distinction, "municipal liability [might] collaps[e] into respondeat superior," for the law would treat similarly (and hold municipalities responsible for) both a police officer's decision about how much force to use when making a particular arrest and a police chief's decision about how much force to use when making a particular kind of arrest. But the distinction is not a clear one. . . .

Nor does the location of "policymaking" authority pose the only conceptually difficult problem. Lower courts must also decide whether a failure to make policy was "deliberately indifferent," rather than "grossly negligent." . . .

Given the basic *Monell* principle, these distinctions may be necessary, for without them, the Court cannot easily avoid a "municipal liability" that "collaps[es] into respondeat superior." But a basic legal principle that requires so many such distinctions to maintain its legal life may not deserve such longevity. . . .

I would ask for further argument that would focus upon the continued viability of *Monell*'s distinction between vicarious municipal liability and municipal liability based upon policy and custom.

Notes and Questions

1. Has the majority changed the *Canton* standard? Imposed a different standard for a different type of municipal "failure to" act? Or merely applied the *Canton* standard to a particular type of "failure to" act? How would the majority answer that question? How would Justice Souter?

2. The majority seems much more concerned about the potential for a flood of claims against municipalities based on a "failure to screen" than based on a "failure to train." Why? Behind every constitutional violation by a municipal officer, isn't there just as plausibly a "failure to train" the officer as a "failure to screen" the officer? Is one of these types of "failure to" claims easier to allege? Harder to litigate?

3. The problem with Brown's claim, according to the majority, is the absence of a connection between the particular constitutional violation Burns committed and what should have been obviously foreseen based on his pre-hiring record.

Why should the Court demand such a level of specificity? And if that level of specificity isn't met here, where if ever will it be met?

4. In what other contexts in civil rights enforcement have we seen the Court demand that judges evaluate issues at a very specific level? Does that requirement tend to help plaintiffs or defendants? Is the Court's insistence on specificity more justified in one context than another?

5. Justice Breyer's observation that *Monell* "has produced a body of law that is neither readily understandable nor easy to apply" is easy to agree with. Does that point alone justify reconsidering the doctrine, even if *Monell* correctly divined congressional intent to rule out respondeat superior? Is it fair to dismiss municipalities' reliance interest? How would municipalities respond if the *Monell* limitations on their liability were eliminated?

6. Recall the discussion in Chapter 1, Section D, of state-law claims that may be brought together with § 1983 claims for the same conduct. The limitations on municipal liability underscore an important advantage of state-law theories: the availability of respondeat superior liability.

CHAPTER 5 PROBLEMS

Problem 5A. We revisit the Clearwater case from Problem 4D to explore the municipal liability issues it raises. Begin by refamiliarizing yourself with the complaint. Then read the City Charter and deposition excerpts that follow below and consider: What arguments can Clearwater make in support of municipal liability? Which (if any) are likely to succeed?

City of Tenleytown Charter (excerpts)

ARTICLE IV: THE COUNCIL

SECTION 400. *Powers Vested in Council.* All powers of the City and the determination of all matters of policy shall be vested in the Council, subject to the provisions of this Charter and the laws of Douglass Commonwealth.

SECTION 411. *The Council; Involvement with Administrative Matters.* Neither the Council nor any of its members shall interfere with the execution by the City Manager of the City Manager's powers and duties, nor in any manner dictate the appointment or removal of any City officers or employees whom the City Manager is empowered to appoint. However, the Council may express its views and freely discuss with the City Manager anything pertaining to the appointment and removal of such officers and employees.

ARTICLE VII: CITY MANAGER

SECTION 701. *City Manager; Powers and Duties.* The City Manager shall be the chief administrative officer of the City. The City Manager shall be responsible to the Council for the administration of City affairs placed in the City Manager's charge by or under this Charter. The City Manager shall be responsible for the faithful execution of all laws. Subject to any Civil Services Rules adopted by the Council, the City Manager shall appoint all officers and employees of the City; and, when the City Manager deems it necessary for the good of the service, the City Manager may suspend, demote, discharge, remove, or discipline any City officer or employee who is appointed by the City Manager.

SECTION 702. *Removal by Council.* The Council may remove the City Manager from office at any time.

(Source Note: The City of Tenleytown Charter is based on, and some of the text is quoted from, the City Charter of San Jose, California.)

Transcript of Deposition of Lee G. Slater (excerpt)

Q. Mr. Slater, what is your role on the City Council?

A. Chairman.

Q. And what does that role entail?

A. Well, I'm the closest thing to a mayor we've got. I lead the Council, and as goes the Council, so goes the City.

Q. And when the Council makes a decision, it is fair to say it's your decision?

A. Well, not if I'm not in the majority. But usually I am, and when I am, then I take full responsibility for the decisions of the Council.

Q. You stand behind all the decisions you vote for?

A. Absolutely.

Q. The substance and the reasoning?

A. Absolutely. I am a man of my word.

Q. So is it fair to say that whenever the City takes an action, the buck stops with you?

A. Well, not whenever. When we make policy, pass legislation, approve the budget, yes, I'm the leader in that process. But there are a thousand little things that go on in running a city that neither I nor the Council could possibly be personally involved with. I mean, there's a limit to what one man can do.

Q. Can you give me an example of something that the City does that the City Council wouldn't decide?

A. Well, take this reservoir inspection thing. We as council members aren't the experts in that kind of thing, we've got no technical expertise, so that's why we have a Sanitation Inspector. If there was a problem in that respect, it's really on her.

Q. And if she's fired?

A. Well, that's the City Manager's responsibility. The Council doesn't concern itself with personnel.

Q. But you are responsible for approving personnel actions that are submitted to you?

A. Yes, we do that.

> Defense counsel: I'm going to object to that last question. It calls for a legal conclusion, and Mr. Slater is not a lawyer.
>
> Plaintiff's counsel: Are you saying the Chair of the Council doesn't know what the responsibilities of the Council are?
>
> Defense counsel: Well, as a practical matter, but they have a staff attorney for legal matters.
>
> Plaintiff's counsel: I'm asking for his testimony as a lay witness.
>
> Defense counsel: That testimony is irrelevant.
>
> Plaintiff's counsel: I understand your position. May I continue?

Q. So, Mr. Slater, is there a formal vote taken to approve the personnel actions?

A. Well, it's not formal, but there's an understanding among us. We have a great deal of confidence in our City Manager, Penny Pincher.

Q. So when you approve a personnel action, formal vote or no, it's an official action of the Council, like any other action?

A. Well, it doesn't get the same kind of debate or consideration as other actions.

Q. But approving a personnel decision is still an official act of the Council?

> Defense counsel: Same objection as before.
>
> Plaintiff's counsel: Are you instructing your client not to answer?
>
> Defense counsel: No. Go ahead, Lee.

A. That's right, they are official acts.

Q. And you stand behind all the Council's decisions in which you join?

A. That's right.

Q. Just like you told me before?

A. That's right.

Q. Did the Council consider the NOPA for the firing of Marcia Clearwater on February 1 of this year?

A. Yes.

Q. Would you tell me what happened with respect to that NOPA on that day?

A. As usual, the Council had a series of personnel actions submitted by Penny.

Q. Were those presented orally or in writing?

A. Oh, we always just get the forms. The clerk passes them around.

Q. And was Ms. Clearwater's NOPA distributed in this way?

A. Yes.

Q.   To each member of the Council?

A.   Well, the packet of personnel forms is passed down the row.

Q.   And then what happened?

A.   Nothing. We flip through them. If no one has any objection, they are approved.

Q.   Was anything said about the Clearwater action?

A.   I don't recall, but nothing like that, a sensitive personnel matter, would be discussed openly at the meeting.

Q.   Did Ms. Pincher say anything at the February 1 Council meeting?

A.   No.

Q.   Why did you approve the Clearwater action?

A.   Well, we have great confidence in Penny. She's been terrific at keeping our costs down.

Q.   So the reason Ms. Pincher gave is the reason the Council approved it?

>   Defense counsel: Objection. Calls for speculation.
>   Plaintiff's counsel: I'll rephrase.

Q.   Mr. Slater, is the reason Ms. Pincher gave on the form to fire Ms. Clearwater the reason that you approved it?

A.   I guess you could say that, yes.

Problem 5B.   Washton George is stopped and cited for jaywalking in the Township of Deanwood by Officer Adam John of the Deanwood Police Department (DPD). George is furious, as jaywalking is not an infraction that is often ticketed in Deanwood. George protests loudly. Officer John says, "Tell the judge if you want to contest the ticket." George continues to yell at John but does not touch him. In response, John shocks George with a Taser (a weapon that discharges electrified barbs into the subject's body). George experiences excruciating pain and muscle spasms. Officer John leaves.

DPD is an agency of Deanwood, so a claim against DPD is a claim against the Township. DPD's Use of Force Policy (UFP) identifies four categories of force:

1.   Contact controls—low-level tactics (e.g., firm grip, escorting) to gain cooperation.

2.   Compliance techniques—actions (e.g., control holds, joint locks, or tackling) that may cause discomfort until control is achieved but will not generally cause injury.

3.   Defensive tactics—actions to force a subject into submission in the face of a threat to officers or others; these may cause significant pain but are unlikely to result in death. Examples include baton strikes and pepper spray.

4.   Deadly force—force likely to cause death or serious injury; usable only against a subject who poses immediate threat of death or serious injury to officers or others.

The UFP also provides: "When dealing with a non-cooperative, agitated civilian who does not pose a threat to himself or others, officers should employ contact controls and if necessary compliance techniques, but not defensive tactics or deadly force if there is no threat." Officers' training on use of force is based exclusively on the UFP. The policy does not mention Tasers.

George finds a lawyer to sue for the use of the Taser. The lawyer determines that relevant precedent is sufficiently unclear on the use of force against a suspect yelling at an officer that Officer John will probably succeed in claiming qualified immunity. So the lawyer decides to sue just the Township of Deanwood for damages for excessive force under § 1983. Assuming that what happened to George violated the Constitution, is the claim likely to succeed? On what theory or theories of municipal liability?

(*Source Note: The UFP is based on General Order 901.07 of the District of Columbia Metropolitan Police Department.*)

PART III

ENFORCING STATUTORY RIGHTS

We now turn from constitutional rights to rights created by federal statutes, including statutes that reach beyond "state actors." Our focus remains not on the details of the substantive rights protected (for instance, whether employment discrimination is prohibited when it constitutes only one of several motivating factors for a decision, or what business reasons can justify discriminatory treatment) but rather on enforcement of those statutory rights by individual litigants through civil actions. Which statutory provisions can be enforced through private civil actions and which cannot? Who are the appropriate defendants? When is an entity liable for the actions of its employees? What remedies are available?

After introducing Reconstruction-era statutory rights and their modern counterparts (Chapter 6), the remainder of Part III is organized according to the means by which statutory rights can be enforced. Chapter 7 covers two federal laws that are enforceable by "implied rights of action"—that is, causes of action that the Court has *inferred* from statutory provisions establishing a substantive protection, rather than causes of action *explicitly* provided in the statutory text. Chapter 8 covers the use of 42 U.S.C. § 1983 to enforce federal laws that lack either an express or implied cause of action. Although Part III does not provide a comprehensive catalogue of federal civil rights statutes, students will become acquainted with some of the major ones, including 42 U.S.C. §§ 1981 and 1982, Titles VI and VII of the Civil Rights Act of 1964, and Title IX of the Education Amendments of 1972.

Prominent throughout the materials in these chapters is the Court's struggle to balance, on one hand, the expansive aims of the civil rights statutes and the *Marbury* principle that rights require remedies with, on the other hand, concerns about fairness to defendants, the proper institutional role of the judiciary, and federalism.

Introduction to Statutory Remedies for Private Discrimination

As we've seen, 42 U.S.C. § 1983 is the primary vehicle for the private civil enforcement of constitutional rights, which apply only against "state actors" (Chapter 1). Discrimination by private actors is regulated not by the Constitution but by a series of federal laws passed in the mid-nineteenth and mid-twentieth centuries (and parallel antidiscrimination laws at the state and local levels). This chapter introduces several federal laws that provide a remedy for discrimination not only against state actors but also against private actors. What differentiates the group of laws in this chapter from those examined throughout the rest of Part III is that courts applied the laws covered in this chapter without seriously questioning the existence of a cause of action to enforce them—either because the laws were widely assumed to be enforceable by their own terms (the Reconstruction-era statutes) or because of an explicit statutory cause of action (Title VII).

The substantive scope of antidiscrimination statutes and provisions concerning their enforcement can be difficult to disentangle, so we'll inevitably touch on some of the substantive protections at issue, but we do not attempt comprehensive coverage of employment discrimination law, which is properly the subject of its own course or its own large unit in a course on employment law broadly. Our focus will remain on issues of enforcement: against whom; in what circumstances; and subject to what defenses can individuals bring civil actions to enforce laws barring private discrimination? Our consideration of these questions mirrors our study (in Parts I and II) of constitutional-rights enforcement through private civil actions and will facilitate comparisons across doctrines.

This chapter is divided into two sections, one covering statutory remedies from the Reconstruction era and one covering a key modern analogue to one of those laws: Title VII of the Civil Rights Act of 1964.

A. RECONSTRUCTION-ERA CIVIL RIGHTS LAWS

We begin with post-Civil War antidiscrimination laws. Ironically, the Court did not answer key questions about Reconstruction-era antidiscrimination laws until Congress was, in the mid-*twentieth* century, finally returning its attention to the long-ignored and long-tolerated scourge of race discrimination.

1. MODERN INTERPRETATION OF 42 U.S.C. §§ 1981 AND 1982

The Reconstruction Congress was concerned not only about rights violations "under color" of law (prohibited by § 1983) but also with private discrimination. Two Reconstruction-era statutes, now codified at 42 U.S.C. §§ 1981 and 1982, arguably reflect the latter focus—but were not recognized as such until a century after their passage.

Section 1981 originally (before its amendment in 1991, discussed below) provided:

> All persons within the jurisdiction of the United States shall have the same right in every State and Territory to make and enforce contracts, to sue, be parties, give evidence, and to the full and equal benefit of all laws and proceedings for the security of persons and property as is enjoyed by white citizens, and shall be subject to like punishment, pains, penalties, taxes, licenses, and exactions of every kind, and to no other.

Section 1982 provides:

> All citizens of the United States shall have the same right, in every State and Territory, as is enjoyed by white citizens thereof to inherit, purchase, lease, sell, hold, and convey real and personal property.

As Professor George Rutherglen recounts, for many years these provisions were given narrowing constructions and generally overshadowed in practice by other claims. Then, "[a]fter nearly a century of virtually complete neglect," Professor Rutherglen notes, "sections 1981 and 1982 suddenly came back to life in *Jones v. Mayer.*" George Rutherglen, *The Improbable History of Section 1981: Clio Still Bemused and Confused*, 55 Sup. Ct. Rev. 303, 322-30 (2003).

Jones v. Alfred H. Mayer Co.
392 U.S. 409 (1968)

■ *Mr. Justice* STEWART *delivered the opinion of the Court....*

On September 2, 1965, the petitioners filed a complaint . . . alleging that the respondents had refused to sell them a home in the Paddock Woods community of St. Louis County for the sole reason that petitioner Joseph Lee Jones is a Negro. Relying in part upon § 1982, the petitioners sought injunctive and other relief. The District Court sustained the respondents' motion to dismiss the complaint, and the Court of Appeals for the Eighth Circuit affirmed, concluding that § 1982 applies only to state action and does not reach private refusals to sell.... We hold that § 1982 bars all racial discrimination, private as well as public, in the sale or rental of property, and that the statute, thus construed, is a valid exercise of the power of Congress to enforce the Thirteenth Amendment....[13]....

[As a threshold matter, the Court rejected the suggestion that the recently passed Fair Housing Act of 1968 had any effect on § 1982. The Court noted that both the substance and procedures of the two laws were different, and the Court refused to assume that the later law, which did not mention § 1982, had repealed § 1982 without saying so.]

We begin with the language of the statute itself. In plain and unambiguous terms, § 1982 grants to all citizens, without regard to race or color, "the same right" to purchase and lease property "as is enjoyed by white citizens."... [T]hat right can be impaired as effectively by "those who place property on the market" as by the State itself. For, even if the State and its agents lend no support to those who wish to exclude persons from their communities on racial grounds, the fact remains that, whenever property "is placed on the market for whites only, whites have a right denied to Negroes." So long as a Negro citizen who wants to buy or rent a home can be turned away simply because he is not white, he cannot be said to enjoy "the same right * * * as is enjoyed by white citizens * * * to * * * purchase (and) lease * * * real and personal property." 42 U.S.C. § 1982.

On its face, therefore, § 1982 appears to prohibit all discrimination against Negroes in the sale or rental of property—discrimination by private owners as well as discrimination by public authorities. Indeed, even the respondents seem to concede that, if § 1982 "means what it says"—to use the words of the respondents' brief—then it must encompass every racially motivated refusal to sell or rent and cannot be confined to officially sanctioned segregation in housing. Stressing what they consider to be the revolutionary implications of so literal a reading of § 1982, the respondents argue that Congress cannot possibly have intended any such result. Our examination of the relevant history, however, persuades us that Congress meant exactly what it said....

To the Congress that passed the Civil Rights Act of 1866 [section 1 of which included 42 U.S.C. § 1982], it was clear that the right to do these things might be infringed not only by "State or local law" but also by "custom, or prejudice." Thus, when Congress provided in § 1 of the Civil Rights Act that the right to purchase and lease property was to be enjoyed equally throughout the United States by Negro and white citizens alike, it plainly meant to secure that right against interference from any source whatever, whether governmental or private.

Indeed, if § 1 had been intended to grant nothing more than an immunity from governmental interference, then much of § 2 [which prohibited

---

13. [Plaintiffs sought various forms of injunctive relief, including requiring Defendants to sell them the home at issue and prohibiting future discrimination in the sale of homes in Paddock Woods.] ... The fact that 42 U.S.C. § 1982 is couched in declaratory terms and provides no explicit method of enforcement does not, of course, prevent a federal court from fashioning an effective equitable remedy.

discrimination "under color of any law, statute, ordinance, regulation, or custom," and would become the criminal statute 18 U.S.C. § 242] would have made no sense at all. . . .

In attempting to demonstrate the contrary, the respondents rely heavily upon the fact that the Congress which approved the 1866 statute wished to eradicate the recently enacted Black Codes—laws which had saddled Negroes with "onerous disabilities and burdens, and curtailed their rights * * * to such an extent that their freedom was of little value * * *." The respondents suggest that the only evil Congress sought to eliminate was that of racially discriminatory laws in the former Confederate States. But the Civil Rights Act was drafted to apply throughout the country, and its language was far broader than would have been necessary to strike down discriminatory statutes. . . .

For the same Congress that wanted to do away with the Black Codes also had before it an imposing body of evidence pointing to the mistreatment of Negroes by private individuals and unofficial groups, mistreatment unrelated to any hostile state legislation. "Accounts in newspapers North and South, Freedmen's Bureau and other official documents, private reports and correspondence were all adduced" to show that "private outrage and atrocity" were "daily inflicted on freedmen * * *." The congressional debates are replete with references to private injustices against Negroes—references to white employers who refused to pay their Negro workers, white planters who agreed among themselves not to hire freed slaves without the permission of their former masters, white citizens who assaulted Negroes or who combined to drive them out of their communities. . . .

In this setting, it would have been strange indeed if Congress had viewed its task as encompassing merely the nullification of racist laws in the former rebel States. . . .

Senator Trumbull's bill [that became the Civil Rights Act of 1866] would, as he pointed out, "destroy all (the) discriminations" embodied in the Black Codes, but it would do more: It would affirmatively secure for all men, whatever their race or color, what the Senator called the "great fundamental rights": "the right to acquire property, the right to go and come at pleasure, the right to enforce rights in the courts, to make contracts, and to inherit and dispose of property."

As to those basic civil rights, the Senator said, the bill would "break down all discrimination between black men and white men."

That the bill would indeed have so sweeping an effect was seen as its great virtue by its friends and as its great danger by its enemies but was disputed by none. Opponents of the bill charged that it would not only regulate state laws but would directly "determine the persons who [would] enjoy * * * property within the States," threatening the ability of white citizens "to determine who [would] be members of [their] communit[ies] * * *." The bill's advocates did not deny the accuracy of those characterizations. Instead, they defended the propriety of employing federal authority to deal with "the white man . . . [who] would invoke the power of local prejudice" against the Negro. Thus, when the Senate passed the Civil Rights Act on February 2, 1866, it did so fully aware of the breadth of the measure it had approved.

[The legislative history in the House is to similar effect.] . . .

In light of the concerns that led Congress to adopt it and the contents of the debates that proceded its passage, it is clear that the Act was designed to do just what its terms suggest: to prohibit all racial discrimination, whether or not under color of law, with respect to the rights enumerated therein—including the right to purchase or lease property. . . .

The remaining question is whether Congress has power under the Constitution to do what § 1982 purports to do: to prohibit all racial discrimination, private and public, in the sale and rental of property. Our starting point is the Thirteenth Amendment, for it was pursuant to that constitutional provision that Congress originally enacted what is now § 1982. The Amendment consists of two parts. Section 1 states: "Neither slavery nor involuntary servitude, except as a punishment for crime whereby the party shall have been duly convicted, shall exist within the United States, or any place subject to their jurisdiction." Section 2 provides: "Congress shall have power to enforce this article by appropriate legislation." . . .

[T]he majority leaders in Congress—who were, after all, the authors of the Thirteenth Amendment—had no doubt that its Enabling Clause contemplated the sort of positive legislation that was embodied in the 1866 Civil Rights Act. Their chief spokesman, Senator Trumbull . . . had brought the Thirteenth Amendment to the floor of the Senate in 1864. In defending the constitutionality of the 1866 Act, he argued that, if the narrower construction of the Enabling Clause were correct, then "the trumpet of freedom that we have been blowing throughout the land has given an 'uncertain sound,' and the promised freedom is a delusion." . . .

Surely Senator Trumbull was right. Surely Congress has the power under the Thirteenth Amendment rationally to determine what are the badges and the incidents of slavery, and the authority to translate that determination into effective legislation. Nor can we say that the determination Congress has made is an irrational one. For this Court recognized long ago that, whatever else they may have encompassed, the badges and incidents of slavery—its "burdens and disabilities"—included restraints upon "those fundamental rights which are the essence of civil freedom, namely, the same right * * * to inherit, purchase, lease, sell and convey property, as is enjoyed by white citizens." Just as the Black Codes, enacted after the Civil War to restrict the free exercise of those rights, were substitutes for the slave system, so the exclusion of Negroes from white communities became a substitute for the Black Codes. And when racial discrimination herds men into ghettos and makes their ability to buy property turn on the color of their skin, then it too is a relic of slavery.

Negro citizens, North and South, who saw in the Thirteenth Amendment a promise of freedom—freedom to "go and come at pleasure" and to "buy and sell when they please"—would be left with "a mere paper guarantee" if Congress were powerless to assure that a dollar in the hands of a Negro will purchase the same thing as a dollar in the hands of a white man. At the very least, the freedom that Congress is empowered to secure under the Thirteenth Amendment includes the freedom to buy whatever a white man can buy, the right to live wherever a white man can live. If Congress cannot say that being a free man means at least this much, then the Thirteenth Amendment made a promise the Nation cannot keep....

[Opinion of Douglas, J., concurring, omitted.]

▪ *Mr. Justice* HARLAN, *whom Mr. Justice* WHITE *joins, dissenting.*

The decision in this case appears to me to be most ill-considered and ill-advised....

For reasons which follow, I believe that the Court's construction of § 1982 as applying to purely private action is almost surely wrong. . . . Moreover, [the passage of the Fair Housing Act] . . . so diminishes the public importance of this case that by far the wisest course would be for this Court to refrain from decision and to dismiss the writ as improvidently granted....

The Court finds it "plain and unambiguous" that [§ 1982] forbids purely private as well as state authorized discrimination. With all respect, I do not find it so. For me, there is an inherent ambiguity in the term "right," as used in § 1982. The "right" referred to may either be a right to equal status under the law, in which case the statute operates only against state-sanctioned discrimination, or it may be an "absolute" right enforceable against private individuals. To me, the words of the statute, taken alone, suggest the former interpretation, not the latter....

In the course of the debates, Senator Trumbull . . . made a number of statements which can only be taken to mean that the bill was aimed at "state action" alone. For example, on January 29, 1866, Senator Trumbull began by citing a number of recently enacted Southern laws depriving men of rights named in the bill. He stated that "[t]he purpose of the bill under consideration is to destroy all these discriminations, and carry into effect the constitutional amendment." . . .

Many of the legislators who took part in the congressional debates inevitably must have shared the individualistic ethic of their time, which emphasized personal freedom and embodied a distaste for governmental interference which was soon to culminate in the era of laissez-faire. It seems to me that most of these men would have regarded it as a great intrusion on individual liberty for the Government to take from a man the power to refuse for personal reasons to enter into a purely private transaction involving the disposition of property, albeit those personal reasons might reflect racial bias. It should be remembered that racial prejudice was not uncommon in 1866, even outside the South. Although Massachusetts had recently enacted the Nation's first law prohibiting racial discrimination in public accommodations, Negroes could not ride within Philadelphia streetcars or attend public schools with white children in New York City. Only five States accorded equal voting rights to Negroes, and it appears that Negroes were allowed to serve on juries only in Massachusetts. Residential segregation was the prevailing pattern almost everywhere in the North. There were no state "fair housing" laws in 1866, and it appears that none had ever been proposed. In this historical context, I cannot conceive that a bill thought to prohibit purely private discrimination not only in the sale or rental of housing but in all property transactions would not have received a great deal of criticism explicitly directed to this feature. The fact that the 1866 Act received no criticism of this kind is for me strong additional evidence that it was not regarded as extending so far. . . .

* * *

Did the Court's broad interpretation of § 1982 extend to § 1981 as well? The next case answers.

Runyon v. McCrary
427 U.S. 160 (1976)

■ *Mr. Justice* STEWART *delivered the opinion of the Court.*

The principal issue presented by these consolidated cases is whether a federal law, namely, 42 U.S.C. § 1981, prohibits private schools from excluding qualified children solely because they are Negroes. . . .

Bobbe's School [in Arlington, Virginia, a suburb of Washington] opened in 1958 and grew from an initial enrollment of five students to 200 in 1972. A day camp was begun in 1967 and has averaged 100 children per year. The [nearby Fairfax County, Va.] Fairfax-Brewster School commenced operations in 1955 and opened a summer day camp in 1956. A total of 223 students were enrolled at the school during the 1972-1973 academic year, and 236 attended the day camp in the summer of 1972. Neither school has ever accepted a Negro child for any of its programs.

In response to a mailed brochure addressed "resident" and an advertisement in the "Yellow Pages" of the telephone directory, Mr. and Mrs. Gonzales telephoned and then visited the Fairfax-Brewster School in May 1969. After the visit, they submitted an application for [their son] Colin's admission to the day camp. The school responded with a form letter, which stated that the school was "unable to accommodate (Colin's) application." Mr. Gonzales telephoned the school. Fairfax-Brewster's Chairman of the Board explained that the reason for Colin's rejection was that the school was not integrated. Mr. Gonzales then telephoned Bobbe's School, from which the family had also received in the mail a brochure addressed to "resident." In response to a question concerning that school's admissions policies, he was told that only members of the Caucasian race were accepted. In August 1972, Mrs. McCrary telephoned Bobbe's School in response to an advertisement in the telephone book. She inquired about nursery school facilities for her son, Michael. She also asked if the school was integrated. The answer was no.

[Colin's and Michael's parents sued the proprietors of Bobbe's School, and the Gonzaleses also sued the Fairfax-Brewster School, under § 1981. The Southern Independent School Association sought and was granted permission to intervene as a party defendant. That organization is a nonprofit association representing approximately 400 schools, many of which deny admission on the basis of race. The district court ruled for the plaintiffs and awarded both damages for emotional distress and an injunction against further race discrimination. . . .]

It is worth noting at the outset some of the questions that these cases do not present. They do not present any question of the right of a private social organization to limit its membership on racial or any other grounds. They do not present any question of the right of a private school to limit its student body to boys, to girls, or to adherents of a particular religious faith, since 42 U.S.C. § 1981 is in no way addressed to such categories of selectivity. They do not even present the application of § 1981 to private sectarian schools that practice racial exclusion on religious grounds. Rather, these cases present only two basic questions: whether § 1981 prohibits private, commercially operated, nonsectarian schools from denying admission to prospective students because they are Negroes, and, if so, whether that federal law is constitutional as so applied.

It is now well established that § 1 of the Civil Rights Act of 1866, 42 U.S.C. § 1981, prohibits racial discrimination in the making and enforcement of private contracts.

In *Jones*, the Court held that the portion of § 1 of the Civil Rights Act of 1866 presently codified as 42 U.S.C. § 1982 prohibits private racial discrimination in the sale or rental of real or personal property. Relying on the legislative history of § 1, from which both § 1981 and § 1982 derive, the Court concluded that Congress intended to prohibit "all racial discrimination, private and public, in the sale . . . of property," and that this prohibition was within Congress' power under § 2 of the Thirteenth Amendment . . . .

As the Court indicated in *Jones*, that holding necessarily implied that the portion of § 1 of the 1866 Act presently codified as 42 U.S.C. § 1981 likewise reaches purely private acts of racial discrimination. The statutory holding in *Jones* was that the "(1866) Act was designed to do just what its terms suggest: to prohibit all racial discrimination, whether or not under color of law, with respect to the rights enumerated therein including the right to purchase or lease property." One of the "rights enumerated" in § 1 is "the same right . . . to make and enforce contracts . . . as is enjoyed by white citizens . . . ." Just as in *Jones* a Negro's § 1 right to purchase property on equal terms with whites was violated when a private person refused to sell to the prospective purchaser solely because he was a Negro, so also a Negro's § 1 right to "make and enforce contracts" is violated if a private offeror refuses to extend to a Negro, solely because he is a Negro, the same opportunity to enter into contracts as he extends to white offerees. . . .

It is apparent that the racial exclusion practiced by the Fairfax-Brewster School and Bobbe's Private School amounts to a classic violation of § 1981. The parents of Colin Gonzales and Michael McCrary sought to enter into contractual relationships with Bobbe's School for educational services. Colin Gonzales' parents sought to enter into a similar relationship with the Fairfax-Brewster School. Under those contractual relationships, the schools would have received payments for services rendered, and the prospective students would have received instruction in return for those payments. The educational services of Bobbe's School and the Fairfax-Brewster School were advertised and offered to members of the general public. But neither school offered services on equal basis to white and nonwhite students. . . . The Court of Appeals' conclusion that § 1981 was thereby violated follows inexorably from the language of that statute, as construed in *Jones* [and subsequent cases].

It is noteworthy that Congress in enacting the Equal Employment Opportunity Act of 1972, as amended, specifically considered and rejected an amendment that would have repealed the Civil Rights Act of 1866, as interpreted by this Court in *Jones*, insofar as it affords private-sector employees a right of action based on racial discrimination in employment. There could hardly be a clearer indication of congressional agreement with the view that § 1981 does reach private acts of racial discrimination. . . .

The question remains whether § 1981, as applied, violates constitutionally protected rights of free association and privacy, or a parent's right to direct the education of his children.

In *NAACP v. Alabama*, and similar decisions, the Court has recognized a First Amendment right "to engage in association for the advancement of beliefs and ideas . . . ." That right is protected because it promotes and may well be essential to the "(e)ffective advocacy of both public and private points of view, particularly controversial ones" that the First Amendment is designed to foster.

From this principle it may be assumed that parents have a First Amendment right to send their children to educational institutions that promote the belief that racial segregation is desirable, and that the children have an equal right to attend such institutions. But it does not follow that the practice of excluding racial minorities from such institutions is also protected by the same principle. . . . In any event, as the Court of Appeals noted, "there is no showing that discontinuance of (the) discriminatory admission practices would inhibit in any way the teaching in these schools of any ideas or dogma." . . .

[The Court went on to reject the arguments that parental rights or privacy rights thwart the application of § 1981 here.]

▪ *Mr. Justice* POWELL, *concurring.*

If the slate were clean I might well be inclined to agree with Mr. Justice White that § 1981 was not intended to restrict private contractual choices. . . . It seems to me, however, that [his argument] comes too late.

The applicability of § 1981 to private contracts has been considered maturely and recently, and I do not feel free to disregard these precedents. . . .

Although the range of consequences suggested by the dissenting opinion, go far beyond what we hold today, I am concerned that our decision not be construed more broadly than would be justified. . . .

In certain personal contractual relationships . . . such as those where the offeror selects those with whom he desires to bargain on an individualized basis, or where the contract is the foundation of a close association (such as, for example, that between an employer and a private tutor, babysitter, or housekeeper), there is reason to assume that, although the choice made by the offeror is selective, it reflects "a purpose of exclusiveness" other than the desire to bar members of the Negro race. Such a purpose, certainly in most cases, would invoke associational rights long respected.

The case presented on the record before us does not involve this type of personal contractual relationship. . . . The schools extended a public offer open, on its face, to any child meeting certain minimum qualifications who chose to accept. They advertised in the "Yellow Pages" of the telephone directories and engaged extensively in general mail solicitations to attract students. The schools are operated strictly on a commercial basis, and one fairly could construe their open-end invitations as offers that matured into binding contracts when accepted by those who met the academic, financial, and other racially neutral specified conditions as to qualifications for entrance. There is no reason to assume that the schools had any special reason for exercising an option of personal choice among those who responded to their public offers. A small kindergarten or music class, operated on the basis of personal invitations extended to a limited number of preidentified students, for example, would present a far different case. . . .

[Section] 1981, as interpreted by our prior decisions, does reach certain acts of racial discrimination that are "private" in the sense that they involve no state action. But choices, including those involved in entering into a contract, that are "private" in the sense that they are not part of a commercial relationship offered generally or widely, and that reflect the selectivity exercised by an individual entering into a personal relationship, certainly were never intended to be restricted by the 19th century Civil Rights Acts. The open offer to the public generally involved in the cases before us is simply not a "private" contract in this sense. Accordingly, I join the opinion of the Court.

■ *Mr. Justice STEVENS, concurring.*

For me the problem in these cases is whether to follow a line of authority which I firmly believe to have been incorrectly decided.

Jones and its progeny have unequivocally held that § 1 of the Civil Rights Act of 1866 prohibits private racial discrimination. There is no doubt in my mind that that construction of the statute would have amazed the legislators who voted for it. . . .

But *Jones* has been decided and is now an important part of the fabric of our law. Although I recognize the force of Mr. Justice White's argument that the construction of § 1982 does not control § 1981, it would be most incongruous to give those two sections a fundamentally different construction. . . .

The policy of the Nation as formulated by the Congress in recent years has moved constantly in the direction of eliminating racial segregation in all sectors of society. This Court has given a sympathetic and liberal construction to such legislation. For the Court now to overrule *Jones* would be a significant step backwards, with effects that would not have arisen from a correct decision in the first instance. Such a step would be so clearly contrary to my understanding of the mores of today that I think the Court is entirely correct in adhering to *Jones.* . . .

▪ *Mr. Justice* WHITE, *with whom Mr. Justice* REHNQUIST *joins, dissenting.*

We are urged here to extend the meaning and reach of 42 U.S.C. § 1981 so as to establish a general prohibition against a private individual's or institution's refusing to enter into a contract with another person because of that person's race. Section 1981 has been on the books since 1870. . . . The majority's belated discovery of a congressional purpose which escaped this Court only a decade after the statute was passed and which escaped all other federal courts for almost 100 years is singularly unpersuasive. . . .

On its face the statute gives "(a)ll persons" (plainly including Negroes) the *"same right* . . . to make . . . contracts . . . as is enjoyed by white citizens." (Emphasis added.) The words "right . . . enjoyed by white citizens" clearly refer to rights existing apart from this statute. Whites had at the time when § 1981 was first enacted, and have (with few exceptions mentioned below) no right to make a contract with an unwilling private person, no matter what that person's motivation for refusing to contract. Indeed it is and always has been central to the very concept of a "contract" that there be "assent by the parties who form the contract to the terms thereof," Restatement of Contracts § 19(b) (1932). The right to make contracts, enjoyed by white citizens, was therefore always a right to enter into binding agreements only with willing second parties. Since the statute only gives Negroes the "same rights" to contract as is enjoyed by whites, the language of the statute confers no right on Negroes to enter into a contract with an unwilling person no matter what that person's motivation for refusing to contract. What is conferred by 42 U.S.C. § 1981 is the right which was enjoyed by whites "to make contracts" with other willing parties and to "enforce" those contracts in court. Section 1981 would thus invalidate any state statute or court-made rule of law which would have the effect of disabling Negroes or any other class of persons from making contracts or enforcing contractual obligations or otherwise giving less weight to their obligations than is given to contractual obligations running to whites. The statute by its terms does not require any private individual or institution to enter into a contract or perform any other act under any circumstances; and it consequently fails to supply a cause of action by respondent students against petitioner schools based on the latter's racially motivated decision not to contract with them.

The legislative history of 42 U.S.C. § 1981 confirms that the statute means what it says and no more, i.e., that it outlaws any legal rule disabling any person from making or enforcing a contract, but does not prohibit private racially motivated refusals to contract.

[Justice White argues at length about the legislative history of § 1981; a key premise of his argument is that the provision originates from an entirely different statute than the majority believes.]

The majority's holding that 42 U.S.C. § 1981 prohibits all racially motivated contractual decisions . . . threatens to embark the Judiciary on a treacherous course. Whether such conduct should be condoned or not, whites and blacks will undoubtedly choose to form a variety of associational relationships pursuant to contracts which exclude members of the other race. Social clubs, black and white, and associations designed to further the interests of blacks or whites are but two examples. Lawsuits by members of the other race attempting to gain admittance to such an association are not pleasant to contemplate. As the associational or contractual relationships become more private, the pressures to hold § 1981 inapplicable to them will increase. Imaginative judicial construction of the word "contract" is foreseeable; Thirteenth Amendment limitations on Congress' power to ban "badges and incidents of slavery" may be discovered; the doctrine of the right to association may be bent to cover a given situation. In any event, courts will be called upon to balance sensitive policy considerations against each other considerations which have never been addressed by any Congress all under the guise of "construing" a statute. This is a task appropriate for the Legislature, not for the Judiciary. . . .

Notes and Questions

1. Who gives the more persuasive account of the legislative history in *Jones*, the majority or the dissent? Is legislative history best analyzed by using the words of legislators or the historical context of the legislation? If you find the answers to these questions murky or subjective, are you persuaded by the view of later Justices (in particular Justice Scalia) that legislative history is not a sound guide to statutory interpretation at all?

2. If §§ 1981 and 1982 don't mean what the Court says they mean in these two cases, of what value are they today?

3. As foreshadowed in the introduction to this chapter, the question of whether §§ 1981 and 1982—which do not by their terms specify how they are to be enforced—contain private causes of action was thought to be sufficiently obvious that it received scant attention from the Court. Footnote 13 of *Jones* simply declared § 1982 enforceable, at least by injunctive relief. The year after *Jones*, the Court found that § 1982 authorized damages as well, explaining, "The existence of a statutory right implies the existence of all necessary and appropriate remedies." *Sullivan v. Little Hunting Park, Inc.*, 396 U.S. 229, 239 (1969). (Three Justices dissented, arguing that certiorari should have been dismissed as improvidently granted, but they did not argue that a damages remedy should be rejected.) Regarding § 1981, the recognition of a cause of action was presented as a fait accompli in a portion of an opinion a few years later in which the entire Court joined: "Although this Court has not specifically so held, it is well settled among the federal Courts of Appeals—and we now join them—that § 1981 affords a federal remedy against discrimination in private employment on the basis of race. An individual who establishes a cause of action under § 1981 is entitled to both equitable and legal relief, including compensatory and, under certain circumstances, punitive damages." *Johnson v. Ry. Exp. Agency, Inc.*, 421 U.S. 454, 459-60 (1975). Now recall how questions regarding the existence of an implicit cause of action sharply divided the Court in *Bivens* (Chapter 2), decided in 1971, right in the midst of the cases cited in this paragraph. Why was the

enforceability of §§ 1981 and 1982 so obvious to the same Justices who fought bitterly over *Bivens*?

4. Given the passage of the Fair Housing Act (FHA) in 1968, the decision in *Jones* had far less practical significance than its sweeping holding might otherwise have suggested. Why did the Court bother to decide the case over Justice Harlan's objection that it shouldn't have waded unnecessarily into a difficult dispute? What countervailing interests support the Court's action in deciding the case?

5. Consider the following analysis:

> [Plaintiff's] argument . . . assumes that social prejudices may be overcome by legislation, and that equal rights cannot be secured to the negro except by an enforced commingling of the two races. We cannot accept this proposition. If the two races are to meet upon terms of social equality, it must be the result of natural affinities, a mutual appreciation of each other's merits, and a voluntary consent of individuals. . . . Legislation is powerless to eradicate racial instincts, or to abolish distinctions based upon physical differences, and the attempt to do so can only result in accentuating the difficulties of the present situation.

Now re-read Justice White's view of § 1981 from his *Runyon* dissent:

> Since the statute only gives Negroes the "same rights" to contract as is enjoyed by whites, the language of the statute confers no right on Negroes to enter into a contract with an unwilling person no matter what that person's motivation for refusing to contract. What is conferred by 42 U.S.C. § 1981 is the right which was enjoyed by whites "to make contracts" with other willing parties and to "enforce" those contracts in court. . . .
>
> The majority's holding that 42 U.S.C. § 1981 prohibits all racially motivated contractual decisions . . . threatens to embark the Judiciary on a treacherous course. Whether such conduct should be condoned or not, whites and blacks will undoubtedly choose to form a variety of associational relationships pursuant to contracts which exclude members of the other race. Social clubs, black and white, and associations designed to further the interests of blacks or whites are but two examples.

Are these two passages comparable in reasoning? Do you recognize the first passage, which comes from the majority opinion in an infamous case? If you find the reasoning analogous to Justice White's, does the comparison diminish your regard for Justice White's position?

6. Notice when the two defendant schools in *Runyon* were founded. Why might one-race private schools have been particularly in demand at that time? Consider also the intervention of the Southern Independent School Association in the *Runyon* dispute. What does that move suggest about the stakes of the case? Professor George Rutherglen points out:

> Congress had not legislated on the subject of segregated private schools, proba-
> bly because such "white academies" had multiplied in response to court-ordered

busing to desegregate the public schools. Congress had little reason to expose itself to further controversy on this issue by expanding the scope of desegregation decrees.

George Rutherglen, *The Improbable History of Section 1981: Clio Still Bemused and Confused*, 55 Sup. Ct. Rev. 303, 339-40 (2003). Accordingly, addressing the use of private schools to perpetuate segregation fell to the Court.

7. Sean F. Reardon & John T. Yun, *Private School Racial Enrollments and Segregation* (2002), considered private school segregation a quarter-century after *Runyon*:

> Black-white segregation is greater among private schools than among public schools. Although 78% of the private school students in the nation were white in 1997-98, the average black private school student was enrolled in a school that was only 34% white. For comparison, note that among public schools, 64% of students were white and the average black public school student attended a school that was 33% white. In other words, black private school students are as racially isolated as are black public school students. . . .
>
> White students are more racially isolated in private schools than in public schools. In public schools 47% of white students attend schools that are 90-100% white, while in private schools 64% of white students attend schools that are 90-100% white. In private schools, white students attend schools that are, on average, almost nine-tenths (88%) white and only 12% minority, whereas white students in public schools attend schools that average four-fifths (81%) white and one-fifth (19%) minority.

Id. at 3-4. What factors other than intentional discrimination might explain the study's findings? Assuming discrimination is still occurring, why might § 1981 be harder to enforce in private schools than the Fourteenth Amendment is in public schools?

8. In trying to cabin the reach of the majority opinion, Justice Powell gives examples of particularly "private" contracts to which he believes § 1981 would not apply. What is the foundation of this distinction as a matter of statutory interpretation? How advisable is it as a matter of policy? How administrable is it? Does the Court's difficulty in enforcing *Brown* (which we'll study in detail later, in Chapter 12) influence whether you view Justice Powell's position as reflecting a lingering discomfort with a fully racially integrated society or a pragmatic attempt to insulate the Court and its progressive ruling from political backlash? In assessing Justice Powell's motivations, you might consider the importance of desegregation litigation to his position on municipal liability in *Monell* (Chapter 5).

9. Relatedly, the question of which transactions are so "private" that they must be beyond the reach of antidiscrimination law arose in a particularly modern context in *Fair Housing Council of San Fernando Valley v. Roommate.com, LLC*, 666 F.3d 1216 (9th Cir. 2012). There, a website that helped people find roommates was sued under the FHA and California antidiscrimination law for enabling site users to list preferences regarding the sex, sexual orientation,

and familial status of their roommates. The FHA prohibits, with respect to the "sale or rental of a dwelling," both discrimination and the publication of discriminatory ads based on sex or familial status; California law applies a similar prohibition to discrimination and ads based on sexual orientation. The court interpreted "dwelling" (and the parallel term under state law) not to include *portions of* a single-family home or apartment, so as to avoid the constitutional concerns it thought would arise if antidiscrimination laws applied to selecting a roommate:

> Aside from immediate family or a romantic partner, it's hard to imagine a relationship more intimate than that between roommates, who share living rooms, dining rooms, kitchens, bathrooms, even bedrooms.
>
> Because of a roommate's unfettered access to the home, choosing a roommate implicates significant privacy and safety considerations. The home is the center of our private lives. Roommates note our comings and goings, observe whom we bring back at night, hear what songs we sing in the shower, see us in various stages of undress and learn intimate details most of us prefer to keep private. Roommates also have access to our physical belongings and to our person. . . . Taking on a roommate means giving him full access to the space where we are most vulnerable.
>
> Equally important, we are fully exposed to a roommate's belongings, activities, habits, proclivities and way of life. This could include matter we find offensive (pornography, religious materials, political propaganda); dangerous (tobacco, drugs, firearms); annoying (jazz, perfume, frequent overnight visitors, furry pets); habits that are incompatible with our lifestyle (early risers, messy cooks, bathroom hogs, clothing borrowers). When you invite others to share your living quarters, you risk becoming a suspect in whatever illegal activities they engage in. . . .
>
> Holding that the FHA applies inside a home or apartment would allow the government to restrict our ability to choose roommates compatible with our lifestyles. This would be a serious invasion of privacy, autonomy and security.
>
> For example, women will often look for female roommates because of modesty or security concerns. As roommates often share bathrooms and common areas, a girl may not want to walk around in her towel in front of a boy. She might also worry about unwanted sexual advances or becoming romantically involved with someone she must count on to pay the rent.
>
> An orthodox Jew may want a roommate with similar beliefs and dietary restrictions, so he won't have to worry about finding honey-baked ham in the refrigerator next to the potato latkes. . . . The same is true of individuals of other faiths that call for dietary restrictions or rituals inside the home.

Note that the court's statutory interpretation excludes the selection of roommates from *all* the protections of the FHA, including the prohibition on race discrimination. Should that be of concern, or should intimate-association rights cover that type of choice also? If you are uncomfortable with that aspect of the majority's holding, does it assuage your concern that §§ 1981 and 1982 provide additional protection against race discrimination?

Would the constitutional logic in *Roommate.com* cover any of Justice Powell's examples in his *Runyon* concurrence? Or would those have to be excluded from § 1981's coverage on some other rationale?

10. A happy epilogue to *Runyon v. McCrary*: Michael McCrary went on to play defensive end in the National Football League and won a Super Bowl with the Baltimore Ravens in 2001. That same year, he received the NFL's "Man of the Year" award for community service—an award named for Byron "Whizzer" White, who was a star running back in the NFL thirty-five years before he wrote his dissent in Michael McCrary's case.

Note: Additional Reconstruction-Era Civil Rights Laws

Two other Reconstruction-era protections deserve mention, although we will not cover them in detail.

1. Criminal prohibitions

Congress provided criminal as well as civil liability for civil rights violators. Specifically, in the provisions now set out in 18 U.S.C. §§ 241 and 242, Congress criminalized both private conspiracies and actions "under color of . . . law" to deprive individuals of their constitutional rights. As we saw in the *Classic* and *Screws* cases (Chapter 1, Section A), § 242 uses "under color" language similar to that of § 1983.

Probably the most famous application of the criminal civil rights protections was to prosecute the individuals who murdered civil rights workers Michael Henry Schwerner, James Earl Chaney, and Andrew Goodman in 1964 in Philadelphia, Mississippi. *See United States v. Price*, 383 U.S. 787 (1966).

The government also charged under § 242 the police officers who beat Los Angeles driver Rodney King in an incident in 1991 that was captured on video and quickly garnered national attention and outrage; two of the four officers were convicted. *See Koon v. United States*, 518 U.S. 81 (1996).

The Criminal Section of the Civil Rights Division of the Justice Department enforces 18 U.S.C. §§ 241 and 242.

2. Civil conspiracy

In what is now 42 U.S.C. § 1985(3), Congress provided:

> If two or more persons in any State or Territory conspire or go in disguise on the highway or on the premises of another, for the purpose of depriving, either directly or indirectly, any person or class of persons of the equal protection of the laws, or of equal privileges and immunities under the laws; or for the purpose of preventing or hindering the constituted authorities of any State or Territory from giving or securing to all persons within such State or Territory the equal protection of the laws; or if two or more persons conspire to prevent by force, intimidation, or threat, any citizen who is lawfully entitled to vote, from giving his support or advocacy in a legal manner, toward or in favor of the election of any lawfully qualified person [in a

presidential or congressional election]; or to injure any citizen in person or property on account of such support or advocacy . . . the party so injured or deprived may have an action for the recovery of damages occasioned by such injury or deprivation, against any one or more of the conspirators.

Although the circumstances to which this provision applies are narrow—in particular, they must involve "some racial, or perhaps otherwise class-based, invidiously discriminatory animus," not just opposition to any protected constitutional right, *Bray v. Alexandria Women's Health Clinic*, 506 U.S. 263 (1993) (rejecting abortion clinics' attempt to use § 1985(3) to seek injunction against anti-abortion protestors)—§ 1985(3) continues to see some modern application. For instance, in *Griffin v. Breckenridge*, 403 U.S. 88 (1971), the Court unanimously permitted the use of § 1985(3) by African-Americans detained and brutally beaten with clubs by two Mississippi white men who mistook them for civil rights workers.

More recently, the plaintiffs in *Ziglar v. Abbasi*, 137 S. Ct. 1843 (2017), which we read in Chapter 2, invoked § 1985(3) alongside *Bivens* in seeking redress for harsh post-September 11 detentions. The Supreme Court held that this claim failed on qualified immunity grounds, which prompted Justice Thomas's noteworthy concurrence expressing doubts about qualified immunity doctrine (see Chapter 4).

And § 1985(3) was the basis for a civil complaint filed in 2017 that began as follows:

1. Over the weekend of August 11 and 12, 2017, hundreds of neo-Nazis and white supremacists traveled from near and far to descend upon the college town of Charlottesville, Virginia, in order to terrorize its residents, commit acts of violence, and use the town as a backdrop to showcase for the media and the nation a neo-nationalist agenda.

2. Plaintiffs in this action are University of Virginia undergraduates, law students and staff, persons of faith, ministers, parents, doctors, and businesspersons—white, brown, and black; Christian and Jewish; young and old. . . . Each Plaintiff in this action was injured as a result of the events in Charlottesville on August 11 and 12. One Plaintiff suffered a stroke. Two plaintiffs were struck in a car attack. Others suffered and continue to suffer deep and debilitating psychological and emotional distress that prevents them from resuming their former lives or from enjoying the basic sense of peace, safety, and tranquility that most in this country can take for granted.

3. Defendants are the individuals and organizations that conspired to plan, promote, and carry out the violent events in Charlottesville. They are neo-Nazis, Klansmen, white supremacists, and white nationalists. They embrace and espouse racist, anti-Semitic, sexist, homophobic, and xenophobic ideologies. Defendants brought with them to Charlottesville the imagery of the Holocaust, of slavery, of Jim Crow, and of fascism. They also brought with them semi-automatic weapons, pistols, mace, rods, armor, shields, and torches. They chanted "Jews will not replace us," "blood and soil," and "this is our town now." Starting at least as early as the beginning of 2017 and continuing through today, they have joined together for the purpose of inciting violence and instilling fear within the community of Charlottesville and beyond, wherever their messages are received.

Complaint, *Sines v. Kessler*, Dkt. 1, No. 3:17-cv-00072 (W.D. Va. filed Oct. 12, 2017).

2. DEVELOPMENT OF § 1981 POST-*RUNYON*

Runyon appeared to be in jeopardy in *Patterson v. McLean Credit Union*, 491 U.S. 164 (1989). That case concerned an African-American bank teller who alleged that she had been harassed because of her race. After the case was argued, the Supreme Court directed the parties to brief and argue the question whether *Runyon* should be reconsidered—a controversial move that caused four Justices to dissent from the reargument order. After reargument, the Court decided that stare decisis counseled against overruling *Runyon*. Nonetheless, the Court went on to hold that § 1981's protection of the "the right . . . to make . . . contracts" did not extend to the bank teller's claim of race-based harassment, because "the right to make contracts does not extend, as a matter of either logic or semantics, to conduct by the employer after the contract relation has been established, including breach of the terms of the contract or imposition of discriminatory working conditions. Such postformation conduct does not involve the right to make a contract, but rather implicates the performance of established contract obligations and the conditions of continuing employment . . . ." Concurring in part and dissenting in part, Justice Brennan, joined by Justices Marshall, Blackmun, and Stevens, protested the majority's "cramped" interpretation of § 1981 and would have held that the statute applied to race-based harassment.

The same year as *Patterson*, the Court restricted § 1981 in another respect, by holding in *Jett v. Dallas Indep. Sch. Dist.*, 491 U.S. 701, 733 (1989), that § 1981 did not apply to governmental actors, because such claims were the exclusive province of § 1983. Once again, Justice Brennan, joined by Justices Marshall, Blackmun, and Stevens, dissented from the narrow construction of § 1981. The dissenters noted the irony of *Jett*'s holding in light of the course of the Court's treatment of § 1981: "It is strange, indeed, simultaneously to question whether § 1981 creates a cause of action on the basis of private conduct (*Patterson*) and whether it creates one for governmental conduct . . .—and hence to raise the possibility that this landmark civil rights statute affords no civil redress at all."

Two years later, Congress responded to these decisions. In the Civil Rights Act of 1991 (also discussed below in connection with its amendments to Title VII), Congress added these two new subsections to § 1981:

> (b) "Make and enforce contracts" defined
> For purposes of this section, the term "make and enforce contracts" includes the making, performance, modification, and termination of contracts, and the enjoyment of all benefits, privileges, terms, and conditions of the contractual relationship.

> (c) Protection against impairment
> The rights protected by this section are protected against impairment by nongovernmental discrimination and impairment under color of State law.

The 1991 Act ended the debate over the fate of *Runyon* by endorsing its holding in § 1981(c). The Act also legislatively overruled *Patterson*'s restriction on race-based harassment claims in § 1981(b).

In specifying that § 1981 applies to "nongovernmental discrimination and impairment under color of State law," one might have thought Congress clearly overruled *Jett* as well, but that question has been the subject of differing opinions in the circuit courts, with the vast majority, surprisingly, holding that *Jett* survives § 1981(c). *Compare Buntin v. City of Boston*, 857 F.3d 69, 74 (1st Cir. 2017) (noting that, in contrast to the extensive discussion of *Patterson* in the legislative history of the 1991 Act, "[n]either of the House Reports mentioned *Jett* even in passing," and joining nine other circuits in reaffirming *Jett*), *with Fed'n of African Am. Contractors v. City of Oakland*, 96 F.3d 1204, 1214 (9th Cir. 1996) (holding that § 1981 must cover both private and governmental discrimination "[b]ecause § 1981(c) affords identical protection against 'impairment by nongovernmental discrimination' and 'impairment under color of State law'"). It is unclear what the final six words ("and impairment under color of State law") could mean if not that § 1981 may be asserted against state actors. Despite the persistence of this circuit split for more than twenty years, the Supreme Court has never resolved it. Why do you think that might be?

Meanwhile, the Supreme Court has extended § 1981 to another kind of claim: retaliation for complaining of race discrimination. *See CBOCS West, Inc. v. Humphries*, 553 U.S. 442, 451 (2008). The Court's holding rested on the legislative history of the 1991 Civil Rights Act and a comparison to § 1982, which nearly four decades earlier had been held to encompass a retaliation claim. Dissenting, Justice Scalia, joined by Justice Thomas, argued that the decision had no basis in the text of § 1981.

Regarding retaliation and harassment claims, then, § 1981 has come increasingly to resemble its modern counterpart for employment law claims, Title VII— albeit only for claims of race discrimination. We now turn to a comparison of both §§ 1981 and 1982 to overlapping antidiscrimination statutes passed a century later.

3. TWENTIETH-CENTURY COUNTERPARTS OF §§ 1981 AND 1982

The Fair Housing Act of 1968 went further in many ways than § 1982 and unsurprisingly has become the primary vehicle for enforcement of equal opportunity in housing. Among other things, the FHA prohibits refusing to sell or rent a dwelling, refusing to negotiate for the sale or rental of a dwelling, or discriminating in the terms or conditions or provisions of services or facilities in connection with the sale or rental of a dwelling, on the basis of race, color, religion, sex, familial status, or national origin. 42 U.S.C. § 3604(a)-(b). The FHA also prohibits advertising a dwelling for sale or rental in a manner that indicates a preference or limitation based on race, color, religion, sex, disability, familial status, or national origin. *Id.* § 3604(c).

Among the key differences between the FHA and § 1982 are:

- The FHA applies not only to race discrimination but also to discrimination based on color, religion, sex, familial status, or national origin.
- The FHA applies to housing advertisements as well as rental or sale arrangements themselves.

- The FHA does not cover (except as to advertising) "any single-family house sold or rented by an owner" (with certain exceptions to this exception) or "rooms or units in dwellings containing living quarters occupied or intended to be occupied by no more than four families living independently of each other, if the owner actually maintains and occupies one of such living quarters as his residence." 42 U.S.C. § 3603(b).
- The FHA exempts religious organizations and private clubs. 42 U.S.C. § 3607.
- The FHA provides two different parallel remedies—an administrative complaint procedure with the federal Department of Housing & Urban Development and a private right of action. 42 U.S.C. §§ 3610 & 3613.
- The FHA prohibits not only intentional discrimination ("disparate treatment") but also practices that have a disparate *impact* on the basis of a prohibited ground. *See Texas Dep't of Hous. & Cmty. Affairs v. Inclusive Communities Project, Inc.*, 135 S. Ct. 2507, 2525 (2015).

In light of these differences, why do you think Congress didn't either repeal § 1982 or meld § 1982 and the FHA into a single unified scheme? Why might Congress have wanted to retain the differences in coverage for discrimination based on race?

Just as § 1982 has declined in importance in the face of a more comprehensive modern statute, so too have some applications of § 1981 been eclipsed. Title VII of the Civil Rights Act of 1964 (42 U.S.C. § 2000e et seq.), bans employment discrimination not just on the basis of race, but also based on color, religion, sex, or national origin. (Certain other applications of § 1981 overlap other portions of the 1964 Civil Rights Act—such as Title VI, which prohibits race discrimination in federally funded programs, see Chapter 7, and Title II, which prohibits discrimination in public accommodations.)

Among the key differences between Title VII and § 1981 are:

- Title VII applies not only to race discrimination but also to discrimination based on color, religion, sex, and national origin.
- Title VII prohibits not just intentional discrimination ("disparate treatment") but also practices that have a disparate *impact* on the basis of a prohibited ground. *Compare* 42 U.S.C. § 2000e-2(k) (disparate impact provision of Title VII), *with Gen. Bldg. Contractors Ass'n, Inc. v. Pennsylvania*, 458 U.S. 375, 391 (1982) ("§ 1981, like the Equal Protection Clause, can be violated only by purposeful discrimination.").
- Title VII does not cover employers with fewer than fifteen employees. 42 U.S.C. § 2000e(b).
- Title VII creates a complex administrative scheme and exhaustion requirement, under which a complainant must file a charge with the Equal Employment Opportunity Commission and await its conciliation efforts and adjudication before the complainant can sue in court. 42 U.S.C. § 2000e-5.

- Title VII applies to governmental employers, *see Fitzpatrick v. Bitzer*, 427 U.S. 445, 447-48 (1976) (states); 42 U.S.C. § 2000e-16 (federal government), whereas (as noted in Section A.2, above) most circuits have held that § 1981 does not.
- Title VII claims may not be brought against individuals, such as a harassing supervisor; instead, plaintiffs must sue the corporations or entities that employ them, but these defendants are not always liable for the actions of their employees. (We examine Title VII rules for employer liability in Section B of this chapter.) By contrast, individuals have been held to be proper defendants under § 1981.

Why do you think Congress decided to maintain two parallel schemes for the prohibition on race discrimination in employment? Why would Congress choose a mandatory administrative regime for the enforcement of Title VII as opposed to the dual-track remedies available to plaintiffs under the FHA?

Note that unlike §§ 1981 and 1982, Title VII and the FHA both provide express causes of action. 42 U.S.C. § 2000e-5 (Title VII); 42 U.S.C. § 3613 (FHA).

In light of Title VII and the FHA, which do you think is used more frequently today, § 1981 or § 1982?

B. ENFORCING TITLE VII

Title VII is among the most important U.S. civil rights laws, and decisions interpreting its substantive provisions merit their own separate unit or course. In keeping with the focus of this book, we will examine the aspect of Title VII most critical to *enforcement* of its substantive antidiscrimination mandate: When can an employer be held liable for the discriminatory acts of its employees? This question is of even greater consequence than the vicarious liability question regarding municipal defendants under § 1983. In contrast to § 1983 litigation, which may be brought against either an offending official or a local government (under different standards), Title VII liability, courts of appeals have held, is available only against an employer. *See, e.g., Fantini v. Salem State Coll.*, 557 F.3d 22, 31 (1st Cir. 2009) (cataloguing and joining circuit consensus to this effect). Accordingly, the framework for employer liability determines not just whether the plaintiff can sue a deep pocket, but whether employees challenging discrimination by other employees (usually, supervisors)— rather than discrimination pursuant to an official corporate policy—can obtain any relief at all.

Note that in contrast to Title VII, § 1981 has been recognized as providing for individual liability. *See, e.g., Shott v. Katz*, 829 F.3d 494, 497 (7th Cir. 2016); *Whidbee v. Garzarelli Food Specialties, Inc.*, 223 F.3d 62, 75 (2d Cir. 2000) (collecting cases). Accordingly, race-discrimination plaintiffs may in some circumstances use § 1981 to name the individual responsible for the alleged discrimination and thereby avoid the limitations on Title VII liability explored in this section. However, as described in the previous section, § 1981 applies only to race discrimination.

1. THE TITLE VII FRAMEWORK FOR VICARIOUS LIABILITY

The Supreme Court began to address employers' liability for their employees' discriminatory conduct in *Meritor Savings Bank, FSB v. Vinson*, 477 U.S. 57 (1986). There, a bank teller alleged that she was coerced into a sexual relationship with and raped several times by her manager, Taylor.

Justice Rehnquist's opinion for the Court in *Meritor* was significant chiefly in recognizing that the creation of a hostile work environment based on a prohibited ground was actionable as discrimination under Title VII even if the plaintiff did not suffer a tangible employment consequence like demotion or discharge. *Meritor* also began to define the contours of employer liability for the actions of its employees:

> Although the District Court concluded that respondent had not proved a violation of Title VII, it nevertheless went on to consider the question of the bank's liability. Finding that "the bank was without notice" of Taylor's alleged conduct, and that notice to Taylor was not the equivalent of notice to the bank, the court concluded that the bank therefore could not be held liable for Taylor's alleged actions. The Court of Appeals took the opposite view, holding that an employer is strictly liable for a hostile environment created by a supervisor's sexual advances, even though the employer neither knew nor reasonably could have known of the alleged misconduct. The court held that a supervisor, whether or not he possesses the authority to hire, fire, or promote, is necessarily an "agent" of his employer for all Title VII purposes, since "even the appearance" of such authority may enable him to impose himself on his subordinates. . . .
>
> This debate over the appropriate standard for employer liability has a rather abstract quality about it given the state of the record in this case. . . .
>
> We therefore decline the parties' invitation to issue a definitive rule on employer liability, but we do agree with the EEOC that Congress wanted courts to look to agency principles for guidance in this area. While such common-law principles may not be transferable in all their particulars to Title VII, Congress' decision to define "employer" to include any "agent" of an employer, 42 U.S.C. § 2000e(b), surely evinces an intent to place some limits on the acts of employees for which employers under Title VII are to be held responsible. For this reason, we hold that the Court of Appeals erred in concluding that employers are always automatically liable for sexual harassment by their supervisors. *See generally* Restatement (Second) of Agency §§ 219-237. For the same reason, absence of notice to an employer does not necessarily insulate that employer from liability.
>
> Finally, we reject petitioner's view that the mere existence of a grievance procedure and a policy against discrimination, coupled with respondent's failure to invoke that procedure, must insulate petitioner from liability. While those facts are plainly relevant, the situation before us demonstrates why they are not necessarily dispositive. Petitioner's general nondiscrimination policy did not address sexual harassment in particular, and thus did not alert employees to their employer's interest in correcting that form of discrimination. Moreover, the bank's grievance procedure apparently required an employee to complain first to her supervisor, in this case Taylor. Since Taylor was the alleged perpetrator, it is not altogether surprising

that respondent failed to invoke the procedure and report her grievance to him. Petitioner's contention that respondent's failure should insulate it from liability might be substantially stronger if its procedures were better calculated to encourage victims of harassment to come forward.

Justice Marshall, joined by Justices Brennan, Blackmun, and Stevens, concurred in the judgment for the plaintiff, but would have reached the employer-liability question:

> The answer supplied by general Title VII law, like that supplied by federal labor law, is that the act of a supervisory employee or agent is imputed to the employer. Thus, for example, when a supervisor discriminatorily fires or refuses to promote a black employee, that act is, without more, considered the act of the employer. The courts do not stop to consider whether the employer otherwise had "notice" of the action, or even whether the supervisor had actual authority to act as he did.

Justice Stevens concurred briefly to say he found no inconsistency between the majority opinion and the concurrence.

Twelve years after *Meritor*, the Court again faced the subject of employer liability for a supervisor's misconduct. This time it provided much more thorough treatment.

Burlington Industries, Inc. v. Ellerth
524 U.S. 742 (1998)

■ *Justice KENNEDY delivered the opinion of the Court. . . .*

From March 1993 until May 1994, [Kimberly] Ellerth worked as a salesperson in one of Burlington's divisions in Chicago, Illinois. During her employment, she alleges, she was subjected to constant sexual harassment by her supervisor, one Ted Slowik [who was Ellerth's supervisor's supervisor]. . . .

Against a background of repeated boorish and offensive remarks and gestures which Slowik allegedly made, Ellerth places particular emphasis on three alleged incidents where Slowik's comments could be construed as threats to deny her tangible job benefits. In the summer of 1993, while on a business trip, Slowik invited Ellerth to the hotel lounge, an invitation Ellerth felt compelled to accept because Slowik was her boss. When Ellerth gave no encouragement to remarks Slowik made about her breasts, he told her to "loosen up" and warned, "you know, Kim, I could make your life very hard or very easy at Burlington."

In March 1994, when Ellerth was being considered for a promotion, Slowik expressed reservations during the promotion interview because she was not "loose enough." The comment was followed by his reaching over and rubbing her knee. Ellerth did receive the promotion; but when Slowik called to announce it, he told Ellerth, "you're gonna be out there with men who work in factories, and they certainly like women with pretty butts/legs."

In May 1994, Ellerth called Slowik, asking permission to insert a customer's logo into a fabric sample. Slowik responded, "I don't have time for you right now, Kim . . . —unless you want to tell me what you're wearing." Ellerth told Slowik she had to go and ended the call. A day or two later, Ellerth called Slowik to ask permission again. This time he denied her request, but added something along the lines of, "are you wearing shorter skirts yet, Kim, because it would make your job a whole heck of a lot easier." . . .

During her tenure at Burlington, Ellerth did not inform anyone in authority about Slowik's conduct, despite knowing Burlington had a policy against sexual harassment. In fact, she chose not to inform her immediate supervisor (not Slowik) because " 'it would be his duty as my supervisor to report any incidents of sexual harassment.' " On one occasion, she told Slowik a comment he made was inappropriate.

[Ultimately, Ellerth quit and, after exhausting her remedies with the EEOC, sued. The district court dismissed because she had not proved that Burlington knew or should have known about the harassment.] . . . The Court of Appeals en banc reversed in a decision which produced eight separate opinions and no consensus for a controlling rationale. . . . We granted certiorari to assist in defining the relevant standards of employer liability.

At the outset, we assume an important proposition . . . : A trier of fact could find in Slowik's remarks numerous threats to retaliate against Ellerth if she denied some sexual liberties. The threats, however, were not carried out or fulfilled. Cases based on threats which are carried out are referred to often as quid pro quo cases, as distinct from bothersome attentions or sexual remarks that are sufficiently severe or pervasive to create a hostile work environment. . . .

Title VII forbids "an employer—(1) to fail or refuse to hire or to discharge any individual, or otherwise to discriminate against any individual with respect to his compensation, terms, conditions, or privileges of employment, because of such individual's . . . sex." 42 U.S.C. § 2000e-2(a)(1).

"Quid pro quo" and "hostile work environment" do not appear in the statutory text. The terms . . . were mentioned in this Court's decision in *Meritor*.

In *Meritor*, the terms served a specific and limited purpose. There we considered whether the conduct in question constituted discrimination in the terms or conditions of employment in violation of Title VII. We assumed, and with adequate reason, that if an employer demanded sexual favors from an employee in return for a job benefit, discrimination with respect to terms or conditions of employment was explicit. Less obvious was whether an employer's sexually demeaning behavior altered terms or conditions of employment in violation of Title VII. We distinguished between quid pro quo claims and hostile environment claims, and said both were cognizable under Title VII, though the latter requires harassment that is severe or pervasive. The principal significance of the distinction is to instruct that Title VII is violated by either explicit or constructive alterations in the terms or conditions of employment and to explain the latter must be severe or pervasive. The distinction was not discussed for its bearing upon an employer's liability for an employee's discrimination. . . .

To the extent they illustrate the distinction between cases involving a threat which is carried out and offensive conduct in general, the terms are relevant when there is a threshold question whether a plaintiff can prove discrimination in violation of Title VII. When a plaintiff proves that a tangible employment action resulted from a refusal to submit to a supervisor's sexual demands, he or she establishes that the employment decision itself constitutes a change in the terms and conditions of employment that is actionable under Title VII. For any sexual harassment preceding the employment decision to be actionable, however, the conduct must be severe or pervasive. Because Ellerth's claim involves only unfulfilled threats, it should be categorized as a hostile work environment claim which requires a showing of severe or pervasive conduct. For purposes of this case, we accept the District Court's finding that the alleged conduct was severe or pervasive. . . .

We must decide, then, whether an employer has vicarious liability when a supervisor creates a hostile work environment by making explicit threats to alter a subordinate's terms or conditions of employment, based on sex, but does not fulfill the threat. We turn to principles of agency law, for the term "employer" is defined under Title VII to include "agents." In express terms, Congress has directed federal courts to interpret Title VII based on agency principles. . . .

[T]he Restatement (Second) of Agency is a useful beginning point for a discussion of general agency principles. . . .

Section 219(1) of the Restatement sets out a central principle of agency law: "A master is subject to liability for the torts of his servants committed while acting in the scope of their employment." . . .

As Courts of Appeals have recognized, a supervisor acting out of gender-based animus or a desire to fulfill sexual urges may not be actuated by a purpose to serve the employer. The harassing supervisor often acts for personal motives, motives unrelated and even antithetical to the objectives of the employer. . . . The general rule is that sexual harassment by a supervisor is not conduct within the scope of employment.

Scope of employment does not define the only basis for employer liability under agency principles. In limited circumstances, agency principles impose liability on employers even where employees commit torts outside the scope of employment. The principles are set forth in the much-cited § 219(2) of the Restatement:

> "(2) A master is not subject to liability for the torts of his servants acting outside the scope of their employment, unless:
>> "(a) the master intended the conduct or the consequences, or
>> "(b) the master was negligent or reckless, or
>> "(c) the conduct violated a non-delegable duty of the master, or
>> "(d) the servant purported to act or to speak on behalf of the principal and
> there was reliance upon apparent authority, or he was aided in accomplishing the tort by the existence of the agency relation."

Subsection (a) addresses direct liability, where the employer acts with tortious intent, and indirect liability, where the agent's high rank in the company makes him or her the employer's alter ego. None of the parties contend Slowik's rank imputes liability under this principle. There is no contention, furthermore, that a nondelegable duty is involved. See § 219(2)(c). So, for our purposes here, subsections (a) and (c) can be put aside.

Subsections (b) and (d) are possible grounds for imposing employer liability on account of a supervisor's acts and must be considered. Under subsection (b), an employer is liable when the tort is attributable to the employer's own negligence. § 219(2)(b). Thus, although a supervisor's sexual harassment is outside the scope of employment because the conduct was for personal motives, an employer can be liable, nonetheless, where its own negligence is a cause of the harassment. An employer is negligent with respect to sexual harassment if it knew or should have known about the conduct and failed to stop it. Negligence sets a minimum standard for employer liability under Title VII; but Ellerth seeks to invoke the more stringent standard of vicarious liability.

Section 219(2)(d) concerns vicarious liability for intentional torts committed by an employee when the employee uses apparent authority (the apparent authority standard), or when the employee "was aided in accomplishing the tort by the existence of the agency relation" (the aided in the agency relation standard). . . .

When a party seeks to impose vicarious liability based on an agent's misuse of delegated authority, the Restatement's aided in the agency relation rule, rather than the apparent authority rule, appears to be the appropriate form of analysis.

We turn to the aided in the agency relation standard. In a sense, most workplace tortfeasors are aided in accomplishing their tortious objective by the existence of the agency relation: Proximity and regular contact may afford a captive pool of potential victims. Were this to satisfy the aided in the agency relation standard, an employer would be subject to vicarious liability not only for all supervisor harassment, but also for all co-worker harassment, a result enforced by neither the EEOC nor any court of appeals to have considered the issue. The aided in the agency relation standard, therefore, requires the existence of something more than the employment relation itself.

At the outset, we can identify a class of cases where, beyond question, more than the mere existence of the employment relation aids in commission of the harassment: when a supervisor takes a tangible employment action against the subordinate. . . .

In the context of this case, a tangible employment action would have taken the form of a denial of a raise or a promotion. . . . A tangible employment action constitutes a significant change in employment status, such as hiring, firing, failing to promote, reassignment with significantly different responsibilities, or a decision causing a significant change in benefits.

When a supervisor makes a tangible employment decision, there is assurance the injury could not have been inflicted absent the agency relation. A tangible employment action in most cases inflicts direct economic harm. As a general proposition, only a supervisor, or other person acting with the authority of the company, can cause this sort of injury. A co-worker can break a co-worker's arm as easily as a supervisor, and anyone who has regular contact with an employee can inflict psychological injuries by his or her offensive conduct. But one co-worker (absent some elaborate scheme) cannot dock another's pay, nor can one co-worker demote another. Tangible employment actions fall within the special province of the supervisor. The supervisor has been empowered by the company as a distinct class of agent to make economic decisions affecting other employees under his or her control.

Tangible employment actions are the means by which the supervisor brings the official power of the enterprise to bear on subordinates. A tangible employment decision requires an official act of the enterprise, a company act. The decision in most cases is documented in official company records, and may be subject to review by higher level supervisors. The supervisor often must obtain the imprimatur of the enterprise and use its internal processes.

For these reasons, a tangible employment action taken by the supervisor becomes for Title VII purposes the act of the employer. Whatever the exact contours of the aided in the agency relation standard, its requirements will always be met when a supervisor takes a tangible employment action against a subordinate....

Whether the agency relation aids in commission of supervisor harassment which does not culminate in a tangible employment action is less obvious. . . . On the one hand, a supervisor's power and authority invests his or her harassing conduct with a particular threatening character, and in this sense, a supervisor always is aided by the agency relation. On the other hand, there are acts of harassment a supervisor might commit which might be the same acts a coemployee would commit, and there may be some circumstances where the supervisor's status makes little difference....

Although *Meritor* suggested the limitation on employer liability stemmed from agency principles, the Court acknowledged other considerations might be relevant as well. For example, Title VII is designed to encourage the creation of antiharassment policies and effective grievance mechanisms. Were employer liability to depend in part on an employer's effort to create such procedures, it would effect Congress' intention to promote conciliation rather than litigation in the Title VII context, and the EEOC's policy of encouraging the development of grievance procedures. To the extent limiting employer liability could encourage employees to report harassing conduct before it becomes severe or pervasive, it would also serve Title VII's deterrent purpose....

In order to accommodate the agency principles of vicarious liability for harm caused by misuse of supervisory authority, as well as Title VII's equally basic policies of encouraging forethought by employers and saving action by objecting employees, we adopt the following holding . . . [:] An employer is subject to vicarious liability to a victimized employee for an actionable hostile environment created by a supervisor with immediate (or successively higher) authority over the employee. When no tangible employment action is taken, a defending employer may raise an affirmative defense to liability or damages, subject to proof by a preponderance of the evidence. The defense comprises two necessary elements: (a) that the employer exercised reasonable care to prevent and correct promptly any sexually harassing behavior, and (b) that the plaintiff employee unreasonably failed to take advantage of any preventive or corrective opportunities provided by the employer or to avoid harm otherwise. While proof that an employer had promulgated an antiharassment policy with complaint procedure is not necessary in every instance as a matter of law, the need for a stated policy suitable to the employment circumstances may appropriately be addressed in any case when litigating the first element of the defense. And while proof that an employee failed to fulfill the corresponding obligation of reasonable care to avoid harm is not limited to showing any unreasonable failure to use any complaint procedure provided by the employer, a demonstration of such failure will normally suffice to satisfy the employer's burden under the second element of the defense. No affirmative defense is available, however, when the supervisor's harassment culminates in a tangible employment action, such as discharge, demotion, or undesirable reassignment. . . .

Although Ellerth has not alleged she suffered a tangible employment action at the hands of Slowik, which would deprive Burlington of the availability of the affirmative defense, this is not dispositive. In light of our decision, Burlington is still subject to vicarious liability for Slowik's activity, but Burlington should have an opportunity to assert and prove the affirmative defense to liability. . . .

[Opinion of Ginsburg, J., concurring in the judgment, omitted.]

■ *Justice THOMAS, with whom Justice SCALIA joins, dissenting.*

The Court today manufactures a rule that employers are vicariously liable if supervisors create a sexually hostile work environment, subject to an affirmative defense that the Court barely attempts to define. This rule applies even if the employer has a policy against sexual harassment, the employee knows about that policy, and the employee never informs anyone in a position of authority about the supervisor's conduct. . . . An employer should be liable if, and only if, the plaintiff proves that the employer was negligent in permitting the supervisor's conduct to occur. . . .

When a supervisor inflicts an adverse employment consequence upon an employee who has rebuffed his advances, the supervisor exercises the specific authority granted to him by his company. His acts, therefore, are the company's acts and are properly chargeable to it.

If a supervisor creates a hostile work environment, however, he does not act for the employer. As the Court concedes, a supervisor's creation of a hostile work environment is neither within the scope of his employment, nor part of his apparent authority. Indeed, a hostile work environment is antithetical to the interest of the employer. In such circumstances, an employer should be liable only if it has been negligent. That is, liability should attach only if the employer either knew, or in the exercise of reasonable care should have known, about the hostile work environment and failed to take remedial action.

Sexual harassment is simply not something that employers can wholly prevent without taking extraordinary measures—constant video and audio surveillance, for example—that would revolutionize the workplace in a manner incompatible with a free society. Indeed, such measures could not even detect incidents of harassment such as the comments Slowik allegedly made to respondent in a hotel bar. The most that employers can be charged with, therefore, is a duty to act reasonably under the circumstances. . . .

Rejecting a negligence standard, the Court instead imposes a rule of vicarious employer liability, subject to a vague affirmative defense, for the acts of supervisors who wield no delegated authority in creating a hostile work environment. This rule is a whole-cloth creation that draws no support from the legal principles on which the Court claims it is based. Compounding its error, the Court fails to explain how employers can rely upon the affirmative defense, thus ensuring a continuing reign of confusion in this important area of the law. . . .

Section 219(2)(d) of the Restatement provides no basis whatsoever for imposing vicarious liability for a supervisor's creation of a hostile work environment. . . . [L]iability under § 219(2)(d) depends upon the plaintiff's belief that the agent acted in the ordinary course of business or within the scope of his apparent authority. In this day and age, no sexually harassed employee can reasonably believe that a harassing supervisor is conducting the official business of the company or acting on its behalf. . . .

Thus although the Court implies that it has found guidance in both precedent and statute . . . its holding is a product of willful policymaking, pure and simple. . . .

Notes and Questions

1. *Ellerth* invokes and defines several Title VII terms of art, including quid pro quo harassment, hostile work environment, and tangible actions. Understanding these is vital to understanding the meaning of the decision.

   a. What is the difference between a "quid pro quo" and a "hostile environment" in terms of the type of harassment described by each? The Court explains that a quid pro quo violates Title VII in and of itself; by contrast, a hostile environment must rise to a certain threshold of seriousness before it constitutes a Title VII violation. What is that threshold? Note that this question is analytically distinct from the question of whether the employer is vicariously liable: The quid-pro-quo/hostile environment distinction is relevant to whether a Title VII violation exists in the first place.

   b. What distinguishes a "tangible" employment action from other employment actions? Under *Ellerth*, what are the implications for the employer's liability when a "tangible" action occurs?

2. In the absence of a "tangible" action, when is the employer liable for the acts of its supervisory employees?

3. What are the two elements of the *Ellerth* defense? Must the employer establish both to protect itself from liability?

4. Justice Thomas argues for a negligence standard in place of the rules set forth by the majority. Is the employee better off under the majority's standard or Justice Thomas's? Does negligence remain a basis for employer liability under the majority's standard?

5. Consider the content of the "unreasonably failed to take advantage" standard. What circumstances might render a failure to take advantage of a corrective opportunity "reasonable"?

6. The dissent charges the majority with imposing its own freewheeling policy judgment on Title VII. It seems hard to argue that the majority's standard— cobbled together from pieces of the Restatement and exceptions created to further particular congressional purposes—clearly followed from the text of the statute. Is Justice Thomas's proposed rule superior in this regard? How if at all could the Court have avoided making a policy choice of some kind?

7. Put yourself in the shoes of counsel for a large corporation. Looking at *Ellerth* alone, what would you do to shore up your ability to defend against claims of sexual harassment? How confident are you that your chosen course of action would enable your company to avoid liability? How does your answer to these questions affect your view of Justice Thomas's critique that the majority announces a vague standard that will create confusion?

8. How does the majority answer Justice Thomas's concern that preventing sexual harassment is effectively impossible without widespread employee surveillance—and perhaps not even then? Does the majority disagree with that premise, or with Justice Thomas's conclusion about the rule that should follow from it?

9. Federal statutes other than Title VII provide protections against employment discrimination based on age (the Age Discrimination in Employment Act) and disability (the Americans with Disabilities Act). These are generally construed in parallel with Title VII. For instance, although hostile work environment claims arise more often under Title VII, courts have applied *Ellerth* to hostile work environment claims based on disability, *see Silk v. City of Chicago*, 194 F.3d 788, 804 (7th Cir. 1999), and age, *see Stapp v. Curry Cty. Bd. of Cty. Comm'rs*, 672 Fed. App'x 841, 843 (10th Cir. 2016).

10. Recall from Chapter 1, Section D, that parallel state employment-discrimination statutes may sweep more broadly than Title VII, reaching more types of discrimination. States courts also differ regarding whether to follow the Supreme Court's *Ellerth* approach to vicarious liability. Some states have adopted *Ellerth*. *See, e.g., Frieler v. Carlson Mktg. Grp., Inc.*, 751 N.W.2d 558,

568 (Minn. 2008); *Aguas v. State*, 107 A.3d 1250, 1253 (N.J. 2015). Others have held that state common law or the wording of the state statute requires different results, which may be more or less employee-friendly than *Ellerth. Compare Zsigo v. Hurley Med. Ctr.*, 716 N.W.2d 220, 221 (Mich. 2006) (rejecting, as a matter of state common law, the aided-by-the-agency-relation rule from the Restatement (Second) of Agency § 219(2)(d)), *with State Dep't of Health Servs. v. Super. Ct.*, 79 P.3d 556, 563, 565-66 (Cal. 2003) (holding that state employment discrimination law does not incorporate agency principles, and applying common law doctrine of avoidable consequences to identify affirmative defense for employers similar to, but stricter than, *Ellerth*, and applicable only to reduce damages, not to shield the employer from liability).

Note: The "Severe or Pervasive" Requirement

The "severe or pervasive" requirement is relevant to whether, for a hostile environment claim, a Title VII violation has occurred, not whether an employer is liable for it.

Faragher v. City of Boca Raton, 524 U.S. 775 (1998), provided the following gloss on the "severe or pervasive" standard:

> [I]n order to be actionable under the statute, a sexually objectionable environment must be both objectively and subjectively offensive, one that a reasonable person would find hostile or abusive, and one that the victim in fact did perceive to be so. We directed courts to determine whether an environment is sufficiently hostile or abusive by "looking at all the circumstances," including the "frequency of the discriminatory conduct; its severity; whether it is physically threatening or humiliating, or a mere offensive utterance; and whether it unreasonably interferes with an employee's work performance." Most recently, we explained that Title VII does not prohibit "genuine but innocuous differences in the ways men and women routinely interact with members of the same sex and of the opposite sex." A recurring point in these opinions is that "simple teasing," offhand comments, and isolated incidents (unless extremely serious) will not amount to discriminatory changes in the "terms and conditions of employment."
>
> These standards for judging hostility are sufficiently demanding to ensure that Title VII does not become a "general civility code." Properly applied, they will filter out complaints attacking "the ordinary tribulations of the workplace, such as the sporadic use of abusive language, gender-related jokes, and occasional teasing." We have made it clear that conduct must be extreme to amount to a change in the terms and conditions of employment[.]

What is the appropriate reference point for judging severity and pervasiveness? If the *Ellerth* case arose today, in the wake of the revelations and allegations beginning in the fall of 2017 concerning sexual harassment by many influential and powerful men in a variety of professions, could Burlington plausibly assert that what happened to Kim Ellerth was relatively minor in comparison to the conduct of other sexual harassers and predators? Should such an argument be able to defeat a showing of severity or pervasiveness?

Courts applying the "severe or pervasive" requirement have reached varying results that are difficult to reconcile. In *Boyer-Liberto v. Fontainebleau Corp.*, 786 F.3d 264 (4th Cir. 2015) (en banc), the court noted that "viable hostile work environment claims often involve repeated conduct" but nonetheless held that, where an African-American waitress at a hotel nightclub was twice called a "porch monkey" and threatened with the loss of her job by a restaurant manager, a reasonable jury could find the conduct sufficiently "severe" to constitute a hostile environment. The majority characterized this slur as "about as odious as the use of" the n-word and recognized that a single, very serious incident could be sufficiently "severe" to create a hostile environment if a racial slur is directed at the plaintiff.

In *Zetwick v. Cty. of Yolo*, 850 F.3d 436, 438 (9th Cir. 2017), a female county correctional officer alleged that she had been hugged by the male county sheriff more than a hundred times over an eight-year period and was once kissed by him at an awards ceremony "ostensibly to congratulate Zetwick on her recent marriage to a sheriff's deputy" and "[t]he kiss landed on or, because Zetwick turned her head, partially on the lips." The plaintiff also alleged that the sheriff hugged other female officers but greeted male officers with a handshake, and that the sheriff once asked another female officer (not the plaintiff) how much she weighed and stared at the officer in a sexually suggestive manner. The sheriff argued that even the plaintiff described the hugs as the kind one might give a relative or friend; that the plaintiff hugged other male colleagues; and that the sheriff did not become aware of the plaintiff's discomfort until she filed a claim against him. The court held that the plaintiff had created a dispute sufficient to survive summary judgment.

In *Webb v. Kroger Ltd. Partnership I*, 2017 WL 607584 (W.D. Va. Feb. 14, 2017), the court granted summary judgment to the employer, holding that the plaintiff, a grocery-store supervisor, failed as a matter of law to reach the "severe or pervasive" threshold where she alleged that her manager made daily comments about her make-up, weight, and whether she was "taking care of [her] husband"; told the plaintiff she needed medication when she was not acting "feminine enough"; asked if she was "having PMS"; made comments about how "women use their womanly ways to get what they want" and how women should "stay home and raise babies"; made comments about how women in the store and parking lot looked; asked another female employee when he would see her legs in a skirt; once "popped" another female employee on the buttocks; and once stated, when yet another female employee was putting a bandage on her boyfriend's cut, something to the effect of, "that's exactly where men like to see women, on their knees in front of them." The court reasoned that the touching of an employee's buttocks and the "on their knees" comment were the most serious incidents, but they were isolated, and the rest of the comments "may have been more pervasive, but are far less severe," falling into the category of "offhand comments" or "simple teasing." The court explained, "Some rolling with the punches is a fact of workplace life. . . . While [Title VII] protects against sexual harassment, it does not reach mere boorishness or crude behavior."

What generalizations can you make from these cases about the meaning of "severe or pervasive"? About sexual harassment litigation generally?

Given the fact-intensive nature of the "severe or pervasive" analysis and the *Ellerth* defense, shouldn't a jury always decide these issues? What would be the costs of applying summary judgment more sparingly in this context?

Note: Title VII Remedies

Originally, Title VII provided only for equitable relief, not damages, but equitable relief was defined to include not only reinstatement and the cessation of unlawful discriminatory practices but also compensatory remedies like back pay and "front pay" (i.e., compensation for loss of future earnings). 42 U.S.C. § 2000e-5(g).

The Civil Rights Act of 1991 expanded the range of remedies for intentional discrimination (not disparate impact) to include additional types of compensatory damages (such as emotional harm, inconvenience, and other non-pecuniary losses) and punitive damages. Punitive damages are capped, may not be awarded against a governmental employer, and require a showing of "malice or . . . reckless indifference to the federally protected rights of an aggrieved individual." Confusingly, the provision of the 1991 Civil Rights Act adding these remedies has been codified as 42 U.S.C. § 1981a, which is distinct from 42 U.S.C. § 1981.

2. Applying *Ellerth*

The following cases illustrate how *Ellerth* works in practice, how courts treat supervisor harassment differently from coworker harassment, and how the standard may be evolving in light of changing societal understandings.

(a) **Elaborating on *Ellerth*.** Decided the same day as *Ellerth*, *Faragher v. City of Boca Raton*, 524 U.S. 775 (1998), announced the same rule flowing from the same agency principles; it also offered further guidance regarding some of the concepts central to *Ellerth*.

Faragher was an ocean lifeguard employed by the City of Boca Raton, Florida. Her two immediate supervisors, Terry and Silverman, created a "sexually hostile atmosphere" (as found by the district court after a bench trial) that included frequent uninvited touching of female lifeguards, lewd remarks to and about female lifeguards, suggestions that female lifeguards should have sex with the supervisors, lewd gestures, and Silverman's statement to Faragher, "Date me or clean the toilets for a year."

The district court entered judgment for Faragher on her Title VII claim; the Eleventh Circuit reversed because, among other things, the City did not know of the harassment.

The Supreme Court ordered that the district court's judgment for Faragher be reinstated. Justice Souter's opinion for the majority restated the holding in *Ellerth* and elaborated on the rationale for holding employers vicariously liable (subject to a defense):

> [I]n implementing Title VII it makes sense to hold an employer vicariously liable for some tortious conduct of a supervisor made possible by abuse of his supervisory authority, and . . . the aided-by-agency-relation principle embodied in § 219(2)(d)

of the Restatement provides an appropriate starting point for determining liability for the kind of harassment presented here. . . . [T]here is a sense in which a harassing supervisor is always assisted in his misconduct by the supervisory relationship. The agency relationship affords contact with an employee subjected to a supervisor's sexual harassment, and the victim may well be reluctant to accept the risks of blowing the whistle on a superior. When a person with supervisory authority discriminates in the terms and conditions of subordinates' employment, his actions necessarily draw upon his superior position over the people who report to him, or those under them, whereas an employee generally cannot check a supervisor's abusive conduct the same way that she might deal with abuse from a co-worker. When a fellow employee harasses, the victim can walk away or tell the offender where to go, but it may be difficult to offer such responses to a supervisor, whose "power to supervise—[which may be] to hire and fire, and to set work schedules and pay rates—does not disappear . . . when he chooses to harass through insults and offensive gestures rather than directly with threats of firing or promises of promotion." Estrich, *Sex at Work*, 43 Stan. L. Rev. 813, 854 (1991). Recognition of employer liability when discriminatory misuse of supervisory authority alters the terms and conditions of a victim's employment is underscored by the fact that the employer has a greater opportunity to guard against misconduct by supervisors than by common workers; employers have greater opportunity and incentive to screen them, train them, and monitor their performance.

Applying these principles, the Court held that the City could not make out the *Ellerth* affirmative defense on these facts:

> The District Court found that the City had entirely failed to disseminate its policy against sexual harassment among the beach employees and that its officials made no attempt to keep track of the conduct of supervisors like Terry and Silverman. The record also makes clear that the City's policy did not include any assurance that the harassing supervisors could be bypassed in registering complaints. Under such circumstances, we hold as a matter of law that the City could not be found to have exercised reasonable care to prevent the supervisors' harassing conduct. Unlike the employer of a small work force, who might expect that sufficient care to prevent tortious behavior could be exercised informally, those responsible for city operations could not reasonably have thought that precautions against hostile environments in any one of many departments in far-flung locations could be effective without communicating some formal policy against harassment, with a sensible complaint procedure.

As in *Ellerth*, Justice Thomas, joined by Justice Scalia, dissented and advocated for a negligence standard.

In what ways does *Faragher* illuminate the meaning of *Ellerth*? What concrete steps does it suggest employers ought to take? To what extent does it ameliorate the vagueness Justice Thomas found in *Ellerth*'s description of the rule?

(b) Fulfilled threats and "tangible" actions. One curiosity of the *Ellerth* majority's definition of "quid pro quo" is that it focuses on the fulfillment of threats. What if a person is asked to perform a sexual act or lose her job, and she accedes to the demand? The threat (of firing, for instance) has not been "carried out," yet the trade of a sexual act for continued employment literally constitutes a "quid pro quo" (Latin meaning "something for something"). Does acceding to a sexual demand under threat of firing constitute a "tangible" action within the meaning of *Ellerth*? Or is an employee who accedes to a concrete demand limited to a hostile work environment claim that may be defeated via the *Ellerth* defense?

Although the Supreme Court has never addressed these questions, the Courts of Appeals for the Second and Ninth Circuits have held that a "tangible employment action" occurs where a plaintiff accedes to a supervisor's demand for a sexual favor in order to avoid being fired. *Holly D. v. Cal. Inst. of Tech.*, 339 F.3d 1158, 1167 (9th Cir. 2003); *Jin v. Met. Life Ins. Co.*, 310 F.3d 84, 94 (2d Cir. 2002). The Second Circuit reasoned in *Jin*:

> Requiring an employee to engage in unwanted sex acts is one of the most pernicious and oppressive forms of sexual harassment that can occur in the workplace. . . . [T]his type of conduct—a classic quid pro quo for which courts have traditionally held employers liable—fits squarely within the definition of "tangible employment action" that the Supreme Court announced in *Faragher* and *Ellerth*.
>
> Here, Jin presented evidence that Morabito ordered her to submit to demeaning sexual acts, explicitly threatened to fire her if she did not submit, and then allowed her to keep her job after she submitted. Essentially, according to Jin, he used his authority to impose on her the added job requirement that she submit to weekly sexual abuse in order to retain her employment.
>
> The Court's analysis of agency principles in *Ellerth* illuminates why the facts at hand meet the tangible employment action threshold. It was Morabito's empowerment by MetLife as an agent who could make economic decisions affecting employees under his control that enabled him to force Jin to submit to his weekly sexual abuse. Another co-worker could not have so compelled Jin's acquiescence because a mere co-worker lacked the authority to either terminate or retain Jin based on her response to sexual demands. Also, that Morabito as a supervisor could require Jin to report to his private office where he could make his threats and carry on his abuses further supports the claim that his empowerment was as the company's agent.

Several district court decisions have taken a contrary view, *see, e.g., Santiero v. Denny's Restaurant Store*, 786 F. Supp. 2d 1228, 1234 (S.D. Tex. 2011), as has Judge Brown of the D.C. Circuit, *Lutkewitte v. Gonzales*, 436 F.3d 248, 271 (D.C. Cir. 2006) (Brown, J., concurring in the judgment). Judge Brown argued in *Lutkewitte*:

> For the current framework to be internally consistent, tangibility should be determined from the employer's perspective. If a supervisor threatens an employee, and she submits in order to avoid adverse consequences, the supervisor has not committed an "official act" but merely threatened to do so. The employer has no way of knowing that its delegated authority has been brandished in such a way as to coerce sexual submission. While it may still be liable in such a situation, *Faragher* and *Ellerth* dictate that it be given the opportunity to defend its conduct and demonstrate that any negligence was committed by the employee.

Is the Second and Ninth Circuits' position faithful to *Ellerth*? Why or why not? If Judge Brown is correct, what are the real-world consequences for the scope of Title VII?

(c) Supervisor versus coworker harassment.   In the racial harassment case *Vance v. Ball State University*, 570 U.S. 421 (2013), the Court explained that an employer is liable for harassment by a supervisor on different terms than it is liable for harassment by a coworker:

> [W]e have held that an employer is directly liable for an employee's unlawful harassment if the employer was negligent with respect to the offensive behavior. *Faragher*. Courts have generally applied this rule to evaluate employer liability when a coworker harasses the plaintiff.
>
> In *Ellerth* and *Faragher*, however, we held that different rules apply where the harassing employee is the plaintiff's "supervisor." In those instances, an employer may be *vicariously* liable for its employees' creation of a hostile work environment.

No Justice disagreed with this distinction; the debate between the majority and dissent concerned the narrower question of how to define a "supervisor" for purposes of the *Ellerth* defense.

Thus, after *Vance*, it is clear that an employer's liability for a hostile work environment depends on whether it was created by a supervisor (in which case the *Ellerth* framework applies) or by a coworker (in which case the plaintiff must show that the employer was negligent).

What reasons might justify applying a different standard for employer liability when the hostile environment was created by a coworker as opposed to a supervisor? Do you find the distinction persuasive?

(d) Harassment of employees by third parties.   Employers can be liable under a hostile-environment theory where the severe or pervasive harassment was perpetrated by a third party, like the employer's customer, rather than by other employees. Courts generally require plaintiffs in such cases to make a showing of negligence—that is, that the employer knew or should have known and failed to take corrective action—rather than applying the *Ellerth* framework. *See, e.g., Freeman v. Dal-Tile Corp.*, 750 F.3d 413, 422-23 (4th Cir. 2014) (harassment by independent contractor); *Watson v. Blue Circle, Inc.*, 324 F.3d 1252, 1259 (11th Cir. 2003) (harassment by employer's customers); *Turnbull v. Topeka State Hosp.*, 255 F.3d 1238, 1244 (10th Cir. 2001) (therapist was assaulted by patient).

Considering such conduct from the perspective of an employee, why should the law treat harassment by customers like harassment by coworkers rather than harassment by supervisors, particularly if employees are expected to cater to customers in a way they probably aren't to coworkers? Considering the issue from the perspective of the employer, it looks quite different: How do customers compare to the other two groups in terms of the employer's degree of control over them? Should courts adopt an employee's or employer's perspective when deciding which rules should govern new Title VII contexts? What considerations justify your answer? What considerations cut the other way?

(e) *Ellerth* evolving?   When is an employee's failure to complain about a hostile work environment reasonable? *Minarsky v. Susquehanna County*, 895 F.3d 303 (3d Cir. 2018), provides a new perspective on that question. Sheri Minarsky worked for a county Veterans Affairs Department, where she reported to Thomas Yadlosky. Her allegations included the following:

> Yadlosky would attempt to kiss her on the lips before he left each Friday, and would approach her from behind and embrace her, "pull[ing] [her] against him." When Minarsky was at her computer or the printer, Yadlosky would purportedly massage her shoulders or touch her face. She testified that these advances were unwanted, and happened frequently—nearly every week. As they worked together, alone, others were seldom present to observe Yadlosky's conduct, other than during the holiday season each year, when Yadlosky asked Minarsky and other female employees to kiss him under mistletoe.
>
> Yadlosky engaged in other non-physical conduct that Minarsky found disturbing. . . . He called her at home on her days off under the pretense of a work-related query but proceeded to ask personal questions. Yadlosky allegedly became hostile if she avoided answering these calls. He sent sexually explicit messages from his work email to Minarsky's work email, to which Minarsky did not respond.

For four years, Minarksy did not report Yadlosky's conduct. Ultimately, Minarsky emailed Yadlosky to express her discomfort. She also told a coworker, whose supervisor overheard the conversation and reported it to the County Commissioners. They fired Yadlosky.

A district court granted summary judgment against Minarsky on her Title VII claim for hostile work environment, holding that the County satisfied both prongs of *Ellerth*. The Third Circuit reversed. Its analysis of the second prong of the *Ellerth* test is notable. Although the County maintained a written anti-harassment policy and permitted employees to report harassment to a supervisor or (if the supervisor was the problem) the Chief Clerk or a County Commissioner, and the County ultimately fired Yadlosky, the Third Circuit found that summary judgment regarding the reasonableness of Minarsky's four-year delay in reporting was inappropriate:

> [O]ur case precedent has routinely found the passage of time coupled with the failure to take advantage of the employer's anti-harassment policy to be unreasonable, as did the District Court here.
>
> Nevertheless, we cannot ignore Minarsky's testimony as to why she did not report Yadlosky's conduct, and we believe that a jury could find that she did not act unreasonably under the circumstances.[12]

---

12. This appeal comes to us in the midst of national news regarding a veritable firestorm of allegations of rampant sexual misconduct that has been closeted for years, not reported by the victims. It has come to light, years later, that people in positions of power and celebrity have exploited their authority to make unwanted sexual advances. In many such instances, the harasser wielded control over the harassed individual's employment or work environment. In nearly all of the instances, the victims asserted a plausible fear of serious adverse consequences had they spoken up at the time that the conduct occurred. While the policy underlying *Faragher-Ellerth* places the onus on the harassed employee to report her harasser, and would fault her for not calling out this conduct so as to prevent it, a jury could conclude that the employee's non-reporting was understandable, perhaps even reasonable. That is, there may be a certain fallacy that underlies the notion that reporting sexual misconduct will end it. Victims do not always view it in this way. Instead, they anticipate negative consequences or fear that the harassers will face no reprimand; thus, more often than not, victims choose not to report the harassment.

Recent news articles report that studies have shown that not only is sex-based harassment in the workplace pervasive, but also the failure to report is widespread. Nearly one-third of American women have experienced unwanted sexual advances from male coworkers, and nearly a quarter of American women have experienced such advances from men who had influence over the conditions of their employment, according to an ABC News/Washington Post poll from October of 2017. Most all of the women who experienced harassment report that the male harassers faced no consequences.

Additionally, three out of four women who have been harassed fail to report it. A 2016 Equal Employment Opportunity Commission (EEOC) Select Task Force study found that approximately 75 percent of those who experienced harassment never reported it or filed a complaint, but instead would "avoid the harasser, deny or downplay the gravity of the situation, or attempt to ignore, forget, or endure the behavior." Those employees who faced harassing behavior did not report this experience "because they fear[ed] disbelief of their claim, inaction on their claim, blame, or social or professional retaliation."

Although we have often found that a plaintiff's outright failure to report persistent sexual harassment is unreasonable as a matter of law, particularly when the opportunity to make such complaints exists, we write to clarify that a mere failure to report one's harassment is not per se unreasonable. Moreover, the passage of time is just one factor in the analysis. Workplace sexual harassment is highly circumstance-specific, and thus the reasonableness of a plaintiff's actions is a paradigmatic question for the jury, in certain cases. If a plaintiff's genuinely held, subjective belief of potential retaliation from reporting her harassment appears to be well-founded, and a jury could find that this belief is objectively reasonable, the trial court should not find that the defendant has proven the second *Faragher-Ellerth* element as a matter of law. Instead, the court should leave the issue for the jury to determine at trial.

Here, Minarsky asserts several countervailing forces that prevented her from reporting Yadlosky's conduct to [the Chief Clerk] or a County Commissioner: her fear of Yadlosky's hostility on a day-to-day basis and retaliation by having her fired; her worry of being terminated by the Chief Clerk; and the futility of reporting, since others knew of his conduct, yet it continued. All of these factors were aggravated by the pressing financial situation she faced with her daughter's cancer treatment. . . .

Appellees argue that the superior-subordinate dynamic is unremarkable, because all *Faragher-Ellerth* cases involve a power imbalance wherein the harasser controls the working conditions of the harassed. We disagree that this is irrelevant; the degree of control and specific power dynamic can offer context to the plaintiff's subjectively held fear of speaking up . . . .

Second, when Minarsky attempted to assert herself in the workplace, she alleges that Yadlosky became "nasty," which deepened her fear of defending herself or disclosing Yadlosky's misconduct. For example, if she tried to request personal days off or ignored his phone calls on days she was not working, he became ill-tempered. . . .

Third, . . . Yadlosky discouraged her from using the anti-harassment policy by underscoring that she could not trust the Commissioners or the Chief Clerk—those to whom she would report the harassment. . . .

Fourth, Minarsky discovered that the County had known of Yadlosky's behavior [toward other women employees] and merely slapped him on the wrist, without more—bolstering Minarsky's claim that she feared the County would ignore any report she made. . . . A jury could find that Minarsky reasonably believed that availing herself of the anti-harassment policy would be futile, if not detrimental.

Fifth, a reasonable jury could consider the pernicious nature of the harassment compounded with its frequency and duration to contextualize Minarsky's actions. . . . Rather than view this merely as Minarsky's idle delay in reporting, a jury could consider the aggravating effect of prolonged, agonizing harassment as a way to credit Minarsky's fear of worsening her situation. . . .

A jury could consider this evidence and find her reaction to be objectively reasonable. We therefore cannot uphold the District Court's conclusion that Minarsky's behavior was unreasonable as a matter of law.

What do you think drove the result in *Minarsky*: the particular facts, or society's growing understanding since 2017 of the nature and extent of sexual harassment in the nation's workplaces? A combination of these? Do you expect future plaintiffs to successfully argue #MeToo? How will defense attorneys seeks to distinguish *Minarsky*?

More generally, does Title VII need updating in terms of when employer liability is available? Or would a series of decisions like *Minarsky* be sufficient to bring the twenty-year-old *Ellerth* framework into the modern era?

CHAPTER 6 PROBLEMS

Problem 6A. J'mae Carter and Ray Ronaldgan are new employees at the Douglass Commonwealth Department of Education (DCDOE), a state agency. They both start the same day, June 1. Their supervisor is Harman S. Trury, who is white. Carter is African-American. Ronaldgan is white. Trury has divided his staff into teams, which he has whimsically named after animals—the Giraffes, the Lions, the Monkeys, and so forth. Trury assigns Carter to the "Monkeys," whose members are all African-American. Trury assigns Ronaldgan to the "Lions." Ronaldgan and Carter meet at the end of their first week and compare their experiences. They discover the Lions have more responsibility than the Monkeys.

The next day, Ronaldgan texts Carter, "Wanna go out Friday?" She replies, "You're sweet, but no thanks. Focusing on work and the gym, no time for dates! LOL." He then texts her a picture of his genitalia, with the message, "Look what you're missing!" She is taken aback and doesn't respond. He texts her again with a similar picture and the message, "Did you get my text? Or is it so big it can't go through? LOL!" To the second message, she responds, "Ray, please stop." He stops for a week, then resumes sending Carter similar messages throughout their first month of work.

DCDOE policy, which is distributed to all employees at the beginning of every fiscal year on October 1, states that "all conduct that violates Title VII of the Civil Rights Act of 1964 is prohibited" and that Title VII violations should be reported "immediately to the state Equal Employment Opportunity" (EEO) office.

Carter complains to Trury about being assigned to the all-black "Monkeys" team with lesser responsibility and about Ronaldgan's graphic texts. Trury laughs off the complaints, saying the animal names are "just for fun," the different level of work responsibility is happenstance, and that it seems she is successfully ignoring Ronaldgan so she doesn't need Trury's help.

Feeling demoralized by her work assignments and the team name, and uncomfortable with Ronaldgan's continued graphic texts, Carter quits. After exhausting her administrative remedies, she sues DCDOE under Title VII and 42 U.S.C. § 1981. Are Carter's claims likely to succeed?

Problem 6B.   The town of Penn Quarter is home to many federal buildings, including the headquarters of the FBI. The Penn Quarter Police Department (PQPD) employs Sergeant Taylor Zachary as its federal security liaison to coordinate security operations between PQPD and federal officers that protect federal buildings. Zachary's supervisor at PQPD is Lieutenant Hayes Rutherford.

After a short while working together, Rutherford starts staring at Zachary whenever he passes her in the hallway. After this happens regularly for a few weeks, Zachary asks why Rutherford is looking at her like that. Rutherford responds that Zachary is beautiful. Embarrassed, Zachary hurries away.

The following week, Rutherford leaves Zachary flowers on her desk. Feeling uncomfortable, Zachary throws the flowers in the trash. The week after that, Rutherford leaves a cookie on Zachary's desk every day, with suggestive notes like "Eat me!" and "Sugar for my sugar!" Over the course of several months, Rutherford continues to indicate his interest in Zachary in similar ways, and she ignores the advances. The unwanted attention from Rutherford causes Zachary sleepless nights and exacerbates ulcers that she suffers.

After enduring four months of unwanted advances, Zachary reads the PQPD personnel policy. There is a strict policy against workplace harassment. PQPD also has a procedure for complaining about harassment: An employee may complain either to her immediate supervisor or to that person's supervisor. PQPD policy requires that, "in order to facilitate prompt resolution of issues," all complaints must be raised within three months of the beginning of the harassing conduct. Zachary decides to try complaining anyway.

Because of the cooperative federal-local arrangement, Rutherford's supervisor is an employee of the U.S. Department of Homeland Security (DHS), Special Agent Arthur Chester. Zachary goes directly to Chester with her concerns about Rutherford's behavior. Chester listens politely to Zachary's concerns but says nothing.

The next day, Zachary learns that she is being transferred out of her role as federal security liaison and into new role focused on handling protest permits for PQPD, with the same level of pay and benefits. Angry to have been transferred out of a role she liked, she demands an explanation from Chester. Chester says that he made the recommendation to Rutherford to transfer her "to avoid further discomfort for anyone."

After exhausting her administrative remedies under Title VII, Zachary sues Rutherford and Penn Quarter for violating Title VII.

1. What conduct can Zachary sue for? What remedies can she seek? What defenses will each defendant raise? Will they succeed?

2. *(Reviewing Chapters 2, 4, and 5.)* Imagine Zachary also raises constitutional claims against Rutherford, the town of Penn Quarter, Chester, and DHS for violating her constitutional equal protection rights by discriminating based on sex. (Assume that no Title VII claim lies against DHS because it is not Zachary's employer.) What are the causes of action against each of these defendants? Before reaching the merits, what obstacles must Zachary overcome? What more information do you need to know to determine which of these claims might succeed? Compare Zachary's chances of success on her constitutional claims with her chances on the Title VII claims.

Implied Rights of Action

Thus far, we have mainly studied civil rights causes of action that Congress explicitly provided by statute, such as § 1983 (Chapter 1) and Title VII (Chapter 6). We have also studied one cause of action (*Bivens*, in Chapter 2) that the Court recognized without reference to a statute, and two (§§ 1981 and 1982, in Chapter 6) whose existence the Court basically took for granted with little or no analysis. This chapter examines the Court's considered approach to recognizing causes of actions arising from civil rights statutes that don't explicitly create them ("implied rights of action")—and how the Court has gone about defining the contours of such actions.

Implied rights of action have been recognized for statutes of all kinds. The most important implied rights of action in the civil rights context arise from Title VI of the Civil Rights Act of 1964 and Title IX of the Education Amendments of 1972 (which are generally referred to simply as "Title VI" and "Title IX" respectively, even though they are sections of different laws).

Particularly for students who have not studied Congress's Spending Power, a brief description of that power will help students understand the operation of Titles VI and IX. Both laws prohibit discrimination—based on race, color, or national origin, in the case of Title VI, and based on sex, in the case of Title IX—in all (Title VI) or some (Title IX) programs receiving federal funds.

Title VI, 42 U.S.C. § 2000d, provides:

> No person in the United States shall, on the ground of race, color, or national origin, be excluded from participation in, be denied the benefits of, or be subjected to discrimination under any program or activity receiving Federal financial assistance.

Title IX, 20 U.S.C. § 1681(a), provides:

> No person in the United States shall, on the basis of sex, be excluded from participation in, be denied the benefits of, or be subjected to discrimination under any education program or activity receiving Federal financial assistance [with a number of specified exceptions].

The exceptions in Title IX include, among others, traditionally single-sex schools, the military, religious schools, boys' and girls' clubs like the Boy and Girl Scouts, fraternities and sororities, and beauty pageants.

The following passages, excerpted from cases we'll study in this chapter, discuss how Titles VI and IX operate as "spending conditions" on the use of federal funds. (The discussion of Title IX here applies to Title VI as well.)

> The two statutes operate in the same manner, conditioning an offer of federal funding on a promise by the recipient not to discriminate, in what amounts essentially to a contract between the Government and the recipient of funds.
>
> That contractual framework distinguishes Title IX from Title VII, which is framed in terms not of a condition but of an outright prohibition. Title VII applies to all employers without regard to federal funding[.]

Gebser v. Lago Vista Indep. Sch. Dist., 524 U.S. 274, 286 (1998).

> [Title IX] was enacted under the Spending Clause of the Constitution, U.S. Const. art. I, § 8, cl. 1 ("The Congress shall have Power To lay and collect Taxes . . . to . . . provide for the . . . general Welfare of the United States"). As a federal spending program, [Title IX] operates "much in the nature of a contract: in return for federal funds, the States agree to comply with federally imposed conditions." . . .
>
> Because of the mutuality required in a contractual relationship of this type—the federal grant in exchange for state agreement to attached conditions—the legitimacy of the attached conditions rests "on whether the State voluntarily and knowingly accepts the terms of the 'contract.'" Thus, Spending Clause legislation . . . presents a state with a choice: the state can either comply with certain congressionally mandated conditions in exchange for federal funds or not comply and decline the funds. . . .
>
> As a general proposition . . . when Congress acts pursuant to its spending power, there is no categorical prohibition against its attaching conditions to grants made to the states.
>
> This mechanism for exercising power under the Spending Clause, however, must have limits. Otherwise, Congress "could render academic the Constitution's other grants and limits of federal authority." Indeed, an unlimited Spending Clause power could circumvent the entire constitutional structure. . . .
>
> [One limitation is that] if the grant or expenditure is, when made to the states, accompanied by conditions, the conditions must be stated "unambiguously."

Litman v. George Mason Univ., 186 F.3d 544, 551-52 (4th Cir. 1999).

The cases deciding whether Titles VI and IX create implied rights of action and defining the contours of such actions rely in part on the characteristics of spending conditions.

The first section of the chapter covers the question of when the Court will recognize an implied right of action. The second section examines the contours of private civil actions under Titles VI and IX.

A. RECOGNIZING A CAUSE OF ACTION

The Supreme Court's test for recognizing an implied right of action has evolved significantly over time. When it recognized causes of action to enforce Titles VI and IX, the Court was far more open to finding such actions than it is today.

1. FINDING IMPLIED RIGHTS OF ACTION FOR TITLES VI AND IX

Although it is not a civil rights case, *Cort v. Ash*, 422 U.S. 66 (1975), is a useful starting place for our study of implied rights of action, because it exemplified the Court's approach to discerning implied rights of action when the Court considered that question regarding Titles VI and IX in the 1970s. The issue in *Cort* was whether a federal criminal statute prohibiting certain election contributions or expenditures by corporations created an implied right of action under which a corporation's shareholders could sue its directors. The Court found no cause of action, applying this multi-factor test:

> In determining whether a private remedy is implicit in a statute not expressly providing one, several factors are relevant. First, is the plaintiff "one of the class for whose especial benefit the statute was enacted"—that is, does the statute create a federal right in favor of the plaintiff? Second, is there any indication of legislative intent, explicit or implicit, either to create such a remedy or to deny one? Third, is it consistent with the underlying purposes of the legislative scheme to imply such a remedy for the plaintiff? And finally, is the cause of action one traditionally relegated to state law, in an area basically the concern of the States, so that it would be inappropriate to infer a cause of action based solely on federal law?

Note that the focus of the first three considerations is legislative intent. The fourth factor requires a judgment based on history and policy. Given the focus on these questions rather than statutory text, you may not be surprised that the Supreme Court ultimately abandoned the *Cort* approach. But long before it did so, the Court decided whether Titles VI and IX implied private rights of action. We begin with these cases, the first of which predates *Cort* and the second of which applies *Cort*.

Lau v. Nichols
414 U.S. 563 (1974)

■ *Mr. Justice DOUGLAS delivered the opinion of the Court.*

The San Francisco, California, school system was integrated in 1971 as a result of a federal court decree. The District Court found that there are 2,856 students of Chinese ancestry in the school system who do not speak English. Of those who have that language deficiency, about 1,000 are given supplemental courses in the English language. About 1,800, however, do not receive that instruction.

This class suit brought by non-English-speaking Chinese students against officials responsible for the operation of the San Francisco Unified School District seeks relief against the unequal educational opportunities, which are alleged to violate, inter alia, the Fourteenth Amendment. No specific remedy is urged upon us. Teaching English to the students of Chinese ancestry who do not speak the language is one choice. Giving instructions to this group in Chinese is another. There may be others. Petitioners ask only that the Board of Education be directed to apply its expertise to the problem and rectify the situation. . . .

[T]here is no equality of treatment merely by providing students with the same facilities, textbooks, teachers, and curriculum; for students who do not understand English are effectively foreclosed from any meaningful education.

Basic English skills are at the very core of what these public schools teach. Imposition of a requirement that, before a child can effectively participate in the educational program, he must already have acquired those basic skills is to make a mockery of public education. We know that those who do not understand English are certain to find their classroom experiences wholly incomprehensible and in no way meaningful.

We do not reach the Equal Protection Clause argument which has been advanced but rely solely on § 601 [in Title VI] of the Civil Rights Act of 1964, 42 U.S.C. § 2000d . . . .

That section bans discrimination based "on the ground of race, color, or national origin," in "any program or activity receiving Federal financial assistance." The school district involved in this litigation receives large amounts of federal financial assistance. The Department of Health, Education, and Welfare (HEW), which has authority to promulgate regulations prohibiting discrimination in federally assisted school systems, 42 U.S.C. § 2000d-1, in 1968 issued one guideline that "(s)chool systems are responsible for assuring that students of a particular race, color, or national origin are not denied the opportunity to obtain the education generally obtained by other students in the system." In 1970 HEW made the guidelines more specific, requiring school districts that were federally funded "to rectify the language deficiency in order to open" the instruction to students who had "linguistic deficiencies."

By § 602 of the Act HEW is authorized to issue rules, regulations, and orders to make sure that recipients of federal aid under its jurisdiction conduct any federally financed projects consistently with § 601. . . .

Discrimination among students on account of race or national origin that is prohibited includes "discrimination . . . in the availability or use of any academic . . . or other facilities of the grantee or other recipient." 45 C.F.R. § 80.5(b) (HEW regulation).

Discrimination is barred which has that effect even though no purposeful design is present: a recipient "may not . . . utilize criteria or methods of administration which have the effect of subjecting individuals to discrimination" or have "the effect of defeating or substantially impairing accomplishment of the objectives of the program as respect individuals of a particular race, color, or national origin." Id., § 80.3(b)(2).

It seems obvious that the Chinese-speaking minority receive fewer benefits than the English-speaking majority from respondents' school system which denies them a meaningful opportunity to participate in the educational program—all earmarks of the discrimination banned by the regulations. In 1970 HEW issued clarifying guidelines, which include the following:

"Where inability to speak and understand the English language excludes national origin-minority group children from effective participation in the educational program offered by a school district, the district must take affirmative steps to rectify the language deficiency in order to open its instructional program to these students."

"Any ability grouping or tracking system employed by the school system to deal with the special language skill needs of national origin-minority group children must be designed to meet such language skill needs as soon as possible and must not operate as an educational deadend or permanent track."

Respondent school district contractually agreed to "comply with title VI of the Civil Rights Act of 1964 . . . and all requirements imposed by or pursuant to the Regulation" of HEW (45 CFR pt. 80) which are "issued pursuant to that title . . ." and also immediately to "take any measures necessary to effectuate this agreement." . . . Senator Humphrey, during the floor debates on the Civil Rights Act of 1964, said:

"Simple justice requires that public funds, to which all taxpayers of all races contribute, not be spent in any fashion which encourages, entrenches, subsidizes, or results in racial discrimination."

We accordingly reverse the judgment of the Court of Appeals and remand the case for the fashioning of appropriate relief.

Mr. Justice WHITE concurs in the result.

■ *Mr. Justice STEWART, with whom THE CHIEF JUSTICE and Mr. Justice BLACKMUN join, concurring in the result.*

It is uncontested that more than 2,800 schoolchildren of Chinese ancestry attend school in the San Francisco Unified School District system even though they do not speak, understand, read, or write the English language, and that as to some 1,800 of these pupils the respondent school authorities have taken no significant steps to deal with this language deficiency. The petitioners do not contend, however, that the respondents have affirmatively or intentionally contributed to this inadequacy, but only that they have failed to act in the face of changing social and linguistic patterns. Because of this laissez-faire attitude on the part of the school administrators, it is not entirely clear that § 601 of the Civil Rights Act of 1964, 42 U.S.C. § 2000d, standing alone, would render illegal the expenditure of federal funds on these schools. For that section provides that "(n)o person in the United States shall, on the ground of race, color, or national origin, be excluded from participation in, be denied the benefits of, or be subjected to discrimination under any program or activity receiving Federal financial assistance."

On the other hand, the interpretive guidelines published by the Office for Civil Rights of the Department of Health, Education, and Welfare in 1970 clearly indicate that affirmative efforts to give special training for non-English-speaking pupils are required by Tit. VI as a condition to receipt of federal aid to public schools . . . .

The critical question is, therefore, whether the regulations and guidelines promulgated by HEW go beyond the authority of § 601. [We have held] that the validity of a regulation promulgated under a general authorization provision such as § 602 of Tit. VI "will be sustained so long as it is 'reasonably related to the purposes of the enabling legislation.'" I think the guidelines here fairly meet that test. Moreover, in assessing the purposes of remedial legislation we have found that departmental regulations and "consistent administrative construction" are "entitled to great weight." The Department has reasonably and consistently interpreted § 601 to require affirmative remedial efforts to give special attention to linguistically deprived children.

For these reasons I concur in the result reached by the Court.

[Opinion of Blackmun, J., joined by Burger, C.J., concurring in the result, omitted.]

Notes and Questions

1. What is the basis for the Court's holding in *Lau*—§ 601, § 602, or the regulations? Some combination of these?

2. What does the majority say about whether the plaintiffs have a private cause of action? What is the majority's assumption about the relationship between rights and remedies?

3. Justice Stewart is much clearer than the majority about where he locates the right being enforced. What consequences flow from his theory? Which government entity's power would be expanded under his view?

* * *

In permitting a private suit to enforce Title VI, *Lau* was cryptic about precisely where the cause of action was found and why. The next case faces these questions squarely in the context of the similarly worded Title IX.

Cannon v. University of Chicago
441 U.S. 677 (1979)

■ *Mr. Justice STEVENS delivered the opinion of the Court.*

Petitioner's complaints allege that her applications for admission to medical school were denied by the respondents because she is a woman. Accepting the truth of those allegations for the purpose of its decision, the Court of Appeals held that petitioner has no right of action against respondents that may be asserted in a federal court. We granted certiorari to review that holding.

Only two facts alleged in the complaints are relevant to our decision. First, petitioner was excluded from participation in the respondents' medical education programs because of her sex. Second, these education programs were receiving federal financial assistance at the time of her exclusion. These facts, admitted *arguendo* by respondents' motion to dismiss the complaints, establish a violation of § 901(a) of Title IX of the Education Amendments of 1972 (hereinafter Title IX).[2]

That section, in relevant part, provides:

> "No person in the United States shall, on the basis of sex, be excluded from participation in, be denied the benefits of, or be subjected to discrimination under any education program or activity receiving Federal financial assistance . . . ."

The statute does not, however, expressly authorize a private right of action by a person injured by a violation of § 901. [For that reason, the district court dismissed the case.] . . .

The Court of Appeals agreed that the statute did not contain an implied private remedy. . . .

As our recent cases—particularly *Cort v. Ash*—demonstrate, the fact that a federal statute has been violated and some person harmed does not automatically give rise to a private cause of action in favor of that person. Instead, before concluding that Congress intended to make a remedy available to a special class of litigants, a court must carefully analyze the four factors that *Cort* identifies as indicative of such an intent. . . .

First, the threshold question under *Cort* is whether the statute was enacted for the benefit of a special class of which the plaintiff is a member. That question is answered by looking to the language of the statute itself. . . .

The language in these statutes—which expressly identifies the class Congress intended to benefit—contrasts sharply with statutory language customarily found in criminal statutes, such as that construed in *Cort*, and other laws enacted for the protection of the general public.[13] There would be far less reason to infer a private remedy in favor of individual persons if Congress, instead of drafting Title IX with an unmistakable focus on the benefited class, had written it simply as a ban on discriminatory conduct by recipients of federal funds or as a prohibition against the disbursement of public funds to educational institutions engaged in discriminatory practices. . . .

---

2. . . . Both medical schools receive federal aid, and both have policies against admitting applicants who are more than 30 years old (petitioner was 39 years old at the time she applied), at least if they do not have advanced degrees. . . . These policies, it is alleged, prevented petitioner from being asked to an interview at the medical schools. . . . Because the incidence of interrupted higher education is higher among women than among men, it is further claimed, the age and advanced-degree criteria operate to exclude women from consideration even though the criteria are not valid predictors of success in medical schools or in medical practice. As such, the existence of the criteria either makes out or evidences a violation of the medical school's duty under Title IX to avoid discrimination on the basis of sex. . . .

13. Not surprisingly, the right- or duty-creating language of the statute has generally been the most accurate indicator of the propriety of implication of a cause of action. . . .

Second, the *Cort* analysis requires consideration of legislative history. . . . [T]he history of Title IX rather plainly indicates that Congress intended to create such a remedy.

Title IX was patterned after Title VI of the Civil Rights Act of 1964. Except for the substitution of the word "sex" in Title IX to replace the words "race, color, or national origin" in Title VI, the two statutes use identical language to describe the benefited class. Both statutes provide the same administrative mechanism for terminating federal financial support for institutions engaged in prohibited discrimination. Neither statute expressly mentions a private remedy for the person excluded from participation in a federally funded program. The drafters of Title IX explicitly assumed that it would be interpreted and applied as Title VI had been during the preceding eight years.

In 1972 when Title IX was enacted, the critical language in Title VI had already been construed as creating a private remedy. . . . It is always appropriate to assume that our elected representatives, like other citizens, know the law; in this case, because of their repeated references to Title VI and its modes of enforcement, we are especially justified in presuming both that those representatives were aware of the prior interpretation of Title VI and that that interpretation reflects their intent with respect to Title IX. . . .

Finally, the very persistence—before 1972 and since, among judges and executive officials, as well as among litigants and their counsel, and even implicit in decisions of this Court[33]—of the assumption that both Title VI and Title IX created a private right of action for the victims of illegal discrimination and the absence of legislative action to change that assumption provide further evidence that Congress at least acquiesces in, and apparently affirms, that assumption. . . .

Third, under *Cort*, a private remedy should not be implied if it would frustrate the underlying purpose of the legislative scheme. On the other hand, when that remedy is necessary or at least helpful to the accomplishment of the statutory purpose, the Court is decidedly receptive to its implication under the statute.

Title IX, like its model Title VI, sought to accomplish two related, but nevertheless somewhat different, objectives. First, Congress wanted to avoid the use of federal resources to support discriminatory practices; second, it wanted to provide individual citizens effective protection against those practices. Both of these purposes were repeatedly identified in the debates on the two statutes.

The first purpose is generally served by the statutory procedure for the termination of federal financial support for institutions engaged in discriminatory practices. That remedy is, however, severe and often may not provide an appropriate means of accomplishing the second purpose if merely an isolated

---

33. Since 1972, the Court has twice reached the merits in suits brought by private litigants to enforce Title VI [including *Lau v. Nichols*]. In both cases it determined that Title VI justified at least some of the relief sought by the private litigants. Although in neither case did the Court in terms address the question of whether Title VI provides a cause of action, in both the issue had been explicitly raised by the parties at one level of the litigation or another. These cases are accordingly consistent, at least, with the widely accepted assumption that Title VI creates a private cause of action. . . .

violation has occurred. In that situation, the violation might be remedied more efficiently by an order requiring an institution to accept an applicant who had been improperly excluded. Moreover, in that kind of situation it makes little sense to impose on an individual, whose only interest is in obtaining a benefit for herself, or on HEW, the burden of demonstrating that an institution's practices are so pervasively discriminatory that a complete cut-off of federal funding is appropriate. The award of individual relief to a private litigant who has prosecuted her own suit is not only sensible but is also fully consistent with—and in some cases even necessary to—the orderly enforcement of the statute....

Fourth, the final inquiry suggested by *Cort* is whether implying a federal remedy is inappropriate because the subject matter involves an area basically of concern to the States. No such problem is raised by a prohibition against invidious discrimination of any sort, including that on the basis of sex. Since the Civil War, the Federal Government and the federal courts have been the "*'primary* and powerful reliances'" in protecting citizens against such discrimination. Moreover, it is the expenditure of federal funds that provides the justification for this particular statutory prohibition. There can be no question but that this aspect of the *Cort* analysis supports the implication of a private federal remedy....

Respondents' principal argument against implying a cause of action under Title IX is that it is unwise to subject admissions decisions of universities to judicial scrutiny at the behest of disappointed applicants on a case-by-case basis. They argue that this kind of litigation is burdensome and inevitably will have an adverse effect on the independence of members of university committees.

This argument is not original to this litigation. It was forcefully advanced in both 1964 and 1972 by the congressional opponents of Title VI and Title IX, and squarely rejected by the congressional majorities that passed the two statutes. In short, respondents' principal contention is not a legal argument at all; it addresses a policy issue that Congress has already resolved.

History has borne out the judgment of Congress. Although victims of discrimination on the basis of race, religion, or national origin have had private Title VI remedies available at least since 1965, respondents have not come forward with any demonstration that Title VI litigation has been so costly or voluminous that either the academic community or the courts have been unduly burdened. Nothing but speculation supports the argument that university administrators will be so concerned about the risk of litigation that they will fail to discharge their important responsibilities in an independent and professional manner....

The fact that other provisions of a complex statutory scheme create express remedies has not been accepted as a sufficient reason for refusing to imply an otherwise appropriate remedy under a separate section. Rather, the Court has generally avoided this type of "excursion into extrapolation of legislative intent," unless there is other, more convincing, evidence that Congress meant to exclude the remedy....

When Congress intends private litigants to have a cause of action to support their statutory rights, the far better course is for it to specify as much when it creates those rights. But the Court has long recognized that under certain limited circumstances the failure of Congress to do so is not inconsistent with an intent on its part to have such a remedy available to the persons benefited by its legislation. Title IX presents the atypical situation in which *all* of the circumstances that the Court has previously identified as supportive of an implied remedy are present. We therefore conclude that petitioner may maintain her lawsuit, despite the absence of any express authorization for it in the statute. . . .

Mr. Chief Justice BURGER *concurs in the judgment.*

■ Mr. Justice REHNQUIST, *with whom Mr. Justice* STEWART *joins, concurring.* . . .

[T]he Court's opinion demonstrates that Congress, at least during the period of the enactment of the several Titles of the Civil Rights Act tended to rely to a large extent on the courts to *decide* whether there should be a private right of action, rather than determining this question for itself. . . .

I fully agree with the Court's statement that "[w]hen Congress intends private litigants to have a cause of action to support their statutory rights, the far better course is for it to specify as much when it creates those rights." . . . Not only is it "far better" for Congress to so specify when it intends private litigants to have a cause of action, but for this very reason this Court in the future should be extremely reluctant to imply a cause of action absent such specificity on the part of the Legislative Branch.

■ Mr. Justice WHITE, *with whom Mr. Justice* BLACKMUN *joins, dissenting.* . . .

The Court recognizes that because Title IX was explicitly patterned after Title VI of the Civil Rights Act of 1964, it is difficult to infer a private cause of action in the former but not in the latter. [I would infer one in neither case.] Rather, the legislative history, like the terms of Title VI itself, makes it abundantly clear that the Act was and is a mandate to federal agencies to eliminate discrimination in federally funded programs. Although there was no intention to cut back on private remedies existing under 42 U.S.C. § 1983 to challenge discrimination occurring under color of state law, there is no basis for concluding that Congress contemplated the creation of private remedies either against private parties who previously had been subject to no constitutional or statutory obligation not to discriminate, or against federal officials or agencies involved in funding allegedly discriminatory programs.

The Court argues that because funding termination, authorized by § 602, 42 U.S.C. § 2000d-1, is a drastic remedy, Congress must have contemplated private suits in order directly and less intrusively to terminate the discrimination allegedly being practiced by the recipient institutions. But the Court's conclusion does not follow from its premise because funding termination was not contemplated as the only—or even the primary—agency action to end discrimination. Rather, Congress considered termination of financial assistance to be a remedy of last resort, and expressly obligated federal agencies to take measures to terminate discrimination without resorting to termination of funding. . . .

Far from conferring new private authority to enforce the federal policy of nondiscrimination, Title VI contemplated agency action to be the principal mechanism for achieving this end. The proponents of Title VI stressed that it did not "confer sweeping new authority, of undefined scope, to Federal departments and agencies," but instead was intended to require the exercise of existing authority to end discrimination by fund recipients, and to furnish the procedure for this purpose. Thus, § 601 states the federal policy of nondiscrimination, and § 602 mandates that the agencies achieve compliance by refusing to grant or continue assistance or by "any other means authorized by law." Under § 602, cutting off funds is forbidden unless the agency determines "that compliance cannot be secured by voluntary means." . . .

To be sure, Congress contemplated that there would be litigation brought to enforce Title VI. The "other means" provisions of § 602 include agency suits to enforce contractual antidiscrimination provisions and compliance with agency regulations, as well as suits brought by the Department of Justice under Title IV of the 1964 Act, where the recipient is a public entity. Congress also knew that there would be private suits to enforce § 601; but these suits were not authorized by § 601 itself but by 42 U.S.C. § 1983. Every excerpt from the legislative history cited by the Court shows full awareness that private suits could redress discrimination contrary to the Constitution and Title VI, if the discrimination were imposed by public agencies; not one statement suggests contemplation of lawsuits against recipients not acting under color of state law. . . .

■ *Mr. Justice POWELL, dissenting.*

I agree with Mr. Justice White that even under the standards articulated in our prior decisions, it is clear that no private action should be implied here. . . . But as mounting evidence from the courts below suggests, and the decision of the Court today demonstrates, the mode of analysis we have applied in the recent past cannot be squared with the doctrine of the separation of powers. The time has come to reappraise our standards for the judicial implication of private causes of action.

Under Art. III, Congress alone has the responsibility for determining the jurisdiction of the lower federal courts. As the Legislative Branch, Congress also should determine when private parties are to be given causes of action under legislation it adopts. As countless statutes demonstrate, including Titles of the Civil Rights Act of 1964, Congress recognizes that the creation of private actions is a legislative function and frequently exercises it. When Congress chooses not to provide a private civil remedy, federal courts should not assume the legislative role of creating such a remedy and thereby enlarge their jurisdiction. . . .

Whether every disappointed applicant for admission to a college or university receiving federal funds has the right to a civil-court remedy under Title IX is likely to be a matter of interest to many of the thousands of rejected applicants. It certainly is a question of vast importance to the entire higher educational community of this country. But . . . respect for our constitutional system dictates that the issue should have been resolved by the elected representatives in Congress after public hearings, debate, and legislative decision. It is not a question properly to be decided by relatively uninformed federal judges who are isolated from the political process.

In recent history, the Court has tended to stray from the Art. III and separation-of-powers principle of limited jurisdiction. This, I believe, is evident from a review of the more or less haphazard line of cases that led to our decision in *Cort v. Ash*. The "four factor" analysis of that case is an open invitation to federal courts to legislate causes of action not authorized by Congress. It is an analysis not faithful to constitutional principles and should be rejected. Absent the most compelling evidence of affirmative congressional intent, a federal court should not infer a private cause of action. . . .

Notes and Questions

1. Accepting the majority's premise that the implied-right-of-action question turns on congressional intent, what is the most persuasive evidence the Court cites in support of intent to create a cause of action?

2. What is the role of the funding-withdrawal mechanism in the Court's decision? Is the Court overstepping its authority in making assumptions about the shortcomings of Congress's *explicit* remedy to justify finding an *implicit* one?

3. Two of the separate opinions—Justice Rehnquist's and Justice Powell's—express discomfort with the whole enterprise of inferring causes of action. Why do they differ as to the result they reach here? How would the majority respond to the argument that Congress should just say what it means and not rely on or expect the courts to create enforcement mechanisms not specified in the statute?

4. What would be the effect of adopting Justice White's approach to the statute? Which recipients of federal funds would be subject to Title IX suits, and would would not?

5. In some respects, at the heart of this case is a clash between text and history. The text of the statute does not specify a private cause of action, yet it's understandable why Congress would have thought it was creating one, or authorizing the Court to create one, in light of precedent. How should proponents of judicial restraint approach this conflict? How does the majority approach it?

6. The private causes of action in Titles VI and IX are not subject to an exhaustion requirement. *See Fitzgerald v. Barnstable School Comm.*, 555 U.S. 246 (2009). Should the Court have created one, in light of the fact that the explicit remedies provided in the statutes lie with federal agencies, not the courts?

7. The Court's analogy between Titles VI and IX has proved durable. Throughout its jurisprudence, it has continued to treat interpretations of one as equally applicable to the other.

2. A NEW APPROACH TO IMPLIED RIGHTS OF ACTION

As the introductory discussion of *Cort* foreshadows, the Supreme Court has in recent years taken a very different view of implied rights of action—one more in line with the Court's increasing emphasis on statutory text and skepticism of legislative intent as a guide to statutory interpretation. Additionally, the unease expressed by Justices Powell and Rehnquist with the entire project of judicially inferring causes of action has come to be shared by a majority of the Court. One manifestation of that view is the Court's increasing hostility toward *Bivens* (see Chapter 2)—another type of "implied" cause of action (albeit implied in the Constitution itself). The next case reflects the effect of these jurisprudential trends on the interpretation of Title VI (and by analogy, Title IX).

Alexander v. Sandoval
532 U.S. 275 (2001)

■ *Justice SCALIA delivered the opinion of the Court.*

This case presents the question whether private individuals may sue to enforce disparate-impact regulations promulgated under Title VI of the Civil Rights Act of 1964.

The Alabama Department of Public Safety (Department), of which petitioner James Alexander is the director, accepted grants of financial assistance from the United States Department of Justice (DOJ) and Department of Transportation (DOT) and so subjected itself to the restrictions of Title VI of the Civil Rights Act of 1964. Section 601 of that Title provides that no person shall, "on the ground of race, color, or national origin, be excluded from participation in, be denied the benefits of, or be subjected to discrimination under any program or activity" covered by Title VI. Section 602 authorizes federal agencies "to effectuate the provisions of [§ 601] . . . by issuing rules, regulations, or orders of general applicability," 42 U.S.C. § 2000d-1, and the DOJ in an exercise of this authority promulgated a regulation forbidding funding recipients to "utilize criteria or methods of administration which have the effect of subjecting individuals to discrimination because of their race, color, or national origin . . . ." 28 CFR § 42.104(b)(2) (2000). See also 49 CFR § 21.5(b)(2) (2000) (similar DOT regulation).

The State of Alabama amended its Constitution in 1990 to declare English "the official language of the state of Alabama." Pursuant to this provision and, petitioners have argued, to advance public safety, the Department decided to administer state driver's license examinations only in English. Respondent Sandoval, as representative of a class, brought suit . . . to enjoin the English-only policy, arguing that it violated the DOJ regulation because it had the effect of subjecting non-English speakers to discrimination based on their national origin. . . .

Although Title VI has often come to this Court, it is fair to say (indeed, perhaps an understatement) that our opinions have not eliminated all uncertainty regarding its commands. For purposes of the present case, however, it is clear from our decisions, from Congress's amendments of Title VI, and from the parties' concessions that three aspects of Title VI must be taken as given. First, private individuals may sue to enforce § 601 of Title VI and obtain both injunctive relief and damages. . . .

Second, it is similarly beyond dispute—and no party disagrees—that § 601 prohibits only intentional discrimination. . . .

Third, we must assume for purposes of deciding this case that regulations promulgated under § 602 of Title VI may validly proscribe activities that have a disparate impact on racial groups, even though such activities are permissible under § 601 [because the petitioners have not challenged the regulations].

Respondents assert that the issue in this case, like the first two described above, has been resolved by [*Cannon*]. . . . [But] *Cannon* was decided on the assumption that the University of Chicago had intentionally discriminated against petitioner. It therefore *held* that Title IX created a private right of action to enforce its ban on intentional discrimination, but had no occasion to consider whether the right reached regulations barring disparate-impact discrimination. . . .

Nor does it follow straightaway from the three points we have taken as given that Congress must have intended a private right of action to enforce disparate-impact regulations. We do not doubt that regulations applying § 601's ban on intentional discrimination are covered by the cause of action to enforce that section. . . . The Title VI regulations at issue in *Lau*, similar to the ones at issue here, forbade funding recipients to take actions which had the effect of discriminating on the basis of race, color, or national origin. Unlike our later cases, however, the Court in *Lau* interpreted § 601 itself to proscribe disparate-impact discrimination, saying that it "rel[ied] solely on § 601 . . . to reverse the Court of Appeals," and that the disparate-impact regulations simply "[made] sure that recipients of federal aid . . . conduct[ed] any federally financed projects consistently with § 601."[5]

We must face now the question avoided by *Lau*, because we have since rejected *Lau*'s interpretation of § 601 as reaching beyond intentional discrimination. It is clear now that the disparate-impact regulations do not simply apply § 601—since they indeed forbid conduct that § 601 permits—and therefore clear that the private right of action to enforce § 601 does not include a private right to enforce these regulations. That right must come, if at all, from the independent force of § 602. As stated earlier, we assume for purposes of this decision that § 602 confers the authority to promulgate disparate-impact regulations; the question remains whether it confers a private right of action to enforce them.

---

5. It is true, as the dissent points out, that three Justices who concurred in the result in *Lau* relied on regulations promulgated under § 602 to support their position. But the five Justices who made up the majority did not . . . .

If not, we must conclude that a failure to comply with regulations promulgated under § 602 that is not also a failure to comply with § 601 is not actionable.

Implicit in our discussion thus far has been a particular understanding of the genesis of private causes of action. Like substantive federal law itself, private rights of action to enforce federal law must be created by Congress. The judicial task is to interpret the statute Congress has passed to determine whether it displays an intent to create not just a private right but also a private remedy. Statutory intent on this latter point is determinative. Without it, a cause of action does not exist and courts may not create one, no matter how desirable that might be as a policy matter, or how compatible with the statute. . . .

[We disagree] with the Government that our cases interpreting statutes enacted prior to *Cort v. Ash* have given "dispositive weight" to the "expectations" that the enacting Congress had formed "in light of the 'contemporary legal context.'" Only three of our legion implied-right-of-action cases have found this sort of "contemporary legal context" relevant, and two of those involved Congress's enactment (or reenactment) of the verbatim statutory text that courts had previously interpreted to create a private right of action. See [e.g.] *Cannon*. We have never accorded dispositive weight to context shorn of text. In determining whether statutes create private rights of action, as in interpreting statutes generally, legal context matters only to the extent it clarifies text.

We therefore begin (and find that we can end) our search for Congress's intent with the text and structure of Title VI. Section 602 authorizes federal agencies "to effectuate the provisions of [§ 601] . . . by issuing rules, regulations, or orders of general applicability." 42 U.S.C. § 2000d-1. It is immediately clear that the "rights-creating" language so critical to the Court's analysis in *Cannon* of § 601 is completely absent from § 602. Whereas § 601 decrees that "[n]o person . . . shall . . . be subjected to discrimination," the text of § 602 provides that "[e]ach Federal department and agency . . . is authorized and directed to effectuate the provisions of [§ 601]." Far from displaying congressional intent to create new rights, § 602 limits agencies to "effectuat[ing]" rights already created by § 601. And the focus of § 602 is twice removed from the individuals who will ultimately benefit from Title VI's protection. Statutes that focus on the person regulated rather than the individuals protected create "no implication of an intent to confer rights on a particular class of persons." Section 602 is yet a step further removed: It focuses neither on the individuals protected nor even on the funding recipients being regulated, but on the agencies that will do the regulating. . . . So far as we can tell, this authorizing portion of § 602 reveals no congressional intent to create a private right of action.

Nor do the methods that § 602 goes on to provide for enforcing its authorized regulations manifest an intent to create a private remedy; if anything, they suggest the opposite. Section 602 empowers agencies to enforce their regulations either by terminating funding to the "particular program, or part thereof," that has violated the regulation or "by any other means authorized by law." No enforcement action may be taken, however, "until the department or agency concerned has advised the appropriate person or persons of the failure to comply with the requirement and has determined that compliance cannot be secured by voluntary means." And every agency enforcement action is subject to judicial review. If an agency attempts to terminate program funding, still more restrictions apply. The agency head must "file with the committees of the House and Senate having legislative jurisdiction over the program or activity involved a full written report of the circumstances and the grounds for such action." And the termination of funding does not "become effective until thirty days have elapsed after the filing of such report." Whatever these elaborate restrictions on agency enforcement may imply for the private enforcement of rights created *outside* of § 602, they tend to contradict a congressional intent to create privately enforceable rights through § 602 itself. The express provision of one method of enforcing a substantive rule suggests that Congress intended to preclude others. Sometimes the suggestion is so strong that it precludes a finding of congressional intent to create a private right of action, even though other aspects of the statute (such as language making the would-be plaintiff "a member of the class for whose benefit the statute was enacted") suggest the contrary. . . . In the present case, the claim of exclusivity for the express remedial scheme does not even have to overcome such obstacles. The question whether § 602's remedial scheme can overbear other evidence of congressional intent is simply not presented, since we have found no evidence anywhere in the text to suggest that Congress intended to create a private right to enforce regulations promulgated under § 602.

Both the Government and respondents argue that the *regulations* contain rights-creating language and so must be privately enforceable, but that argument skips an analytical step. Language in a regulation may invoke a private right of action that Congress through statutory text created, but it may not create a right that Congress has not. Thus, when a statute has provided a general authorization for private enforcement of regulations, it may perhaps be correct that the intent displayed in each regulation can determine whether or not it is privately enforceable. But it is most certainly incorrect to say that language in a regulation can conjure up a private cause of action that has not been authorized by Congress. Agencies may play the sorcerer's apprentice but not the sorcerer himself. . . .

Neither as originally enacted nor as later amended does Title VI display an intent to create a freestanding private right of action to enforce regulations promulgated under § 602. We therefore hold that no such right of action exists. . . . The judgment of the Court of Appeals is reversed.

▨ *Justice* STEVENS, *with whom Justice* SOUTER, *Justice* GINSBURG, *and Justice* BREYER *join, dissenting.* . . .

Today, in a decision unfounded in our precedent and hostile to decades of settled expectations, a majority of this Court carves out an important exception to the right of private action long recognized under Title VI. . . .

When this Court faced an identical case 27 years ago, all the Justices believed that private parties could bring lawsuits under Title VI and its implementing regulations to enjoin the provision of governmental services in a manner that discriminated against non-English speakers. *See Lau.* While five Justices saw no need to go beyond the command of § 601, Chief Justice Burger, Justice Stewart, and Justice Blackmun relied specifically and exclusively on the regulations to support the private action. There is nothing in the majority's opinion in *Lau,* or in earlier opinions of the Court, that is not fully consistent with the analysis of the concurring Justices or that would have differentiated between private actions to enforce the text of § 601 and private actions to enforce the regulations promulgated pursuant to § 602.

Five years later, we more explicitly considered whether a private right of action exists to enforce the guarantees of Title VI and its gender-based twin, Title IX. *See Cannon.* . . . *Cannon* was itself a disparate-impact case. In that case, the plaintiff brought suit against two private universities challenging medical school admissions policies that set age limits for applicants. Plaintiff, a 39-year-old woman, alleged that these rules had the effect of discriminating against women because the incidence of interrupted higher education is higher among women than among men. In providing a shorthand description of her claim in the text of the opinion, we ambiguously stated that she had alleged that she was denied admission "because she is a woman," but we appended a lengthy footnote setting forth the details of her disparate-impact claim. Other than the short-hand description of her claim, there is not a word in the text of the opinion even suggesting that she had made the improbable allegation that the University of Chicago and Northwestern University had intentionally discriminated against women. . . .

[T]o the extent that the majority denies relief to the respondents merely because they neglected to mention 42 U.S.C. § 1983 in framing their Title VI claim, this case is something of a sport. Litigants who in the future wish to enforce the Title VI regulations against state actors in all likelihood must only reference § 1983 to obtain relief. . . .

The majority's statutory analysis does violence to both the text and the structure of Title VI. Section 601 does not stand in isolation, but rather as part of an integrated remedial scheme. Section 602 exists for the sole purpose of forwarding the antidiscrimination ideals laid out in § 601. The majority's persistent belief that the two sections somehow forward different agendas finds no support in the statute. Nor does Title VI anywhere suggest, let alone state, that for the purpose of determining their legal effect, the "rules, regulations, [and] orders of general applicability" adopted by the agencies are to be bifurcated by the Judiciary into two categories based on how closely the courts believe the regulations track the text of § 601. . . .

For three decades, we have treated § 602 as granting the responsible agencies the power to issue broad prophylactic rules aimed at realizing the vision laid out in § 601, even if the conduct captured by these rules is at times broader than that which would otherwise be prohibited. . . .

This understanding is firmly rooted in the text of Title VI. As § 602 explicitly states, the agencies are authorized to adopt regulations to "effectuate" § 601's antidiscrimination mandate. The plain meaning of the text reveals Congress' intent to provide the relevant agencies with sufficient authority to transform the statute's broad aspiration into social reality. So too does a lengthy, consistent, and impassioned legislative history.

This legislative design reflects a reasonable—indeed inspired—model for attacking the often-intractable problem of racial and ethnic discrimination. On its own terms, the statute supports an action challenging policies of federal grantees that explicitly or unambiguously violate antidiscrimination norms (such as policies that on their face limit benefits or services to certain races). With regard to more subtle forms of discrimination (such as schemes that limit benefits or services on ostensibly race-neutral grounds but have the predictable and perhaps intended consequence of materially benefiting some races at the expense of others), the statute does not establish a static approach but instead empowers the relevant agencies to evaluate social circumstances to determine whether there is a need for stronger measures. Such an approach builds into the law flexibility, an ability to make nuanced assessments of complex social realities, and an admirable willingness to credit the possibility of progress.

The "effects" regulations at issue in this case represent the considered judgment of the relevant agencies that discrimination on the basis of race, ethnicity, and national origin by federal contractees are significant social problems that might be remedied, or at least ameliorated, by the application of a broad prophylactic rule. Given the judgment underlying them, the regulations are inspired by, at the service of, and inseparably intertwined with § 601's antidiscrimination mandate. Contrary to the majority's suggestion, they "appl[y]" § 601's prohibition on discrimination just as surely as the intentional discrimination regulations the majority concedes are privately enforceable. . . .

At the time Congress was considering Title VI, it was normal practice for the courts to infer that Congress intended a private right of action whenever it passed a statute designed to protect a particular class that did not contain enforcement mechanisms which would be thwarted by a private remedy. Indeed, the very year Congress adopted Title VI, this Court specifically stated that "it is the duty of the courts to be alert to provide such remedies as are necessary to make effective the congressional purpose." Assuming, as we must, that Congress was fully informed as to the state of the law, the contemporary context presents important evidence as to Congress' intent—evidence the majority declines to consider. . . .

[The Court] attaches significance to the fact that the "rights-creating" language in § 601 that defines the classes protected by the statute is not repeated in § 602. But, of course, there was no reason to put that language in § 602 because it is perfectly obvious that the regulations authorized by § 602 must be designed to protect precisely the same people protected by § 601. Moreover, it is self-evident that, linguistic niceties notwithstanding, any statutory provision whose stated purpose is to "effectuate" the eradication of racial and ethnic discrimination has as its "focus" those individuals who, absent such legislation, would be subject to discrimination.

[And] the Court repeats the argument advanced and rejected in *Cannon* that the express provision of a fund cutoff remedy "suggests that Congress intended to preclude others." In *Cannon,* we carefully explained why the presence of an explicit mechanism to achieve one of the statute's objectives (ensuring that federal funds are not used "to support discriminatory practices") does not preclude a conclusion that a private right of action was intended to achieve the statute's other principal objective ("to provide individual citizens effective protection against those practices"). . . . In today's decision, the Court does not grapple with—indeed, barely acknowledges—our rejection of this argument in *Cannon.*

Like much else in its opinion, the present majority's unwillingness to explain its refusal to find the reasoning in *Cannon* persuasive suggests that today's decision is the unconscious product of the majority's profound distaste for implied causes of action rather than an attempt to discern the intent of the Congress that enacted Title VI of the Civil Rights Act of 1964. . . .

Notes and Questions

1. What must a plaintiff show after *Sandoval* to use an implied cause of action to enforce a regulation? How easy is that showing to make?

2. What is "rights creating language," and what is its role in reflecting congressional intent, according to the majority? According to the dissent? How has the significance of rights-creating language transformed since *Cannon*'s reference to it in its footnote 13?

3. What if anything remains of the *Cort v. Ash* approach (exemplified by *Cannon*) after *Sandoval*?

4. As between the majority and the dissent, which has the more persuasive understanding of *Lau*? Of *Cannon*?

5. As Justice Stevens protests, the 1964 Congress legislated against a set of background legal rules quite different from those of *Sandoval.* And, of course, the opinions of Justices Powell and Rehnquist in *Cannon,* suggesting that Congress should not expect the Court to find implied rights of action going forward, came fifteen years too late to provide guidance to the 1964 Congress. Shouldn't *that* Congress have been entitled to rely on the law at that time—just as qualified immunity permits officers to rely on the law at the time they acted? How do you think the majority would respond to this criticism?

6. How far does *Sandoval* go? What are its implications beyond agency-created rights? Under what circumstances can you imagine the methodology of *Sandoval* yielding a future holding that *Congress* created an implied cause of action?

7. As we saw in Chapter 1, Section D, there are important differences between federal civil rights law and the civil rights laws in some states. The approach to implied rights of action is no exception. Even after *Sandoval,* some state courts asking whether their own statutes imply a cause of action have continued to use

an inquiry more like *Cort v. Ash. See, e.g., Shumate v. Drake Univ.*, 846 N.W.2d 503, 508 (Iowa 2014) (declining to reconsider four-factor test after *Sandoval*); *Asylum Hill Problem Solving Revitalization Ass'n v. King*, 890 A.2d 522, 527-28 (Conn. 2006) (continuing to apply three-factor test adapted from *Cort*).

B. THE CONTOURS OF ACTIONS UNDER TITLES VI AND IX

Although *Sandoval* mostly, if not entirely, shuts the door on future pleas to recognize implied rights of action, whether in statutes or regulations, *Sandoval* does not cast doubt on the rights of action the Court has already recognized to enforce Titles VI and IX.

Once recognized, the implied rights of actions to enforce Titles VI and IX prompted additional questions. Were damages available? Against which defendants? In what circumstances? This section explores the Court's answers to these questions.

1. WHAT REMEDIES ARE AVAILABLE?

In *Lau* and *Cannon*, plaintiffs challenged ongoing policies that they claimed violated Titles VI or IX. But some plaintiffs seek redress for past harms alone. May they obtain damages?

Franklin v. Gwinnett County Public Schools
503 U.S. 60 (1992)

▪ *Justice* WHITE *delivered the opinion of the Court.*

This case presents the question whether the implied right of action under Title IX of the Education Amendments of 1972, 20 U.S.C. §§ 1681-1688, which this Court recognized in *Cannon v. University of Chicago*, supports a claim for monetary damages.

Petitioner Christine Franklin was a student at North Gwinnett High School in Gwinnett County, Georgia, between September 1985 and August 1989. Respondent Gwinnett County School District operates the high school and receives federal funds. According to the complaint . . ., Franklin was subjected to continual sexual harassment beginning in the autumn of her tenth grade year (1986) from Andrew Hill, a sports coach and teacher employed by the district. Among other allegations, Franklin avers that Hill . . . forcibly kissed her on the mouth in the school parking lot, that he telephoned her at her home and asked if she would meet him socially, and that, on three occasions in her junior year, Hill interrupted a class, requested that the teacher excuse Franklin, and took her to a private office where he subjected her to coercive intercourse. The complaint further alleges that though they became aware of and investigated Hill's sexual harassment of Franklin and other female students, teachers and administrators took no action to halt it and discouraged Franklin from pressing charges against Hill. On April 14, 1988, Hill resigned on the condition that all matters pending against him be dropped. The school thereupon closed its investigation.

In this action, the District Court dismissed the complaint on the ground that Title IX does not authorize an award of damages. The Court of Appeals affirmed. . . .

In *Cannon*, the Court held that Title IX is enforceable through an implied right of action. We have no occasion here to reconsider that decision. Rather, in this case we must decide what remedies are available in a suit brought pursuant to this implied right. As we have often stated, the question of what remedies are available under a statute that provides a private right of action is "analytically distinct" from the issue of whether such a right exists in the first place. Thus, although we examine the text and history of a statute to determine whether Congress intended to create a right of action, we presume the availability of all appropriate remedies unless Congress has expressly indicated otherwise. This principle has deep roots in our jurisprudence. . . .

From the earliest years of the Republic, the Court has recognized the power of the Judiciary to award appropriate remedies to redress injuries actionable in federal court, although it did not always distinguish clearly between a right to bring suit and a remedy available under such a right. In *Marbury v. Madison*, for example, Chief Justice Marshall observed that our Government "has been emphatically termed a government of laws, and not of men. It will certainly cease to deserve this high appellation, if the laws furnish no remedy for the violation of a vested legal right." This principle originated in the English common law, and Blackstone described it as "a general and indisputable rule, that where there is a legal right, there is also a legal remedy, by suit or action at law, whenever that right is invaded." . . .

We now address whether Congress intended to limit application of this general principle in the enforcement of Title IX. Because the cause of action was inferred by the Court in *Cannon*, the usual recourse to statutory text and legislative history in the period prior to that decision necessarily will not enlighten our analysis. Respondents and the United States fundamentally misunderstand the nature of the inquiry, therefore, by needlessly dedicating large portions of their briefs to discussions of how the text and legislative intent behind Title IX are "silent" on the issue of available remedies. Since the Court in *Cannon* concluded that this statute supported no express right of action, it is hardly surprising that Congress also said nothing about the applicable remedies for an implied right of action. . . .

Our reading of the two amendments to Title IX enacted after *Cannon* leads us to conclude that Congress did not intend to limit the remedies available in a suit brought under Title IX. In the Rehabilitation Act Amendments of 1986, 42 U.S.C. § 2000d-7, Congress abrogated the States' Eleventh Amendment immunity under Title IX, Title VI, § 504 of the Rehabilitation Act of 1973, and the Age Discrimination Act of 1975. This statute cannot be read except as a validation of

Cannon's holding. A subsection of the 1986 law provides that in a suit against a State, "remedies (including remedies both at law and in equity) are available for such a violation to the same extent as such remedies are available for such a violation in the suit against any public or private entity other than a State." While it is true that this saving clause says nothing about the nature of those other available remedies, absent any contrary indication in the text or history of the statute, we presume Congress enacted this statute with the prevailing traditional rule in mind.

In addition to the Rehabilitation Act Amendments of 1986, Congress also enacted the Civil Rights Restoration Act of 1987. Without in any way altering the existing rights of action and the corresponding remedies permissible under Title IX, Title VI, § 504 of the Rehabilitation Act, and the Age Discrimination Act, Congress broadened the coverage of these antidiscrimination provisions in this legislation. . . . Congress made no effort to restrict the right of action recognized in *Cannon* and ratified in the 1986 Act or to alter the traditional presumption in favor of any appropriate relief for violation of a federal right. We cannot say, therefore, that Congress has limited the remedies available to a complainant in a suit brought under Title IX.

Respondents and the United States nevertheless suggest three reasons why we should not apply the traditional presumption in favor of appropriate relief in this case.

First, respondents argue that an award of damages violates separation of powers principles because it unduly expands the federal courts' power into a sphere properly reserved to the Executive and Legislative Branches. In making this argument, respondents misconceive the difference between a cause of action and a remedy. Unlike the finding of a cause of action, which authorizes a court to hear a case or controversy, the discretion to award appropriate relief involves no such increase in judicial power. Federal courts cannot reach out to award remedies when the Constitution or laws of the United States do not support a cause of action. Indeed, properly understood, respondents' position invites us to *abdicate* our historic judicial authority to award appropriate relief in cases brought in our court system. It is well to recall that such authority historically has been thought necessary to provide an important safeguard against abuses of legislative and executive power, as well as to ensure an independent Judiciary. Moreover, selective abdication of the sort advocated here would harm separation of powers principles in another way, by giving judges the power to render inutile causes of action authorized by Congress through a decision that *no* remedy is available.

Next, . . . respondents and the United States contend that the normal presumption in favor of all appropriate remedies should not apply because Title IX was enacted pursuant to Congress' Spending Clause power. [We have previously] observed that remedies were limited under such Spending Clause statutes when the alleged violation was *unintentional*. Respondents and the United States maintain that this presumption should apply equally to *intentional* violations. We disagree. The point of not permitting monetary damages for an unintentional violation is that the receiving entity of federal funds lacks notice that it will be liable for a monetary award. This notice problem does not arise in a case such as this, in which intentional discrimination is alleged. Unquestionably, Title IX placed on the Gwinnett County Public Schools the duty not to discriminate on the basis of sex, and "when a supervisor sexually harasses a subordinate because of the subordinate's sex, that supervisor 'discriminate[s]' on the basis of sex." *Meritor*. We believe the same rule should apply when a teacher sexually harasses and abuses a student. Congress surely did not intend for federal moneys to be expended to support the intentional actions it sought by statute to proscribe. . . .

Finally, the United States asserts that the remedies permissible under Title IX should nevertheless be limited to backpay and prospective relief. In addition to diverging from our traditional approach to deciding what remedies are available for violation of a federal right, this position conflicts with sound logic. . . . [I]n this case the equitable remedies suggested by respondent and the Federal Government are clearly inadequate. Backpay does nothing for petitioner, because she was a student when the alleged discrimination occurred. Similarly, because Hill—the person she claims subjected her to sexual harassment—no longer teaches at the school and she herself no longer attends a school in the Gwinnett system, prospective relief accords her no remedy at all. The Government's answer that administrative action helps other similarly situated students in effect acknowledges that its approach would leave petitioner remediless. . . .

■ *Justice* SCALIA, *with whom* THE CHIEF JUSTICE *and Justice* THOMAS *join, concurring in the judgment.*

The substantive right at issue here is one that Congress did not expressly create, but that this Court found to be "implied." *Cannon*. Quite obviously, the search for what was Congress' *remedial* intent as to a right whose very existence Congress did not expressly acknowledge is unlikely to succeed . . . .

In my view, when rights of action are judicially "implied," categorical limitations upon their remedial scope may be judicially implied as well. Although we have abandoned the expansive rights-creating approach exemplified by *Cannon*—and perhaps ought to abandon the notion of implied causes of action entirely—causes of action that came into existence under the *ancien regime* should be limited by the same logic that gave them birth. To require, with respect to a right that is not consciously and intentionally created, that any limitation of remedies must be express, is to provide, in effect, that the most questionable of private rights will also be the most expansively remediable. As the United States puts it, "[w]hatever the merits of 'implying' rights of action may be, there is no justification for treating [congressional] silence as the equivalent of the broadest imaginable grant of remedial authority."

I nonetheless agree with the Court's disposition of this case. Because of legislation enacted subsequent to *Cannon*, it is too late in the day to address whether a judicially implied exclusion of damages under Title IX would be appropriate. The Rehabilitation Act Amendments of 1986 must be read, in my view, not only "as a validation of *Cannon*'s holding," but also as an implicit acknowledgment that damages are available. I therefore concur in the judgment.

Notes and Questions

1. *Franklin* represents a rare show of unanimity in the area of implied rights of action. Why was even the conservative wing of the Court willing to recognize a damages remedy? What other indicia of congressional intent have we seen suffice to signify Congress's satisfaction with the Court's interpretive work?

2. Is the Court's recognition of judicial authority to develop remedies a natural extension of the principles espoused in *Bivens* (see Chapter 2)? If not, what's the difference? If so, why was the Court willing to expand the implied remedy for a Title IX violation in the same period it was contracting the availability of the implied *Bivens* remedy for constitutional violations?

3. Consider the parallels between Justice Rehnquist's concurrence in *Cannon* and Justice Scalia's in *Franklin*. In light of the results in these cases, how likely is Congress to get the message they are trying to send?

4. Note the Court's reliance on *Meritor*, a Title VII case (Chapter 6, Section B). Are decisions about Title VII a sound basis for interpreting Title IX? Why or why not? The Court would reconsider that connection in our next principal case.

Note: Titles VI and IX and Sovereign Immunity

Congress's enactment of 42 U.S.C. § 2000d-7 in the Rehabilitation Act Amendments of 1986 played an important role in *Franklin*. That statute merits brief consideration in its own right. It provides:

> (1) A State shall not be immune under the Eleventh Amendment of the Constitution of the United States from suit in Federal court for a violation of section 504 of the Rehabilitation Act of 1973, title IX of the Education Amendments of 1972, the Age Discrimination Act of 1975, title VI of the Civil Rights Act of 1964, or the provisions of any other Federal statute prohibiting discrimination by recipients of Federal financial assistance.

> (2) In a suit against a State for a violation of a statute referred to in paragraph (1), remedies (including remedies both at law and in equity) are available for such a violation to the same extent as such remedies are available for such a violation in the suit against any public or private entity other than a State.

42 U.S.C. § 2000d-7(a).

Franklin states (albeit in conclusory fashion) that Congress, in this provision, "abrogated the States' Eleventh Amendment immunity under Title IX [and] Title VI." That summary conclusion has been a subject of subsequent litigation in the lower courts.

In *Litman v. George Mason Univ.*, 186 F.3d 544 (4th Cir. 1999), a Virginia state university argued in defending against a Title IX suit that "there is nothing in the text that even remotely suggests that Virginia's public universities must waive the Eleventh Amendment as a condition of receiving federal funds. Indeed, the statute does not even contain the word waiver. [GMU] argues that a statute must say something like 'as a condition of receiving federal funds under this Act, the States agree to waive their Eleventh Amendment immunity' and that absent such explicit language, the mere receipt of Title IX funds cannot effect a waiver" (some internal quotation marks omitted). The Fourth Circuit rejected the school's argument: "There can be no doubt that GMU is able 'to ascertain what is expected of it' in return for federal education funds."

Litman has been widely followed; the Supreme Court itself subsequently reiterated *Franklin*'s characterization of the Rehabilitation Act Amendments. *See Alexander v. Sandoval*, 532 U.S. 275, 280 (2001). Thus, Congress successfully required waiver of states' sovereign immunity for claims under Titles VI and IX.

What does the lingering dispute on this point even after *Franklin* reveal about the strength of the clear statement rule for spending conditions requiring the waiver of sovereign immunity (see Chapter 3, Section B.3)?

Note: Punitive Damages for Implied Rights

In *Barnes v. Gorman*, 536 U.S. 181 (2002), the Court considered whether punitive damages were available for violations of the Rehabilitation Act and the Americans with Disabilities Act (ADA). The ADA incorporates the remedies applicable to the Rehabilitation Act, which in turn incorporates the remedies applicable to Title VI, so the question before the Court was whether the implied cause of action of Title VI (and therefore also Title IX) includes punitive damages. In an opinion by Justice Scalia, the Court answered no, reasoning:

> [A] remedy is "appropriate relief," *Franklin*, only if the funding recipient is on notice that, by accepting federal funding, it exposes itself to liability of that nature. A funding recipient is generally on notice that it is subject not only to those remedies explicitly provided in the relevant legislation, but also to those remedies traditionally available in suits for breach of contract. Thus we have held that under Title IX, which contains no express remedies, a recipient of federal funds is nevertheless subject to suit for compensatory damages, and injunction, forms of relief traditionally available in suits for breach of contract. Like Title IX, Title VI mentions no remedies—indeed, it fails to mention even a private right of action (hence this Court's decision finding an implied right of action in *Cannon*). But punitive damages, unlike compensatory damages and injunction, are generally not available for breach of contract.

Justice Stevens, joined by Justices Ginsburg and Breyer, concurred in the judgment on narrower grounds.

Is *Barnes* consistent with *Franklin*'s approach to the question of what relief is available under implied rights of action? In light of the absence of an express cause of action in the first place, why should a funding recipient be more surprised by an award of punitive damages than by an award of compensatory damages or an injunction? Why is contract law the appropriate model for the permissible scope of remedies? In what ways does a Spending Clause arrangement resemble, and in what ways does it deviate from, an ordinary contract?

2. INSTITUTIONAL LIABILITY UNDER TITLES VI AND IX

As plaintiffs began to seek redress for violations not flowing directly from policies and practices of institutions receiving federal funding, the Court was required to confront the question of what showing must be made to hold an institution liable for acts it did not direct. As in Title VII, this question is crucial to private civil enforcement of Titles VI and IX, as courts have held that individuals are not proper defendants under those statutes. *See, e.g., Kinman v. Omaha Pub. Sch. Dist.*, 171 F.3d 607, 611 (8th Cir. 1999) (joining several circuits in holding that "because they are not grant recipients, school officials may not be sued in their individual capacity under Title IX" (citing cases from the First, Fifth, Seventh, and Eleventh Circuits)). Thus, in many instances, rules for institutional liability determine whether private civil actions can be used to redress violations of Titles VI or IX at all.

Gebser v. Lago Vista Independent School District
524 U.S. 274 (1998)

▪ *Justice O'CONNOR delivered the opinion of the Court.*

The question in this case is when a school district may be held liable in damages in an implied right of action under Title IX of the Education Amendments of 1972, for the sexual harassment of a student by one of the district's teachers. We conclude that damages may not be recovered in those circumstances unless an official of the school district who at a minimum has authority to institute corrective measures on the district's behalf has actual notice of, and is deliberately indifferent to, the teacher's misconduct.

In the spring of 1991, when petitioner Alida Star Gebser was an eighth-grade student at a middle school in respondent Lago Vista Independent School District (Lago Vista), she joined a high school book discussion group led by Frank Waldrop, a teacher at Lago Vista's high school. Lago Vista received federal funds at all pertinent times. During the book discussion sessions, Waldrop often made sexually suggestive comments to the students. . . . [H]e began to direct more of his suggestive comments toward Gebser, including during the substantial amount of time that the two were alone in his classroom. He initiated sexual contact with Gebser in the spring, when, while visiting her home ostensibly to give her a book, he kissed and fondled her. The two had sexual intercourse on a number of occasions during the remainder of the school year. Their relationship continued through the summer and into the following school year, and they often had intercourse during class time, although never on school property.

Gebser did not report the relationship to school officials, testifying that while she realized Waldrop's conduct was improper, she was uncertain how to react and she wanted to continue having him as a teacher. In October 1992, the parents of two other students complained to the high school principal about Waldrop's comments in class. The principal arranged a meeting, at which, according to the principal, Waldrop indicated that he did not believe he had made offensive remarks but apologized to the parents and said it would not happen again. . . . A couple of months later, in January 1993, a police officer discovered Waldrop and Gebser engaging in sexual intercourse and arrested Waldrop. Lago Vista terminated his employment, and subsequently, the Texas Education Agency revoked his teaching license. During this time, the district had not promulgated or distributed an official grievance procedure for lodging sexual harassment complaints; nor had it issued a formal anti-harassment policy.

Gebser and her mother filed suit against Lago Vista and Waldrop . . . .

Petitioners, joined by the United States as amicus curiae, would invoke standards used by the Courts of Appeals in Title VII cases involving a supervisor's sexual harassment of an employee in the workplace. In support of that approach, they point to a passage in *Franklin* in which we stated: "Unquestionably, Title IX placed on the Gwinnett County Public Schools the duty not to discriminate on the basis of sex, and 'when a supervisor sexually harasses a subordinate because of the subordinate's sex, that supervisor "discriminate[s]" on the basis of sex.' *Meritor Sav. Bank, FSB v. Vinson*. We believe the same rule should apply when a teacher sexually harasses and abuses a student." *Meritor* directs courts to look to common law agency principles when assessing an employer's liability under Title VII for sexual harassment of an employee by a supervisor. Petitioners and the United States submit that, in light of *Franklin*'s comparison of teacher-student harassment with supervisor-employee harassment, agency principles should likewise apply in Title IX actions. . . .

Meritor's rationale for concluding that agency principles guide the liability inquiry under Title VII rests on an aspect of that statute not found in Title IX: Title VII, in which the prohibition against employment discrimination runs against "an employer," 42 U.S.C. § 2000e-2(a), explicitly defines "employer" to include "any agent," § 2000e(b). Title IX contains no comparable reference to an educational institution's "agents," and so does not expressly call for application of agency principles.

In this case, moreover, petitioners seek not just to establish a Title IX violation but to recover damages based on theories of respondeat superior and constructive notice. It is that aspect of their action, in our view, that is most critical to resolving the case. Unlike Title IX, Title VII contains an express cause of action, § 2000e-5(f). . . . With respect to Title IX, however, the private right of action is judicially implied, and there is thus no legislative expression of the scope of available remedies, including when it is appropriate to award monetary damages. . . .

[Title IX] condition[s] an offer of federal funding on a promise by the recipient not to discriminate, in what amounts essentially to a contract between the Government and the recipient of funds.

That contractual framework distinguishes Title IX from Title VII, which is framed in terms not of a condition but of an outright prohibition. . . .

Title IX's contractual nature has implications for our construction of the scope of available remedies. When Congress attaches conditions to the award of federal funds under its spending power, as it has in Title IX and Title VI, we examine closely the propriety of private actions holding the recipient liable in monetary damages for noncompliance with the condition. *See Franklin*. Our central concern in that regard is with ensuring that "the receiving entity of federal funds [has] notice that it will be liable for a monetary award." *Franklin*. . . . If a school district's liability for a teacher's sexual harassment rests on principles of constructive notice or respondeat superior, it will likewise be the case that the recipient of funds was unaware of the discrimination. It is sensible to assume that Congress did not envision a recipient's liability in damages in that situation.

Most significantly, Title IX contains important clues that Congress did not intend to allow recovery in damages where liability rests solely on principles of vicarious liability or constructive notice. Title IX's express means of enforcement—by administrative agencies—operates on an assumption of actual notice to officials of the funding recipient. The statute entitles agencies who disburse education funding to enforce their rules implementing the nondiscrimination mandate through proceedings to suspend or terminate funding or through "other means authorized by law." 20 U.S.C. § 1682. Significantly, however, an agency may not initiate enforcement proceedings until it "has advised the appropriate person or persons of the failure to comply with the requirement and has determined that compliance cannot be secured by voluntary means." The administrative regulations implement that obligation, requiring resolution of compliance issues "by informal means whenever possible" and prohibiting commencement of enforcement proceedings until the agency has determined that voluntary compliance is unobtainable and "the recipient . . . has been notified of its failure to comply and of the action to be taken to effect compliance."

In the event of a violation, a funding recipient may be required to take "such remedial action as [is] deem[ed] necessary to overcome the effects of [the] discrimination." . . .

Presumably, a central purpose of requiring notice of the violation "to the appropriate person" and an opportunity for voluntary compliance before administrative enforcement proceedings can commence is to avoid diverting education funding from beneficial uses where a recipient was unaware of discrimination in its programs and is willing to institute prompt corrective measures. The scope of private damages relief proposed by petitioners is at odds with that basic objective. When a teacher's sexual harassment is imputed to a school district or when a school district is deemed to have "constructively" known of the teacher's harassment, by assumption the district had no actual knowledge of the teacher's conduct. Nor, of course, did the district have an opportunity to take action to end the harassment or to limit further harassment.

It would be unsound, we think, for a statute's express system of enforcement to require notice to the recipient and an opportunity to come into voluntary compliance while a judicially implied system of enforcement permits substantial liability without regard to the recipient's knowledge or its corrective actions upon receiving notice. Moreover, an award of damages in a particular case might well exceed a recipient's level of federal funding. Where a statute's express enforcement scheme hinges its most severe sanction on notice and unsuccessful efforts to obtain compliance, we cannot attribute to Congress the intention to have implied an enforcement scheme that allows imposition of greater liability without comparable conditions.

Because the express remedial scheme under Title IX is predicated upon notice to an "appropriate person" and an opportunity to rectify any violation, 20 U.S.C. § 1682, we conclude, in the absence of further direction from Congress, that the implied damages remedy should be fashioned along the same lines. An "appropriate person" under § 1682 is, at a minimum, an official of the recipient entity with authority to take corrective action to end the discrimination. Consequently, in cases like this one that do not involve official policy of the recipient entity, we hold that a damages remedy will not lie under Title IX unless an official who at a minimum has authority to address the alleged discrimination and to institute corrective measures on the recipient's behalf has actual knowledge of discrimination in the recipient's programs and fails adequately to respond.

We think, moreover, that the response must amount to deliberate indifference to discrimination. The administrative enforcement scheme presupposes that an official who is advised of a Title IX violation refuses to take action to bring the recipient into compliance. The premise, in other words, is an official decision by the recipient not to remedy the violation. That framework finds a rough parallel in the standard of deliberate indifference. Under a lower standard, there would be a risk that the recipient would be liable in damages not for its own official decision but instead for its employees' independent actions. Comparable considerations led to our adoption of a deliberate indifference standard for claims under § 1983 alleging that a municipality's actions in failing to prevent a deprivation of federal rights was the cause of the violation. *See Board of Comm'rs of Bryan Cty. v. Brown; Canton v. Harris.*

Applying the framework to this case is fairly straightforward, as petitioners do not contend they can prevail under an actual notice standard. The only official alleged to have had information about Waldrop's misconduct is the high school principal. That information, however, consisted of a complaint from parents of other students charging only that Waldrop had made inappropriate comments during class, which was plainly insufficient to alert the principal to the possibility that Waldrop was involved in a sexual relationship with a student. . . . Justice Stevens points out in his dissenting opinion that Waldrop of course had knowledge of his own actions. Where a school district's liability rests on actual notice principles, however, the knowledge of the wrongdoer himself is not pertinent to the analysis.

Petitioners focus primarily on Lago Vista's asserted failure to promulgate and publicize an effective policy and grievance procedure for sexual harassment claims. They point to Department of Education regulations requiring each funding recipient to "adopt and publish grievance procedures providing for prompt and equitable resolution" of discrimination complaints, 34 C.F.R. § 106.8(b), and to notify students and others that "it does not discriminate on the basis of sex in the educational programs or activities which it operates," § 106.9(a). Lago Vista's alleged failure to comply with the regulations, however, does not establish the requisite actual notice and deliberate indifference. And in any event, the failure to promulgate a grievance procedure does not itself constitute "discrimination" under Title IX. . . .

Until Congress speaks directly on the subject . . . we will not hold a school district liable in damages under Title IX for a teacher's sexual harassment of a student absent actual notice and deliberate indifference. . . .

▪ Justice STEVENS, with whom Justice SOUTER, Justice GINSBURG, and Justice BREYER join, dissenting. . . .

[T]he majority's policy judgment about the appropriate remedy in this case thwarts the purposes of Title IX. . . .

The Court . . . holds that the law does not provide a damages remedy for the Title IX violation alleged in this case because no official of the school district with "authority to institute corrective measures on the district's behalf" had actual notice of Waldrop's misconduct. That holding is at odds with settled principles of agency law, under which the district is responsible for Waldrop's misconduct because "he was aided in accomplishing the tort by the existence of the agency relation." Restatement (Second) of Agency § 219(2)(d).[9] This case presents a paradigmatic example of a tort that was made possible, that was effected, and that was repeated over a prolonged period because of the powerful influence that Waldrop had over Gebser by reason of the authority that his employer, the school district, had delegated to him. As a secondary school teacher, Waldrop exercised even greater authority and control over his students than employers and supervisors exercise over their employees. His gross misuse of that authority allowed him to abuse his young student's trust. . . .

The reason why the common law imposes liability on the principal in such circumstances is the same as the reason why Congress included the prohibition against discrimination on the basis of sex in Title IX: to induce school boards to adopt and enforce practices that will minimize the danger that vulnerable students will be exposed to such odious behavior. The rule that the Court has crafted creates the opposite incentive. As long as school boards can insulate themselves from knowledge about this sort of conduct, they can claim immunity from damages liability. Indeed, the rule that the Court adopts would preclude a damages remedy even if every teacher at the school knew about the harassment but did not have "authority to institute corrective measures on the district's behalf." It is not my function to determine whether this newly fashioned rule is wiser than the established common-law rule. It is proper, however, to suggest that the Court bears the burden of justifying its rather dramatic departure from settled law, and to explain why its opinion fails to shoulder that burden. . . .

---

9. The Court suggests that agency principles are inapplicable to this case because Title IX does not expressly refer to an "agent," as Title VII does. Title IX's focus on the protected class rather than the fund recipient fully explains the statute's failure to mention "agents" of the recipient, however. . . .

[T]he Court suggests that the school district did not have fair notice when it accepted federal funding that it might be held liable "'for a monetary award'" under Title IX. The Court cannot mean, however, that respondent was not on notice that sexual harassment of a student by a teacher constitutes an "intentional" violation of Title IX for which damages are available, because we so held shortly before Waldrop began abusing Gebser. . . . Moreover, the nondiscrimination requirement set out in Title IX is clear, and this Court held that sexual harassment constitutes intentional sex discrimination long before the sexual abuse in this case began. Normally, of course, we presume that the citizen has knowledge of the law. . . .

The Court reasons that because administrative proceedings to terminate funding cannot be commenced until after the grant recipient has received notice of its noncompliance and the agency determines that voluntary compliance is not possible, there should be no damages liability unless the grant recipient has actual notice of the violation (and thus an opportunity to end the harassment).

The fact that Congress has specified a particular administrative procedure to be followed when a subsidy is to be terminated, however, does not illuminate the question of what the victim of discrimination on the basis of sex must prove in order to recover damages in an implied private right of action. . . .

The majority's inappropriate reliance on Title IX's administrative enforcement scheme to limit the availability of a damages remedy leads the Court to require not only actual knowledge on the part of "an official who at a minimum has authority to address the alleged discrimination and to institute corrective measures on the recipient's behalf," but also that official's "refus[al] to take action," or "deliberate indifference" toward the harassment. Presumably, few Title IX plaintiffs who have been victims of intentional discrimination will be able to recover damages under this exceedingly high standard. . . .

A theme that seems to underlie the Court's opinion is a concern that holding a school district liable in damages might deprive it of the benefit of the federal subsidy—that the damages remedy is somehow more onerous than a possible termination of the federal grant. It is possible, of course, that in some cases the recoverable damages, in either a Title IX action or a state-law tort action, would exceed the amount of a federal grant. That is surely not relevant to the question whether the school district or the injured student should bear the risk of harm—a risk against which the district, but not the student, can insure. It is not clear to me why the well-settled rules of law that impose responsibility on the principal for the misconduct of its agents should not apply in this case. As a matter of policy, the Court ranks protection of the school district's purse above the protection of immature high school students that those rules would provide. Because those students are members of the class for whose special benefit Congress enacted Title IX, that policy choice is not faithful to the intent of the policymaking branch of our Government. . . .

[Dissenting opinion of Ginsburg, J., joined by Souter and Breyer, JJ., omitted.]

Notes and Questions

1. What is the test for holding a school district liable for a Title IX violation? Where does it come from? Text? Legislative history? Tradition? Somewhere else?

2. What is the role of notice in the Court's opinion? How does it limit liability for Title IX violations? What is the rationale for imposing this limit?

3. Consider the Court's comparisons and contrasts to two other bodies of law we have studied—Title VII and municipal liability under § 1983. What reasons does the Court give for its treatment of each, and are these reasons persuasive? How does the rule the Court applies here differ from the rules for holding an employer liable in those other contexts? Which rule is the most administrable?

4. What incentives does the majority's rule create for a school district? If you were counsel to a district, how would you respond to this decision? Would implementing a policy against harassment be useful in protecting your client?

5. Justice Stevens thinks administrative mechanisms are irrelevant to the question of when an institution should be liable via an implied private right of action. Why? If Congress wanted the wrongdoing entity to have notice of the problem so it could self-correct, why shouldn't the Court respect that choice?

6. Responding to Justice Stevens's point that Waldrop had notice of his own actions, the majority declares that "the knowledge of the wrongdoer himself is not pertinent to the analysis"? Why should that be? Doesn't he meet the definition of someone with authority to rectify the violation? As between the student victim and the school-district employer, who is in a better position to ensure that someone with such authority does not abuse it? How has the Court's approach to notice changed since *Franklin*?

7. Which side of the debate, the majority or the dissent, has the more persuasive claim to judicial restraint, and why?

* * *

When the harasser is not employed by the institution receiving federal funds but is instead the victim's fellow student, is a private Title IX action available? The Court has held that it can be.

Davis v. Monroe County Board of Education
526 U.S. 629 (1999)

■ *Justice O'Connor delivered the opinion of the Court. . . .*

We consider here whether a private damages action may lie against the school board in cases of student-on-student harassment. We conclude that it may, but only where the funding recipient acts with deliberate indifference to known acts of harassment in its programs or activities. Moreover, we conclude that such an action will lie only for harassment that is so severe, pervasive, and objectively offensive that it effectively bars the victim's access to an educational opportunity or benefit. . . .

[According to the complaint,] Petitioner's minor daughter, LaShonda, was allegedly the victim of a prolonged pattern of sexual harassment by one of her fifth-grade classmates at Hubbard Elementary School, a public school in Monroe County, Georgia. According to petitioner's complaint, the harassment began in December 1992, when the classmate, G.F., attempted to touch LaShonda's breasts and genital area and made vulgar statements such as "'I want to get in bed with you'" and "'I want to feel your boobs.'" Similar conduct allegedly occurred on or about January 4 and January 20, 1993. LaShonda reported each of these incidents to her mother and to her classroom teacher, Diane Fort. Petitioner, in turn, also contacted Fort, who allegedly assured petitioner that the school principal, Bill Querry, had been informed of the incidents. Petitioner contends that, notwithstanding these reports, no disciplinary action was taken against G.F.

G.F.'s conduct allegedly continued for many months. In early February, G.F. purportedly placed a door stop in his pants and proceeded to act in a sexually suggestive manner toward LaShonda during physical education class. LaShonda reported G.F.'s behavior. . . . Approximately one week later, G.F. again allegedly engaged in harassing behavior. . . . Again, LaShonda allegedly reported the incident to the teacher . . . .

Petitioner alleges that G.F. once more directed sexually harassing conduct toward LaShonda in physical education class in early March, and that LaShonda reported the incident. . . . In mid-April 1993, G.F. allegedly rubbed his body against LaShonda in the school hallway in what LaShonda considered a sexually suggestive manner, and LaShonda again reported the matter to Fort.

The string of incidents finally ended in mid-May, when G.F. was charged with, and pleaded guilty to, sexual battery for his misconduct. The complaint alleges that LaShonda had suffered during the months of harassment, however; specifically, her previously high grades allegedly dropped as she became unable to concentrate on her studies, and, in April 1993, her father discovered that she had written a suicide note. . . .

Nor was LaShonda G.F.'s only victim; it is alleged that other girls in the class fell prey to G.F.'s conduct. At one point, in fact, a group composed of LaShonda and other female students tried to speak with Principal Querry about G.F.'s behavior. According to the complaint, however, a teacher denied the students' request with the statement, "'If [Querry] wants you, he'll call you.'"

Petitioner alleges that no disciplinary action was taken in response to G.F.'s behavior toward LaShonda [even after she spoke with Fort and Principal Querry]. When petitioner inquired as to what action the school intended to take against G.F., Querry simply stated, "'I guess I'll have to threaten him a little bit harder.'" Yet, petitioner alleges, at no point during the many months of his reported misconduct was G.F. disciplined for harassment. . . . Nor, according to the complaint, was any effort made to separate G.F. and LaShonda. . . .

[R]espondents urge that Title IX provides no notice that recipients of federal educational funds could be liable in damages for harm arising from student-on-student harassment. Respondents contend, specifically, that the statute only proscribes misconduct by grant recipients, not third parties. Respondents argue, moreover, that it would be contrary to the very purpose of Spending Clause legislation to impose liability on a funding recipient for the misconduct of third parties, over whom recipients exercise little control.

We agree with respondents that a recipient of federal funds may be liable in damages under Title IX only for its own misconduct. . . . We disagree with respondents' assertion, however, that petitioner seeks to hold the Board liable for G.F.'s actions instead of its own. Here, petitioner attempts to hold the Board liable for its own decision to remain idle in the face of known student-on-student harassment in its schools. In *Gebser*, we concluded that a recipient of federal education funds may be liable in damages under Title IX where it is deliberately indifferent to known acts of sexual harassment by a teacher. . . .

Gebser . . . established that a recipient intentionally violates Title IX, and is subject to a private damages action, where the recipient is deliberately indifferent to known acts of teacher-student discrimination. Indeed, whether viewed as "discrimination" or "subject[ing]" students to discrimination, Title IX "[u]nquestionably . . . placed on [the Board] the duty not" to permit teacher-student harassment in its schools, *Franklin*, and recipients violate Title IX's plain terms when they remain deliberately indifferent to this form of misconduct.

We consider here whether the misconduct identified in *Gebser*—deliberate indifference to known acts of harassment—amounts to an intentional violation of Title IX, capable of supporting a private damages action, when the harasser is a student rather than a teacher. We conclude that, in certain limited circumstances, it does. As an initial matter, in *Gebser* we expressly rejected the use of agency principles in the Title IX context, noting the textual differences between Title IX and Title VII. Additionally, the regulatory scheme surrounding Title IX has long provided funding recipients with notice that they may be liable for their failure to respond to the discriminatory acts of certain nonagents. The Department of Education requires recipients to monitor third parties for discrimination in specified circumstances and to refrain from particular forms of interaction with outside entities that are known to discriminate. . . .

This is not to say that the identity of the harasser is irrelevant. On the contrary, both the "deliberate indifference" standard and the language of Title IX narrowly circumscribe the set of parties whose known acts of sexual harassment can trigger some duty to respond on the part of funding recipients. Deliberate indifference makes sense as a theory of direct liability under Title IX only where the funding recipient has some control over the alleged harassment. A recipient cannot be directly liable for its indifference where it lacks the authority to take remedial action. . . .

The statute's plain language confines the scope of prohibited conduct based on the recipient's degree of control over the harasser and the environment in which the harassment occurs. If a funding recipient does not engage in harassment directly, it may not be liable for damages unless its deliberate indifference "subject[s]" its students to harassment. That is, the deliberate indifference must, at a minimum, "cause [students] to undergo" harassment or "make them liable or vulnerable" to it. Random House Dictionary of the English Language 1415 (1966) (defining "subject" as "to cause to undergo the action of something specified; expose" or "to make liable or vulnerable; lay open; expose"). Moreover, because the harassment must occur "under" "the operations of" a funding recipient, *see* 20 U.S.C. § 1681(a); § 1687 (defining "program or activity"), the harassment must take place in a context subject to the school district's control, Random House Dictionary of the English Language, *supra*, at 1543 (defining "under" as "subject to the authority, direction, or supervision of").

These factors combine to limit a recipient's damages liability to circumstances wherein the recipient exercises substantial control over both the harasser and the context in which the known harassment occurs. Only then can the recipient be said to "expose" its students to harassment or "cause" them to undergo it "under" the recipient's programs. We agree with the dissent that these conditions are satisfied most easily and most obviously when the offender is an agent of the recipient. We rejected the use of agency analysis in *Gebser*, however, and we disagree that the term "under" somehow imports an agency requirement into Title IX. As noted above, the theory in *Gebser* was that the recipient was directly liable for its deliberate indifference to discrimination. Liability in that case did not arise because the "teacher's actions [were] treated" as those of the funding recipient; the district was directly liable for its own failure to act. The terms "subjec[t]" and "under" impose limits, but nothing about these terms requires the use of agency principles.

Where, as here, the misconduct occurs during school hours and on school grounds—the bulk of G.F.'s misconduct, in fact, took place in the classroom—the misconduct is taking place "under" an "operation" of the funding recipient. In these circumstances, the recipient retains substantial control over the context in which the harassment occurs. More importantly, however, in this setting the Board exercises significant control over the harasser.... On more than one occasion, this Court has recognized the importance of school officials' "comprehensive authority . . . , consistent with fundamental constitutional safeguards, to prescribe and control conduct in the schools." . . . The common law, too, recognizes the school's disciplinary authority. We thus conclude that recipients of federal funding may be liable for "subject[ing]" their students to discrimination where the recipient is deliberately indifferent to known acts of student-on-student sexual harassment and the harasser is under the school's disciplinary authority....

The dissent consistently mischaracterizes this standard to require funding recipients to "remedy" peer harassment, and to "ensur[e] that . . . students conform their conduct to" certain rules. Title IX imposes no such requirements. On the contrary, the recipient must merely respond to known peer harassment in a manner that is not clearly unreasonable. This is not a mere "reasonableness" standard, as the dissent assumes. In an appropriate case, there is no reason why courts, on a motion to dismiss, for summary judgment, or for a directed verdict, could not identify a response as not "clearly unreasonable" as a matter of law....

We believe . . . that the standard set out here is sufficiently flexible to account both for the level of disciplinary authority available to the school and for the potential liability arising from certain forms of disciplinary action. A university might not, for example, be expected to exercise the same degree of control over its students that a grade school would enjoy, and it would be entirely reasonable for a school to refrain from a form of disciplinary action that would expose it to constitutional or statutory claims. . . .

The requirement that recipients receive adequate notice of Title IX's proscriptions also bears on the proper definition of "discrimination" in the context of a private damages action. We have elsewhere concluded that sexual harassment is a form of discrimination for Title IX purposes and that Title IX proscribes harassment with sufficient clarity to satisfy [the] notice requirement and serve as a basis for a damages action. *See Gebser*; *Franklin*. Having previously determined that "sexual harassment" is "discrimination" in the school context under Title IX, we are constrained to conclude that student-on-student sexual harassment, if sufficiently severe, can likewise rise to the level of discrimination actionable under the statute. The statute's other prohibitions, moreover, help give content to the term "discrimination" in this context. Students are not only protected from discrimination, but also specifically shielded from being "excluded from participation in" or "denied the benefits of" any "education program or activity receiving Federal financial assistance." § 1681(a). The statute makes clear that, whatever else it prohibits, students must not be denied access to educational benefits and opportunities on the basis of gender. We thus conclude that funding recipients are properly held liable in damages only where they are deliberately indifferent to sexual harassment, of which they have actual knowledge, that is so severe, pervasive, and objectively offensive that it can be said to deprive the victims of access to the educational opportunities or benefits provided by the school. . . .

Whether gender-oriented conduct rises to the level of actionable "harassment" thus "depends on a constellation of surrounding circumstances, expectations, and relationships," including, but not limited to, the ages of the harasser and the victim and the number of individuals involved. Courts, moreover, must bear in mind that schools are unlike the adult workplace and that children may regularly interact in a manner that would be unacceptable among adults. Indeed, at least early on, students are still learning how to interact appropriately with their peers. It is thus understandable that, in the school setting, students often engage in insults, banter, teasing, shoving, pushing, and gender-specific conduct that is upsetting to the students subjected to it. Damages are not available for simple acts of teasing and name-calling among school children, however, even where these comments target differences in gender. Rather, in the context of student-on-student harassment, damages are available only where the behavior is so severe, pervasive, and objectively offensive that it denies its victims the equal access to education that Title IX is designed to protect. . . .

The fact that it was a teacher who engaged in harassment in *Franklin* and *Gebser* is relevant. The relationship between the harasser and the victim necessarily affects the extent to which the misconduct can be said to breach Title IX's guarantee of equal access to educational benefits and to have a systemic effect on a program or activity. Peer harassment, in particular, is less likely to satisfy these requirements than is teacher-student harassment.

Applying this standard to the facts at issue here, we conclude that the Eleventh Circuit erred in dismissing petitioner's complaint. Petitioner alleges that her daughter was the victim of repeated acts of sexual harassment by G.F. over a 5-month period, and there are allegations in support of the conclusion that G.F.'s misconduct was severe, pervasive, and objectively offensive. The harassment was not only verbal; it included numerous acts of objectively offensive touching, and, indeed, G.F. ultimately pleaded guilty to criminal sexual misconduct. Moreover, the complaint alleges that there were multiple victims who were sufficiently disturbed by G.F.'s misconduct to seek an audience with the school principal. Further, petitioner contends that the harassment had a concrete, negative effect on her daughter's ability to receive an education. The complaint also suggests that petitioner may be able to show both actual knowledge and deliberate indifference on the part of the Board, which made no effort whatsoever either to investigate or to put an end to the harassment. . . .

▪ *Justice* KENNEDY, *with whom* THE CHIEF JUSTICE, *Justice* SCALIA, *and Justice* THOMAS *join, dissenting.* . . .

The only certainty flowing from the majority's decision is that scarce resources will be diverted from educating our children and that many school districts, desperate to avoid Title IX peer harassment suits, will adopt whatever federal code of student conduct and discipline the Department of Education sees fit to impose upon them. The Nation's schoolchildren will learn their first lessons about federalism in classrooms where the Federal Government is the ever-present regulator. . . . This federal control of the discipline of our Nation's schoolchildren is contrary to our traditions and inconsistent with the sensible administration of our schools. . . .

Schools cannot be held liable for peer sexual harassment because Title IX does not give them clear and unambiguous notice that they are liable in damages for failure to remedy discrimination by their students. As the majority acknowledges, Title IX prohibits only misconduct by grant recipients, not misconduct by third parties. The majority argues, nevertheless, that a school "subjects" its students to discrimination when it knows of peer harassment and fails to respond appropriately.

The mere word "subjected" cannot bear the weight of the majority's argument. As we recognized in *Gebser*, the primary purpose of Title IX is "to prevent recipients of federal financial assistance from using the funds in a discriminatory manner." We stressed in *Gebser* that Title IX prevents discrimination by the grant recipient, whether through the acts of its principals or the acts of its agents. . . .

In any event, a plaintiff cannot establish a Title IX violation merely by showing that she has been "subjected to discrimination." Rather, a violation of Title IX occurs only if she is "subjected to discrimination under any education program or activity," 20 U.S.C. § 1681(a), where "program or activity" is defined as "all of the operations of" a grant recipient, § 1687.

Under the most natural reading of this provision, discrimination violates Title IX only if it is authorized by, or in accordance with, the actions, activities, or policies of the grant recipient. *See* Webster's Third New International Dictionary 2487 (1981) (defining "under" as "required by: in accordance with: bound by"); American Heritage Dictionary 1395 (New College ed. 1981) (defining "under" as "[w]ith the authorization of; attested by; by virtue of"); Random House Dictionary of the English Language 2059 (2d ed. 1987) (defining "under" as "authorized, warranted, or attested by" or "in accordance with"). This reading reflects the common legal usage of the term "under" to mean pursuant to, in accordance with, or as authorized or provided by.

It is not enough, then, that the alleged discrimination occur in a "context subject to the school district's control." The discrimination must actually be "controlled by"—that is, be authorized by, pursuant to, or in accordance with, school policy or actions. . . .

I am aware of no basis in law or fact . . . for attributing the acts of a student to a school and, indeed, the majority does not argue that the school acts through its students. Discrimination by one student against another therefore cannot be "under" the school's program or activity as required by Title IX. . . .

A public school does not control its students in the way it controls its teachers or those with whom it contracts. Most public schools do not screen or select students, and their power to discipline students is far from unfettered. . . .

Perhaps even more startling than its broad assumptions about school control over primary and secondary school students is the majority's failure to grapple in any meaningful way with the distinction between elementary and secondary schools, on the one hand, and universities on the other. . . .

A university's power to discipline its students for speech that may constitute sexual harassment is also circumscribed by the First Amendment. . . .

The only guidance the majority gives schools in distinguishing between the "simple acts of teasing and name-calling among school children," said not to be a basis for suit even when they "target differences in gender," and actionable peer sexual harassment is, in reality, no guidance at all. . . . Is equal access denied when a girl who tires of being chased by the boys at recess refuses to go outside? When she cannot concentrate during class because she is worried about the recess activities? When she pretends to be sick one day so she can stay home from school? It appears the majority is content to let juries decide. . . .

The majority's inability to provide any workable definition of actionable peer harassment simply underscores the myriad ways in which an opinion that purports to be narrow is, in fact, so broad that it will support untold numbers of lawyers who will prove adept at presenting cases that will withstand the defendant school districts' pretrial motions. . . .

The majority seems oblivious to the fact that almost every child, at some point, has trouble in school because he or she is being teased by his or her peers. The girl who wants to skip recess because she is teased by the boys is no different from the overweight child who skips gym class because the other children tease her about her size in the locker room; or the child who risks flunking out because he refuses to wear glasses to avoid the taunts of "four-eyes"; or the child who refuses to go to school because the school bully calls him a "scaredy-cat" at recess. Most children respond to teasing in ways that detract from their ability to learn. The majority's test for actionable harassment will, as a result, sweep in almost all of the more innocuous conduct it acknowledges as a ubiquitous part of school life.

The string of adjectives the majority attaches to the word "harassment"— "severe, pervasive, and objectively offensive"—likewise fails to narrow the class of conduct that can trigger liability, since the touchstone for determining whether there is Title IX liability is the effect on the child's ability to get an education. Indeed, the Court's reliance on the impact on the child's educational experience suggests that the "objective offensiveness" of a comment is to be judged by reference to a reasonable child at whom the comments were aimed. Not only is that standard likely to be quite expansive, it also gives schools—and juries—little guidance, requiring them to attempt to gauge the sensitivities of, for instance, the average seven-year-old. . . .

In the context of teacher harassment, the *Gebser* notice standard imposes some limit on school liability. Where peer harassment is the discrimination, however, it imposes no limitation at all. In most cases of student misbehavior, it is the teacher who has authority, at least in the first instance, to punish the student and take other measures to remedy the harassment. The anomalous result will be that, while a school district cannot be held liable for a teacher's sexual harassment of a student without notice to the school board (or at least to the principal), the district can be held liable for a teacher's failure to remedy peer harassment. The threshold for school liability, then, appears to be lower when the harasser is a student than when the harasser is a teacher who is an agent of the school. The absurdity of this result confirms that it was neither contemplated by Congress nor anticipated by the States. . . .

A school faced with a peer sexual harassment complaint in the wake of the majority's decision may well be beset with litigation from every side. One student's demand for a quick response to her harassment complaint will conflict with the alleged harasser's demand for due process. Another student's demand for a harassment-free classroom will conflict with the alleged harasser's claim to a mainstream placement under the [Individuals with Disabilities Education Act] or with his state constitutional right to a continuing, free public education. On college campuses, and even in secondary schools, a student's claim that the school should remedy a sexually hostile environment will conflict with the alleged harasser's claim that his speech, even if offensive, is protected by the First Amendment. In each of these situations, the school faces the risk of suit, and maybe even multiple suits, regardless of its response. . . .

In the final analysis, this case is about federalism. Yet the majority's decision today says not one word about the federal balance. Preserving our federal system is a legitimate end in itself. It is, too, the means to other ends. It ensures that essential choices can be made by a government more proximate to the people than the vast apparatus of federal power. Defining the appropriate role of schools in teaching and supervising children who are beginning to explore their own sexuality and learning how to express it to others is one of the most complex and sensitive issues our schools face. Such decisions are best made by parents and by the teachers and school administrators who can counsel with them. The delicacy and immense significance of teaching children about sexuality should cause the Court to act with great restraint before it displaces state and local governments. . . .

Notes and Questions

1. Responding to the dissent's concerns about the breadth of the Court's holding, the majority identifies several limitations on liability for peer-on-peer harassment as compared to teacher-student harassment. What are these limitations? Do they answer the dissent's objections? How important are bright lines to the dissent's conception of an appropriate rule?

2. Consider the importance of "control" and "authority to take corrective action" in the factual contexts of *Gebser* and *Davis*. In which context is the school more likely to have control, a teacher-student relationship or a peer-to-peer relationship? In which context are a greater number of officials likely authorized to take corrective action? How do your answers to these questions affect your view of the breadth of the holding in *Davis*?

3. What's the difference between the "severe *or* persuasive" requirement for Title VII harassment claims and the "severe, pervasive, *and objectively offensive*" standard for Title IX? Where do these adjectives come from? How clear is their meaning?

4. Courts tend to consider the question whether a particular school employee is authorized to take corrective action to be a question of fact. *See Murrell v. Sch. Dist. No. 1*, 186 F.3d 1238, 1247 (10th Cir. 1999) ("We decline simply to name job titles that would or would not adequately satisfy this requirement. . . . Because officials' roles vary among school districts, deciding who exercises substantial control for the purposes of Title IX liability is necessarily a fact-based inquiry."); *accord Doe v. Sch. Bd. of Broward Cty.*, 604 F.3d 1248, 1256 (11th Cir. 2010). Is that treatment likely to assuage Justice Kennedy's concern about *Davis*'s breadth?

5. The dissent accuses the majority of putting school officials in an impossible position, given the school's competing legal obligations to both the victim of school bullying and the perpetrator. How often is that conflict likely to arise, and how difficult should these obligations be to reconcile? In concrete terms: Do you think courts will require schools to accommodate a student with a disability in a manner that enables the student to subject other students to "severe, pervasive, and objectively offensive" harassment?

6. Consider the issue of notice. How has the notion of notice evolved from *Gebser* to *Davis*? It might be useful after *Davis* to conceive of this line of cases as discussing two *different* types of notice—the notice required to open the door to

any liability for the district under Title IX and the notice required to establish liability *in an individual case*. What is the difference between these two types of notice? Who must receive each type? How is each conveyed? What is the relevance of each type to Title IX cases going forward?

7. A claim for peer-on-peer harassment can arise not only under Titles VI and IX but also under § 1983, because even though the harassing student is not acting "under color" of law, the district can be liable for failing to supervise the students under its authority. (See Chapter 5 for the standards for this type of claim.) For an example of a case proceeding under this theory, see *T.E. v. Pine Bush Cent. Sch. Dist.*, 58 F. Supp. 3d 332, 376-79 (S.D.N.Y. 2014).

Applications

1. Extending Title IX to retaliation claims. In *Jackson v. Birmingham Board of Education*, 544 U.S. 167 (2005), the Court held that the Title IX implied right of action extends to retaliation for complaining about discrimination as well as discriminatory acts themselves. Justice O'Connor's opinion for the Court explained that retaliation *is* in effect discrimination:

> Retaliation against a person because that person has complained of sex discrimination is another form of intentional sex discrimination encompassed by Title IX's private cause of action. Retaliation is, by definition, an intentional act. It is a form of "discrimination" because the complainant is being subjected to differential treatment. Moreover, retaliation is discrimination "on the basis of sex" because it is an intentional response to the nature of the complaint: an allegation of sex discrimination. We conclude that when a funding recipient retaliates against a person because he complains of sex discrimination, this constitutes intentional "discrimination" "on the basis of sex," in violation of Title IX.

The majority went on to reject objections based on *Sandoval* and on the purported lack of notice to funding recipients that they could be liable for such claims:

> The [defendant] contends that our decision in *Alexander v. Sandoval* compels a holding that Title IX's private right of action does not encompass retaliation. . . . *Sandoval* held that private parties may not invoke Title VI regulations to obtain redress for disparate-impact discrimination because Title VI itself prohibits only intentional discrimination.
>
> The [defendant] cites a Department of Education regulation prohibiting retaliation "against any individual for the purpose of interfering with any right or privilege secured by [Title IX]," 34 CFR § 100.7(e) (2004), and contends that Jackson, like the petitioners in *Sandoval*, seeks an "impermissible extension of the statute" when he argues that Title IX's private right of action encompasses retaliation. This argument, however, entirely misses the point. We do not rely on regulations extending Title IX's protection beyond its statutory limits; indeed, we do not rely on the Department of Education's regulation at all, because the statute itself contains the necessary prohibition. . . . In step with *Sandoval*, we hold that Title IX's private right of action encompasses suits for retaliation, because retaliation falls within the statute's prohibition of intentional discrimination on the basis of sex. . . .

The [defendant] insists that we should not interpret Title IX to prohibit retaliation because it was not on notice that it could be held liable for retaliating against those who complain of Title IX violations. We disagree. Funding recipients have been on notice that they could be subjected to private suits for intentional sex discrimination under Title IX since 1979, when we decided *Cannon*. . . .

[T]he Board should have been put on notice by the fact that our cases since *Cannon*, such as *Gebser* and *Davis*, have consistently interpreted Title IX's private cause of action broadly to encompass diverse forms of intentional sex discrimination. Indeed, retaliation presents an even easier case than deliberate indifference. It is easily attributable to the funding recipient, and it is always—by definition—intentional.

Justice Thomas, joined by Chief Justice Rehnquist and Justices Scalia and Kennedy, dissented:

[The Court's] holding is contrary to the plain terms of Title IX, because retaliatory conduct is not discrimination on the basis of sex. Moreover, we require Congress to speak unambiguously in imposing conditions on funding recipients through its spending power. And, in cases in which a party asserts that a cause of action should be implied, we require that the statute itself evince a plain intent to provide such a cause of action. Section 901 of Title IX meets none of these requirements.

From Justice Thomas's summary of the ways he believed the majority contravened the Court's prior holdings, you might think that *Jackson* represented a major turn in the jurisprudence of implied rights of action. It didn't. Why not? What aspects of the majority's reasoning cabined the case's reach merely to the addition of retaliation claims to Title IX rather than broader changes to the Court's approach to implied rights of action?

If discrimination by definition includes retaliation, why do statutes like Title VII list them separately? *Compare* 42 U.S.C. § 2000e-2(a) (barring discrimination), *with id.* § 2000e-3(a) (barring retaliation). The Court has nonetheless read prohibitions on retaliation into bans on discrimination in the Age Discrimination in Employment Act, *see Gomez-Perez v. Potter*, 553 U.S. 474, 491 (2008), and (as noted in Chapter 6) 42 U.S.C. § 1981.

2. Liability for deliberate indifference after the fact. Where a school is sued for a student's being sexually assaulted by another student, the *Gebser-Davis* test, especially the actual notice requirement, seems to suggest that the school's deliberate indifference must precede the assault. Not necessarily, some courts of appeals have ruled. For instance, in *Farmer v. Kansas State University*, 918 F.3d 1094 (10th Cir. 2019), plaintiffs "allege[d] that KSU violated Title IX's ban against sex discrimination by being deliberately indifferent *after* Plaintiffs reported to KSU that other students had raped them, and that deliberate indifference caused Plaintiffs subsequently to be deprived of educational benefits that were available to other students." Specifically, one of the plaintiffs alleged that she was "living in fear that she would run into her attacker, missed classes, struggled in school, secluded herself from friends, withdrew from KSU activities in which she had previously taken a leadership role, fell into a deep depression, slept excessively, and engaged in self-destructive behaviors such as excessive drinking and slitting her wrist"; the other plaintiff alleged that her grades plummeted, leading to the loss of her academic scholarship, and she "is always afraid, apprehensive, and hyper-alert, on-campus and off. Every man who passes her on the sidewalk terrifies her. At least once a day on-campus, Sara is overcome by panic, anxious that any passing man could be one of the student-assailants. She is constantly on the lookout for [one of the student-assailants]. Recently, walking to the K-State library she passed a man who turned toward her. She jumped, screamed, and began to cry."

KSU argued that the plaintiffs were required to allege that its deliberate indifference subjected them to *further* harassment. The court held otherwise:

> *Davis* . . . clearly indicates that Plaintiffs can state a viable Title IX claim by alleging alternatively either that KSU's deliberate indifference to their reports of rape caused Plaintiffs " 'to undergo' harassment or 'ma[d]e them liable or vulnerable' to it." . . . To underscore that a Title IX plaintiff is not required to allege that she suffered actual additional incidents of sexual harassment, the Supreme Court in *Davis* referred to the Random House Dictionary definition of "subject" to include, "to make liable . . . ; lay open; expose." . . .
>
> Once a funding recipient, like KSU, has actual knowledge of sexual harassment that is severe, pervasive and objectively offensive enough to deprive a student of access to the educational benefits and resources the recipient offers, the recipient cannot, acting with deliberate indifference, turn a blind eye to that harassment. Critically, then, KSU's alleged liability stems directly from its own conduct, its own deliberate indifference to known student-on-student sexual harassment occurring in its programs and activities that is sufficiently severe, pervasive, and objectively offensive enough to deprive a student of access to the educational opportunities the recipient provides. KSU is wrong to contend that, by holding it liable for its own deliberate indifference to the serious rape charges, we are requiring the university to remediate the harm caused by the student rapists rather than KSU itself. . . .
>
> Plaintiffs can state a viable Title IX claim for student-on-student harassment by alleging that the funding recipient's deliberate indifference caused them to be "vulnerable to" further harassment without requiring an allegation of subsequent actual sexual harassment.

Applying these rules to the facts alleged, the court concluded:

> Plaintiffs have [stated a claim] by alleging, among other things, that KSU's deliberate indifference caused them objectively to fear encountering their unchecked assailants on campus, which in turn caused Plaintiffs to stop participating in the educational opportunities KSU offered its students.

Does this holding apply *Davis* or extend it? Would it support a claim based on a plaintiff's being made vulnerable to harassment where the plaintiff had not been subjected to *any* harassment either before or after the school's deliberate indifference? What would such a plaintiff have to show?

What effect are holdings like *Farmer* likely to have on schools' incentives in responding to severe, pervasive, objectively offensive peer-on-peer harassment or assault?

CHAPTER 7 PROBLEMS

Problem 7A.   Return to Problem 2C in Chapter 2. Now imagine that Ibrahim Lincoln sues Agent Harding G. Warren under INDA, asserting an implied right of action for damages. Will the court recognize this cause of action? Why or why not?

Problem 7B.   Garfield James is an African-American student at Kingman Park College (KPC), a private school that receives federal funds.

During his first semester at KPC, James lives in an on-campus dorm in a single-occupancy room. One day in October, he finds a note taped to his dorm-room door that reads, "Monkey go back to Africa!" James, shocked and intimidated, does not report it. One day in November, he finds a banana is nailed to his dorm-room door. Just after Thanksgiving, he finds another note on his door, saying, "Go home already!"

In early December, James reports the incidents to the dean of residential life, Adam Quincy. Dean Quincy expresses dismay and sympathy but says that without evidence pointing to the culprit, there's nothing he can do but give James the option to move out of the dorm at the end of the semester. James asks Dean Quincy to ask for an investigation by campus police. Quincy says that he'll try but campus police are very busy. In the meantime, the deadline for mid-year housing transfers is approaching, so James needs to decide whether to move off campus or pay for a second semester in the dorms. Deeply uncomfortable now in the dorm, James decides to move off campus.

Off campus, James is much happier in his immediate environment, but he misses some of the social aspects of campus life. He had been planning to rush KPC's social-service fraternity, but its members live together in on-campus housing, so he decides not to do so. In February, after James has moved, he receives a call from campus police, who inform him that because he no longer lives in the dorms, and nothing has happened since he moved out, the police cannot spare the resources to investigate.

More and more, James keeps to himself, going onto campus as little as possible. He becomes depressed. He loses contact with what few friends he had made at KPC. His second semester grades decline. At the end of his first year at KPC, he sues the school under Title VI. Will James be able to hold the school liable?

Problem 7C.   Mt. Pleasant Law Center (MPLC), which receives federal funds, has second- and third-year students teach sections of a required writing class for 1Ls. The students are overseen by the Board of Student Assistants, which is made up exclusively of other students.

MPLC 2L Vin Calidge runs one of the sections. Whenever he calls on a woman in class, he compliments her appearance, as in "You're looking lovely today," or "Yes, beautiful?" After his first semester teaching, out of Calidge's fourteen students, twelve note in their course evaluations that Calidge frequently remarks on the appearance of the women but not of the men. The course evaluations are read every semester by the faculty who oversee the writing class.

After Calidge's second semester teaching (with no change in his classroom manner), several of Calidge's students complain to the MPLC Registrar's Office. The complaint is never passed on. The school has no procedure for receiving complaints at the Registrar's Office or passing them along from the Registrar to other administrators.

One of Calidge's students complains to the Board of Student Assistants that she is uncomfortable speaking in section because she knows Calidge would make a comment on her appearance if she does. The student does not mention that Calidge is doing this to every woman in the class; she only happens to speak about her own experience.

The head of the Board of Student Assistants calls the MPLC general counsel to ask what to do. The general counsel replies that if further complaints of this type are received, then that will show it's more than an isolated complaint and the Board should take action.

At the end of Calidge's third semester teaching (he is now a 3L), a group of female students whose appearances Calidge has remarked upon in class sue MPLC for violating Title IX by failing to remove Calidge from teaching.

Is the suit likely to succeed? Why or why not?

Enforcement of Federal Statutory Rights via § 1983

Justice White's *Cannon* dissent and Justice Stevens's *Sandoval* dissent in the previous chapter argue that those decisions regarding implied rights of action were erroneous or unwise in part because the rights at issue in those cases could be enforced instead via 42 U.S.C. § 1983. This chapter explores the availability of § 1983 for those purposes and for enforcing statutory rights generally. The first two sections trace the development of the Court's jurisprudence for determining when § 1983 can be used to enforce a statutory right. The last two sections address related questions— when statutory violations can be enjoined without resort to § 1983 (and without an implied right of action), and when statutes can foreclose the use of § 1983 to enforce constitutional rights.

Note one key difference between implied rights of action and § 1983: Implied rights can be used against non-governmental funding recipients (like the defendants in *Cannon*), but because § 1983 requires the defendant to be acting "under color" of law, only governmental defendants (or private defendants who qualify as "state actors," as discussed in Chapter 1, Section B) can be sued.

A. RECOGNIZING § 1983 STATUTORY ENFORCEMENT ACTIONS

Return once again to the text of § 1983 (emphasis added):

> Every person who, under color of any statute, ordinance, regulation, custom, or usage, of any State or Territory or the District of Columbia, subjects, or causes to be subjected, any citizen of the United States or other person within the jurisdiction thereof to the deprivation of any rights, privileges, or immunities secured by the Constitution *and laws*, shall be liable to the party injured in an action at law, suit in equity, or other proper proceeding for redress . . . .

Chapters 1, 3, 4, and 5 examined the use of § 1983 in enforcing "rights . . . secured by the Constitution." What about rights "secured by . . . laws"? For starters, did Congress's addition of the words "and laws" authorize the use of § 1983 to enforce federal statutes as well as constitutional provisions? If so, which "laws" can § 1983 enforce? Any of them?

1. THE BASIS FOR § 1983 ENFORCEMENT OF STATUTORY RIGHTS

Maine v. Thiboutot
448 U.S. 1 (1980)

■ *Mr. Justice* BRENNAN *delivered the opinion of the Court.* . . .

Respondents brought this suit in the Maine Superior Court alleging that petitioners, the State of Maine and its Commissioner of Human Services, violated § 1983 by depriving respondents of welfare benefits to which they were entitled under the federal Social Security Act. . . . The petitioners present [the question] whether § 1983 encompasses claims based on purely statutory violations of federal law . . . .

The question before us is whether the phrase "and laws," as used in § 1983, means what it says, or whether it should be limited to some subset of laws. Given that Congress attached no modifiers to the phrase, the plain language of the statute undoubtedly embraces respondents' claim that petitioners violated the Social Security Act. . . .

[P]etitioners nevertheless persist in suggesting that the phrase "and laws" should be read as limited to civil rights or equal protection laws. Petitioners suggest that when § 1 of the Civil Rights Act of 1871, which accorded jurisdiction and a remedy for deprivations of rights secured by "the Constitution of the United States," was divided by the 1874 statutory revision into a remedial section, Rev. Stat. § 1979, and jurisdictional sections, Rev. Stat. §§ 563(12) and 629(16), Congress intended that the same change made in § 629(16) be made as to each of the new sections as well. Section 629(16), the jurisdictional provision for the circuit courts and the model for the current jurisdictional provision, 28 U.S.C. § 1343(3), applied to deprivations of rights secured by "the Constitution of the United States or of any right secured by any law providing for equal rights." On the other hand, the remedial provision, the predecessor of § 1983, was expanded to apply to deprivations of rights secured by "the Constitution and laws," and § 563(12), the provision granting jurisdiction to the district courts, to deprivations of rights secured by "the Constitution of the United States, or of any right secured by any law of the United States." . . .

[T]he legislative history does not permit a definitive answer. There is no express explanation offered for the insertion of the phrase "and laws." On the one hand, a principal purpose of the added language was to "ensure that federal legislation providing specifically for equality of rights would be brought within the ambit of the civil action authorized by that statute." On the other hand, there are no indications that that was the only purpose, and Congress' attention was specifically directed to this new language. Representative Lawrence, in a speech to the House of Representatives that began by observing that the revisers had very often changed the meaning of existing statutes, referred to the civil rights statutes as "possibly [showing] verbal modifications bordering on legislation." He went on to read to Congress the original and revised versions. In short, Congress was aware of what it was doing, and the legislative history does not demonstrate that the plain language was not intended. Petitioners' arguments amount to the claim that had Congress been more careful, and had it fully thought out the relationship among the various sections, it might have acted differently. That argument, however, can best be addressed to Congress, which, it is important to note, has remained quiet in the face of our many pronouncements on the scope of § 1983....

■ *Mr. Justice* POWELL, *with whom* THE CHIEF JUSTICE *and Mr. Justice* REHNQUIST *join, dissenting.*

The Court holds today, almost casually, that 42 U.S.C. § 1983 creates a cause of action for deprivations under color of state law of any federal statutory right....

If we were forbidden to look behind the language in legislative enactments, there might be some force to the suggestion that "and laws" must be read to include all federal statutes.[1] But the "plain meaning" rule is not as inflexible as the Court imagines....

Blind reliance on plain meaning is particularly inappropriate where, as here, Congress inserted the critical language without explicit discussion when it revised the statutes in 1874. Indeed, not a single shred of evidence in the legislative history of the adoption of the 1874 revision mentions this change....

Section 1983 derives from § 1 of the Civil Rights Act of 1871, which provided a cause of action for deprivations of constitutional rights only. "Laws" were not mentioned. The phrase "and laws" was added in 1874, when Congress consolidated the laws of the United States into a single volume under a new subject-matter arrangement. Consequently, the intent of Congress in 1874 is central to this case.

In addition to creating a cause of action, § 1 of the 1871 Act conferred concurrent jurisdiction upon "the district or circuit courts of the United States. . . . " In the 1874 revision, the remedial portion of § 1 was codified as § 1979 of the Revised Statutes, which provided for a cause of action in terms identical to the present § 1983. The jurisdictional portion of § 1 was divided

---

1. The "plain meaning" of "and laws" may be more elusive than the Court admits. One might expect that a statute referring to all rights secured either by the Constitution or by the laws would employ the disjunctive "or." . . .

[A] natural reading of the conjunctive "and" in § 1983 would require that the right at issue be secured both by the Constitution and by the laws. In 1874, this would have included the rights set out in the Civil Rights Act of 1866, which had been incorporated in the Fourteenth Amendment and re-enacted in the Civil Rights Act of 1870. The legislative history does not suggest that the Court should adopt such a limited construction. But an advocate of "plain meaning" hardly can ignore the ambiguity.

into § 563(12), conferring district court jurisdiction, and § 629(16), conferring circuit court jurisdiction. Although §§ 1979, 563(12), and 629(16) came from the same source, each was worded differently. Section 1979 referred to deprivations of rights "secured by the Constitution and laws"; § 563(12) described rights secured "by the Constitution of the United States, or . . . by any law of the United States"; and § 629(16) encompassed rights secured "by the Constitution of the United States, or . . . by any law providing for equal rights of citizens of the United States." When Congress merged the jurisdiction of circuit and district courts in 1911, the narrower language of § 629(16) was adopted and ultimately became the present 28 U.S.C. § 1343(3).

In my view, the legislative history unmistakably shows that the variations in phrasing introduced in the 1874 revision were inadvertent, and that each section was intended to have precisely the same scope. Moreover, the only defensible interpretation of the contemporaneous legislative record is that the reference to "laws" in each section was intended "to do no more than ensure that federal legislation providing specifically for equality of rights would be brought within the ambit of the civil action authorized by [§ 1979]." . . .

The Revision Commission, which worked for six years on the project, submitted to Congress a draft that did contain substantive changes. But a Joint Congressional Committee, which was appointed in early 1873 to transform the draft into a bill, concluded that it would be "utterly impossible to carry the measure through, if it was understood that it contained new legislation." Therefore, the Committee employed Thomas Jefferson Durant to "strike out . . . modifications of the existing law" "wherever the meaning of the law had been changed." On December 10, 1873, Durant's completed work was introduced in the House with the solemn assurance that the bill "embodies the law as it is."

The House met in a series of evening sessions to review the bill and to restore original meaning where necessary. During one of these sessions, Representative Lawrence delivered the speech upon which the Court now relies. Lawrence explained that the revisers often had separated existing statutes into substantive, remedial, and criminal sections to accord with the new organization of the statutes by topic. He read both the original and revised versions of the civil rights statutes to illustrate the arrangement, and "possibly [to] show verbal modifications bordering on legislation." After reading § 1979 without mentioning the addition of "and laws," Lawrence stated that "[a] comparison of all these will present a fair specimen of the manner in which the work has been done, and from these all can judge of the accuracy of the translation." . . . Nothing in this sequence of remarks supports the decision of the Court today. There was no mention of the addition of "and laws" nor any hint that the reach of § 1983 was to be extended. If Lawrence had any such intention, his statement to the House was a singularly disingenuous way of proposing a major piece of legislation.

In context, it is plain that Representative Lawrence did not mention changes "bordering on legislation" as a way of introducing substantive changes in § 1 of the 1871 Act. Rather, he was emphasizing that the revision was not intended to modify existing statutes, and that his reading might reveal errors that should be eliminated. . . .

The Court's opinion does not consider the nature or scope of the litigation it has authorized. In practical effect, today's decision means that state and local governments, officers, and employees now may face liability whenever a person believes he has been injured by the administration of any federal-state cooperative program, whether or not that program is related to equal or civil rights.

Even a cursory survey on the United States Code reveals that literally hundreds of cooperative regulatory and social welfare enactments may be affected. The States now participate in the enforcement of federal laws governing migrant labor, noxious weeds, historic preservation, wildlife conservation, anadromous fisheries, scenic trails, and strip mining. Various statutes authorize federal-state cooperative agreements in most aspects of federal land management. In addition, federal grants administered by state and local governments now are available in virtually every area of public administration. Unemployment, Medicaid, school lunch subsidies, food stamps, and other welfare benefits may provide particularly inviting subjects of litigation. Federal assistance also includes a variety of subsidies for education, housing, health care, transportation, public works, and law enforcement. Those who might benefit from these grants now will be potential § 1983 plaintiffs.

No one can predict the extent to which litigation arising from today's decision will harass state and local officials; nor can one foresee the number of new filings in our already overburdened courts. But no one can doubt that these consequences will be substantial. And the Court advances no reason to believe that any Congress—from 1874 to the present day—intended this expansion of federally imposed liability on state defendants. . . .

Today's decision confers upon the courts unprecedented authority to oversee state actions that have little or nothing to do with the individual rights defined and enforced by the civil rights legislation of the Reconstruction Era. This result cannot be reconciled with the purposes for which § 1983 was enacted. . . .

In my view, the Court's decision today significantly expands the concept of "civil rights" and creates a major new intrusion into state sovereignty under our federal system. . . .

Notes and Questions

1. This case presents a classic clash between textualism and other methods of interpretation, with an additional twist: the possibility that the content of the text itself was inadvertent. What should a textualist do in such situations—assume that the legislature knew what it was doing or heed evidence to the contrary? How does that evidence stack up in this case?

2. Justice Powell predicts a flood of new litigation if § 1983 is deployed to enforce federal laws. Why should that be, unless federal laws are routinely being violated? And if they are, why shouldn't there be a remedy?

3. If the majority is right that "and laws" always meant what it means here, why did it take the Supreme Court more than 100 years to say so?

4. Justice Powell warns that "literally hundreds of cooperative regulatory and social welfare enactments may be affected" by the Court's holding. That may be true in the modern era, but it wouldn't have been in 1874, when the scope of the federal government was much smaller. How does this change in the potential scope of the phrase "and laws" over time bear on the question of statutory interpretation? Should the broad modern scope counsel against the majority's approach, as Justice Powell contends? Or does the fact that "and laws" would have referred to many fewer laws in 1874 support the majority's view that Congress didn't add this phrase by accident?

2. THE LIMITS OF *THIBOUTOT*

How far does the *Thiboutot* holding extend? Does enforcement of the rights guaranteed by the Constitution "and laws" mean *all* parts of *all* federal laws? No, answered the Supreme Court in a pair of cases decided the year after *Thiboutot*.

Pennhurst State School & Hospital v. Halderman, 451 U.S. 1 (1981), demonstrated one important condition for enforceability: Congress must have created a substantive "right." At issue in *Pennhurst* was whether a state hospital could be sued for alleged violations of the Developmentally Disabled Assistance and Bill of Rights Act, which established a federal-state grant program through which the federal government provided aid to participating states for programs to care for and treat people with developmental disabilities. As with other Spending Clause programs, state participation was voluntary, but the federal money came with conditions about how states must treat beneficiaries. For instance, the Act instructed that "appropriate treatment" should be provided in the "least restrictive" environment. In an opinion by Justice Rehnquist, the Court rejected hospital patients' effort to enforce that requirement:

> The Act . . . lists a variety of conditions for the receipt of federal funds. Under § 6005, for example, the Secretary "as a condition of providing assistance" shall require that "each recipient of such assistance take affirmative action" to hire qualified handicapped individuals. Each State, in turn, shall "as a condition" of receiving assistance submit to the Secretary a plan to evaluate the services provided under the Act. § 6009. Each State shall also "as a condition" of receiving assistance "provide the Secretary satisfactory assurances that each program . . . which receives funds from the State's allotment . . . has in effect for each developmentally disabled person who receives services from or under the program a habilitation plan." § 6011(a). And § 6012(a) conditions aid on a State's promise to "have in effect a system to protect and advocate the rights of persons with developmental disabilities."
>
> At issue here . . . is § 6010, the "bill of rights" provision. It states in relevant part:
>
>> "Congress makes the following findings respecting the rights of persons with developmental disabilities:
>>
>> "(1) Persons with developmental disabilities have a right to appropriate treatment, services, and habilitation for such disabilities.
>>
>> "(2) The treatment, services, and habilitation for a person with developmental disabilities should be designed to maximize the developmental potential of the person and should be provided in the setting that is least restrictive of the person's personal liberty.

"(3) The Federal Government and the States both have an obligation to assure that public funds are not provided to any institutio[n] ... that—(A) does not provide treatment, services, and habilitation which is appropriate to the needs of such person; or (B) does not meet the following minimum standards ...."

Noticeably absent from § 6010 is any language suggesting that § 6010 is a "condition" for the receipt of federal funding under the Act. Section 6010 thus stands in sharp contrast to §§ 6005, 6009, 6011, and 6012....

We are persuaded that § 6010, when read in the context of other more specific provisions of the Act, does no more than express a congressional preference for certain kinds of treatment. It is simply a general statement of "findings" and, as such, is too thin a reed to support the rights and obligations read into it by the court below....

[T]he court below failed to recognize the well-settled distinction between congressional "encouragement" of state programs and the imposition of binding obligations on the States.

Dissenting in part, Justice White, joined by Justices Brennan and Marshall, argued that § 6010 did in fact impose obligations on funding recipients: "Section 6010(3), for example, obligates the Federal and State Governments not to spend the public funds on programs that do not carry out the basic requirement of § 6010(1) and, more specifically, do not meet minimum standards with respect to certain aspects of treatment and custody." The dissenters also found that the legislative history supported treating the requirements of § 6010 as rights-creating.

The same year as *Pennhurst*, the Supreme Court recognized another important limitation on enforceability in *Middlesex County Sewerage Authority v. National Sea Clammers Ass'n*, 453 U.S. 1 (1981). There, an association of fishermen sued various federal, state and local officials for alleged violations of the Federal Water Pollution Control Act (FWPCA) and Marine Protection, Research, and Sanctuaries Act (MPRSA), among other claims. One of the questions before the Court was whether these federal laws could be enforced via § 1983.

Writing for the Court, Justice Powell first recounted the basis on which the district court had dismissed the complaint:

With respect to the claims based on alleged violations of the FWPCA, the court noted that respondents had failed to comply with the 60-day notice requirement of the "citizen suit" provision in ... the Act. This provision allows suits under the Act by private citizens, but authorizes only prospective relief, and the citizen plaintiffs first must give notice to the EPA, the State, and any alleged violator. Because respondents did not give the requisite notice, the court refused to allow them to proceed with a claim under the Act independent of the citizen-suit provision.... The court applied the same analysis to respondents' claims under the MPRSA, which contains similar citizen-suit and notice provisions.

The majority decided that the district court had been correct to hold the plaintiffs to the procedures provided in the FWPCA and MPRSA, and that these statutes could not be enforced under § 1983:

[W]hen "a state official is alleged to have violated a federal statute which provides its own comprehensive enforcement scheme, the requirements of that enforcement procedure may not be bypassed by bringing suit directly under § 1983." As discussed above, the FWPCA and MPRSA do provide quite comprehensive enforcement mechanisms. It is hard to believe that Congress intended to preserve the

§ 1983 right of action when it created so many specific statutory remedies, including the two citizen-suit provisions.[31]

We therefore conclude that the existence of these express remedies demonstrates not only that Congress intended to foreclose implied private actions but also that it intended to supplant any remedy that otherwise would be available under § 1983.

In a partial concurrence and partial dissent, Justice Stevens, joined by Justice Blackmun, disagreed that § 1983 enforcement was foreclosed, arguing that "rules are meant to be obeyed, and those who violate them should be held responsible for their misdeeds. Since the earliest days of the common law, it has been the business of courts to fashion remedies for wrongs."

Notes and Questions

1. What are the implications of *Pennhurst*'s limitation on § 1983 enforcement of federal statutes? What kinds of statutory provisions can be enforced? How much guidance does *Pennhurst* provide regarding which are enforceable and which are not?

2. What is the textual basis for the majority's approach in *Pennhurst*? Given *Thiboutot*'s rigid textualism, why shouldn't "and laws" mean "and any laws"? Is there some buyer's remorse here on the part of the *Thiboutot* majority as the Justices contemplate how sweeping that decision could be if every provision of every federal law is enforceable?

3. Justice Stevens's dissent in *Sea Clammers* chides the majority with the simple and intuitive proposition that rules are meant to be obeyed and therefore must be enforced. Does the majority foreclose enforcement of the environmental statutes at issue? What is the practical difference between Justice Stevens's approach and the majority's?

4. What is the difference between the question considered in *Pennhurst* and the one considered in *Sea Clammers*? How do they relate to each other?

3. THE TWO-PART TEST FOR ENFORCEABILITY OF STATUTORY RIGHTS

Two subsequent cases synthesized the holdings in *Pennhurst* and *Sea Clammers* into a unified framework for analyzing statutory enforceability under § 1983.

In *Wright v. City of Roanoke Redevelopment & Housing Authority*, 479 U.S. 418 (1987), the Court considered whether § 1983 could be used to enforce the Brooke Amendment to the Housing Act of 1937, which imposed a ceiling on rents charged to public housing tenants. The plaintiffs in *Wright* were public housing tenants who claimed that the housing authority of Roanoke, Virginia, had violated the Brooke Amendment's rent ceiling by overbilling them for utilities. The district court

---

31. . . . [C]ontrary to Justice Stevens' argument, we do not suggest that the burden is on a plaintiff to demonstrate congressional intent to preserve § 1983 remedies.

granted summary judgment for the City and the court of appeals affirmed, ruling that tenants' rights under the Brooke Amendment are enforceable only by the U.S. Department of Housing and Urban Development (HUD). Justice White's opinion for the Court reversed:

> *Thiboutot* held that § 1983 was available to enforce violations of federal statutes by agents of the State. *Pennhurst* and *Sea Clammers*, however, recognized two exceptions to the application of § 1983 to remedy statutory violations: where Congress has foreclosed such enforcement of the statute in the enactment itself and where the statute did not create enforceable rights, privileges, or immunities within the meaning of § 1983. In *Pennhurst*, a § 1983 action did not lie because the statutory provisions were thought to be only statements of "findings" indicating no more than a congressional preference—at most a "nudge in the preferred directio[n]," and not intended to rise to the level of an enforceable right. In *Sea Clammers*, an intent to foreclose resort to § 1983 was found in the comprehensive remedial scheme provided by Congress, a scheme that itself provided for private actions and left no room for additional private remedies under § 1983. Similarly, *Smith v. Robinson*, 468 U.S. 992 (1984), held that allowing a plaintiff to circumvent the Education of the Handicapped Act's administrative remedies would be inconsistent with Congress' carefully tailored scheme, which itself allowed private parties to seek remedies for violating federal law. Under these cases, if there is a state deprivation of a "right" secured by a federal statute, § 1983 provides a remedial cause of action unless the state actor demonstrates by express provision or other specific evidence from the statute itself that Congress intended to foreclose such private enforcement. "We do not lightly conclude that Congress intended to preclude reliance on § 1983 as a remedy" for the deprivation of a federally secured right. *Smith*. . . .
>
> In both *Sea Clammers* and *Smith v. Robinson*, the statutes at issue themselves provided for private judicial remedies, thereby evidencing congressional intent to supplant the § 1983 remedy. There is nothing of that kind found in the Brooke Amendment or elsewhere in the Housing Act. Indeed, the only private remedy provided for is the local grievance procedures which the Act now requires. These procedures are not open to class grievances; and even if tenants may grieve about a PHA's utility allowance schedule, which petitioners dispute, the existence of a state administrative remedy does not ordinarily foreclose resort to § 1983. *See Patsy*.
>
> The Court of Appeals and respondents rely on HUD's authority to audit, enforce annual contributions contracts, and cut off federal funds. But these generalized powers are insufficient to indicate a congressional intention to foreclose § 1983 remedies. . . .
>
> [I]t is said that tenants may sue on their lease in state courts and enforce their Brooke Amendment rights in that litigation. Perhaps they could, but the state-court remedy is hardly a reason to bar an action under § 1983, which was adopted to provide a federal remedy for the enforcement of federal rights. . . .
>
> [R]espondent asserts that neither the Brooke Amendment nor the interim regulations gave the tenants any specific or definable rights to utilities, that is, no enforceable rights within the meaning of § 1983. We perceive little substance in this claim. The Brooke Amendment [imposed] . . . mandatory limitation focusing on the individual family and its income. The intent to benefit tenants is undeniable. . . .
>
> Respondent nevertheless asserts that the provision for a "reasonable" allowance for utilities is too vague and amorphous to confer on tenants an enforceable "right"

within the meaning of § 1983 and that the whole matter of utility allowances must be left to the discretion of the PHA, subject to supervision by HUD. The regulations, however, defining the statutory concept of "rent" as including utilities, have the force of law, they specifically set out guidelines that the PHAs were to follow in establishing utility allowances, and they require notice to tenants and an opportunity to comment on proposed allowances. In our view, the benefits Congress intended to confer on tenants are sufficiently specific and definite to qualify as enforceable rights under *Pennhurst* and § 1983, rights that are not, as respondent suggests, beyond the competence of the judiciary to enforce.

In dissent, Justice O'Connor, joined by Chief Justice Rehnquist and Justices Powell and Scalia, framed the inquiry in these terms:

> Whether a federal statute confers substantive rights is not an issue unique to § 1983 actions. In implied right of action cases, the Court also has asked . . . whether "the statute create[s] a federal right in favor of the plaintiff." In determining whether a statute creates enforceable rights, the "key to the inquiry is the intent of the Legislature." *Sea Clammers*. We have looked first to the statutory language, to determine whether it is "phrased in terms of the persons benefited," *Cannon*, and is cast in mandatory rather than precatory terms. *See Pennhurst*. We then have reviewed the legislative history of the statute and other traditional aids of statutory interpretation to determine congressional intent to create enforceable rights. *See Sea Clammers*.

Justice O'Connor argued that the Brooke Amendment's legislative history did not support finding an intent to create a "statutory right" to a limit on utility payments and that such a right would be ill-suited to judicial enforcement because the "provisions remained subject to the exercise of wide discretion by the local housing authorities, thereby rendering it difficult or impossible to determine whether a violation occurred."

The standard for § 1983 enforceability of statutory rights further crystalized in *Wilder v. Virginia Hospital Ass'n*, 496 U.S. 498 (1990). There, an association of hospitals claimed that state officials failed to apply adequate reimbursement rates for Medicaid services that the hospitals had provided. The Medicaid Act provision at issue, known as the Boren Amendment, required "reimbursement according to rates that a 'State finds, and makes assurances satisfactory to the Secretary, are reasonable and adequate to meet the costs which must be incurred by efficiently and economically operated facilities.'" 42 U.S.C. § 1396a(a)(13)(A). The Court held the provision enforceable in an opinion by Justice Brennan, who began by restating the relevant inquiry:

> In *Thiboutot*, we held that § 1983 provides a cause of action for violations of federal statutes as well as the Constitution. We have recognized two exceptions to this rule. A plaintiff alleging a violation of a federal statute will be permitted to sue under § 1983 unless (1) "the statute [does] not create enforceable rights, privileges, or immunities within the meaning of § 1983," or (2) "Congress has foreclosed such enforcement of the statute in the enactment itself." *Wright*.[9] Petitioners argue first

---

9. This is a different inquiry than that involved in determining whether a private right of action can be implied from a particular statute. In implied right of action cases, we employ the four-factor *Cort [v. Ash]* test to determine "whether Congress intended to create the private remedy asserted" for the violation of statutory rights. The test reflects a concern, grounded in separation of powers, that

that the Boren Amendment does not create any "enforceable rights" and second, that Congress has foreclosed enforcement of the Act under § 1983. We address these contentions in turn. . . .

[The first] inquiry turns on whether "the provision in question was intend[ed] to benefit the putative plaintiff." If so, the provision creates an enforceable right unless it reflects merely a "congressional preference" for a certain kind of conduct rather than a binding obligation on the governmental unit, *Pennhurst*, or unless the interest the plaintiff asserts is "'too vague and amorphous'" such that it is "'beyond the competence of the judiciary to enforce.'" (quoting *Wright*). Under this test, we conclude that the Act creates a right enforceable by health care providers under § 1983 . . . .

There can be little doubt that health care providers are the intended beneficiaries of the Boren Amendment. The provision establishes a system for reimbursement of providers and is phrased in terms benefiting health care providers: It requires a state plan to provide for "payment . . . of the *hospital* services, *nursing facility* services, and services in an *intermediate care facility* for the mentally retarded provided under the plan." 42 U.S.C. § 1396a(a)(13)(A) (emphasis added). The question in this case is whether the Boren Amendment imposes a "binding obligation" on the States that gives rise to enforceable rights. . . .

In light of *Pennhurst* and *Wright*, we conclude that the Boren Amendment imposes a binding obligation on States participating in the Medicaid program to adopt reasonable and adequate rates and that this obligation is enforceable under § 1983 by health care providers. The Boren Amendment is cast in mandatory rather than precatory terms: The state plan "*must*" "provide for payment . . . of hospital[s]" according to rates the State finds are reasonable and adequate. 42 U.S.C. § 1396a(a)(13)(A) (emphasis added). . . .

Petitioners also argue that Congress has foreclosed enforcement of the Medicaid Act under § 1983. We find little merit in this argument. "'We do not lightly conclude that Congress intended to preclude reliance on § 1983 as a remedy' for the deprivation of a federally secured right." *Wright*. The burden is on the State to show "by express provision or other specific evidence from the statute itself that Congress intended to foreclose such private enforcement." *Wright*. . . .

The Medicaid Act . . . authorizes the Secretary to withhold approval of plans, or to curtail federal funds to States whose plans are not in compliance with the Act. In addition, the Act requires States to adopt a procedure for postpayment claims review to "ensure the proper and efficient payment of claims and management of the program." By regulation, the States are required to adopt an appeals procedure by which individual providers may obtain administrative review of reimbursement rates. . . .

This administrative scheme cannot be considered sufficiently comprehensive to demonstrate a congressional intent to withdraw the private remedy of § 1983. In *Wright*, we concluded that the "generalized powers" of the Department of Housing and Urban Development (HUD) to audit and cut off federal funds were insufficient to foreclose reliance on § 1983 to vindicate federal rights.

Congress rather than the courts controls the availability of remedies for violations of statutes. Because § 1983 provides an "alternative source of express congressional authorization of private suits," *Sea Clammers*, these separation-of-powers concerns are not present in a § 1983 case. Consistent with this view, we recognize an exception to the general rule that § 1983 provides a remedy for violation of federal statutory rights only when Congress has affirmatively withdrawn the remedy. *See Wright*.

Chief Justice Rehnquist's dissent, joined by Justices O'Connor, Scalia, and Kennedy, found no congressional intent to create an enforceable right in particular rates because the provision invoked was "simply a part of the thirteenth listed requirement for such plans," and because of "the absence in the statute of any express 'focus' on providers as a beneficiary class of the provision." Moreover, the dissenters argued, the structure of the statute reflected Congress's commitment only to a particular process for setting rates, not to any particular outcomes.

Notes and Questions

1. In light of *Wright* and *Wilder*, what is the structure of the § 1983 statutory enforceability analysis? What two questions are asked? What factors determine the answers to each question?

2. After *Wright* and *Wilder*, what is required for a *Sea Clammers* "foreclosure" argument to succeed?

3. In light of the Court's § 1983 enforceability jurisprudence, is all the work the Court did in *Cannon* (Chapter 7) to find an implied right of action under Title IX irrelevant? In what circumstances would an implied right of action be more useful than § 1983? (Hint: Think about which types of defendants can be sued under each.)

4. The dissenters in *Wright* compare the § 1983 inquiry to the private right of action inquiry we studied in Chapter 7. Is that an apt comparison? Why or why not? Keep this analogy in mind; it will make an important reappearance.

B. THE CONTEMPORARY TEST FOR § 1983 ENFORCEABILITY

The Court further clarified what makes a right "enforceable" in the two cases that define the test today: *Blessing v. Freestone* and *Gonzaga University v. Doe*.

Blessing v. Freestone
520 U.S. 329 (1997)

▪ *Justice O'CONNOR delivered the opinion of the Court. . . .*

Arizona participates in the federal Aid to Families with Dependent Children (AFDC) program, which provides subsistence welfare benefits to needy families. To qualify for federal AFDC funds, the State must certify that it will operate a child support enforcement program that conforms with the numerous requirements set forth in Title IV-D of the Social Security Act, and will do so pursuant to a detailed plan that has been approved by the Secretary of Health and Human Services. . . .

If a State does not "substantially comply" with the requirements of Title IV-D, the Secretary is authorized to penalize the State by reducing its AFDC grant by up to five percent. The Secretary has interpreted "substantial compliance" as: (a) full compliance with requirements that services be offered statewide and that certain recipients be notified monthly of the support collected, as well as with reporting, recordkeeping, and accounting rules; (b) 90 percent compliance with case opening and case closure criteria; and (c) 75 percent compliance with most remaining program requirements. . . .

[Arizona has a poor record of enforcing child support obligations; it obtains regular child support payments for fewer than five percent of the parents it serves. Several Arizona AFDC participants sued Arizona officials under § 1983 for violating Title IV-D. Arizona's failings, plaintiffs claimed, resulted from staff shortages, high caseloads, unmanageable backlogs, and accounting and recordkeeping deficiencies. The district court, holding that Congress had foreclosed private enforcement of Title IV-D, granted summary judgment to defendants. The court of appeals reversed, holding the title enforceable.] . . .

In order to seek redress through § 1983, . . . plaintiff must assert the violation of a federal *right*, not merely a violation of federal *law*. We have traditionally looked at three factors when determining whether a particular statutory provision gives rise to a federal right. First, Congress must have intended that the provision in question benefit the plaintiff. *Wright*. Second, the plaintiff must demonstrate that the right assertedly protected by the statute is not so "vague and amorphous" that its enforcement would strain judicial competence. *Id.* Third, the statute must unambiguously impose a binding obligation on the States. In other words, the provision giving rise to the asserted right must be couched in mandatory, rather than precatory, terms. *Wilder*.

Even if a plaintiff demonstrates that a federal statute creates an individual right, there is only a rebuttable presumption that the right is enforceable under § 1983. Because our inquiry focuses on congressional intent, dismissal is proper if Congress "specifically foreclosed a remedy under § 1983." Congress may do so expressly, by forbidding recourse to § 1983 in the statute itself, or impliedly, by creating a comprehensive enforcement scheme that is incompatible with individual enforcement under § 1983. . . .

Without distinguishing among the numerous rights that might have been created by this federally funded welfare program, the Court of Appeals agreed in sweeping terms that "Title IV-D creates enforceable rights in families in need of Title IV-D services." The Court of Appeals did not specify exactly which "rights" it was purporting to recognize, but it apparently believed that federal law gave respondents the right to have the State substantially comply with Title IV-D in all respects. We disagree.

As an initial matter, the lower court's holding that Title IV-D "creates enforceable rights" paints with too broad a brush. It was incumbent upon respondents to identify with particularity the rights they claimed, since it is impossible to determine whether Title IV-D, as an undifferentiated whole, gives rise to undefined "rights." Only when the complaint is broken down into manageable analytic bites can a court ascertain whether each separate claim satisfies the various criteria we have set forth for determining whether a federal statute creates rights. . . .

The Court of Appeals did not engage in such a methodical inquiry. As best we can tell, the Court of Appeals seemed to think that respondents had a right to require the Director of Arizona's child support agency to bring the State's program into substantial compliance with Title IV-D. But the requirement that a State operate its child support program in "substantial compliance" with Title IV-D was not intended to benefit individual children and custodial parents, and therefore it does not constitute a federal right. Far from creating an individual entitlement to services, the standard is simply a yardstick for the Secretary to measure the systemwide performance of a State's Title IV-D program. Thus, the Secretary must look to the aggregate services provided by the State, not to whether the needs of any particular person have been satisfied. A State substantially complies with Title IV-D when it provides most mandated services (such as enforcement of support obligations) in only 75 percent of the cases reviewed during the federal audit period. States must aim to establish paternity in 90 percent of all eligible cases, but may satisfy considerably lower targets so long as their efforts are steadily improving. It is clear, then, that even when a State is in "substantial compliance" with Title IV-D, any individual plaintiff might still be among the 10 or 25 percent of persons whose needs ultimately go unmet. Moreover, even upon a finding of substantial noncompliance, the Secretary can merely reduce the State's AFDC grant by up to five percent; she cannot, by force of her own authority, command the State to take any particular action or to provide any services to certain individuals. In short, the substantial compliance standard is designed simply to trigger penalty provisions that increase the frequency of audits and reduce the State's AFDC grant by a maximum of five percent. As such, it does not give rise to individual rights. . . .

We do not foreclose the possibility that some provisions of Title IV-D give rise to individual rights. The lower court did not separate out the particular rights it believed arise from the statutory scheme, and we think the complaint is less than clear in this regard. . . . We think that this defect is best addressed by sending the case back for the District Court to construe the complaint in the first instance, in order to determine exactly what rights, considered in their most concrete, specific form, respondents are asserting. . . .

Because we leave open the possibility that Title IV-D may give rise to some individually enforceable rights, we pause to consider petitioner's final argument that no remand is warranted because the statute contains "a remedial scheme that is 'sufficiently comprehensive . . . to demonstrate congressional intent to preclude the remedy of suits under § 1983.'" *Wilder* (quoting *Sea Clammers*). . . .

Only twice have we found a remedial scheme sufficiently comprehensive to supplant § 1983: in *Sea Clammers*, and *Smith*. In *Sea Clammers*, we focused on the "unusually elaborate enforcement provisions" of the Federal Water Pollution Control Act, which placed at the disposal of the Environmental Protection Agency a panoply of enforcement options, including noncompliance orders, civil suits, and criminal penalties. We emphasized that several provisions of the Act authorized private persons to initiate enforcement actions. . . . Likewise, in *Smith*, the review scheme in the Education of the Handicapped Act permitted aggrieved individuals to invoke "carefully tailored" local administrative procedures followed by federal judicial review. . . .

The enforcement scheme that Congress created in Title IV-D is far more limited than those in *Sea Clammers* and *Smith*. Unlike the federal programs at issue in those cases, Title IV-D contains no private remedy—either judicial or administrative—through which aggrieved persons can seek redress. The only way that Title IV-D assures that States live up to their child support plans is through the Secretary's oversight. The Secretary can audit only for "substantial compliance" on a programmatic basis. Furthermore, up to 25 percent of eligible children and custodial parents can go without most of the services enumerated in Title IV-D before the Secretary can trim a State's AFDC grant. . . . To the extent that Title IV-D may give rise to individual rights, therefore, we agree with the Court of Appeals that the Secretary's oversight powers are not comprehensive enough to close the door on § 1983 liability. . . .

■ *Justice* SCALIA, *with whom Justice* KENNEDY *joins, concurring.*

[An agreement between the federal government and a State] is "in the nature of a contract": The State promises to provide certain services to private individuals, in exchange for which the Federal Government promises to give the State funds. In contract law, when such an arrangement is made (A promises to pay B money, in exchange for which B promises to provide services to C), the person who receives the benefit of the exchange of promises between the two others (C) is called a third-party beneficiary. Until relatively recent times, the third-party beneficiary was generally regarded as a stranger to the contract, and could not sue upon it; that is to say, if, in the example given above, B broke his promise and did not provide services to C, the only person who could enforce the promise in court was the other party to the contract, A. This appears to have been the law at the time § 1983 was enacted. If so, the ability of persons in respondents' situation to compel a State to make good on its promise to the Federal Government was not a "righ[t] . . . secured by the . . . laws" under § 1983. While it is of course true that newly enacted laws are automatically embraced within § 1983, it does not follow that the question of what rights those new laws (or, for that matter, old laws) secure is to be determined according to modern notions rather than according to the understanding of § 1983 when it was enacted. Allowing third-party beneficiaries of commitments to the Federal Government to sue is certainly a vast expansion.

It must be acknowledged that *Wright* and *Wilder* permitted beneficiaries of federal-state contracts to sue under § 1983, but the argument set forth above was not raised. I am not prepared without further consideration to reject the possibility that third-party-beneficiary suits simply do not lie. I join the Court's opinion because . . . it leaves that possibility open.

* * *

Just a few years after *Blessing*, the Court further adjusted the test for finding an enforceable right. The new decision took its cues from the Court's decision the previous year in *Alexander v. Sandoval* (Chapter 7) and from the approach of Justice O'Connor's dissent in *Wright*. The result was a test that retained the two-step structure from *Wright* and *Wilder* but rendered the inquiry at the first step (the enforceable-right question) much harder for plaintiffs to satisfy than it was in *Wright* and *Wilder*.

Gonzaga University v. Doe
536 U.S. 273 (2002)

■ *Chief Justice* REHNQUIST *delivered the opinion of the Court.*

The question presented is whether a student may sue a private university for damages under 42 U.S.C. § 1983 to enforce provisions of the Family Educational Rights and Privacy Act of 1974 (FERPA or Act), which prohibit the federal funding of educational institutions that have a policy or practice of releasing education records to unauthorized persons. We hold such an action foreclosed because the relevant provisions of FERPA create no personal rights to enforce under 42 U.S.C. § 1983.

Respondent John Doe is a former undergraduate in the School of Education at Gonzaga University, a private university in Spokane, Washington. He planned to graduate and teach at a Washington public elementary school. Washington at the time required all of its new teachers to obtain an affidavit of good moral character from a dean of their graduating college or university. In October 1993, Roberta League, Gonzaga's "teacher certification specialist," overheard one student tell another that respondent engaged in acts of sexual misconduct against Jane Doe, a female undergraduate. League launched an investigation and contacted the state agency responsible for teacher certification, identifying respondent by name and discussing the allegations against him. Respondent did not learn of the investigation, or that information about him had been disclosed, until March 1994, when he was told by League and others that he would not receive the affidavit required for certification as a Washington schoolteacher.

Respondent then sued Gonzaga and League (petitioners) in state court. He alleged violations of Washington tort and contract law, as well as a pendent violation of § 1983 for the release of personal information to an "unauthorized person" in violation of FERPA.[1] A jury found for respondent on all counts, awarding him $1,155,000, including $150,000 in compensatory damages and $300,000 in punitive damages on the FERPA claim. . . .

Congress enacted FERPA under its spending power to condition the receipt of federal funds on certain requirements relating to the access and disclosure of student educational records. The Act directs the Secretary of Education to withhold

---

1. The Washington Court of Appeals and the Washington Supreme Court found petitioners to have acted "under color of state law" for purposes of § 1983 when they disclosed respondent's personal information. . . . Although the petition for certiorari challenged this holding, we agreed to review only the question posed in the first paragraph of this opinion. . . . We therefore assume without deciding that the relevant disclosures occurred under color of state law.

federal funds from any public or private "educational agency or institution" that fails to comply with these conditions. As relevant here, the Act provides:

> "No funds shall be made available under any applicable program to any educational agency or institution which has a policy or practice of permitting the release of education records (or personally identifiable information contained therein . . .) of students without the written consent of their parents to any individual, agency, or organization."

20 U.S.C. § 1232g(b)(1).

The Act directs the Secretary of Education to enforce this and other of the Act's spending conditions. The Secretary is required to establish an office and review board within the Department of Education for "investigating, processing, reviewing, and adjudicating violations of [the Act]." Funds may be terminated only if the Secretary determines that a recipient institution "is failing to comply substantially with any requirement of [the Act]" and that such compliance "cannot be secured by voluntary means." . . .

[U]nless Congress "speak[s] with a clear voice," and manifests an "unambiguous" intent to confer individual rights, federal funding provisions provide no basis for private enforcement by § 1983. . . .

[S]ome courts [have] interpret[ed] *Blessing* as allowing plaintiffs to enforce a statute under § 1983 so long as the plaintiff falls within the general zone of interest that the statute is intended to protect, something less than what is required for a statute to create rights enforceable directly from the statute itself under an implied private right of action. Fueling this uncertainty is the notion that our implied private right of action cases have no bearing on the standards for discerning whether a statute creates rights enforceable by § 1983. . . .

We now reject the notion that our cases permit anything short of an unambiguously conferred right to support a cause of action brought under § 1983. Section 1983 provides a remedy only for the deprivation of "rights, privileges, or immunities secured by the Constitution and laws" of the United States. Accordingly, it is *rights,* not the broader or vaguer "benefits" or "interests," that may be enforced under the authority of that section. This being so, we further reject the notion that our implied right of action cases are separate and distinct from our § 1983 cases. To the contrary, our implied right of action cases should guide the determination of whether a statute confers rights enforceable under § 1983.

We have recognized that whether a statutory violation may be enforced through § 1983 "is a different inquiry than that involved in determining whether a private right of action can be implied from a particular statute." *Wilder.* But the inquiries overlap in one meaningful respect—in either case we must first determine whether Congress *intended to create a federal right.* Thus we have held that "[t]he question whether Congress . . . intended to create a private right of action [is] definitively answered in the negative" where a "statute by its terms grants no private rights to any identifiable class." For a statute to create such private rights, its text must be "phrased in terms of the persons benefited." *Cannon.* We have recognized, for example, that Title VI of the Civil Rights Act of 1964 and Title IX of the Education Amendments of 1972 create individual rights because those statutes are phrased "with an *unmistakable focus* on the benefited class." *Id.* (emphasis added). But even where a statute is phrased in such explicit rights-creating terms, a plaintiff suing under an implied right of action still must show that the statute manifests an intent "to create not just a private *right* but also a private *remedy*." *Sandoval* (emphases added).

Plaintiffs suing under § 1983 do not have the burden of showing an intent to create a private remedy because § 1983 generally supplies a remedy for the vindication of rights secured by federal statutes. Once a plaintiff demonstrates that a statute confers an individual right, the right is presumptively enforceable by § 1983. But the initial inquiry—determining whether a statute confers any right at all—is no different from the initial inquiry in an implied right of action case, the express purpose of which is to determine whether or not a statute "confer[s] rights on a particular class of persons." This makes obvious sense, since § 1983 merely provides a mechanism for enforcing individual rights "secured" elsewhere, *i.e.,* rights independently "secured by the Constitution and laws" of the United States. "[O]ne cannot go into court and claim a 'violation of § 1983'—for § 1983 by itself does not protect anyone against anything."

A court's role in discerning whether personal rights exist in the § 1983 context should therefore not differ from its role in discerning whether personal rights exist in the implied right of action context. Both inquiries simply require a determination as to whether or not Congress intended to confer individual rights upon a class of beneficiaries. Compare *Wright* (statute must be "intended to rise to the level of an enforceable right"), with *Sandoval* (statute must evince "congressional intent to create new rights"). Accordingly, where the text and structure of a statute provide no indication that Congress intends to create new individual rights, there is no basis for a private suit, whether under § 1983 or under an implied right of action.

Justice Stevens disagrees with this conclusion principally because separation-of-powers concerns are, in his view, more pronounced in the implied right of action context as opposed to the § 1983 context. But we fail to see how relations between the branches are served by having courts apply a multifactor balancing test to pick and choose which federal requirements may be enforced by § 1983 and which may not. Nor are separation-of-powers concerns within the Federal Government the only guideposts in this sort of analysis. See *Will v. Michigan Dept. of State Police* ("[I]f Congress intends to alter the 'usual constitutional balance between the States and the Federal Government,' it must make its intention to do so 'unmistakably clear in the language of the statute.'").

With this principle in mind, there is no question that FERPA's nondisclosure provisions fail to confer enforceable rights. To begin with, the provisions entirely lack the sort of "rights-creating" language critical to showing the requisite congressional intent to create new rights. *Sandoval*; *Cannon*. Unlike the individually focused terminology of Titles VI and IX ("No person . . . shall . . . be subjected to discrimination"), FERPA's provisions speak only to the Secretary of Education, directing that "[n]o funds shall be made available" to any "educational agency or institution" which has a prohibited "policy or practice." This focus is two steps removed from the interests of individual students and parents and clearly does not confer the sort of "*individual* entitlement" that is enforceable under § 1983. *Blessing*. As we said in *Cannon*: "There would be far less reason to infer a private remedy in favor of individual persons if Congress, instead of drafting Title IX with an unmistakable focus on the benefited class, had written it simply as a ban on discriminatory conduct by recipients of federal funds or as a prohibition against the disbursement of public funds to educational institutions engaged in discriminatory practices." See also *Sandoval* ("Statutes that focus on the person regulated rather than the individuals protected create 'no implication of an intent to confer rights on a particular class of persons.'").

FERPA's nondisclosure provisions further speak only in terms of institutional policy and practice, not individual instances of disclosure. See §§ 1232g(b)(1)-(2) (prohibiting the funding of "any educational agency or institution which has a *policy or practice* of permitting the release of education records" (emphasis added)). Therefore, as in *Blessing*, they have an "aggregate" focus, they are not concerned with "whether the needs of any particular person have been satisfied," and they cannot "give rise to individual rights." Recipient institutions can further avoid termination of funding so long as they "comply substantially" with the Act's requirements. This, too, is not unlike *Blessing*, which found that Title IV-D failed to support a § 1983 suit in part because it only required "substantial compliance" with federal regulations....

Our conclusion that FERPA's nondisclosure provisions fail to confer enforceable rights is buttressed by the mechanism that Congress chose to provide for enforcing those provisions. Congress expressly authorized the Secretary of Education to "*deal with violations*" of the Act (emphasis added), and required the Secretary to "establish or designate [a] review board" for investigating and adjudicating such violations. Pursuant to these provisions, the Secretary created the Family Policy Compliance Office (FPCO) "to act as the Review Board required under the Act [and] to enforce the Act with respect to all applicable programs." The FPCO permits students and parents who suspect a violation of the Act to file individual written complaints. If a complaint is timely and contains required information, the FPCO will initiate an investigation, notify the educational institution of the charge, and request a written response. If a violation is found, the FPCO distributes a notice of factual findings and a "statement of the specific steps that the agency or institution must take to comply" with FERPA. These administrative procedures squarely distinguish this case from *Wright* and *Wilder*, where an aggrieved individual lacked any federal review mechanism, and further counsel against our finding a congressional intent to create individually enforceable private rights....

In sum, if Congress wishes to create new rights enforceable under § 1983, it must do so in clear and unambiguous terms....

▪ *Justice BREYER, with whom Justice SOUTER joins, concurring in the judgment.*

The ultimate question, in respect to whether private individuals may bring a lawsuit to enforce a federal statute, through 42 U.S.C. § 1983 or otherwise, is a question of congressional intent. In my view, the factors set forth in this Court's § 1983 cases are helpful indications of that intent. See, *e.g., Blessing*. But the statute books are too many, the laws too diverse, and their purposes too complex, for any single legal formula to offer more than general guidance. I would not, in effect, predetermine an outcome through the use of a presumption—such as the majority's presumption that a right is conferred only if set forth "unambiguously" in the statute's "text and structure."

At the same time, I do not believe that Congress intended private judicial enforcement of this statute's "school record privacy" provisions. The Court mentions most of the considerations I find persuasive . . . .

■ *Justice* STEVENS, *with whom Justice* GINSBURG *joins, dissenting.* . . .

[The provision at issue] plainly meets the standards we articulated in *Blessing* for establishing a federal right: It is directed to the benefit of individual students and parents; the provision is binding on States, as it is "couched in mandatory, rather than precatory, terms"; and the right is far from "'vague and amorphous.'" Indeed, the right at issue is more specific and clear than rights previously found enforceable under § 1983 in *Wright* and *Wilder*, both of which involved plaintiffs' entitlement to "reasonable" amounts of money. As such, the federal right created by § 1232g(b) is "presumptively enforceable by § 1983." . . .

[T]he Court contrasts FERPA's "[n]o funds shall be made available" language with "individually focused terminology" characteristic of federal antidiscrimination statutes, such as "[n]o person . . . shall . . . be subjected to discrimination." But the sort of rights-creating language idealized by the Court has *never* been present in our § 1983 cases; rather, such language ordinarily gives rise to an implied cause of action. See *Cannon*. None of our four most recent cases involving whether a Spending Clause statute created rights enforceable under § 1983 . . . involved the sort of "no person shall" rights-creating language envisioned by the Court. And in two of those cases—*Wright* and *Wilder*—we concluded that individual rights enforceable under § 1983 existed. . . .

As our cases recognize, Congress can rebut the presumption of enforcement under § 1983. . . . [But the] administrative avenues [described by the majority] fall far short of what is necessary to overcome the presumption of enforceability. . . .[5] . . .

A requirement that Congress intend a "right to support a cause of action," as opposed to simply the creation of an individual federal right, makes sense in the implied right of action context. As we have explained, our implied right of action cases "reflec[t] a concern, grounded in separation of powers, that

---

5. The Court does not test FERPA's administrative scheme against the "comprehensive enforcement scheme," standard for rebutting the presumptive enforceability of a federal right, because it concludes that there is no federal right to trigger this additional analysis. Yet, at the same time, the Court imports "enforcement scheme" considerations into the initial question whether the statute creates a presumptively enforceable right. Folding such considerations into the rights question renders the rebuttal inquiry superfluous. Moreover, the Court's approach is inconsistent with our past cases, which have kept separate the inquiries whether there is a right and whether an enforcement scheme rebuts presumptive enforceability. . . .

Congress rather than the courts controls the availability of remedies for violations of statutes." However, imposing the implied right of action framework upon the § 1983 inquiry is not necessary: The separation-of-powers concerns present in the implied right of action context "are not present in a § 1983 case," because Congress expressly authorized private suits in § 1983 itself. *Wilder*. Nor is it consistent with our precedent, which has always treated the implied right of action and § 1983 inquiries as separate. . . .

[O]ur implied right of action cases do not necessarily cleanly separate out the "right" question from the "cause of action" question. For example, in the discussion of rights-creating language in *Cannon*, which the Court characterizes as pertaining only to whether there is a right, *Cannon*'s reasoning is explicitly based on whether there is "reason to infer a private remedy," and the "propriety of implication of a cause of action." Because *Cannon* and other implied right of action cases do not clearly distinguish the questions of "right" and "cause of action," it is inappropriate to use these cases to determine whether a statute creates rights enforceable under § 1983. . . .

Moreover, by circularly defining a right actionable under § 1983 as, in essence, "a right which Congress intended to make enforceable," the Court has eroded—if not eviscerated—the long-established principle of presumptive enforceability of rights under § 1983. . . .

Notes and Questions

1. You might wonder about the relationship among *Wright*, *Wilder*, *Blessing*, and *Gonzaga*. Were *Wright* and *Wilder* overruled by the later cases? Was *Blessing* eclipsed by *Gonzaga*? In fact, courts of appeals today regularly refer to the "*Blessing-Gonzaga*" approach for determining enforceability and treat *Wright* and *Wilder* as good law but rarely invoke them. Is that the path you would have predicted based on your reading of *Blessing* and *Gonzaga*?

2. Do *Blessing* and *Gonzaga* reject enforceability because they have changed the *Wright-Wilder* framework? Because they apply that framework more strictly? Because different statutory provisions are at issue? Some combination of these?

3. What does the "*Blessing-Gonzaga*" framework consist of? How many steps are there? What considerations go into each step? Which party bears the burden at each step?

4. Which aspect of the *Blessing-Gonzaga* analysis is most challenging for plaintiffs to satisfy and why?

5. What do you make of the factor that the majority says "buttresses" its conclusion in *Gonzaga*? Does that discussion clarify the inquiry or confuse it? Does the majority indicate the role of the "buttressing" factor in the formal test for § 1983 statutory enforceability?

6. What is the significance of *Blessing*'s requirement that § 1983 enforceability be determined provision-by-provision rather than at a broader level? Will that

requirement result in more provisions being held enforceable, or fewer? What is its likely effect on the volume of § 1983 statutory-enforceability litigation?

7. Recall Justice Stevens's dissent in *Sandoval* (Chapter 7). Did he turn out to be correct that the effect of that decision could be avoided by pleading a case under § 1983? Why or why not?

8. Which is easier today, the test for finding an implied right of action or the test for § 1983 enforceability of a statute? Why?

9. Consider Justice Stevens's objection to the linkage of implied-right jurisprudence to § 1983-enforceability jurisprudence. Why does he think judicial restraint in one of these areas is more appropriate? What is the majority's response?

Applications

As noted, *Blessing* and *Gonzaga* together define the contours of the § 1983 statutory-enforceability inquiry today. Consider these examples of the *Blessing-Gonzaga* test in practice:

1. Adoption Assistance and Child Welfare Act, 42 U.S.C. § 673(a)(3). This Spending Clause program provides federal payments to participating states, which in turn provide financial assistance to help families adopting special-needs children. After Oregon notified families receiving payments under this statute that the state would be imposing a 7.5 percent across-the-board reduction in payments because of budget shortfalls, a group of families sued to enforce a statutory right under § 673(a)(3) to individualized payment determinations based on their needs.

In *ASW v. Oregon*, 424 F.3d 970 (9th Cir. 2005), the court held § 673(a)(3) enforceable via § 1983:

> Our initial inquiry is whether the text and structure of the Act contains the requisite "rights-creating" language that evinces a congressional intent to confer an entitlement to individualized payment determinations. We conclude that it does.
>
> Section 671 requires Oregon to have a plan that mandates that adoption assistance will be provided in accordance with § 673. Section 673(a)(3) requires that the amount of adoption assistance payments be determined "through agreement between the adoptive parents and the State . . . which . . . take[s] into consideration the circumstances of the adopting parents and the needs of the child being adopted." Furthermore, the amount of the payment may only be readjusted "with the concurrence of the adopting parents, depending upon changes" in the circumstances of the adopting parents and the needs of the child. This language evinces a clear intent to create a federal right. The statutory text unambiguously requires the State to engage in an individualized process with each family that takes into account their unique requirements in determining the amount of their adoption assistance payments throughout the duration of their participation in the program. Just as "[Title VI and Title IX] create individual rights because those statutes are phrased with an unmistakable focus on the benefitted class," *Gonzaga Univ.*, these particular statutory provisions are unambiguously framed in terms of the specific individuals benefitted and contain explicit duty creating language. . . .

The second and third prongs of the *Blessing* test are also satisfied. The right to individualized payment determinations that reflect the unique circumstances of the parents and the special needs of their adopted child is a concrete and objective right, the enforcement of which does not "strain judicial competence." *Blessing*. Furthermore, there is no ambiguity as to what Oregon was required to do under § 673(a)(3) as a condition of receiving federal funding. . . . *Cf. Pennhurst* (holding that the phrases "appropriate treatment" and "least restrictive" were too vague to be enforceable as the State did not agree to any specific terms and conditions as a prerequisite to receiving federal funding).

We are not persuaded by the fact that . . . the Eleventh Circuit reviewed a different provision of [the statute] . . . and concluded that it did not create the right the plaintiffs were seeking to enforce. We do not look at the Act in its entirety and determine at that level of generality whether it creates individual rights. *See Blessing*. Instead, we review only the particular statutory provision at issue.

Because Plaintiffs have asserted a federal right presumptively enforceable under § 1983, the burden falls on the State to rebut this presumption by showing that Congress has "specifically foreclosed a remedy under § 1983" either expressly "or impliedly, by creating a comprehensive enforcement scheme that is incompatible with individual enforcement under § 1983." *Blessing*. . . .

[W]e do "not lightly conclude that Congress intended to preclude reliance on § 1983 as a remedy for the deprivation of a federally secured right." The Act provides that disputes over adoption assistance benefits may be heard before the State agency, but does not mention nor preclude federal review. The mere availability of administrative review mechanisms to protect Plaintiffs' interests cannot defeat their ability to invoke § 1983. *See Blessing*. . . .

[T]he Act does not include a comprehensive enforcement mechanism incompatible with a § 1983 action. It simply provides the beneficiary with an "opportunity for a fair hearing before the State agency" to contest individual benefit claims under the Act. 42 U.S.C. § 671(a)(12). . . .

We conclude therefore that Plaintiffs may proceed with an action under § 1983 on their claim that they were entitled to individualized payment determinations.

2. U.S. Housing Act, 42 U.S.C. § 1437p. The USHA is a federal grant program providing funds to local public housing authorities (PHAs), in exchange for which PHAs agree to comply with a variety of conditions, which relate to (among other things) rent calculation, leases, tenant selection, and demolition or disposition of housing projects. In 2006, the City Council of Washington, D.C., approved a redevelopment plan to demolish and replace the historic Barry Farm public housing property, which was purchased in 1867 and developed as one of the first communities for African-American homeowners after the Civil War. Barry Farm residents who would be displaced sued the D.C. Housing Authority, arguing that the demolition violated a provision of the USHA, § 1437p, placing certain conditions on demolitions.

In *Barry Farm Tenants v. D.C. Housing Authority*, 311 F. Supp. 3d 57 (D.D.C. 2018), the court held this provision unenforceable under § 1983:

The plaintiffs' core allegation underlying this claim is that DCHA "was prohibited from taking any action to demolish Barry Farm without obtaining HUD's [i.e., the U.S. Department of Housing and Urban Development's] approval, as such actions were contrary to its obligation 'to maintain and operate the property as housing for low-income families'. . . . [Its] actions and omissions have resulted in the de facto demolition of units within Barry Farm in violation of 42 U.S.C. § 1437p and 24 C.F.R. § 970.25." The plaintiffs acknowledge that "[t]his express prohibition is not contained in the current text of the [USHA] itself, but in the HUD regulations promulgated thereunder." . . .

It is well-settled that "[l]anguage in a regulation may invoke a private right of action that Congress through statutory text created, but it may not create a right that Congress has not." *Sandoval.* Therefore, the Court considers which specific provisions in Section 1437p could conceivably give rise to an enforceable constructive demolition claim. There are two subsections in Section 1437p potentially relevant to plaintiffs' claims. Subsection (a)(1)(A) and Subsection (a)(3) provide in relevant part:

> [U]pon receiving an application by a public housing agency for authorization, with or without financial assistance under this subchapter, to demolish . . . a public housing project . . . the Secretary [of HUD] shall approve the application, if the [PHA] certifies—(1) in the case of—(A) an application proposing demolition of a public housing project . . . , that—(i) the project . . . is obsolete as to physical condition, location, or other factors, making it unsuitable for housing purposes; and (ii) no reasonable program of modification is cost-effective to return the public housing project . . . to useful life; and . . . (3) that the [PHA] has specifically authorized the demolition or disposition in the public housing agency plan, and has certified that the actions contemplated in the public housing agency plan comply with this section[.]

42 U.S.C. § 1437p(a). Subsection (b) requires that the HUD Secretary reject an application if it lacks any of the necessary certifications. § 1437p(b).

Section 1437p(a)(1)(A) and (a)(3) are directed at the HUD Secretary, mandating that the Secretary approve a PHA's demolition application if the PHA makes the required certifications. These subsections . . . do not mention the public housing residents at all.

Indeed, the subsections relevant to the plaintiffs' constructive demolition claim read like "an administrative checklist" of the certifications that the PHA must make for the Secretary to approve the application for demolition. The provision is focused on the entity regulated—HUD—and not the public housing residents. See § 1437p(a)(1)(A), (a)(3); *see also Sandoval* ("Statutes that focus on the person regulated rather than the individuals protected create no implication of an intent to confer rights on a particular class of persons."). While the relevant subsections list the information that a PHA must certify in a demolition application, they command action only from the HUD Secretary. . . .

Like the relevant subsections of Section 1437p, the [FERPA] provisions [in *Gonzaga*] lacked "rights-creating language" and spoke "only to the Secretary of Education" in directing that no funds shall be made available to an institution that discloses private records in violation of the Act. As with the relevant subsections of Section 1437p, the focus of the provision was "removed" from the interests of the affected individuals, and thus did not confer an enforceable individual entitlement under Section 1983. . . .

Citing the "Declaration of Policy" section of the amended USHA, the plaintiffs argue that the new statute elevates the rights of public housing residents. However, the Court cannot use a "blanket approach" in determining whether a statute creates enforceable rights. *Blessing.* The Court must, as it did here, examine the "precise statutory provision at issue" for such "rights-creating" language. And as discussed above, the specific provisions at issue do not contain rights-creating language. . . .

Because the Court finds that Congress did not intend for these specific provisions to benefit the plaintiffs, the Court does not need to consider the remaining two *Blessing* factors.

What factor or factors are most important to the § 1983 statutory-enforceability inquiry? What is the role of the specific statutory terms Congress uses? How much does the syntax of the statutory provision matter?

Note: Federal Statutory Rights and Qualified Immunity

We learned in Chapter 4 that qualified immunity is a defense to § 1983 liability. How does it apply when a § 1983 claim is based on the violation of a statute instead of the Constitution?

This question does not seem to arise frequently, as qualified immunity is not generally asserted as a defense to the enforcement of statutory rights via § 1983.

The Supreme Court has explained: "[O]fficials sued for violations of rights conferred by a statute or regulation . . . become liable for damages only to the extent that there is a clear violation of the statutory rights that give rise to the cause of action for damages." *Davis v. Scherer*, 468 U.S. 183, 194 n. 12 (1984).

Does the sentence quoted mean that a defendant loses immunity merely by violating an enforceable statute in a "clear" way? Or must the specific statute have previously been held enforceable under § 1983 in order for the plaintiff to defeat qualified immunity?

At least one circuit has taken the former approach: "[The view] that Defendants are entitled to qualified immunity because it is not 'clearly established' that the statutory provisions at issue are privately enforceable [is] incorrect. . . . [W]hether a federal statute is privately enforceable and whether an official is entitled to qualified immunity for a violation of that statute are two separate inquiries. There need not be 'clearly established law' showing that a statute is privately enforceable." *Henry A. v. Willden*, 678 F.3d 991, 1006 n.7 (9th Cir. 2012). *Accord Del A. v. Edwards*, 855 F.2d 1148, 1152 (5th Cir.), *vacated for reh'g en banc*, 862 F.2d 1107 (1988), *appeal dismissed*, 867 F.2d 842 (1989).

Presumably the intuition behind this approach is that the command of a statute itself is "clearly established law" (statutes being clearer and more specific than the Constitution), so overcoming qualified immunity does not depend on a prior holding that the statute in question is enforceable via § 1983.

Is that approach persuasive? Should courts give qualified immunity more teeth in this context? If so, what should a plaintiff be required to show to overcome this defense?

C. ENFORCING STATUTORY RIGHTS USING INHERENT EQUITABLE POWER

We have seen how some statutes have been held to imply a cause of action (Chapter 7). And we have seen thus far in this chapter how some statutes have been held enforceable via § 1983. We now turn to yet another, somewhat related avenue for enforcement of statutes: federal courts' inherent equitable power.

You may recall that we identified inherent equitable power as the simplest mechanism to sue for an injunction to stop *federal* officials from violating the *Constitution* (Chapter 2, Section A). The Supreme Court has recently made clear that it may also be used to enforce federal *statutes*, and against *state* officials as well federal ones.

The Court arrived at this announcement in a strangely incidental manner. For many years, the courts of appeals explicitly (and to some extent the Supreme Court implicitly) recognized a different source of authority—the Constitution's Supremacy Clause, Art. VI, cl. 2, which provides that federal law trumps state law and which is the basis for federal preemption of state laws—as providing a cause of action to enforce federal statutory provisions, as long as the plaintiff sought only an injunction. The value to plaintiffs of this cause of action was that it enabled plaintiffs to enforce statutes without the limitations the Court had imposed on statutory enforceability via § 1983.

The Supreme Court did not squarely address until recently whether such an action in fact existed. In *Armstrong v. Exceptional Child Center, Inc.*, 135 S. Ct. 1378 (2015), the Court held, without disagreement on this point, that a Supremacy Clause cause of action does *not* exist. But in the course of discussing the Supremacy Clause, the Court identified a different source of remedial authority—inherent equitable power—that operates in much the same way as the Supremacy Clause had for many years been assumed to. However, the Court made clear that the use of inherent equitable power can be foreclosed by Congress with respect to any given statute. The Court then considered the conditions under which such foreclosure occurs.

Armstrong v. Exceptional Child Center, Inc.
135 S. Ct. 1378 (2015)

■ *Justice* SCALIA *delivered the opinion of the Court, except as to Part IV [which was joined by Chief Justice* ROBERTS *and Justices* THOMAS *and* ALITO].

We consider whether Medicaid providers can sue to enforce § (30)(A) of the Medicaid Act.

Medicaid is a federal program that subsidizes the States' provision of medical services to "families with dependent children and of aged, blind, or disabled individuals, whose income and resources are insufficient to meet the costs of necessary medical services." Like other Spending Clause legislation, Medicaid offers the States a bargain: Congress provides federal funds in exchange for the States' agreement to spend them in accordance with congressionally imposed conditions.

In order to qualify for Medicaid funding, the State of Idaho adopted, and the Federal Government approved, a Medicaid "plan," which Idaho administers through its Department of Health and Welfare. Idaho's plan includes "habilitation services"—in-home care for individuals who [otherwise would need care in a hospital or other facility at state expense.] Providers of these services are reimbursed by the Department of Health and Welfare.

Section 30(A) of the Medicaid Act requires Idaho's plan to:

"provide such methods and procedures relating to the utilization of, and the payment for, care and services available under the plan . . . as may be necessary to safeguard against unnecessary utilization of such care and services and to assure that payments are consistent with efficiency, economy, and quality of care and are sufficient to enlist enough providers so that care and services are available under the plan at least to the extent that such care and services are available to the general population in the geographic area. . . ."

Respondents are providers of habilitation services to persons covered by Idaho's Medicaid plan. They sued [state officials] claiming that Idaho violates § 30(A) by reimbursing providers of habilitation services at rates lower than § 30(A) permits. They asked the court to enjoin petitioners to increase these rates. [The district court granted summary judgment to plaintiffs, and the court of appeals affirmed the use of the Supremacy Clause to enjoin a violation of a federal statute.] . . .

The Supremacy Clause, Art. VI, cl. 2, reads:

"This Constitution, and the Laws of the United States which shall be made in Pursuance thereof; and all Treaties made, or which shall be made, under the Authority of the United States, shall be the supreme Law of the Land; and the Judges in every State shall be bound thereby, any Thing in the Constitution or Laws of any State to the Contrary notwithstanding."

It is apparent that this Clause creates a rule of decision: Courts "shall" regard the "Constitution," and all laws "made in Pursuance thereof," as "the supreme Law of the Land." They must not give effect to state laws that conflict with federal laws. It is equally apparent that the Supremacy Clause is not the "'source of any federal rights,'" and certainly does not create a cause of action. It instructs courts what to do when state and federal law clash, but is silent regarding who may enforce federal laws in court, and in what circumstances they may do so.

Hamilton wrote that the Supremacy Clause "only declares a truth, which flows immediately and necessarily from the institution of a Federal Government." The Federalist No. 33. And Story described the Clause as "a positive affirmance of that, which is necessarily implied." These descriptions would have been grossly inapt if the Clause were understood to give affected parties a constitutional (and hence congressionally unalterable) right to enforce federal laws against the States. And had it been understood to provide such significant private rights against the States, one would expect to find that mentioned in the preratification historical record, which contained ample discussion of the Supremacy Clause by both supporters and opponents of ratification. We are aware of no such mention, and respondents have not provided any. Its conspicuous absence militates strongly against their position. . . .

If the Supremacy Clause includes a private right of action, then the Constitution requires Congress to permit the enforcement of its laws by private actors, significantly curtailing its ability to guide the implementation of federal law. It would be strange indeed to give a clause that makes federal law supreme a reading that limits Congress's power to enforce that law, by imposing mandatory private enforcement—a limitation unheard-of with regard to state legislatures. . . .

Respondents contend that our preemption jurisprudence—specifically, the fact that we have regularly considered whether to enjoin the enforcement of state laws that are alleged to violate federal law—demonstrates that the Supremacy Clause creates a cause of action for its violation. They are incorrect. It is true enough that we have long held that federal courts may in some circumstances grant injunctive relief against state officers who are violating, or planning to violate, federal law. *See, e.g., Ex parte Young.* But that has been true not only with respect to violations of federal law by state officials, but also with respect to violations of federal law by federal officials. Thus, the Supremacy Clause need not be (and in light of our textual analysis above, cannot be) the explanation. What our cases demonstrate is that, "in a proper case, relief may be given in a court of equity . . . to prevent an injurious act by a public officer." *Carroll v. Safford*, 3 How. 441, 463 (1845).

The ability to sue to enjoin unconstitutional actions by state and federal officers is the creation of courts of equity, and reflects a long history of judicial review of illegal executive action, tracing back to England. It is a judge-made remedy, and we have never held or even suggested that, in its application to state officers, it rests upon an implied right of action contained in the Supremacy Clause. That is because, as even the dissent implicitly acknowledges, it does not. . . .

[Plaintiffs cannot proceed in equity in this case.] . . . In our view the Medicaid Act implicitly precludes private enforcement of § 30(A), and respondents cannot, by invoking our equitable powers, circumvent Congress's exclusion of private enforcement.

Two aspects of § 30(A) establish Congress's "intent to foreclose" equitable relief. First, the sole remedy Congress provided for a State's failure to comply with Medicaid's requirements—for the State's "breach" of the Spending Clause contract—is the withholding of Medicaid funds by the Secretary of Health and Human Services. 42 U.S.C. § 1396c. As we have elsewhere explained, the "express provision of one method of enforcing a substantive rule suggests that Congress intended to preclude others." *Alexander v. Sandoval.*

The provision for the Secretary's enforcement by withholding funds might not, by itself, preclude the availability of equitable relief. But it does so when combined with the judicially unadministrable nature of § 30(A)'s text. It is difficult to imagine a requirement broader and less specific than § 30(A)'s mandate that state plans provide for payments that are "consistent with efficiency, economy, and quality of care," all the while "safeguard[ing] against unnecessary utilization of . . . care and services." Explicitly conferring enforcement of this judgment-laden standard upon the Secretary alone establishes, we think, that Congress "wanted to make the agency remedy that it provided exclusive," thereby achieving "the expertise, uniformity, widespread consultation, and resulting administrative guidance that can accompany agency decisionmaking," and avoiding "the comparative risk of inconsistent interpretations and misincentives that can arise out of an occasional inappropriate application of the statute in a private action." The sheer complexity associated with enforcing § 30(A), coupled with the express provision of an administrative remedy, shows that the Medicaid Act precludes private enforcement of § 30(A) in the courts.

The dissent agrees with us that the Supremacy Clause does not provide an implied right of action, and that Congress may displace the equitable relief that is traditionally available to enforce federal law. It disagrees only with our conclusion that such displacement has occurred here.

The dissent insists that, "because Congress is undoubtedly aware of the federal courts' long-established practice of enjoining preempted state action, it should generally be presumed to contemplate such enforcement unless it affirmatively manifests a contrary intent." But a "long-established practice" does not justify a rule that denies statutory text its fairest reading. Section 30(A), fairly read in the context of the Medicaid Act, "display[s] a[n] intent to foreclose" the availability of equitable relief. . . .

[T]he dissent speaks as though we leave these plaintiffs with no resort. That is not the case. Their relief must be sought initially through the Secretary rather than through the courts. The dissent's complaint that the sanction available to the Secretary (the cut-off of funding) is too massive to be a realistic source of relief seems to us mistaken. We doubt that the Secretary's notice to a State that its compensation scheme is inadequate will be ignored.

IV [Plurality Opinion]

The last possible source of a cause of action for respondents is the Medicaid Act itself. They do not claim that, and rightly so. Section 30(A) lacks the sort of rights-creating language needed to imply a private right of action. *Sandoval.* It is phrased as a directive to the federal agency charged with approving state Medicaid plans, not as a conferral of the right to sue upon the beneficiaries of the State's decision to participate in Medicaid. The Act says that the "Secretary shall approve any plan which fulfills the conditions specified in subsection (a)," the subsection that includes § 30(A). We have held that such language "reveals no congressional intent to create a private right of action." *Sandoval.* And again, the explicitly conferred means of enforcing compliance with § 30(A) by the Secretary's withholding funding, suggests that other means of enforcement are precluded. *Sandoval.*

Spending Clause legislation like Medicaid "is much in the nature of a contract." The notion that respondents have a right to sue derives, perhaps, from the fact that they are beneficiaries of the federal-state Medicaid agreement, and that intended beneficiaries, in modern times at least, can sue to enforce the obligations of private contracting parties. We doubt, to begin with, that providers are intended beneficiaries (as opposed to mere incidental beneficiaries) of the Medicaid agreement, which was concluded for the benefit of the infirm whom the providers were to serve, rather than for the benefit of the providers themselves. More fundamentally, however, the modern jurisprudence permitting intended beneficiaries to sue does not generally apply to contracts between a private party and the government—much less to contracts between two governments. Our precedents establish that a private right of action under federal law is not created by mere implication, but must be "unambiguously conferred." *Gonzaga.* Nothing in the Medicaid Act suggests that Congress meant to change that for the commitments made under § 30(A). . . .

▧ *Justice* BREYER, *concurring in part and concurring in the judgment.*

Like all other Members of the Court, . . . I would ask whether "federal courts may in [these] circumstances grant injunctive relief against state officers who are violating, or planning to violate, federal law." I believe the answer to this question is no.

That answer does not follow from the application of a simple, fixed legal formula separating federal statutes that may underlie this kind of injunctive action from those that may not. . . . Rather, I believe that several characteristics of the federal statute before us, when taken together, make clear that Congress intended to foreclose respondents from bringing this particular action for injunctive relief.

For one thing, as the majority points out, § 30(A) of the Medicaid Act, sets forth a federal mandate that is broad and nonspecific. But, more than that, § 30(A) applies its broad standards to the setting of rates. The history of ratemaking demonstrates that administrative agencies are far better suited to this task than judges. . . .

Reading § 30(A) underscores the complexity and nonjudicial nature of the rate-setting task. That provision requires State Medicaid plans to "assure that payments are consistent with efficiency, economy, and quality of care and are sufficient to enlist enough providers" to assure "care and services" equivalent to that "available to the general population in the geographic area." The methods that a state agency, such as Idaho's Department of Health and Welfare, uses to make this kind of determination may involve subsidiary determinations of, for example, the actual cost of providing quality services, including personnel and total operating expenses; changes in public expectations with respect to delivery of services; inflation; a comparison of rates paid in neighboring States for comparable services; and a comparison of any rates paid for comparable services in other public or private capacities. . . .

I recognize that courts might in particular instances be able to resolve rate-related requests for injunctive relief quite easily. But I see no easy way to separate in advance the potentially simple sheep from the more harmful rate-making goats. In any event, this case, I fear, belongs in the latter category. . . .

▧ *Justice* SOTOMAYOR, *with whom Justice* KENNEDY, *Justice* GINSBURG, *and Justice* KAGAN *join, dissenting.*

Suits in federal court to restrain state officials from executing laws that assertedly conflict with the Constitution or with a federal statute are not novel. To the contrary, this Court has adjudicated such requests for equitable relief since the early days of the Republic. Nevertheless, today the Court holds that Congress has foreclosed private parties from invoking the equitable powers of the federal courts to require States to comply with § 30(A) of the Medicaid Act. It does so without pointing to the sort of detailed remedial scheme we have previously deemed necessary to establish congressional intent to preclude resort to equity. Instead, the Court relies on Congress' provision for agency enforcement of § 30(A)—an enforcement mechanism of the sort we have already definitively determined not to foreclose private actions—and on the mere fact that § 30(A) contains relatively broad language. As I cannot agree that these statutory provisions demonstrate the requisite congressional intent to restrict the equitable authority of the federal courts, I respectfully dissent. . . .

Most important for purposes of this case is not the mere existence of this equitable authority, but the fact that it is exceedingly well established— supported, as the Court puts it, by a "long history." Congress may, if it so chooses, either expressly or implicitly preclude *Ex parte Young* enforcement actions with respect to a particular statute or category of lawsuit. But because Congress is undoubtedly aware of the federal courts' long-established practice of enjoining preempted state action, it should generally be presumed to contemplate such enforcement unless it affirmatively manifests a contrary intent. . . .

In this respect, equitable preemption actions differ from suits brought by plaintiffs invoking 42 U.S.C. § 1983 or an implied right of action to enforce a federal statute. Suits for "redress designed to halt or prevent the constitutional violation rather than the award of money damages" seek "traditional forms of relief." By contrast, a plaintiff invoking § 1983 or an implied statutory cause of action may seek a variety of remedies—including damages—from a potentially broad range of parties. Rather than simply pointing to background equitable principles authorizing the action that Congress presumably has not overridden, such a plaintiff must demonstrate specific congressional intent to create a statutory right to these remedies. *See Gonzaga Univ.*; *Alexander v. Sandoval.* For these reasons, the principles that we have developed to determine whether a statute creates an implied right of action, or is enforceable through § 1983, are not transferable to the *Ex parte Young* context.

In concluding that Congress has "implicitly preclude[d] private enforcement of § 30(A)," the Court ignores this critical distinction and threatens the vitality of our *Ex parte Young* jurisprudence. . . .

[T]he Court cites 42 U.S.C. § 1396c, which authorizes the Secretary of Health and Human Services to withhold federal Medicaid payments to a State in whole or in part if the Secretary determines that the State has failed to comply with the obligations set out in § 1396a, including § 30(A). But . . . § 1396c provides no specific procedure that parties actually affected by a State's violation of its statutory obligations may invoke in lieu of *Ex parte Young*—leaving them without any other avenue for seeking relief from the State. Nor will § 1396c always provide a particularly effective means for redressing a State's violations: If the State has violated § 30(A) by refusing to reimburse medical providers at a level "sufficient to enlist enough providers so that care and services are available" to Medicaid beneficiaries to the same extent as they are available to "the general population," agency action resulting in a reduced flow of federal funds to that State will often be self-defeating. Far from rendering § 1396c "superfluous," then, *Ex parte Young* actions would seem to be an anticipated and possibly necessary supplement to this limited agency-enforcement mechanism. . . .

Section 1396c also parallels other provisions scattered throughout the Social Security Act that likewise authorize the withholding of federal funds to States that fail to fulfill their obligations. Yet, we have consistently authorized judicial enforcement of the Act. . . .

Notes and Questions

1. What factors are relevant to whether a statute may be enforced via courts' inherent equitable power? Does the Court explain which factors might be dispositive? Whether the factors discussed in *Armstrong* are exclusive? What do you suppose accounts for the Court's cageyness on these points?

2. Why do you think Justice Breyer refrained from joining Part IV? What do you think the plurality is driving at in that section?

3. What is at the heart of Justice Sotomayor's dispute with the majority? Is it the meaning of § 30(A)? The standard applied to analyze § 30(A)? The nature of federal courts' equitable power? Something else?

4. Although this case is not formally about § 1983 enforceability or implied rights of action, what implications might this decision have for those inquiries if *Armstrong*'s approach is subsequently folded into the *Blessing-Gonzaga* analysis?

D. STATUTORY FORECLOSURE OF CONSTITUTIONAL CLAIMS

So far, we have seen how § 1983 can be used to enforce a statute and how statutes can be enforced via courts' traditional equitable power. In both inquiries, a (or the) key question is whether Congress intended to foreclose these modes of enforcement for a given statute. We conclude our chapter on the interaction between § 1983 and other federal statutes by examining a different type of foreclosure: when a federal statute other than § 1983 forecloses the use of § 1983 (and *Bivens*) to enforce *constitutional* rights.

For instance, in *Brown v. General Services Administration*, 425 U.S. 820 (1976), the Court considered whether an African-American GSA employee who complained of employment discrimination could bring a constitutional equal protection claim instead of complying with the procedures of Title VII. The Court held that he could not, in an opinion by Justice Stewart:

> Title VII of the Civil Rights Act of 1964 forbids employment discrimination based on race, color, religion, sex, or national origin. Until it was amended in 1972 by the Equal Employment Opportunity Act, however, Title VII did not protect federal employees. Although federal employment discrimination clearly violated both the Constitution, and statutory law, before passage of the 1972 Act, the effective availability of either administrative or judicial relief was far from sure. Charges of racial discrimination were handled parochially within each federal agency. . . .
>
> Section 717 of the Civil Rights Act of 1964 proscribes federal employment discrimination and establishes an administrative and judicial enforcement system. Section 717(a) provides that all personnel actions affecting federal employees and applicants for federal employment "shall be made free from any discrimination based on race, color, religion, sex, or national origin."
>
> Sections 717(b) and (c) establish complementary administrative and judicial enforcement mechanisms designed to eradicate federal employment discrimination.

Subsection (b) delegates to the Civil Service Commission full authority to enforce the provisions of subsection (a) . . . .

Section 717(c) permits an aggrieved employee to file a civil action in a federal district court to review his claim of employment discrimination. Attached to that right, however, are certain preconditions. Initially, the complainant must seek relief in the agency that has allegedly discriminated against him. . . .

Sections 706(f) through (k), which are incorporated "as applicable" by § 717(d), govern such issues as venue, the appointment of attorneys, attorneys' fees, and the scope of relief. . . .

The balance, completeness, and structural integrity of § 717 are inconsistent with the petitioner's contention that the judicial remedy afforded by § 717(c) was designed merely to supplement other putative judicial relief. His view fails, in our estimation, to accord due weight to the fact that unlike these other supposed remedies, § 717 does not contemplate merely judicial relief. Rather, it provides for a careful blend of administrative and judicial enforcement powers. Under the petitioner's theory, . . . [t]he crucial administrative role that each agency together with the Civil Service Commission was given by Congress in the eradication of employment discrimination would be eliminated "by the simple expedient of putting a different label on (the) pleadings." It would require the suspension of disbelief to ascribe to Congress the design to allow its careful and thorough remedial scheme to be circumvented by artful pleading.

Justice Marshall took no part in the decision. Dissenting, Justice Stevens, joined by Justice Brennan, pointed out that "the General Subcommittee on Labor of the House Committee on Education and Labor rejected an amendment which would have explicitly provided that § 717 would be the exclusive remedy for federal employees."

(You may wonder why, in light of *Brown*, the Court in *Davis v. Passman*, 442 U.S. 228 (1979), recognized a federal employee's *Bivens* claim for employment discrimination in violation of the Fifth Amendment's equal protection guarantee (Chapter 2). In a footnote, *Davis* explained that the position from which plaintiff was fired was exempt from § 717.)

The Court returned to the question of foreclosure of constitutional claims in *Smith v. Robinson*, 468 U.S. 992 (1984). There, a school district cut off funding for a special education program for a child with cerebral palsy. His parents brought claims under the Education of the Handicapped Act (EHA) along with other statutory claims and constitutional due process and equal protection claims. The plaintiffs won. Attorneys' fees were available for the § 1983 claims but not for the EHA claims. The dispute over whether the plaintiffs could obtain fees reached the Supreme Court. Writing for the Court, Justice Blackmun concluded that fees were unavailable because of the interaction between the EHA and § 1983:

[Petitioners'] § 1983 claims were not based on alleged violations of the EHA, but on independent claims of constitutional deprivations. As the Court of Appeals recognized, however, petitioners' constitutional claims, a denial of due process and a denial of a free appropriate public education as guaranteed by the Equal Protection Clause, are virtually identical to their EHA claims. The question to be asked, therefore, is whether Congress intended that the EHA be the exclusive avenue through which a plaintiff may assert those claims. . . .

We have little difficulty concluding that Congress intended the EHA to be the exclusive avenue through which a plaintiff may assert an equal protection claim to a publicly financed special education. The EHA is a comprehensive scheme set up by Congress to aid the States in complying with their constitutional obligations to provide public education for handicapped children. Both the provisions of the statute and its legislative history indicate that Congress intended handicapped children with constitutional claims to a free appropriate public education to pursue those claims through the carefully tailored administrative and judicial mechanism set out in the statute. . . .

In light of the comprehensive nature of the procedures and guarantees set out in the EHA and Congress' express efforts to place on local and state educational agencies the primary responsibility for developing a plan to accommodate the needs of each individual handicapped child, we find it difficult to believe that Congress also meant to leave undisturbed the ability of a handicapped child to go directly to court with an equal protection claim to a free appropriate public education. Not only would such a result render superfluous most of the detailed procedural protections outlined in the statute, but, more important, it would also run counter to Congress' view that the needs of handicapped children are best accommodated by having the parents and the local education agency work together to formulate an individualized plan for each handicapped child's education. No federal district court presented with a constitutional claim to a public education can duplicate that process.

We do not lightly conclude that Congress intended to preclude reliance on § 1983 as a remedy for a substantial equal protection claim. Since 1871, when it was passed by Congress, § 1983 has stood as an independent safeguard against deprivations of federal constitutional and statutory rights. *See Patsy; Monroe.* Nevertheless, § 1983 is a statutory remedy and Congress retains the authority to repeal it or replace it with an alternative remedy. The crucial consideration is what Congress intended. *See Brown v. GSA.*

In this case, we think Congress' intent is clear. Allowing a plaintiff to circumvent the EHA administrative remedies would be inconsistent with Congress' carefully tailored scheme.

Dissenting, Justice Brennan, joined by Justices Marshall and Stevens, argued that because "[r]epeals by implication . . . are strongly disfavored," the EHA and § 1983 must be harmonized by permitting § 1983 to be asserted alongside the EHA once the EHA's administrative review provisions have been complied with.

The Court's most recent discussion of foreclosure in the constitutional context provided more structure to the analysis. *Fitzgerald v. Barnstable School Committee,* 555 U.S. 246 (2009), was a peer-on-peer sexual harassment case. The Fitzgeralds' daughter, a kindergartener, was subjected to repeated harassment on the school bus by a third-grade boy who bullied her into lifting her skirt and, later, pulling down her underwear and spreading her legs. When the Fitzgeralds complained, the principal proposed remedial measures including transferring their daughter to a different bus or leaving rows of empty seats between the kindergarteners and older students on the original bus. The Fitzgeralds felt that these proposals punished their daughter instead of the boy and countered with alternative proposals, including transferring the boy to a different bus or placing a monitor on the original bus. The school superintendent did not act on these proposals. The Fitzgeralds sued the district and its superintendent under Title IX, § 1983 (for a denial of equal protection), and state law. The district court dismissed the § 1983 and state-law claims and granted summary judgment to the district on the Title IX claim. As relevant here, the First Circuit affirmed the dismissal of the § 1983 claim, holding under *Sea Clammers* and *Smith* that Title IX's implied private remedy was "sufficiently comprehensive" to preclude the use of § 1983. In a unanimous opinion by Justice Alito, the Supreme Court reversed:

> In determining whether a subsequent statute precludes the enforcement of a federal right under § 1983, we have placed primary emphasis on the nature and extent of that statute's remedial scheme. See *Sea Clammers.*
>
> [In *Sea Clammers* and *Smith,*] the statutes at issue required plaintiffs to comply with particular procedures and/or to exhaust particular administrative remedies prior to filing suit. Offering plaintiffs a direct route to court via § 1983 would have circumvented these procedures and given plaintiffs access to tangible benefits—such as damages, attorney's fees, and costs—that were unavailable under the statutes. . . .
>
> [Title IX's] only express enforcement mechanism, is an administrative procedure resulting in the withdrawal of federal funding from institutions that are not in compliance. In addition, this Court has recognized an implied private right of action. *Cannon.* In a suit brought pursuant to this private right, both injunctive relief and damages are available. *Franklin.*
>
> These remedies—withdrawal of federal funds and an implied cause of action—stand in stark contrast to the "unusually elaborate," "carefully tailored," and "restrictive" enforcement schemes of the statutes at issue [in *Sea Clammers* and *Smith*]. Unlike those statutes, Title IX has no administrative exhaustion requirement and no notice provisions. Under its implied private right of action, plaintiffs can file directly in court, *Cannon,* and can obtain the full range of remedies, see *Franklin.* As a result, parallel and concurrent § 1983 claims will neither circumvent required procedures, nor allow access to new remedies. . . .
>
> This Court has never held that an implied right of action had the effect of precluding suit under § 1983, likely because of the difficulty of discerning congressional intent in such a situation. Mindful that we should "not lightly conclude that Congress intended to preclude reliance on § 1983 as a remedy for a substantial equal protection claim," *Smith,* we see no basis for doing so here.
>
> A comparison of the substantive rights and protections guaranteed under Title IX and under the Equal Protection Clause lends further support to the conclusion that Congress did not intend Title IX to preclude § 1983 constitutional suits. Title IX's protections are narrower in some respects and broader in others. . . .
>
> Title IX reaches institutions and programs that receive federal funds, which may include nonpublic institutions, but it has consistently been interpreted as not authorizing suit against school officials, teachers, and other individuals. The Equal Protection Clause reaches only state actors, but § 1983 equal protection claims may be brought against individuals as well as municipalities and certain other state entities.
>
> Title IX exempts from its restrictions several activities that may be challenged on constitutional grounds. For example, Title IX exempts elementary and secondary schools from its prohibition against discrimination in admissions; it exempts military service schools and traditionally single-sex public colleges from all of its provisions. Some exempted activities may form the basis of equal protection claims.

Even where particular activities and particular defendants are subject to both Title IX and the Equal Protection Clause, the standards for establishing liability may not be wholly congruent. For example, a Title IX plaintiff can establish school district liability by showing that a single school administrator with authority to take corrective action responded to harassment with deliberate indifference. *Gebser.* A plaintiff stating a similar claim via § 1983 for violation of the Equal Protection Clause by a school district or other municipal entity must show that the harassment was the result of municipal custom, policy, or practice. *Monell.*

In light of the divergent coverage of Title IX and the Equal Protection Clause, as well as the absence of a comprehensive remedial scheme . . . we conclude that Title IX was not meant to be an exclusive mechanism for addressing gender discrimination in schools, or a substitute for § 1983 suits as a means of enforcing constitutional rights. Accordingly, we hold that § 1983 suits based on the Equal Protection Clause remain available to plaintiffs alleging unconstitutional gender discrimination in schools.

Notes and Questions

1. It might strike you intuitively as strange that a mere *statute* should be able to foreclose enforcement of a *constitutional* right. Doesn't that turn the hierarchy of U.S. law upside down? This apparent anomaly can be explained by recalling that § 1983 is itself a federal statute, just like the statutes that the Court has found foreclose the use of § 1983 for constitutional enforcement. Framed in this way, the question is not whether a statute can foreclose enforcement of the Constitution (to which it may seem like the answer should be "no"), but whether Congress can establish one statutory mechanism for enforcing some rights while establishing different statutory mechanisms for others (to which a "yes" answer may seem more reasonable).

   Still, the recognition that Congress can alter, limit, and potentially withdraw mechanisms for enforcement of constitutional rights raises significant questions about the bare minimum enforcement mechanisms the Constitution itself demands. How far could Congress go in restricting the right to sue over constitutional violations? Could it preclude particular remedies entirely? Prevent all constitutional enforcement via private civil action? If § 1983 didn't exist, would the Court feel compelled to create it? Would the result be a jurisprudence that resembles *Bivens* (Chapter 2), or something else?

2. Under what circumstances will the Supreme Court recognize that Congress has foreclosed the use of § 1983 for a particular constitutional claim? What two factors drive the Court's analysis? How has its approach evolved over the past forty years? Has finding foreclosure of this type become easier or harder?

3. How does the test for this type of foreclosure resemble, and how does it differ from, the test for discerning congressional foreclosure of *statutory* enforcement via § 1983? In analyzing foreclosure generally, why has the Court repeatedly invoked *Sea Clammers* (about the foreclosure of § 1983 enforceability for a statutory right) and *Smith* (about the foreclosure of § 1983 enforceability for a constitutional right) in tandem and without differentiating between them?

CHAPTER 8 PROBLEMS

Problem 8A. The Privacy Act provides: "It shall be unlawful for any Federal, State or local government agency to deny to any individual any right, benefit, or privilege provided by law because of such individual's refusal to disclose his social security account number." Pub. L. No. 93-579, § 7(a)(1), at 5 U.S.C. § 552a note. No enforcement mechanism of any kind is provided.

1. Is this provision enforceable via § 1983?

2. *(Reviewing Chapter 7.)* Does this provision create an implied right of action?

Problem 8B. Before its repeal in 2015, a provision of the No Child Left Behind Act (then at 20 U.S.C. § 6316(e)(1)) provided that where a school failed to meet certain federal benchmarks for two consecutive years, "the local educational agency serving such school shall . . . arrange for the provision of supplemental educational services to eligible children in the school from a provider . . . that is selected by the parents and approved for that purpose by the State educational agency in accordance with reasonable criteria . . . that the State educational agency shall adopt." The statute provided that the Secretary of Education could cut off federal education funds to a district for lack of compliance.

1. Prior to repeal of this provision, was the right to supplemental educational services enforceable under § 1983?

2. Could a plaintiff denied supplemental education services seek injunctive relief under courts' inherent equitable power?

Problem 8C. Return to Problem 2C in Chapter 2. Setting aside the question of whether Ibrahim Lincoln can assert a *Bivens* cause of action, what if the government defended against his equal protection claim by arguing that INDA foreclosed it? Would that argument succeed? Why or why not?

PART IV

REMEDIES

In a successful § 1983 suit, the defendant is "liable to the party injured in an action at law, suit in equity, or other proper proceeding for redress." In 1871, an "action at law" generally referred to damages, and "suit in equity" authorized an injunction. A century later, Congress added a separate statutory provision entitling winning plaintiffs to recover their attorneys' fees as well.

In this final section of the book, we explore these remedies and their limitations. What types of injuries are compensable in damages (Chapter 9)? Under what circumstances may attorneys' fees be awarded and how are they measured (Chapter 10)? Under what circumstances can a court hear a suit seeking an injunction (Chapter 11)? How and when can injunctions be deployed as tools of structural reform to reshape massive government institutions like schools and prisons—and how effective are such injunctions (Chapter 12)?

(Note that although many of the topics in this final part of the book are relevant to most or all of the causes of action we have studied throughout the book, Chapter 9, covering damages, is devoted to constitutional enforcement lawsuits, because for most of the other causes of action we have studied (Chapters 6 and 7), damages are either straightforwardly specified by statute (Title VII) or were considered in the Court's development of the cause of action itself (Titles VI and IX).)

As we'll see, the constraints on the types of remedies available in various circumstances—and, in particular, the narrowing of plaintiffs' opportunities to seek injunctive relief—constitute as significant an obstacle to effective civil rights litigation as the defenses and limitations on liability we have studied so far.

Damages

In a variety of contexts, the Court has looked to tort-law principles to help resolve ambiguities in or supply background norms for civil rights statutes—including § 1983 (e.g., common law immunities), and Title VII (e.g., the derivation of the *Ellerth* defense). Perhaps nowhere in the jurisprudence of civil rights enforcement is the common law's influence so strong as in the rules governing what types of damages are available under § 1983 and how they are measured.

Damages are "a sum of money awarded to a person injured by the tort of another." Restatement (Second) of Torts § 902. Damages are intended to "make the plaintiff whole" or, to put it another way, "to compensate the victim with an amount of money equal to the losses suffered." John C.P. Goldberg, *Two Conceptions of Tort Damages: Fair v. Full Compensation*, 55 DePaul L. Rev. 435, 435 (2006).

There are three categories of damages: compensatory, nominal, and punitive. Compensatory damages are monetary relief intended to provide "compensation, indemnity or restitution for harm." Restatement (Second) of Torts § 903. Compensatory damages are available for, among other things: personal harms like "bodily harm and emotional distress; loss or impairment of earning capacity; reasonable medical and other expenses; and harm to property or business," *id.* § 924; death, *id.* § 925; and the conversion or destruction of property or any other legally protected interest, *id.* § 927. An injured plaintiff is entitled to recover damages for past, present, and future harm resulting from the defendant's tortious act. *Id.* § 910. This includes recovery for reasonable expenditures. *Id.* § 919.

Nominal damages are a small amount of money awarded to a plaintiff who is able to establish a cause of action but is unable to demonstrate that the alleged tort caused any harm for which compensation would be appropriate. *Id.* § 907.

Punitive damages are awarded to punish a defendant for especially outrageous conduct; they aim to deter future wrongdoing. *Id.* § 908(1).

Tort-law damages principles provide the basis for the Court's jurisprudence on damages and § 1983. As you study how the Court imported tort concepts into the § 1983 context, keep in mind the purposes of each. John C.P. Goldberg, *Twentieth-Century Tort Theory*, 91 Geo. L.J. 513, 517 (2003), notes: "The tort suit, if successful, ordinarily entailed that the court would order the tortfeasor to provide redress to the victim, usually in the form of money damages. Tort was thus conceived of as a law of personal redress rather than a law of public regulation or punishment." Is § 1983 merely "a law of personal redress rather than a law of public regulation"?

Damages' broader role as a deterrent and the effectiveness of damages suits as impact litigation are considered in Section C of the Prologue. This is a good point at which to review that short section (or read it for the first time, if you haven't yet).

A. COMPENSATORY AND NOMINAL DAMAGES

What is necessary to obtain compensatory damages under § 1983? Is a violation of the Constitution enough?

Carey v. Piphus
435 U.S. 247 (1978)

■ *Mr. Justice POWELL delivered the opinion of the Court.*

[A high school student believed to have been smoking marijuana on school grounds and an elementary school student who violated a school rule by wearing an earring in one ear were both suspended for twenty days by the Chicago Public Schools. They sued for violations of their procedural due process rights and sought injunctive and declaratory relief and damages. The district court held that both students had been suspended in violation of due process but declined to award damages because plaintiffs had provided no evidence of their injuries. The court of appeals reversed, holding that the district court should have considered evidence submitted regarding the pecuniary value of each day of school missed, though such damages could not be awarded on remand if the defendants showed that the plaintiffs would have been suspended anyway had appropriate procedures been provided. Even if the plaintiffs would have been suspended anyway, the court of appeals further instructed, some damages should still be awarded because plaintiffs had been denied due process.] ...

The Members of the Congress that enacted § 1983 did not address directly the question of damages, but the principle that damages are designed to compensate persons for injuries caused by the deprivation of rights hardly could have been foreign to the many lawyers in Congress in 1871. . . . To the extent that Congress intended that awards under § 1983 should deter the deprivation of constitutional rights, there is no evidence that it meant to establish a deterrent more formidable than that inherent in the award of compensatory damages.[11]

---

11. This is not to say that exemplary or punitive damages might not be awarded in a proper case under § 1983 with the specific purpose of deterring or punishing violations of constitutional rights. . . . We also note that the potential liability of § 1983 defendants for attorney's fees, provides additional—and by no means inconsequential—assurance that agents of the State will not deliberately ignore due process rights.

It is less difficult to conclude that damages awards under § 1983 should be governed by the principle of compensation than it is to apply this principle to concrete cases. But over the centuries the common law of torts has developed a set of rules to implement the principle that a person should be compensated fairly for injuries caused by the violation of his legal rights. These rules, defining the elements of damages and the prerequisites for their recovery, provide the appropriate starting point for the inquiry under § 1983 as well.

It is not clear, however, that common-law tort rules of damages will provide a complete solution to the damages issue in every § 1983 case. In some cases, the interests protected by a particular branch of the common law of torts may parallel closely the interests protected by a particular constitutional right. In such cases, it may be appropriate to apply the tort rules of damages directly to the § 1983 action. In other cases, the interests protected by a particular constitutional right may not also be protected by an analogous branch of the common law torts. *See Monroe; Bivens.* In those cases, the task will be the more difficult one of adapting common-law rules of damages to provide fair compensation for injuries caused by the deprivation of a constitutional right.

Although this task of adaptation will be one of some delicacy—as this case demonstrates—it must be undertaken. . . .

In this case, the Court of Appeals held that if petitioners can prove on remand that "[respondents] would have been suspended even if a proper hearing had been held," then respondents will not be entitled to recover damages to compensate them for injuries caused by the suspensions. The court thought that in such a case, the failure to accord procedural due process could not properly be viewed as the cause of the suspensions. The court suggested that in such circumstances, an award of damages for injuries caused by the suspensions would constitute a windfall, rather than compensation, to respondents. We do not understand the parties to disagree with this conclusion. Nor do we.

The parties do disagree as to the further holding of the Court of Appeals that respondents are entitled to recover substantial—although unspecified—damages to compensate them for "the injury which is 'inherent in the nature of the wrong,'" even if their suspensions were justified and even if they fail to prove that the denial of procedural due process actually caused them some real, if intangible, injury. Respondents, elaborating on this theme, submit that the holding is correct because injury fairly may be "presumed" to flow from every denial of procedural due process. Their argument is that in addition to protecting against unjustified deprivations, the Due Process Clause also guarantees the "feeling of just treatment" by the government. They contend that the deprivation of protected interests without procedural due process, even where the premise for the deprivation is not erroneous, inevitably arouses strong feelings of mental and emotional distress in the individual who is denied this "feeling of just treatment." . . .

[I]t is not reasonable to assume that every departure from procedural due process, no matter what the circumstances or how minor, inherently is . . . likely to cause distress. . . . Where the deprivation of a protected interest is substantively justified but procedures are deficient in some respect, there may well be those who suffer no distress over the procedural irregularities. Indeed, . . . a person may not even know that procedures were deficient until he enlists the aid of counsel to challenge a perceived substantive deprivation.

Moreover, where a deprivation is justified but procedures are deficient, whatever distress a person feels may be attributable to the justified deprivation rather than to deficiencies in procedure. . . .

Finally, we foresee no particular difficulty in producing evidence that mental and emotional distress actually was caused by the denial of procedural due process itself. Distress is a personal injury familiar to the law, customarily proved by showing the nature and circumstances of the wrong and its effect on the plaintiff. In sum, then, although mental and emotional distress caused by the denial of procedural due process itself is compensable under § 1983, we hold that neither the likelihood of such injury nor the difficulty of proving it is so great as to justify awarding compensatory damages without proof that such injury actually was caused.

The Court of Appeals believed, and respondents urge, that cases dealing with awards of damages for racial discrimination, the denial of voting rights and the denial of Fourth Amendment rights, support a presumption of damages where procedural due process is denied. Many of the cases relied upon do not help respondents because they held or implied that some actual, if intangible, injury must be proved before compensatory damages may be recovered. . . . More importantly, the elements and prerequisites for recovery of damages appropriate to compensate injuries caused by the deprivation of one constitutional right are not necessarily appropriate to compensate injuries caused by the deprivation of another. As we have said, these issues must be considered with reference to the nature of the interests protected by the particular constitutional right in question. For this reason, and without intimating an opinion as to their merits, we do not deem the cases relied upon to be controlling. . . .

Common-law courts traditionally have vindicated deprivations of certain "absolute" rights that are not shown to have caused actual injury through the award of a nominal sum of money. By making the deprivation of such rights actionable for nominal damages without proof of actual injury, the law recognizes the importance to organized society that those rights be scrupulously observed; but at the same time, it remains true to the principle that substantial damages should be awarded only to compensate actual injury or, in the case of exemplary or punitive damages, to deter or punish malicious deprivations of rights. . . .

We therefore hold that if, upon remand, the District Court determines that respondents' suspensions were justified, respondents nevertheless will be entitled to recover nominal damages not to exceed one dollar from petitioners. . . .

Mr. Justice MARSHALL concurs in the result.

Mr. Justice BLACKMUN took no part in the consideration or decision of this case.

Notes and Questions

1. What constraint has the Court placed on damages in § 1983 cases?

2. How important is the rule the Court has imposed? Won't future plaintiffs just make sure to present the right kind of evidence? Or is the vague nature of the "feeling of just treatment" combined with the question of causation—did the plaintiffs feel distress because they lacked process or because they were suspended?—likely to make the required showing difficult?

3. How much do you expect *Carey v. Piphus* matters outside the context of procedural due process? For what other constitutional claims might damages be difficult to prove?

4. What do you make of the Court's treatment of race discrimination, the denial of voting rights, and Fourth Amendment violations? How does the requirement of proven harm apply to those types of claims? How should it?

5. Consider the premise of the Court's analysis—that the starting place for § 1983 damages is the analogy to tort law. In light of the history of § 1983 and the nature of the rights at issue, how persuasive is that premise? How does it square with *Monroe* (Chapter 1)? With *Bivens* (Chapter 2)?

6. Of what use are nominal damages, which may be, for instance, $1? Are there any reasons a plaintiff not tangibly injured might bring a case for such damages alone? Are there any reasons an impact litigator might do so?

* * *

The next case required the Court to address more directly the tension between the tort model of damages and the purposes of § 1983. Recall Justice Harlan's suggestion, in his *Monroe v. Pape* concurrence (Chapter 1), that the Congress that enacted § 1983 may have considered the violation of a constitutional right to be "significantly different from and more serious than a violation of a state right," and so believed that the former "deserves a different remedy even though the same act may constitute both a state tort and the deprivation of a constitutional right." Does this intuition about the special value of constitutional rights translate into additional damages for a § 1983 claim?

Memphis Community School District v. Stachura
477 U.S. 299 (1986)

■ *Justice POWELL delivered the opinion of the Court....*

[Respondent Edward Stachura is a tenured teacher in the Memphis, Michigan, public schools, where he taught seventh grade science. In response to his teaching methods regarding the unit on human reproduction and inaccurate rumors about the use of sexually explicit material, the school board suspended him.

After he sued the district and its officials for due process and First Amendment violations, he was reinstated. Respondent's constitutional claims for damages went to trial.]

[A]t respondent's request and over petitioners' objection, the court charged that damages also could be awarded based on the value or importance of the constitutional rights that were violated[.]

The jury found petitioners liable, and awarded a total of $275,000 in compensatory damages and $46,000 in punitive damages. The District Court [reduced the award slightly, and the court of appeals affirmed.]

Petitioners challenge the jury instructions authorizing damages for violation of constitutional rights on the ground that those instructions permitted the jury to award damages based on its own unguided estimation of the value of such rights. . . .

We have repeatedly noted that 42 U.S.C. § 1983 creates "'a species of tort liability' in favor of persons who are deprived of 'rights, privileges, or immunities secured' to them by the Constitution." *Carey*. Accordingly, when § 1983 plaintiffs seek damages for violations of constitutional rights, the level of damages is ordinarily determined according to principles derived from the common law of torts. . . .

"[T]he basic purpose" of § 1983 damages is "to compensate persons for injuries that are caused by the deprivation of constitutional rights." *Carey*. . . .

The instructions at issue here cannot be squared with *Carey*, or with the principles of tort damages on which *Carey* and § 1983 are grounded. The jurors in this case were told that, in determining how much was necessary to "compensate [respondent] for the deprivation" of his constitutional rights, they should place a money value on the "rights" themselves by considering such factors as the particular right's "importance ... in our system of government," its role in American history, and its "significance ... in the context of the activities" in which respondent was engaged. These factors focus, not on compensation for provable injury, but on the jury's subjective perception of the importance of constitutional rights as an abstract matter. *Carey* establishes that such an approach is impermissible. The constitutional right transgressed in *Carey*—the right to due process of law—is central to our system of ordered liberty. We nevertheless held that no compensatory damages could be awarded for violation of that right absent proof of actual injury. *Carey* thus makes clear that the abstract value of a constitutional right may not form the basis for § 1983 damages.[11] . . .

Section 1983 presupposes that damages that compensate for actual harm ordinarily suffice to deter constitutional violations. Moreover, damages based on the "value" of constitutional rights are an unwieldy tool for ensuring compliance with the Constitution. History and tradition do not afford any sound guidance concerning the precise value that juries should place on constitutional

---

11. We did approve an award of nominal damages for the deprivation of due process in *Carey*. Our discussion . . . makes clear that nominal damages, and not damages based on some undefinable "value" of infringed rights, are the appropriate means of "vindicating" rights whose deprivation has not caused actual, provable injury . . . .

protections. Accordingly, were such damages available, juries would be free to award arbitrary amounts without any evidentiary basis, or to use their unbounded discretion to punish unpopular defendants. Such damages would be too uncertain to be of any great value to plaintiffs, and would inject caprice into determinations of damages in § 1983 cases. We therefore hold that damages based on the abstract "value" or "importance" of constitutional rights are not a permissible element of compensatory damages in such cases.

Respondent further argues that the challenged instructions authorized a form of "presumed" damages—a remedy that is both compensatory in nature and traditionally part of the range of tort law remedies. . . . Presumed damages are a substitute for ordinary compensatory damages, not a supplement for an award that fully compensates the alleged injury. When a plaintiff seeks compensation for an injury that is likely to have occurred but difficult to establish, some form of presumed damages may possibly be appropriate. In those circumstances, presumed damages may roughly approximate the harm that the plaintiff suffered and thereby compensate for harms that may be impossible to measure. . . . [T]he instructions at issue in this case did not serve this purpose, but instead called on the jury to measure damages based on a subjective evaluation of the importance of particular constitutional values. Since such damages are wholly divorced from any compensatory purpose, they cannot be justified as presumed damages.[14] Moreover, no rough substitute for compensatory damages was required in this case, since the jury was fully authorized to compensate respondent for both monetary and nonmonetary harms caused by petitioners' conduct. . . .

Justice BRENNAN and Justice STEVENS join the opinion of the Court and also join Justice MARSHALL's opinion concurring in the judgment.

---

14. For the same reason, *Nixon v. Herndon*, 273 U.S. 536 (1927), and similar cases do not support the challenged instructions. In *Nixon*, the Court held that a plaintiff who was illegally prevented from voting in a state primary election suffered compensable injury. This holding did not rest on the "value" of the right to vote as an abstract matter; rather, the Court recognized that the plaintiff had suffered a particular injury—his inability to vote in a particular election—that might be compensated through substantial money damages.

Nixon followed a long line of cases . . . authorizing substantial money damages as compensation for persons deprived of their right to vote in particular elections. Although these decisions sometimes speak of damages for the value of the right to vote, their analysis shows that they involve nothing more than an award of presumed damages for a nonmonetary harm that cannot easily be quantified:

"In the eyes of the law th[e] right [to vote] is so valuable that damages are presumed from the wrongful deprivation of it without evidence of actual loss of money, property, or any other valuable thing, and the amount of the damages is a question peculiarly appropriate for the determination of the jury, because each member of the jury has personal knowledge of the value of the right."

The "value of the right" in the context of these decisions is the money value of the particular loss that the plaintiff suffered—a loss of which "each member of the jury has personal knowledge." It is not the value of the right to vote as a general, abstract matter, based on its role in our history or system of government. . . .

■ *Justice MARSHALL, with whom Justice BRENNAN, Justice BLACKMUN, and Justice STEVENS join, concurring in the judgment.*

I agree with the Court that this case must be remanded for a new trial on damages. . . . I write separately to emphasize that the violation of a constitutional right, in proper cases, may itself constitute a compensable injury. . . .

Following *Carey*, the Courts of Appeals have recognized that invasions of constitutional rights sometimes cause injuries that cannot be redressed by a wooden application of common-law damages rules. In *Hobson v. Wilson*, 237 U.S. App. D.C. 219 (1984), plaintiffs claimed that defendant Federal Bureau of Investigation agents had invaded their First Amendment rights to assemble for peaceable political protest, to associate with others to engage in political expression, and to speak on public issues free of unreasonable government interference. The District Court found that the defendants had succeeded in diverting plaintiffs from, and impeding them in, their protest activities. The Court of Appeals for the District of Columbia Circuit held that that injury to a First Amendment-protected interest could itself constitute compensable injury wholly apart from any "emotional distress, humiliation and personal indignity, emotional pain, embarrassment, fear, anxiety and anguish" suffered by plaintiffs. The court warned, however, that that injury could be compensated with substantial damages only to the extent that it was "reasonably quantifiable"; damages should not be based on "the so-called inherent value of the rights violated."

I believe that the *Hobson* court correctly stated the law. When a plaintiff is deprived, for example, of the opportunity to engage in a demonstration to express his political views, "[i]t is facile to suggest that no damage is done." Loss of such an opportunity constitutes loss of First Amendment rights "'in their most pristine and classic form.'" There is no reason why such an injury should not be compensable in damages. At the same time, however, the award must be proportional to the actual loss sustained. . . .

The Court therefore properly remands for a new trial on damages. I do not understand the Court, however, to hold that deprivations of constitutional rights can never themselves constitute compensable injuries. Such a rule would be inconsistent with the logic of *Carey*, and would defeat the purpose of § 1983 by denying compensation for genuine injuries caused by the deprivation of constitutional rights.

Notes and Questions

1. What category of damages did the Court reject in *Stachura*? How does this holding differ from the holding in *Carey*?

2. What disagreement, if any, exists between Justice Marshall and the majority? What types of damages is he trying to preserve and why?

3. Consider footnote 14 of the Court's opinion, distinguishing cases about voting rights. What tangible harm does a person sustain when wrongfully denied the right to vote? How is the measurement of that harm less abstract or arbitrary than what the jury was asked to figure out here?

4. Is the problem with the jury instruction here merely semantic? If you represented the plaintiff on remand, how might you ask for the same amount of
damages again?

5. One can imagine harms that are constitutionally grave but minimally compensable
under *Stachura*. For instance, if the police break into your house and search it
without a warrant, that strikes at the core interest the Fourth Amendment was
meant to protect, yet if no tangible harm results, damages will be limited to the
emotional distress you felt at the intrusion. What mechanisms could address this
type of mismatch between amount of compensation and seriousness of violation?

6. In deciding this case, how does the Court prioritize the goals of compensation
and deterrence? In the various cases we have studied, have the Court's relative
valuations of these two goals remained consistent? In what contexts has the
Court taken a different view of these goals from that in *Stachura*, and why?

Note: Damages and the Role of Insurers

The effects of civil rights enforcement through private damages actions turn not only
on what types of damages are available but also on who pays them. John Rappaport,
How Private Insurers Regulate Public Police, 130 Harv. L. Rev. 1539 (2017), examines
the role of insurers in regulating police conduct. Professor Rappaport points out that
insurers of municipalities have a financial incentive to reduce the amount that municipalities pay in litigation and therefore to reduce constitutional violations by police.
Professor Rappaport identifies several important implications of insurers' interest in
police conduct. Perhaps most significant is insurers' role in regulating constitutional
norms through police trainings and follow-up audits of insured municipalities.

Recall from Chapter 4 that individual officer-defendants are nearly always
indemnified by their employers when held liable for constitutional violations.
From the perspective of the plaintiff, the money is the same whether it comes from
the defendant or somewhere else. From the perspective of public accountability,
though, does it matter that defendants are in some instances twice removed from
paying judgments—the defendant passes the cost on to the government employer,
and the employer passes it on to the insurer? Does this arrangement dissipate whatever deterrent value § 1983 damages have? Or will government entities still feel the
pinch of too many constitutional violations when their insurance premiums rise?

A more optimistic view is that, whereas governments may not even keep track
of, much less learn from, the constitutional violations their employees commit (see
Prologue, Section C), Professor Rappaport's work suggests that insurers are more
responsive—offering trainings to protect their bottom line, for instance. Might the
involvement of insurers actually enhance the deterrent value of damages?

B. PUNITIVE DAMAGES

We have seen how the Court has adapted principles of compensatory and nominal
damages from the common law. What about punitive damages?

In *Smith v. Wade*, 461 U.S. 30 (1983), a prisoner at a Missouri institution claimed that the defendant, a guard, placed him in danger by housing him with two prisoners who beat and sexually assaulted him. The court instructed the jury that it could award punitive damages under § 1983 if it found "a reckless or callous disregard of, or indifference to, the rights or safety of others." The guard argued that punitive damages depended on showing an intent to injure. The Court, in an opinion by Justice Brennan, rejected that argument and endorsed the jury instruction that had been given:

> [A survey of historical practice regarding ordinary tort cases reveals that t]he large majority of state and lower federal courts were in agreement that punitive damage awards did not require a showing of actual malicious intent; they permitted punitive awards on variously stated standards of negligence, recklessness, or other culpable conduct short of actual malicious intent. The same rule applies today. . . .
>
> [Smith argues] that an actual intent standard is preferable to a recklessness standard because it is less vague. . . . Recklessness or callous indifference, he argues, is too uncertain a standard to achieve deterrence rationally and fairly. A prison guard, for example, can be expected to know whether he is acting with actual ill will or intent to injure, but not whether he is being reckless or callously indifferent.
>
> Smith's argument, if valid, would apply to ordinary tort cases as easily as to § 1983 suits; hence, it hardly presents an argument for adopting a different rule under § 1983. In any event, the argument is unpersuasive. While, arguendo, an intent standard may be easier to understand and apply to particular situations than a recklessness standard, we are not persuaded that a recklessness standard is too vague to be fair or useful. . . .
>
> More fundamentally, Smith's argument for certainty in the interest of deterrence overlooks the distinction between a standard for punitive damages and a standard of liability in the first instance. Smith seems to assume that prison guards and other state officials look mainly to the standard for punitive damages in shaping their conduct. We question the premise; we assume, and hope, that most officials are guided primarily by the underlying standards of federal substantive law—both out of devotion to duty, and in the interest of avoiding liability for compensatory damages. At any rate, the conscientious officer who desires clear guidance on how to do his job and avoid lawsuits can and should look to the standard for actionability in the first instance. The need for exceptional clarity in the standard for punitive damages arises only if one assumes that there are substantial numbers of officers who will not be deterred by compensatory damages; only such officers will seek to guide their conduct by the punitive damages standard. The presence of such officers constitutes a powerful argument against raising the threshold for punitive damages. . . .
>
> Smith contends that even if § 1983 does not ordinarily require a showing of actual malicious intent for an award of punitive damages, such a showing should be required in this case. He argues that the deterrent and punitive purposes of punitive damages are served only if the threshold for punitive damages is higher in every case than the underlying standard for liability in the first instance. In this case, . . . both [the constitutional merits standard and the punitive damages standard] apply a standard of reckless or callous indifference to Wade's rights. Hence, Smith argues, the district judge erred in not requiring a higher standard for punitive damages, namely, actual malicious intent.
>
> This argument incorrectly assumes that, simply because the instructions specified the same threshold of liability for punitive and compensatory damages, the two

forms of damages were equally available to the plaintiff. The argument overlooks a key feature of punitive damages—that they are never awarded as of right, no matter how egregious the defendant's conduct. . . . Hence, it is not entirely accurate that punitive and compensatory damages were awarded in this case on the same standard. To make its punitive award, the jury was required to find not only that Smith's conduct met the recklessness threshold (a question of ultimate fact), but also that his conduct merited a punitive award of $5,000 in addition to the compensatory award (a discretionary moral judgment).

Accordingly, the Court concluded:

[A] jury may be permitted to assess punitive damages in an action under § 1983 when the defendant's conduct is shown to be motivated by evil motive or intent, or when it involves reckless or callous indifference to the federally protected rights of others. We further hold that this threshold applies even when the underlying standard of liability for compensatory damages is one of recklessness.

In dissent, Justice Rehnquist, joined by Chief Justice Burger and Justice Powell, first disputed the majority's account of the historical practice, then argued:

It is anomalous, and counter to deep-rooted legal principles and common-sense notions, to punish persons who meant no harm, and to award a windfall, in the form of punitive damages, to someone who already has been fully compensated. These peculiarities ought to be carefully limited—not expanded to every case where a jury may think a defendant was too careless, particularly where a vaguely-defined, elastic standard like "reckless indifference" gives free reign to the biases and prejudices of juries. . . .

One of the principal themes of our immunity decisions is that the threat of liability must not deter an official's "willingness to execute his office with the decisiveness and the judgment required by the public good." . . . Precisely the same reasoning applies to liability for punitive damages. Because punitive damages generally are not subject to any relation to actual harm suffered, and because the recklessness standard is so imprecise, the remedy poses an even greater threat to the ability of officials to take decisive, efficient action. . . . It would have been difficult for the Court to have fashioned a more effective Damoclean sword than the open-ended, standardless and unpredictable liability it creates today.

Justice O'Connor also dissented.

Can punitive damages be awarded against a municipality? No, explained Justice Blackmun for the Court in *City of Newport v. Fact Concerts, Inc.*, 453 U.S. 247 (1981):

Given that municipal immunity from punitive damages was well established at common law by 1871, we proceed on the familiar assumption that "Congress would have specifically so provided had it wished to abolish the doctrine." *Pierson.* Nothing in the legislative debates suggests that, in enacting § 1 of the Civil Rights Act, the 42d Congress intended any such abolition. . . .

Punitive damages by definition are not intended to compensate the injured party, but rather to punish the tortfeasor whose wrongful action was intentional or malicious, and to deter him and others from similar extreme conduct. Regarding retribution, it remains true that an award of punitive damages against a municipality "punishes" only the taxpayers, who took no part in the commission of the tort. . . . Neither reason nor justice suggests that such retribution should be visited upon the shoulders of blameless or unknowing taxpayers. . . .

Respondent argues vigorously that deterrence is a primary purpose of § 1983, and that because punitive awards against municipalities for the malicious conduct of their policymaking officials will induce voters to condemn official misconduct through the electoral process, the threat of such awards will deter future constitutional violations. . . .

[But there is] no reason to suppose that corrective action, such as the discharge of offending officials who were appointed and the public excoriation of those who were elected, will not occur unless punitive damages are awarded against the municipality. The Court recently observed in a related context: "The more reasonable assumption is that responsible superiors are motivated not only by concern for the public fisc but also by concern for the Government's integrity." *Carlson v. Green*. This assumption is no less applicable to the electorate at large. And if additional protection is needed, the compensatory damages that are available against a municipality may themselves induce the public to vote the wrongdoers out of office.

Justice Brennan, joined by Justices Marshall and Stevens, dissented, arguing that the issue decided by the Court had not been properly preserved for the Court's review.

Notes and Questions

1. What is the standard for awarding punitive damages under § 1983? What requirement did the Court reject and why?

2. The Court's decision in *Fact Concerts* contains echoes of the debates over municipal liability generally. How consistent are the assumptions underlying *Fact Concerts* with those supporting the decisions in *Owen* and *Monell* (Chapter 5)?

3. Why might the availability of punitive damages against an individual defendant be insufficient to deter violations by the defendant's employer? How have municipal leaders generally reacted when video footage has shown law enforcement acting in a reckless or callous manner? How do the limitations on compensatory damages in *Carey* and *Stachura* affect your view of the appropriate rule?

CHAPTER 9 PROBLEMS

Problem 9A. Consider a Fourth Amendment case in which a pedestrian is unconstitutionally stopped and frisked by a police officer without reasonable suspicion. Nothing illegal is found. The encounter lasts five minutes. What kinds of damages could the pedestrian seek against the officer? How likely is such a case to be brought?

Problem 9B. Kalorama University (KU) is a state school with a large population of students whose native language is not English. In response to a tide of anti-immigrant sentiment nationwide, the school imposes the following rule on KU undergraduate admissions: "All applicants must disclose if English is their first language. Admissions officers may consider whether the school has the resources to handle the number of non-native speakers who have applied and, if not, exercise their discretion to reject a portion of non-native English-speaking applicants on that basis."

Francisco Piriz is a high school senior who immigrated to the United States from Mexico at age 5. He is a star student and captain of the debate team. English is not his first language. He hopes to study history in college.

Piriz applies to KU, his first choice. He is eligible for in-state tuition there. As required, Piriz discloses that he is not a native English speaker. Piriz's grades and scores are in the top quartile among KU applicants.

Piriz is rejected at KU but gets into Takoma Park Tech (TPT), which is ranked five spots higher than KU in well-regarded college rankings but is outside Piriz's home state. Piriz's school counselor tells him that none of her students in ten years has been admitted to TPT but rejected at KU. KU's admission rate was 40 percent for all applicants but 10 percent for applicants identifying as non-native speakers. Nearly all the applicants who identified as non-native speakers were Latino immigrants. Piriz is sure he was rejected because he is a non-native speaker. Piriz feels both angry and depressed.

Piriz decides to attend TPT. As an out-of-state student there, Piriz will pay higher tuition than he would have at KU. He plans to apply to transfer to KU after his first year at TPT.

Meanwhile, Piriz wants to sue KU for compensation and approaches you for legal help. Your research reveals evidence showing that the Chancellor of KU adopted the language policy for discriminatory reasons. You conclude that Piriz has a viable § 1983 claim against the Chancellor in his individual capacity for an equal protection violation.

What damages can Piriz seek? How will they be measured?

Attorneys' Fees

We turn now to a type of remedy that has no effect on the formal *enforceability* of constitutional and civil rights but an important practical effect on whether such rights *will in fact be enforced*: attorneys' fees.

Although the default rule in the United States (in contrast to Britain) is that a victorious litigant does not recover legal fees from the losing party, Congress has created an exception to this rule to help civil rights plaintiffs attract counsel to litigate cases that may be of great benefit to the public but yield insufficient damages to entice lawyers to take such cases on a contingency basis.

42 U.S.C. § 1988(b) provides (with the key terms italicized):

> In any action or proceeding to enforce a provision of sections 1981, 1981a, 1982, 1983, 1985, and 1986 of this title, title IX of Public Law 92-318 [20 U.S.C. § 1681 et seq.], the Religious Freedom Restoration Act of 1993 [42 U.S.C. § 2000bb et seq.], the Religious Land Use and Institutionalized Persons Act of 2000 [42 U.S.C. § 2000cc et seq.], title VI of the Civil Rights Act of 1964 [42 U.S.C. § 2000d et seq.], or section 13981 of this title, the court, *in its discretion,* may allow the *prevailing party,* other than the United States, *a reasonable attorney's fee as part of the costs . . . .*

Title VII of the Civil Rights Act of 1964 has a similar attorneys' fees provision, as does Title II of that Act, which prohibits discrimination in public accommodations and which is the subject of one of the early Supreme Court cases interpreting fee-shifting statutes. The Supreme Court has interpreted all these statutes as establishing the same basic rules for fees.

Section A of this chapter covers the prerequisites for an award of fees. Section B examines how fees are calculated. Section C explores the complex practical and ethical implications of settlement offers that require plaintiffs to waive their right to attorneys' fees.

A. THE MEANING OF "PREVAILING PARTY" AND "DISCRETION"

Our first several cases (three discussed in abbreviated form and one set out as a principal case) reflect how and why Congress came to enact these provisions, and they define two of the crucial statutory phrases — "prevailing party" and "in its discretion."

Newman v. Piggie Park Enterprises, Inc., 390 U.S. 400 (1968), was a public accommodations case under Title II of the Civil Rights Act of 1964 to enjoin race discrimination at six South Carolina restaurants. The court of appeals held that the successful plaintiffs were entitled to attorneys' fees only to the extent that the defendants' arguments had been advanced "for purposes of delay and not in good faith." In a brief per curiam opinion, the Court rejected this "subjective standard" for awarding fees:

> When the Civil Rights Act of 1964 was passed, it was evident that enforcement would prove difficult and that the Nation would have to rely in part upon private litigation as a means of securing broad compliance with the law. A Title II suit is thus private in form only. When a plaintiff brings an action under that Title, he cannot recover damages. If he obtains an injunction, he does so not for himself alone but also as a "private attorney general," vindicating a policy that Congress considered of the highest priority. If successful plaintiffs were routinely forced to bear their own attorneys' fees, few aggrieved parties would be in a position to advance the public interest by invoking the injunctive powers of the federal courts. Congress therefore enacted the provision for counsel fees — not simply to penalize litigants who deliberately advance arguments they know to be untenable but, more broadly, to encourage individuals injured by racial discrimination to seek judicial relief under Title II.
>
> It follows that one who succeeds in obtaining an injunction under that Title should ordinarily recover an attorney's fee unless special circumstances would render such an award unjust. Because no such circumstances are present here, the District Court on remand should include reasonable counsel fees as part of the costs to be assessed against the respondents.

In *Alyeska Pipeline Service Co. v. Wilderness Society*, 421 U.S. 240 (1975), the Court considered whether plaintiffs could be awarded fees for prevailing absent a statute authorizing such an award. Environmental groups had sued to prevent the Secretary of the Interior from issuing permits necessary for the construction of an oil pipeline. The court of appeals awarded attorneys' fees to the successful plaintiffs based on the court's inherent equitable power. The Supreme Court, in an opinion by Justice White, held that the fee award was impermissible:

> In the United States, the prevailing litigant is ordinarily not entitled to collect a reasonable attorneys' fee from the loser. We are asked to fashion a far-reaching exception to this "American Rule"; but having considered its origin and development, we are convinced that it would be inappropriate for the Judiciary, without legislative guidance, to reallocate the burdens of litigation in the manner and to the extent urged by respondents and approved by the Court of Appeals.
>
> At common law, costs were not allowed; but for centuries in England there has been statutory authorization to award costs, including attorneys' fees. Although the

matter is in the discretion of the court, counsel fees are regularly allowed to the prevailing party. . . .

In 1796, this Court appears to have ruled that the Judiciary itself would not create a general rule, independent of any statute, allowing awards of attorneys' fees in federal courts. In *Arcambel v. Wiseman*, 3 U.S. (3 Dall.) 306, the inclusion of attorneys' fees as damages was overturned on the ground that "(t)he general practice of the United States is in oposition (sic) to it; and even if that practice were not strictly correct in principle, it is entitled to the respect of the court, till it is changed, or modified, by statute." This Court has consistently adhered to that early holding. . . .

[I]t would be difficult, indeed, for the courts, without legislative guidance, to consider some statutes important and others unimportant and to allow attorneys' fees only in connection with the former. If the statutory limitation of right-of-way widths involved in this case is a matter of the gravest importance, it would appear that a wide range of statutes would arguably satisfy the criterion of public importance and justify an award of attorneys' fees to the private litigant. . . . Moreover, should courts, if they were to embark on the course urged by respondents, opt for awards to the prevailing party, whether plaintiff or defendant, or only to the prevailing plaintiff? Should awards be discretionary or mandatory? Would there be a presumption operating for or against them in the ordinary case?

[The American Rule] is deeply rooted in our history and in congressional policy; and it is not for us to invade the legislature's province by redistributing litigation costs in the manner suggested by respondents and followed by the Court of Appeals.

Justices Brennan and Marshall each dissented, focusing on what Justice Marshall referred to as "well-established power of federal equity courts to award attorneys' fees when the interests of justice so require."

In response to *Alyeska*, the following year, Congress enacted the Civil Rights Attorney's Fees Awards Act of 1976, codified as 42 U.S.C. § 1988(b), quoted above.

The Court next considered the possibility of fee-shifting in favor of *defendants*. In *Christiansburg Garment Co. v. EEOC*, 434 U.S. 412 (1978), the defendant in an unsuccessful Title VII action sought attorneys' fees and argued that the *Piggie Park* standard for awards to prevailing plaintiffs applied to prevailing defendants as well. Justice Stewart's opinion for a unanimous Court rejected that view:

Section 706(k) of Title VII of the Civil Rights Act of 1964 provides:

"In any action or proceeding under this title the court, in its discretion, may allow the prevailing party. . . . reasonable attorney's fee . . . ."

It can . . . be taken as established, as the parties in this case both acknowledge, that under § 706(k) of Title VII a prevailing plaintiff ordinarily is to be awarded attorney's fees in all but special circumstances. . . .

Relying on what it terms "the plain meaning of the statute," the company argues that the language of § 706(k) admits of only one interpretation: "A prevailing defendant is entitled to an award of attorney's fees on the same basis as a prevailing plaintiff." But the permissive and discretionary language of the statute does not even invite, let alone require, such a mechanical construction. The terms of § 706(k) provide no indication whatever of the circumstances under which either a plaintiff or a defendant should be entitled to attorney's fees. And a moment's reflection reveals that there are at least two strong equitable considerations counseling an attorney's fee award to a prevailing Title VII plaintiff that are wholly absent in the case of a prevailing Title VII defendant.

First, as emphasized so forcefully in *Piggie Park*, the plaintiff is the chosen instrument of Congress to vindicate "a policy that Congress considered of the highest priority." Second, when a district court awards counsel fees to a prevailing plaintiff, it is awarding them against a violator of federal law. As the Court of Appeals clearly perceived, "these policy considerations which support the award of fees to a prevailing plaintiff are not present in the case of a prevailing defendant." A successful defendant seeking counsel fees under § 706(k) must rely on quite different equitable considerations. . . .

[We hold that] a district court may in its discretion award attorney's fees to a prevailing defendant in a Title VII case upon a finding that the plaintiff's action was frivolous, unreasonable, or without foundation, even though not brought in subjective bad faith.

In applying these criteria, it is important that a district court resist the understandable temptation to engage in post hoc reasoning by concluding that, because a plaintiff did not ultimately prevail, his action must have been unreasonable or without foundation. This kind of hindsight logic could discourage all but the most airtight claims, for seldom can a prospective plaintiff be sure of ultimate success. . . . Decisive facts may not emerge until discovery or trial. The law may change or clarify in the midst of litigation. . . .

[A]ssessing attorney's fees against plaintiffs simply because they do not finally prevail would substantially add to the risks inhering in most litigation and would undercut the efforts of Congress to promote the vigorous enforcement of the provisions of Title VII.

Together, *Piggie Park*, *Alyeska*, and *Christiansburg* set out the basic ground rules for fee-shifting under the civil rights statutes, including the requirement that a fee award be authorized by Congress and the asymmetrical treatment of plaintiffs and defendants. The next case interprets a key prerequisite for fee-shifting: When does a plaintiff "prevail"?

Buckhannon Board & Care Home v. West Virginia Department of Health & Human Resources
532 U.S. 598 (2001)

■ *Chief Justice* REHNQUIST *delivered the opinion of the Court.*

Numerous federal statutes allow courts to award attorney's fees and costs to the "prevailing party." The question presented here is whether this term includes a party that has failed to secure a judgment on the merits or a court-ordered consent decree, but has nonetheless achieved the desired result because the lawsuit brought about a voluntary change in the defendant's conduct. We hold that it does not.

[Buckhannon Board and Care Home, Inc., which operates assisted-living facilities, failed an inspection by West Virginia state authorities because some of the residents were incapable of "self-preservation," i.e., moving themselves out of dangers such as fire. Buckhannon challenged the state's "self-preservation" requirement as a violation of the Fair Housing Amendments Act of 1988 (FHAA), and the Americans with Disabilities Act (ADA).

The state then amended its law to remove the "self-preservation" requirement. The court dismissed Buckhannon's case as moot.]

Petitioners requested attorney's fees as the "prevailing party" under the FHAA and ADA [which have fee provisions substantially the same as the one in § 1988]. Petitioners argued that they were entitled to attorney's fees under the "catalyst theory," which posits that a plaintiff is a "prevailing party" if it achieves the desired result because the lawsuit brought about a voluntary change in the defendant's conduct. Although most Courts of Appeals recognize the "catalyst theory," the Court of Appeals for the Fourth Circuit rejected it . . . .

In designating those parties eligible for an award of litigation costs, Congress employed the term "prevailing party," a legal term of art. Black's Law Dictionary 1145 (7th ed. 1999) defines "prevailing party" as "[a] party in whose favor a judgment is rendered, regardless of the amount of damages awarded <in certain cases, the court will award attorney's fees to the prevailing party>. — Also termed successful party." This view that a "prevailing party" is one who has been awarded some relief by the court can be distilled from our prior cases. . . .

Our "[r]espect for ordinary language requires that a plaintiff receive at least some relief on the merits of his claim before he can be said to prevail." . . . In addition to judgments on the merits, we have held that settlement agreements enforced through a consent decree may serve as the basis for an award of attorney's fees. Although a consent decree does not always include an admission of liability by the defendant, it nonetheless is a court-ordered "chang[e] [in] the legal relationship between [the plaintiff] and the defendant." These decisions, taken together, establish that enforceable judgments on the merits and court-ordered consent decrees create the "material alteration of the legal relationship of the parties" necessary to permit an award of attorney's fees.

We think, however, the "catalyst theory" falls on the other side of the line from these examples. It allows an award where there is no judicially sanctioned change in the legal relationship of the parties. Even under a limited form of the "catalyst theory," a plaintiff could recover attorney's fees if it established that the "complaint had sufficient merit to withstand a motion to dismiss for lack of jurisdiction or failure to state a claim on which relief may be granted." This is not the type of legal merit that our prior decisions, based upon plain language and congressional intent, have found necessary. . . . A defendant's voluntary change in conduct, although perhaps accomplishing what the plaintiff sought to achieve by the lawsuit, lacks the necessary judicial imprimatur on the change. Our precedents thus counsel against holding that the term "prevailing party" authorizes an award of attorney's fees without a corresponding alteration in the legal relationship of the parties. . . .

Petitioners nonetheless argue that the legislative history of the Civil Rights Attorney's Fees Awards Act supports a broad reading of "prevailing party" which includes the "catalyst theory." We doubt that legislative history could overcome what we think is the rather clear meaning of "prevailing party" — the term actually used in the statute. Since we resorted to such history in [prior cases], however, we do likewise here.

The House Report to § 1988 states that "[t]he phrase 'prevailing party' is not intended to be limited to the victor only after entry of a final judgment following a full trial on the merits," H.R. Rep. No. 94-1558, p. 7 (1976), while the Senate Report explains that "parties may be considered to have prevailed when they vindicate rights through a consent judgment or without formally obtaining relief," S. Rep. No. 94-1011, p. 5 (1976). . . . We think the legislative history cited by petitioners is at best ambiguous as to the availability of the "catalyst theory" for awarding attorney's fees. Particularly in view of the "American Rule" that attorney's fees will not be awarded absent "explicit statutory authority," such legislative history is clearly insufficient to alter the accepted meaning of the statutory term.

Petitioners finally assert that the "catalyst theory" is necessary to prevent defendants from unilaterally mooting an action before judgment in an effort to avoid an award of attorney's fees. They also claim that the rejection of the "catalyst theory" will deter plaintiffs with meritorious but expensive cases from bringing suit. We are skeptical of these assertions, which are entirely speculative and unsupported by any empirical evidence (e.g., whether the number of suits brought in the Fourth Circuit has declined, in relation to other Circuits . . .).

Petitioners discount the disincentive that the "catalyst theory" may have upon a defendant's decision to voluntarily change its conduct, conduct that may not be illegal. "The defendants' potential liability for fees in this kind of litigation can be as significant as, and sometimes even more significant than, their potential liability on the merits," and the possibility of being assessed attorney's fees may well deter a defendant from altering its conduct. . . .

We have also stated that "[a] request for attorney's fees should not result in a second major litigation," and have accordingly avoided an interpretation of the fee-shifting statutes that would have "spawn[ed] a second litigation of significant dimension." Among other things, a "catalyst theory" hearing would require analysis of the defendant's subjective motivations in changing its conduct, an analysis that "will likely depend on a highly factbound inquiry and may turn on reasonable inferences from the nature and timing of the defendant's change in conduct." Although we do not doubt the ability of district courts to perform the nuanced "three thresholds" test required by the "catalyst theory" — whether the claim was colorable rather than groundless; whether the lawsuit was a substantial rather than an insubstantial cause of the defendant's change in conduct; whether the defendant's change in conduct was motivated by the plaintiff's threat of victory rather than threat of expense — it is clearly not a formula for "ready administrability." . . .

■ *Justice SCALIA, with whom Justice THOMAS joins, concurring.*

I join the opinion of the Court in its entirety, and write to respond at greater length to the contentions of the dissent. . . .

The dissent points out that the Prison Litigation Reform Act of 1995 limits attorney's fees to an amount "proportionately related to the court ordered relief for the violation." This shows that sometimes Congress does explicitly "tightly bind fees to judgments," inviting (the dissent believes) the conclusion that "prevailing party" does not fasten fees to judgments. That conclusion does not follow from the premise. What this statutory provision demonstrates, at most, is that use of the phrase "prevailing party" is not the only way to impose a requirement of court-ordered relief. That is assuredly true. But it would be no more rational to reject the normal meaning of "prevailing party" because some statutes produce the same result with different language, than it would be to conclude that, since there are many synonyms for the word "jump," the word "jump" must mean something else.

It is undoubtedly true, as the dissent points out by quoting a nonlegal dictionary, that the word "prevailing" can have other meanings in other contexts. . . . But when "prevailing party" is used by courts or legislatures in the context of a lawsuit, it is a term of art. . . . Words that have acquired a specialized meaning in the legal context must be accorded their legal meaning. . . .

The dissent distorts the term "prevailing party" beyond its normal meaning for policy reasons, but even those seem to me misguided. They rest upon the presumption that the catalyst theory applies when "the suit's merit led the defendant to abandon the fray, to switch rather than fight on, to accord plaintiff sooner rather than later the principal redress sought in the complaint." As the dissent would have it, by giving the term its normal meaning the Court today approves the practice of denying attorney's fees to a plaintiff with a proven claim of discrimination, simply because the very merit of his claim led the defendant to capitulate before judgment. That is not the case. . . . What the dissent's stretching of the term produces is something more, and something far less reasonable: an award of attorney's fees when the merits of the plaintiff's case remain unresolved—when, for all one knows, the defendant only "abandon[ed] the fray" because the cost of litigation—either financial or in terms of public relations—would be too great. In such a case, the plaintiff may have "prevailed" as Webster's defines that term— "gain[ed] victory by virtue of strength or superiority." But I doubt it was greater strength in financial resources, or superiority in media manipulation, rather than superiority in legal merit, that Congress intended to reward.

It could be argued, perhaps, that insofar as abstract justice is concerned, there is little to choose between the dissent's outcome and the Court's: If the former sometimes rewards the plaintiff with a phony claim (there is no way of knowing), the latter sometimes denies fees to the plaintiff with a solid case whose adversary slinks away on the eve of judgment. But it seems to me the evil of the former far outweighs the evil of the latter. There is all the difference in the world between a rule that denies the extraordinary boon of attorney's fees to some plaintiffs who are no less "deserving" of them than others who receive them, and a rule that causes the law to be the very instrument of wrong—exacting the payment of attorney's fees to the extortionist. . . .

■ *Justice GINSBURG, with whom Justice STEVENS, Justice SOUTER, and Justice BREYER join, dissenting.* . . .

The Court's insistence that there be a document filed in court—a litigated judgment or court-endorsed settlement—upsets long-prevailing Circuit precedent applicable to scores of federal fee-shifting statutes. The decision allows a defendant to escape a statutory obligation to pay a plaintiff's counsel fees, even though the suit's merit led the defendant to abandon the fray, to switch rather than fight on, to accord plaintiff sooner rather than later the principal redress sought in the complaint. Concomitantly, the Court's constricted definition of "prevailing party," and consequent rejection of the "catalyst theory," impede access to court for the less well heeled, and shrink the incentive Congress created for the enforcement of federal law by private attorneys general. . . .

One can entirely agree with Black's Law Dictionary that a party "in whose favor a judgment is rendered" prevails, and at the same time resist, as most Courts of Appeals have, any implication that only such a party may prevail. In prior cases, we have not treated Black's Law Dictionary as preclusively definitive; instead, we have accorded statutory terms, including legal "term [s] of art," a contextual reading. . . .

The spare "prevailing party" language of the fee-shifting provision [at issue] . . . contrast[s] with prescriptions that so tightly bind fees to judgments as to exclude the application of a catalyst concept. The Prison Litigation Reform Act of 1995, for example, directs that fee awards to prisoners under § 1988 be "proportionately related to the court ordered relief for the violation." That statute, by its express terms, forecloses an award to a prisoner on a catalyst theory. But the FHAA and ADA fee-shifting prescriptions, modeled on 42 U.S.C. § 1988 unmodified, do not similarly staple fee awards to "court ordered relief." Their very terms do not foreclose a catalyst theory. . . .

I would "assume . . . that Congress intends the words in its enactments to carry 'their ordinary, contemporary, common meaning.'" In everyday use, "prevail" means "gain victory by virtue of strength or superiority: win mastery: triumph." Webster's Third New International Dictionary 1797 (1976). There are undoubtedly situations in which an individual's goal is to obtain approval of a judge, and in those situations, one cannot "prevail" short of a judge's formal declaration. In a piano competition or a figure skating contest, for example, the person who prevails is the person declared winner by the judges. However, where the ultimate goal is not an arbiter's approval, but a favorable alteration of actual circumstances, a formal declaration is not essential. Western democracies, for instance, "prevailed" in the Cold War even though the Soviet Union never formally surrendered. Among television viewers, John F. Kennedy "prevailed" in the first debate with Richard M. Nixon during the 1960 Presidential contest, even though moderator Howard K. Smith never declared a winner.

A lawsuit's ultimate purpose is to achieve actual relief from an opponent. Favorable judgment may be instrumental in gaining that relief. Generally, however, "the judicial decree is not the end but the means. At the end of the rainbow lies not a judgment, but some action (or cessation of action) by the defendant . . . ." On this common understanding, if a party reaches the "sought-after destination," then the party "prevails" regardless of the "route taken." . . .

In this case, Buckhannon's purpose in suing West Virginia officials was not narrowly to obtain a judge's approbation. The plaintiffs' objective was to stop enforcement of a rule requiring Buckhannon to evict [elderly residents] as the price of remaining in business. If Buckhannon achieved that objective on account of the strength of its case . . . then Buckhannon is properly judged a party who prevailed. . . .

Under the catalyst rule that held sway until today, plaintiffs who obtained the relief they sought through suit on genuine claims ordinarily qualified as "prevailing parties," so that courts had discretion to award them their costs and fees. Persons with limited resources were not impelled to "wage total law" in order to assure that their counsel fees would be paid. They could accept relief, in money or of another kind, voluntarily proffered by a defendant who sought to avoid a recorded decree. And they could rely on a judge then to determine, in her equitable discretion, whether counsel fees were warranted and, if so, in what amount.[10]

Congress appears to have envisioned that very prospect. The Senate Report on the 1976 Civil Rights Attorney's Fees Awards Act states: "[F]or purposes of the award of counsel fees, parties may be considered to have prevailed when they vindicate rights through a consent judgment or without formally obtaining relief." S. Rep. No. 94-1011, at 5. In support, the Report cites cases in which parties recovered fees in the absence of any court-conferred relief. The House Report corroborates: "[A]fter a complaint is filed, a defendant might voluntarily cease the unlawful practice. *A court should still award fees* even though it might conclude, as a matter of equity, that *no formal relief*, such as an injunction, is needed." H.R. Rep. No. 94-1558, at 7 (emphases added). These Reports, Courts of Appeals have observed, are hardly ambiguous. . . .

In opposition to the argument that defendants will resist change in order to stave off an award of fees, one could urge that the catalyst rule may lead defendants promptly to comply with the law's requirements: the longer the litigation, the larger the fees. Indeed, one who knows noncompliance will be expensive might be encouraged to conform his conduct to the legal requirements before litigation is threatened. . . . [W]hy should this Court's fee-shifting rulings drive a plaintiff prepared to accept adequate relief, though out-of-court and unrecorded, to litigate on and on? And if the catalyst rule leads defendants to negotiate not only settlement terms but also allied counsel fees, is that not a consummation to applaud, not deplore? . . .

The concurring opinion adds another argument against the catalyst rule: That opinion sees the rule as accommodating the "extortionist" who obtains relief because of "greater strength in financial resources, or superiority in media manipulation, rather than superiority in legal merit." This concern overlooks both the character of the rule and the judicial superintendence Congress ordered for all fee allowances. . . . Congress assigned responsibility for awarding fees not to automatons unable to recognize extortionists, but to judges expected and instructed to exercise "discretion." So viewed, the catalyst rule provided no berth for nuisance suits, or "thinly disguised forms of extortion." . . .

---

10. Given the protection furnished by the catalyst rule, aggrieved individuals were not left to worry, and wrongdoers were not led to believe, that strategic maneuvers by defendants might succeed in averting a fee award. Apt here is Judge Friendly's observation construing a fee-shifting statute kin to the provisions before us: "Congress clearly did not mean that where [a Freedom of Information Act] suit had gone to trial and developments made it apparent that the judge was about to rule for the plaintiff, the Government could abort any award of attorney fees by an eleventh hour tender of the information."

Notes and Questions

1. Return to the language of § 1988(b) (and parallel provisions of Titles II and VII): "[T]he court, in its discretion, may allow the prevailing party, other than the United States, a reasonable attorney's fee as part of the costs." How has the Court interpreted the phrases "prevailing party" and "in its discretion"? Does a court have "discretion" to award fees in the ordinary sense of that term? Does "prevailing party" have the same meaning for plaintiffs and defendants?

2. If the Court in *Christiansburg* had ruled for the defendant, what would the effect on civil rights litigation have likely been?

3. How does *Buckhannon*'s approach to statutory interpretation differ from that of the first three cases discussed in this chapter? Do the majority and dissent disagree about that approach, or is their dispute about its application? Which is more consistent with the Supreme Court's approach to interpreting civil rights statutes generally—the approach of *Piggie Park* and *Christiansburg* or the approach of *Buckhannon*?

4. If you were frustrated with the Supreme Court's text-defying approach to interpreting the Eleventh Amendment (Chapter 3), how do *Piggie Park* and *Christiansburg* affect your view about appropriate methods of statutory interpretation? Is it possible to generalize that some methods of statutory interpretation are better for civil rights plaintiffs than others? If so, which ones?

5. When should a textualist look to a legal dictionary and when to a general dictionary? How do the various opinions in *Buckhannon* address that question?

6. Both the majority and dissenting blocs in *Buckhannon* charge that the other side's rule will produce perverse incentives. What are those incentives and how plausible is each side's prediction about them? Are these predictions inconsistent? If one side of the debate seems correct to you, is it because that side's account of the incentives seems more plausible, because that side is focusing on the more important set of incentives, or something else?

7. Does Justice Scalia's approach to § 1988 in *Buckhannon* put him at odds with *Piggie Park* and *Christiansburg*? Would he overrule those cases?

8. Both before and after *Buckhannon*, the Court has construed "prevailing party" narrowly in other situations. For instance, the Court rejected "prevailing" status for a plaintiff who prevailed through administrative proceedings rather than in court. *N.C. Dep't of Trans. v. Crest St. Community Council, Inc.*, 479 U.S. 6 (1986). And the Court has rejected "prevailing" status for a party that obtained a preliminary injunction but ultimately lost on the merits. *Sole v. Wyner*, 551 U.S. 74 (2007). What incentives do these results create?

9. Among the most important questions *Buckhannon* leaves open is how formal a settlement must be to establish that the plaintiff "prevailed." *Buckhannon* states that "court-ordered consent decrees" count. How about a settlement that is not

entered as an order of a court? Does that fail the *Buckhannon* test because it is not court-ordered, as a consent decree or a judgment is? *See John T. ex rel. Paul T. v. Del. Cty. Intermediate Unit*, 318 F.3d 545, 560 (3d Cir. 2003) ("no court has endorsed the agreement with a 'judicial imprimatur'"). Or does it qualify as a "material alteration of the legal relationship of the parties" because it is, like any contract, enforceable in court? *See Barrios v. Cal. Interscholastic Fed'n*, 277 F.3d 1128, 1134 (9th Cir. 2002) ("the legal relationship is altered because the plaintiff can force the defendant to do something he otherwise would not have to do"). Most circuits that have considered the question do not treat a settling plaintiff as a "prevailing party" absent a court order.

10. What effect has *Buckhannon* had on civil rights enforcement by private civil action? One answer comes from a survey of 221 public interest organizations in 2004, reported in Catherine R. Albiston & Laura Beth Nielsen, *The Procedural Attack on Civil Rights: The Empirical Reality of* Buckhannon *for the Private Attorney General*, 54 UCLA L. Rev. 1087, 1092 (2007), which found: "[P]ublic interest organizations that litigate paradigmatic public interest cases, such as class actions seeking injunctive relief against government actors, are the most likely to be affected by *Buckhannon*. . . . *Buckhannon* encourages strategic capitulation [by defendants to avoid paying fees], makes settlement more difficult, and discourages both public interest organizations and private counsel from taking on enforcement actions."

Note: Fee Awards Against Federal Actors

The Supreme Court has never recognized an attorneys' fees remedy as part of *Bivens* (Chapter 2). There *is* a general provision for fee awards against the federal government, the Equal Access to Justice Act (EAJA), which provides in pertinent part:

> Except as otherwise specifically provided by statute, a court shall award to a prevailing party other than the United States fees and other expenses, in addition to any costs . . . , incurred by that party in any civil action (other than cases sounding in tort), including proceedings for judicial review of agency action, brought by or against the United States in any court having jurisdiction of that action, unless the court finds that the position of the United States was substantially justified or that special circumstances make an award unjust.

28 U.S.C. § 2412(d)(1)(A). The exception for cases in which "the court finds that the position of the United States was substantially justified" is capacious. The Supreme Court has held that "substantially justified" in this context means "not 'justified to a high degree,' but rather 'justified in substance or in the main' — that is, justified to a degree that could satisfy a reasonable person." *Pierce v. Underwood*, 487 U.S. 552, 565 (1988). Further, "a position can be justified even though it is not correct, and we believe it can be substantially (i.e., for the most part) justified if a reasonable person could think it correct, that is, if it has a reasonable basis in law and fact." *Id.* at 565 n.2. Because the government's position must merely be "reasonable," an award of fees against the government is not the norm.

Can *Bivens* plaintiffs obtain fees under EAJA? The consensus view is that they cannot. A leading case on this point reasoned as follows:

[U]nlike in § 1988, which provides for fees from the actual defendant, the EAJA provides for fees only from the United States, which of course is never a party to a *Bivens* action. . . . Federal agents are sued in their individual capacities rather than their official capacities in *Bivens* actions; thus, a *Bivens* action is not a "civil action . . . against the United States" under § 2412(d).

Kreines v. United States, 33 F.3d 1105, 1109 (9th Cir. 1994).

The unavailability of fee-shifting is another regard in which *Bivens* is less robust than § 1983.

B. DETERMINING THE AMOUNT OF FEE AWARDS

Whereas the Court has provided definitive (if sometimes controversial) interpretations of "discretion" and "prevailing party," the Court's instructions on how to calculate a "reasonable attorney's fee" leave much more to the judgment of the district court. And the question of what is "reasonable" is not entirely separable from whether and to what degree a party has "prevailed."

Hensley v. Eckerhart
461 U.S. 424 (1983)

■ *Justice POWELL delivered the opinion of the Court.*

[Individuals involuntarily confined at Fulton State Hospital in Missouri challenged their treatment, conditions at the hospital, the process for placement in maximum security, and the lack of compensation for work performed there. The process claim was resolved by consent decree; the compensation claim became moot as a result of a voluntary change in practices; and the treatment and conditions claim went to trial. The court found in favor of plaintiffs in five of the six areas challenged. Plaintiffs sought $150,000 in fees. Defendants opposed the request, arguing, among other things, that Plaintiffs should not be compensated for hours spent in pursuit of unsuccessful claims.] . . .

The purpose of § 1988 is to ensure "effective access to the judicial process" for persons with civil rights grievances. H.R. Rep. No. 94-1558, p. 1 (1976). Accordingly, a prevailing plaintiff "'should ordinarily recover an attorney's fee unless special circumstances would render such an award unjust.'"

The amount of the fee, of course, must be determined on the facts of each case. On this issue the House Report simply refers to twelve factors set forth in *Johnson v. Georgia Highway Express, Inc.*, 488 F.2d 714 (CA5 1974).[3] . . . One

___

3. The twelve factors are: (1) the time and labor required; (2) the novelty and difficulty of the questions; (3) the skill requisite to perform the legal service properly; (4) the preclusion of employment by the attorney due to acceptance of the case; (5) the customary fee; (6) whether the fee

of the factors in *Johnson*, "the amount involved and the results obtained," indicates that the level of a plaintiff's success is relevant to the amount of fees to be awarded. The importance of this relationship is confirmed in varying degrees by the other cases cited approvingly in the Senate Report. . . .

The most useful starting point for determining the amount of a reasonable fee is the number of hours reasonably expended on the litigation multiplied by a reasonable hourly rate. This calculation provides an objective basis on which to make an initial estimate of the value of a lawyer's services. The party seeking an award of fees should submit evidence supporting the hours worked and rates claimed. Where the documentation of hours is inadequate, the district court may reduce the award accordingly.

The district court also should exclude from this initial fee calculation hours that were not "reasonably expended." S. Rep. No. 94-1011, p. 6 (1976). Cases may be overstaffed, and the skill and experience of lawyers vary widely. Counsel for the prevailing party should make a good faith effort to exclude from a fee request hours that are excessive, redundant, or otherwise unnecessary, just as a lawyer in private practice ethically is obligated to exclude such hours from his fee submission. "In the private sector, 'billing judgment' is an important component in fee setting. It is no less important here. Hours that are not properly billed to one's client also are not properly billed to one's adversary pursuant to statutory authority."

The product of reasonable hours times a reasonable rate does not end the inquiry. There remain other considerations that may lead the district court to adjust the fee upward or downward, including the important factor of the "results obtained."[9] This factor is particularly crucial where a plaintiff is deemed "prevailing" even though he succeeded on only some of his claims for relief. In this situation two questions must be addressed. First, did the plaintiff fail to prevail on claims that were unrelated to the claims on which he succeeded? Second, did the plaintiff achieve a level of success that makes the hours reasonably expended a satisfactory basis for making a fee award?

In some cases a plaintiff may present in one lawsuit distinctly different claims for relief that are based on different facts and legal theories. In such a suit, even where the claims are brought against the same defendants — often an institution and its officers, as in this case — counsel's work on one claim will be unrelated to his work on another claim. Accordingly, work on an unsuccessful claim cannot be deemed to have been "expended in pursuit of the ultimate result achieved." . . .

In other cases the plaintiff's claims for relief will involve a common core of facts or will be based on related legal theories. Much of counsel's time will be

---

is fixed or contingent; (7) time limitations imposed by the client or the circumstances; (8) the amount involved and the results obtained; (9) the experience, reputation, and ability of the attorneys; (10) the "undesirability" of the case; (11) the nature and length of the professional relationship with the client; and (12) awards in similar cases. . . .

9. The district court also may consider other factors identified in *Johnson v. Georgia Highway Express, Inc.*, 488 F.2d 714, 717-719 (CA5 1974), though it should note that many of these factors usually are subsumed within the initial calculation of hours reasonably expended at a reasonable hourly rate.

devoted generally to the litigation as a whole, making it difficult to divide the hours expended on a claim-by-claim basis. Such a lawsuit cannot be viewed as a series of discrete claims. Instead the district court should focus on the significance of the overall relief obtained by the plaintiff in relation to the hours reasonably expended on the litigation.

Where a plaintiff has obtained excellent results, his attorney should recover a fully compensatory fee. Normally this will encompass all hours reasonably expended on the litigation, and indeed in some cases of exceptional success an enhanced award may be justified. In these circumstances the fee award should not be reduced simply because the plaintiff failed to prevail on every contention raised in the lawsuit. Litigants in good faith may raise alternative legal grounds for a desired outcome, and the court's rejection of or failure to reach certain grounds is not a sufficient reason for reducing a fee. The result is what matters.[11]

If, on the other hand, a plaintiff has achieved only partial or limited success, the product of hours reasonably expended on the litigation as a whole times a reasonable hourly rate may be an excessive amount. This will be true even where the plaintiff's claims were interrelated, nonfrivolous, and raised in good faith. Congress has not authorized an award of fees whenever it was reasonable for a plaintiff to bring a lawsuit or whenever conscientious counsel tried the case with devotion and skill. Again, the most critical factor is the degree of success obtained. . . .

A request for attorney's fees should not result in a second major litigation. . . .

On remand the District Court should determine the proper amount of the attorney's fee award in light of these standards. . . .

[Concurring opinion of Burger, C.J., omitted.]

■ Justice BRENNAN, with whom Justice MARSHALL, Justice BLACKMUN, and Justice STEVENS join, concurring in part and dissenting in part.

The Court today holds that "the extent of a plaintiff's success is a crucial factor in determining the proper amount of an award of attorney's fees under 42 U.S.C. § 1988." I agree with the Court's carefully worded statement because it is fully consistent with the purpose of § 1988 as well as the interpretation of that statute reached by the courts of appeals. I also agree that plaintiffs may receive attorney's fees for cases in which " 'they succeed on any significant issue in litigation which achieves some of the benefit the parties sought in bringing suit,' " and that plaintiffs may receive fees for all hours reasonably spent litigating a case even if they do not prevail on every claim or legal theory.

---

11. We agree with the District Court's rejection of "a mathematical approach comparing the total number of issues in the case with those actually prevailed upon." Such a ratio provides little aid in determining what is a reasonable fee in light of all the relevant factors. Nor is it necessarily significant that a prevailing plaintiff did not receive all the relief requested. For example, a plaintiff who failed to recover damages but obtained injunctive relief, or vice versa, may recover a fee award based on all hours reasonably expended if the relief obtained justified that expenditure of attorney time.

Regretfully, however, I do not join the Court's opinion. In restating general principles of the law of attorney's fees, the Court omits a number of elements crucial to the calculation of attorney's fees under § 1988. . . .

Furthermore, whether one considers all the relevant factors or merely the relationship of fees to results obtained, the District Court in this case awarded a fee that was well within the court's zone of discretion under § 1988, and it explained the amount of the fee meticulously. . . .

[O]n many occasions awarding counsel fees that reflect the full market value of their time will require paying more than their customary hourly rates. Most attorneys paid an hourly rate expect to be paid promptly and without regard to success or failure. Customary rates reflect those expectations. Attorneys who take cases on contingency, thus deferring payment of their fees until the case has ended and taking upon themselves the risk that they will receive no payment at all, generally receive far more in winning cases than they would if they charged an hourly rate. The difference, however, reflects the time-value of money and the risk of nonrecovery usually borne by clients in cases where lawyers are paid an hourly rate. Courts applying § 1988 must also take account of the time-value of money and the fact that attorneys can never be 100% certain they will win even the best case.

Therefore, district courts should not end their fee inquiries when they have multiplied a customary hourly rate times the reasonable number of hours expended, and then checked the product against the results obtained. They should also consider both delays in payment and the pre-litigation likelihood that the claims which did in fact prevail would prevail. These factors are potentially relevant in every case. Even if the results obtained do not justify awarding fees for all the hours spent on a particular case, no fee is reasonable unless it would be adequate to induce other attorneys to represent similarly situated clients seeking relief comparable to that obtained in the case at hand. . . .

Notes and Questions

1. As between the standards advocated by the majority and by the dissent, which is more faithful to Congress's intent in § 1988? Which is more administrable?

2. Justice Brennan argues that the "lodestar" — courts' shorthand for the *Hensley* formula of reasonable hourly rate multiplied by hours reasonably spent — sometimes undervalues an attorney's work. When does he think that will be the case, and why? Do you agree? What values and assumptions guide your answer?

3. Some civil actions to enforce civil rights are brought not by private firms but by nonprofit organizations that do not charge their clients for their services. How if at all should the Court account for these arrangements in the lodestar calculation?

    In *Blum v. Stenson*, 465 U.S. 886 (1984), the Court "granted certiorari to consider whether it was proper for the District Court to use prevailing market rates in awarding attorney's fees to nonprofit legal services organizations." The Court, in an opinion by Justice Powell, determined unanimously that it was:

> [P]etitioner urges this Court to require that all fee awards under § 1988 be calculated according to the cost of providing legal services rather than according to the prevailing market rate. . . . Because market rates incorporate operating expenses that may exceed the expenses of nonprofit legal services organizations, and include an element of profit unnecessary to attract nonprofit counsel, the Solicitor General argues that fee awards based on market rates "confer an unjustified windfall or subsidy upon legal services organizations." . . .
>
> In enacting the statute, Congress directed that attorney's fees be calculated according to standards currently in use under other fee-shifting statutes . . . [and cited with approval cases in which] fee awards were calculated according to prevailing market rates. None . . . made any mention of a cost-based standard. Petitioner's argument that the use of market rates violates congressional intent, therefore, is flatly contradicted by the legislative history of § 1988.
>
> It is also clear from the legislative history that Congress did not intend the calculation of fee awards to vary depending on whether plaintiff was represented by private counsel or by a nonprofit legal services organization. . . .[11]

As the Court envisioned in footnote 11, nonprofit attorneys do in practice turn to their private-sector counterparts for fee schedules on which to base claims about an appropriate market rate.

* * *

Not infrequently in civil rights enforcement, the damages are quite low relative to the fee award. In such cases, should the amount of damages exert a gravitational force on the amount of the fee award?

City of Riverside v. Rivera
477 U.S. 561 (1986)

▪ Justice BRENNAN announced the judgment of the Court and delivered an opinion in which Justice MARSHALL, Justice BLACKMUN, and Justice STEVENS join.

The issue presented in this case is whether an award of attorney's fees under 42 U.S.C. § 1988 is per se "unreasonable" within the meaning of the statute if it exceeds the amount of damages recovered by the plaintiff in the underlying civil rights action.

Respondents, eight Chicano individuals, attended a party on the evening of August 1, 1975, at the Riverside, California, home of respondents Santos and Jennie Rivera. A large number of unidentified police officers, acting without a

---

11. . . . [In figuring out what the "market rate" is for a nonprofit lawyer,] the rates charged in private representations may afford relevant comparisons. . . . [T]he burden is on the fee applicant to produce satisfactory evidence—in addition to the attorney's own affidavits—that the requested rates are in line with those prevailing in the community for similar services by lawyers of reasonably comparable skill, experience and reputation. . . .

warrant, broke up the party using tear gas and, as found by the District Court, "unnecessary physical force." Many of the guests, including four of the respondents, were arrested. The District Court later found that "[t]he party was not creating a disturbance in the community at the time of the break-in." Criminal charges against the arrestees were ultimately dismissed for lack of probable cause.

[The partygoers sued the City of Riverside, the police chief, and thirty individual police officers under several federal and state law theories, including 42 U.S.C. § 1983 for violations of their First, Fourth, and Fourteenth Amendment rights. The court granted summary judgment in favor of seventeen of the individual officers. The rest proceeded to trial, where the jury returned a total of thirty-seven individual verdicts in favor of the plaintiffs and awarded $33,350 in compensatory and punitive damages.]

Respondents also sought attorney's fees and costs under § 1988 [for approximately 2,000 hours of work at $125 an hour]. . . . The District Court found both the hours and rates reasonable, and awarded respondents $245,456.25 in attorney's fees. . . . [After the award was vacated and remanded in light of the Court's decision in *Hensley*,] the District Court held two additional hearings, reviewed additional briefing, and reexamined the record as a whole. The court made extensive findings of fact and conclusions of law, and again concluded that respondents were entitled to an award of $245,456.25 in attorney's fees, based on the same total number of hours expended on the case and the same hourly rates. . . . [The court of appeals affirmed.] . . .

Petitioners argue that the District Court failed properly to follow *Hensley* in calculating respondents' fee award. We disagree. The District Court carefully considered the results obtained by respondents pursuant to the instructions set forth in *Hensley*, and concluded that respondents were entitled to recover attorney's fees for all hours expended on the litigation. First, the court found that "[t]he amount of time expended by counsel in conducting this litigation was reasonable and reflected sound legal judgment under the circumstances." The court also determined that counsel's excellent performances in this case entitled them to be compensated at prevailing market rates, even though they were relatively young when this litigation began.

The District Court then concluded that it was inappropriate to adjust respondents' fee award downward to account for the fact that respondents had prevailed only on some of their claims, and against only some of the defendants. The court first determined that "it was never actually clear what officer did what until we had gotten through with the whole trial," so that "[u]nder the circumstances of this case, it was reasonable for plaintiffs initially to name thirty-one individual defendants . . . as well as the City of Riverside as defendants in this action." . . .

The court then found that the lawsuit could not "be viewed as a series of discrete claims," *Hensley*:

> "All claims made by plaintiffs were based on a common core of facts. The claims on which plaintiffs did not prevail were closely related to the claims on which they did prevail. The time devoted to claims on which plaintiffs did not prevail cannot reasonably be separated from time devoted to claims on which plaintiffs did."

The District Court also considered the amount of damages recovered, and determined that the size of the damages award did not imply that respondents' success was limited:

"[T]he size of the jury award resulted from (a) the general reluctance of jurors to make large awards against police officers, and (b) the dignified restraint which the plaintiffs exercised in describing their injuries to the jury. For example, although some of the actions of the police would clearly have been insulting and humiliating to even the most insensitive person and were, in the opinion of the Court, intentionally so, plaintiffs did not attempt to play up this aspect of the case."

The court paid particular attention to the fact that the case "presented complex and interrelated issues of fact and law," and that "[a] fee award in this civil rights action will . . . advance the public interest":

"Counsel for plaintiffs . . . served the public interest by vindicating important constitutional rights. Defendants had engaged in lawless, unconstitutional conduct, and the litigation of plaintiffs' case was necessary to remedy defendants' misconduct. Indeed, the Court was shocked at some of the acts of the police officers in this case and was convinced from the testimony that these acts were motivated by a general hostility to the Chicano community in the area where the incident occurred. The amount of time expended by plaintiffs' counsel in conducting this litigation was clearly reasonable and necessary to serve the public interest as well as the interests of plaintiffs in the vindication of their constitutional rights." . . .

Based on our review of the record, we agree with the Court of Appeals that the District Court's findings were not clearly erroneous. We conclude that the District Court correctly applied the factors announced in *Hensley* in calculating respondents' fee award, and that the court did not abuse its discretion in awarding attorney's fees for all time reasonably spent litigating the case.

Petitioners, joined by the United States as amicus curiae, maintain that *Hensley*'s lodestar approach is inappropriate in civil rights cases where a plaintiff recovers only monetary damages. In these cases, so the argument goes, use of the lodestar may result in fees that exceed the amount of damages recovered and that are therefore unreasonable. Likening such cases to private tort actions, petitioners and the United States submit that attorney's fees in such cases should be proportionate to the amount of damages a plaintiff recovers. Specifically, they suggest that fee awards in damages cases should be modeled upon the contingent-fee arrangements commonly used in personal injury litigation. In this case, assuming a 33% contingency rate, this would entitle respondents to recover approximately $11,000 in attorney's fees.

The amount of damages a plaintiff recovers is certainly relevant to the amount of attorney's fees to be awarded under § 1988. It is, however, only one of many factors that a court should consider in calculating an award of attorney's fees. We reject the proposition that fee awards under § 1988 should necessarily be proportionate to the amount of damages a civil rights plaintiff actually recovers.

As an initial matter, we reject the notion that a civil rights action for damages constitutes nothing more than a private tort suit benefiting only the individual plaintiffs whose rights were violated. Unlike most private tort litigants, a civil rights plaintiff seeks to vindicate important civil and constitutional rights that cannot be valued solely in monetary terms. And, Congress has determined that "the public as a whole has an interest in the vindication of the rights conferred by the statutes enumerated in § 1988, over and above the value of a civil rights remedy to a particular plaintiff. . . ." Regardless of the form of relief he actually obtains, a successful civil rights plaintiff often secures important social benefits that are not reflected in nominal or relatively small damages awards. In this case, for example, the District Court found that many of petitioners' unlawful acts were "motivated by a general hostility to the Chicano community," and that this litigation therefore served the public interest . . . .

In addition, the damages a plaintiff recovers contributes significantly to the deterrence of civil rights violations in the future. This deterrent effect is particularly evident in the area of individual police misconduct, where injunctive relief generally is unavailable.

Congress expressly recognized that a plaintiff who obtains relief in a civil rights lawsuit "'does so not for himself alone but also as a "private attorney general," vindicating a policy that Congress considered of the highest importance.'" House Report, at 2 (quoting *Piggie Park*). "If the citizen does not have the resources, his day in court is denied him; the congressional policy which he seeks to assert and vindicate goes unvindicated; and the entire Nation, not just the individual citizen, suffers." 122 Cong. Rec. 33313 (1976) (remarks of Sen. Tunney).

Because damages awards do not reflect fully the public benefit advanced by civil rights litigation, Congress did not intend for fees in civil rights cases, unlike most private law cases, to depend on obtaining substantial monetary relief. . . .

A rule that limits attorney's fees in civil rights cases to a proportion of the damages awarded would seriously undermine Congress' purpose in enacting § 1988. Congress enacted § 1988 specifically because it found that the private market for legal services failed to provide many victims of civil rights violations with effective access to the judicial process. See House Report, at 3. These victims ordinarily cannot afford to purchase legal services at the rates set by the private market. Moreover, the contingent fee arrangements that make legal services available to many victims of personal injuries would often not encourage lawyers to accept civil rights cases, which frequently involve substantial expenditures of time and effort but produce only small monetary recoveries. . . .

This case illustrates why the enforcement of civil rights laws cannot be entrusted to private-sector fee arrangements. . . . In light of the difficult nature of the issues presented by this lawsuit and the low pecuniary value of the many of the rights respondents sought to vindicate, it is highly unlikely that the prospect of a fee equal to a fraction of the damages respondents might recover would have been sufficient to attract competent counsel.[10] . . .

---

10. The United States suggests that "[t]he prospect of recovering $11,000 for representing [respondents] in a damages suit (assuming a contingency rate of 33%) is likely to attract a substantial number of attorneys." . . . We reject the United States' suggestion that the prospect of working nearly 2,000 hours at a rate of $5.65 an hour, to be paid more than 10 years after the work began, is "likely to attract a substantial number of attorneys."

■ *Justice POWELL, concurring in the judgment.*

I join only the Court's judgment. The plurality opinion reads our decision in *Hensley v. Eckerhart* more expansively than I would, and more expansively than is necessary to decide this case. For me affirmance — quite simply — is required by the District Court's detailed findings of fact, which were approved by the Court of Appeals. On its face, the fee award seems unreasonable. But I find no basis for this Court to reject the findings made and approved by the courts below. . . .

[T]he District Judge who presided throughout this protracted litigation found that the claims of respondents rested on a "common core of facts," and involved related legal theories. Since the suit was premised on one episode, the only significant variation in the facts supporting the claims against the several defendants concerned the extent of the participation by the various police officers. Petitioners offer no persuasive reason to question the District Court's express finding that "[t]he time devoted to claims on which plaintiffs did not prevail cannot reasonably be separated from time devoted to claims on which plaintiffs did prevail." . . .

[Opinion of Burger, C.J., dissenting, omitted.]

■ *Justice REHNQUIST, with whom THE CHIEF JUSTICE, Justice WHITE, and Justice O'CONNOR join, dissenting. . . .*

In April 1981, the District Court made its initial fee award of $245,456.25. . . . [After the award was vacated in light of *Hensley,*] the District Court convened a hearing, at which the court promptly announced: "I tell you now that I will not change the award. I will simply go back and be more specific about it." The court ultimately proved true to its word. After reviewing the record and the submissions of the parties, the court convened a second hearing, at which it approved exactly the same award as before: $245,456.25 in attorney's fees. The only noticeable change was that, the second time around, the court created a better "paper trail" by including in its order a discussion of those factors in *Hensley* . . . .

It is obvious to me that the District Court viewed *Hensley* not as a constraint on its discretion, but instead as a blueprint for justifying, in an after-the-fact fashion, a fee award it had already decided to enter solely on the basis of the "lodestar." . . .

Indeed, on the basis of some of the statements made by the District Court in this case, I reluctantly conclude that the court may have attempted to make up to respondents in attorney's fees what it felt the jury had wrongfully withheld from them in damages. . . .

If jurors are reluctant to make large awards against police officers, this is a fact of life that plaintiffs, defendants, and district courts must live with, and a district court simply has no business trying to correct what it regards as an unfortunate tendency in the award of damages by granting inflated attorney's fees.

The analysis of whether the extraordinary number of hours put in by respondents' attorneys in this case was "reasonable" must be made in light of both the traditional billing practices in the profession, and the fundamental principle that the award of a "reasonable" attorney's fee under § 1988 means a fee that would have been deemed reasonable if billed to affluent plaintiffs by their own attorneys....

If A has a claim for contract damages in the amount of $10,000 against B, and retains an attorney to prosecute the claim, it would be both extraordinary and unjustifiable, in the absence of any special arrangement, for the attorney to put in 200 hours on the case and send the client a bill for $25,000. Such a bill would be "unreasonable," regardless of whether A obtained a judgment against B for $10,000 or obtained a take-nothing judgment. And in such a case, where the prospective recovery is limited, it is exactly this "billing judgment" which enables the parties to achieve a settlement; any competent attorney, whether prosecuting or defending a contract action for $10,000, would realize that the case simply cannot justify a fee in excess of the potential recovery on the part of either the plaintiff's or the defendant's attorney....

The plurality . . . "reject[s] the proposition that fee awards under § 1988 should necessarily be proportionate to the amount of damages a civil rights plaintiff actually recovers." I agree with the plurality that the importation of the contingent-fee model to govern fee awards under § 1988 is not warranted by the terms and legislative history of the statute. But I do not agree with the plurality if it means to reject the kind of "proportionality" that I have previously described. Nearly 2,000 attorney-hours spent on a case in which the total recovery was only $33,000, in which only $13,300 of that amount was recovered for the federal claims, and in which the District Court expressed the view that, in such cases, juries typically were reluctant to award substantial damages against police officers, is simply not a "reasonable" expenditure of time. The snippets of legislative history which the plurality relies upon to dismiss any relationship between the amount of time put in on a case and the amount of damages awarded are wholly unconvincing. One may agree with all of the glowing rhetoric contained in the plurality's opinion about Congress' noble purpose in authorizing attorney's fees under § 1988 without concluding that Congress intended to turn attorneys loose to spend as many hours as possible to prepare and try a case that could reasonably be expected to result only in a relatively minor award of monetary damages....

Notes and Questions

1. What rule does *Rivera* reject? How would you describe the rule the plurality adopts?

2. One might boil down the dispute between the plurality and the dissent to the question whether incentivizing low-damages cases like this one was an accidental byproduct of § 1988 or one of its key goals. How do Justices Brennan and Rehnquist justify their divergent answers to that question? What are the guiding values and assumptions behind each position?

3. The Court continued to grapple with the implications of the widespread contingency-fee model. In *Blanchard v. Bergeron*, 489 U.S. 87 (1989), the Court unanimously held that the lodestar approach governed the calculation of fees under § 1988 even where it produced a fee that substantially exceeded the amount provided in the contingent-fee agreement between plaintiff and his counsel. In *Venegas v. Mitchell*, 495 U.S. 82 (1990), the Court unanimously held that § 1988 does not invalidate contingent-fee contracts that would require a prevailing plaintiff to pay his attorney more than the statutory fee award against the defendant. Finally, in *City of Burlington v. Dague*, 505 U.S. 557 (1992), the Court held, per Justice Scalia, that enhancement of a fee award based on the ex ante risk of losing the case is not permitted under the fee-shifting statutes (including, the Court stated, § 1988, although *Dague* was not a civil rights case). The majority in *Dague* relied on several factors: its view that "an enhancement for contingency would likely duplicate in substantial part factors already subsumed in the lodestar"; the Court's prior treatment of contingency agreements in *Blanchard* and *Venegas*; and the unadministrability of a rule permitting courts to use likelihood of success as a basis for fee enhancement. Dissenting, Justice Blackmun (joined by Justice Stevens) and Justice O'Connor both argued that a "reasonable" fee was one that considered the realities of the legal market, including the problem that in the absence of enhancements for winning unlikely victories, lawyers would lack incentive to take on riskier cases.

Considering these three cases together with *Rivera*, how have the contingent-fee model and the workings of the legal market influenced the Court's attorney-fee jurisprudence? How did the operation of the legal market factor into Congress's decision to enact fee-shifting provisions in the first place? Should that relationship inform how the Court considers market forces in interpreting fee-shifting statutes?

4. The *Rivera* dissenters accuse the district court of using the fee award to compensate for a jury award that the court thought insufficient. Is it clear that the Congress that enacted § 1988 would have disliked that result? Isn't the judge better situated than the jury to see the big picture of how a particular civil rights case serves the public interest and therefore to make an award accordingly? Could that have been why Congress gave the judge "discretion" to discern the award — discretion that the Court has wrongly cabined by focusing on the lodestar? Or is Justice Rehnquist's objection to the blurring of the institutional roles of the judge and the jury insurmountable?

5. Consider the relationship between *Rivera* and *Stachura* (Chapter 9), decided the same year. The latter forbids juries from awarding damages based on the abstract value of a constitutional right and limits plaintiffs to traditional categories of tort damages. Does *Rivera*'s allowance of large fee awards in small-damage cases make up for rules like the one in *Stachura* limiting compensatory damages in the first place? After all, from the standpoint of deterrence, a dollar out of the defendant's pocket as part of a fee award is no different than a dollar in compensatory damages. Then again, if the real problem — as the district court thought here — is that ordinary tort damages are too small to address some kinds of constitutional violations, why isn't increasing damages, rather than compensating via fee awards, the most straightforward solution? Which is the better rule from the plaintiff's perspective? From the perspective of the Congress that passed the Fees Act? As between high fee awards and enhancements in compensatory damages based on the value of a right, which method of supplementing the amount of a judgment is more easily calculable?

6. Regardless of the Justices' views on proportionality, why shouldn't the Court simply have vacated the award here in light of the district judge's bald declaration that he was determined to adhere to his prior fee award notwithstanding *Hensley*? Does the Court's failure to address this apparent act of judicial defiance send a troubling message to district courts? Why might the plurality have chosen to ignore the district court's apparent disregard for the Court's prior order to reconsider?

Note: Fee Awards and Nominal Damages

In *Farrar v. Hobby*, 506 U.S. 103 (1992), the administrators of decedent Farrar's estate sought $17 million in compensatory damages from Texas officials for alleged due process violations in connection with the closing of a school that Farrar operated. The trial court awarded only nominal damages but granted $280,000 in attorneys' fees. The court of appeals reversed the fee award on the ground that plaintiffs had not "prevailed." The Supreme Court, in an opinion by Justice Thomas, affirmed the court of appeals but disagreed with its approach:

> When a court awards nominal damages, it neither enters judgment for defendant on the merits nor declares the defendant's legal immunity to suit. . . . A plaintiff may demand payment for nominal damages no less than he may demand payment for millions of dollars in compensatory damages. A judgment for damages in any amount, whether compensatory or nominal, modifies the defendant's behavior for the plaintiff's benefit by forcing the defendant to pay an amount of money he otherwise would not pay. As a result, the Court of Appeals for the Fifth Circuit erred in holding that petitioners' nominal damages award failed to render them prevailing parties.
>
> Although the "technical" nature of a nominal damages award or any other judgment does not affect the prevailing party inquiry, it does bear on the propriety of fees awarded under § 1988. . . . Indeed, "the most critical factor" in determining the reasonableness of a fee award "is the degree of success obtained." In this case, petitioners received nominal damages instead of the $17 million in compensatory damages that they sought. This litigation accomplished little beyond giving petitioners "the moral satisfaction of knowing that a federal court concluded that [their] rights had been violated" in some unspecified way. . . .
>
> In some circumstances, even a plaintiff who formally "prevails" under § 1988 should receive no attorney's fees at all. . . . In a civil rights suit for damages . . . the awarding of nominal damages also highlights the plaintiff's failure to prove actual, compensable injury. . . . When a plaintiff recovers only nominal damages because of his failure to prove an essential element of his claim for monetary relief, the only reasonable fee is usually no fee at all. . . .

Concurring, Justice O'Connor suggested that while the outcome in this case was clear, fee awards might be appropriate in other nominal damages cases, because "[n]ominal relief does not necessarily a nominal victory make. But . . . substantial difference between the judgment recovered and the recovery sought suggests that the victory is in fact purely technical. Here that suggestion is quite strong. Joseph Farrar asked for 17 million dollars; he got one. It is hard to envision a more dramatic difference." Concurring in part and dissenting in part, Justice White, joined by Justices Blackmun, Stevens, and Souter, agreed that Farrar had "prevailed" but thought it preferable to remand rather than to declare that no fee award was appropriate.

Does *Farrar* contradict either *Buckhannon* regarding the meaning of "prevailing party" or *Hensley* and *Rivera* on the question of a reasonable fee? How do you square a presumption about when a "reasonable fee is no fee at all" with the case-specific approach of *Hensley*? Or do the extreme facts make *Farrar* essentially an anomaly?

C. FEE WAIVERS

Probably the thorniest question of fees law is what happens when defendants offer plaintiffs a settlement conditioned on fee waiver, or, in a damages case, offer a "lump sum" settlement that covers all relief including damages and fees. These practices raise both statutory questions and ethical ones.

Evans v. Jeff D.
475 U.S. 717 (1986)

■ *Justice* STEVENS *delivered the opinion of the Court. . . .*

[Plaintiffs, a class of disabled children, sued Idaho officials for constitutional and statutory violations over deficiencies in state health and educational programs. They were represented by Charles Johnson of the Idaho Legal Aid Society. After more than two years of litigation, on the eve of trial, Defendants proposed a settlement, which (in plaintiffs' own view) "offered virtually all of the injunctive relief [they] had sought in their complaint" but required them to waive fees. The district court was required to approve the settlement because it resolved a class action suit.] . . . Originally, this waiver was unacceptable to the Idaho Legal Aid Society, which had instructed Johnson to reject any settlement offer conditioned upon a waiver of fees, but Johnson ultimately determined that his ethical obligation to his clients mandated acceptance of the proposal. . . .

After the stipulation was signed, Johnson filed a written motion requesting the District Court to approve the settlement "except for the provision on costs and attorney's fees," and to allow respondents to present a bill of costs and fees for consideration by the court. At the oral argument on that motion, Johnson contended that petitioners' offer had exploited his ethical duty to his clients — that he was "forced," by an offer giving his clients "the best result [they] could have gotten in this court or any other court," to waive his attorney's fees. The District Court [nonetheless approved the settlement]. . . .

[The court of appeals] invalidated the fee waiver and left standing the remainder of the settlement; it then instructed the District Court to "make its own determination of the fees that are reasonable" and remanded for that limited purpose.

In explaining its holding, the Court of Appeals emphasized . . . that the strong federal policy embodied in the Fees Act normally requires an award of fees to prevailing plaintiffs in civil rights actions, including those who have prevailed through settlement. The court added that "[w]hen attorney's fees are negotiated as part of a class action settlement, a conflict frequently exists between the class lawyers' interest in compensation and the class members' interest in relief." "To avoid this conflict," the Court of Appeals . . . "disapproved simultaneous negotiation of settlements and attorney's fees" absent a showing of "unusual circumstances." . . .

To begin with, the Court of Appeals' decision rested on an erroneous view of the District Court's power to approve settlements in class actions. . . . [T]he power to approve or reject a settlement negotiated by the parties before trial does not authorize the court to require the parties to accept a settlement to which they have not agreed. . . . The options available to the District Court were essentially the same as those available to respondents: it could have accepted the proposed settlement; it could have rejected the proposal and postponed the trial to see if a different settlement could be achieved; or it could have decided to try the case. The District Court could not enforce the settlement on the merits and award attorney's fees any more than it could, in a situation in which the attorney had negotiated a large fee at the expense of the plaintiff class, preserve the fee award and order greater relief on the merits. The question we must decide, therefore, is whether the District Court had a duty to reject the proposed settlement because it included a waiver of statutorily authorized attorney's fees.

That duty, whether it takes the form of a general prophylactic rule or arises out of the special circumstances of this case, derives ultimately from the Fees Act rather than from the strictures of professional ethics. Although respondents contend that Johnson, as counsel for the class, was faced with an "ethical dilemma" when petitioners offered him relief greater than that which he could reasonably have expected to obtain for his clients at trial (if only he would stipulate to a waiver of the statutory fee award), and although we recognize Johnson's conflicting interests between pursuing relief for the class and a fee for the Idaho Legal Aid Society, we do not believe that the "dilemma" was an "ethical" one in the sense that Johnson had to choose between conflicting duties under the prevailing norms of professional conduct. Plainly, Johnson had no ethical obligation to seek a statutory fee award. His ethical duty was to serve his clients loyally and competently. Since the proposal to settle the merits was more favorable than the probable outcome of the trial, Johnson's decision to recommend acceptance was consistent with the highest standards of our profession. The District Court, therefore, correctly concluded that approval of the settlement involved no breach of ethics in this case.

The defect, if any, in the negotiated fee waiver must be traced not to the rules of ethics but to the Fees Act.[15] . . .

The text of the Fees Act provides no support for the proposition that Congress intended to ban all fee waivers offered in connection with substantial relief on the merits. On the contrary, the language of the Act, as well as its legislative history, indicates that Congress bestowed on the "prevailing party" (generally plaintiffs) a statutory eligibility for a discretionary award of attorney's fees in specified civil rights actions. It did not prevent the party from waiving this eligibility any more than it legislated against assignment of this right to an attorney, such as effectively occurred here. . . . Thus, while it is undoubtedly true that Congress expected fee shifting to attract competent counsel to represent citizens deprived of their civil rights, it neither bestowed fee awards upon attorneys nor rendered them nonwaivable or nonnegotiable; instead, it added them to the arsenal of remedies available to combat violations of civil rights, a goal not invariably inconsistent with conditioning settlement on the merits on a waiver of statutory attorney's fees.

In fact, we believe that a general proscription against negotiated waiver of attorney's fees in exchange for a settlement on the merits would itself impede vindication of civil rights, at least in some cases, by reducing the attractiveness of settlement. . . .

Most defendants are unlikely to settle unless the cost of the predicted judgment, discounted by its probability, plus the transaction costs of further litigation, are greater than the cost of the settlement package. If fee waivers cannot be negotiated, the settlement package must either contain an attorney's fee component of potentially large and typically uncertain magnitude, or else the parties must agree to have the fee fixed by the court. Although either of these alternatives may well be acceptable in many cases, there surely is a significant number in which neither alternative will be as satisfactory as a decision to try the entire case.

The adverse impact of removing attorney's fees and costs from bargaining might be tolerable if the uncertainty introduced into settlement negotiations were small. But it is not. The defendants' potential liability for fees in this kind of litigation can be as significant as, and sometimes even more significant than, their potential liability on the merits. . . .

Indeed, in this very case "[c]ounsel for defendants view[ed] the risk of an attorney's fees award as the most significant liability in the case." Undoubtedly there are many other civil rights actions in which potential liability for attorney's fees may overshadow the potential cost of relief on the merits and darken prospects for settlement if fees cannot be negotiated.

The unpredictability of attorney's fees may be just as important as their magnitude when a defendant is striving to fix its liability. . . . The consequence of

---

15. Even state bar opinions holding it unethical for defendants to request fee waivers in exchange for relief on the merits of plaintiffs' claims are bottomed ultimately on § 1988 [citing ethics opinions from D.C., New York, and Maine]. For the sake of completeness, it should be mentioned that the bar is not of one mind on this ethical judgment [citing opinions from the D.C. Circuit and Georgia permitting fee waivers].

[the] succession of necessarily judgmental decisions [by the court applying the *Hensley* approach] for the ultimate fee award is inescapable: a defendant's liability for his opponent's attorney's fees in a civil rights action cannot be fixed with a sufficient degree of confidence to make defendants indifferent to their exclusion from negotiation. It is therefore not implausible to anticipate that parties to a significant number of civil rights cases will refuse to settle if liability for attorney's fees remains open, thereby forcing more cases to trial, unnecessarily burdening the judicial system, and disserving civil rights litigants. Respondents' own waiver of attorney's fees and costs to obtain settlement of their educational claims is eloquent testimony to the utility of fee waivers in vindicating civil rights claims. We conclude, therefore, that it is not necessary to construe the Fees Act as embodying a general rule prohibiting settlements conditioned on the waiver of fees in order to be faithful to the purposes of that Act. . . .

What the outcome of this settlement illustrates is that the Fees Act has given the victims of civil rights violations a powerful weapon that improves their ability to employ counsel, to obtain access to the courts, and thereafter to vindicate their rights by means of settlement or trial. For aught that appears, it was the "coercive" effect of respondents' statutory right to seek a fee award that motivated petitioners' exceptionally generous offer. Whether this weapon might be even more powerful if fee waivers were prohibited in cases like this is another question,[34] but it is in any event a question that Congress is best equipped to answer. . . .

■ *Justice* BRENNAN, *with whom Justice* MARSHALL *and Justice* BLACKMUN *join, dissenting.* . . .

[B]y awarding attorney's fees Congress sought to attract competent counsel to represent victims of civil rights violations. Congress' primary purpose was to enable "private attorneys general" to protect the public interest by creating economic incentives for lawyers to represent them. The Court's assertion that the Fees Act was intended to do nothing more than give individual victims of civil rights violations another remedy is thus at odds with the whole thrust of the legislation. Congress determined that the public as a whole has an interest in the vindication of the rights conferred by the civil rights statutes over and above the value of a civil rights remedy to a particular plaintiff. . . .

Having concluded that the Fees Act merely creates another remedy to vindicate the rights of individual plaintiffs, the Court asks whether negotiated waivers

---

34. We are cognizant of the possibility that decisions by individual clients to bargain away fee awards may, in the aggregate and in the long run, diminish lawyers' expectations of statutory fees in civil rights cases. If this occurred, the pool of lawyers willing to represent plaintiffs in such cases might shrink, constricting the "effective access to the judicial process" for persons with civil rights grievances which the Fees Act was intended to provide. H.R. Rep. No. 94-1558, p. 1 (1976). That the "tyranny of small decisions" may operate in this fashion is not to say that there is any reason or documentation to support such a concern at the present time. Comment on this issue is therefore premature at this juncture. We believe, however, that as a practical matter the likelihood of this circumstance arising is remote.

of statutory attorney's fees are "invariably inconsistent" with the availability of such fees as a remedy for individual plaintiffs. Not surprisingly, the Court has little difficulty knocking down this frail straw man. But the proper question is whether permitting negotiated fee waivers is consistent with Congress' goal of attracting competent counsel. It is therefore necessary to consider the effect on this goal of allowing individual plaintiffs to negotiate fee waivers. . . .

It seems obvious that allowing defendants in civil rights cases to condition settlement of the merits on a waiver of statutory attorney's fees will diminish lawyers' expectations of receiving fees and decrease the willingness of lawyers to accept civil rights cases. . . .[7] . . .

As a formal matter, of course, the statutory fee belongs to the plaintiff, and thus technically the decision to waive entails a sacrifice only by the plaintiff. As a practical matter, however, waiver affects only the lawyer. Because "a vast majority of the victims of civil rights violations" have no resources to pay attorney's fees, H.R. Rep. 1, lawyers cannot hope to recover fees from the plaintiff and must depend entirely on the Fees Act for compensation.[10]

The plaintiff thus has no real stake in the statutory fee and is unaffected by its waiver. Consequently, plaintiffs will readily agree to waive fees if this will help them to obtain other relief they desire. As summed up by the Legal Ethics Committee of the District of Columbia Bar:

> "Defense counsel . . . are in a uniquely favorable position when they condition settlement on the waiver of the statutory fee: They make a demand for a benefit that the plaintiff's lawyer cannot resist as a matter of ethics and one in which the plaintiff has no interest and therefore will not resist."

Of course, from the lawyer's standpoint, things could scarcely have turned out worse. He or she invested considerable time and effort in the case, won, and has exactly nothing to show for it. . . .

And, of course, once fee waivers are permitted, defendants will seek them as a matter of course, since this is a logical way to minimize liability. Indeed, defense counsel would be remiss not to demand that the plaintiff waive statutory attorney's fees. A lawyer who proposes to have his client pay more than is

---

7. It is especially important to keep in mind the fragile nature of the civil rights bar. Even when attorney's fees are awarded, they do not approach the large sums which can be earned in ordinary commercial litigation. It is therefore cost inefficient for private practitioners to devote much time to civil rights cases. . . . Instead, civil rights plaintiffs must depend largely on legal aid organizations for assistance. These organizations, however, are short of resources and also depend heavily on statutory fees.

10. Nor can attorneys protect themselves by requiring plaintiffs to sign contingency agreements or retainers at the outset of the representation. Amici legal aid societies inform us that they are prohibited by statute, court rule, or Internal Revenue Service regulation from entering into fee agreements with their clients. Moreover, even if such agreements could be negotiated, the possibility of obtaining protection through contingency fee arrangements is unavailable in the very large proportion of civil rights cases which, like this case, seek only injunctive relief. . . . Of course, none of the parties has seriously suggested that civil rights attorneys can protect themselves through private arrangements. After all, Congress enacted the Fees Act because, after *Alyeska*, it found such arrangements wholly inadequate.

necessary to end litigation has failed to fulfill his fundamental duty zealously to represent the best interests of his client. Because waiver of fees does not affect the plaintiff, a settlement offer is not made less attractive to the plaintiff if it includes a demand that statutory fees be waived. Thus, in the future, we must expect settlement offers routinely to contain demands for waivers of statutory fees.

The cumulative effect this practice will have on the civil rights bar is evident. It does not denigrate the high ideals that motivate many civil rights practitioners to recognize that lawyers are in the business of practicing law, and that, like other business people, they are and must be concerned with earning a living. The conclusion that permitting fee waivers will seriously impair the ability of civil rights plaintiffs to obtain legal assistance is embarrassingly obvious. . . .

[To justify its result, the Court reasons] that, unless fee waivers are permitted, "parties to a significant number of civil rights cases will refuse to settle. . . ." This is a wholly inadequate justification for the Court's result.

First, the effect of prohibiting fee waivers on settlement offers is just not an important concern in the context of the Fees Act. I agree with the Court that encouraging settlements is desirable policy. But it is judicially created policy, applicable to litigation of any kind and having no special force in the context of civil rights cases. . . . [E]ven if prohibiting fee waivers does discourage some settlements, a judicial policy favoring settlement cannot possibly take precedence over this express congressional policy. We must implement Congress' agenda, not our own.

In an attempt to justify its decision to elevate settlement concerns, the Court argues that . . . "'[s]ome plaintiffs will receive compensation in settlement where, on trial, they might not have recovered, or would have recovered less than what was offered.'" . . .

The fact that fee waivers may produce some settlement offers that are beneficial to a few individual plaintiffs is hardly "consistent with the purposes of the Fees Act," if permitting fee waivers fundamentally undermines what Congress sought to achieve. Each individual plaintiff who waives his right to statutory fees in order to obtain additional relief for himself makes it that much more difficult for the next victim of a civil rights violation to find a lawyer willing or able to bring his case. As obtaining legal assistance becomes more difficult, the "benefit" the Court so magnanimously preserves for civil rights plaintiffs becomes available to fewer and fewer individuals, exactly the opposite result from that intended by Congress. . . .

Second, even assuming that settlement practices are relevant, the Court greatly exaggerates the effect that prohibiting fee waivers will have on defendants' willingness to make settlement offers. This is largely due to the Court's failure to distinguish the fee waiver issue from the issue of simultaneous negotiation of fees and merits claims. The Court's discussion mixes concerns over a defendant's reluctance to settle because total liability remains uncertain with reluctance to settle because the cost of settling is too high. However, it is a prohibition on simultaneous negotiation, not a prohibition on fee waivers, that makes it difficult for the defendant to ascertain his total liability at the time he agrees to settle the merits. . . .

I would . . . permit simultaneous negotiation of fees and merits claims, since this would not contravene the purposes of the Fees Act. . . .

Notes and Questions

1. After *Jeff D.*, what limits, if any, prevent defendants from offering, and plaintiffs from accepting, fee waivers as part of every settlement proposal?

2. Both the majority and the dissent agree that the issue is one of statutory interpretation, not ethics. Yet ethics rules obviously shape how the statute is applied in practice. Should state bars that agree with Justice Brennan prohibit defense counsel from seeking fee waivers in order to protect the integrity of the Fees Act and the intent of Congress? Or has the Supreme Court essentially ruled that Congress would not want plaintiffs to have this "protection," and so bar associations would contravene the will of Congress by intervening? What are the federalism implications of bar regulations implementing Justice Brennan's view? Would such rules be preempted by § 1988? Note that the New York bar committee withdrew its restrictive rulings in light of *Jeff D.*

3. Leaving Congress out of it, what is the right ethical answer? What duty does a defense attorney violate by counseling a repeat-player institutional defendant to insist on fee waivers? Isn't that approach in defendants' long-term interests?

4. Regarding fees and settlement, isn't a plaintiff's attorney always to some extent negotiating against her client? Is there any way around that problem?

5. The effect of *Jeff D.* on the civil rights bar has been significant but not uniform. Julie Davies, *Federal Civil Rights Practice in the 1990s: The Dichotomy Between Reality and Theory*, 48 Hastings L.J. 197, 204, 215-21 (1997), surveyed thirty-five civil rights practitioners practicing in a range of subfields of civil rights litigation and representing a range of practice settings, including nonprofits, solo practitioners, and private firms of various sizes. A majority of survey participants reported that requests for fee waivers were not much of a problem in their practice because they "very quickly developed fee agreements with clients which offer some protection from waivers in the form of financial disincentives," such as a retainer that requires a client who accepts a fee waiver to pay most or all of the lodestar. "Attorneys also discourage fee waivers by exercising caution in client selection and by educating clients about the importance of fees in a civil rights practice to prepare clients in the event of a settlement offer contingent on a waiver." Nonetheless, "in cases where settlement offers are made, defendants enter the arena with newfound leverage. Given low damages and high litigation costs, plaintiffs' attorneys often recognize that it is in the best interests of their clients, and indeed themselves, to accept settlements that result in the attorney making an amount much less than his or her hourly rate."

   Professor Davies found that fee waivers were particularly an issue for non-profit organizations: "It is difficult for non-profit attorneys to protect themselves against requests for fee waivers through contingency or other fee agreements because these agreements may imperil their tax-exempt status." Ultimately, because of the rise in lump-sum settlement offers by defendants, Professor Davies concluded, plaintiffs' lawyers approach civil rights claims more like ordinary tort claims — that is, claims in which lawyers do not expect fee-shifting.

Based on these findings, what aspects of the majority's and dissent's respective predictions about *Jeff D.* have been borne out in practice? Are the results consistent with the congressional purpose behind the Fees Act? Good for civil rights plaintiffs as a group?

CHAPTER 10 PROBLEMS

Problem 10A. You represent a plaintiff whose handgun was seized by local police during a traffic stop of her motor home, pursuant to a state law that prohibits the possession of guns in vehicles. You sue under the Second Amendment seeking injunctive relief requiring the gun to be returned and damages for the seizure "in an amount to be determined by the jury appropriate to the evidence adduced at trial." Early in the case, prior to discovery, the police return the gun, and the state legislature repeals the law. Still, you fight on, seeking damages for your client.

The case takes years, including an interlocutory appeal on the novel issue of whether Second Amendment precedents concerning the home apply to a home that is also a vehicle. The client's damages are modest — she seeks compensation only for emotional distress and the loss of opportunity to use her gun for recreation while it was confiscated. On principle, neither the plaintiff nor the defendants will agree to settle.

The case ultimately goes to trial, and the jury awards the client $5,000. At the outset of the representation, anticipating that the fee award might be higher than the damages amount, you put in the retainer agreement a fee provision saying that the client owes you any attorneys' fees the court awards her.

You move for attorneys' fees. Taking into account all the time you spent investigating the facts and the law, taking discovery, briefing dispositive motions, litigating the appeal, trying the case, and so forth, and your reasonable hourly rate, you calculate your lodestar at $200,000. The district court holds that your client was a prevailing party but awards only $20,000 in fees. The court reasons that, given the small damages, the case must have been filed mainly for law reform reasons, but because the state legislature changed the law on its own and "catalyst" fees are barred, the amount of litigation was not reasonable for the scope of the result achieved. The court also compares your case to *Farrar* and opines that $5,000 was barely more than a "nominal" victory.

You wish to appeal the ruling on fees, but shortly after the verdict, the plaintiff leaves town for her annual summer cross-country trip in her motor home and is "off the grid." You cannot reach her before the deadline to appeal.

1. Can you ethically pursue the appeal? Why or why not?
2. If you do pursue the appeal, what arguments can you make that the court erred regarding the amount of the fees? How do you rate your chances of success?
3. What precautions could you take to avoid this conundrum in the future?

Problem 10B.   You file an Eighth Amendment claim on behalf of a prisoner who has been kept in solitary confinement, you contend, for an unconstitutionally long time. The complaint seeks both damages and injunctive relief. After filing the complaint, you seek a preliminary injunction requiring your client to be sent back to the general prison population and not to be returned to solitary absent certain conditions. The judge grants your motion, and the prison complies but appeals the injunction. Meanwhile, prison officials move to dismiss the damages claim on qualified immunity grounds. The district court denies the motion. The officials appeal, and the court of appeals consolidates the two appeals. The court of appeals affirms the preliminary injunction but reverses the denial of immunity, holding that the client has shown a constitutional violation but not a violation of "clearly established" law.

By the time the appeal is decided and the case returned to the district court for further proceedings, two years have passed since the filing of the complaint. The client has completed his sentence, and he has been released from prison. Because of the injunction, he was never returned to solitary. Upon his release, the defendants move to dismiss the case and to dissolve the preliminary injunction as moot. The motion is granted.

You move for attorneys' fees.

1. What are your arguments for prevailing party status and what do you expect the defendants to argue in response?
2. If you are a prevailing party, what portion of your work do you expect to obtain a fee award for, and why?

Equitable Relief and Justiciability

To the impact litigator as well as to civil rights plaintiffs, injunctive relief—a court order to cease or refrain from unlawful conduct or to take legally required action—can be more valuable than damages. For the impact litigator, injunctive relief provides an opportunity to halt government practices and policies directly, rather than indirectly through an award of damages that may or may not provide a meaningful deterrent to the appropriate officials. (It is also not subject to the defense of qualified immunity. *See Wood v. Strickland*, 420 U.S. 308, 314 n.6 (1975).) Plaintiffs in some circumstances may likewise be more interested in injunctive relief than damages—for instance, because of a pressing need to halt injurious conduct or because the nature of the injuries at issue might not support a significant damages award (for reasons discussed in Chapter 9).

In this chapter, we'll examine threshold issues governing when a civil rights plaintiff may obtain an injunction. What shape injunctions may take when aimed at reforming a major government instiution like a school district or a prison is a question that we'll consider separately when we study institutional reform litigation in Chapter 12.

Aside from the merits of the underlying claim, the availability of injunctive relief is governed, broadly speaking, by two doctrines: equitable discretion and justiciability.

Equitable discretion refers to a court's exercise of judgment in deciding whether or not to issue an injunction. Four factors guide this judgment: the strength of the case on the merits; whether in the absence of relief the plaintiff faces irreparable harm (that is, harm not redressable later by a montary award); the balance of equities; and the public interest. *Winter v. Nat. Res. Def. Council, Inc.*, 555 U.S. 7, 20, 32 (2008). Although the application of these factors involves some legal nuance—for instance, some but not all circuits have adopted a "sliding scale" approach, under which "the elements of the preliminary injunction test are balanced, so that a stronger showing of one element may offset a weaker showing of another," *Hernandez v. Sessions*, 872 F.3d 976, 990 (9th Cir. 2017)—these factors are by their nature fact-specific or directly tied to the merits of the case. Therefore, studying applications of the factors governing equitable discretion will not be broadly illuminating about the contours of civil rights litigation.

By contrast, the other doctrine relevant to the availability of injunctive relief—justiciability—is governed by general legal rules that shape civil rights litigation to a significant degree. In fact, it might not be an exaggeration to say that rules regarding standing to seek injunctive relief (standing being the most influential of the justiciability rules) constitute the greatest single limitation on the scope and effectiveness of civil rights litigation. Our study of the conditions necessary for injunctive relief will therefore focus on the major justiciability doctrines.

Justiciability is the question whether a case is fit for judicial resolution. The major justiciability doctrines flow from Article III's statement that federal courts adjudicate "cases" or "controversies," as opposed to answering abstract legal questions through "advisory opinions"—a practice that some state judicial systems permit but that the federal system does not. *See Muskrat v. United States*, 219 U.S. 346 (1911) (tracing the prohibition on advisory opinions back to the 1790s, including Chief Justice Jay's letter refusal to answer legal questions posed by the Washington Administration outside the context of a case).

The two most significant justiciability doctrines are *standing* (whether the plaintiff has a personal stake in the outcome of the case by virtue of a specific injury that has befallen or threatens the plaintiff, that is caused by the defendant, and that a court ruling can fix), and *mootness* (whether, in light of changed circumstances, the controversy is still "live" such that the court can grant meaningful relief). We'll examine each in detail. We also cover, as a subset of standing, the question of *ripeness* (whether judicial resolution would be premature because the controversy is insufficiently concrete), and additional "prudential" limitations on standing. The political question doctrine—a justiciability rule barring the adjudication of controversies that the Constitution has committed to the political branches—arises less frequently and so is left to courses on Federal Courts and Constitutional Law.

Although justiciability questions arise in many contexts and so not all of the cases we'll read here are civil rights cases, the central question this chapter seeks to answer is how justiciability doctrines (in particular, standing, but to some degree mootness also) affect the availability of injunctive relief to enforce civil rights. These doctrines rarely come up when a civil rights plaintiff seeks damages, because damages claims by their nature involve an allegation of a specific, past harm for which the plaintiff seeks compensation, and the court can always grant meaningful relief—money. When a plaintiff seeks an injunction, by contrast, standing regularly poses a major obstacle, and if the circumstances change during the litigation, mootness can also create difficulties for the plaintiff. We will not separately discuss declaratory relief, which is subject to the same justiciability limitations as injunctive relief and which is generally covered in Federal Courts courses.

Section A provides a general introduction to the doctrines of standing and mootness by presenting a case addressing both doctrines on the same set of facts. Section A also introduces ripeness and prudential principles of standing. Sections B and C explore the standing and mootness inquiries, respectively, in more detail, with particular attention to the civil rights context. Section A can stand alone, without Sections B or C, in providing an overview of justiciability. Section B can also be read in isolation, for a lesson focusing just on the basics of standing and the most significant applications of standing for civil rights enforcement.

A. INTRODUCTION TO JUSTICIABILITY

Friends of the Earth, Inc. v. Laidlaw Environmental Services
528 U.S. 167 (2000)

■ Justice GINSBURG delivered the opinion of the Court.

[In 1986, Laidlaw Environmental Services bought a hazardous waste incinerator facility in Roebuck, South Carolina, that included a wastewater treatment plant. In accordance with the federal Clean Water Act, Laidlaw received a National Pollutant Discharge Elimination System (NPDES) permit that placed limits on Laidlaw's discharge of pollutants, including mercury, into rivers. Laidlaw violated its permit's mercury limits on 489 occasions between 1987 and 1995. The Clean Water Act permits private civil actions to enforce limits imposed by NPDES permits. Three environmental groups sued Laidlaw for noncompliance with its permit. The district court granted judgment for plaintiffs and imposed a civil penalty, payable to the government, of $405,800. The court denied injunctive relief because it found Laidlaw had come into substantial compliance with its permit. The court of appeals reversed, holding that the case became moot because the only remedy granted—civil penalties payable to the government—would not redress any injury to the plaintiff organizations. Laidlaw represented that after the appellate decision but before the grant of certiorari, the Roebuck facility was closed, but plaintiffs disputed the effect of the closure on the chance of future violations because Laidlaw retained its permit.] . . .

The Constitution's case-or-controversy limitation on federal judicial authority, Art. III, § 2, underpins both our standing and our mootness jurisprudence, but the two inquiries differ in respects critical to the proper resolution of this case, so we address them separately. . . .

[T]o satisfy Article III's standing requirements, a plaintiff must show (1) it has suffered an "injury in fact" that is (a) concrete and particularized and (b) actual or imminent, not conjectural or hypothetical; (2) the injury is fairly traceable to the challenged action of the defendant; and (3) it is likely, as opposed to merely speculative, that the injury will be redressed by a favorable decision. An association has standing to bring suit on behalf of its members when its members would otherwise have standing to sue in their own right, the interests at stake are germane to the organization's purpose, and neither the claim asserted nor the relief requested requires the participation of individual members in the lawsuit.

Laidlaw contends first that FOE lacked standing from the outset even to seek injunctive relief, because the plaintiff organizations failed to show that any of their members had sustained or faced the threat of any "injury in fact" from Laidlaw's activities. In support of this contention Laidlaw points to the District Court's finding, made in the course of setting the penalty amount, that there had been "no demonstrated proof of harm to the environment" from Laidlaw's mercury discharge violations.

The relevant showing for purposes of Article III standing, however, is not injury to the environment but injury to the plaintiff. . . . Focusing properly on injury to the plaintiff, the District Court found that FOE had demonstrated sufficient injury to establish standing. For example, FOE member Kenneth Lee Curtis averred in affidavits that he lived a half-mile from Laidlaw's facility; that he occasionally drove over the North Tyger River, and that it looked and smelled polluted; and that he would like to fish, camp, swim, and picnic in and near the river between 3 and 15 miles downstream from the facility, as he did when he was a teenager, but would not do so because he was concerned that the water was polluted by Laidlaw's discharges. Curtis reaffirmed these statements in extensive deposition testimony. For example, he testified that he would like to fish in the river at a specific spot he used as a boy, but that he would not do so now because of his concerns about Laidlaw's discharges.

Other members presented evidence to similar effect. . . . [A member of one plaintiff organization] Angela Patterson attested that she lived two miles from the facility; that before Laidlaw operated the facility, she picnicked, walked, birdwatched, and waded in and along the North Tyger River because of the natural beauty of the area; that she no longer engaged in these activities in or near the river because she was concerned about harmful effects from discharged pollutants; and that she and her husband would like to purchase a home near the river but did not intend to do so, in part because of Laidlaw's discharges. . . . [Another] member Gail Lee attested that her home, which is near Laidlaw's facility, had a lower value than similar homes located farther from the facility, and that she believed the pollutant discharges accounted for some of the discrepancy. . . . [Other members presented similar evidence.] . . .

[T]he affidavits and testimony presented by FOE in this case assert that Laidlaw's discharges, and the affiant members' reasonable concerns about the effects of those discharges, directly affected those affiants' recreational, aesthetic, and economic interests. These submissions present dispositively more than the mere "general averments" and "conclusory allegations" found inadequate in [prior precedent]. Nor can the affiants' conditional statements—that they would use the nearby North Tyger River for recreation if Laidlaw were not discharging pollutants into it—be [considered too speculative]. . . .

[I]t is undisputed that Laidlaw's unlawful conduct—discharging pollutants in excess of permit limits—was occurring at the time the complaint was filed. . . . Unlike the dissent, we see nothing "improbable" about the proposition that a company's continuous and pervasive illegal discharges of pollutants into a river would cause nearby residents to curtail their recreational use of that waterway and would subject them to other economic and aesthetic harms. The proposition is entirely reasonable, the District Court found it was true in this case, and that is enough for injury in fact.

Laidlaw argues next that even if FOE had standing to seek injunctive relief, it lacked standing to seek civil penalties. Here the asserted defect is not injury but redressability. Civil penalties offer no redress to private plaintiffs, Laidlaw argues, because they are paid to the Government . . . .

It can scarcely be doubted that, for a plaintiff who is injured or faces the threat of future injury due to illegal conduct ongoing at the time of suit, a sanction that effectively abates that conduct and prevents its recurrence provides a form of redress. Civil penalties can fit that description. To the extent that they encourage defendants to discontinue current violations and deter them from committing future ones, they afford redress to citizen plaintiffs who are injured or threatened with injury as a consequence of ongoing unlawful conduct. . . .

Satisfied that FOE had standing under Article III to bring this action, we turn to the question of mootness.

The only conceivable basis for a finding of mootness in this case is Laidlaw's voluntary conduct—either its achievement by August 1992 of substantial compliance with its NPDES permit or its more recent shutdown of the Roebuck facility. It is well settled that "a defendant's voluntary cessation of a challenged practice does not deprive a federal court of its power to determine the legality of the practice." "[I]f it did, the courts would be compelled to leave '[t]he defendant . . . free to return to his old ways.'" In accordance with this principle, the standard we have announced for determining whether a case has been mooted by the defendant's voluntary conduct is stringent: "A case might become moot if subsequent events made it absolutely clear that the allegedly wrongful behavior could not reasonably be expected to recur." The "heavy burden of persua[ding]" the court that the challenged conduct cannot reasonably be expected to start up again lies with the party asserting mootness.

[In holding this case moot] . . . the Court of Appeals confused mootness with standing. . . . [A] defendant claiming that its voluntary compliance moots a case bears the formidable burden of showing that it is absolutely clear the allegedly wrongful behavior could not reasonably be expected to recur. By contrast, in a lawsuit brought to force compliance, it is the plaintiff's burden to establish standing by demonstrating that, if unchecked by the litigation, the defendant's allegedly wrongful behavior will likely occur or continue, and that the "threatened injury [is] certainly impending." . . . [Thus,] there are circumstances in which the prospect that a defendant will engage in (or resume) harmful conduct may be too speculative to support standing, but not too speculative to overcome mootness.

Furthermore, if mootness were simply "standing set in a time frame," the exception to mootness that arises when the defendant's allegedly unlawful activity is "capable of repetition, yet evading review," could not exist. When, for example, a mentally disabled patient files a lawsuit challenging her confinement in a segregated institution, her postcomplaint transfer to a community-based program will not moot the action, despite the fact that she would have lacked initial standing had she filed the complaint after the transfer. Standing admits of no similar exception; if a plaintiff lacks standing at the time the action commences, the fact that the dispute is capable of repetition yet evading review will not entitle the complainant to a federal judicial forum. . . .

The facility closure, like Laidlaw's earlier achievement of substantial compliance with its permit requirements, might moot the case, but . . . only if one or the other of these events made it absolutely clear that Laidlaw's permit violations could not reasonably be expected to recur. The effect of both Laidlaw's compliance and the facility closure on the prospect of future violations is a disputed factual matter. . . . These issues have not been aired in the lower courts; they remain open for consideration on remand. . . . [*The Court reversed the appellate court's order to dismiss the case as moot.*]

[*Concurring opinions of Stevens, J., and Kennedy, J., omitted.*]

■ *Justice* SCALIA, *with whom Justice* THOMAS *joins, dissenting. . . .*

Plaintiffs, as the parties invoking federal jurisdiction, have the burden of proof and persuasion as to the existence of standing. The plaintiffs in this case fell far short of carrying their burden of demonstrating injury in fact. The Court cites affiants' testimony asserting that their enjoyment of the North Tyger River has been diminished due to "concern" that the water was polluted, and that they "believed" that Laidlaw's mercury exceedances had reduced the value of their homes. These averments alone cannot carry the plaintiffs' burden of demonstrating that they have suffered a "concrete and particularized" injury. . . .

Ongoing "concerns" about the environment are not enough, for "[i]t is the *reality* of the threat of repeated injury that is relevant to the standing inquiry, not the plaintiff's subjective apprehensions." At the very least, in the present case, one would expect to see evidence supporting the affidavits' bald assertions regarding decreasing recreational usage and declining home values, as well as evidence for the improbable proposition that Laidlaw's violations, even though harmless to the environment, are somehow responsible for these effects. Plaintiffs here have made no attempt at such a showing, but rely entirely upon unsupported and unexplained affidavit allegations of "concern." . . .

The Court's treatment of the redressability requirement . . . is equally cavalier. . . .

The Court's opinion reads as though the only purpose and effect of the redressability requirement is to assure that the plaintiff receive *some* of the benefit of the relief that a court orders. That is not so. If it were, a federal tort plaintiff fearing repetition of the injury could ask for tort damages to be paid not only to himself but to other victims as well, on the theory that those damages would have at least some deterrent effect beneficial to him. . . .

If the Court had undertaken the necessary inquiry into whether significant deterrence of the plaintiffs' feared injury was "likely," it would have had to reason something like this: Strictly speaking, no polluter is deterred by a penalty for past pollution; he is deterred by the *fear* of a penalty for *future* pollution. That fear . . . will be substantial under an emissions program such as the federal scheme here, which is regularly and notoriously enforced; it will be even higher when a prospective polluter subject to such a regularly enforced program has, as here, been the object of public charges of pollution and a suit. . . . The deterrence on which the plaintiffs must rely for standing in the present case is the marginal increase in Laidlaw's fear of future penalties that will be achieved by adding federal penalties for Laidlaw's past conduct.

I cannot say for certain that this marginal increase is zero; but I can say for certain that it is entirely speculative whether it will make the difference between these plaintiffs' suffering injury in the future and these plaintiffs' going unharmed. In fact, the assertion that it will "likely" do so is entirely farfetched. . . .

Notes and Questions

1. What are the required elements for standing? What types of showings are needed to make out each element?

2. What are the differences between standing and mootness?

3. The costs associated with justiciability limits are easy to discern: Rights may go unredressed and violations of law unchecked. What are the benefits of justiciability to the legal system? What's wrong with advisory opinions? And shouldn't a party's willingness to put in the time, effort, and (often) money to litigate a case demonstrate that the party has a concrete stake in its outcome?

   Before joining the Supreme Court, then-Judge Scalia touted standing's importance to the separation of powers:

   > [T]he judicial doctrine of standing is a crucial and inseparable element of that principle, whose disregard will inevitably produce—as it has during the past few decades—an overjudicialization of the processes of self-governance. . . .
   >
   > [The degree to which a plaintiff cares about a problem, or the fact that] he may be a more ardent proponent of constitutional regularity or of the necessity of the governmental act that has been wrongfully omitted . . . does not establish that he has been harmed distinctively—only that he assesses the harm as more grave, which is a fair subject for democratic debate in which he may persuade the rest of us. Since our readiness to be persuaded is no less than his own (we are harmed just as much) there is no reason to remove the matter from the political process and place it in the courts.

   Antonin Scalia, *The Doctrine of Standing as an Essential Element of the Separation of Powers*, 17 Suffolk U. L. Rev. 881, 881, 894-95 (1983).

   In what ways does this justification of justiciability track arguments about judicial restraint generally, and what aspects of the argument are specific to the virtues of justiciability doctrine? If you agree that some principles of judicial restraint are advisable in order to respect the separation of powers, do you think standing and mootness impose the appropriate degree of restraint and apply in the appropiate cases? As you learn more about justiciability, you might return to this question and consider whether justiciability doctrines serve their putative functions.

4. Professor James Pfander provides a provocactive originalist counter-narrative:

While Justice Scalia was quite insistent that the injury-in-fact requirement was a crucial element of Article III standing limits, the term did not appear in the Court's decisions until 1970. . . . That alone suggests that the requirement was not part of what Article III meant when it restricted the judicial power to specified cases and controversies. . . .

Congress assigned a number of non-contentious matters to the federal courts in the early Republic. These ex parte proceedings did not require the plaintiff to set forth a personal injury in fact; rather, the party would typically file a petition in federal court, seeking to assert or register a claim of right under federal law. Nor was the plaintiff obliged to name a defendant; the proceeding assumed that the court would test the sufficiency of the plaintiff's factual showing. . . . Prominent among early examples of non-contentious jurisdiction, Congress assigned the federal courts responsibility for passing on ex parte petitions by aliens who sought naturalized citizenship under federal law. . . .

Federal courts in the late eighteenth and early nineteenth centuries took up these non-contentious matters without suggesting that the absence of injuries in fact and adverse parties barred federal adjudication. . . . Unlike modern definitions, [Chief Justice] Marshall explained that the key to the presence of a "case" in Article III lay in a party's "assertion of his rights in the form prescribed by law." This formulation clearly encompasses the submission of an ex parte claim of right, such as a naturalization petition, and makes no mention of the need for an injury or an opposing party.

James E. Pfander, *Scalia's Legacy: Originalism and Change in the Law of Standing*, 6 Brit. J. Am. Legal Stud. 85, 101-02 (2017).

5. Professor Richard Fallon observes that "the idea that rulings on standing often represent concealed judgments on the merits has acquired the status of folk wisdom." Richard H. Fallon, Jr., *The Linkage Between Justiciability and Remedies— and Their Connections to Substantive Rights*, 92 Va. L. Rev. 633, 634-35 (2006). What opportunities do you see in the doctrine for Justices to import their views of the merits, or their preferences on whether to hear the case on the merits, into the standing decision?

Note: Prudential Principles of Standing

In addition to the constitutional requirements of standing—the three elements that the Court has identified as necessary to create a "case" or "controversy" under Article III—the Court has also identified three "prudential" principles that it sometimes invokes to restrict standing further.

First, the Court has said it will not hear cases asserting "generalized grievances"—meaning that plaintiffs cannot sue based on a general interest in having the government follow the law. The main application of this principle is to bar most types of cases in which standing is based merely on the plaintiff's status as a taxpayer who does not want the government to use the plaintiff's taxes for purposes asserted to be unlawful. *See, e.g., Ariz. Christian Sch. Tuition Org. v. Winn*, 563 U.S. 125, 130 (2011). The generalized-grievance principle is not about how many people an asserted harm affects. For instance, the Court held that Massachusetts had standing to sue the federal Environmental Protection Agency over its failure to regulate greenhouse gases, as Massachusetts claimed the Clean Air Act required; because the threatened injury (that coastal Massachusetts land would be lost to flooding) was sufficiently concrete, the fact "[t]hat these climate-change risks are 'widely shared' does not minimize Massachusetts' interest in the outcome of this litigation." *Massachusetts v. EPA*, 549 U.S. 497, 522 (2007). Thus, the generalized-grievance prohibition focuses on the specificity of the harm to the plaintiff, not how many people share the injury.

Second, the Court has restricted plaintiffs' ability to raise the rights of a party not before the Court ("third party standing"). For instance, the Court has held non-justiciable public defenders' attempt to raise the rights of their hypothetical future clients, *Kowalski v. Tesmer*, 543 U.S. 125, 127 (2004), and a death-row inmate's challenge to the death sentence of a fellow inmate, *Whitmore v. Arkansas*, 495 U.S. 149, 151 (1990). However, the Court does permit a plaintiff to raise the rights of a third party if the plaintiff has a close relationship to the third party, *e.g., Singleton v. Wulff*, 428 U.S. 106, 118 (1976) (plurality opinion) (doctors permitted to assert their patients' rights); if the third parties are unlikely to be able to assert their own rights, *e.g., Powers v. Ohio*, 499 U.S. 400, 415 (1991) (litigants may assert the rights of prospective jurors not to be excluded from juries on the basis of their race); or where First Amendment is at issue, *e.g., Brockett v. Spokane Arcades, Inc.*, 472 U.S. 491; 503 (1985).

Third, the Court has sometimes required, almost exclusively in administrative law cases, that the plaintiff be within the "zone of interests" protected by the statute invoked. *See* Erwin Chemerinsky, Federal Jurisdiction § 2.3.6, at 112 (7th ed. 2016). The Court has recently framed this requirement as a matter of statutory interpretation, specifically "whether [the plaintiff] falls within the class of plaintiffs whom Congress has authorized to sue under" the statute at issue. *Lexmark Int'l, Inc. v. Static Control Components, Inc.*, 572 U.S. 118, 128 (2014). It therefore rarely arises in civil rights cases, where (assuming a cause of action has been recognized) the eligible plaintiffs are usually clear.

The applicability (or at least the terminology) of prudential standing principles is in flux. The Court's unanimous 2014 decision in *Lexmark* endorsed the view that "'prudential standing' is a misnomer" and noted that such non-constitutional limits on standing are in tension with federal courts' "virtually unflagging" obligation to decide cases within their jurisdiction. Thus, *Lexmark* suggested that prudential principles might be modified or recharacterized as elements of the constitutional standing analysis. Regardless, civil rights litigators must be aware of the substance of "prudential" limitations, however they might evolve.

Note: Ripeness and Pre-Enforcement Challenges

Like mootness, ripeness is a doctrine about the timing of adjudication. Unlike mootness, however, the ripeness doctrine is often in practice indistinguishable from, or a subset of, the standing requirement that the plaintiff be facing a concrete rather than a hypothetical injury. *See* Erwin Chemerinsky, *Federal Jurisdiction*

§ 2.4.1, at 124-25 (7th ed. 2016). A case is "unripe" when adjudication is premature, because, for instance, it is uncertain whether the plaintiff's injury will materialize. That uncertainty also defeats the injury prong of standing.

One way to conceive of ripeness as independent is to narrow its focus to the question of when a law or regulation can be challenged prior to its being *enforced against the plaintiff. See id.* at 120. "[I]t is not necessary that [a plaintiff] first expose himself to actual arrest or prosecution to be entitled to challenge a statute that he claims deters the exercise of his constitutional rights." *Steffel v. Thompson*, 415 U.S. 452, 459 (1974). Few would-be plaintiffs would want to run the risk of criminal prosecution and punishment if their challenge to the law fails. But the threat of enforcement still must be sufficiently "imminent" to make the dispute "concrete."

Susan B. Anthony List v. Driehaus, 573 U.S. 149 (2014), illustrates how the Court balances the availability of pre-enforcement challenges with the necessary "concreteness" for standing. (Even in this circumstance, the Court analyzed the pre-enforcement challenge in terms of *standing* rather than (as the courts below had done) *ripeness*; the Court explained that in this case they "boil down to the same question.")

During the 2010 election season, a pro-life advocacy group called Susan B. Anthony List ("SBA List") accused Rep. Steve Driehaus, who was then seeking reelection, of having voted for "taxpayer-funded abortion" when he voted for the Affordable Care Act of 2010. Rep. Driehaus brought an administrative complaint to the Ohio Elections Commission under an Ohio law that made it a crime for any person to "[m]ake a false statement concerning the voting record of a candidate or public official" or to "[p]ost, publish, circulate, distribute, or otherwise disseminate a false statement concerning a candidate, either knowing the same to be false or with reckless disregard of whether it was false or not." In response, SBA List filed suit challenging the Ohio law under the First Amendment. Driehaus lost the election and dropped his complaint to the Commission, but SBA List continued to pursue its facial challenge to the law. The case was dismissed as nonjusticiable, and the Sixth Circuit affirmed, reasoning that the injury was too speculative because SBA List had not been held to have violated the law in Driehaus's case and had not claimed that it intended to make false statements in the future.

The Supreme Court reversed and held, in an opinion by Justice Thomas for a unanimous Court, that SBA List had standing to challenge the Ohio law:

> [A]n actual arrest, prosecution, or other enforcement action is not a prerequisite to challenging the [enforcement of a] law. Instead, we have permitted preenforcement review under circumstances that render the threatened enforcement sufficiently imminent. Specifically, we have held that a plaintiff satisfies the injury-in-fact requirement where he alleges "an intention to engage in a course of conduct arguably affected with a constitutional interest, but proscribed by a statute, and there exists a credible threat of prosecution thereunder." Several of our cases illustrate the circumstances under which plaintiffs may bring a preenforcement challenge consistent with Article III.
>
> In *Steffel* [*v. Thompson*], for example, police officers threatened to arrest petitioner and his companion for distributing handbills protesting the Vietnam

War. Petitioner left to avoid arrest; his companion remained and was arrested and charged with criminal trespass. Petitioner sought a declaratory judgment that the trespass statute was unconstitutional as applied to him.

We determined that petitioner had alleged a credible threat of enforcement: He had been warned to stop handbilling and threatened with prosecution if he disobeyed; he stated his desire to continue handbilling (an activity he claimed was constitutionally protected); and his companion's prosecution showed that his "concern with arrest" was not "'chimerical.'" . . .

In *Babbitt* [*v. Farm Workers*], we considered a preenforcement challenge to a statute that made it an unfair labor practice to encourage consumers to boycott an "agricultural product . . . by the use of dishonest, untruthful and deceptive publicity." The plaintiffs contended that the law "unconstitutionally penalize[d] inaccuracies inadvertently uttered in the course of consumer appeals."

Building on *Steffel,* we explained that a plaintiff could bring a preenforcement suit when he "has alleged an intention to engage in a course of conduct arguably affected with a constitutional interest, but proscribed by a statute, and there exists a credible threat of prosecution thereunder." We found those circumstances present in *Babbitt.* In that case, the law "on its face proscribe[d] dishonest, untruthful, and deceptive publicity." The plaintiffs had "actively engaged in consumer publicity campaigns in the past" and alleged "an intention to continue" those campaigns in the future. And although they did not "plan to propagate untruths," they argued that "'erroneous statement is inevitable in free debate.'" We concluded that the plaintiffs' fear of prosecution was not "imaginary or wholly speculative," and that their challenge to the consumer publicity provision presented an Article III case or controversy.

Applying these principles, the Court found standing to challenge the Ohio law. On remand, the district court held the law unconstitutional, and the Sixth Circuit affirmed. *Susan B. Anthony List v. Driehaus,* 814 F.3d 466 (6th Cir. 2016).

What is the test for standing to bring a pre-enforcement challenge to a law?

It is important both to know what courts and litigants mean when they inquire into ripeness—they are asking whether adjudication is premature—and also to recognize that the doctrine overlaps with standing to such a degree that most or all questions of ripeness may be, and increasingly are, analyzed in terms of the injury prong of standing.

We now turn to a more detailed look at standing.

B. STANDING

As noted, the purpose of the standing requirement is to ensure that the plaintiff has a concrete stake in a case heard by a federal court. The constitutional elements of standing are: (1) the plaintiff has suffered an injury, that is (2) caused by the defendant's conduct, and (3) would be redressed by a court decision in the plaintiff's favor.

Standing plays a major role in restricting the availability of injunctive relief, in large part because of the decision in *City of Los Angeles v. Lyons.* The Court held there that standing must be demonstrated for each type of relief sought, so standing to sue for damages based on past harm does not entitle the plaintiff to seek an injunction against future harm of the same type. Further, the Court limited standing to seek an injunction to plaintiffs who could demonstrate that they *likely* faced future injury—a requirement that *Lyons* and subsequent cases have applied strictly. We begin with a discussion of the injury requirement and *Lyons* jurisprudence, followed by the other two constitutional elements of standing—causation and redressability.

1. INJURY AND THE "*LYONS* PROBLEM"

Lyons had two important forerunners taking a narrow view of judicial power to issue injunctions.

In *O'Shea v. Littleton*, 414 U.S. 488 (1974), seventeen black and two white residents of Cairo, Illinois, brought a civil rights class action charging that the local judges engaged in a pattern of illegal bond setting, sentencing, and jury-fee practices in criminal cases and that police and prosecutors intentionally discriminated based on race in the enforcement of criminal laws by applying them more harshly to black residents than to white residents. In an opinion by Justice White, the Court held that the plaintiffs lacked standing:

> Plaintiffs in the federal courts "must allege some threatened or actual injury resulting from the putatively illegal action before a federal court may assume jurisdiction." . . . The injury or threat of injury must be both "real and immediate," not "conjectural" or "hypothetical." Moreover, if none of the named plaintiffs purporting to represent a class establishes the requisite of a case or controversy with the defendants, none may seek relief on behalf of himself or any other member of the class.
>
> In the complaint that began this action, the sole allegations of injury are that . . . petitioners "have denied and continue to deny to plaintiffs and members of their class their constitutional rights" by illegal bond-setting, sentencing, and jury-fee practices. . . . Past exposure to illegal conduct does not in itself show a present case or controversy regarding injunctive relief, however, if unaccompanied by any continuing, present adverse effects. . . .
>
> Of course, past wrongs are evidence bearing on whether there is a real and immediate threat of repeated injury. But here the prospect of future injury rests on the likelihood that respondents will again be arrested for and charged with violations of the criminal law and will again be subjected to bond proceedings, trial, or sentencing before petitioners. Important to this assessment is the absence of allegations that any relevant criminal statute of the State of Illinois is unconstitutional on its face or as applied or that respondents have been or will be improperly charged with violating criminal law. . . . Apparently, the proposition is that if respondents proceed to violate an unchallenged law and if they are charged, held to answer, and tried in any proceedings before petitioners, they will be subjected to the discriminatory practices that petitioners are alleged to have followed. But it seems to us that attempting to anticipate whether and when these respondents will be charged with crime and will be made to appear before either petitioner takes us into the area of speculation and conjecture. The nature of respondents' activities is not described in detail and no specific threats are alleged to have been made against them. . . .

> What [plaintiffs] seek is an injunction aimed at controlling or preventing the occurrence of specific events that might take place in the course of future state criminal trials. . . . Apparently the order would contemplate interruption of state proceedings to adjudicate assertions of noncompliance by petitioners. This seems to us nothing less than an ongoing federal audit of state criminal proceedings . . . .
>
> A federal court should not intervene to establish the basis for future intervention that would be so intrusive and unworkable.

Justice Blackmun concurred in part. Justice Douglas, joined by Justices Brennan and Marshall, dissented:

> What has been alleged here is not only wrongs done to named plaintiffs, but a recurring pattern of wrongs . . . to weight the scales of justice repeatedly on the side of white prejudices and against black protests, fears, and suffering. This is a more pervasive scheme for suppression of blacks and their civil rights than I have ever seen. It may not survive a trial. But if this case does not present a "case or controversy" involving the named plaintiffs, then that concept has been so watered down as to be no longer recognizable.

Two years later, *Rizzo v. Goode*, 423 U.S. 362 (1976), returned to themes similar to those that drove the decision in *O'Shea*. In *Rizzo*, plaintiffs in two class actions alleged a pattern of unconstitutional police mistreatment of minority citizens of Philadelphia and Philadelphia residents in general. In one case, two particular officers, not named as parties, were identified as having violated plaintiffs' rights in three instances. In the other case, another two constitutional violations were identified. The district court ordered the police department "to submit to (the District) Court for its approval a comprehensive program for improving the handling of citizen complaints alleging police misconduct." A citizen complaint procedure was then developed through negotiations among the parties and incorporated into the district court's final judgment. The court of appeals affirmed.

In an opinion by Justice Rehnquist, the Supreme Court reversed, first "entertain[ing] serious doubts whether on the facts as found there was made out the requisite Art. III case or controversy" in light of *O'Shea*. The Court went on to hold that, in any event, the district court's injunction was improper because it rested on an amorphous theory of liability—"a constitutional 'duty' on the part of petitioners . . . to 'eliminate' future police misconduct"—and violated principles of federalism by "inject[ing] [the court] . . . into the internal disciplinary affairs of this state agency."

Justice Blackmun, joined by Justices Brennan and Marshall, dissented, contending that "the District Court here, with detailed, careful, and sympathetic findings, ascertained the existence of violations of citizens' constitutional rights, of a pattern of that type of activity, of its likely continuance and recurrence, and of an official indifference as to doing anything about it." Justice Stevens took no part.

It is debatable (and the *Lyons* majority and dissent would in fact debate) the extent to which the sweeping rule of *Lyons* naturally followed from *O'Shea* and *Rizzo*.

City of Los Angeles v. Lyons
461 U.S. 95 (1983)

■ *Justice* WHITE *delivered the opinion of the Court....*

The complaint alleged that on October 6, 1976, at 2 A.M., [Adolph] Lyons was stopped by the defendant officers for a traffic or vehicle code violation and that although Lyons offered no resistance or threat whatsoever, the officers, without provocation or justification, seized Lyons and applied a "chokehold"[1]—either the "bar arm control" hold or the "carotid-artery control" hold or both—rendering him unconscious and causing damage to his larynx.

Counts I through IV of the complaint sought damages against the officers and the City. Count V, with which we are principally concerned here, sought a preliminary and permanent injunction against the City barring the use of the control holds. That count alleged that the city's police officers, "pursuant to the authorization, instruction and encouragement of defendant City of Los Angeles, regularly and routinely apply these choke holds in innumerable situations where they are not threatened by the use of any deadly force whatsoever," that numerous persons have been injured as the result of the application of the chokeholds, that Lyons and others similarly situated are threatened with irreparable injury in the form of bodily injury and loss of life, and that Lyons "justifiably fears that any contact he has with Los Angeles police officers may result in his being choked and strangled to death without provocation, justification or other legal excuse."...

The District Court found that Lyons had been stopped for a traffic infringement and that without provocation or legal justification the officers involved had applied a "department-authorized chokehold which resulted in injuries to the plaintiff." The court further found that the department authorizes the use of the holds in situations where no one is threatened by death or grievous bodily harm, that officers are insufficiently trained, that the use of the holds involves a high risk of injury or death as then employed, and that their continued use in situations where neither death nor serious bodily injury is threatened "is unconscionable in a civilized society."... A preliminary injunction was entered enjoining "the use of both the carotid-artery and bar arm holds under circumstances which do not threaten death or serious bodily injury." An improved training program and regular reporting and record keeping were also ordered. The Court of Appeals affirmed in a brief per curiam opinion....

---

1. The police control procedures at issue in this case are referred to as "control holds," "chokeholds," "strangleholds," and "neck restraints." All these terms refer to two basic control procedures: the "carotid" hold and the "bar arm" hold. In the "carotid" hold, an officer positioned behind a subject places one arm around the subject's neck and holds the wrist of that arm with his other hand. The officer, by using his lower forearm and bicep muscle, applies pressure concentrating on the carotid arteries located on the sides of the subject's neck. The "carotid" hold is capable of rendering the subject unconscious by diminishing the flow of oxygenated blood to the brain. The "bar arm" hold, which is administered similarly, applies pressure at the front of the subject's neck. "Bar arm" pressure causes pain, reduces the flow of oxygen to the lungs, and may render the subject unconscious.

[Lyons'] first amended complaint alleged that 10 chokehold-related deaths had occurred. By May, 1982, there had been five more such deaths. . . .

It goes without saying that those who seek to invoke the jurisdiction of the federal courts must satisfy the threshhold requirement imposed by Article III of the Constitution by alleging an actual case or controversy. Plaintiffs must demonstrate a "personal stake in the outcome" in order to "assure that concrete adverseness which sharpens the presentation of issues" necessary for the proper resolution of constitutional questions. Abstract injury is not enough. The plaintiff must show that he "has sustained or is immediately in danger of sustaining some direct injury" as the result of the challenged official conduct and the injury or threat of injury must be both "real and immediate," not "conjectural" or "hypothetical."

In *O'Shea v. Littleton*, we dealt with a case brought by a class of plaintiffs claiming that they had been subjected to discriminatory enforcement of the criminal law. . . . [We held that the] complaint [failed] to allege a case or controversy. Although it was claimed in that case that particular members of the plaintiff class had actually suffered from the alleged unconstitutional practices, we observed that "[p]ast exposure to illegal conduct does not in itself show a present case or controversy regarding injunctive relief . . . if unaccompanied by any continuing, present adverse effects." Past wrongs were evidence bearing on "whether there is a real and immediate threat of repeated injury." But the prospect of future injury rested "on the likelihood that [plaintiffs] will again be arrested for and charged with violations of the criminal law and will again be subjected to bond proceedings, trial, or sentencing before petitioners." . . . We could not find a case or controversy in those circumstances: the threat to the plaintiffs was not "sufficiently real and immediate to show an existing controversy simply because they anticipate violating lawful criminal statutes and being tried for their offenses. . . ."

Another relevant decision for present purposes is *Rizzo v. Goode*, a case in which plaintiffs alleged widespread illegal and unconstitutional police conduct aimed at minority citizens and against City residents in general. . . . The claim of injury rested upon "what one or a small, unnamed minority of policemen might do to them in the future because of that unknown policeman's perception" of departmental procedures. This hypothesis was "even more attenuated than those allegations of future injury found insufficient in *O'Shea* to warrant [the] invocation of federal jurisdiction." The Court also held that plaintiffs' showing at trial of a relatively few instances of violations by individual police officers, without any showing of a deliberate policy on behalf of the named defendants, did not provide a basis for equitable relief. . . .

No extension of *O'Shea* and *Rizzo* is necessary to hold that respondent Lyons has failed to demonstrate a case or controversy with the City that would justify the equitable relief sought. Lyons' standing to seek the injunction requested depended on whether he was likely to suffer future injury from the use of the chokeholds by police officers. Count V of the complaint alleged the traffic stop and choking incident five months before. That Lyons may have been illegally choked by the police on October 6, 1976, while presumably affording Lyons standing to claim damages against the individual officers and perhaps against the City, does nothing to establish a real and immediate threat that he would again be stopped for a traffic violation, or for any other offense, by an officer or officers who would illegally choke him into unconsciousness without any provocation or resistance on his part. The additional allegation in the complaint that the police in Los Angeles routinely apply chokeholds in situations where they are not threatened by the use of deadly force falls far short of the allegations that would be necessary to establish a case or controversy between these parties.

In order to establish an actual controversy in this case, Lyons would have had not only to allege that he would have another encounter with the police but also to make the incredible assertion either, (1) that all police officers in Los Angeles always choke any citizen with whom they happen to have an encounter, whether for the purpose of arrest, issuing a citation or for questioning or, (2) that the City ordered or authorized police officers to act in such manner. Although Count V alleged that the City authorized the use of the control holds in situations where deadly force was not threatened, it did not indicate why Lyons might be realistically threatened by police officers who acted within the strictures of the City's policy. If, for example, chokeholds were authorized to be used only to counter resistance to an arrest by a suspect, or to thwart an effort to escape, any future threat to Lyons from the City's policy or from the conduct of police officers would be no more real than the possibility that he would again have an encounter with the police and that either he would illegally resist arrest or detention or the officers would disobey their instructions and again render him unconscious without any provocation.[7]

Under *O'Shea* and *Rizzo*, these allegations were an insufficient basis to provide a federal court with jurisdiction to entertain Count V of the complaint.[8]

---

7. The centerpiece of Justice Marshall's dissent is that Lyons had standing to challenge the City's policy because to recover damages he would have to prove that what allegedly occurred on October 6, 1976, was pursuant to City authorization. We agree completely that for Lyons to succeed in his damages action, it would be necessary to prove that what happened to him—that is, as alleged, he was choked without any provocation or legal excuse whatsoever—was pursuant to a City policy. . . . [H]owever, it does not follow that Lyons had standing to seek the injunction prayed for in Count V. . . .

[T]o have a case or controversy with the City that could sustain Count V, Lyons would have to credibly allege that he faced a realistic threat from the future application of the City's policy. Justice Marshall nowhere confronts this requirement—the necessity that Lyons demonstrate that he, himself, will not only again be stopped by the police but will be choked without any provocation or legal excuse. Justice Marshall plainly does not agree with that requirement, and he was in dissent in *O'Shea*. We are at issue in that respect.

8. As previously indicated, Lyons alleged that he feared he would be choked in any future encounter with the police. The reasonableness of Lyons' fear is dependent upon the likelihood of a recurrence of the allegedly unlawful conduct. It is the reality of the threat of repeated injury that is relevant to the standing inquiry, not the plaintiff's subjective apprehensions. The emotional consequences of a prior act simply are not a sufficient basis for an injunction absent a real and immediate threat of future injury by the defendant. Of course, emotional upset is a relevant consideration in a damages action.

[The court of appeals erred in holding otherwise and distinguishing *O'Shea* and *Rizzo*.] . . .

First, the Court of Appeals thought that Lyons was more immediately threatened than the plaintiffs in those cases since, according to the Court of Appeals, Lyons need only be stopped for a minor traffic violation to be subject to the strangleholds. But even assuming that Lyons would again be stopped for a traffic or other violation in the reasonably near future, it is untenable to assert, and the complaint made no such allegation, that strangleholds are applied by the Los Angeles police to every citizen who is stopped or arrested regardless of the conduct of the person stopped. We cannot agree that the "odds," that Lyons would not only again be stopped for a traffic violation but would also be subjected to a chokehold without any provocation whatsoever are sufficient to make out a federal case for equitable relief. We note that five months elapsed between October 6, 1976, and the filing of the complaint, yet there was no allegation of further unfortunate encounters between Lyons and the police.

Of course, it may be that among the countless encounters between the police and the citizens of a great city such as Los Angeles, there will be certain instances in which strangleholds will be illegally applied and injury and death unconstitutionally inflicted on the victim. As we have said, however, it is no more than conjecture to suggest that in every instance of a traffic stop, arrest, or other encounter between the police and a citizen, the police will act unconstitutionally and inflict injury without provocation or legal excuse. And it is surely no more than speculation to assert either that Lyons himself will again be involved in one of those unfortunate instances, or that he will be arrested in the future and provoke the use of a chokehold by resisting arrest, attempting to escape, or threatening deadly force or serious bodily injury.

Second, the Court of Appeals viewed *O'Shea* and *Rizzo* as cases in which the plaintiffs sought "massive structural" relief against the local law enforcement systems and therefore that the holdings in those cases were inapposite to cases such as this where the plaintiff, according to the Court of Appeals, seeks to enjoin only an "established," "sanctioned" police practice assertedly violative of constitutional rights. *O'Shea* and *Rizzo*, however, cannot be so easily confined. . . . If Lyons has made no showing that he is realistically threatened by a repetition of his experience of October, 1976, then he has not met the requirements for seeking an injunction in a federal court, whether the injunction contemplates intrusive structural relief or the cessation of a discrete practice. . . .

There was no finding that Lyons faced a real and immediate threat of again being illegally choked. The City's policy was described as authorizing the use of the strangleholds "under circumstances where no one is threatened with death or grievous bodily harm." That policy was not further described, but the record before the court contained the department's existing policy with respect to the employment of chokeholds. Nothing in that policy, contained in a Police Department manual, suggests that the chokeholds, or other kinds of force for that matter, are authorized absent some resistance or other provocation by the arrestee or other suspect.[9] On the contrary, police officers were instructed to use chokeholds only when lesser degrees of force do not suffice and then only "to gain control of a suspect who is violently resisting the officer or trying to escape." ...

Contrary to the view of the Court of Appeals, it is not at all "difficult" under our holding "to see how anyone can ever challenge police or similar administrative practices." The legality of the violence to which Lyons claims he was once subjected is at issue in his suit for damages and can be determined there.

Absent a sufficient likelihood that he will again be wronged in a similar way, Lyons is no more entitled to an injunction than any other citizen of Los Angeles; and a federal court may not entertain a claim by any or all citizens who no more than assert that certain practices of law enforcement officers are unconstitutional. ...

[R]ecognition of the need for a proper balance between state and federal authority counsels restraint in the issuance of injunctions against state officers engaged in the administration of the states' criminal laws in the absence of irreparable injury which is both great and immediate. ... In exercising their equitable powers federal courts must recognize "[t]he special delicacy of the adjustment to be preserved between federal equitable power and State administration of its own law." ...

▪ *Justice* MARSHALL, *with whom Justice* BRENNAN, *Justice* BLACKMUN *and Justice* STEVENS *join, dissenting.*

The District Court found that the City of Los Angeles authorizes its police officers to apply life-threatening chokeholds to citizens who pose no threat of violence, and that respondent, Adolph Lyons, was subjected to such a chokehold. The Court today holds that a federal court is without power to enjoin the enforcement of the City's policy, no matter how flagrantly unconstitutional it may be. Since no one can show that he will be choked in the future, no one—not even a person who, like Lyons, has almost been choked to death—has standing to challenge the continuation of the policy. The City is free to continue the policy indefinitely as long as it is willing to pay damages for the injuries and deaths that result. I dissent from this unprecedented and unwarranted approach to standing. ...

Respondent Adolph Lyons is a 24-year-old Negro male who resides in Los Angeles. According to the uncontradicted evidence in the record, at about

---

9. The dissent notes that a LAPD training officer stated that the police are authorized to employ the control holds whenever an officer "feels" that there is about to be a bodily attack. The dissent's emphasis on the word "feels" apparently is intended to suggest that LAPD officers are authorized to apply the holds whenever they "feel" like it. If there is a distinction between permitting the use of the holds when there is a "threat" of serious bodily harm, and when the officer "feels" or believes there is about to be a bodily attack, the dissent has failed to make it clear. The dissent does not, because it cannot, point to any written or oral pronouncement by the LAPD or any evidence showing a pattern of police behavior that would indicate that the official policy would permit the application of the control holds on a suspect that was not offering, or threatening to offer, physical resistance.

2:30 A.M. on October 6, 1976, Lyons was pulled over to the curb by two officers of the Los Angeles Police Department (LAPD) for a traffic infraction because one of his taillights was burned out. The officers greeted him with drawn revolvers as he exited from his car. Lyons was told to face his car and spread his legs. He did so. He was then ordered to clasp his hands and put them on top of his head. He again complied. After one of the officers completed a pat-down search, Lyons dropped his hands, but was ordered to place them back above his head, and one of the officers grabbed Lyons' hands and slammed them onto his head. Lyons complained about the pain caused by the ring of keys he was holding in his hand. Within five to ten seconds, the officer began to choke Lyons by applying a forearm against his throat. As Lyons struggled for air, the officer handcuffed him, but continued to apply the chokehold until he blacked out. When Lyons regained consciousness, he was lying face down on the ground, choking, gasping for air, and spitting up blood and dirt. He had urinated and defecated. He was issued a traffic citation and released. . . .

Although the City instructs its officers that use of a chokehold does not constitute deadly force, since 1975 no less than 16 persons have died following the use of a chokehold by an LAPD police officer. Twelve have been Negro males.[3] The evidence submitted to the District Court established that for many years it has been the official policy of the City to permit police officers to employ chokeholds in a variety of situations where they face no threat of violence. In reported "altercations" between LAPD officers and citizens the chokeholds are used more frequently than any other means of physical restraint. Between February 1975 and July 1980, LAPD officers applied chokeholds on at least 975 occasions, which represented more than three-quarters of the reported altercations.

It is undisputed that chokeholds pose a high and unpredictable risk of serious injury or death. Chokeholds are intended to bring a subject under control by causing pain and rendering him unconscious. Depending on the position of the officer's arm and the force applied, the victim's voluntary or involuntary reaction, and his state of health, an officer may inadvertently crush the victim's larynx, trachea, or thyroid. The result may be death caused by either cardiac arrest or asphyxiation. An LAPD officer described the reaction of a person to being choked as "do[ing] the chicken," in reference apparently to the reactions of a chicken when its neck is wrung. The victim experiences extreme pain. His face turns blue as he is deprived of oxygen, he goes into spasmodic convulsions, his eyes roll back, his body wriggles, his feet kick up and down, and his arms move about wildly.

Although there has been no occasion to determine the precise contours of the City's chokehold policy, the evidence submitted to the District Court provides some indications. LAPD training officer Terry Speer testified that an officer is authorized to deploy a chokehold whenever he "feels that there's about to be a bodily attack made on him." A training bulletin states that "[c]ontrol holds . . . allow officers to subdue any resistance by the suspects." . . .

---

3. Thus in a City where Negro males constitute 9% of the population, they have accounted for 75% of the deaths resulting from the use of chokeholds. . . .

Moreover, the officers are taught to maintain the chokehold until the suspect goes limp, despite substantial evidence that the application of a chokehold invariably induces a "flight or flee" syndrome, producing an involuntary struggle by the victim which can easily be misinterpreted by the officer as willful resistance that must be overcome by prolonging the chokehold and increasing the force applied. In addition, officers are instructed that the chokeholds can be safely deployed for up to three or four minutes. Robert Jarvis, the City's expert who has taught at the Los Angeles Police Academy for the past twelve years, admitted that officers are never told that the bar-arm control can cause death if applied for just two seconds. Of the nine deaths for which evidence was submitted to the District Court, the average duration of the choke where specified was approximately 40 seconds. . . .

It is simply disingenuous for the Court to assert that its decision requires "[n]o extension" of *O'Shea v. Littleton* and *Rizzo v. Goode*. In contrast to this case *O'Shea* and *Rizzo* involved disputes focusing solely on the threat of future injury which the plaintiffs in those cases alleged they faced. In *O'Shea* the plaintiffs did not allege past injury and did not seek compensatory relief. In *Rizzo*, the plaintiffs sought only declaratory and injunctive relief and alleged past instances of police misconduct only in an attempt to establish the substantiality of the threat of future injury. . . .

By contrast, Lyons' request for prospective relief is coupled with his claim for damages based on past injury. In addition to the risk that he will be subjected to a chokehold in the future, Lyons has suffered past injury. Because he has a live claim for damages, he need not rely solely on the threat of future injury to establish his personal stake in the outcome of the controversy. In the cases relied on by the majority, the Court simply had no occasion to decide whether a plaintiff who has standing to litigate a dispute must clear a separate standing hurdle with respect to each form of relief sought.

The Court's decision likewise finds no support in the fundamental policy underlying the Article III standing requirement—the concern that a federal court not decide a legal issue if the plaintiff lacks a sufficient "personal stake in the outcome of the controversy. . . ."

Because Lyons has a claim for damages against the City, and because he cannot prevail on that claim unless he demonstrates that the City's chokehold policy violates the Constitution, his personal stake in the outcome of the controversy adequately assures an adversary presentation of his challenge to the constitutionality of the policy. Moreover, the resolution of this challenge will be largely dispositive of his requests for declaratory and injunctive relief. No doubt the requests for injunctive relief may raise additional questions. But these questions involve familiar issues relating to the appropriateness of particular forms of relief, and have never been thought to implicate a litigant's standing to sue. The denial of standing separately to seek injunctive relief therefore cannot be justified by the basic concern underlying the Article III standing requirement.

Our cases uniformly state that the touchstone of the Article III standing requirement is the plaintiff's personal stake in the underlying dispute, not in the particular types of relief sought. Once a plaintiff establishes a personal stake in a dispute, he has done all that is necessary to "invok[e] the court's authority . . . to challenge the action sought to be adjudicated." . . .

The federal practice has been to reserve consideration of the appropriate relief until after a determination of the merits, not to foreclose certain forms of relief by a ruling on the pleadings. The prayer for relief is no part of the plaintiff's cause of action. Rather, "[t]he usual rule is that where legal rights have been invaded and a cause of action is available, a federal court may use any available remedy to make good the wrong done." . . .

The principles of federalism . . . do not preclude the limited preliminary injunction issued in this case. Unlike the permanent injunction at issue in *Rizzo*, the preliminary injunction involved here entails no federal supervision of the LAPD's activities. The preliminary injunction merely forbids the use of chokeholds absent the threat of deadly force, permitting their continued use where such a threat does exist. This limited ban takes the form of a preventive injunction, which has traditionally been regarded as the least intrusive form of equitable relief. Moreover, the City can remove the ban by obtaining approval of a training plan. . . .

The Court's decision removes an entire class of constitutional violations from the equitable powers of a federal court. It immunizes from prospective equitable relief any policy that authorizes persistent deprivations of constitutional rights as long as no individual can establish with substantial certainty that he will be injured, or injured again, in the future. The Chief Justice asked in *Bivens* (dissenting opinion), "what would be the judicial response to a police order authorizing 'shoot to kill' with respect to every fugitive?" His answer was that it would be "easy to predict our collective wrath and outrage." We now learn that wrath and outrage cannot be translated into an order to cease the unconstitutional practice, but only an award of damages to those who are victimized by the practice and live to sue and to the survivors of those who are not so fortunate. Under the view expressed by the majority today, if the police adopt a policy of "shoot to kill," or a policy of shooting one out of ten suspects, the federal courts will be powerless to enjoin its continuation. The federal judicial power is now limited to levying a toll for such a systematic constitutional violation.

Notes and Questions

1. What is the majority's test for standing to seek injunctive relief? What would Lyons have had to show to meet it?

2. There are several strands to disentangle in this complex and consequential decision—the Court's decision to require standing for each form of relief, the Court's skepticism about the alleged extent of the city's practice, the Court's requirement that Lyons demonstrate that he personally was likely to face another chokehold, the high bar that the Court set for such a showing, and the Court's concern for federalism. What role does each of these factors play in the Court's holding? Are all of them necessary to the result?

3. What reason does the majority give for requiring standing to seek injunctive relief distinct from standing to pursue damages? On what grounds does the dissent oppose that requirement?

4. The majority leans heavily on *O'Shea* and *Rizzo*, which it claims not to be extending. To what extent is the outcome here dictated by those decisions?

5. The court of appeals had distinguished *O'Shea* and *Rizzo* because they involved more intrusive relief into government entities' operations. Is the scope of relief relevant to the majority's holding here? Why or why not?

6. Federalism figures prominently in *O'Shea*, *Rizzo*, and *Lyons*, as it does throughout debates about civil rights enforcement doctrines. As Professor (and later Judge) Michael McConnell has summarized federalism's main postulates:

> Three important advantages of decentralized decision making emerge from an examination of the founders' arguments and the modern literature. First, decentralized decision making is better able to reflect the diversity of interests and preferences of individuals in different parts of the nation. Second, allocation of decision making authority to a level of government no larger than necessary will prevent mutually disadvantageous attempts by communities to take advantage of their neighbors. And third, decentralization allows for innovation and competition in government.

Michael W. McConnell, *Federalism: Evaluating the Founders' Design*, 54 U. Chi. L. Rev. 1484, 1493 (1987); *see also* Steven G. Calabresi & Lucy D. Bickford, *Federalism and Subsidiarity: Perspectives from U.S. Constitutional Law*, 55 Nomos 123 (2012) (arguing for "[s]ubsidiarity"—"the idea that matters should be decided at the lowest or least centralized competent level of government"); James F. Blumstein, *Federalism and Civil Rights: Complementary and Competing Paradigms*, 47 Vand. L. Rev. 1251, 1252-53 (1994) ("[F]ederalism seeks to empower geographically-based minorities in a political manner. This political empowerment insulates, to some extent, geographically-based minorities from political subordination at the hands of majoritarian national constituencies and institutions").

To what extent is federalism the basis for decision in *O'Shea*, *Rizzo*, and *Lyons*? What is its role in these cases otherwise? How do the results of each case serve the values of federalism? What values are subordinated to federalism?

7. How much of the majority's decision in *Lyons* do you attribute to its skepticism of Lyons's allegations and of the district court's findings? Do you think courts today would have such a difficult time crediting the plaintiff's case in light of the incidents captured on video in the past several years of police shootings of unarmed black men? Note that the plaintiff's race appears near the beginning of Justice Marshall's dissent; the majority never mentions it. How does the factual debate between the majority and dissent in *Lyons* affect your view of the value of diversity on the Court?

8. The standing requirement derives, as the majority explains, from the concern that issues will be inadequately presented unless both sides of a dispute have a concrete stake in it. From that perspective, the Court argues, Lyons's stake in the claim for injunctive relief is too abstract because the likelihood of his experiencing another chokehold is low. How does Justice Marshall answer the majority's concern about Lyons's personal interest? Why might Lyons have a stake in the injunctive relief claim even absent a high likelihood of *personally* experiencing a chokehold?

9. Consider the tort-law theory that the appropriate level of precaution to take against a given danger is a function of the danger's magnitude and its likelihood of occurring. Viewed through that lens, perhaps even a low likelihood that Lyons will be subjected to another chokehold justifies taking the threat quite seriously for purposes of evaluating his standing. Based on the majority's reasoning, how do you imagine the majority would respond to this argument?

10. Consider Justice Marshall's famous and chilling claim that the federal judiciary has been reduced to "levying a toll" for even egregious constitutional violations. Is that a fair characterization of the result the majority has reached? If not, why not? If so, how far do you think Justice Marshall's critique goes—doesn't it call into question the value of damages generally as a remedy for civil rights violations? One can imagine even large awards being of little consequence relative to the budget of a large city like Los Angeles, Chicago, or New York. Recall our prior discussions of the value of damages—both their monetary value (Chapter 9) and strategic value (Section C of the Prologue). In light of *Lyons*, should Congress be studying whether our system of civil rights enforcement relies too heavily on damages?

11. If you find yourself siding with Justice Marshall regarding whether Lyons may seek an injunction, how far would you go? Same result for any black resident of L.A., regardless of past exposure to chokeholds? Same result for any resident of L.A. of any race? An Angelino without a driver's license? Someone who lives elsewhere entirely? If you agree with Justice Marshall, must you also oppose the results in *Rizzo* and/or *O'Shea*?

12. You might think that if the standing problem here is insufficient probability—no single individual is sufficiently likely to be subjected to a chokehold in the future—then the solution lies in the class action device, which permits a small number of named plaintiffs to sue on behalf of a large group of unnamed ones. But as Justice White noted in *O'Shea*, courts have held that the named plaintiff in a class action must demonstrate standing without reliance on the absent class members. If that rule were relaxed, to what extent and under what circumstances would the harshness of the *Lyons* rule be ameliorated?

13. Practicing civil rights litigators regularly refer to potential cases as having a "*Lyons* problem" and refrain from seeking injunctive relief on that basis. What solutions or workarounds can you imagine civil rights litigators pursuing in such circumstances?

Applications

Compare *Lyons* to these two subsequent environmental cases, which relied on or distinguished it:

1. *Lujan v. Defenders of Wildlife*, 504 U.S. 555 (1992). The Endangered Species Act of 1973 instructs the Secretary of the Interior to identify, based on specified critera, species threatened with extinction. Other federal agencies must consult with the Secretary to make sure their actions are not likely to further jeopardize identified species. In 1986, a new regulation limited the consultation requirement to actions taken in the United States or on the high seas. Conservation organizations challenged the regulation. The Supreme Court, per Justice Scalia, held that they lacked standing. Regarding injury, the Court reasoned:

> Respondents' claim to injury is that the lack of consultation with respect to certain funded activities abroad "increas[es] the rate of extinction of endangered and threatened species." Of course, the desire to use or observe an animal species, even for purely esthetic purposes, is undeniably a cognizable interest for purpose of standing. "But the 'injury in fact' test requires more than an injury to a cognizable interest. It requires that the party seeking review be himself among the injured." . . .
>
> With respect to this aspect of the case, the Court of Appeals focused on the affidavits of two [members of the one of the plaintiff organizations]—Joyce Kelly and Amy Skilbred. Ms. Kelly stated that she traveled to Egypt in 1986 and "observed the traditional habitat of the endangered nile crocodile there and intend[s] to do so again, and hope[s] to observe the crocodile directly". . . . Ms. Skilbred averred that she traveled to Sri Lanka in 1981 and "observed th[e] habitat" of "endangered species such as the Asian elephant and the leopard" . . . [and] she "intend[s] to return to Sri Lanka in the future and hope[s] to be more fortunate in spotting at least the endangered elephant and leopard." When Ms. Skilbred was asked at a subsequent deposition if and when she had any plans to return to Sri Lanka, she reiterated that "I intend to go back to Sri Lanka," but confessed that she had no current plans: "I don't know [when]. There is a civil war going on right now. I don't know. Not next year, I will say. In the future."
>
> We shall assume for the sake of argument that these affidavits contain facts showing that certain agency-funded projects threaten listed species—though that is questionable. They plainly contain no facts, however, showing how damage to the species will produce "imminent" injury to Mses. Kelly and Skilbred. That the women "had visited" the areas of the projects before the projects commenced proves nothing. As we have said in a related context, " 'Past exposure to illegal conduct does not in itself show a present case or controversy regarding injunctive relief . . . if unaccompanied by any continuing, present adverse effects.' " *Lyons*. And the affiants' profession of an "inten[t]" to return to the places they had visited before—where they will presumably, this time, be deprived of the opportunity to observe animals of the endangered species—is simply not enough. Such "some day" intentions—without any description of concrete plans, or indeed even any specification of when the some day will be—do not support a finding of the "actual or imminent" injury that our cases require.

In a portion of the opinion speaking only for a plurality, Justice Scalia also found that the plaintiffs failed to demonstrate that the requested injunction would redress their injuries. Justice Kennedy, joined by Justice Souter, concurred in the judgment. Justice Stevens concurred in the judgment on the merits, but he would have found standing.

Justice Blackmun, joined by Justice O'Connor, dissented, arguing that the plaintiffs had raised genuine issues of fact as to whether Kelly or Skilbred would in fact be injured and therefore should not have lost at summary judgment. Further, the dissenters "fear[ed] the Court's demand for detailed descriptions of future conduct will do little to weed out those who are genuinely harmed from those who are not. More likely, it will resurrect a code-pleading formalism in federal court summary judgment practice, as federal courts . . . will demand more and more particularized showings of future harm. . . . A nurse turned down for a job on grounds of her race had better be prepared to show on what date she was prepared to start work, that she had arranged daycare for her child, and that she would not have accepted work at another hospital instead."

2. _Friends of the Earth, supra,_ Section A. In holding that the plaintiff organizations had standing to seek redress for Laidlaw's mercury discharges into the North Tyger River based on the organizations' members' concrete plans to use the area for recreation, the Court, per Justice Ginsburg, distinguished _Lyons_:

> In _Lyons_, we held that a plaintiff lacked standing to seek an injunction against the enforcement of a police chokehold policy because he could not credibly allege that he faced a realistic threat from the policy. In the footnote from _Lyons_ cited by the dissent, we noted that "[t]he reasonableness of Lyons' fear is dependent upon the likelihood of a recurrence of the allegedly unlawful conduct," and that his "subjective apprehensions" that such a recurrence would even take place were not enough to support standing. Here, in contrast, it is undisputed that Laidlaw's unlawful conduct—discharging pollutants in excess of permit limits—was occurring at the time the complaint was filed. Under _Lyons_, then, the only "subjective" issue here is "[t]he reasonableness of [the] fear" that led the affiants to respond to that concededly ongoing conduct by refraining from use of the North Tyger River and surrounding areas. Unlike the dissent, we see nothing "improbable" about the proposition that a company's continuous and pervasive illegal discharges of pollutants into a river would cause nearby residents to curtail their recreational use of that waterway and would subject them to other economic and aesthetic harms. The proposition is entirely reasonable, the District Court found it was true in this case, and that is enough for injury in fact.

Dissenting, Justice Scalia, joined by Justice Thomas, thought _Lyons_ required a more substantial showing: "At the very least, in the present case, one would expect to see evidence supporting the affidavits' bald assertions regarding decreasing recreational usage and declining home values, as well as evidence for the improbable proposition that Laidlaw's violations . . . are somehow responsible for these effects."

Are _Lujan_ and _Friends of the Earth_ faithful applications of _Lyons_? Are they consistent with one another? What do these cases reflect about the strictness of the _Lyons_ standard? About the importance of judges' factual assumptions about what is "likely"?

* * *

Lyons continues to cast a long shadow over civil rights litigation, even where neither federalism concerns nor police practices are implicated.

In late 2005, the New York Times revealed that, following the attacks of September 11, 2001, the Bush Administration began secretly conducting warrantless surveillance of telephone and email communications of individuals and organizations within the United States. A group of organizational and individual plaintiffs sued to enjoin the program as unconstitutional and a violation of the Foreign Intelligence Surveillance Act of 1978 (FISA). The government invoked a privilege for "state secrets" to prevent discovery of the contours of the program. The plaintiffs—lawyers, journalists, and academics (or organizations thereof) who regularly spoke with individuals suspected of terrorism—nonetheless claimed their communications would likely be monitored because they fell within the scope of the program, as revealed in public statements by administration officials: communications "where one party to the communication is located outside the United States and the NSA has 'a reasonable basis to conclude that one party to the communication is a member of al Qaeda, affiliated with al Qaeda, or a member of an organization affiliated with al Qaeda, or working in support of al Qaeda.'" The district court held that the plaintiffs had standing and enjoined the warrantless surveillance program in August 2006, but in *ACLU v. NSA*, 493 F.3d 644 (6th Cir. 2007), a splintered panel of the Sixth Circuit with no majority opinion vacated and ordered the case dismissed for lack of standing. The Supreme Court denied certiorari.

Meanwhile, the administration went to Congress to seek additional surveillance powers. The resulting legislation, the FISA Amendments Act, was enacted in 2008. It was quickly challenged in court, with a theory of standing similar to the one pursued in *ACLU v. NSA*. This challenge did reach the Supreme Court.

Clapper v. Amnesty International
568 U.S. 398 (2013)

■ *Justice* ALITO *delivered the opinion of the Court.*

In 1978, after years of debate, Congress enacted the Foreign Intelligence Surveillance Act (FISA) to authorize and regulate certain governmental electronic surveillance of communications for foreign intelligence purposes. . . .

Congress authorized judges of the Foreign Intelligence Surveillance Court (FISC) to approve electronic surveillance for foreign intelligence purposes if there is probable cause to believe that "the target of the electronic surveillance is a foreign power or an agent of a foreign power," and that each of the specific "facilities or places at which the electronic surveillance is directed is being used, or is about to be used, by a foreign power or an agent of a foreign power." . . .

When Congress enacted the FISA Amendments Act of 2008 (FISA Amendments Act), it left much of FISA intact, but it "established a new and independent source of intelligence collection authority, beyond that granted in traditional FISA." As relevant here, § 702 of FISA, 50 U.S.C. § 1881a, which was enacted as part of the FISA Amendments Act, supplements pre-existing FISA authority by creating a new framework under which the Government may seek the FISC's authorization of certain foreign intelligence surveillance targeting the communications of non-U.S. persons located abroad. Unlike traditional FISA surveillance, § 1881a does not require the Government to demonstrate probable cause that the target of the electronic surveillance is a foreign power or agent of a foreign power. And, unlike traditional FISA, § 1881a does not require the Government to specify the nature and location of each of the particular facilities or places at which the electronic surveillance will occur. . . .

Respondents are attorneys and human rights, labor, legal, and media organizations whose work allegedly requires them to engage in sensitive and sometimes privileged telephone and e-mail communications with colleagues, clients, sources, and other individuals located abroad. Respondents believe that some of the people with whom they exchange foreign intelligence information are likely targets of surveillance under § 1881a. Specifically, respondents claim that they communicate by telephone and e-mail with people the Government "believes or believed to be associated with terrorist organizations," "people located in geographic areas that are a special focus" of the Government's counterterrorism or diplomatic efforts, and activists who oppose governments that are supported by the United States Government. Respondents claim that § 1881a compromises their ability to locate witnesses, cultivate sources, obtain information, and communicate confidential information to their clients. Respondents also assert that they "have ceased engaging" in certain telephone and e-mail conversations. According to respondents, the threat of surveillance will compel them to travel abroad in order to have in-person conversations. In addition, respondents declare that they have undertaken "costly and burdensome measures" to protect the confidentiality of sensitive communications.

[Respondents filed a facial challenge to the FISA Amendments Act. The district court dismissed for lack of standing. The Second Circuit reversed.] . . .

To establish Article III standing, an injury must be "concrete, particularized, and actual or imminent; fairly traceable to the challenged action; and redressable by a favorable ruling." "Although imminence is concededly a somewhat elastic concept, it cannot be stretched beyond its purpose, which is to ensure that the alleged injury is not too speculative for Article III purposes—that the injury is *certainly* impending." . . . "[A]llegations of *possible* future injury" are not sufficient.

Respondents assert that they can establish injury in fact that is fairly traceable to § 1881a because there is an objectively reasonable likelihood that their communications with their foreign contacts will be intercepted under § 1881a at some point in the future. This argument fails. [The] "objectively reasonable likelihood" standard is inconsistent with our requirement that "threatened injury must be certainly impending to constitute injury in fact." Furthermore, respondents' argument rests on their highly speculative fear that: (1) the Government will decide to target the communications of non-U.S. persons with whom they communicate; (2) in doing so, the Government will choose to invoke its authority under § 1881a rather than utilizing another method of surveillance; (3) the Article III judges who serve on the Foreign Intelligence Surveillance Court will conclude that the Government's proposed surveillance procedures satisfy

§ 1881a's many safeguards and are consistent with the Fourth Amendment; (4) the Government will succeed in intercepting the communications of respondents' contacts; and (5) respondents will be parties to the particular communications that the Government intercepts. [This] highly attenuated chain of possibilities does not satisfy the requirement that threatened injury must be certainly impending. Moreover, even if respondents could demonstrate injury in fact, the second link in the above-described chain of contingencies—which amounts to mere speculation about whether surveillance would be under § 1881a or some other authority—shows that respondents cannot [show any injury would be] satisfy the fairly traceable to § 1881a.

First, it is speculative whether the Government will imminently target communications to which respondents are parties. Section 1881a expressly provides that respondents, who are U.S. persons, cannot be targeted for surveillance under § 1881a. . . . Accordingly, respondents' theory necessarily rests on their assertion that the Government will target *other individuals*—namely, their foreign contacts.

Yet respondents have no actual knowledge of the Government's § 1881a targeting practices. Instead, respondents merely speculate and make assumptions about whether their communications with their foreign contacts will be acquired under § 1881a. For example, journalist Christopher Hedges states: "I have no choice but to *assume* that any of my international communications *may* be subject to government surveillance, and I have to make decisions . . . in light of that *assumption*." Similarly, attorney Scott McKay asserts that, "[b]ecause of the [FISA Amendments Act], we now have to *assume* that every one of our international communications *may* be monitored by the government." "The party invoking federal jurisdiction bears the burden of establishing" standing—and, at the summary judgment stage, such a party "can no longer rest on . . . 'mere allegations,' but must 'set forth' by affidavit or other evidence 'specific facts.'" Respondents, however, have set forth no specific facts demonstrating that the communications of their foreign contacts will be targeted. Moreover, because § 1881a at most *authorizes*—but does not *mandate* or *direct*—the surveillance that respondents fear, respondents' allegations are necessarily conjectural. . . .

Second, even if respondents could demonstrate that the targeting of their foreign contacts is imminent, respondents can only speculate as to whether the Government will seek to use § 1881a-authorized surveillance (rather than other methods) to do so. . . .

Third, even if respondents could show that the Government will seek the Foreign Intelligence Surveillance Court's authorization to acquire the communications of respondents' foreign contacts under § 1881a, respondents can only speculate as to whether that court will authorize such surveillance. In the past, we have been reluctant to endorse standing theories that require guesswork as to how independent decisionmakers will exercise their judgment. . . .

Fourth, even if the Government were to obtain the Foreign Intelligence Surveillance Court's approval to target respondents' foreign contacts under § 1881a, it is unclear whether the Government would succeed in acquiring the communications of respondents' foreign contacts. And fifth, even if the Government were to conduct surveillance of respondents' foreign contacts, respondents can only speculate as to whether *their own communications* with their foreign contacts would be incidentally acquired.

In sum, respondents' speculative chain of possibilities does not establish that injury based on potential future surveillance is certainly impending or is fairly traceable to § 1881a.[5]

Respondents' alternative argument—namely, that they can establish standing based on the measures that they have undertaken to avoid § 1881a-authorized surveillance—fares no better. Respondents assert that they are suffering ongoing injuries that are fairly traceable to § 1881a because the risk of surveillance under § 1881a requires them to take costly and burdensome measures to protect the confidentiality of their communications. Respondents claim, for instance, that the threat of surveillance sometimes compels them to avoid certain e-mail and phone conversations, to "tal[k] in generalities rather than specifics," or to travel so that they can have in-person conversations. . . .

[Allowing plaintiffs to] establish standing by asserting that they suffer present costs and burdens that are based on a fear of surveillance, so long as that fear is not "fanciful, paranoid, or otherwise unreasonable[,]" . . . improperly waters down the fundamental requirements of Article III. . . . [R]espondents cannot manufacture standing merely by inflicting harm on themselves based on their fears of hypothetical future harm that is not certainly impending. Any ongoing injuries that respondents are suffering are not fairly traceable to § 1881a.

If the law were otherwise, an enterprising plaintiff would be able to secure a lower standard for Article III standing simply by making an expenditure based on a nonparanoid fear. . . . [R]espondents could, "for the price of a plane ticket, . . . transform their standing burden from one requiring a showing of actual or imminent . . . interception to one requiring a showing that their subjective fear of such interception is not fanciful, irrational, or clearly unreasonable." Thus, allowing respondents to bring this action based on costs they incurred in response to a speculative threat would be tantamount to accepting a repackaged version of respondents' first failed theory of standing.

Another reason that respondents' present injuries are not fairly traceable to § 1881a is that even before § 1881a was enacted, they had a similar incentive to engage in many of the countermeasures that they are now taking. For instance, respondent Scott McKay's declaration describes [his] "knowledge" that thousands of communications involving one of his clients were monitored in the past. But this surveillance was conducted pursuant to FISA authority that predated § 1881a. Thus, because the Government was allegedly conducting

---

5. Our cases do not uniformly require plaintiffs to demonstrate that it is literally certain that the harms they identify will come about. In some instances, we have found standing based on a "substantial risk" that the harm will occur, which may prompt plaintiffs to reasonably incur costs to mitigate or avoid that harm. But to the extent that the "substantial risk" standard is relevant and is distinct from the "clearly impending" requirement, respondents fall short of even that standard, in light of the attenuated chain of inferences necessary to find harm here. . . .

surveillance of Mr. McKay's client before Congress enacted § 1881a, it is difficult to see how the safeguards that Mr. McKay now claims to have implemented can be traced to § 1881a.

Because respondents do not face a threat of certainly impending interception under § 1881a, the costs that they have incurred to avoid surveillance are simply the product of their fear of surveillance. . . . "[A]llegations of a subjective 'chill' are not an adequate substitute for a claim of specific present objective harm or a threat of specific future harm." . . .

[Finally], " '[t]he assumption that if respondents have no standing to sue, no one would have standing, is not a reason to find standing.' " . . .

We hold that respondents lack Article III standing because they cannot demonstrate that the future injury they purportedly fear is certainly impending and because they cannot manufacture standing by incurring costs in anticipation of non-imminent harm. . . .

■ *Justice* BREYER, *with whom Justice* GINSBURG, *Justice* SOTOMAYOR, *and Justice* KAGAN *join, dissenting.*

The plaintiffs' standing depends upon the likelihood that the Government, acting under the authority of 50 U.S.C. § 1881a, will harm them by intercepting at least some of their private, foreign, telephone, or e-mail conversations. In my view, this harm is not "speculative." Indeed it is as likely to take place as are most future events that commonsense inference and ordinary knowledge of human nature tell us will happen. . . .

First, the plaintiffs have engaged, and continue to engage, in electronic communications of a kind that the 2008 amendment, but not the prior Act, authorizes the Government to intercept. These communications include discussions with family members of those detained at Guantanamo, friends and acquaintances of those persons, and investigators, experts and others with knowledge of circumstances related to terrorist activities. . . .

Second, the plaintiffs have a strong *motive* to engage in, and the Government has a strong *motive* to listen to, conversations of the kind described. A lawyer representing a client normally seeks to learn the circumstances surrounding the crime (or the civil wrong) of which the client is accused. . . . Journalists and human rights workers have strong similar motives to conduct conversations of this kind. At the same time, the Government has a strong motive to conduct surveillance of conversations that contain material of this kind. The Government, after all, seeks to learn as much as it can reasonably learn about suspected terrorists. . . .

Third, the Government's *past behavior* shows that it has sought, and hence will in all likelihood continue to seek, information about alleged terrorists and detainees through means that include surveillance of electronic communications. . . . [P]laintiff Scott McKay states that the Government (under the authority of the pre-2008 law) "intercepted some 10,000 telephone calls and 20,000 email communications involving [his client] Mr. Al-Hussayen."

Fourth, the Government has the *capacity* to conduct electronic surveillance of the kind at issue. *[Justice Breyer here cites a string of sources for the proposition that the government's technological capacity is quite broad.]* Of course, to exercise this capacity the Government must have intelligence court authorization. But the Government rarely files requests that fail to meet the statutory criteria. See Letter from Ronald Weich, Assistant Attorney General, to Joseph R. Biden, Jr., 1 (Apr. 30, 2012) (In 2011, of the 1,676 applications to the intelligence court, two were withdrawn by the Government, and the remaining 1,674 were approved, 30 with some modification). . . .

[W]e need only assume that the Government is doing its job (to find out about, and combat, terrorism) in order to conclude that there is a high probability that the Government will intercept at least some electronic communication to which at least some of the plaintiffs are parties. The majority is wrong when it describes the harm threatened plaintiffs as "speculative."

The majority more plausibly says that the plaintiffs have failed to show that the threatened harm is "*certainly impending.*" But, as the majority appears to concede [at footnote 5], *certainty* is not, and never has been, the touchstone of standing. The future is inherently uncertain. Yet federal courts frequently entertain actions for injunctions and for declaratory relief aimed at preventing future activities that are reasonably likely or highly likely, but not absolutely certain, to take place. . . .

[C]ourts have often found *probabilistic* injuries sufficient to support standing. In *Duke Power Co. v. Carolina Environmental Study Group, Inc.,* for example, the plaintiffs, a group of individuals living near a proposed nuclear powerplant, challenged . . . a statute that limited the plant's liability in the case of a nuclear accident. . . . The Court found standing in part due to "our generalized concern about exposure to radiation and the apprehension flowing from the *uncertainty* about the health and genetic consequences of even small emissions." . . .

How could the law be otherwise? Suppose that a federal court faced a claim by homeowners that (allegedly) unlawful dam-building practices created a high risk that their homes would be flooded. Would the court deny them standing on the ground that the risk of flood was only 60, rather than 90, percent? . . .

In some standing cases, the Court has found that a reasonable probability of *future* injury comes accompanied with *present* injury that takes the form of reasonable efforts to mitigate the threatened effects of the future injury or to prevent it from occurring. Thus, in *Monsanto Co. v. Geertson Seed Farms*, plaintiffs, a group of conventional alfalfa growers, challenged an agency decision to deregulate genetically engineered alfalfa. They claimed that deregulation would harm them because their neighbors would plant the genetically engineered seed, bees would obtain pollen from the neighbors' plants, and the bees would then (harmfully) contaminate their own conventional alfalfa with the genetically modified gene. The lower courts had found a "reasonable probability" that this injury would occur.

Without expressing views about that probability, we found standing because the plaintiffs would suffer present harm by trying to combat the threat.

The plaintiffs . . . would have to take "measures to minimize the likelihood of potential contamination and to ensure an adequate supply of non-genetically-engineered alfalfa." . . .

Virtually identical circumstances are present here. Plaintiff McKay, for example, points out that, when he communicates abroad about, or in the interests of, a client (*e.g.*, a client accused of terrorism), he must "make an assessment" whether his "client's interests would be compromised" should the Government "acquire the communications." If so, he must either forgo the communication or travel abroad. . . . See also *Friends of the Earth* (holding that plaintiffs who curtailed their recreational activities on a river due to reasonable concerns about the effect of pollutant discharges into that river had standing). . . .

In sum, as the Court concedes, the word "certainly" in the phrase "certainly impending" does not refer to absolute certainty. As our case law demonstrates, what the Constitution requires is something more akin to "reasonable probability" or "high probability." The use of some such standard is all that is necessary here to ensure the actual concrete injury that the Constitution demands. . . .

Notes and Questions

1. Has *Amnesty International* merely applied *Lyons* or extended it? If the latter, in what way(s) has *Lyons* been extended?

2. The majority repeats a principle of standing law that the Court has espoused for decades: "[T]he assumption that if respondents have no standing to sue, no one would have standing, is not a reason to find standing." This principle might be the most extreme aspect of the standing doctrine; the Court is acknowledging that some injuries—potentially some constitutional violations, even—are effectively beyond the reach of the courts. How can this result be reconciled with the rule of law? What values might the majority invoke to justify it?

3. Consider plaintiffs' attempt to frame their injuries as reasonable responses to the possibility of surveillance rather than a likelihood of actually being surveilled. The majority views this analytical move as asserting "a repackaged version of respondents' first failed theory of standing." But in *Friends of the Earth* (on which the *Amnesty International* plaintiffs relied), changes in plaintiffs' conduct in response to the defendants' mercury discharges in a river were the crux of plaintiffs' successful standing theory. What's the difference? Does the Court now consider any actions by plaintiffs "self-inflicted" and therefore not a basis to find injury? Or is the Court making a judgment that the plaintiffs' conduct in one case was more reasonable than in the other? What standard governs such a judgment?

4. People often take precautions against dangers that seem remote—think of all the types of perils for which people buy insurance. In light of the human tendency to guard against even low-probability risks, what's wrong with finding injury based on the plaintiffs' precautionary steps here?

5. One of the majority's most significant concerns is manipulation of the standing analysis—that if plaintiffs could point to their own conduct as evidence of harm, then they could, in the majority's words, "for the price of a plane ticket" effectively purchase standing. Does the dissent answer this concern? Then again, wouldn't purchasing a plane ticket have solved the standing deficiency in *Lujan*? Why is this tactic more acceptable in one context than the other?

Applications

1. Defining the standard.   The majority and dissent debate the formulation of the *Lyons* likelihood standard: Is it a "certainly impending" injury or a "substantial risk" of injury? In light of the majority's determination in footnote 5 that plaintiffs fail under either formulation, the "certainly impending" formulation could be characterized as dicta.

The Justices may have lost interest in this debate. In *Department of Commerce v. New York*, 139 S. Ct. 2551 (2019), discussed in more detail in the next note, the Court considered a challenge to the decision by the U.S. Department of Commerce to add to the decennial census a question about individuals' citizenship. The Court stated that "future injuries . . . 'may suffice if the threatened injury is certainly impending, or there is a substantial risk that the harm will occur.'" The Court used the same formulation in *Susan B. Anthony List v. Driehaus*, 573 U.S. 149 (2014).

Do these decisions show that the standards are interchangeable? If so, why not just return to the "substantial risk" formulation? If not, what is the purpose of including both a higher and a lower standard in the disjunctive, permitting plaintiffs to satisfy either one?

2. A jurisprudence of "predictable effect"?   After the Court's sweeping rejection of speculative injuries in *Amnesty International*, the standing discussion in *Department of Commerce v. New York*, 139 S. Ct. 2551 (2019), may seem surprising. That case, as noted, was a challenge to the proposed addition of a citizenship question to the census. Plaintiffs were states, counties, cities, and non-governmental organizations who claimed that inclusion of this question would depress the response rate and cause various types of injury. The Court's analysis of standing, with which no Justice disagreed, proceeded as follows in an opinion by Chief Justice Roberts:

> Respondents assert a number of injuries—diminishment of political representation, loss of federal funds, degradation of census data, and diversion of resources—all of which turn on their expectation that reinstating a citizenship question will depress the census response rate and lead to an inaccurate population count. Several States with a disproportionate share of noncitizens, for example, anticipate losing a seat in Congress or qualifying for less federal funding if their populations are undercounted. . . .
>
> The District Court concluded that the evidence at trial established a sufficient likelihood that the reinstatement of a citizenship question would result in noncitizen households responding to the census at lower rates than other groups, which in turn would cause them to be undercounted and lead to many of respondents'

asserted injuries. For purposes of standing, these findings of fact were not so suspect as to be clearly erroneous.

We therefore agree that at least some respondents have Article III standing. Several state respondents here have shown that if noncitizen households are undercounted by as little as 2%—lower than the District Court's 5.8% prediction—they will lose out on federal funds that are distributed on the basis of state population. That is a sufficiently concrete and imminent injury to satisfy Article III, and there is no dispute that a ruling in favor of respondents would redress that harm.

The Government contends, however, that any harm to respondents is not fairly traceable to the Secretary's decision, because such harm depends on the independent action of third parties choosing to violate their legal duty to respond to the census. The chain of causation is made even more tenuous, the Government argues, by the fact that such intervening, unlawful third-party action would be motivated by unfounded fears that the Federal Government will itself break the law by using noncitizens' answers against them for law enforcement purposes. The Government invokes our steady refusal to "endorse standing theories that rest on speculation about the decisions of independent actors," *Amnesty Int'l*, particularly speculation about future unlawful conduct, *Lyons*.

But we are satisfied that, in these circumstances, respondents have met their burden of showing that third parties will likely react in predictable ways to the citizenship question, even if they do so unlawfully and despite the requirement that the Government keep individual answers confidential. The evidence at trial established that noncitizen households have historically responded to the census at lower rates than other groups, and the District Court did not clearly err in crediting the Census Bureau's theory that the discrepancy is likely attributable at least in part to noncitizens' reluctance to answer a citizenship question. Respondents' theory of standing thus does not rest on mere speculation about the decisions of third parties; it relies instead on the predictable effect of Government action on the decisions of third parties.

How does this analysis square with *Lyons* and *Amnesty International*? The Court notes that *Lyons* involved "speculation about future unlawful conduct," but so does this case—as the Court notes, it's unlawful not to answer the census. And even if that type of violation is qualitatively different than the type of traffic infraction the Justices were thinking about in *Lyons*, the plaintiffs in *Amnesty International* did not need to engage in criminal activity at all for the harm they feared to materialize, and yet the Court refused to speculate about possible harms. Further, the Court's reliance on how "noncitizen households have historically responded to the census" and "the predictable effect of Government action on the decisions of third parties" seems in conflict with the reasoning of prior cases, which have held that historical harm is no guarantee of future harm and that something close to "certainty" is required in speculating about future events.

One way to reconcile these cases is to posit that the Court simply made a different predictive judgment—based on detailed district court findings—about the likelihood of a census undercount as compared to the likelihood that particular individuals will be surveilled by a secret government program. Are there any consistent metrics by which the Court assesses likelihood? Or is it all ad hoc judgments? In light of *Department of Commerce*, what litigation strategies should plaintiffs seeking injunctive relief pursue?

3. Reframing the injury.   *ACLU v. Clapper,* 785 F.3d 787 (2d Cir. 2015), concerned a challenge to the NSA's "telephone metadata program" under which the NSA "collects in bulk 'on an ongoing daily basis' the metadata associated with telephone calls made by and to Americans, and aggregates those metadata into a repository or data bank that can later be queried." (Telephone metadata, the court explained, "do not include the voice content of telephone conversations" but do include "details about telephone calls, including, for example, the length of a call, the phone number from which the call was made, and the phone number called" as well as, sometimes, "information about a caller's general location.")

The court of appeals explained the privacy implications of the case in these terms:

> That telephone metadata do not directly reveal the content of telephone calls, however, does not vitiate the privacy concerns arising out of the government's bulk collection of such data. Appellants and amici take pains to emphasize the startling amount of detailed information metadata can reveal—"information that could traditionally only be obtained by examining the contents of communications" and that is therefore "often a proxy for content." For example, a call to a single-purpose telephone number such as a "hotline" might reveal that an individual is: a victim of domestic violence or rape; a veteran; suffering from an addiction of one type or another; contemplating suicide; or reporting a crime. Metadata can reveal civil, political, or religious affiliations; they can also reveal an individual's social status, or whether and when he or she is involved in intimate relationships.

The government claimed that § 215 of the USA PATRIOT Act, a broad post-September 11 national security statute, authorized the program. Before considering the merits, the court of appeals assessed plaintiffs' standing:

> Americans first learned about the telephone metadata program that appellants now challenge on June 5, 2013, when the British newspaper The Guardian published a FISC order leaked by former government contractor Edward Snowden. The order directed Verizon Business Network Services, Inc., a telephone company, to produce to the NSA . . . call detail records, every day, on all telephone calls made through its systems or using its services where one or both ends of the call are located in the United States.
>
> After the order was published, the government acknowledged that it was part of a broader program of bulk collection of telephone metadata from other telecommunications providers carried out pursuant to § 215. It is now undisputed that the government has been collecting telephone metadata information in bulk under § 215 since at least May 2006, when the FISC first authorized it to do so . . . .
>
> The government has disclosed additional FISC orders reauthorizing the program. FISC orders must be renewed every 90 days, and the program has therefore been renewed 41 times since May 2006. Most recently, the program was reauthorized by the FISC on February 26, 2015; that authorization expires on June 1, 2015. . . .
>
> On June 11, 2013, the [ACLU and its New York affiliate]—current and former Verizon customers, respectively—sued the government officials responsible for administering the telephone metadata program, challenging the program on

both statutory and constitutional grounds and seeking declaratory and injunctive relief. . . .

Appellants in this case have . . . established standing to sue, as the district court correctly held. Appellants here need not speculate that the government has collected, or may in the future collect, their call records. To the contrary, the government's own orders demonstrate that appellants' call records are indeed among those collected as part of the telephone metadata program. Nor has the government disputed that claim. It argues instead that any alleged injuries here depend on the government's reviewing the information collected, and that appellants have not shown anything more than a "speculative prospect that their telephone numbers would ever be used as a selector to query, or be included in the results of queries of, the telephony metadata."

But the government's argument misapprehends what is required to establish standing in a case such as this one. Appellants . . . alleg[e] injury from the very collection of their telephone metadata. . . . "[A] violation of the [Fourth] Amendment is fully accomplished at the time of an unreasonable governmental intrusion." If the telephone metadata program is unlawful, appellants have suffered a concrete and particularized injury fairly traceable to the challenged program and redressable by a favorable ruling.

Amnesty International does not hold otherwise. There, the Supreme Court, reversing our decision, held that respondents had not established standing because they could not show that the government was surveilling them, or that such surveillance was "certainly impending." Instead, the Supreme Court stated that respondents' standing arguments were based on a "speculative chain of possibilities" . . . .

Here, appellants' alleged injury requires no speculation whatsoever as to how events will unfold under § 215—appellants' records (among those of numerous others) have been targeted for seizure by the government; the government has used the challenged statute to effect that seizure; the orders have been approved by the FISC; and the records have been collected. *Amnesty International*'s "speculative chain of possibilities" is, in this context, a reality.

On the merits, the court held that § 215 did not authorize the telephone metadata program and reversed the dismissal of the case. However, in light of the then-ongoing debate in Congress over the reauthorization of the USA PATRIOT Act, which was set to expire a few weeks after the court's decision, the court remanded to the district court to consider the appropriate relief.

Congress subsequently allowed certain provisions of the USA PATRIOT Act, including § 215, to expire on June 1, 2015. The following day, Congress enacted the USA FREEDOM Act, which reinstated some but not all of the surveillance authority granted under the prior statute and required that bulk collection of call records under § 215 end within 180 days. *See* Pub. L. No. 114-23, 129 Stat. 268, §§ 103, 109.

Does *ACLU v. Clapper* demonstrate that the *Amnesty International* standard is reasonable because it does not doom all challenges to national security surveillance? Or does the fact that a major national-security leak was required to enable plaintiffs to establish standing highlight the standard's unreasonable strictness?

4. Overcoming the *Lyons* problem.   Where the injury cannot be reframed, as in *ACLU v. Clapper*, what does it take for plaintiffs to overcome a *Lyons* problem? Here are two examples:

(a) *Floyd v. City of New York*, 283 F.R.D. 153, 169-70 (S.D.N.Y. 2012), was a landmark challenge to the New York Police Department's practice of stopping and frisking a great many civilians; the plaintiffs charged that the practice was both racially skewed and driven by numerical goals rather than the individualized suspicion required by the Fourth Amendment. The court found standing to seek injunctive relief:

> David Ourlicht, the fourth plaintiff, indisputably does have standing[;] . . . "the presence of one party with standing is sufficient to satisfy Article III's case-or-controversy requirement." First, unlike Lyons, who alleged only one past instance of unconstitutional police behavior, Ourlicht was stopped by NYPD officers three times in 2008 and once again in 2010, after this lawsuit was filed. "The possibility of recurring injury ceases to be speculative when actual repeated incidents are documented." Second, unlike [Lyons] . . . Ourlicht's risk of future injury does not depend on his being arrested for unlawful conduct and so he cannot avoid that injury by following the law. The risk of injury is not based on a string of unlikely contingencies: according to his sworn affidavit, Ourlicht was stopped and frisked while going about his daily life—walking down the sidewalk, sitting on a bench, getting into a car.
>
> Finally, . . . the frequency of alleged injuries inflicted by the practices at issue here creates a likelihood of future injury sufficient to address any standing concerns. In *Lyons*, the police department's challenged policies were responsible for ten deaths; here, the police department has conducted over 2.8 million stops over six years and its paperwork indicates that, at the very least, 60,000 of the stops were unconstitutional (because they were based on nothing more than a person's "furtive movement"). Every day, the NYPD conducted 1200 stops; every day, the NYPD conducted nearly thirty facially unlawful stops based on nothing more than "subjective, promiscuous appeals to an ineffable intuition." In the face of these widespread practices, Ourlicht's risk of future injury is "'real and immediate,' not 'conjectural' or 'hypothetical,'" and he satisfies Article III's standing requirements.

(b) *In re Navy Chaplaincy*, 697 F.3d 1171, 1176-77 (D.C. Cir. 2012), involved a claim of "denominational discrimination" by "non-liturgical Protestant" military chaplains, who challenged the Navy's policy of basing promotions on the secret votes of a small selection board led by the Chief of Chaplains. "Relying on statistical analysis by their expert and other evidence, [plaintiffs] assert that non-liturgical Protestant chaplains are promoted to higher ranks at significantly lower rates than are liturgical Protestant and Catholic chaplains, and that candidates are more likely to be recommended for promotion when they share the denomination of the chaplains who sit on the selection board." The district court denied standing, but the court of appeals reversed. There was no question that plaintiffs would be considered for promotion in the future; the key dispute concerned whether they were likely to face discrimination. The court held that the likelihood that the challenged policies would result in discrimination was "sufficiently non-speculative" because, unlike in *Lyons*, "plaintiffs ha[d] identified concrete and consistently-implemented policies claimed to produce [the alleged] injury." The Court reasoned that "chaplains inclined to vote on the basis of their religious preferences may be more likely to do so under the cover of secret ballots. Moreover, it goes without saying that the small size of selection boards gives potentially biased chaplains more influence over the outcome of the proceedings."

Are these cases consistent with *Lyons* and *Amnesty International* in terms of the amount of speculation in which they are willing to engage? Does *Floyd* offer plaintiffs in police cases a reliable theory on which to distinguish *Lyons* in the future, or is *Floyd* the exception that proves the strictness of the rule? Is *Floyd's* use of statistics in demonstrating the likelihood Ourlicht will be stopped again in tension with *Lyons'* rejection of a theory of likelihood based on "the odds" of a future violation, or is it distinguishable because the particular "odds" in *Floyd* were so much higher? Does the secrecy of the procedures in *Navy Chaplaincy*, which weighed in plaintiffs' favor there, look different after *Amnesty International*, which afforded plaintiffs no allowance for the aspects of the government's surveillance practices they were in no position to know?

2. CAUSATION AND REDRESSABILITY

We consider causation and redressability together, because they often overlap: "[I]f the defendant is the cause of the plaintiff's injury, then it is likely that halting the defendant's behavior will stop the injury." Erwin Chemerinsky, *Federal Jurisdiction* § 2.3.3, at 78 (7th ed. 2016).

Warth v. Seldin, 422 U.S. 490 (1975), illustrates how claims of injury that are too attenuated from the challenged conduct are insufficient to support causation. In *Warth*, a nonprofit organization and several residents of Rochester, New York, alleged that the zoning practices of the neighboring suburb of Penfield had the effect of excluding low-income and minority would-be residents from Penfield. The court rejected standing on a variety of grounds. As to a group of plaintiffs who alleged that they attempted to find housing for themselves in Penfield but were unable to do so, the Court held that the failure to establish causation doomed justiciability:

> None of them has ever resided in Penfield; each claims at least implicitly that he desires, or has desired, to do so. Each asserts, moreover, that he made some effort, at some time, to locate housing in Penfield that was at once within his means and adequate for his family's needs. Each claims that his efforts proved fruitless. We may assume, as petitioners allege, that respondents' actions have contributed, perhaps substantially, to the cost of housing in Penfield. But there remains the question whether petitioners' inability to locate suitable housing in Penfield reasonably can be said to have resulted, in any concretely demonstrable way, from respondents' alleged constitutional and statutory infractions. Petitioners must allege facts from which it reasonably could be inferred that, absent the respondents' restrictive zoning practices, there is a substantial probability that they would have been able to purchase or lease in Penfield and that, if the court affords the relief requested, the asserted inability of petitioners will be removed.
>
> We find the record devoid of the necessary allegations. . . .
>
> [B]y their own admission, realization of petitioners' desire to live in Penfield always has depended on the efforts and willingness of third parties to build low- and moderate-cost housing. The record specifically refers to only two such

efforts . . . [and] the record is devoid of any indication that these projects, or other like projects, would have satisfied petitioners' needs at prices they could afford, or that, were the court to remove the obstructions attributable to respondents, such relief would benefit petitioners. Indeed, petitioners' descriptions of their individual financial situations and housing needs suggest precisely the contrary—that their inability to reside in Penfield is the consequence of the economics of the area housing market, rather than of respondents' assertedly illegal acts. In short, the facts alleged fail to support an actionable causal relationship between Penfield's zoning practices and petitioners' asserted injury.

Justice Douglas dissented, charging that the majority "reads the complaint and the record with antagonistic eyes" out of a desire to avoid the sensitive subject matter of the case. Justice Brennan, joined by Justices White and Marshall, dissented as well, arguing that the majority required too detailed a level of proof of causation prior to discovery.

Standing also failed for lack of causation in *Allen v. Wright*, 468 U.S. 737 (1984), in which parents of African-American schoolchildren in districts undergoing desegregation sued the IRS for its alleged laxness in enforcing a provision of federal tax law denying tax-exempt status to racially discriminatory private schools. The plaintiffs alleged that the agency's lackluster enforcement permitted the expansion of discriminatory private schools, which as a result could enroll more white students fleeing public school systems implementing desegregation orders and thereby diminish the effectiveness of those orders in enabling African-American students who remained in the public school system to receive "a desegregated education." The Court rejected this theory of standing:

> The diminished ability of respondents' children to receive a desegregated education would be fairly traceable to unlawful IRS grants of tax exemptions only if there were enough racially discriminatory private schools receiving tax exemptions in respondents' communities for withdrawal of those exemptions to make an appreciable difference in public school integration. Respondents have made no such allegation. It is, first, uncertain how many racially discriminatory private schools are in fact receiving tax exemptions. Moreover, it is entirely speculative . . . whether withdrawal of a tax exemption from any particular school would lead the school to change its policies. It is just as speculative whether any given parent of a child attending such a private school would decide to transfer the child to public school as a result of any changes in educational or financial policy made by the private school once it was threatened with loss of tax-exempt status. It is also pure speculation whether, in a particular community, a large enough number of the numerous relevant school officials and parents would reach decisions that collectively would have a significant impact on the racial composition of the public schools.
>
> The links in the chain of causation between the challenged Government conduct and the asserted injury are far too weak for the chain as a whole to sustain respondents' standing.

Justice Marshall did not participate. Dissenting, Justice Brennan argued that the majority ignored plaintiffs' identification of thirty-two specific private schools that discriminated and continued to receive tax-exempt status; eighteen of these were in one city, Memphis, that was under court order to desegregate. Thus, Justice Brennan argued, "there can be little doubt that the respondents have identified communities containing 'enough racially discriminatory private schools receiving tax exemptions . . . to make an appreciable difference in public school integration.'"

Justice Stevens's dissent, joined by Justice Blackmun, added that causation was satisfied by reference to general principles as well:

> [W]hen something becomes more expensive, less of it will be purchased. . . . If racially discriminatory private schools lose the "cash grants" that flow from the operation of the statutes, the education they provide will become more expensive and hence less of their services will be purchased. . . . Thus, the laws of economics . . . compel the conclusion that the injury respondents have alleged—the increased segregation of their children's schools because of the ready availability of private schools that admit whites only—will be redressed if these schools' operations are inhibited through the denial of preferential tax treatment.

Both the *Lyons* line of cases and the Court's analysis of the causation and redressability prongs of standing prohibit plaintiffs from relying on excessive speculation. They differ insofar as one analysis (*Lyons*) concerns speculation about whether the claimed injury will occur, whereas the other (causation) concerns speculation about the link between a recognized injury and the defendants' conduct.

Is speculation or attenuation more justifiable in one context than the other? What's wrong with speculation, anyway? Judgments about how likely certain events are to occur drive judicial decisionmaking all the time—from tort law (was this injury foreseeable?) to the Fourth Amendment (would a reasonable person have believed that evidence of a crime would be found in this particular place?). Is speculation somehow less justifiable in the context of standing analysis? The Court seems to think so; why?

What principles guide the Court's judgment about when speculation is permissible in establishing standing? Or are the three prongs of the standing test sufficiently malleable that the Justices are free to import their own intuitions about how the world works and their own inclinations about whether the courts ought to hear particular cases?

C. MOOTNESS AND ITS EXCEPTIONS

Standing is generally a greater obstacle than mootness to civil rights suits seeking injunctive relief, because the plaintiff bears the burden of establishing standing, and there are no exceptions to the standing requirements. Still, mootness can pose substantial challenges as well.

The basic rule of mootness is simple: A case becomes moot when the issues are not "live," meaning that "it is impossible for a court to grant any effectual relief whatever to the prevailing party." *Chafin v. Chafin*, 568 U.S. 165, 172 (2013) (citation and internal quotation marks omitted).

For instance, in *DeFunis v. Odegaard*, 416 U.S. 312 (1974) (per curiam), the Court held that a law student's challenge to the consideration of race in the admissions process at the University of Washington Law School had become moot, because as a result of a lower court ruling in his favor, he was admitted to the school, and by the time the case reached the Supreme Court he was in his final term of law school, so the case's outcome would not affect his ability to obtain his degree:

> [A]ll parties agree that DeFunis is now entitled to complete his legal studies at the University of Washington and to receive his degree from that institution. A determination by this Court of the legal issues tendered by the parties is no longer necessary to compel that result, and could not serve to prevent it. . . . The controversy between the parties has thus clearly ceased to be "definite and concrete" and no longer "touch(es) the legal relations of parties having adverse legal interests." . . .
>
> There is a line of decisions in this Court standing for the proposition that the "voluntary cessation of allegedly illegal conduct does not deprive the tribunal of power to hear and determine the case, i.e., does not make the case moot." . . . But mootness in the present case depends not at all upon a "voluntary cessation" of the admissions practices that were the subject of this litigation. It depends, instead, upon the simple fact that DeFunis is now in the final quarter of the final year of his course of study, and the settled and unchallenged policy of the Law School to permit him to complete the term for which he is now enrolled.

Justice Brennan, joined by Justices Douglas, White, and Marshall, dissented, raising the possibility that unforeseen circumstances such as the plaintiff's illness or academic failure could prevent him from completing his studies and thus the case was not necessarily moot. Justice Douglas added a separate dissent.

Legal fights over mootness often play out in the context of the mootness exceptions, which recognize that adjudication may sometimes be permissible even if the named plaintiff's controversy is no longer "live." *Friends of the Earth*, in Section A, is one such example, applying the "voluntary cessation" exception. *Friends of the Earth* also mentions a separate exception for harms that are so brief in duration that they are classified as "capable of repetition yet evading review." A third category of exceptions, not mentioned in *Friends of the Earth*, pertains to class actions. We'll cover each of these in turn.

(Some treatments of mootness recognize a fourth exception, known as the "collateral consequences" exception, for the lingering effects of criminal convictions, such as where a habeas petitioner has been released from prison but remains subject to restrictions asssociated with his conviction. We won't address this exception separately, as it boils down to an application of the primary rule: Where a person continues to suffer consequences as a result of the challenged conduct, a court could grant effective relief by eliminating those consequences, so the case falls outside the definition of mootness. *See* Erwin Chemerinsky, *Federal Jurisdiction* § 2.5.2, at 141 (7th ed. 2016).)

1. THE VOLUNTARY CESSATION EXCEPTION

As both *DeFunis* and *Friends of the Earth* reflect, courts will not dismiss a case for mootness resulting from the defendant's "voluntary cessation" of the challenged conduct absent a strong showing that it will not recur. *Friends of the Earth* explained the rationale for this exception and the showing required to overcome it:

> It is well settled that "a defendant's voluntary cessation of a challenged practice does not deprive a federal court of its power to determine the legality of the practice." "[I]f it did, the courts would be compelled to leave '[t]he defendant . . . free to return to his old ways.'" In accordance with this principle, the standard we have announced for determining whether a case has been mooted by the defendant's voluntary conduct is stringent: "A case might become moot if subsequent events made it absolutely clear that the allegedly wrongful behavior could not reasonably be expected to recur." The "heavy burden of persua[ding]" the court that the challenged conduct cannot reasonably be expected to start up again lies with the party asserting mootness.

This principle was applied in *Lyons* (Section B.1) where, after the district court enjoined the chokehold practices challenged there and the appeals court affirmed (but before the Supreme Court reviewed the case), the Los Angeles Police Department imposed a moratorium on one type of chokehold challenged and prohibited the other. Justice White's majority opinion disposed of the mootness question easily (and without dissent on this point):

> Lyons [argues] that in light of changed conditions, an injunctive decree is now unnecessary because he is no longer subject to a threat of injury. He urges that the preliminary injunction should be vacated. The City, on the other hand, while acknowledging that subsequent events have significantly changed the posture of this case, . . . asserts that the case is not moot because the moratorium is not permanent and may be lifted at any time.
>
> We agree with the City that the case is not moot, since the moratorium by its terms is not permanent. Intervening events have not "irrevocably eradicated the effects of the alleged violation."

The Court went on to the issue its landmark holding on standing, discussed above.

What is the standard for overcoming the voluntary cessation rule? Why is it so strict? How do you reconcile such a strong presumption in favor of justiciability here with the Court's presumption against justiciability in the standing context?

A strategic puzzler: Why do you think it was the *plaintiff* who argued for mootness and vacatur of the injunction, while the defendant argued the contrary? (Hint: Which party had sought Supreme Court review? Which side did the parties likely expect to win?)

2. CAPABLE OF REPETITION YET EVADING REVIEW

Courts will also decide otherwise moot cases if the controversy is "capable of repetition yet evading review" (CORYER). Though principally known for its substantive holding recognizing a constitutional right to obtain an abortion, *Roe v. Wade*, 410 U.S. 113 (1973), is a classic example of the CORYER exception. Justice Blackmun's majority opinion explained:

> [The defendant] suggests that Roe's case must now be moot because she and all other members of her class are no longer subject to any 1970 pregnancy.

The usual rule in federal cases is that an actual controversy must exist at stages of appellate or certiorari review, and not simply at the date the action is initiated.

But when, as here, pregnancy is a significant fact in the litigation, the normal 266-day human gestation period is so short that the pregnancy will come to term before the usual appellate process is complete. If that termination makes a case moot, pregnancy litigation seldom will survive much beyond the trial stage, and appellate review will be effectively denied. Our law should not be that rigid. Pregnancy often comes more than once to the same woman, and in the general population, if man is to survive, it will always be with us. Pregnancy provides a classic justification for a conclusion of nonmootness. It truly could be "capable of repetition, yet evading review."

We, therefore, agree with the District Court that Jane Roe had standing to undertake this litigation, that she presented a justiciable controversy, and that the termination of her 1970 pregnancy has not rendered her case moot.

No Justice disagreed on this point.

A key limit to the CORYER principle is that the *specific plaintiffs themselves* must face the possibility of repetition. In keeping with the Court's distaste for speculation in the context of justiciability, the Court in *United States v. Sanchez-Gomez*, 138 S. Ct. 1532 (2018), rejected the application of CORYER because it depended on too many assumptions about parties' future conduct. The issue in *Sanchez-Gomez* was the constitutionality of a blanket policy of subjecting all federal in-custody criminal defendants to shackling of their hands and feet at pretrial court appearances. Several criminal defendants objected to being shackled. The district court denied relief, and the defendants appealed. Although their criminal cases ended while the appeal was pending, the court of appeals nonetheless reached the merits and held the policy unconstitutional. The Supreme Court, in a unanimous opinion by Chief Justice Roberts, vacated and remanded with instructions to dismiss the case as moot, holding (among other things) that the CORYER exception to mootness did not apply:

> Sanchez-Gomez and Patricio-Guzman are no longer in pretrial custody. Their criminal cases, arising from their illegal entry into the United States, ended in guilty pleas well before the Court of Appeals issued its decision. Respondents contend, however, that the claims brought by Sanchez-Gomez and Patricio-Guzman fall within the "exception to the mootness doctrine for a controversy that is capable of repetition, yet evading review." A dispute qualifies for that exception only "if (1) the challenged action is in its duration too short to be fully litigated prior to its cessation or expiration, and (2) there is a reasonable expectation that the same complaining party will be subjected to the same action again." The parties do not contest that the claims at issue satisfy the first prong of that test, but they sharply disagree as to the second.
>
> Respondents argue that Sanchez-Gomez and Patricio-Guzman meet the second prong because they will again violate the law, be apprehended, and be returned to pretrial custody. But we have consistently refused to "conclude that the case-or-controversy requirement is satisfied by" the possibility that a party "will be prosecuted for violating valid criminal laws." *O'Shea*. We have instead "assume[d] that [litigants] will conduct their activities within the law and so avoid prosecution and conviction as well as exposure to the challenged course of conduct." *Ibid*.
>
> Respondents argue that this usual refusal to assume future criminal conduct is unwarranted here given the particular circumstances of Sanchez-Gomez's and Patricio-Guzman's offenses. They cite two civil cases—*Honig v. Doe* and

Turner v. Rogers—in which this Court concluded that the expectation that a litigant would repeat the misconduct that gave rise to his claims rendered those claims capable of repetition. Neither case, however, supports a departure from the settled rule.

Honig involved a disabled student's challenge to his suspension from school for disruptive behavior. We found that given his "inability to conform his conduct to socially acceptable norms" or "govern his aggressive, impulsive behavior," it was "reasonable to expect that [the student would] again engage in the type of misconduct that precipitated this suit" and "be subjected to the same unilateral school action for which he initially sought relief." In *Turner*, we determined that an indigent person repeatedly held in civil contempt for failing to make child support payments, who was at the time over $13,000 in arrears, and whose next hearing was only five months away, was destined to find himself in civil contempt proceedings again. The challenged denial of appointed counsel at his contempt hearing was thus capable of repetition.

Respondents contend that Sanchez-Gomez and Patricio-Guzman, like the challengers in *Honig* and *Turner*, are likely to find themselves right back where they started if we dismiss their case as moot. Respondents cite a Sentencing Commission report finding that in 2013 thirty-eight percent of those convicted and sentenced for an illegal entry or illegal reentry offense "were deported and subsequently illegally reentered at least one time." Respondents emphasize the economic and familial pressures that often compel individuals such as Sanchez-Gomez and Patricio-Guzman to repeatedly attempt to enter the United States. And respondents note that both men, after their release, actually did cross the border into the United States, were apprehended again, and were charged with new illegal entry offenses. . . .

Honig and *Turner* are inapposite. Our decisions in those civil cases rested on the litigants' inability, for reasons beyond their control, to prevent themselves from transgressing and avoid recurrence of the challenged conduct. In *Honig*, such incapacity was the very reason the school sought to expel the student. And in *Turner*, the indigent individual's large outstanding debt made him effectively incapable of satisfying his imminent support obligations. Sanchez-Gomez and Patricio-Guzman, in contrast, are "able—and indeed required by law"—to refrain from further criminal conduct. Their personal incentives to return to the United States, plus the elevated rate of recidivism associated with illegal entry offenses, do not amount to an inability to obey the law. We have consistently refused to find the case or controversy requirement satisfied where, as here, the litigants simply "anticipate violating lawful criminal statutes." *O'Shea.*

Is the Court saying that it was more likely that Roe would become pregnant (and that Honig would be unable to control himself and Turner would be unable to pay) than that Sanchez-Gomez and Patricio-Guzman would reoffend? Or are certain types of predictions disfavored? Which ones?

3. CLASS ACTION EXCEPTIONS

The third exception (or, really, category of exceptions) to mootness arises from the special status of class actions. Although full coverage of class actions is left to courses on Civil Procedure, we touch on class actions briefly here to the extent they provide an important strategic tool for civil rights litigators to address justiciability.

A class action is a type of civil case in which an individual plaintiff or a small group of plaintiffs (the "named plaintiffs") seek to represent a much larger group of "similarly situated" individuals who would be difficult to name as plaintiffs. If a court "certifies a class" (i.e., permits a case to proceed as a class action), then all members defined as part of the class—including both the named plaintiffs and the absent class members on whose behalf they litigate—are bound by the result of the case, whether a win or a loss. Both damages and injunctive relief can be available through class actions, depending on which class-action criteria are met. The criteria for certifying a class action are set out in Federal Rule of Civil Procedure 23, which requires, at a minimum, that the class is sufficiently large that it would be impractical to join everyone by name, that one or more issues of fact or law are common to class members, that the named plaintiffs' claims are typical of the class members' claims, and that the named plaintiffs and their counsel will adequately represent the interests of the absent class members. Additional criteria apply depending on the type of relief sought.

As noted earlier in the chapter, the class action device does *not* help establish standing: One or more named plaintiffs themselves must have standing, and the fact that they seek to represent a large group is irrelevant to that inquiry. *O'Shea.* But the certification or even attempted certification of a class action *can* defeat mootness.

First, the Supreme Court has held that the mootness of the named plaintiffs' claims does not render a case moot if a class has been certified and the harm is "inherently transitory"—that is, of such limited duration that it might escape judicial review if mootness were judged based on the named plaintiff alone. In *Sosna v. Iowa*, 419 U.S. 393 (1975), the plaintiff was a married woman whose petition for divorce was denied by an Iowa court because she did not meet a state requirement that she live in the state for a year before filing the petition. She filed a class action challenging the durational residency requirement as a violation of equal protection, and she obtained class certification. By the time the Supreme Court heard the case, the plaintiff had obtained a divorce elsewhere and in any event had lived in Iowa for more than a year, so the law no longer barred her from obtaining a divorce in Iowa. The Court, per Justice Rehnquist, held that class certification saved the case from mootness, because upon certification "the class of unnamed persons described in the certification acquired a legal status separate from the interest asserted by appellant," and the controversy "remains very much alive" as to the class members even though "because of the passage of time, no single challenger will remain subject to its restrictions for the period necessary to see such a lawsuit to its conclusion." The Court cautioned, however, "that the same exigency that justifies this doctrine serves to identify its limits. In cases in which the alleged harm would not dissipate during the normal time required for resolution of the controversy, the general principles of Art. III jurisdiction require that the plaintiff's personal stake in the litigation continue throughout the entirety of the litigation." On the merits, the Court upheld the challenged law. Justice Marshall, joined by Justice Brennan, dissented on the merits. Only Justice White dissented on justiciability, arguing that the existence of a class was insufficient to justify adjudicating the case: "None of the anonymous members of the class is present to direct counsel and ensure that class interests are being properly served. For all practical purposes, this case has become one-sided and has lost the adversary quality necessary to satisfy the constitutional 'case or controversy' requirement."

The Court followed *Sosna* in *County of Riverside v. McLaughlin*, 500 U.S. 44 (1991), a challenge to the amount of time between warrantless arrests in a California county and the judicial determination of probable cause that is constitutionally required to justify continued detention. The district court certified a class action. When the case reached the Supreme Court, the County argued that the suit had become moot, but Justice O'Connor's opinion for the Court rejected that view:

> It is true, of course, that the claims of the named plaintiffs have since been rendered moot; eventually, they either received probable cause determinations or were released. Our cases leave no doubt, however, that by obtaining class certification, plaintiffs preserved the merits of the controversy for our review. In factually similar cases we have held that "the termination of a class representative's claim does not moot the claims of the unnamed members of the class." *See, e.g., Sosna.* That the class was not certified until after the named plaintiffs' claims had become moot does not deprive us of jurisdiction. We recognized . . . that "[s]ome claims are so inherently transitory that the trial court will not have even enough time to rule on a motion for class certification before the proposed representative's individual interest expires."

On the merits, the Court held that the Constitution requires a probable-cause hearing within forty-eight hours of arrest. Four Justices dissented on the merits, but no one disagreed as to mootness.

Second, even if class certification has been *denied* when the named plaintiff's case becomes moot, the named plaintiff retains a personal stake in appealing the denial of certification. If certification is subsequently obtained, then the class can take advantage of the exception to mootness for certified classes. The leading case on this situation is *U.S. Parole Commission v. Geraghty*, 445 U.S. 388 (1980). There, a federal prisoner brought a class action challenging federal parole guidelines. The district court denied class certification and ruled against the plaintiff on the merits. While plaintiff's appeal was pending, he was released from prison. The court of appeals held that the plaintiff's release did not render moot the question of whether class certification had been erroneously denied, and the Supreme Court affirmed in an opinion by Justice Blackmun:

> A plaintiff who brings a class action presents two separate issues for judicial resolution. One is the claim on the merits; the other is the claim that he is entitled to represent a class. "The denial of class certification stands as an adjudication of one of the issues litigated." . . .
>
> [T]he purpose of the "personal stake" requirement is to assure that the case is in a form capable of judicial resolution. The imperatives of a dispute capable of judicial resolution are sharply presented issues in a concrete factual setting and self-interested parties vigorously advocating opposing positions. We conclude that these elements can exist with respect to the class certification issue notwithstanding the fact that the named plaintiff's claim on the merits has expired. The question whether class certification is appropriate remains as a concrete, sharply presented issue. In

Sosna v. Iowa it was recognized that a named plaintiff whose claim on the merits expires after class certification may still adequately represent the class. Implicit in that decision was the determination that vigorous advocacy can be assured through means other than the traditional requirement of a "personal stake in the outcome." Respondent here continues vigorously to advocate his right to have a class certified.

We therefore hold that an action brought on behalf of a class does not become moot upon expiration of the named plaintiff's substantive claim, even though class certification has been denied. The proposed representative retains a "personal stake" in obtaining class certification sufficient to assure that Art. III values are not undermined. If the appeal results in reversal of the class certification denial, and a class subsequently is properly certified, the merits of the class claim then may be adjudicated pursuant to the holding in *Sosna*.

Justice Powell, joined by Chief Justice Burger and Justices Stewart and Rehnquist, dissented:

> Art. III contains no exception for class actions. Thus, we have held that a putative class representative who alleges no individual injury "may [not] seek relief on behalf of himself or any other member of the class." *O'Shea*. Only after a class has been certified in accordance with Rule 23 can it "acquir[e] a legal status separate from the interest asserted by [the named plaintiff]." *Sosna*. . . .
>
> The Court makes no effort to identify any injury to respondent that may be redressed by, or any benefit to respondent that may accrue from, a favorable ruling on the certification question. . . .
>
> [C]lass certification issues are "ancillary to the litigation of substantive claims." . . . A motion for class certification, like a motion to join additional parties or to try the case before a jury instead of a judge, seeks only to present a substantive claim in a particular context. Such procedural devices generally have no value apart from their capacity to facilitate a favorable resolution of the case on the merits. . . .
>
> In any realistic sense, the only persons before this Court who appear to have an interest are the defendants and a lawyer who no longer has a client.

Several appellate courts have extended this mootness exception to circumstances in which class certification has been sought but not yet ruled on when the named plaintiffs' claims become moot. *See, e.g., Gayle v. Warden Monmouth County Corr. Inst.*, 838 F.3d 297, 305 (3d Cir. 2016); *Primax Recoveries, Inc. v. Sevilla*, 324 F.3d 544, 546-47 (7th Cir. 2003); *Zeidman v. J. Ray McDermott & Co.*, 651 F.2d 1030, 1051 (5th Cir. 1981). The logic is straightforward: If named plaintiffs have a personal stake in class certification sufficient to sustain their attempt to obtain certification *after a denial*, that same stake exists *as soon as they have filed* the motion for class certification, regardless of whether it has been acted upon. However, some courts have held (albeit with little analysis) that they may not hear cases in which the named plaintiff's case became moot when a class certification motion had been filed but not yet ruled on. *See Slayman v. FedEx Ground Package Sys., Inc.*, 765 F.3d 1033, 1048 (9th Cir. 2014) (relying on pre-*Geraghty* circuit precedent without citation to or discussion of *Geraghty*); *Inmates of Lincoln Intake & Det. Facility by Windes v. Boosalis*, 705 F.2d 1021, 1023 (8th Cir. 1983) (citing but not discussing *Geraghty*).

An example of how civil rights litigators use class actions in planning for the likelihood of mootness is *J.D. v. Azar*, 925 F.3d 1291 (D.C. Cir. 2019). That case challenged the Trump Administration's policy of refusing to permit undocumented, unaccompanied immigrant minors in federal custody to leave the facilities at which they were held to access abortion services held to access abortion services (even if the pregnancy at issue was the result of rape). Learning about specific minors in those circumstances was extremely difficult for counsel, both because of the minors' custodial status and because of language barriers. The case was originally filed on behalf of a single minor plaintiff (known as "J.D." or "Jane Doe"), who sought class certification, a preliminary injunction for the class, and a temporary restraining order (TRO) for herself given the time-sensitivity of her need for an abortion. The district court granted the TRO quickly, and the plaintiff was able to obtain an abortion before the court ruled on class certification and the classwide injunction. Plaintiffs' counsel then identified and joined three additional plaintiffs in the same circumstances. One of the new plaintiffs, Jane Roe, was an additional proposed class representative, but each of the new plaintiffs obtained an abortion pursuant to a TRO or was released from government custody before the district court ruled on the class certification and injunction motions. Ultimately, the court certified the class and enjoined the government from obstructing abortion access for any unaccompanied immigrant minors in its custody and from disclosing the minors' pregnancies or abortion decisions to their families or others. The government appealed, and the court of appeals affirmed class certification, invoking the inherently transitory exception of *Sosna* and *Riverside* to reject the government's argument that mootness defeated the class's entitlement to relief:

> [T]he "inherently transitory" exception to mootness requires us to determine (i) whether the individual claim might end before the district court has a reasonable amount of time to decide class certification, and (ii) whether some class members will retain a live claim at every stage of litigation. . . .
>
> Doe and Roe have demonstrated that the exception applies in this case. The claims at issue likely will, or at least might, end quickly. The average length of custody for a minor was 41 days in fiscal year 2017 . . . [and] "the length of time that pregnant [minors] will remain in [government] custody is uncertain and unpredictable." . . .
>
> The government . . . stresses that Doe's and Roe's claims remained live long enough for the district court to decide their merits through temporary restraining order applications. The district court "necessarily ha[d] time to take action" on the certification request because it had enough time to decide the merits. No case law supports this argument. We reject its upshot as unworkable and inequitable: that some class actions would evaporate because the irreparable harm to individual plaintiffs was clear enough to warrant immediate relief but the class definition issue was complex enough to require discovery. Relatedly, we fear that accepting the argument would vitiate the mootness exception. Courts may issue temporary relief in virtually every case; a judge sometimes will sign a restraining order on the day the plaintiff files her complaint. Indeed, there would have been no need to apply the exception in . . . [*Riverside*], because the lower courts could have granted interim relief releasing detainees from pretrial custody. Accordingly, we find irrelevant the issuance of emergency relief in this case.
>
> As for the second question, the district court found—and the government does not dispute—that some class members will have live claims at every stage of litigation. [The government] continues to keep pregnant minors, and the plaintiffs

represent that about a dozen expressed an interest in abortion or related information during the first six months after the issuance of the injunction.

[T]he plaintiffs have established both requirements of the "inherently transitory" exception.

On the merits, the court affirmed the injunction as to abortion access and vacated and remanded for more factual development regarding the injunction against disclosure of information.

Note that the doctrines governing "inherently transitory" harms and harms "capable of repetition yet evading review" involve similar concepts but differ in two crucial respects: whether they can be asserted outside of the class action context (only CORYER can) and whether the possibility of repetition of the harm must apply to the specific named plaintiffs themselves (required only for CORYER).

The Supreme Court's approach to mootness in the class action context has the obvious advantage of preventing certain time-limited types of claims from falling through the judicial cracks. Does that benefit outweigh the values served by justiciability? For instance, once the named plaintiff no longer has a stake in the outcome, who drives the litigation? For whose purposes?

Contrast the Court's class-action mootness exceptions with the principle of standing law that "[t]he assumption that if respondents have no standing to sue, no one would have standing, is not a reason to find standing." *Amnesty Int'l*. What might justify the inconsistency between standing and mootness doctrines in terms of how each weighs the interest in judicial resolution against the values served by justiciability limitations? Should the Court adopt a uniform approach to this question?

Finally, consider the logistics of invoking the class-action exceptions to mootness. What steps must lawyers take to preserve class claims in cases like *Riverside* where the harm may occur and end within a period of days? What if the rights at issue concern an individual's treatment during criminal procedings? If the named plaintiff must, at the moment of filing, have standing (as several plantiffs did in *Riverside*), but federal courts will abstain from issues pending in a state criminal proceeding (see Chapter 1, Section C), how can unconstitutional practices in criminal trials be challenged?

CHAPTER 11 PROBLEMS

Problem 11A.   Return to Problem 9B in Chapter 9. Can Piriz seek an injunction to have the native-speaker policy lifted for when he reapplies to KU as a transfer student next year? Why or why not?

Problem 11B.   In a tight race for mayor in the City of Columbia Heights, the police union has come out in favor of candidate Cleve Groverland over his opponent Lynn Frankevelt. To try to tip the scales in favor of their union's preferred candidate, Officers Millie Morefill and Taft Howard plan to disrupt the polling place at Tubman Elementary School, which is in an overwhelmingly pro-Frankevelt precinct. The plan is that Morefill will work security for the polls in the morning and hide drugs throughout the school, then Howard will come by in the afternoon with a police dog who will smell the drugs and alert, thereby giving Howard an excuse to summon a team of officers to search the school. The search will slow the voting process and create long lines that will make it impossible for everyone to vote before the polls close.

Another officer learns of the plan and informs Frankevelt, who sues to enjoin it.

1. Does she have standing? Based on what threatened injury?

2. If she doesn't, whom would you recommend she find to challenge the rogue officers' plan and why?

Problem 11C. Same scenario as 11B, but now imagine that no one learns of the plan in advance. Instead, it works, creating chaos and halting the lines as police search for the (planted) drugs. When the line finally starts moving again after the chaos, only an hour remains before the polls are scheduled to close. But a police officer figures out what has happened and shares her discovery with a local paper, which tweets it out to the public. There are 500 people still in line outside the polling station.

Upon learning why the line has been held up, Joe Orgebush, the last voter in line, calls his lawyer, who rushes to court alleging various constitutional violations and seeking a TRO requiring that all voters in line when the polls close be allowed to vote.

1. Does Orgebush have standing? What additional facts do you need to know to figure it out?

2. *(Reviewing Chapter 9.)* A judge declines to issue the injunction, the polls close on time, and Orgebush and nine other people are turned away from the closed polling place. Frankevelt, whom Orgebush had intended to vote for, loses by one hundred votes. Frankevelt and Orgebush both sue Morefill and Howard for damages. What damages, if any, can each recover?

Problem 11D. Recall from Section C in this chapter that in *United States v. Sanchez-Gomez*, 138 S. Ct. 1532 (2018)—a challenge by criminal defendants to a blanket policy of subjecting all federal in-custody criminal defendants to shackling of their hands and feet at pretrial court appearances—the Supreme Court refused to apply the CORYER exception to save the challenge from mootness once the cases of the criminal defendants challenging the policy had ended. Because the challenge arose in the context of criminal cases, the class action device was unavailable.

Imagine you are an impact litigator in the same jurisdiction in which *Sanchez-Gomez* arose.

1. How might you design a *civil* action to challenge the same policy? Consider both the legal obstacles you would face in terms of justiciability and the logistical ones in finding an appropriate client and taking timely action in court.

2. *(Reviewing Chapter 1.)* What is the effect of abstention on your proposed lawsuit? Can you design your suit to avoid it?

Institutional Reform

As we near the end of our study, we return to where we started: impact litigation seeking institutional reform. This use of impact litigation has played an important but contested role in shaping some of our society's government-run institutions. Unlike lawsuits for damages or injunctions targeted at a specific law or policy, institutional reform litigation can, when successful, result in far-reaching court orders that entail years or even decades of judicial supervision of the defendant institutions. Whether courts are qualified and constitutionally authorized to undertake such supervision and whether institutional reform litigation tends to be successful in reforming institutions are the main questions this chapter will consider as we examine institutional reform litigation in two key contexts in which it is used: schools (Section A) and prisons (Section B).

An early and influential account of institutional reform litigation makes this case for its importance:

> The fundamental ground of traditional reservations about constitutional adjudication is that the courts may be called upon to act counter to the popular will as expressed in legislation. . . . [But courts'] target is generally administrative rather than legislative action, action that is thus derivative rather than a direct expression of the legislative mandate. Moreover, one may ask whether democratic theory really requires deference to majoritarian outcomes whose victims are . . . [individuals like prisoners who] have no alternative access to the levers of power in the system. . . .
>
> Moreover, an amalgam of less tangible institutional factors will continue to operate to shape judicial performance . . . : general expectations as to the competence and conscientiousness of federal judges; professional traditions of conduct and performance; the accepted, often tacit, canons and leeways of office. These are amorphous. They mark no sharp boundaries. Their flexibility and vagueness can be abused. But other kinds of constraint are no less vulnerable; and the historical experience is that egregious violation has invariably activated a countervailing response. . . .
>
> In my view, judicial action only achieves . . . legitimacy by responding to, indeed by stirring, the deep and durable demand for justice in our society.

Abram Chayes, *The Role of the Judge in Public Law Litigation*, 89 Harv. L. Rev. 1281, 1314-16 (1976).

What are the key assumptions and needs justifying institutional reform litigation in Chayes's view? Consider, as you read this chapter, how they stack up against the assumptions and interests invoked to argue that institutional reform cases represent an inappropriate use of the judicial power.

A. SCHOOL DESEGREGATION

We begin by picking up the story of *Brown* where the Prologue (Section A) left off. We proceed chronologically through the history of desegregation litigation—its tepid beginnings, a brief period of vigorous judicial activity, and a long period of retrenchment.

1. "ALL DELIBERATE SPEED"

After the Court's landmark ruling holding school segregation unconstitutional in 1954, the Court heard reargument the next Term regarding remedy. Chief Justice Warren's unanimous opinion for the Court in *Brown v. Board of Education*, 349 U.S. 294 (1955) ("*Brown II*"), ordered that remedies be devised by the district courts because they were most familiar with local conditions. But the Court's remand instructions were notoriously self-contradictory. On one hand, the Court admonished that "the vitality of these constitutional principles [announced in *Brown I*] cannot be allowed to yield simply because of disagreement with them." And the Court authorized district courts to consider a broad range of factors relevant to relief, including physical facilities, transportation, personnel, and school district boundaries. On the other hand, the Court hedged, "courts may find that additional time is necessary to carry out the ruling in an effective manner." The ambiguous decision is summed up by the oxymoronic phrase for which it is best known (in italics): Lower courts were to issue orders necessary "to admit to public schools on a racially nondiscriminatory basis with *all deliberate speed* the parties to these cases."

Progress in implementing *Brown* was slow, uneven, and beset with obstacles, as Dean Erwin Chemerinsky summarizes:

> After *Brown*, southern states used every imaginable technique to obstruct desegregation. Some school systems attempted to close public schools rather than desegregate. Some school boards adopted so-called "freedom of choice" plans which allowed students to choose the school where they would enroll and resulted in continued segregation. In some places, school systems outright disobeyed desegregation orders. The phrase "massive resistance" appropriately describes what occurred during the decade after *Brown*. . . .
>
> The result of this massive resistance was that a decade after *Brown*, little desegregation had occurred. In the South, just 1.2% of African-American school children were attending schools with whites. In South Carolina, Alabama, and Mississippi, not one African-American child attended a public school with a white child in the 1962-1963 school year. In North Carolina, only one-fifth of one percent (or 0.2%)

of the African-American students attended desegregated schools in 1961, and the figure did not rise above 1% until 1965. Similarly, in Virginia in 1964, only 1.63% of African Americans were attending desegregated schools. . . .

Finally, by the mid-1960s, desegregation began to proceed. By 1968, the integration rate rose to 32% and by 1972-1973, 91.3% of southern schools were desegregated. . . .

Many factors explain the delay between *Brown* and any results in desegregation. Efforts to thwart *Brown* had to be defeated. The 1964 Civil Rights Act, in which Title VI tied federal funds to eliminating desegregation, played a crucial role. But so did renewed attention by the Supreme Court to segregated schools. For a decade after *Brown*, the Court largely stayed out of the desegregation effort. It was not until 1964 that the Court lamented that "[t]here has been entirely too much deliberation and not enough speed" in achieving desegregation. . . .

[T]he Court finally attempted to provide guidance to lower courts in structuring remedies to desegregate schools in *Swann v. Charlotte-Mecklenburg Board of Education*.

Erwin Chemerinsky, *The Segregation and Resegregation of American Public Education: The Courts' Role*, 81 N.C. L. Rev. 1597, 1602-04 (2003) (quoting *Griffin v. County School Board*, 377 U.S. 218, 229 (1964)).

2. "BROAD POWER TO FASHION A REMEDY"

Swann v. Charlotte-Mecklenburg Board of Education
402 U.S. 1 (1971)

■ *Mr. Chief Justice BURGER delivered the opinion for a unanimous Court.*

[The Charlotte-Mecklenburg school system encompasses the City of Charlotte and surrounding Mecklenburg County, North Carolina, serving more than 84,000 pupils in 107 schools. Approximately 71 percent of students in the district are white and 29 percent African-American. About two-third of the black students attended schools at which 99 percent or 100 percent of the student body was black. The district court found that this arrangement resulted from discriminatory actions of the school board. The court's far-reaching remedy focused on altering school attendance zones. The most controversial aspect of the plan was its treatment of elementary schools: The plan created groupings of elementary schools that paired two or three predominately white suburban schools with an inner-city, predominantly black school and bused all the inner-city students to the suburban schools for grades 1-4 and suburban students to the inner-city schools for grades 5-6.]. . . .

Over the 16 years since *Brown II*, many difficulties were encountered in implementation of the basic constitutional requirement that the State not discriminate between public school children on the basis of their race. Nothing in our national experience prior to 1955 prepared anyone for dealing with changes and adjustments of the magnitude and complexity encountered since then. Deliberate resistance of some to the Court's mandates has impeded the good-faith efforts of others to bring school systems into compliance. The detail and nature of these dilatory tactics have been noted frequently by this Court and other courts.

By the time the Court considered *Green v. County School Board*, in 1968, very little progress had been made in many areas where dual school systems had historically been maintained by operation of state laws. In *Green*, the Court was confronted with a record of a freedom-of-choice program that the District Court had found to operate in fact to preserve a dual system more than a decade after *Brown II*. While acknowledging that a freedom-of-choice concept could be a valid remedial measure in some circumstances, its failure to be effective in *Green* required that: "The burden on a school board today is to come forward with a plan that promises realistically to work now . . . until it is clear that state imposed segregation has been completely removed."

This was plain language, yet the 1969 Term of Court brought fresh evidence of the dilatory tactics of many school authorities. . . .

The objective today remains to eliminate from the public schools all vestiges of state-imposed segregation. Segregation was the evil struck down by *Brown I* as contrary to the equal protection guarantees of the Constitution. That was the violation sought to be corrected by the remedial measures of *Brown II*. That was the basis for the holding in *Green* that school authorities are "clearly charged with the affirmative duty to take whatever steps might be necessary to convert to a unitary system in which racial discrimination would be eliminated root and branch."

If school authorities fail in their affirmative obligations under these holdings, judicial authority may be invoked. Once a right and a violation have been shown, the scope of a district court's equitable powers to remedy past wrongs is broad, for breadth and flexibility are inherent in equitable remedies. . . .

In seeking to define even in broad and general terms how far this remedial power extends it is important to remember that judicial powers may be exercised only on the basis of a constitutional violation. Remedial judicial authority does not put judges automatically in the shoes of school authorities whose powers are plenary. Judicial authority enters only when local authority defaults. . . .

As with any equity case, the nature of the violation determines the scope of the remedy. In default by the school authorities of their obligation to proffer acceptable remedies, a district court has broad power to fashion a remedy that will assure a unitary school system. . . .

In *Green*, we pointed out that existing policy and practice with regard to faculty, staff, transportation, extracurricular activities, and facilities were among the most important indicia of a segregated system. Independent of student assignment, where it is possible to identify a "white school" or a "Negro school" simply by reference to the racial composition of teachers and staff, the quality of school buildings and equipment, or the organization of sports activities, a prima facie case of violation of substantive constitutional rights under the Equal Protection Clause is shown. . . .

The central issue in this case is that of student assignment, and there are essentially four problem areas: [whether racial quotas are permissible remedies;

whether all single-race schools must be eliminated; what limits apply to court-ordered rearrangement of attendance zones; and what limits apply to court-ordered transportation of students.]

(1) Racial Balances or Racial Quotas . . . .

Our objective . . . is to see that school authorities exclude no pupil of a racial minority from any school, directly or indirectly, on account of race; it does not and cannot embrace all the problems of racial prejudice, even when those problems contribute to disproportionate racial concentrations in some schools. . . .

If we were to read the holding of the District Court to require, as a matter of substantive constitutional right, any particular degree of racial balance or mixing, that approach would be disapproved and we would be obliged to reverse. The constitutional command to desegregate schools does not mean that every school in every community must always reflect the racial composition of the school system as a whole. . . .

[But here w]e see therefore that the use made of mathematical ratios was no more than a starting point in the process of shaping a remedy, rather than an inflexible requirement. From that starting point the District Court proceeded to frame a decree that was within its discretionary powers, as an equitable remedy for the particular circumstances. . . . Awareness of the racial composition of the whole school system is likely to be a useful starting point in shaping a remedy to correct past constitutional violations. In sum, the very limited use made of mathematical ratios was within the equitable remedial discretion of the District Court.

(2) One-Race Schools.

The record in this case reveals the familiar phenomenon that in metropolitan areas minority groups are often found concentrated in one part of the city. In some circumstances certain schools may remain all or largely of one race until new schools can be provided or neighborhood patterns change. Schools all or predominantly of one race in a district of mixed population will require close scrutiny to determine that school assignments are not part of state-enforced segregation. . . .

No per se rule can adequately embrace all the difficulties of reconciling the competing interests involved; but in a system with a history of segregation the need for remedial criteria of sufficient specificity to assure a school authority's compliance with its constitutional duty warrants a presumption against schools that are substantially disproportionate in their racial composition. . . . [School authorities] have the burden of showing that such school assignments are genuinely nondiscriminatory. . . .

(3) Remedial Altering of Attendance Zones.

The maps submitted in these cases graphically demonstrate that one of the principal tools employed by school planners and by courts to break up the dual school system has been a frank—and sometimes drastic—gerrymandering of school districts and attendance zones. An additional step was pairing, "clustering," or "grouping" of schools with attendance assignments made deliberately to accomplish the transfer of Negro students out of formerly segregated Negro schools and transfer of white students to formerly all-Negro schools. More often than not, these zones are neither compact nor contiguous; indeed they may be on opposite ends of the city. As an interim corrective measure, this cannot be said to be beyond the broad remedial powers of a court. . . .

The remedy for . . . segregation may be administratively awkward, inconvenient, and even bizarre in some situations and may impose burdens on some; but all awkwardness and inconvenience cannot be avoided in the interim period when remedial adjustments are being made to eliminate the dual school systems. . . .

In this area, we must of necessity rely to a large extent, as this Court has for more than 16 years, on the informed judgment of the district courts in the first instance and on courts of appeals. We hold that the pairing and grouping of non-contiguous school zones is a permissible tool and such action is to be considered in light of the objectives sought. . . .

(4) Transportation of Students . . . .

The District Court's conclusion that assignment of children to the school nearest their home serving their grade would not produce an effective dismantling of the dual system is supported by the record.

Thus the remedial techniques used in the District Court's order were within that court's power to provide equitable relief; implementation of the decree is well within the capacity of the school authority. . . .

The trips for elementary school pupils average about seven miles and the District Court found that they would take "not over 35 minutes at the most." This system compares favorably with the transportation plan previously operated in Charlotte under which each day 26,600 students on all grade levels were transported an average of 15 miles one way for an average trip requiring over an hour. In these circumstances, we find no basis for holding that the local school authorities may not be required to employ bus transportation as one tool of school desegregation. Desegregation plans cannot be limited to the walk-in school. . . .

In *Green*, this Court used the term "feasible" and by implication, "workable," "effective," and "realistic" in the mandate to develop "a plan that promises realistically to work, and . . . to work now." On the facts of this case, we are unable to conclude that the order of the District Court is not reasonable, feasible and workable. . . .

At some point, these school authorities and others like them should have achieved full compliance with this Court's decision in *Brown I*. The systems would then be "unitary" . . . .

It does not follow that the communities served by such systems will remain demographically stable, for in a growing, mobile society, few will do so. Neither school authorities nor district courts are constitutionally required to make year-by-year adjustments of the racial composition of student bodies once the affirmative duty to desegregate has been accomplished and racial discrimination through official action is eliminated from the system. This does not mean that federal courts are without power to deal with future problems; but in the absence of a showing that either the school authorities or some other agency of the State has deliberately attempted to fix or alter demographic patterns to affect the racial composition of the schools, further intervention by a district court should not be necessary. . . .

Notes and Questions

1. According to *Swann*, what is the test for whether a district court is properly exercising its remedial authority? What practical limitations does this test impose? How closely tailored must remedies be to the violations they are addressing?

2. Note that *Swann*, like both *Brown* decisions, was unanimous. Can you identify tensions within the *Swann* opinion that might reflect attempts to reconcile competing concerns among the Justices?

3. What is the meaning of *Brown*, according to *Swann*? As you read this chapter, note the evolution of the Court's account of what *Brown* achieved.

4. Consider *Swann*'s effectiveness as impact litigation. The busing remedy approved there proved massively controversial and helped spur (or accelerate) a demographic phenomenon dubbed "white flight." Dean Chemerinsky explains this trend and how it complicated subsequent desegregation efforts:

> White families moved to suburban areas to avoid being part of desegregation orders affecting cities. In virtually every urban area, the inner city was increasingly comprised of racial minorities. By contrast, the surrounding suburbs were almost exclusively white and what little minority population did reside in suburbs was concentrated in towns that were almost exclusively African-American. School district lines parallel town borders, meaning that racial separation of cities and suburbs results in segregated school systems. For example, by 1980, whites constituted less than one-third of the students enrolled in the public schools in Baltimore, Dallas, Detroit, Houston, Los Angeles, Miami, Memphis, New York, and Philadelphia. . . .
>
> *Swann* focused exclusively on remedies within a school district. The holding did not address interdistrict remedies. When a school system is comprised predominantly of minority students, there is a limit to how much desegregation can be achieved without an interdistrict remedy.

Erwin Chemerinsky, *The Segregation and Resegregation of American Public Education: The Courts' Role*, 81 N.C. L. Rev. 1597, 1605-06 (2003).

Taking account of the possibility of backlash, would the most prudent course for the plaintiffs' attorneys in *Swann* have been to seek a narrower remedy than the plan ultimately approved by the Supreme Court? Counseling against such caution was the serious possibility that less robust remedies would have been ineffective. But as you evaluate the legacy of *Swann* and the strategic choices impact litigators must make, the next case provides an important cautionary tale.

3. The *Swann* consensus fractures

Milliken v. Bradley ("Milliken I")
418 U.S. 717 (1974)

■ *Mr. Chief Justice* Burger *delivered the opinion of the Court....*

[The Detroit branch of the NAACP along with individual students and parents sued the Detroit Board of Education and various Michigan state officials for maintaining a segregated school system. After a forty-one-day trial, the district court found that both Detroit and Michigan had committed constitutional violations by using zoning, transportation, and construction choices to maintain a dual system in Detroit and obstructing efforts to integrate the schools.]

[Regarding remedy], the District Court issued its findings and conclusions on the three Detroit-only plans submitted by the city Board and the respondents. It found that the best of the three plans "would make the Detroit school system more identifiably Black . . . thereby increasing the flight of Whites from the city and the system." From this the court concluded that the plan "would not accomplish desegregation . . . within the corporate geographical limits of the city." Accordingly, the District Court held that it "must look beyond the limits of the Detroit school district for a solution to the problem," and that "(s)chool district lines are simply matters of political convenience and may not be used to deny constitutional rights." . . .

[T]he court designated 53 of the 85 suburban school districts plus Detroit as the "desegregation area" and appointed a panel to prepare and submit "an effective desegregation plan" for the Detroit schools that would encompass the entire desegregation area. . . .

[The Court of Appeals affirmed in substantial part], concluding that "the only feasible desegregation plan involves the crossing of the boundary lines between the Detroit School District and adjacent or nearby school districts for the limited purpose of providing an effective desegregation plan." It reasoned that such a plan would be appropriate because of the State's violations, and could be implemented because of the State's authority to control local school districts. . . .

[T]he District Court's approach . . . raises the fundamental question, not presented in *Swann*, as to the circumstances in which a federal court may order desegregation relief that embraces more than a single school district. The court's analytical starting point was its conclusion that school district lines are no more than arbitrary lines on a map drawn "for political convenience." Boundary lines may be bridged where there has been a constitutional violation calling for inter-district relief, but the notion that school district lines may be casually ignored or treated as a mere administrative convenience is contrary to the history of public education in our country. No single tradition in public education is more deeply rooted than local control over the operation of schools; local autonomy has long been thought essential both to the maintenance of community concern and support for public schools and to quality of the educational process. . . . [L]ocal control over the educational process affords citizens an opportunity to participate in decision-making, permits the structuring of school programs to fit local needs, and encourages "experimentation, innovation, and a healthy competition for educational excellence." . . .

[T]he interdistrict remedy approved by the two courts [below] could disrupt and alter the structure of public education in Michigan. The metropolitan remedy would require, in effect, consolidation of 54 independent school districts historically administered as separate units into a vast new super school district. Entirely apart from the logistical and other serious problems attending large-scale transportation of students, the consolidation would give rise to an array of other problems in financing and operating this new school system. Some of the more obvious questions would be: What would be the status and authority of the present popularly elected school boards? Would the children of Detroit be within the jurisdiction and operating control of a school board elected by the parents and residents of other districts? What board or boards would levy taxes for school operations in these 54 districts constituting the consolidated metropolitan area? What provisions could be made for assuring substantial equality in tax levies among the 54 districts, if this were deemed requisite? What provisions would be made for financing? Would the validity of long-term bonds be jeopardized unless approved by all of the component districts as well as the State? What body would determine that portion of the curricula now left to the discretion of local school boards? Who would establish attendance zones, purchase school equipment, locate and construct new schools, and indeed attend to all the myriad day-to-day decisions that are necessary to school operations affecting potentially more than three-quarters of a million pupils? . . .

[A]bsent a complete restructuring of the laws of Michigan relating to school districts the District Court will become first, a de facto "legislative authority" to resolve these complex questions, and then the "school superintendent" for the entire area. This is a task which few, if any, judges are qualified to perform and one which would deprive the people of control of schools through their elected representatives. . . .

The controlling principle consistently expounded in our holdings is that the scope of the remedy is determined by the nature and extent of the constitutional violation. *Swann.* Before the boundaries of separate and autonomous school districts may be set aside by consolidating the separate units for remedial purposes or by imposing a cross-district remedy, it must first be shown that there has been a constitutional violation within one district that produces a significant segregative effect in another district. Specifically, it must be shown that racially discriminatory acts of the state or local school districts, or of a single school district have been a substantial cause of interdistrict segregation. Thus an interdistrict remedy might be in order where the racially discriminatory acts of one or more school districts caused racial segregation in an adjacent district, or where district lines have been deliberately drawn on the basis of race. In such circumstances an interdistrict remedy would be appropriate to eliminate the interdistrict segregation directly caused by the constitutional violation. Conversely, without an interdistrict violation and interdistrict effect, there is no constitutional wrong calling for an interdistrict remedy.

The record before us, voluminous as it is, contains evidence of de jure segregated conditions only in the Detroit schools; indeed, that was the theory on which the litigation was initially based and on which the District Court took evidence. With no showing of significant violation by the 53 outlying school districts and no evidence of any interdistrict violation or effect, the court went beyond the original theory of the case as framed by the pleadings and mandated a metropolitan area remedy. To approve the remedy ordered by the court would impose on the outlying districts, not shown to have committed any constitutional violation, a wholly impermissible remedy based on a standard not hinted at in *Brown I* and *II* or any holding of this Court. . . .

The constitutional right of the Negro respondents residing in Detroit is to attend a unitary school system in that district. Unless petitioners drew the district lines in a discriminatory fashion, or arranged for white students residing in the Detroit district to attend schools in Oakland and Macomb Counties, they were under no constitutional duty to make provisions for Negro students to do so. The view of the dissenters, that the existence of a dual system in Detroit can be made the basis for a decree requiring cross-district transportation of pupils, cannot be supported on the grounds that it represents merely the devising of a suitably flexible remedy for the violation of rights already established by our prior decisions. It can be supported only by drastic expansion of the constitutional right itself, an expansion without any support in either constitutional principle or precedent. . . .

[*Concurring opinion of Stewart, J., and dissenting opinion of Douglas, J., omitted.*]

■ *Mr. Justice* WHITE, *with whom Mr. Justice* DOUGLAS, *Mr. Justice* BRENNAN, *and Mr. Justice* MARSHALL *join, dissenting.* . . .

The core of my disagreement is that deliberate acts of segregation and their consequences will go unremedied, not because a remedy would be infeasible or unreasonable in terms of the usual criteria governing school desegregation cases, but because an effective remedy would cause what the Court considers to be undue administrative inconvenience to the State. The result is that the State of Michigan, the entity at which the Fourteenth Amendment is directed, has successfully insulated itself from its duty to provide effective desegregation remedies by vesting sufficient power over its public schools in its local school districts. If this is the case in Michigan, it will be the case in most States. . . .

I am surprised that the Court, sitting at this distance from the State of Michigan, claims better insight than the Court of Appeals and the District Court as to whether an interdistrict remedy for equal protection violations practiced by the State of Michigan would involve undue difficulties for the State in the management of its public schools. In the area of what constitutes an acceptable desegregation plan, "we must of necessity rely to a large extent, as this Court has for more than 16 years, on the informed judgment of the district courts in the first instance and on courts of appeals." *Swann*. Obviously, whatever difficulties there might be, they are surmountable; for the Court itself concedes that, had there been sufficient evidence of an interdistrict violation, the District Court could have fashioned a single remedy for the districts implicated rather than a different remedy for each district in which the violation had occurred or had an impact.

I am even more mystified as to how the Court can ignore the legal reality that the constitutional violations, even if occurring locally, were committed by governmental entities for which the State is responsible and that it is the State that must respond to the command of the Fourteenth Amendment. An interdistrict remedy for the infringements that occurred in this case is well within the confines and powers of the State, which is the governmental entity ultimately responsible for desegregating its schools. . . .

■ *Mr. Justice* MARSHALL, *with whom Mr. Justice* DOUGLAS, *Mr. Justice* BRENNAN, *and Mr. Justice* WHITE *join, dissenting.*

In *Brown v. Board of Education*, this Court held that segregation of children in public schools on the basis of race deprives minority group children of equal educational opportunities and therefore denies them the equal protection of the laws under the Fourteenth Amendment. This Court recognized then that remedying decades of segregation in public education would not be an easy task. Subsequent events, unfortunately, have seen that prediction bear bitter fruit. . . .

After 20 years of small, often difficult steps toward that great end, the Court today takes a giant step backwards. Notwithstanding a record showing widespread and pervasive racial segregation in the educational system provided by the State of Michigan for children in Detroit, this Court holds that the District Court was powerless to require the State to remedy its constitutional violation in any meaningful fashion. Ironically purporting to base its result on the principle that the scope of the remedy in a desegregation case should be determined by the nature and the extent of the constitutional violation, the Court's answer is to provide no remedy at all for the violation proved in this case, thereby guaranteeing that Negro children in Detroit will receive the same separate and inherently unequal education in the future as they have been unconstitutionally afforded in the past. . . .

The rights at issue in this case are too fundamental to be abridged on grounds as superficial as those relied on by the majority today. We deal here with the right of all of our children, whatever their race, to an equal start in life and to an equal opportunity to reach their full potential as citizens. Those children who have been denied that right in the past deserve better than to see fences thrown up to deny them that right in the future. Our Nation, I fear, will be ill served by the Court's refusal to remedy separate and unequal education, for unless our children begin to learn together, there is little hope that our people will ever learn to live together. . . .

Our prior cases have not minced words as to what steps responsible officials and agencies must take in order to remedy segregation in the public schools. Not only must distinctions on the basis of race be terminated for the future, but school officials are also "clearly charged with the affirmative duty to take whatever steps might be necessary to convert to a unitary system in which racial discrimination would be eliminated root and branch." . . .

Under our decisions, it was clearly proper for the District Court to take into account the so-called "white flight" from the city schools which would be forthcoming from any Detroit-only decree. The court's prediction of white flight was well supported by expert testimony based on past experience in other cities undergoing desegregation relief. . . . One cannot ignore the white-flight problem, for where legally imposed segregation has been established, the District Court has the responsibility to see to it not only that the dual system is terminated at once but also that future events do not serve to perpetuate or re-establish segregation. See *Swann*.

We held in *Swann*, that where de jure segregation is shown, school authorities must make "every effort to achieve the greatest possible degree of actual desegregation." This is the operative standard. . . . If these words have any meaning at all, surely it is that school authorities must, to the extent possible, take all practicable steps to ensure that Negro and white children in fact go to school together. This is, in the final analysis, what desegregation of the public schools is all about.

Because of the already high and rapidly increasing percentage of Negro students in the Detroit system, as well as the prospect of white flight, a Detroit-only plan simply has no hope of achieving actual desegregation. Under such a plan white and Negro students will not go to school together. Instead, Negro children will continue to attend all-Negro schools. The very evil that *Brown I* was aimed at will not be cured, but will be perpetuated for the future.

Under a Detroit-only decree, Detroit's schools will clearly remain racially identifiable in comparison with neighboring schools in the metropolitan community. . . . The message of this action will not escape the Negro children in the city of Detroit. It will be of scant significance to Negro children who have for years been confined by de jure acts of segregation to a growing core of all-Negro schools surrounded by a ring of all-white schools that the new dividing line between the races is the school district boundary. . . .

It is a hollow remedy indeed where "after supposed 'desegregation' the schools remained segregated in fact." We must do better than "substitute . . . one segregated school system for another segregated school system." To suggest, as does the majority, that a Detroit-only plan somehow remedies the effects of de jure segregation of the races is, in my view, to make a solemn mockery of *Brown I*'s holding that separate educational facilities are inherently unequal and of *Swann*'s unequivocal mandate that the answer to de jure segregation is the greatest possible degree of actual desegregation. . . .

Today's holding, I fear, is more a reflection of a perceived public mood that we have gone far enough in enforcing the Constitution's guarantee of equal justice than it is the product of neutral principles of law. In the short run, it may seem to be the easier course to allow our great metropolitan areas to be divided up each into two cities—one white, the other black—but it is a course, I predict, our people will ultimately regret. I dissent.

Notes and Questions

1. *Milliken I* exposed the fragility of the *Swann* consensus and, with four Nixon appointees now on the Court, represented a significant shift in the Court's remedial jurisprudence. To what extent does *Milliken* repudiate the premises of *Swann*? Can the two be harmonized?

2. What is the central holding of *Milliken* about the remedial power of the federal courts?

3. What role does each of the following factors play in the disagreement between the majority and dissenters in *Milliken*: history, the judicial role, federalism, and the meaning of *Brown* itself? In light of your answer, to what extent are the lessons of *Milliken* generalizable outside the desegregation context?

4. Ultimately, in spite of the 1974 decision, the *Milliken* litigation resulted in a massive remedial order (discussed in Chapter 3). But as Judge Nathaniel Jones has explained, *Milliken* was in a broader sense a Pyrrhic victory:

> *Milliken II* provided immense benefits to all children in the urban district, which was heavily composed of minority students. . . . The decision also proved to be the basis for a number of subsequent courts to order ancillary relief, with states being required to contribute substantial sums of money. . . .
>
> Despite the benefits that flowed from the litigation, it was clear that the decision regarding interdistrict relief was a severe setback. . . .
>
> In the long term, [the original trial judge in *Milliken*] has been proven correct. His findings that a desegregation order limited only to Detroit would not stand for long and that multi-district metropolitan desegregation was necessary for an effective remedy have both been borne out. . . . What is now happening, with devastating effect, is that segregation is retaking American schools.

Nathaniel R. Jones, *The Judicial Betrayal of Blacks—Again: The Supreme Court's Destruction of the Hopes Raised by* Brown v. Board of Education, 32 Fordham Urb. L.J. 109, 125-27 (2004).

What lessons do the course and consequences of the *Milliken* litigation provide for impact litigators?

4. TERMINATING DESEGREGATION DECREES

A 2003 report from the Civil Rights Project at Harvard University provided this summary of the history of desegregation from the 1970s to 1991:

> A closely divided Supreme Court was stalemated on desegregation policy for a long period and left the law basically unchanged between the mid-1970s and 1991. The legal standards in place during this time allowed civil rights organizations to almost always win a lawsuit claiming unconstitutional racial segregation in a school district because almost all urban school districts had discriminated in relatively overt ways over time. . . .
>
> The Reagan Administration, however, brought a shift in the position of the Justice Department, which took a stance of strong opposition to desegregation litigation, opposing even the continuation of existing desegregation plans. The Administration

developed theories that desegregation had failed and that existing desegregation orders should be cancelled after only a few years. The Justice Department began to advocate such a policy in the federal courts in the mid-1980s.

Erica Frankenberg, Chungmei Lee & Gary Orfield, *A Multiracial Society with Segregated Schools: Are We Losing the Dream?* 17-18 (2003).

Beginning in the 1990s, the Supreme Court took an accommodating position toward school districts seeking to end court-ordered desegregation plans.

Board of Education of Oklahoma City v. Dowell, 498 U.S. 237 (1991), written by Chief Justice Rehnquist, reversed a court of appeals decision holding that strict conditions must be met before a federal court's 1972 desegregation decree for Oklahoma City could be ended. The Court explained:

> Such decrees . . . are not intended to operate in perpetuity. Local control over the education of children allows citizens to participate in decisionmaking, and allows innovation so that school programs can fit local needs. *Milliken I.* The legal justification for displacement of local authority by an injunctive decree in a school desegregation case is a violation of the Constitution by the local authorities. Dissolving a desegregation decree after the local authorities have operated in compliance with it for a reasonable period of time properly recognizes that "necessary concern for the important values of local control of public school systems dictates that a federal court's regulatory control of such systems not extend beyond the time required to remedy the effects of past intentional discrimination."

The Court ordered the case remanded to the district court to reconsider dissolving the decree based on "whether the Board had complied in good faith with the desegregation decree since it was entered, and whether the vestiges of past discrimination had been eliminated to the extent practicable."

Justice Marshall, joined by Justices Blackmun and Stevens, dissented:

> I believe a desegregation decree cannot be lifted so long as conditions likely to inflict the stigmatic injury condemned in *Brown I* persist and there remain feasible methods of eliminating such conditions. . . .
>
> The Court has indicated that "the ultimate end to be brought about" by a desegregation remedy is "a unitary, nonracial system of public education." We have suggested that this aim is realized once school officials have "eliminate[d] from the public schools *all* vestiges of state-imposed segregation," *Swann* . . . .
>
> Consistent with the mandate of *Brown I,* our cases have imposed on school districts an unconditional duty to eliminate *any* condition that perpetuates the message of racial inferiority inherent in the policy of state-sponsored segregation. The racial identifiability of a district's schools is such a condition. Whether this "vestige" of state-sponsored segregation will persist cannot simply be ignored at the point where a district court is contemplating the dissolution of a desegregation decree. In a district with a history of state-sponsored school segregation, racial separation, in my view, *remains* inherently unequal.

Following *Dowell*, "many districts returned to court to seek the end of their desegregation orders. In districts where they did not, some white parents sought to end these desegregation efforts." Frankenberg, Lee & Orfield, *supra*, at 19 (footnotes omitted). In contrast to the courts' slow slog toward implementing desegregation orders decades before, now some district courts "acted on their own initiative and with considerable speed in terminating desegregation orders." *Id.*

The next case reflects how the Court expanded on its new approach to desegregation decrees.

Missouri v. Jenkins
515 U.S. 70 (1995)

■ *Chief Justice* REHNQUIST *delivered the opinion of the Court....*

[In this eighteen-year-old school desegregation litigation, the district court found that Kansas City, Missouri, School District (KCMSD) and the State had operated the KCMSD as a segregated district (i.e., an *intra*district violation). The court's remedial program included the reduction of class sizes; full-day kindergarten; expanded summer school; before- and after-school tutoring; and an early childhood development program. The next year, the court approved a further plan to turn most KCMSD schools into "magnet" schools, both in order to "provide a greater educational opportunity to *all* KCMSD students," and because it believed "that the proposed magnet plan [was] so attractive that it would draw non-minority students from the private schools who have abandoned or avoided the KCMSD, and draw in additional non-minority students from the suburbs." The court also ordered a salary increase for teachers and non-instructional staff.]

The District Court's desegregation plan has been described as the most ambitious and expensive remedial program in the history of school desegregation. The annual cost per pupil at the KCMSD far exceeds that of the neighboring SSD's [suburban school districts] or of any school district in Missouri.... These massive expenditures have financed "high schools in which every classroom will have air conditioning, an alarm system, and 15 microcomputers; a 2,000-square-foot planetarium; green houses and vivariums; a 25-acre farm with an air-conditioned meeting room for 104 people; a Model United Nations wired for language translation; broadcast capable radio and television studios with an editing and animation lab; a temperature controlled art gallery; movie editing and screening rooms; a 3,500-square-foot dust-free diesel mechanics room; 1,875-square-foot elementary school animal rooms for use in a zoo project; swimming pools; and numerous other facilities." ...

With this background, we turn to the present controversy. First, the State has challenged the District Court's requirement that it fund salary increases for KCMSD instructional and noninstructional staff. The State claimed that funding for salaries was beyond the scope of the District Court's remedial authority. Second, the State has challenged the District Court's order requiring it to continue to fund the remedial quality education programs for the 1992-1993 school year. The State contended that ... it had achieved partial unitary status with respect to the quality education programs already in place. As a result, the State argued that the District Court should have relieved it of responsibility for funding those programs. ...

[Our prior cases have synthesized *Swann* and *Milliken I* as follows:]

"In the first place, like other equitable remedies, the nature of the desegregation remedy is to be determined by the nature and scope of the constitutional violation. The remedy must therefore be related to 'the *condition* alleged to offend the Constitution. . . .' Second, the decree must indeed be *remedial* in nature, that is, it must be designed as nearly as possible 'to restore the victims of discriminatory conduct to the position they would have occupied in the absence of such conduct.' Third, the federal courts in devising a remedy must take into account the interests of state and local authorities in managing their own affairs, consistent with the Constitution."

Because "federal supervision of local school systems was intended as a temporary measure to remedy past discrimination," *Dowell*, we also have considered the showing that must be made by a school district operating under a desegregation order for complete or partial relief from that order[:]

> "[a]mong the factors which must inform the sound discretion of the court in ordering partial withdrawal are the following: [1] whether there has been full and satisfactory compliance with the decree in those aspects of the system where supervision is to be withdrawn; [2] whether retention of judicial control is necessary or practicable to achieve compliance with the decree in other facets of the school system; and [3] whether the school district has demonstrated, to the public and to the parents and students of the once disfavored race, its good-faith commitment to the whole of the courts' decree and to those provisions of the law and the Constitution that were the predicate for judicial intervention in the first instance."

The ultimate inquiry is " 'whether the [constitutional violator] ha[s] complied in good faith with the desegregation decree since it was entered, and whether the vestiges of past discrimination ha[ve] been eliminated to the extent practicable.' " . . .

Here, the District Court has found, and the Court of Appeals has affirmed, that this case involved no interdistrict constitutional violation that would support interdistrict relief. Thus, the proper response by the District Court should have been to eliminate to the extent practicable the vestiges of prior *de jure* segregation within the KCMSD . . . .

Instead of seeking to remove the racial identity of the various schools within the KCMSD, the District Court has set out on a program to create a school district that was equal to or superior to the surrounding SSD's. Its remedy has focused on "desegregative attractiveness," coupled with "suburban comparability." . . .

Nothing in *Milliken I* suggests that the District Court in that case could have circumvented the limits on its remedial authority by requiring the State of Michigan, a constitutional violator, to implement a magnet program designed to achieve the same interdistrict transfer of students that we held was beyond its remedial authority. Here, the District Court has done just that: created a magnet district of the KCMSD in order to serve the *inter*district goal of attracting nonminority students from the surrounding SSD's and redistributing them within the KCMSD. The District Court's pursuit of "desegregative attractiveness" is beyond the scope of its broad remedial authority. . . .

The District Court's pursuit of "desegregative attractiveness" cannot be reconciled with our cases placing limitations on a district court's remedial authority. It is certainly theoretically possible that the greater the expenditure per pupil within the KCMSD, the more likely it is that some unknowable number of nonminority students not presently attending schools in the KCMSD will choose to enroll in those schools. Under this reasoning, however, every increased expenditure, whether it be for teachers, noninstructional employees, books, or buildings, will make the KCMSD in some way more attractive, and thereby perhaps induce nonminority students to enroll in its schools. But this rationale is not susceptible to any objective limitation. This case provides numerous examples demonstrating the limitless authority of the District Court operating under this rationale. In short, desegregative attractiveness has been used "as the hook on which to hang numerous policy choices about improving the quality of education in general within the KCMSD." . . .

Similar considerations lead us to conclude that the District Court's order requiring the State to continue to fund the quality education programs because student achievement levels were still "at or below national norms at many grade levels" cannot be sustained. . . .

The basic task of the District Court is to decide whether the reduction in achievement by minority students attributable to prior *de jure* segregation has been remedied to the extent practicable. . . . Although the District Court has determined that "[s]egregation has caused a system wide *reduction* in achievement in the schools of the KCMSD," it never has identified the incremental effect that segregation has had on minority student achievement or the specific goals of the quality education programs.

In reconsidering this order, the District Court . . . should consider that the State's role with respect to the quality education programs has been limited to the funding, not the implementation, of those programs. As all the parties agree that improved achievement on test scores is not necessarily required for the State to achieve partial unitary status as to the quality education programs, the District Court should sharply limit, if not dispense with, its reliance on this factor. Just as demographic changes independent of *de jure* segregation will affect the racial composition of student assignments, so too will numerous external factors beyond the control of the KCMSD and the State affect minority student achievement. So long as these external factors are not the result of segregation, they do not figure in the remedial calculus. Insistence upon academic goals unrelated to the effects of legal segregation unwarrantably postpones the day when the KCMSD will be able to operate on its own. . . .

On remand, the District Court must bear in mind that its end purpose is not only "to remedy the violation" to the extent practicable, but also "to restore state and local authorities to the control of a school system that is operating in compliance with the Constitution." . . .

[Concurring opinion of O'Connor, J., omitted.]

■ *Justice* Thomas, *concurring.*

It never ceases to amaze me that the courts are so willing to assume that anything that is predominantly black must be inferior. . . .

It should by now be clear that the existence of one-race schools is not by itself an indication that the State is practicing segregation. See, *e.g., Swann.* The continuing "racial isolation" of schools after *de jure* segregation has ended may well reflect voluntary housing choices or other private decisions. Here, for instance, the demography of the entire KCMSD has changed considerably since 1954. Though blacks accounted for only 18.9% of KCMSD's enrollment in 1954, by 1983-1984 the school district was 67.7% black. That certain schools are overwhelmingly black in a district that is now more than two-thirds black is hardly a sure sign of intentional state action. . . .

Without a basis in any real finding of intentional government action, the District Court's imposition of liability upon the State of Missouri improperly rests upon a theory that racial imbalances are unconstitutional. . . . In effect, the court found that racial imbalances constituted an ongoing constitutional violation that continued to inflict harm on black students. This position appears to rest upon the idea that any school that is black is inferior, and that blacks cannot succeed without the benefit of the company of whites. . . .

It is clear that the District Court misunderstood the meaning of *Brown I. Brown I* did not say that "racially isolated" schools were inherently inferior; the harm that it identified was tied purely to *de jure* segregation, not *de facto* segregation. . . .

Segregation was not unconstitutional because it might have caused psychological feelings of inferiority. Public school systems that separated blacks and provided them with superior educational resources—making blacks "feel" superior to whites sent to lesser schools—would violate the Fourteenth Amendment, whether or not the white students felt stigmatized, just as do school systems in which the positions of the races are reversed. . . .

Regardless of the relative quality of the schools, segregation violated the Constitution because the State classified students based on their race. Of course, segregation additionally harmed black students by relegating them to schools with substandard facilities and resources. But neutral policies, such as local school assignments, do not offend the Constitution when individual private choices concerning work or residence produce schools with high black populations. The Constitution does not prevent individuals from choosing to live together, to work together, or to send their children to school together, so long as the State does not interfere with their choices on the basis of race. . . .

Not only did the court subscribe to a theory of injury that was predicated on black inferiority, it also married this concept of liability to our expansive approach to remedial powers. We have given the federal courts the freedom to use any measure necessary to reverse problems—such as racial isolation or low educational achievement—that have proven stubbornly resistant to government policies. We have not permitted constitutional principles such as federalism or the separation of powers to stand in the way of our drive to reform the schools.

Thus, the District Court here ordered massive expenditures by local and state authorities, without congressional or executive authorization and without any indication that such measures would attract whites back to KCMSD or raise KCMSD test scores. The time has come for us to put the genie back in the bottle. . . .

Our willingness to unleash the federal equitable power has reached areas beyond school desegregation. Federal courts have used "structural injunctions," as they are known, not only to supervise our Nation's schools, but also to manage prisons, mental hospitals, and public housing. Judges have directed or managed the reconstruction of entire institutions and bureaucracies, with little regard for the inherent limitations on their authority.

Such extravagant uses of judicial power are at odds with the history and tradition of the equity power and the Framers' design. . . .

Federal courts do not possess the capabilities of state and local governments in addressing difficult educational problems. State and local school officials not only bear the responsibility for educational decisions, they also are better equipped than a single federal judge to make the day-to-day policy, curricular, and funding choices necessary to bring a school district into compliance with the Constitution.[5]

Federal courts simply cannot gather sufficient information to render an effective decree, have limited resources to induce compliance, and cannot seek political and public support for their remedies. When we presume to have the institutional ability to set effective educational, budgetary, or administrative policy, we transform the least dangerous branch into the most dangerous one. . . .

To ensure that district courts do not embark on such broad initiatives in the future, we should demand that remedial decrees be more precisely designed to benefit only those who have been victims of segregation. Race-conscious remedies for discrimination not only must serve a compelling governmental interest (which is met in desegregation cases), but also must be narrowly tailored to further that interest. In the absence of special circumstances, the remedy for *de jure* segregation ordinarily should not include educational programs for students who were not in school (or were even alive) during the period of segregation. . . .

This Court should never approve a State's efforts to deny students, because of their race, an equal opportunity for an education. But the federal courts also should avoid using racial equality as a pretext for solving social problems that do not violate the Constitution. . . .

---

5. Certain aspects of this desegregation plan—for example, compensatory educational programs and orders that the State pay for half of the costs—come perilously close to abrogating the State's Eleventh Amendment immunity from federal money damages awards. *See Edelman v. Jordan.* Although we held in *Milliken II* that such remedies did not run afoul of the Eleventh Amendment, it is difficult to see how they constitute purely prospective relief rather than retrospective compensation. Of course, the state treasury inevitably must fund a State's compliance with injunctions commanding prospective relief, but that does not require a State to supply money to comply with orders that have a backward-looking, compensatory purpose.

■ *Justice* SOUTER, *with whom Justice* STEVENS, *Justice* GINSBURG, *and Justice* BREYER *join, dissenting*. . . .

From the start, the District Court has consistently treated salary increases as an important element in remedying the systemwide reduction in student achievement resulting from segregation in the KCMSD. As noted above, the Court does not question this remedial goal. . . . The only issue, then, is whether the salary increases ordered by the District Court have been reasonably related to achieving that goal, keeping in mind the broad discretion enjoyed by the District Court in exercising its equitable powers. . . .

The District Court had evidence in front of it that . . . discontinuing desegregation funding for salary levels would result in their abrupt drop . . . , with the resulting disparity between teacher pay in the district and the nationwide level increasing to as much as 40 to 45 percent, and a mass exodus of competent employees likely taking place. Faced with this evidence, the District Court found that continued desegregation funding of salaries, and small increases in those salaries over time, were essential to the successful implementation of its remedial scheme, including the elevation of student achievement. . . .

[T]he Court does not question the District Court's salary orders insofar as they relate to the objective of raising the level of student achievement in the KCMSD, but rather overlooks that basis for the orders altogether. The Court suggests that the District Court rested its approval of salary increases only on the object of drawing students into the district's schools and rejects the increases for that reason. It seems clear, however, that the District Court and the Court of Appeals both viewed the salary orders as serving two complementary but distinct purposes, and to the extent that the District Court concludes on remand that its salary orders are justified by reference to the quality of education alone, nothing in the Court's opinion precludes those orders from remaining in effect. . . .

We are not dealing here with an interdistrict remedy in the sense that *Milliken I* used the term. In the *Milliken I* litigation, the District Court had ordered 53 surrounding school districts to be consolidated with the Detroit school system. . . . It was this imposition of remedial measures on more than the one wrongdoing school district that we termed an "interdistrict remedy" . . . .

We did not hold, however, that any remedy that takes into account conditions outside of the district in which a constitutional violation has been committed is an "interdistrict remedy," and as such improper in the absence of an "interdistrict violation." To the contrary, by emphasizing that remedies in school desegregation cases are grounded in traditional equitable principles, we left open the possibility that a district court might subject a proven constitutional wrongdoer to a remedy with intended effects going beyond the district of the wrongdoer's violation, when such a remedy is necessary to redress the harms flowing from the constitutional violation.

The Court, nonetheless, reads *Milliken I* quite differently. It reads the case as categorically forbidding imposition of a remedy on a guilty district with intended consequences in a neighboring innocent district, unless the constitutional violation yielded segregative effects in that innocent district.

Today's decision therefore amounts to a redefinition of the terms of *Milliken I* and consequently to a substantial expansion of its limitation on the permissible remedies for prior segregation. . . .

■ Justice GINSBURG, *dissenting*. . . .

The Court stresses that the present remedial programs have been in place for seven years. But compared to more than two centuries of firmly entrenched official discrimination, the experience with the desegregation remedies ordered by the District Court has been evanescent.

In 1724, Louis XV of France issued the Code Noir, the first slave code for the Colony of Louisiana, an area that included Missouri. When Missouri entered the Union in 1821, it entered as a slave State.

Before the Civil War, Missouri law prohibited the creation or maintenance of schools for educating blacks: "No person shall keep or teach any school for the instruction of negroes or mulattoes, in reading or writing, in this State." Act of Feb. 16, 1847, § 1.

Beginning in 1865, Missouri passed a series of laws requiring separate public schools for blacks. The Missouri Constitution first permitted, then required, separate schools. . . .

[These provisions were not repealed until after *Brown*.] . . . Just ten years ago, in June 1985, the District Court issued its first remedial order [governing the KCMSD].

Today, the Court declares illegitimate the goal of attracting nonminority students to the Kansas City, Missouri, School District, and thus stops the District Court's efforts to integrate a school district that was, in the 1984/1985 school year, sorely in need and 68.3% black. Given the deep, inglorious history of segregation in Missouri, to curtail desegregation at this time and in this manner is an action at once too swift and too soon.

Notes and Questions

1. What is the focus of the *Jenkins* inquiry regarding whether a desegregation decree should be ended? How has the focus of the Court's standard for evaluating desegregation remedies evolved?

2. What substantive limitations does *Jenkins* place on the remedial authority of courts? To what extent are these merely concrete applications of principles announced in earlier cases and to what extent does the majority in *Jenkins* break new ground?

3. The majority and (to an even greater extent) Justice Thomas frame much of their reasoning as an institutional-competence critique of the federal courts' ability to manage a school district. How does Justice Souter reframe the institutional competence question? Whose account is more persuasive?

4. After *Milliken I* and *Jenkins*, what is left of the remedial principles articulated in *Swann*?

5. According to Justice Thomas, what is the meaning of *Brown*? How and why does he think courts err in issuing "structural injunctions"? To what extent are his views on these two issues interrelated?

6. Federalism-based critiques of judicial problem-solving need not proceed from suspicion of judges' motives or assumptions of hubris. Rather, as one older critique of institutional reform observes, one of the main concerns is unintended consequences:

> When a judge undertakes systematic relief, he displaces the elected and appointed officials who normally supervise the state or local function that is the object of that litigation.... There is a genuine danger of a judge's "tunnel vision"; concerned with the problem placed before him in the particular lawsuit, for example, appalling conditions in a mental hospital, he has no occasion to be concerned about the impact of his ruling on limited state or local financial resources. Understandably, the judge is likely to say that constitutional rights cannot be denied by an appeal to budget difficulties. As a result, public resources may fund a function or service which is the subject of litigation at the expense of other valuable services not before the court.

A.E. Dick Howard, *The States and the Supreme Court*, 31 Cath. U. L. Rev. 375, 426 (1982). Can courts tailor their remedies to avoid any displacement of local authorities? Or is the answer to critiques like this one that judges act in an institutional reform capacity only when local authorities have proven themselves untrustworthy?

7. Another critique of institutional reform litigation is that even judges themselves are not functionally in charge of their orders; instead, they must hand over day-to-day responsibility to special masters, court-appointed monitors, and other lawyers:

> Under many consent decrees, effective control of the state or local governmental institution is shifted from elected officials to an ad hoc group of lawyers that writes and administers the judicial regime. . . . Consent decrees are plagued by unintended consequences, yet are difficult to modify in light of experience and changing circumstances. It is not unusual for consent decrees to control a state or local agency for 20 or 30 years, and even then, there may be no end in sight.

Ross Sandler & David Schoenbrod, *The Supreme Court, Democracy and Institutional Reform Litigation*, 49 N.Y.L. Sch. L. Rev. 915, 916 (2005).

Is the reliance on experts or outside monitors a feature or a bug of institutional reform? Is it worth trading off judges' constitutional authority for other actors' greater knowledge or capacity to stay more directly engaged with a problem? Or does this problem illustrate that the judiciary is simply the wrong branch to undertake large-scale reforms?

8. The Court's approach to substantive principles of equal protection law has evolved in tandem with the Court's limitations on district courts' remedial authority—with the result that voluntary desegregation efforts undertaken by local school authorities are, like broad remedial court orders, difficult to sustain.

Chiefly, the Court's decision in *Parents Involved in Community Schools v. Seattle School District No. 1*, 551 U.S. 701 (2007), struck down the Seattle and Louisville school districts' consideration of race in public-school assignments to promote more diverse schools. "Racial balance," the plurality opinion cautioned, "is not to be achieved for its own sake." The dissenters chastised the Court for rejecting "local efforts to bring about the kind of racially integrated education that *Brown v. Board of Education* long ago promised."

B. PRISON REFORM

The story of prison reform litigation in many respects parallels that of desegregation litigation. When courts began to address systemic constitutional violations in the nation's prisons, they initially imposed robust remedies with the blessing of the Supreme Court. Then political backlash, combined with an increasingly conservative Court, sharply limited the role of the courts.

The main difference between the two contexts was the primary driver of the shift away from broad remedial orders. In education, the change was judge-driven: Beginning with *Milliken I*, the Supreme Court limited the remedial authority of courts and eased school districts' path out of judicial oversight. Regarding prisons, the signal event was legislative: The passage of the Prison Litigation Reform Act (PLRA) in 1995 created substantial new barriers to judicial involvement in prison conditions.

As in our study of desegregation, this section proceeds mostly chronologically, tracing the rise and subsequent fall of the courts' involvement in institutional reform. The questions raised here echo those addressed in the desegregation cases. What is the proper role of the courts? What is the appropriate balance between federalism and vindicating constitutional rights?

1. "A DARK AND EVIL WORLD"

The next case (begun in the 1960s as *Holt v. Sarver*) was a wide-ranging challenge to the Arkansas prison system and is considered one of the seminal cases on prison reform.

Hutto v. Finney
437 U.S. 678 (1978)

■ *Mr. Justice STEVENS delivered the opinion of the Court.*

After finding that conditions in the Arkansas penal system constituted cruel and unusual punishment, the District Court entered a series of detailed remedial orders [including the one challenged here:] an order placing a maximum limit of 30 days on confinement in punitive isolation . . . .

The routine conditions that the ordinary Arkansas convict had to endure were characterized by the District Court as "a dark and evil world completely alien to the free world." That characterization was amply supported by the evidence.[3] The punishments for misconduct not serious enough to result in punitive isolation were cruel,[4] unusual,[5] and unpredictable.[6] It is the discipline known as "punitive isolation" that is most relevant for present purposes.

Confinement in punitive isolation was for an indeterminate period of time. An average of 4, and sometimes as many as 10 or 11, prisoners were crowded into windowless 8' × 10' cells containing no furniture other than a source of water and a toilet that could only be flushed from outside the cell. At night the prisoners were given mattresses to spread on the floor. Although some prisoners suffered from infectious diseases such as hepatitis and venereal disease, mattresses were removed and jumbled together each morning, then returned to the cells at random in the evening. Prisoners in isolation received fewer than 1,000 calories a day; their meals consisted primarily of 4-inch squares of "grue," a substance created by mashing meat, potatoes, oleo, syrup, vegetables, eggs, and seasoning into a paste and baking the mixture in a pan.

After finding the conditions of confinement unconstitutional, the District Court did not immediately impose a detailed remedy of its own. Instead, it directed the Department of Correction to "make a substantial start" on improving conditions and to file reports on its progress. . . . [After the Department's progress proved unsatisfactory, the court] placed limits on the number of men that could be confined in one cell, required that each have a bunk, discontinued the "grue" diet, and set 30 days as the maximum isolation sentence. . . .

[Petitioners challenge] that portion of the District Court's most recent order that forbids the Department to sentence inmates to more than 30 days in punitive isolation. Petitioners assume that the District Court held that indeterminate sentences to punitive isolation always constitute cruel and unusual punishment. This assumption misreads the District Court's holding.

---

3. . . . Cummins Farm, the institution at the center of this litigation, required its 1,000 inmates to work in the fields 10 hours a day, six days a week, using mule-drawn tools and tending crops by hand. The inmates were sometimes required to run to and from the fields, with a guard in an automobile or on horseback driving them on. They worked in all sorts of weather, so long as the temperature was above freezing, sometimes in unsuitably light clothing or without shoes. The inmates slept together in large, 100-man barracks and some convicts, known as "creepers," would slip from their beds to crawl along the floor, stalking their sleeping enemies. In one 18-month period, there were 17 stabbings, all but 1 occurring in the barracks. Homosexual rape was so common and uncontrolled that some potential victims dared not sleep . . . .

4. Inmates were lashed with a wooden-handled leather strap five feet long and four inches wide. Although it was not official policy to do so, some inmates were apparently whipped for minor offenses until their skin was bloody and bruised.

5. The "Tucker telephone," a hand-cranked device, was used to administer electrical shocks to various sensitive parts of an inmate's body.

6. Most of the guards were simply inmates who had been issued guns. . . . As the District Court found, it was "within the power of a trusty guard to murder another inmate with practical impunity," because trusties with weapons were authorized to use deadly force against escapees. "Accidental shootings" also occurred; and one trusty fired his shotgun into a crowded barracks because the inmates would not turn off their TV. Another trusty beat an inmate so badly the victim required partial dentures.

Read in its entirety, the District Court's opinion makes it abundantly clear that the length of isolation sentences was not considered in a vacuum. In the court's words, punitive isolation "is not necessarily unconstitutional, but it may be, depending on the duration of the confinement and the conditions thereof." . . . A filthy, overcrowded cell and a diet of "grue" might be tolerable for a few days and intolerably cruel for weeks or months.

The question before the trial court was whether past constitutional violations had been remedied. The court was entitled to consider the severity of those violations in assessing the constitutionality of conditions in the isolation cells. . . . The length of time each inmate spent in isolation was simply one consideration among many. We find no error in the court's conclusion that, taken as a whole, conditions in the isolation cells continued to violate the prohibition against cruel and unusual punishment.

In fashioning a remedy, the District Court had ample authority to go beyond earlier orders and to address each element contributing to the violation. The District Court had given the Department repeated opportunities to remedy the cruel and unusual conditions in the isolation cells. If petitioners had fully complied with the court's earlier orders, the present time limit might well have been unnecessary. But taking the long and unhappy history of the litigation into account, the court was justified in entering a comprehensive order to insure against the risk of inadequate compliance.[9] . . .

The order is supported by the interdependence of the conditions producing the violation. . . . Like the Court of Appeals, we find no error in the inclusion of a 30-day limitation on sentences to punitive isolation as a part of the District Court's comprehensive remedy. . . .

[Opinions of Brennan, J., concurring, and Powell, J., concurring in part and dissenting in part, are omitted.]

■ *Mr. Justice* REHNQUIST, *dissenting.* . . .

No person of ordinary feeling could fail to be moved by the Court's recitation of the conditions formerly prevailing in the Arkansas prison system. Yet I fear that the Court has allowed itself to be moved beyond the well-established bounds limiting the exercise of remedial authority by the federal district courts. [As established in our school desegregation cases, remedies must] be related to the condition alleged to offend the Constitution . . . [and] designed as nearly as possible to restore the victims of discriminatory conduct to the position they would have occupied in the absence of such conduct. . . . [T]he federal courts in devising a remedy must take into account the interests of state and local authorities in managing their own affairs. . . .

The District Court's order limiting the maximum period of punitive isolation to 30 days in no way relates to any condition found offensive to the Constitution.

---

9. [S]tate and local authorities have primary responsibility for curing constitutional violations. "If, however '[those] authorities fail in their affirmative obligations . . . judicial authority may be invoked.' *Swann.* Once invoked, 'the scope of a district court's equitable powers to remedy past wrongs is broad, for breadth and flexibility are inherent in equitable remedies.'" . . .

It is, when stripped of descriptive verbiage, a prophylactic rule, doubtless well designed to assure a more humane prison system in Arkansas, but not complying with the limitations set forth in [our school desegregation cases]. . . . The District Court found that the confinement of two prisoners in a single cell on a restricted diet for 30 days did not violate the Eighth Amendment. While the Court today remarks that "the length of confinement cannot be ignored," it does not find that confinement under the conditions described by the District Court becomes unconstitutional on the 31st day. It must seek other justifications for its affirmance of that portion of the District Court's order. . . .

The sole effect of the provision is to grant future offenders against prison discipline greater benefits than the Constitution requires . . . .

Notes and Questions

1. What parallels can you draw between prison reform and desegregation litigation—in terms of their objectives, the institutional competence of the federal courts in these contexts, the federalism implications of court supervision, and the remedial principles applicable to each in the 1970s? What are the differences?

2. How does the *Hutto* majority's approach to courts' remedial discretion compare to the approach in *Swann*? *Milliken I*? As we'll see, changes in the statutory and judicial landscape have significantly curtailed courts' ability to order remedies for constitutional violations in prisons and jails.

3. Justice Rehnquist expressed concern that the district court imposed a "prophylactic rule" rather than tailoring its remedy to a constitutional violation. What remedy would have been appropriate here under his approach?

2. JUDICIAL LIMITS ON REMEDIES FOR PRISON CONDITIONS

Even before (or around the same time when) Congress enacted the PLRA to impose statutory limits on courts' remedial authority, the Supreme Court was backing away from the broad approach of *Hutto*.

One development limiting institutional reform orders was increasing solicitude for efforts by prisons and jails to obtain modifications of prior decrees. For instance, in *Rufo v. Inmates of Suffolk County Jail*, 502 U.S. 367 (1992), litigation begun in 1971 to reform conditions at a nineteenth-century Boston jail (known as the "Charles Street Jail") still used to house pretrial detainees had resulted in a finding of unconstitutional conditions and a 1979 consent decree under which a new facility would be built. One of the key provisions of the decree required creating enough capacity for each detainee to be housed in a separate cell. With the new jail still under construction in 1989 and the jail population rising, the Suffolk County sheriff moved to modify the decree to permit housing two detainees in one cell ("double celling"). The district court denied the motion, given the importance of single celling to the original agreement, and the court of appeals affirmed. The Supreme Court reversed, in an opinion by Justice White holding that the district court had applied too strict a standard to the request to modify the decree. Instead, "[u]nder the flexible standard we adopt today, a party seeking modification of a consent decree must establish that a significant change in facts or law warrants revision of the decree and that the proposed modification is suitably tailored to the changed circumstance." Applying this standard, the Court explained, modification might be appropriate:

> Even if the decree is construed as an undertaking by petitioners to provide single cells for pretrial detainees, to relieve petitioners from that promise based on changed conditions does not necessarily violate the basic purpose of the decree. That purpose was to provide a remedy for what had been found, based on a variety of factors, including double celling, to be unconstitutional conditions obtaining in the Charles Street Jail. If modification of one term of a consent decree defeats the purpose of the decree, obviously modification would be all but impossible. That cannot be the rule. The District Court was thus in error in holding that . . . modification of the single cell requirement was necessarily forbidden.

More generally, the Court observed:

> The upsurge in institutional reform litigation since *Brown v. Board of Education* has made the ability of a district court to modify a decree in response to changed circumstances all the more important. Because such decrees often remain in place for extended periods of time, the likelihood of significant changes occurring during the life of the decree is increased.

Justice Thomas took no part in the decision. Justice O'Connor concurred to caution against deferring to the views of prison officials "who do not have a model record of compliance with previous court orders in this case."

In dissent, Justice Stevens, joined by Justice Blackmun, did not dispute the majority's standard, but argued that the district court had acted within its discretion in refusing to modify the decree: "After a judicial finding of constitutional violation, petitioners were ordered in 1973 to place pretrial detainees in single cells. In return for certain benefits, petitioners committed themselves in 1979 to continued compliance with the single-celling requirement. . . . It was clearly not an abuse of discretion for the District Court to require petitioners to honor this commitment."

Alongside its permissive view on decree modification, the Supreme Court also limited the remedial authority of federal courts in the 1980s and 1990s by narrowing the interpretations of *substantive* rights. For instance, in *Rhodes v. Chapman*, 452 U.S. 337 (1981), a federal court had ordered an Ohio prison to end its practice of housing two prisoners in the same cell because of overcrowding at the facility, but the Supreme Court reversed, holding that, in light of the district court's finding that food, sanitation, and medical care were adequate, double celling at the prison was not "cruel and unusual punishment" in violation of the Eighth Amendment. In *Lewis v. Casey*, 518 U.S. 343 (1996), a federal court had entered a detailed order requiring the Arizona Department of Corrections to improve its prison library system to respect prisoners' constitutional right to access the courts. The order specified the times that libraries were to be kept open, the number of hours of library use to which each inmate was entitled, and the minimal educational requirements for prison librarians, among other things. The Court reversed, holding principally that a constitutional violation of an incarcerated individual's right to access the courts could not be shown unless the plaintiff "demonstrate[d] that the alleged shortcomings in the library or legal assistance program hindered his efforts to pursue a legal claim"; under this definition, plaintiffs had not shown a systemwide constitutional violation that could justify the scope of the district court's order.

Notes and Questions

1. From the perspective of an impact litigator, which is worse, a general willingness on the part of federal courts to modify institutional reform consent decrees at the behest of defendant institutions, or a narrowing of the constitutional rights at stake? What precautions should plaintiffs' attorneys take in setting up their litigation to avoid either result?

2. Should the plaintiffs in these cases have pursued mechanisms for reform other than judicial relief? What alternatives were likely available?

3. Consider whether the result in *Rufo* holds peril for defendants as well as plaintiffs. How will the approach in *Rufo* affect plaintiffs' future willingness to agree to a consent decree (rather than build a more damning record, litigate to judgment, and seek attorneys' fees)? Put more concretely: If plaintiffs can't trust that their bargained-for agreements will be subsequently honored, why should they settle?

4. From an institutional defendant's perspective, what incentives does *Rufo* create? In what ways can defendants create favorable conditions to seek modifications of prior orders?

5. *Rufo* continues to influence litigation over the modification of consent decrees, even beyond the prison context. For instance, *Horne v. Flores*, 557 U.S. 433 (2009), applied *Rufo* to hold that a district court that had ordered Arizona to increase school funding to assist English-language learners pursuant to the Equal Educational Opportunities Act of 1974 had erred in denying state officials' request for relief on the basis of changed circumstances. Justice Alito's majority opinion observed:

> [Such requests] serve[] a particularly important function in what we have termed "institutional reform litigation." *Rufo.* For one thing, injunctions issued in such cases often remain in force for many years, and the passage of time frequently brings about changed circumstances—changes in the nature of the underlying problem, changes in governing law or its interpretation by the courts, and new policy insights—that warrant reexamination of the original judgment.
>
> Second, institutional reform injunctions often raise sensitive federalism concerns. Such litigation commonly involves areas of core state responsibility, such as public education. *See Jenkins.*
>
> Federalism concerns are heightened when, as in these cases, a federal court decree has the effect of dictating state or local budget priorities....
>
> Finally, the dynamics of institutional reform litigation differ from those of other cases....

> Injunctions of this sort bind state and local officials to the policy preferences of their predecessors and may thereby "improperly deprive future officials of their designated legislative and executive powers."

In dissent, Justice Breyer, joined by Justices Stevens, Souter, and Ginsburg, accused the majority of ignoring the lower courts' careful consideration of the alleged changed circumstances and of promulgating a new, heightened (but vague) standard for modifying decrees in "institutional reform" cases.

Should the "institutional reform" context make a difference when a court considers a request to modify an injunction? Why or why not? What values drive your answer?

3. THE PLRA

Professor Margo Schlanger explains the impetus for Congress's enactment of the Prison Litigation Reform Act (PLRA):

> Driven at least in large part by the steep increase in the number of jail and prison inmates, . . . the amount of civil litigation brought by inmates in federal court increased steadily during the 1980s, and more steeply in the early 1990s. In 1995, inmates filed nearly 40,000 new federal civil lawsuits—nineteen percent of the federal civil docket. About fifteen percent of the federal civil trials held that year were in inmate civil rights cases.
>
> But in the mid-1990s, the state officials who were the most frequent targets of the growing inmate docket were finally able to capitalize on the rightward move in American politics and mobilize a major campaign against the lawsuits. Building on years of (noninmate) tort reform drives as well as law-and-order rhetoric, state officials got their proposed legislative solution into the Republican Congress's 1994 Contract with America. . . . The PLRA's passage was aided by its connection to several longstanding political trends. In particular, it marked the overlap of conservatives' discontent with so-called "imperial" judging, tort reformers' concern with the problem of frivolous lawsuits, and new congressional willingness to legislate federal court procedure.

Margo Schlanger, *Inmate Litigation*, 116 Harv. L. Rev. 1555, 1557-59 (2003).

The PLRA could not change the substantive constitutional law governing prison litigation (primarily the Eighth Amendment's prohibition on cruel and unusual punishment). But with regard to litigation procedure, the PLRA represented a "sea change," *id.* at 1627, including in the following areas:

- Prisoners must exhaust all "available" administrative grievance procedures in their institutions; if they do not, their court cases are usually dismissed. 42 U.S.C. § 1997e(a).
- Even indigent prisoners proceeding *in forma pauperis* must pay a filing fee, and under a new "three strikes" provision, prisoners who have had three prior actions dismissed because they are "frivolous, malicious, or fail[] to state a claim upon which relief may be granted" cannot proceed *in forma pauperis* at all unless they face "imminent danger of serious physical injury." 28 U.S.C. § 1915(g).

- Courts must screen prisoner filings and dismiss them (which may occur without notice or an opportunity to respond) if the complaint is "frivolous, malicious, or fails to state a claim upon which relief may be granted; or . . . seeks monetary relief from a defendant who is immune from such relief." 28 U.S.C. § 1915A.

The PLRA imposed the following limitations on remedies:

- Prisoners may not receive court-awarded damages for "mental or emotional injury suffered while in custody without a prior showing of physical injury or the commission of a sexual act." 42 U.S.C. § 1997e(e).
- An injunction to address prison conditions may not issue unless it "is narrowly drawn, extends no further than necessary to correct the violation of the Federal right, and is the least intrusive means necessary to correct the violation of the Federal right." Additionally, in considering such an order, "[t]he court shall give substantial weight to any adverse impact on public safety or the operation of a criminal justice system caused by the relief." 18 U.S.C. § 3626(a)(1)(A).
- Prisoner release orders are specifically forbidden unless "(i) a court has previously entered an order for less intrusive relief that has failed to remedy the deprivation of the Federal right sought to be remedied through the prisoner release order; and (ii) the defendant has had a reasonable amount of time to comply with the previous court orders." 18 U.S.C. § 3626(a)(3)(A). Additionally, to order releases, the court must find that "(i) crowding is the primary cause of the violation of a Federal right; and (ii) no other relief will remedy the violation of the Federal right." 18 U.S.C. § 3626(a)(3)(E).
- These limitations on relief apply even to consent decrees—i.e., court-ordered remedies negotiated by the parties. 18 U.S.C. § 3626(c)(1).
- A defendant or intervenor can move at any time to terminate an injunction on the ground that it does not comply with these limitations. 18 U.S.C. § 3626(b)(2).

From the perspective of an impact litigator, which of these limitations are the most damaging to the ability to obtain relief? From the perspective of an institutional defendant, which are most valuable?

To what extent do these limitations codify the Rehnquist Court's restrictive approach to remedies as exemplified in *Rufo* and *Jenkins*? In what respects are they stricter? Less strict?

In 2015, Professor Schlanger examined the effects of the PLRA after two decades. She found, first, that upon passage of the statute, prison civil rights claims in federal court almost immediately fell by roughly one-third, both in absolute terms and relative to the size of the incarcerated population. *See* Margo Schlanger, *Trends in Prisoner Litigation, As the PLRA Enters Adulthood*, 5 U.C. Irvine L. Rev. 153, 157 & tbl. 1 (2015). After a period of further decline, filings leveled off in the 2000s at around 10 per 1,000 prisoners, down from a high of around 24 filings per 1,000 prisoners in the mid-1990s. *See id.* Prisoners' success rates, too, have fallen. *See id.* at 162-63. Professor Schlanger calculated that the national success rate for plaintiffs in all federal cases ending in federal fiscal year 2012 was 54.5 percent overall; for prisoner civil rights cases, it was 11.1 percent. *See id.* at 165 tbl. 4. Finally, the percentage of jails and prisons covered by court orders and the percentage of the incarcerated population covered by court orders fell substantially—by at least one-third for the first decade or so of the PLRA (the amount of time for which data were available). *See id.* at 169 tbl. 8.

We turn now to a closer look at two of the most significant PLRA limitations on civil rights enforcement suits by incarcerated people: exhaustion and the limitations on injunctive relief.

4. EXHAUSTION UNDER THE PLRA

As noted, the PLRA requires that a prisoner exhaust "such administrative remedies as are available" before suing to challenge prison conditions. 42 U.S.C. § 1997e(a).

What does that mean in practice? Grievance processes vary by jurisdiction. In the federal system, Bureau of Prisons (BOP) regulations provide that, except for grievances involving sexual abuse (and certain other limited circumstances), an incarcerated person must first attempt "informal resolution" with prison staff, pursuant to procedures established at that facility, before filing an administrative grievance, and the deadline for both of these steps together is 20 days from the date of the basis for the grievance. 28 C.F.R. 542.13(a) & 542.14(a). The complainant has 20 days from the date of the Warden's response to appeal an adverse decision to the BOP Regional Director, and then 30 days from that person's response to appeal an adverse decision to the General Counsel of BOP—the final step in the grievance process. 28 C.F.R. 542.15(b). BOP officials "may" (but are not required to) extend these deadlines for "valid reason," such as if the complainant cannot file because of physical inability to prepare a request or appeal. 28 C.F.R. 542.14(b) & 542.15(a). A complaint may be submitted directly to the Regional Director if "the inmate's safety or well-being would be placed in danger if the Request became known at the [inmate's own] institution." 28 C.F.R. 542(d)(1).

In addition to the quick deadlines in the BOP process, incarcerated individuals may face a number of other challenges in completing all the steps of the process: they may lack legal training, not know how quickly they must complete each step, face language barriers, or be restricted in their movements within their institution during the critical time periods.

If an incarcerated person fails to complete the required steps and then tries to sue in court, the exhaustion requirement generally dooms the claim.

The Court recently emphasized the strictness of the exhaustion requirement in *Ross v. Blake*, 136 S. Ct. 1850 (2016), which rejected an exception for "special circumstances":

> [J]udge-made exhaustion doctrines, even if flatly stated at first, remain amenable to judge-made exceptions. But a statutory exhaustion provision stands on a different footing. There, Congress sets the rules—and courts have a role in creating exceptions only if Congress wants them to. For that reason, mandatory exhaustion statutes like the PLRA establish mandatory exhaustion regimes, foreclosing judicial discretion. . . .

We have taken just that approach in construing the PLRA's exhaustion provision—rejecting every attempt to deviate . . . from its textual mandate [including via proposed exceptions for excessive force claims, for constitutional claims, and for cases in which the plaintiff wanted a type of relief that the grievance process did not provide.]

However, the Court noted, the PLRA's text offers prisoners an important qualification:

Under § 1997e(a), the exhaustion requirement hinges on the "availab[ility]" of administrative remedies: An inmate, that is, must exhaust available remedies, but need not exhaust unavailable ones. . . . [T]he ordinary meaning of the word "available" is "'capable of use for the accomplishment of a purpose,' and that which 'is accessible or may be obtained.'" . . .

[W]e note as relevant here three kinds of circumstances in which an administrative remedy, although officially on the books, is not capable of use to obtain relief. . . .

First, . . . an administrative procedure is unavailable when (despite what regulations or guidance materials may promise) it operates as a simple dead end—with officers unable or consistently unwilling to provide any relief to aggrieved inmates. Suppose, for example, that a prison handbook directs inmates to submit their grievances to a particular administrative office—but in practice that office disclaims the capacity to consider those petitions. The procedure is not then "capable of use" for the pertinent purpose. . . . So too if administrative officials have apparent authority, but decline ever to exercise it. . . .

Next, an administrative scheme might be so opaque that it becomes, practically speaking, incapable of use. In this situation, some mechanism exists to provide relief, but no ordinary prisoner can discern or navigate it. . . . The procedures need not be sufficiently "plain" as to preclude any reasonable mistake or debate with respect to their meaning. When an administrative process is susceptible of multiple reasonable interpretations, Congress has determined that the inmate should err on the side of exhaustion. But when a remedy is . . . essentially "unknowable"—so that no ordinary prisoner can make sense of what it demands—then it is also unavailable. . . .

And finally, the same is true when prison administrators thwart inmates from taking advantage of a grievance process through machination, misrepresentation, or intimidation.

Notes and Questions

1. Can you think of any "special circumstances" in which the exhaustion rule should be waived notwithstanding the PLRA's text? Or will litigation over the "availability" question avert any injustices that the exhaustion rule might create?

2. The Supreme Court has observed that the goal of the exhaustion requirement in the PLRA was "to reduce the quantity and improve the quality of prisoner suits." *Porter v. Nussle*, 534 U.S. 516, 524 (2002). Does the statute seem designed to achieve both those goals equally?

3. Does it surprise you that no Justice dissented from *Ross*? How would you explain that result—the obvious correctness of the reasoning, the allure of textualism, or something else?

4. If you were a civil rights attorney who regularly represented prisoners, what would be the most effective steps you could take to help your clients avoid losing court cases because of the exhaustion requirement? When should you take those steps?

5. An "Exceptional" Case

Notwithstanding the PLRA's strict limitations, prison reform litigation still occasionally succeeds. We conclude with the most significant and far-reaching success in recent years—with the caveat that it represents the exception rather than the rule. The analysis reflects how many hurdles plaintiffs must clear under the PLRA to obtain injunctive relief.

Brown v. Plata
563 U.S. 493 (2011)

■ *Justice* Kennedy *delivered the opinion of the Court.* . . .

The degree of overcrowding in California's prisons is exceptional. California's prisons are designed to house a population just under 80,000, but . . . [t]he State's prisons had operated at around 200% of design capacity for at least 11 years. Prisoners are crammed into spaces neither designed nor intended to house inmates. As many as 200 prisoners may live in a gymnasium, monitored by as few as two or three correctional officers. As many as 54 prisoners may share a single toilet. . . .

Prisoners in California with serious mental illness do not receive minimal, adequate care. Because of a shortage of treatment beds, suicidal inmates may be held for prolonged periods in telephone-booth sized cages without toilets. A psychiatric expert reported observing an inmate who had been held in such a cage for nearly 24 hours, standing in a pool of his own urine, unresponsive and nearly catatonic. Prison officials explained they had " 'no place to put him.' " Other inmates awaiting care may be held for months in administrative segregation, where they endure harsh and isolated conditions and receive only limited mental health services. Wait times for mental health care range as high as 12 months. In 2006, the suicide rate in California's prisons was nearly 80% higher than the national average for prison populations; and a court-appointed Special Master found that 72.1% of suicides involved "some measure of inadequate assessment, treatment, or intervention, and were therefore most probably foreseeable and/or preventable."

Prisoners suffering from physical illness also receive severely deficient care. California's prisons were designed to meet the medical needs of a population at 100% of design capacity and so have only half the clinical space needed to treat the current population. A correctional officer testified that, in one prison, up to 50 sick inmates may be held together in a 12- by 20-foot cage for up to five hours awaiting treatment. The number of staff is inadequate, and prisoners face significant delays in access to care. A prisoner with severe abdominal pain died after a 5-week delay in referral to a specialist; a prisoner with "constant and extreme" chest pain died after an 8-hour delay in evaluation by a doctor; and a prisoner died of testicular cancer after a "failure of MDs to work up for cancer in a young man with 17 months of testicular pain." Doctor Ronald Shansky, former medical director of the Illinois state prison system, surveyed death reviews for California prisoners. He concluded that extreme departures from the standard of care were "widespread," and that the proportion of "possibly preventable or preventable" deaths was "extremely high." Many more prisoners, suffering from severe but not life-threatening conditions, experience prolonged illness and unnecessary pain. . . .

[A] three-judge court heard 14 days of testimony and issued a 184-page opinion, making extensive findings of fact. The court ordered California to reduce its prison population to 137.5% of the prisons' design capacity within two years. Assuming the State does not increase capacity through new construction, the order requires a population reduction of 38,000 to 46,000 persons. Because it appears all but certain that the State cannot complete sufficient construction to comply fully with the order, the prison population will have to be reduced to at least some extent. The court did not order the State to achieve this reduction in any particular manner. Instead, the court ordered the State to formulate a plan for compliance and submit its plan for approval by the court.

To incarcerate, society takes from prisoners the means to provide for their own needs. Prisoners are dependent on the State for food, clothing, and necessary medical care. A prison's failure to provide sustenance for inmates "may actually produce physical 'torture or a lingering death.'" . . . A prison that deprives prisoners of basic sustenance, including adequate medical care, is incompatible with the concept of human dignity and has no place in civilized society.

If government fails to fulfill this obligation, the courts have a responsibility to remedy the resulting Eighth Amendment violation. See *Hutto*. Courts must be sensitive to the State's interest in punishment, deterrence, and rehabilitation, as well as the need for deference to experienced and expert prison administrators faced with the difficult and dangerous task of housing large numbers of convicted criminals. Courts nevertheless must not shrink from their obligation to "enforce the constitutional rights of all 'persons,' including prisoners." Courts may not allow constitutional violations to continue simply because a remedy would involve intrusion into the realm of prison administration. . . .

[To impose an order limiting a prison population under the PLRA, a] three-judge court must then find by clear and convincing evidence that "crowding is the primary cause of the violation of a Federal right" and that "no other relief will remedy the violation of the Federal right." As with any award of prospective relief under the PLRA, the relief "shall extend no further than necessary to correct the violation of the Federal right of a particular plaintiff or plaintiffs." The three-judge court must therefore find that the relief is "narrowly drawn, extends no further than necessary . . . , and is the least intrusive means necessary to correct the violation of the Federal right." In making this determination, the three-judge court must give "substantial weight to any adverse impact on public safety or the operation of a criminal justice system caused by the relief." Applying these standards, the three-judge court found a population limit appropriate, necessary, and authorized in this case. . . .

[1]

[Regarding the requirement that crowding be the "primary cause" of the violation, t]he record documents the severe impact of burgeoning demand on the provision of care. At the time of trial, vacancy rates for medical and mental health staff ranged as high as 20% for surgeons, 25% for physicians, 39% for nurse practitioners, and 54.1% for psychiatrists. . . . Even on the assumption that vacant positions could be filled, the evidence suggested there would be insufficient space for the necessary additional staff to perform their jobs. . . . Staff operate out of converted storage rooms, closets, bathrooms, shower rooms, and visiting centers. These makeshift facilities impede the effective delivery of care and place the safety of medical professionals in jeopardy, compounding the difficulty of hiring additional staff.

This shortfall of resources relative to demand contributes to significant delays in treatment. Mentally ill prisoners are housed in administrative segregation while awaiting transfer to scarce mental health treatment beds for appropriate care. . . . Delays are no less severe in the context of physical care. Prisons have backlogs of up to 700 prisoners waiting to see a doctor. . . . Urgent specialty referrals at one prison had been pending for six months to a year.

Crowding also creates unsafe and unsanitary living conditions that hamper effective delivery of medical and mental health care. A medical expert described living quarters in converted gymnasiums or dayrooms, where large numbers of prisoners may share just a few toilets and showers, as "'breeding grounds for disease.'" . . .

The three-judge court acknowledged that the violations were caused by factors in addition to overcrowding and that reducing crowding in the prisons would not entirely cure the violations. . . . The three-judge court nevertheless found that overcrowding was the primary cause in the sense of being the foremost cause of the violation.

This understanding of the primary cause requirement is consistent with the text of the PLRA. The State in fact concedes that it proposed this very definition of primary cause to the three-judge court. "Primary" is defined as "[f]irst or highest in rank, quality, or importance; principal." American Heritage Dictionary. Overcrowding need only be the foremost, chief, or principal cause of the violation. . . .

[One of the district court judges] compared the problem to "'a spider web, in which the tension of the various strands is determined by the relationship among all the parts of the web, so that if one pulls on a single strand, the tension of the entire web is redistributed in a new and complex pattern.'" See also *Hutto* (noting "the interdependence of the conditions producing the violation," including overcrowding). Only a multifaceted approach aimed at many causes, including overcrowding, will yield a solution. . . .

A finding that overcrowding is the "primary cause" of a violation is therefore permissible, despite the fact that additional steps will be required to remedy the violation.

[2]

The three-judge court was also required to find by clear and convincing evidence that "no other relief will remedy the violation of the Federal right."

The State argues that the violation could have been remedied through a combination of new construction, transfers of prisoners out of State, hiring of medical personnel, and continued efforts by the Receiver and Special Master [appointed in these cases]. . . . The evidence at trial, however, supports the three-judge court's conclusion that an order limited to other remedies would not provide effective relief. . . .

Construction of new facilities, in theory, could alleviate overcrowding, but the three-judge court found no realistic possibility that California would be able to build itself out of this crisis. . . .

The three-judge court also rejected additional hiring as a realistic means to achieve a remedy. The State for years had been unable to fill positions necessary for the adequate provision of medical and mental health care, and the three-judge court found no reason to expect a change. . . . The court also concluded that there would be insufficient space for additional staff to work even if adequate personnel could somehow be retained. Additional staff cannot help to remedy the violation if they have no space in which to see and treat patients. . . .

[Remedial efforts have been ongoing for at least nine years.] At one time, it may have been possible to hope that these violations would be cured without a reduction in overcrowding. A long history of failed remedial orders, together with substantial evidence of overcrowding's deleterious effects on the provision of care, compels a different conclusion today. . . .

[3]

The PLRA states that no prospective relief shall issue with respect to prison conditions unless it is narrowly drawn, extends no further than necessary to correct the violation of a federal right, and is the least intrusive means necessary to correct the violation. . . .

The population limit imposed by the three-judge court does not fail narrow tailoring simply because it will have positive effects beyond the plaintiff class. Narrow tailoring requires a " ' "fit" between the [remedy's] ends and the means chosen to accomplish those ends.' " The scope of the remedy must be proportional to the scope of the violation, and the order must extend no further than necessary to remedy the violation. This Court has rejected remedial orders that unnecessarily reach out to improve prison conditions other than those that violate the Constitution. But the precedents do not suggest that a narrow and otherwise proper remedy for a constitutional violation is invalid simply because it will have collateral effects. . . .

This case is unlike cases where courts have impermissibly reached out to control the treatment of persons or institutions beyond the scope of the violation. Even prisoners with no present physical or mental illness may become afflicted, and all prisoners in California are at risk so long as the State continues to provide inadequate care. Prisoners in the general population will become sick, and will become members of the plaintiff classes, with routine frequency; and overcrowding may prevent the timely diagnosis and care necessary to provide effective treatment and to prevent further spread of disease. Relief targeted only at present members of the plaintiff classes may therefore fail to adequately protect future class members who will develop serious physical or mental illness. Prisoners who are not sick or mentally ill do not yet have a claim that they have been subjected to care that violates the Eighth Amendment, but in no sense are they remote bystanders in California's medical care system. They are that system's next potential victims.

A release order limited to prisoners within the plaintiff classes would, if anything, unduly limit the ability of State officials to determine which prisoners should be released. . . .

[4]

In reaching its decision, the three-judge court gave "substantial weight" to any potential adverse impact on public safety from its order. . . .

The PLRA's requirement that a court give "substantial weight" to public safety does not require the court to certify that its order has no possible adverse impact on the public. A contrary reading would depart from the statute's text by replacing the word "substantial" with "conclusive." . . .

The three-judge court credited substantial evidence that prison populations can be reduced in a manner that does not increase crime to a significant degree. Some evidence indicated that reducing overcrowding in California's prisons could even improve public safety. . . .

Expert witnesses produced statistical evidence that prison populations had been lowered without adversely affecting public safety in a number of jurisdictions, including certain counties in California, as well as Wisconsin, Illinois, Texas, Colorado, Montana, Michigan, Florida, and Canada. . . .

The court found that various available methods of reducing overcrowding would have little or no impact on public safety. Expansion of good-time credits would allow the State to give early release to only those prisoners who pose the least risk of reoffending. Diverting low-risk offenders to community programs such as drug treatment, day reporting centers, and electronic monitoring would likewise lower the prison population without releasing violent convicts. The State now sends large numbers of persons to prison for violating a technical term or condition of their parole, and it could reduce the prison population by punishing technical parole violations through community-based programs. This last measure would be particularly beneficial as it would reduce crowding in the reception centers, which are especially hard hit by overcrowding. The court's order took account of public safety concerns by giving the State substantial flexibility to select among these and other means of reducing overcrowding. . . .

[5]

Establishing the population at which the State could begin to provide constitutionally adequate medical and mental health care, and the appropriate time frame within which to achieve the necessary reduction, requires a degree of judgment. The inquiry involves uncertain predictions regarding the effects of population reductions, as well as difficult determinations regarding the capacity of prison officials to provide adequate care at various population levels. Courts have substantial flexibility when making these judgments. "'Once invoked, "the scope of a district court's equitable powers . . . is broad, for breadth and flexibility are inherent in equitable remedies."'" *Hutto* (quoting *Milliken II*, in turn quoting *Swann*). . . .

The medical and mental health care provided by California's prisons falls below the standard of decency that inheres in the Eighth Amendment. This extensive and ongoing constitutional violation requires a remedy, and a remedy will not be achieved without a reduction in overcrowding. The relief ordered by the three-judge court is required by the Constitution and was authorized by Congress in the PLRA. The State shall implement the order without further delay. . . .

■ *Justice* SCALIA, *with whom Justice* THOMAS *joins, dissenting.*

Today the Court affirms what is perhaps the most radical injunction issued by a court in our Nation's history: an order requiring California to release the staggering number of 46,000 convicted criminals.

There comes before us, now and then, a case whose proper outcome is so clearly indicated by tradition and common sense, that its decision ought to shape the law, rather than vice versa. One would think that, before allowing the decree of a federal district court to release 46,000 convicted felons, this Court would bend every effort to read the law in such a way as to avoid that outrageous result. Today, quite to the contrary, the Court disregards stringently drawn provisions of the governing statute, and traditional constitutional limitations upon the power of a federal judge, in order to uphold the absurd.

The proceedings that led to this result were a judicial travesty. I dissent because the institutional reform the District Court has undertaken violates the terms of the governing statute, ignores bedrock limitations on the power of Article III judges, and takes federal courts wildly beyond their institutional capacity. . . .

The plaintiffs do not appear to claim—and it would absurd to suggest—that every single one of those prisoners has personally experienced "torture or a lingering death," as a consequence of that bad medical system. Indeed, it is inconceivable that anything more than a small proportion of prisoners in the plaintiff classes have personally received sufficiently atrocious treatment that their Eighth Amendment right was violated . . . .

[T]he vast majority of inmates most generously rewarded by the release order—the 46,000 whose incarceration will be ended—do not form part of any aggrieved class even under the Court's expansive notion of constitutional violation. Most of them will not be prisoners with medical conditions or severe mental illness; and many will undoubtedly be fine physical specimens who have developed intimidating muscles pumping iron in the prison gym.

Even if I accepted the implausible premise that the plaintiffs have established a systemwide violation of the Eighth Amendment, I would dissent from the Court's endorsement of a decrowding order. That order is an example of what has become known as a "structural injunction." . . .

The drawbacks of structural injunctions have been described at great length elsewhere. See, *e.g., Missouri v. Jenkins* (Thomas, J., concurring). This case illustrates one of their most pernicious aspects: that they force judges to engage in a form of factfinding-as-policymaking that is outside the traditional judicial role. The factfinding judges traditionally engage in involves the determination of past or present facts based (except for a limited set of materials of which courts may take "judicial notice") exclusively upon a closed trial record. . . . When a judge manages a structural injunction, however, he will inevitably be required to make very broad empirical predictions necessarily based in large part upon policy views—the sort of predictions regularly made by legislators and executive officials, but inappropriate for the Third Branch. . . .

The District Court cast these predictions (and the Court today accepts them) as "factual findings," made in reliance on the procession of expert witnesses that testified at trial. Because these "findings" have support in the record, it is difficult to reverse them under a plain-error standard of review. And given that the District Court devoted nearly 10 days of trial and 70 pages of its opinion to this issue, it is difficult to dispute that the District Court has discharged its statutory obligation to give "substantial weight to any adverse impact on public safety."

But the idea that the three District Judges in this case relied solely on the credibility of the testifying expert witnesses is fanciful. *Of course* they were relying largely on their own beliefs about penology and recidivism. And *of course* different district judges, of different policy views, would have "found" that rehabilitation would not work and that releasing prisoners would increase the crime rate. I am not saying that the District Judges rendered their factual findings in bad faith. I am saying that it is impossible for judges to make "factual findings" without inserting their own policy judgments, when the factual findings *are* policy judgments. What occurred here is no more judicial factfinding in the ordinary sense than would be the factual findings that deficit spending will not lower the unemployment rate, or that the continued occupation of Iraq will decrease the risk of terrorism. Yet, because they have been branded "factual findings" entitled to deferential review, the policy preferences of three District Judges now govern the operation of California's penal system. . . .

[S]tructural injunctions do not simply invite judges to indulge policy preferences. They invite judges to indulge *incompetent* policy preferences. Three years of law school and familiarity with pertinent Supreme Court precedents give no insight whatsoever into the management of social institutions. . . .

■ *Justice* ALITO, *with whom* THE CHIEF JUSTICE *joins, dissenting.* . . .

The decree in this case is a perfect example of what the Prison Litigation Reform Act of 1995 was enacted to prevent.

The Constitution does not give federal judges the authority to run state penal systems. Decisions regarding state prisons have profound public safety and financial implications, and the States are generally free to make these decisions as they choose. . . .

Many of the problems . . . plainly could be addressed without releasing prisoners and without incurring the costs associated with a large-scale prison construction program. Sanitary procedures could be improved; sufficient supplies of medicine and medical equipment could be purchased; an adequate system of records management could be implemented; and the number of medical and other staff positions could be increased. Similarly, it is hard to believe that staffing vacancies cannot be reduced or eliminated and that the qualifications of medical personnel cannot be improved by any means short of a massive prisoner release. Without specific findings backed by hard evidence, this Court should not accept the counterintuitive proposition that these problems cannot be ameliorated by increasing salaries, improving working conditions, and providing better training and monitoring of performance.

While the cost of a large-scale construction program may well exceed California's current financial capabilities, a more targeted program, involving the repair and perhaps the expansion of current medical facilities (as opposed to general prison facilities), might be manageable. . . .

The prisoner release ordered in this case is unprecedented, improvident, and contrary to the PLRA. In largely sustaining the decision below, the majority is gambling with the safety of the people of California. . . .

Notes and Questions

1. Does *Plata* show that the PLRA is working as Congress intended, establishing a high bar for screening out meritless cases but permitting meritorious ones to succeed? Or that the PLRA's limitations are so stringent that courts must stretch them to grant relief even for egregious constitutional violations?

2. As between the majority and the dissenters, whose approach do you think is more consistent with the text of the PLRA's limitations on remedial orders? With the congressional intent behind those limitations?

3. The majority notes the "exceptional" nature of the circumstances here. Should only an "exceptional" case justify sweeping relief? How should the balance be struck between the seriousness of the constitutional violations at issue and the institutional competence and federalism concerns raised by the dissenters? Or, as Justice Scalia suggests, should the latter concerns be treated not as factors to be weighed but as limitations on the Court's authority?

4. Consider the role of tailoring of remedies in both the school and prison contexts. Could the Court's modern institutional reform jurisprudence be summed

up by the principle that the remedy must be tailored to the violation? If not, what's missing from that account? If so, is that a satisfactory guideline regarding courts' power to address widespread constitutional violations? How if at all would you modify it?

5. Recall Justice Thomas's concurrence in *Jenkins* in connection with Justice Scalia's dissent in *Plata*. In which sphere are Justice Scalia's and Justice Thomas's institutional competence and federalism concerns more salient, schools or prisons? Why?

6. In connection with the institutional reform critiques of Justices Scalia and Thomas, consider the view of federal appellate Judge Diarmuid O'Scannlain:

> [I]n a democracy such as ours, the legitimate authority does not lie with the attorney prosecuting, or the judge presiding over, any specific piece of institutional reform litigation. It lies with the political branches, particularly with Congress and with the legislatures of individual states. . . .
>
> [Institutional reform cases] tend to involve large and ever-shifting numbers of parties, and "the trial judge has increasingly become the creator and manager of complex forms of ongoing relief" that "require the judge's continuing involvement" and that more closely resemble complicated series of administrative regulations than the injunctions of old. Thus the federal judge became both the creator and the interpreter of any number of social policies, roles that the Founders explicitly gave to different bodies . . . .

Diarmuid F. O'Scannlain, *Access to Justice Within the Federal Courts—A Ninth Circuit Perspective*, 90 Or. L. Rev. 1033, 1038, 1044-45 (2012). How much of the federal judiciary's work since *Brown v. Board of Education* does this critique implicate? *Brown* itself? Should skeptics of institutional reform litigation likewise be skeptical of judicial review generally? How does the *Plata* majority answer these concerns?

7. If you find concerns about judicial overinvolvement persuasive, what alternative do you propose? If courts should not be providing a remedy, what other actors are in a position to do so? How likely is it that they will?

8. Do Justice Scalia's suggestions that the Court ought to "bend every effort" to avoid the majority's result and "shape the law" to "tradition and common sense" "rather than vice versa" cast doubt on his commitment to principle? To the rule of law? Or is he just being honest about what judges in fact do all the time when adjudicating hard cases?

9. A 2015 study, Magnus Lofstrom & Brandon Martin, *Public Safety Realignment: Impacts So Far,* Pub. Policy Inst. of Cal. (Sept. 2015), provides an early report about the effects of the order affirmed in *Plata*. According to Lofstrom and Martin, the California prison population fell by about 27,000 by 2012, but then leveled off and did not reach the court-mandated target until 2015, after the November 2014 passage of Proposition 47 reduced penalties for many drug and property offenses. Violent crime did not increase, but auto thefts rose. Recidivism rates were mostly unchanged. In many respects, the authors

deem the transformation of the California prison system a success. However, some of the decrease in the prison population was achieved by shifting prisoners to county jails, where populations rose "close to historical highs."

A more recent investigative report underscores the dangerous conditions facing those incarcerated in California jails after the *Plata* remedy went into effect, with higher numbers of deaths in California jails since 2011 as jails have struggled with new crowding problems of their own. *See* Jason Pohl & Ryan Gabrielson, *California Tried to Fix Its Prisons. Now County Jails Are More Deadly*, ProPublica, Apr. 24, 2019.

Do these accounts vindicate institutional reformers' and the *Plata* majority's faith in the judicial process? Exemplify the unintended consequences bound to follow from judicial involvement in the affairs of state and local government? Some of each?

10. Recall the questions about impact litigation with which we began our study, in the Prologue. What lessons do you draw from the school and prison cases regarding the value and effectiveness of impact litigation? The ideal conditions in which to pursue it? The power of litigation as compared with other means to seek change?

CHAPTER 12 PROBLEMS

Problem 12A. Capitol Hill Public Schools (CHPS) adopts a school choice plan with a "voluntary desegregation" component. Under the plan, Capitol Hill parents choose the schools their children attend from among all CHPS schools. If a school is oversubscribed, CHPS picks which students to reassign to a second- or third-choice school based on a variety of factors, one of which is whether students will help keep the school within a "target range" of demographics, which is 35-55 percent white, 35-55 percent black, 5-15 percent Latino, and 3-10 percent for the total of all other races.

A group of parents sue CHPS, claiming that the use of race as a factor in school assignments violates equal protection. The district court dismisses the case. The court of appeals reinstates it and remands for further proceedings. The parties engage in discovery and proceed to trial.

By the time the trial concludes, the case has been litigated for three years. Many students have been at the same school for years under the plan. At trial, the district court rules in favor of the plaintiffs and enters an injunction prohibiting the use of race within the school choice plan.

For the following year's school assignments, CHPS stops using race as a factor in school assignments within its school choice plan, but it adds a new factor to the algorithm for deciding which students must be reassigned from their first-choice schools if they are oversubscribed: Students are given priority to stay in a school if they were previously enrolled there.

The plaintiffs move to modify the injunction to enjoin the new factor, arguing that CHPS is acting in bad faith to circumvent the judgment by locking in place previous assignments made under the plan that has been struck down. The district court agrees. It orders CHPS to replace the whole school choice system with a new assignment plan based on neighborhood boundary zones and to reassign all students to their neighborhood schools for the following school year.

CHPS appeals, arguing that the second remedial order exceeds the scope of the district court's authority.

Imagine you represent the plaintiffs. How would you defend the second order? How would CHPS challenge it? Which side do you expect to prevail?

Problem 12B.   A culture of violence prevails at the Palisades City Jail (PCJ). After a PCJ prisoner is granted parole, the prisoner is as a matter of course violently hazed by fellow prisoners between the announcement of the decision and the actual release. The Palisades Sheriff in charge of the jail, Jerry Ford, has never provided any formal training to his guards about how to protect prisoners from violence by other prisoners.

A week before PCJ prisoner Harry Benjamin is to come up for parole, another PCJ prisoner about to be released is beaten so badly he ends up in the hospital.

Benjamin is granted parole, with his release date to occur in three weeks. Later that day, he files a complaint in federal court against Sheriff Ford seeking protection from prisoner violence. Benjamin alleges that given the guards' lack of training and the culture of violence, PCJ cannot protect him, and its inability to do so violates the Eighth Amendment. Benjamin seeks two forms of emergency relief, each asserted in the alternative: He asks the court either to require the Sheriff to house him in the medical ward until his release or to require that the Sheriff immediately conduct training for all PCJ guards on preventing prisoner-on-prisoner violence.

The current PCJ grievance policy states: "All grievances must be mailed to the sheriff, who shall respond within 1000 days." The number appears to be a typo; prior editions of the policy said "10 days." In practice, Sheriff Ford sometimes acts within ten days, but backlogs can arise, and his responses sometimes take up to three months.

1. Would the Sheriff succeed in defending under the PLRA based on a failure to exhaust? Why or why not?

2. Now consider the remedies Benjamin has proposed. What obstacles will he face in seeking each? Based on these obstacles, which is Benjamin more likely to obtain, and which is less likely? If you were his lawyer, is there any other remedy you would propose?

3. *(Reviewing Chapter 11.)* Evaluate Benjamin's standing to sue for injunctive relief.

4. *(Reviewing Chapter 3.)* In what capacity should Benjamin name Sheriff Ford? Why?

5. *(Reviewing Chapter 5.)* Now imagine that Benjamin sues the City of Palisades instead of the Sheriff. Assuming he succeeds on the merits of the constitutional claim, what else must he show to obtain relief against the City? Is it likely he will be able to do so? Why or why not?

Table of Cases

Principal cases are indicated by italics.

Index